DEVELOPMENT PLANNING

Lessons
of
Experience

DEVELOPMENT
PLANNING
Lessons of Experience

ALBERT WATERSTON

Assisted By
C. J. MARTIN, AUGUST T. SCHUMACHER,
AND FRITZ A. STEUBER

The Economic Development Institute
International Bank for Reconstruction and Development
THE JOHNS HOPKINS PRESS   BALTIMORE MARYLAND

Foreword

THIS IS THE sixth publication of the Economic Development Institute. The Institute was established in 1955 by the International Bank for Reconstruction and Development. Its objective is to improve the quality of economic management in government in the less developed countries. At the Institute, senior officials of member governments of the Bank are given an opportunity to study and discuss the practical problems facing them as administrators as well as the broad issues of economic policy which their day-to-day tasks often prevent them from seeing. An effort is made to put before them the growing experience of the Bank and of the international community as a whole in promoting economic development.

Publications of the Economic Development Institute are primarily designed for use by persons working in responsible administrative and advisory capacities in government, financial institutions or other important sectors of the economy of the Bank's less developed member countries. It is hoped that they may also prove informative and useful to educational institutions and to groups and organizations of all kinds concerned with the problems of economic development.

The present publication is related to the training activities of the Economic Development Institute. In connection with his teaching assignment at the Institute, Mr. Waterston probed into the experience of many countries to determine the efficiency and effectiveness of their planning organizations. In co-operation with others, he described in monographs the planning machinery of three countries, Morocco, Pakistan and Yugoslavia. The present study brings together the results of his investigations in these three and many other countries and attempts to derive from them the "lessons of experience" which are bound to be of much interest to planners and others concerned with economic development.

The publications of the Economic Development Institute are the work of individuals. While in every case inestimable benefit has been derived from intimate contact with the work of the Bank, the publications in no sense purport to set forth the official views of the Bank or to be an authoritative statement of its policies in general or in detail.

JOHN H. ADLER
Director
Economic Development Institute

Preface

THIS IS A comparative study of development planning. It attempts to identify when, how and why planning has been successful or unsuccessful, and to draw relevant lessons of experience therefrom. Over a period of seven years, a group in the International Bank for Reconstruction and Development systematically collected a wide variety of materials on the experience of countries which plan their development. The basic raw material was obtained from a core group of some 55 countries in Africa, Asia, Europe and the Americas, including countries with advanced and less advanced, as well as socialized and mixed, economies. The collected data were analyzed and arranged nationally and topically according to a classification system devised for the purpose. In addition to the core group of countries, for which efforts were made to get complete coverage, partial information was obtained for all other countries which have attempted to plan their development. The study therefore draws, as much as was possible, on the experience of well over a hundred countries.

Besides the introductory section, the study comprises 16 Chapters divided into two parts. Part One includes a description and analysis of the planning process as revealed in the experience of the countries under review. Considerable attention is given to problems of plan formulation, although not to details of planning technique. Because problems of implementation have been found to be the most intractable ones in the planning experience of most countries, the greatest emphasis is given to them. Part One lays the substantive foundation for Part Two, which contains an extensive discussion of the experience of countries in setting up organizations and administrative procedures for preparing and implementing development projects, sectoral programs, and regional and national development plans.

Detailed appendices contain, among other things, a comprehensive chronological listing of national plans by country or dependent territory; a comprehensive list of names and addresses of central planning agencies; organization charts of representative central planning agencies; and a list of some 370 references cited in the text which constitute an extensive bibliography on development planning.

The organization of the book was arranged to facilitate its use as a reference work or textbook on development planning. For example, at the end of each chapter, except the Introduction, there is a summary and conclusions section; references cited in footnotes were reduced in size and made identical with the first part of each entry in the list of works cited at the end of the book; an unusually detailed index, consolidating country and topical data not included in the table of contents, simplifies cross reference; and important abbreviations used in the study are listed in the front of the book.

The study is unavoidably incomplete. Several subjects which might have been covered are not. But even if they had been included, the study would still be incomplete because it sought to survey the planning experience in as many countries in the world as possible and to draw such lessons and conclusions as seemed useful. And although the goal was known to be unattainable from the start, it nevertheless seemed worth striving for since the closer it was approached the more there was to learn.

Although theoretical or other points of view found in the literature on planning are presented for each topic covered, the approach is essentially inductive. As was to be expected, wide discrepancies between theory and practice were frequently encountered, and this led to attempts to reconcile the two. Sometimes, the resolution required proposals for changing practice, but at other times it seemed more appropriate to recommend adjustments in theory.

When feasible, published sources were quoted or cited to illustrate prevailing theory and practice. Whenever possible, quotations and citations for a broad cross-section and representative sample of countries were used, but this was not always possible because most of the published material on planning experience concentrates on a very few countries. It was therefore necessary at times to use published material available for one country to illustrate situations which were known to prevail also in others for which no published data could be found. Thus, frequent quotation or citation of published material for a country does not imply that the situation discussed was necessarily limited to the country concerned.

Considerable effort was made to check on the accuracy of the examples cited to illustrate various points. Although some examples may prove, nevertheless, to have been inaccurate originally or to have been overtaken by events, errors in illustrations need not invalidate the points made.

The study considers and discusses the lessons inherent in planning successes, but since unresolved planning problems are both more numerous and more challenging than those which have generally been overcome, most of the study concentrates on them. This may perhaps seem to give the study an unduly pessimistic orientation. If so, it would be the opposite of what is intended. So much experience has now been acquired about which planning mechanisms work well and which do not, that countries forewarned and forearmed are better able than ever before to avoid pitfalls and plan with reasonable assurance of success. It is hoped that this study will prove of some use for these purposes.

The author's debt to others is so great that it is hard to know where to begin and where to end acknowledgements. Cyril J. Martin, August T. Schumacher and Fritz Steuber labored long and hard to accumulate and arrange the basic research materials used in the study and Messrs. Martin and Schumacher also prepared first drafts of several chapters. Richard H. Demuth read the draft manuscript and made many penetrating comments which greatly improved it. Dr. Edward S. Mason of Harvard University also read the draft manuscript and made helpful suggestions. Members of an Informal Advisory Committee, which included Richard H. Demuth (Chairman), John H. Adler, Dragoslav Avramovic, Willem Brakel, Roger A. Chaufournier, John A. Edelman, William M. Gilmartin, Harold N. Graves, Jr., and Andrew M. Kamarck, set up within the World Bank to advise the author, somehow found time from their busy schedules to read and comment, sometimes in considerable detail, on the manuscript. They, as well as Reginald A. Clarke, A. J. Creshkoff, Sylvain R. F. Plasschaert and many other colleagues in the World Bank, were helpful in reading all or parts of the manuscript and commenting thereon. Dr. Gerhard Colm of the National Planning Association and Dr. Richard Goode of the International Monetary Fund also read and commented on individual chapters.

Nor could the study have been carried out without the help of many others. Jeffrey H. Dennis checked the footnotes, prepared the list of works cited and performed many other tasks. Thomas B. Winston greatly improved the form and readability of the report with many editorial suggestions. Miss Mary Philippides started the list of national plans which August T. Schumacher completed. The staff of the Bank's Research Files, especially Bogomir Chokel, made many helpful contributions to this list, and also met many requests for documentary assistance. August T. Schumacher, assisted by Miss Regina Bassani, prepared the list of central planning agencies included in Appendix IV, and, assisted by Jeffrey H. Dennis, compiled the index. Martin L. Loftus, Charles O. Olsen and their staff in the Bank-Fund Joint Library were unfailingly helpful with suggestions and in supplying innumerable books and documents. Miss Regina Bassani not only typed the manuscript, but guided the study from handwritten copy through many stages to the final draft.

To those mentioned, as well as to many others who were not, who helped make this study possible, the author extends his thanks. However, since the final decision about what was to be included in and what was to be excluded from the book was the author's, it seems only fair that he assume full responsibility for all errors and omissions.

ALBERT WATERSTON

Washington, D. C.
June, 1965

CONTENTS

Important Abbreviations Used

AFL-CIO American Federation of Labor—Congress of Industrial Organizations.

AID Agency for International Development (United States).

BAEQ Bureau d'Aménagement de l'Est de Québec, Inc. [Eastern Québec Planning Bureau] (Canada).

CAG Comparative Administrative Group of the American Society for Public Administration.

CAR Corporación Autónima Regional de la Sabana de Bogotá y Valles de Chinqínquira y Ubate [Autonomous Regional Corporation of the Savannah of Bogotá and the Chinqínquira and Ubate Valleys] (Colombia).

Cassa Cassa per il Mezzogiorno [Fund for the South] (Italy).

CD&W Colonial Development and Welfare (United Kingdom).

CIAP Cómite Interamericano de la Alianza para el Progreso [Inter-American Committee for the Alliance for Progress].

CIDE Comisión de Inversiones y Desarrollo Económico [Investments and Economic Development Commission] (Uruguay).

CODESUL Council for the Development of the Extreme South (Brazil).

COEB Gaspé and Magdalen Island Regional Council for Economic Development (Canada).

COMECON Council for Mutual Economic Assistance (Eastern Europe).

COPERE Cómite de Programación Económica y de Reconstrucción [Economic Programing and Reconstruction Committee] (Chile).

COPLAN Development Planning Commission (Brazil).

CORFO Corporación de Fomento de la Producción [Corporation for the Development of Production] (Chile).

CSO Central Statistical Office (Thailand).

CVC Corporación Autónima Regional del Valle del Cauca [Autonomous Regional Corporation of the Cauca Valley] (Colombia).

CVM Corporación Autónima Regional de los Valles de Magdalena y Sinú [Autonomous Regional Corporation of the Valleys of the Magdalena and Sinú] (Colombia).

DAC Development Assistance Committee of the Organization for Economic Co-operation and Development.

DECP   Division de la Coordination Economique et du Plan [Economic Co-ordination and Planning Division] (Morocco).

DVC   Damodar Valley Corporation (India).

EACSO   East African Common Services Organization.

ECA   Economic Commission for Africa.

ECAFE   Economic Commission for Asia and the Far East.

ECE   Economic Commission for Europe.

ECLA   Economic Commission for Latin America.

EEC   European Economic Community (Common Market).

EFTA   European Free Trade Association.

EPU   Economic Planning Unit (Malaya).

FICCI   Federation of the Indian Chambers of Commerce and Industry (India).

FAO   Food and Agriculture Organization.

GDP   Gross Domestic Product.

GNP   Gross National Product.

Gosplan   Central Planning Agency of the Union of Soviet Socialist Republics.

IBRD   International Bank for Reconstruction and Development (World Bank).

IDB   Inter-American Development Bank.

INE   Instituto Nacional de Estadística [National Statistical Institute] (Spain).

LAFTA   Latin American Free Trade Association.

NEC   National Economic Council (Pakistan or the Philippines).

NEDB   National Economic Development Board (Thailand).

NEDC   National Economic Development Council (United Kingdom).

NED   National Economic Development Council (United Kingdom).

NTPC   National Technical Planning Committee (Sudan).

OAS   Organization of American States.

OECD   Organization for European Co-operation and Development.

PAU   Pan American Union.

PEO   Programme Evaluation Organization (India).

PEP   Political and Economic Planning (Published in the United Kingdom).

PIA   Program Implementation Agency (Philippines).

PO   Plan Organization (Iran).

SIECA   Secretariat of the General Treaty for Central American Economic Integration.

SUDENE   Superintendência do Desenvolvimento do Nordeste [Superintendency for the Development of the Northeast] (Brazil).

TAA   Technical Assistance Administration of the United Nations.

TAO   Bureau of Technical Assistance Operations of the United Nations.

TTEC   Thai Technical and Economic Cooperation Office (Thailand).

UAR   United Arab Republic.

UDEAC   Union Douanière et Economique de l'Afrique Centrale [Customs and Economic Union for Central Africa].

UK   United Kingdom.

UN   United Nations.

UNESCO   United Nations Educational, Scientific and Cultural Organization.

US   United States of America.

USSR   Union of Soviet Socialist Republics.

WAPDA   Water and Power Development Authority (Pakistan).

PART ONE

The Development Planning Process

Chapter I

Introduction

SINCE THE END of the Second World War, a considerable literature on development planning has accumulated. Most of it is concerned with how planning ought to be practiced, or more explicitly, how planning would work if it worked as originally conceived or as the writer might wish. While examples from experience have been used to illustrate principles, most authors have chosen to concentrate on theory rather than practice. These writers have generally been as aware as anyone that there was always a gap—often a great one—between the theories they espoused and planning as it is practiced, especially in less developed countries. But mostly they have considered discrepancies between the two as short-run aberrations which would tend to disappear as more planners were trained and acquired experience.

The formal training of planners has reflected these attitudes. In universities in the industrialized countries, as well as in universities and institutes in the less developed countries themselves, to which would-be planners from less developed countries have come to learn the art or, as some may aver, the science of development planning, courses have largely concentrated on techniques for getting the highest possible returns from the allocation of economic resources. These techniques have in the main included such subjects as econometric model-building based on linear or curvilinear programing, the construction of input-output matrices, shadow-pricing methodology, simulation technique, operations research and the theory of games. While this training may be valuable to some, it has thus far proved to be of little practical use to planners in most less developed countries.

This is only partly because of a dearth of reliable statistics without which refined technique cannot work, an absence of technicians capable of joining in the formulation of an econometrically based comprehensive plan, or a failure of government leaders to understand what planning is all about. Of far greater importance is the fact that in most less developed countries the major unresolved planning problems are primarily political and administrative instead of economic. Against these problems, econometric techniques, which constitute the main stock in trade of the modern planner, have thus far made almost no headway.

Even a casual examination of the results achieved from development planning in most less developed countries indicates that they are falling short of what is reasonable to expect. The record is so poor—it has been worsening in fact—that it has sometimes led to disillusionment with planning and the abandonment of plans. Even in India, a citadel of planning, planning has been under unprecedented attack. Indeed, participants in the United Nations Meeting of Experts on Administrative Aspects of National Development Planning, held in Paris in June 1964, went so far as to suggest that national development planning was in crisis.

Perhaps this goes too far. Nevertheless, the record is not one in which planners can take pride. It can hardly be a source of complacency for planners when they reflect how few are the less developed countries which succeed in achieving even modest plan targets. It behooves planners to re-examine their approach to planning in the light of actual experience.

Although national development planning is very young—it has been practiced on a continuing basis for little more than 35 years in the USSR, for less than 20 years in countries which started planning soon after the end of World War II, and for much less than a decade in most of the rest of the world—development planning has already acquired its orthodoxies and high priests.

In the socialized countries, the official doctrine has been that rapid and balanced development could be carried out only through centralized plan formulation and execution. Amidst increasing indications over the last decade that centralized decision-making was seriously interfering with the ability of socialized enterprises to fulfill their plan targets, and clear evidence in Yugoslavia that decentralized implementation was producing far better results than centralized controls, the accepted tenets and ways were retained and expanded in most socialized countries. When these tenets were questioned, at first hesitantly and then more boldly and insistently, they were vigorously defended by the most respected savants. What was needed, they replied, were more, not fewer controls. The theory was good, but practice was bad. Practice had to be brought into line with theory.

But events proved more persuasive than words. Despite valiant efforts to reform the system within the limits laid down by theory, planning problems multiplied. And, as will be seen later, eventually theory gave way. New forms are coming into use. Rigid adherence to precept hallowed by use is being followed by flexible experimentation. What form planning will take is uncertain, except that it will be different from the past.

In the mixed-economy countries, also, a basic credo took root early. It holds that comprehensive development planning, based on econometric techniques, is so superior to any other type that all countries, at all stages of development, would be well advised to use it in preference to any other. The rationale for this belief is discussed in detail in Chapter IV. There is little question that from the theoretical point of view, comprehensive development planning excels. It may also be granted that it works effectively in some countries, especially in the more advanced nations or in those less developed countries that are so firmly committed to development planning that the usual problems seem to be more manageable. It may even be granted that some countries which plan only partially could benefit from the introduction of comprehensive planning. But it must also be said that comprehensive development planning does not work in most less developed countries where it has been tried.

Here, as before, those who believe in the established doctrine argue that what is wrong is practice—not theory. Here, too, those who consider comprehensive planning the "be all and end all" of planning, contend that the many failures only prove the need for more—not less—comprehensive planning. But here, also, the pressure of circumstances is convincing many countries to abandon an "idealized outlook" and adjust practice to needs dictated by realities.

Forced from the chrysalis of theory by the imperative of events, national development planning has emerged as a diverse phenomenon which almost invariably differs in some important respects from one country to another. To an even greater extent, diversity arises because not only the aims of planning but the methods used to formulate and implement plans are closely conditioned by a country's political, economic and social values and institutions, and its stage of development. Since in these respects every country is unique in some way, the results in one country usually differ markedly from those in another even when both have adopted the same planning methods.[1]

Yet, every country has qualities and planning problems which are

[1] UN. TAA. *Introduction to Public Administration in Development Policy, Preliminary survey of the experience of several Latin American countries*, p. 3. [See list of works cited at end of book for full citation for this and succeeding footnotes.]

common to all. It is, therefore, a mistake to believe that the planning experience of one country has no relevance to others—as much a mistake as it is to think that one type of planning is the answer to development in all countries at all times. Indeed, the material in the chapters which follow provides much evidence to support the view that, although methodology and approach may vary greatly from one country to another, certain principles have emerged in the planning experience of socialized and mixed economies, and in the industrially developed and less developed nations, which are valid in any country. One need cite only one example: Experience demonstrates that when a country's leaders in a stable government are strongly devoted to development, inadequacies of the particular form of planning used—or even the lack of any formal planning—will not seriously impede the country's development. Conversely, in the absence of political commitment or stability, the most advanced form of planning will not make a significant contribution toward a country's development.

It is therefore a mistake to imagine that a certain system of planning or a certain kind of plan is the key to national development. Those planners who insist that it is, when most countries do not in practice accept this view, only succeed in separating their activities and their plans from the planning process as it operates in most less developed countries. While planners may be shifting resources about on paper and proving to their own satisfaction that a country's national income can be doubled within a decade, the country may be having great difficulty in maintaining much lower rates of growth.

When planners look up from their plans, they cannot fail to become aware that their theoretical formulations have greatly outstripped practical capabilities. They can then appreciate the advice of one planner to

> survey things as they are, observe what needs to be done, study the means you have to do it with, and then work out practical ways of going about it.[2]

When this sequence is followed, the forms of planning are likely to be quite different from those set by reference to abstract concepts. Thus, it may be found that improvements in budgetary practice should precede the formulation of a comprehensive development plan in some

---

[2] Ionides, Michael G. "The Objects and Implications of Economic Development," p. 15.

countries; or that the establishment of machinery to improve the preparation and execution of projects, and the formulation of sectoral programs may be more important in some countries at some time in their history than the establishment of a central planning office.

The shortage of good, well-prepared projects which is a well-nigh universal feature of the planning experience of less developed countries is now widely recognized as a major impediment to the execution of plans for development. Planners are also beginning to realize that the absence of appropriate policies and measures, more often than the absence of additional investment funds, accounts for shortfalls in plan targets. But the implications of these truths are not yet fully understood by most planners. Thus, they do not comprehend that they must mold their plans to "things as they are." Planners must, of course, try to improve the planning *milieu* in which they work. But to accomplish this, it is of little use to start with a set of theoretical abstractions of planning as it might be and seek to force them upon an inhospitable environment. Theory is important—nay, vital. But an important lesson of experience is that *a priori* abstractions from theory, no matter how penetrating, are only a beginning; to complete the story, there is need for *a posteriori* abstractions from history. The problems of planning

> are not likely to be settled by the continuing elaboration and refinement of purely logical and mathematical analysis. This is because much of the empirical basis of current theorizing appears to consist of *a priori* 'common sense' assumptions or of fragmentary or obsolete data. If theoreticians avoid the discipline of empirical verification for too long, they run the risk that their work will attenuate into a kind of sterile scholasticism. Elegance is not a substitute for evidence . . . . it is never enough to judge theories, decision models, etc., only by their logical validity; they must always also be submitted to such empirical verification as may be possible.[3]

[3] Colm, Gerhard and Geiger, Theodore. "Country Programming as a Guide to Development," p. 66.

Chapter II

The Many Meanings of Planning

> . . . planning . . . is an abstraction. . . . Standing by
> itself, it has no clearly identifiable meaning.[1]

INTRODUCTION

ANYONE WHO has thought much about planning, recognizes it as a
complex and many-sided phenomenon. But it has been defined in
widely divergent ways, often tendentiously. For instance, one writer
who agrees that planning is "big and complicated" nevertheless considers it "not much more than applied common sense," [2] while another
contends that it is "a complex clustering of problems to be 'explored,'
not 'defined.' " [3] Most writers, however, see planning as an organized,
intelligent attempt to select the best available alternatives to achieve
specific goals. It represents

> the rational application of human knowledge to the process of
> reaching decisions which are to serve as the basis of human
> action. . . . The central core of the meaning remains the estab-
> lishment of relationships between means and ends with the object
> of achieving the latter by the most efficient use of the former.[4]

Or as Prime Minister Nehru of India defined it, more simply and
pragmatically:

> Planning is the exercise of intelligence to deal with facts and
> situations as they are and find a way to solve problems.[5]

Planning may be used for a variety of purposes, from the preparation
and execution of programs for putting men on the moon or into outer

---

[1] Skeoch, L. A. and Smith, David C. *Economic Planning: The Relevance of
Western European Experience for Canada*, p. 1.

[2] Morrison, Herbert. *Economic Planning*, p. 15.

[3] Elliott, John E. "Economic Planning Reconsidered," p. 55.

[4] Sociedad Interamericana de Planificación. *Enseñanza de la Planificación en la
América Latina*, pp. 101–102.

[5] Nehru, Jawaharlal. "Strategy of the Third Plan," pp. 33–34.

space, to the management of an enterprise, a city, a region or a nation. It can be temporary, as in planning after a natural disaster, in wartime or during postwar reconstruction. Or it may be for a longer time, as in national planning for economic stability, full employment or economic development.

To plan economically, one need not have a moral purpose; one need only be prudent in the use of scarce resources:

> Planning economically is to plan in such a way that the scarce means at our disposal yields us the greatest satisfaction—however one wishes to define 'satisfaction.' If . . . [someone] . . . chooses one method which yields him less satisfaction for the given amount of expenditure of scarce resources at his disposal than he could have derived from another method, he is not acting economically.[6]

Just as economic planning eschews moral judgments, it has no one approach to all problems. It does not, for example, necessarily involve regimentation, collectivization or industrialization.[7] Nor is its use limited to a particular kind of economy or society. It exists under a variety of political systems. Its scope ranges

> all the way from the relatively limited planning of an essentially private or mixed enterprise economy to the comprehensive, all-embracing planning of a totalitarian economic system . . . . it could quite easily appear in many and diverse situations, as, e.g., capitalistic planning, socialistic planning, democratic planning, totalitarian planning, business planning, government planning, and so on.[8]

Despite the great variety of forms which it may take, all planning has certain common attributes. These include looking ahead, making choices, and, where possible, arranging that future actions for attaining objectives follow fixed paths or, where this is impossible, setting limits to the consequences which may arise from such action. These attributes can be discovered in such diverse kinds of planning as wartime and postwar reconstruction planning, town and country planning, full employment and anticyclical planning, as well as in development planning.

[6] Baldwin, Claude David. *Economic Planning: Its Aims and Implications*, p. 11.
[7] Friedmann, John. "Introduction" (to) The Study and Practice of Planning, p. 329.
[8] Elliott, John E. "Economic Planning Reconsidered," p. 62.

WARTIME PLANNING

During World War II, the United Kingdom and the United States both adopted centralized physical planning and controls over economic activity similar to those found in socialized economies. In both countries, wartime planning supplanted the market to some degree and prevented the forces of supply and demand from determining the prices and quantities of goods and services bought and sold.

In the United Kingdom, aggregate demand greatly exceeded supply. As a result, there were plans and controls for manpower, raw materials, and imports to secure the routing of scarce resources in the required quantities and at the appropriate times to the armed forces, productive units or other places where the planners thought they would do the most good. Consumer goods were rationed to restrict demand to the level of supplies. Because the U.K., as an island, was especially dependent on imports, the use of shipping was also regulated according to plan to insure that available bottoms carried the most important commodities. In effect, Government decisions were substituted for the market and the price mechanism to allocate basic productive resources.

In the United States, the Government experimented with various systems for allocating materials through priority and budgeting systems. Controls were often on a more informal basis than in the United Kingdom and greater reliance was laid on the price system, either through ceiling prices or by subsidies for imports. Nevertheless, government controls, often detailed, extended over a wide range of economic activity. In both countries, it was possible to introduce planning which displaced market forces only because the people in both nations realized that it was essential to winning the war. Even though it was not always good planning, bad effects from mistakes were more than counterbalanced by favorable results arising from the clarity and unity of the planning objective, i.e., winning the war, the complete commitment of the political leadership to that objective and the willingness of people to change their mode of life and undertake sacrifices to reach the common goal. A number of useful lessons emerged from this experience which threw light on what is essential for carrying out plans. As will be seen later, there were also significant lessons to be drawn from the planning methods used. Also it became evident that in times of emergency, governments were not prepared to let the market operate freely to bring forth the output required to meet the emergency.

TOWN AND COUNTRY PLANNING

For countries which had suffered severe damage in World War II, the postwar years brought increased interest and participation in a type of physical planning known as town and country planning. Prewar references to planning, at least in the more advanced countries, usually meant physical planning for efficient and aesthetic use of land, rehabilitation of slum areas or relocation of their population on other sites, establishment of new towns, construction of industrial centers, development of satellite areas or reorganization of transportation systems to meet changed needs. From these beginnings, architects and professional town planners developed a whole series of principles in a "science" of town and country planning which emphasized zoning of land areas, expansion of public utilities and development of housing projects.

After the war, the United Kingdom passed a Town and Country Act and established a Ministry of Town and Country Planning to insure that available land was properly utilized through zoning which would provide adequate "green belts" for recreational and other activities. The Ministry played an important role in the reconstruction era, although its importance declined subsequently. In 1964, the Ministry of Housing and Local Government completed a two and one-half year South East Study which provides a detailed master plan for redeveloping a region containing 18 million people, nearly 40 per cent of the population of England and Wales. The Study is intended to set priorities in allocating land for future homes, shops, industry and schools.

The Netherlands also renewed its interest in physical planning after the war. For a long time before World War II, the Netherlands had relied on physical planning for water control and reclamation. Until 1931, these projects were handled locally, but in 1941, an organization was set up to plan such projects on a national scale. Because of the country's terrain and the need for sea flooding and general water control, much physical planning revolved around waterway and waterworks projects. But there were other fields in which physical planning was also significant. Thus, the scarcity of agricultural land led to planning for its rational use and to the preparation of a master plan for reallocating land. In 1954, a Land Consolidation Act was passed which made possible the improvement of agricultural areas on a large scale. The Zuider Zee Reclamation Project and the Delta Works Plan were important physical planning projects which involved both water control and land reclamation programs. In the postwar period, the reconstruction of Rotterdam and Amsterdam, among other cities, proceeded in accordance with physical plans which included the construction and expansion of ports, industrial centers and residential communities.

The need for a more organized approach to metropolitan planning also has become apparent in developing countries as the migration of rural populations to urban areas has continued, on all continents, in communist and capitalist countries alike. In tropical and subtropical urban areas, crowding, low earning capacity, poor nutrition and lack of sanitation are already creating serious economic and social problems. Moreover, the outlook is that the general growth of populations and improved efficiency in agriculture in the next 20 years will accelerate the movement of people from rural to urban areas in less developed countries. In a report on the problem, the World Health Organization has said that the expected increase in urban population

> clearly justifies the warning that, after the question of keeping world peace, metropolitan planning is probably the most serious single problem faced by man in the second half of the 20th century.[9]

City planning of a special kind has made considerable progress in Brazil. In that country, urban planning has often meant the creation of a whole new city. The outstanding example of such planning is the new national capital of Brasilia. The cities of Belo Horizonte and Goiânia, each the capital of its respective State, were also systematically planned. The planning of Belo Horizonte was especially interesting because it involved the establishment of an industrial area outside the limits of the residential part of the city. In Brazil, as elsewhere, city planning has been considered a branch of architecture, but it is increasingly being influenced by social and economic planning.[10]

Puerto Rico is still another area with a long history of physical

---

[9] *New York Times*, July 21, 1964.
[10] Daland, Robert T. "Chapter V. The Future and Brazilian Planning," pp. 46–48.

planning. As long ago as the 16th century, a Spanish law had set standards to be followed in establishing new towns. In 1821, the Colonial Government had created a board to formulate a general public works plan; in 1860, a master road plan had been published; and in the 1930's, a series of city planning studies had been made. Thus, when the Puerto Rican Planning, Urbanization and Zoning Board came into being in 1942, it could draw on a considerable accumulation of experience with physical planning. The Board differs from previous planning organizations in Puerto Rico because its functions not only cover town and country planning, including the preparation of master plans for land use and the construction of public facilities, but also economic planning. In Puerto Rico, therefore, a close link exists between physical and economic planning.

Similar links are appearing in other, especially more advanced, countries. In the United States, for example, physical planning

> was first claimed by the engineers and a little later by the landscape architects. Then the architects as such entered the contest. Within the last two decades the social scientists and public administrators have begun to challenge the physical design professions. The typical planner today is trained in a variety of disciplines, both in physical design and social science with the object of learning to integrate all the elements necessary to solve some specific social problem.[11]

The typical physical planner in industrial countries is an urban planner. The growing movement of population to cities and the consequent expansion of the fringes of urban life are joining towns into agglomerations of urban areas. The increase in the number of people living in closer proximity than ever before and, at the same time, their higher levels of living and greater mobility, have challenged the ingenuity of the physical planners to design school, hospital, water, sanitation, highway and other facilities and amenities to meet new and continually expanding needs. As the outward movement of town clusters have continued, physical planners have increasingly encountered problems whose solution depends on decisions involving the economy of the region in which they are working. Consequently, physical planning has become increasingly concerned with problems usually reserved to economic planning.

[11] *Ibid.*, p. 50.

ANTICYCLICAL PLANNING

Economic planning is primarily anticyclical or developmental. Anticyclical planning is generally limited to industrially advanced countries with strong private sectors and well-developed markets. The principal aim of anticyclical planning is to achieve, within the prevailing economic and social framework and the limits prescribed by the need to maintain economic stability, a level of effective demand which allows the fullest utilization to be made of capital stocks, labor force and other resources. Policies and measures adopted to attain plan objectives and targets operate largely through the market and demand is controlled mostly through monetary and fiscal measures. While there are times when demand may have to be stimulated to raise it to levels required to utilize excess capacities, it has in practice been necessary more frequently to curb demand which threatened to exceed productive possibilities. Anticyclical planning also aims to increase the rate at which incomes grow. But it lets the private sector determine the direction of growth and it does not attempt to rationalize public investment for the purpose of accelerating the rate of growth. Since there are usually too many rather than too few projects, the problem is not to stimulate growth but to insure that the growth rate does not expand so much that it jeopardizes economic stability through inflation or balance of payments difficulties.

Sweden has engaged in anticyclical planning since 1933. The Netherlands offers, perhaps, the best-known example of effective anticyclical planning. The Dutch recognized that their country's position as a world trader subject to the vicissitudes of world markets could be maintained in the postwar period only through the exercise of economic discipline. The Government also realized that in the circumstances existing in the Netherlands, the greatest benefits could be obtained by providing economic incentives to private enterprise and by limiting its own activities to what was required to maintain economic stability. The system of anticyclical planning which the Netherlands adopted at an early stage after the reconstruction period was well suited for these purposes and for allowing the economy to move forward without undue fluctuations.

The main objectives of Dutch planning are full employment, avoidance of inflation, equilibrium in the balance of payments and some shift of incomes in favor of workers, especially through improvements in education, health and housing. The medium through which these objectives are quantified is an annual plan in which a forecast for the year is made and policies are suggested for achieving plan targets. Instruments used to reach targets consist mainly of appropriate monetary policies applied by the central bank; tax measures and government expenditures operating through the budget; and controls on wages, housing and prices. In the cyclical circumstances which have prevailed in the Netherlands, the use of these policy instruments has been, on the whole, restrictive in character. But they have succeeded both in stabilizing the economy and producing a satisfactory rate of growth.

Techniques employed in anticyclical planning have been refined greatly in the last decade. The impact of Keynesian theory has led to the development of a considerable body of complex economic and mathematical concepts which have been applied to the construction of econometric models and for other purposes. In recent years, economists have been attempting to use similar techniques for development planning. There is little question that development planning can learn from the experience of anticyclical planning, although indiscriminate transference of technique from anticyclical to development planning has sometimes done more harm than good.

DEVELOPMENT PLANNING

National Planning

Superficially, development planning may seem to resemble anticyclical planning. This is largely because they both usually seek to increase employment and incomes. But there are basic differences between the two.

Anticyclical planning seeks to achieve full employment of resources and social and economic progress through existing institutions because, in the more advanced countries where such planning is generally practiced, these institutions operate with acceptable efficiency. The distribution of land, property and incomes is not unduly askew. Government administration functions well or, at least, adequately. The private sector is well developed, entrepreneurs are informed and ready to expand existing capacities or undertake new ventures when opportunities arise. The price system is sufficiently elastic to permit markets to work with reasonable efficiency as mechanisms for allocating investment and other resources in accordance with social demand.

But this is not the situation in most less developed countries. There are usually many glaring imbalances in their economies. There are generally unemployed and underemployed resources, balance of payments difficulties and a variety of bottlenecks which impede production and distribution. Usually, the systems of land tenure and land use are archaic and unproductive, the incidence of taxation is inequitable and the distribution of incomes is lopsided. Government machinery is weak, the domestic private sector, often concentrated in commerce and trade, is typically ill-equipped and reluctant to expand productive capacity or open up new industrial fields, while foreign investment is often limited to the extraction of natural resources to be processed abroad. Prices respond only haphazardly to changes in supply and demand because markets are often rudimentary, imperfectly organized and fettered by many rigidities. There are barriers to the free flow of information, as well as

> restraints of custom, tradition, and ignorance; and entry into markets is limited by a wide variety of monopolistic controls. Capital markets, foreign exchange markets, even labor markets which operate fairly efficiently in developed economies patently do not do so in many less developed countries.[12]

These circumstances make changes in the traditional economic and social structure of most less developed countries a precondition of development. They also explain why many governments in less developed countries are unwilling to let the market allocate investment resources and determine their countries' rate of growth; and they explain why these governments turn instead to planning to attain economic and social progress, the transformation of institutional arrangements they consider to be inimical to the expansion of productive forces and the establishment of a more equitable and balanced society. For while anticyclical planning aims to stimulate demand through the market and existing institutions, development planning seeks to break down structural obstacles (and this often includes the way markets operate) which hinder growth. Development planning therefore goes much further than anticyclical planning:

> In the underdeveloped countries of Asia, Africa, and Latin America, development requires social and cultural change as well as

---

[12] Millikan, Max F. "Criteria for Decision-Making in Economic Planning," p. 29.

economic growth; that is, qualitative transformations must occur concurrently with quantitative increases. There is, in fact, a reciprocal relation between the two, and neither process is likely to continue for long or go very far without the other. Hence, development means change plus growth.[13]

Accelerated economic growth [14] and structural change are thus the two main expressed or implied aims of development planning. But the emphasis given to the second aim varies from country to country. In the socialized countries, profound institutional alterations designed to eradicate political, as well as economic and social, conditions believed to be responsible for backwardness are considered the prerequisite for, if not the key to, generating and sustaining a high level of growth of production and income. In a few countries with mixed economies, institutional change also takes precedence over economic progress. For example, in the opinion of the Vice-Chairman of Indonesia's Supreme Advisory Council,

> countries such as Indonesia must be fully aware of the difference in nature between planning as a feature of society, where the 'target' is to build a new society, and the planning of investment projects, where the 'target' is a specific item of economic development. The second kind of planning must be made *subservient* to the first, which is primary.[15]

It is therefore not surprising to find that, among countries with mixed economics, Indonesia represents an extreme case of institutional adaptation, including extensive nationalization and major alterations in the price system. In the United Arab Republic also, many structural changes were made as part of a program of "Arab socialism." The Government carried out a major agrarian reform which included imposition of ceilings on land holdings and the redistribution of land. It also took over direct control and, to a large extent, ownership of all the main industrial and trading companies, banks and financial institutions.

But in most mixed economies, the degree of structural change is generally less pronounced and more gradual. In fact, in the planning of

[13] Colm, Gerhard and Geiger, Theodore. "Country Programming as a Guide to Development," p. 47.

[14] By "accelerated economic growth" is meant a rate of growth that is higher than would be obtained without planning.

[15] Abdulgani, Roeslan. "The Lessons of Indonesia's Experience of Planning," p. 442.

a few developed countries, the amount of institutional change is so small that the line between development planning, defined as including change as well as growth, and anticyclical planning becomes tenuous. One such country is Japan. On the one hand, Japanese planning resembles anticyclical planning in that the role of government is largely limited to creating favorable conditions for private enterprise operating in a market economy. On the other hand, it resembles development planning in that the Government is expected to supplement private investment by joining with it in such fields as public utilities and by stimulating, fostering and guiding economic activity in a variety of ways.

The ambivalence is due partly to the fact that Japan moved from stabilization planning directly into development planning without shedding all the attributes of the former or taking on all the accouterments of the latter. It has also been partly because Japan has a well-developed private enterprise system which operates effectively in a market economy. There was, therefore, no great urgency to make basic changes in the economic structure. In the Netherlands, also, where steps are being taken to shift from anticyclical to development planning, some elements characteristic of anticyclical planning are likely to be retained and little change in institutional arrangements is to be expected.

But in most countries, especially in less developed nations, the idea is firmly held that development planning can be effective only if it includes basic institutional reforms. Thus, the signatory powers of the Charter for the Alliance for Progress have agreed to carry out comprehensive land and tax reforms. According to two members of the Alliance Committee of Nine, these reforms, among others,

> are deemed essential to lay a foundation for sustained economic and social advance within the countries of Latin America. . . . The dual function of structural reforms—the increase in productivity and the mobilization of resources on the one side and the satisfaction of equity requirements on the other—is critical to rapid development under current conditions in democratic countries. The optimum use of natural resources (and particularly the land) and the tapping of the great potential energies of the human resources (which requires widespread involvement in development by the people of a nation) are at the very foundations of economic advance. People who have relatively little cannot be expected to work hard and accept the discipline of a development

effort, unless they feel that they arc receiving and will continue to receive a fair share of the total returns.[16]

In India, also, the Government is committed through constitutional procedures to a program of radical change referred to as "democratic socialism" and, in Ghana, the Government is committed to institutional changes in the name of "African socialism." The head of the French Planning Commission has recalled that, even in France in 1945,

> the idea of nationalizing the key sectors of the economy [accompanied] the idea of substituting the Plan for certain market mechanisms that had failed before the war to remedy the economic and social consequences of the great crisis of the 1930's.[17]

In some developing countries, the institutional changes made have contributed little or nothing to either economic or social progress. In other countries, changes have been advocated or carried out although they were expected to retard economic expansion for awhile because they were considered prerequisites to execution of a successful program for national development. Land reforms in India and Pakistan are examples. The first head of the Harvard Advisory Group in Pakistan has pointed out that, although the direct economic effects of land reform were probably detrimental to output in the short run, Pakistan's Planning Board felt it was important that the Government reform land tenure practices

> (1) to give evidence of the determination of the government to achieve social justice, a determination which would be essential to any popular support for sacrifices in the interest of development, and (2) to remove the power of the large landowners who in parts of West Pakistan exercised quasi-feudal powers over economic, social and political life, and who opposed most measures of social and economic reform. . . .[18]

But in many less developed countries, little more than lip service is paid to the need for agricultural, tax and administrative reforms which are clearly essential to progress. Vested interests do everything possible to prevent change in the *status quo*. As in countries in other parts of the world,

[16] Perloff, Harvey S. and Saez, Raul. "National Planning and Multinational Planning Under the Alliance for Progress," p. 49.
[17] Massé, Pierre. "French Economic Planning," p. 4.
[18] Bell, David E. "Planning for Development in Pakistan," p. 17.

there are important groups within each of the Latin American countries who are strongly opposed to social reforms and such groups can be expected to resist the implementation of such reforms with all means available to them.[19]

The governments in such countries are frequently unable or unwilling to go far in changing the underlying structure of their societies. They prefer instead to induce change by enlarging the scope of the public sector through increased public investment. Since this may greatly alter the rates of growth of different economic sectors, favoring some as opposed to others, structural changes in the economy can, and do, occur. In societies where development causes many people to move from a near subsistence way of life into a cash economy, from depressed rural areas into more advanced farming regions, or from the country to the cities, social changes are also inevitable. But these changes may cause increased social and political tensions which impede rather than aid the acceleration of the rate of economic and social progress.

The Problem of Definition. Because planning objectives and practices in each country are in some respects different from those in every other country, it is impossible to compose a definition of development planning which satisfies everyone and every need. The variety and range of definitions are great. One can find, at one extreme, a definition broad enough to include practically every country and, at the other extreme, one narrow enough to exclude all but a few. When development planning is defined as

> any action by the State, whose purpose is to raise the rate of economic growth above that which would take place without any conscious effort,[20]

almost any country with an investment project can be considered to be planning; and as will be seen later, when only comprehensive planning based on mathematical models is acceptable as development planning, only a handful of countries can qualify as practitioners of the planning art. It therefore seemed best to avoid these extremes in formulating a definition of development planning for selecting the

[19] Perloff, Harvey S. and Saez, Raul. "National Planning and Multinational Planning Under the Alliance for Progress," p. 49.
[20] UN. TAA. *Economic Planning in Ceylon,* p. 12.

countries to be included in this study. For this purpose, the definition of development planning could, on the one hand, safely exclude countries like the United States or the Federal Republic of Germany which make no pretense whatever at planning for growth and institutional change. On the other hand, it appeared desirable to include countries which, however inadequately, made a deliberate and continuing, albeit intermittent, attempt to translate into action some kind of plan for their development.

But it was considered essential that the Government, not a private or quasi-governmental group, sponsor the planning effort. Thus, India could not be said to have been planning in 1944 when eight leading Indian industrialists issued the so-called Bombay Plan in that year as their contribution to the discussion then going forward about the course of India's future development. The Bombay Plan is historically interesting as a pathfinding private effort, but not as an example of national development planning. Nor could Peru be said to be engaged in planning despite the "National Plan of Economic and Social Development for 1962–71," prepared on its own initiative by Peru's Central Bank, since the Government of Peru has never shown any real interest in the Plan.

Until a government adopts a plan as its own, it is only a proposal. Some governments, in fact, carefully choose to have plans prepared by nongovernmental bodies in order to retain complete freedom to reject the plans. In both Sweden and Finland, for example, plans have been prepared by *ad hoc* commissions appointed by the Government which issued the plans on their own responsibility. Neither Government was under obligation to accept the plan prepared by its commission. Neither commission's proposals could be considered national plans, therefore, unless and until adopted by its Government.

The considerations mentioned in the preceding discussion served as the basis for formulating the following working definition of development planning: a country was considered to be engaged in development planning if its government made a deliberate and continuing attempt to accelerate the rate of economic and social progress and to alter institutional arrangements which were considered to block the attainment of this goal. The attempt had to be a conscious one made by a government and it had to be made often enough to give substance to the government's claim or belief that it was concerting policies and taking action designed to bring about economic and social progress and institutional change. But it was not essential that a country be committed to unremitting or appropriate action, nor was it necessary that its efforts be comprehensive instead of partial or, for obvious reasons, that these efforts be successful. Hence, countries which plan badly have not been excluded. And for good reasons: there are few countries which can claim to be planning well and, what is equally important, there is much to be learned from failure.

The implications of the definition adopted will become more apparent in the pages which follow. Perhaps it will suffice for now to say that it does not deviate fundamentally from those generally accepted. The definition had the effect of encompassing most countries which make some attempt at development planning, including advanced as well as less advanced nations and those with largely socialized as well as those with mixed economies.[21] But it excluded countries like the United States and the Federal Republic of Germany, although there are those who contend that even these countries can be said to engage in development planning.

Regional Planning

Development planning may also be regional in scope. Regions may be political or economic. A political region is a geographic area designated as a governmental administrative unit in a nation or dependent territory; a combination of nations or dependent territories; or a combination of one or more nations with one or more dependent territories. An economic region is an area with common economic and social problems induced by natural or other conditions, like a river basin or an area without adequate supplies of water for agriculture.[22] In either case, regional development planning may be subnational or multinational.

Subnational regional planning was formerly regarded as a part of city planning. In recent years, however, the region has emerged as a fundamental planning unit as planners increasingly recognized that regions often have peculiar characteristics and economic problems which need special consideration. This has led to the establishment of subnational regional planning as an independent discipline with its

---

[21] I.e., those in which private enterprise is permitted to operate in more than one major economic sector.

[22] Within a political or economic region there may be a functional region, whose more restricted boundaries are determined by the area needed to achieve a more limited objective, e.g., colonization.

own orientation and methodology. Subnational regional planning may mean one of three things: [23]

1. It may refer to planning for a city, state, metropolitan area or a depressed part of a country as a separate economy. A special authority may be created with regulatory or fiscal powers to formulate the plan, carry it out and operate completed projects. The Tennessee Valley Authority (TVA) in the Tennessee Valley of the United States, the *Cassa per il Mezzogiorno* (the Cassa) in Southern Italy, the *Superintendência do Desenvolvimento do Nordeste* (SUDENE) in the Northeast of Brazil and the *Corporación Autónima del Valle del Cauca* (CVC) in the Cauca Valley of Colombia are examples.

2. Subnational regional planning may also refer to the preparation of a series of regional plans covering an entire country as part of the process of preparing a national plan. As will be seen later, planning in socialized countries involves the preparation of a whole series of regional plans for republics and subsidiary areas, and their testing for consistency with each other and the national plan. The aggregation of regional plans is supposed to add up to the total allocations of materials, equipment and labor in the over-all plan. In federal nations with mixed economies, like Nigeria and Pakistan, regional plans for each of the regional governments are also prepared and integrated with the national plan.

3. Finally, subnational regional planning may refer to the fitting of projects under a national plan to insure the best possible location of industry and to reduce economic disparities among the regions in a country. In Yugoslavia, for example, the Investment Bank awards investment and other credits to sponsors of projects on the basis of which project is likely to offer the best yield as determined by detailed investment criteria set up by the Bank. For each major project, locational and other studies are made to permit competition to be limited to project sponsors situated in the regions considered best for the project. To insure that depressed regions get an appropriate share of new investment, separate investment credit allocations are made for these areas. Competition for these funds is restricted to sponsors of projects who locate new plans in these regions.

Multinational regional planning also may mean three different things:

[23] Adapted and extended from Higgins, Benjamin. *Some Comments on Regional Planning*, pp. 1–2.

1. It may refer to planning for an economic region which extends beyond the boundaries of one country. For instance, the planning for redevelopment of the Indus River Basin covers portions of both India and Pakistan. This regional plan was adopted by both countries after eight years of negotiations in which the World Bank participated. Another example is the plan which the Committee for Coordination of Investigations of the Lower Mekong Basin is to prepare for the lower Mekong River Basin. The plan will provide a ten-year program for the use of the River's water for navigation, power, irrigation, etc., by Cambodia, Laos, Thailand and South Viet-Nam.[24]

2. Multinational regional planning may also refer to planning for one or more economic sectors of two or more countries. Thus, the European Coal and Steel Community plans for the coal and steel sectors of six European countries through a supernational central agency with power to tax, levy fines, order changes in import tariffs and make judicial reviews. The European Economic Community (Common Market) has also prepared proposals for a common approach by its member countries in specific economic sectors, including agriculture and automobile manufacturing. The Food and Agriculture Organization's Mediterranean Development Project conducted a series of studies and made proposals for the integrated development of agriculture and forestry in ten Mediterranean countries. And in the five Central American countries and Panama, a plan has been prepared to establish a regional telecommunications network and to make their national networks compatible with the regional system.

3. Finally, multinational regional planning may refer to the coordination of national plans or to the setting of integrated targets for the entire economies of several countries which are members of an international regional organization. This kind of regional planning has thus far made the least headway, but promises to make more progress in the future. International organizations like the European Economic Community (EEC) and the European Free Trade Association (EFTA) in Western Europe, the Council of Mutual Economic Assistance (COMECON) in Eastern Europe, the permanent Secretariat of the General Treaty for Central American Economic Integration (SIECA) and the Latin American Free Trade Association (LAFTA)

---

[24] Mainland China, which also has important riparian rights to the Mekong River, will not be a party to the proposed plan. The Mekong also flows through Burma and Nepal, but the topography of the river basin in these countries precludes diversion of its waters there.

in Latin America, and the East African Common Services Organization (EACSO) all of which have been established in recent years, have been giving increasing attention to the desirability of international economic co-operation and integration among their member countries. The EEC has already made projections to 1970 of alternative possible and probable growth rates in the EEC countries. It is also drafting a medium-term economic policy program for 1966–70 which will endeavor

> to set side by side the Member States' long-term plans, programmes, projections and forecasts and endeavour to lend cohesion to the long-term national policies and the various courses of Community actions, and so to lay the technical and political foundations for a consolidated programme.[25]

COMECON [26] has also been attempting, without much success thus far, to co-ordinate the national plans of its member countries. However, plan co-ordination with a view to getting greater specialization among member countries is scheduled to increase with the round of national plans which went into effect in 1965. At the request of the Economic Commission for Africa (ECA) at its fifth session, the Executive Secretary prepared "concrete proposals concerning co-ordination of development plans of African countries." [27] The ECA has advocated since its establishment that countries in the region co-ordinate their plans for the location of industries in order to avoid unnecessary duplication and waste of resources. At an ECA meeting in Nairobi in February 1965, seven countries in East and Central Africa laid the basis for establishing an African Common Market later. The recent establishment of *Union Douanière et Economique de l'Afrique Centrale* (UDEAC) with Cameroun, Congo (Brazzaville), Chad, Central African Republic and Gabon as members, may be a harbinger of other economic groupings in the region. In East Africa, Kenya, Tanganyika (Tanzania) and Uganda have continued economic co-ordination as independent nations through the East African Common Services Organization (EACSO), which in 1961 replaced the East African High Commission, with the three countries as members.

[25] Swan, D. and McLachlan, D. L. "Programming and Competition in the European Communities," p. 88 (as quoted from *Action Programme*, p. 76).

[26] COMECON's active members are the Soviet Union, Poland, Czechoslovakia, East Germany, Hungary, Rumania, Bulgaria and Mongolia.

[27] UN. ECA. *Economic Bulletin for Africa* [*Part B; Special Articles*], p. 66.

Although the EACSO's future is in doubt, there is a possibility that it may lead to attempts to co-ordinate regional economic activity and planning. Finally, in Latin America, intense efforts are being made on many fronts to further hemispheric economic co-operation and integration through regional planning. Indeed, it has been claimed that the evaluation of national plans on the basis of formally established criteria by the Alliance Committee of Nine

> is in effect a beginning of multinational planning. Programs and policies within national plans are . . . tested . . . for consistency with what other Latin American countries are doing, or propose to do, and potential conflicts are brought to the forefront.[28]

SUMMARY AND CONCLUSIONS

In summary, planning has been defined in many ways, but most authorities agree that it is, in essence, an organized, conscious and continual attempt to select the best available alternatives to achieve specific goals. Planning involves the economizing of scarce resources. It has been used for a variety of ends, by different societies and in different ways. It is not limited to totalitarian or socialistic solutions. It can be and is used by democratic and capitalistic countries.

It has been employed in wartime and peacetime. It has a long history in physical planning for towns and rural areas. Planning as anticyclical or stabilization planning has been used effectively in advanced countries like the Netherlands and Sweden. Wartime, town and country, and anticyclical planning have elements in common with development planning and all of them have contributed to development planning in various ways from their experience.

Development planning may appear at times to resemble anticyclical planning, but it is fundamentally different. The basic objective of anticyclical planning is to increase demand within the prevailing economic and social institutional framework of a market economy, while development planning seeks to change that framework in the process of securing an acceleration in the rate of economic and social progress. A shorthand statement of development planning's primary goals is: change plus growth. Some nations which profess to plan their

[28] Perloff, Harvey and Saez, Raul. "National Planning and Multinational Planning Under the Alliance for Progress," p. 51.

development seem to concentrate only on the element of change, while others seem largely to ignore it. But the need for change is widely accepted as important to, if not the very essence of, development planning.

For the purpose of this study, countries were considered to be engaged in development planning if their governments were making a conscious and continuing attempt to increase their rate of economic and social progress and to alter those institutional arrangements which were considered to be obstacles to the achievement of this aim. This definition has the effect of including most countries which make some effort to plan their development and to exclude those which make no pretense at planning.

Development planning includes subnational and multinational regional planning. Subnational regional planning may mean planning for one region, planning for a series of regions covering an entire country or the siting of projects to insure the best possible location of industry and to reduce economic disparities among the regions of a country. Multinational regional planning may refer to planning for an economic region which extends beyond the boundaries of one country. It may also refer to planning for one or more economic sectors of two or more countries; and it may refer to the co-ordination of national plans or to the setting of integrated targets for the economies of several countries which are members of an international regional organization.

Chapter III

The Spread of Development Planning

If planning did not exist, the logic of the
times would demand its invention.—Anonymous

EARLY PLANNING

TODAY, the national plan appears to have joined the national anthem
and the national flag as a symbol of sovereignty and modernity. But it
is only within the last decade, especially in the second half of the
decade, that the diffusion of development planning became world-
wide. Thirty-five years ago, no country was engaged in long-term
development planning on a continuing basis, although earlier examples
of planned development of a nation or a region can be found in the first
decades of this century, as well as in earlier periods going back to
antiquity. In ancient times, construction of highway networks, terraces
for agriculture, or irrigation and flood control systems involved a
considerable amount of development planning in Mesopotamia, Baby-
lonia, Egypt, India and China, as well as in pre-Columbian Indian
civilizations of Mexico, and Central and South America. In modern
times, development plans made their first appearance in colonial and
other dependent territories. The Belgian Government introduced a
public investment plan for the Belgian Congo's railways and mines in
1906 and a more extensive program of public works, which was carried
out over a period of years, in 1920. What appears to have been the first
outline of an integrated development plan in modern times was
advanced by the British Governor of the Gold Coast, now Ghana, in
1919 to cover a ten-year period.[1] But the widespread acceptance of
development planning as a means of accelerating the rate of economic
growth and achieving other development objectives is of very recent
origin.

---

[1] The so-called [Sir Gordon] Guggisberg Plan for 1920–30. See, Greenstreet,
D. K. "The Guggisberg Ten-Year Development Plan," pp. 18–26.

Prior to World War II, the Soviet Union was the only country engaged in systematic development planning, having adopted its First Five-Year Plan in 1929. The Soviet leaders considered planning a corollary to socialism, the means for creating

the material and technical basis of Communism and the highest standard of living in the world through the establishment of high and stable rates of growth and of optimal interrelationships in the development of the economy.[2]

The advent of planning in the USSR seems to have made an impression on Indian leaders long before political leaders in most other countries. As early as 1933, Shri M. Visveswaraya, one-time Chief Administrator of Mysore and a leader in the industrialization of southern India, prepared a ten-year plan for doubling India's national income.[3] When a Conference of Ministers of Industries, meeting in 1938 under the chairmanship of the President of the Indian National Congress, established a National Planning Committee, the Committee revived the idea of planning to double the national income in a decade. As in the USSR, the problem of economic backwardness was viewed mainly as one of "catching-up" with the advanced countries. The resolution setting up the National Planning Committee stated that catching-up was a matter of industrialization, and industrialization one of planning:

the problems of poverty and unemployment, of National Defence and of economic regeneration in general cannot be solved without industrialisation. As a step toward such industrialisation, a comprehensive scheme of National Planning should be formulated.[4]

Although World War II interrupted the work of the Committee, its activities made the Indian people and Government keenly aware of the need for planning. This awareness, and the agitation it produced, led the British Government in 1941 to appoint a high level government planning committee in India and to replace it in 1943 by an even higher level reconstruction committee of the Cabinet with the Viceroy as Chairman. Then in 1944, a Department of Planning and Development was set up. At the request of this Department, the Central and Provincial Governments prepared a number of projects to be under-

[2] Bor, Mikhail Zakharovich. "The Organization and Practice of National Economic Planning in the Union of Soviet Socialist Republics," p. 113.

[3] Visveswaraya, M. *Planned Economy for India.*

[4] Ghosh, O. K. *Problems of Economic Planning in India,* p. 46.

taken after the war. In 1944, also, eight leading Indian industrialists issued a plan, known as the Bombay Plan, which proposed doubling per capita income and trebling the national income in 15 years.[5] But the exigencies of war and the Indian political situation prevented the preparation and execution of development plans. Little was accomplished until partition of the country in August 1947 and attainment of independence gave new impetus to planning in both India and Pakistan.[6]

The history of development planning in the Philippines is generally similar. Interest in planning there became active as early as 1934, when the economic implications of impending independence were being discussed. In that year, the Philippines Economic Association issued a report advocating planned development of agriculture, fishing, industry, mineral resources, transportation and trade. In 1935, two months after the establishment of the Commonwealth, the transitional stage before independence, a National Economic Council was created to prepare development plans. Stimulated by the "New Deal" Government in the United States, with its ideas of planned mobilization and redistribution of production facilities and purchasing power, as well as regional planning through the Tennessee Valley Authority, interest in planned development in the Philippines intensified through the second half of the 1930's. But here, also, the outbreak of war interrupted attempts to give effect to planning proposals.

The war interfered with the growth of development planning almost everywhere, the exception being the Caribbean. Following recommendations made by a Royal Commission, appointed in 1938 to investigate civil disturbances and other grave problems created in the West Indies by a drastic decline in prices of that region's most important cash crops, the British Government in 1940 passed a Colonial Development and Welfare (CD&W) Act, superseding a Colonial Development Act passed in 1929, which provided for funds to be allocated to colonial development. The 1940 Act covered all British colonies, but during the war years shortages of materials and personnel made it impossible to carry out proposals for colonial development except in the West Indies. In nearby Puerto Rico, Governor Tugwell, appointed by the New Deal Government in the United States, and one of its staunchest exponents, strongly advocated planned development

[5] *Ibid.*, p. 48.
[6] *Ibid.*, pp. 47–48.

to reduce unemployment on the island through the increase of jobs and expanding production. Development planning started by a Planning Board established in 1942 was vigorously advanced through the war years. But the Caribbean was an exception; in most places the war hindered incipient development planning. Nevertheless, the war was a turning point for planning.

POSTWAR PLANNING

The experience of World War II, when the industrialized free-enterprise economies had used physical planning to insure that scarce materials and other commodities went to priority production, demonstrated that when the people of a country were moved by a common aim under emergency conditions, ambitious plans could be carried out. And after the war ended, continued shortages made it necessary for most countries to retain wartime planning measures for several years.

Europe. France became the first country in Western Europe to attack its reconstruction and development problems through a multi-annual plan. In France, pressure exerted by members of the postwar provisional Government to substitute planning to a considerable extent for market forces, which before the war had failed to remedy the effects of the great depression of the 1930's, led in 1945–46 to the preparation of the First (Monnet) Plan of Modernization and Equipment. From the Government's point of view, no other choice was feasible:

> France in 1945 had not only to rebuild the ruins of the war and to repair the damage of the Occupation period. It had to make good the lag it had suffered in relation to the other great industrial nations, not only during the wartime years of intensive technological innovation but also during the earlier period 1930–40. Modernization or decadence—that was the dilemma on which the authors of the First Plan centered their project.[7]

The coming of the European Recovery Program, or Marshall Plan, in 1948 soon increased the number of European nations with plans. Under the Marshall Plan, each participating country was required to prepare comprehensive four-year and annual plans embracing its

[7] Massé, Pierre. "French Economic Planning," p. 4.

resources and their utilization, which became the basis for governmental policy and action. During the Marshall Plan period, the United States actively supported the formulation of plans in these countries, a role which it considered consistent with its responsibility for providing aid for the reconstruction of Wesern Europe.

When the Marshall Plan ended, with its goals more or less accomplished, some of the countries involved retained and expanded their planning activities. Through its second and succeeding four-year plans, France sought to influence the rate and composition of investment in order to bring about a continuing high rate of economic expansion, while the Netherlands continued with annual plans directed primarily toward the maintenance of monetary and balance of payments stability and, secondarily, toward encouraging a level of economic activity appropriate to its resources. Meanwhile, in Eastern Europe, the countries which had come under Russian influence began planning on the Soviet model to expedite the rehabilitation and expansion of their nationalized economies.

Asia and the Middle East. At the end of the war, Asian countries which either had, or were about to, become independent, embraced planning to a much greater extent than countries in any other region. In the Philippines, a Joint Philippine-American Finance Commission, established to recommend measures which would allow the Philippines to recover from the effects of the war and to attain a rapid rate of economic growth, included in its 1947 report a five-year plan for capital investments for the 1947–51 period. This section of the report, known as the Hibben Plan, was the first of a long series of development plans in the Philippines. Some countries, outside as well as inside Asia, felt so strongly about the need for planning their development that they adopted a practice followed in the socialized countries of incorporating in their constitutions a requirement for planning. Thus, Burma which, like the Philippines, had established a central planning agency, the National Planning Board, before independence, adopted in Section 41 of its Constitution a provision that

the economic life of the Union shall be planned with the aim of increasing the public wealth, of improving the material conditions of the people and raising their cultural level, of consolidating the independence of the Union and strengthening its defensive capacity.

When Egypt entered into its abortive union with Syria, the provisional constitution for the UAR provided that the national economy would be organized in accordance with plans conforming to principles of social justice and aiming at a rapid improvement in the standard of living.[8]

In India, a vigorous resurgence of interest in planning followed the cessation of the war. Soon after the Interim Government was established in September 1946, an Advisory Planning Board was appointed to propose measures for co-ordinating planning activities, setting planning objectives and priorities and creating planning machinery. Among other proposals, the Board recommended that a central planning commission be established. But it was not until a Working Committee of the Indian Congress Party made a similar recommendation in January 1950 that the creation of the Indian Planning Commission was announced in February 1950, within a month of the promulgation of India's Constitution. Meanwhile, early in 1948, a few months after the partition of India, Pakistan had created a Development Board with authority to co-ordinate development plans, recommend priorities, watch the progress of development projects and report to the Cabinet on such progress. Pakistan was partly influenced by a desire to make more secure its economic independence from India, with which it engaged in what a high official has described as "a kind of 'growthmanship' rivalry."[9] But the deplorably low standard of living in the new nation also contributed to the Government's decision to engage in planning to speed up the country's development. Indeed, the resolution of the Working Committee of the Indian Congress Party which explained why planning was essential for India could also have been applied to Pakistan:

> The need for a comprehensive plan has become a matter of compelling urgency in India now owing to the ravages of the Second World War and the economic and political consequence of the partition of the country which followed the wake of the achievement of freedom and the steady worsening of the economic situation in India and the world.[10]

Development planning in Asia received new impetus through the newly formed Colombo Plan for Cooperative Economic Development

[8] National Bank of Egypt. *Economic Bulletin,* p. 6.

[9] Hasan, Said (Deputy Chairman, Pakistan Planning Commission). *Dawn,* August 14, 1963.

[10] Ghosh, O. K. *Problems of Economic Planning in India,* p. 50.

in South and Southeast Asia. In May 1950, member countries (at the time consisting of Ceylon, India, Pakistan, Malaya, Singapore, North Borneo and Sarawak) drew up six-year development plans for the period July 1951 to June 1957 to constitute a blueprint of the Colombo Plan. Although none of these plans were carefully prepared or carried out and some were replaced before their term ended, e.g., in India by the First Five-Year Plan in 1952 and in Pakistan by its First Five Year Plan in 1955, they captured the imagination of Asian political leaders and gave the region a lead in development planning which it has not lost. The conquest of Mainland China by a Communist regime brought the Soviet variety of planning to the largest country in Asia. Today, every Asian nation outside the Middle East, except Sikkim, has prepared a development plan of some kind.

Colonial Planning. The effectiveness of wartime planning in the United Kingdom and elsewhere, as well as the pioneering results of development planning in the West Indies in carrying out projects and programs under the CD&W Act of 1940, convinced the British Government that development planning for the colonies was desirable. In 1945, when a victorious end to the war was in sight, another Colonial Development and Welfare (CD&W) Act was passed which more than doubled the amount which the United Kingdom had previously been prepared to make available for colonial development. To give effect to the Act, the Colonial Office required the colonies to prepare and submit ten-year development plans for 1946–56, on the basis of which CD&W funds were to be apportioned. Because of postwar uncertainties and personnel shortages, most of the plans were not prepared and accepted before the end of the 1940's or the early 1950's. But then, a major shift had taken place in the purposes which the British Government sought to accomplish through the ten-year plans. The primary purpose of the Colonial Development Act of 1929 had been to help solve the unemployment problem in the United Kingdom. In contrast, the CD&W Act of 1940 had as its main purpose improvement of the welfare of the colonial territories. This was also the original purpose of the CD&W Act of 1945, but after the financial crisis of 1947 in the United Kingdom, increased output and income from which each territory could finance most of its own development became a main British objective of colonial development.

Other European colonial powers also adopted development planning for their colonies. More for strategic than for economic reasons,

France had pursued a policy designed to make the economies of its colonies complementary to that of metropolitan France in order to fit them into an "integrated autarkic imperial economy." [11] To this end, a Colonial Development Fund had been created in 1935 to provide investment resources for the colonies over a 15-year period. After the war, a ten-year colonial development plan, known as the *Plan Pleven,* was prepared for the years 1946 to 1956 which confirmed the prewar policy of integrated development. With the advent of the Marshall Plan, the *Plan Pleven* was replaced by the French four-year plans, covering the entire French Union.[12] Morocco, Algeria and Tunisia had special status as part of the territory of France. They had been excluded from the *Plan Pleven* for the colonial territories, but their plans were included as regional plans within the over-all four-year plans, eligible for Marshall Plan financing.

While most of the British CD&W plans had been prepared by the Colonial Governments in the territories, the French plans were usually prepared in Paris. Portugal drew up plans for its territories in Lisbon. In 1948–49 a Belgian mission, in co-operation with the colonial administration, prepared a Ten-Year Plan for the period 1950–59 for the balanced social and economic development of the Belgian Congo. A Ten-Year Plan for 1950–59 was also prepared for the Belgian Trusteeship Territory of Ruanda-Urundi; while the Netherlands, without Indonesia, concentrated on the preparation of a development plan for Surinam. At the request of the Netherlands and Surinam Governments, preliminary studies by Surinam's central planning agency were reviewed by a survey mission of the World Bank, in September 1951. On the basis of the mission's proposals, a Ten-Year Development Plan was issued by the Surinam Government in 1952 and a revised version was adopted in October 1954.

The World Bank. The World Bank has been an important agency, from about 1950, in starting or accelerating organized national developmental planning in many countries. As a result of recommendations by its survey and other missions, many countries and dependent territories have either established or reorganized central planning agencies, or prepared national development plans based on World Bank recommendations. In Iran, where planning activity began in 1946

---

[11] Niculescu, Barbu. *Colonial Planning, A Comparative Study,* p. 71.
[12] Plans for French Overseas Departments are still included in a section of the French National Plan.

with a Planning Committee of Iran's Central Bank and two government planning committees established to prepare plans for utilizing Iran's petroleum earnings for economic expansion, World Bank advice resulted in Iran's engagement of foreign consultants who helped prepare projects for implementing the country's First Seven-Year Plan of 1948. The World Bank also has furnished countries with resident advisers and other technical assistance to help prepare and implement national development plans and programs. In 1964, the Bank established a West African Office and an East African Office to help African countries prepare projects and programs, initially in agriculture and transportation.

Aid and Planning. The spread of development planning has also been stimulated by Western countries providing loans and grants. Whether or not these countries have favored planning for their own economies, they have accepted planning in recipient countries and often insisted on the formulation of plans before they extended aid to less developed countries. Thus, countries like the Republic of Korea, the Republic of China (Taiwan) and Afghanistan started to prepare plans mainly to meet requirements of donor countries which supply foreign aid. The United States has taken a strong stand in advocating development planning in less developed countries. In his State of the Union Address to the Congress of January 30, 1961, the late President Kennedy proposed that all United States foreign aid be extended on the basis of "orderly planning for national and regional development instead of a piecemeal approach." The Charter of the Alliance for Progress, the Program set up in 1961 by 20 nations in the Western Hemisphere as a co-operative effort to improve education, housing, health and economic growth in Latin America, requested Latin American countries to create or strengthen their long-term development planning machinery and facilitate the preparation and execution of long-term plans. In response, nine Latin American countries which previously had no central planning agencies, established such bodies and most Latin American countries started or intensified development planning activities. All Latin American nations now have national planning bodies engaged in some form of development planning.

Africa. Development planning in Africa, which had been greatly stimulated by the colonial powers, particularly by the British CD&W Act of 1945 and by French postwar plans, took a new importance as new States emerged on that continent. By the beginning of 1965, 35 independent African nations had formulated development plans. Among Africa's independent nations, only Ruanda had not formulated a development plan. But planning in Africa has not been restricted to the newer emergent nations. Ethiopia has had two five-year plans and, at the end of 1964, the Union of South Africa issued its first Six-Year Economic Development Programme for 1964–69.

Among the new nations of Africa, the limited purview of colonial planning was broadened to encompass nothing less than the full realization of economic potentialities. Thus, while Nigeria's planners agree that a significant amount of development took place in the ten years preceding independence, they believe it is nevertheless

> true to say that nature's rich endowment—in the shape of the country's lands, rivers, its underground wealth, the resources of its ocean front, and, above all, its virile population have scarcely yet been developed to a degree sufficient to alleviate the poverty of the bulk of the people.[13]

One planning objective in Nigeria, therefore, is the development of these natural endowments to support a continual improvement in her people's living standard. But

> the basic objective of planning in Nigeria is not merely to accelerate the rate of economic growth and the rate at which the level of living of the population can be raised; it is also to give her an increasing measure of control over her own destiny

by making the country less dependent on foreign assistance, foreign private capital and sudden changes in prices of her primary exports.[14]

These aspirations, which are by no means peculiar to Nigeria, have been given increased urgency by beliefs commonly encountered in developing countries that the breach between rich and poor countries has been widening, and that only planned development in the less advanced countries can halt or reverse the trend. As seen through Egyptian eyes,

> unprecedented prosperity in Europe and other developed countries which began shortly after the Second World War enhanced the desire of the rest of the world to achieve higher standards of

[13] Nigeria. Federal Ministry of Economic Development. *National Development Plan, 1962–1968*, p. 1.
[14] *Ibid.*, p. 3.

living. The widening gap in the standard of living between developed and under-developed countries raised more than one question concerning the means of . . . reaching the stage of mass consumption. . . . To cut through the vicious circle of poverty, economic planning was entrusted with the difficult job of upsetting the elements of stagnation and initiating a series of new invest-ments that may result in a new rising spiral of prosperity.[15]

Recent Developments. In the last few years, national development planning has also been adopted by most industrialized countries. After a long period of debate, the United Kingdom has begun to plan for development. In the spring of 1947, the Labour Government in power in the United Kingdom had established an Economic Planning Board composed of industrialists and labor unionists and a Central Economic Planning Staff in the Treasury to prepare long-term programs for man-power and resources. But except for a Four-Year Plan for 1948/49 to 1952/53 prepared for the Organization for European Economic Co-operation in 1948, no plans were published. The question of planning vs. free enterprise has been raised frequently as an aftermath of wartime planning, with the anti-planners generally in the ascendancy until the mid-1950's. But sentiment changed as the largely short-run policies (mostly fiscal and monetary) failed to increase production, productivity, and income while maintaining employment, price stability, and a bal-ance of payments surplus. There was, moreover, a growing belief that French planning without controls could also be employed in the United Kingdom. These factors brought a revival of prosposals for planning in the second half of the 1950's. In 1962, the Conservative Government in power established a National Economic Development Council (NEDC) which was charged with studying ways of removing obstacles to growth.[16] NEDC issued reports which included (a) five-year national accounts projections for 1961–66 and 1966–70 based on a growth tar-get of 4 per cent per annum (a rate substantially higher than the rate of 2.5 per cent which has prevailed in recent years in the United King-dom), and (b) a consideration of the policy implications involved in attaining the 4 per cent growth rate. When the Labour Government took office in 1964, it established a Ministry of Economic Affairs which immediately started working on a five-year development plan. In ad-

[15] National Bank of Egypt. *Economic Bulletin*, p. 5.
[16] Worswick, G.D.N. "A Technically Advanced Country: England," pp. 294–322 gives an excellent account of the background and the developments which led to the creation of the NEDC.

dition, planning machinery was set up for Northern Ireland and six English regions. Planning agencies are also to be established for South West England and for Scotland and Wales. The likelihood is therefore that planning will play an increasingly important role in the United Kingdom.

Italy [17] and Belgium,[18] using the French planning system as a model, are also planning their development on a national scale.[19] The Netherlands is preparing a five-year plan. Norway, which since 1954 has sought to rationalize and co-ordinate investment and economic policy through a system of four-year "national budgets," prepared by temporary secretariats in the Ministry of Finance, has now set up a permanent planning secretariat in the Ministry of Finance. In Sweden, where similar *ad hoc* Royal Commissions of experts have issued on their own responsibility economic forecasts since 1948 in the form of multiannual national budgets, a permanent Council of Economic Planning has been established under the chairmanship of the Minister of Finance, with a permanent secretariat in the Ministry of Finance. Most of the less industrialized countries in Europe have also turned to planning as an essential element for their development. Portugal began to plan its development in 1952, Eire in 1958, and Cyprus, Finland, Greece, Iceland, Malta, Northern Ireland, Turkey and Spain in the 1960's. In Finland, a special commission appointed by the Government, published a plan for 1960–70 with targets and recommendations of policy measures deemed necessary to fulfill the targets.[20] And in Denmark, the Government prepared a plan for the development of public investment for three fiscal years beginning in 1965. Outside of Europe, Japan approved its first five-year development plan in 1955; and Canada established a 28-member Economic Council of Canada which has made forecasts of the expected rates of growth in incomes and output in 1965–70, on the basis of what the economy can be expected to do and what it could do if resources are used efficiently. The gap between the two, "points to the problems." [21]

Among the more important industrialized nations, only the Federal

[17] A national Economic Planning Committee started work in the autumn of 1962. A five-year plan for the period 1965–69 has been prepared and approved.

[18] A Program for Economic Expansion for 1962–65 was approved by the Belgium Senate in June 1963.

[19] Belgian planning also borrowed the Netherlands' technique of basing the plan on an analysis of prospective trends.

[20] UN. ECE. "Long-Term Planning in Western Europe," p. 59.

[21] "Canada's Planners Walk a Tightrope," *Business Week*, p. 148.

Republic of Germany and the United States have not taken steps to engage in national development planning. It remains to be seen whether Germany can long resist the pressures which have made the other regular members of the European Economic Community, or European Common Market, resort to national planning. These pressures are likely to increase when the European Economic Community begins to co-ordinate the medium-term economic policies of its member countries in a program scheduled to start January 1, 1966. As the result of greater interdependence which the program is likely to foster within the Community, Germany may find it undesirable to forego the possible advantages which co-ordinated planning gives to its trading partners in the Common Market. Several State governments in Germany already engage in planning and the Federal Ministries of Transport, Post Offices and Health have each prepared multiannual investment programs in their fields of activity. In addition, the Government has recently established a four-year framework for its annual budget. The Federal Government plays a strong role in the economy. Between 1948 and 1957, public investment exceeded 40 per cent of total new investment. A series of Government measures passed to promote investment in certain sectors and exports has also increased the extent of Government intervention in the economy.[22] The Government has also established a Council of Economic Advisers to report annually on the possibilities for achieving the Government's economic objectives, including a steady and appropriate rate of growth. It may be, therefore, that only a doctrinal vocabulary separates Germany from planning.

In the United States, the Kennedy Administration had indicated that it aimed to increase the annual growth rate in the United States in the 1960's from 2.5 per cent prevailing in 1953–60 to 4 per cent or more. Dr. Walter W. Heller, then Chairman of the U.S. Council of Economic Advisers, said that the United States'

> commitment to growth is clearly reflected in its 1961 pledge in concert with the other 19 members of the OECD to seek an increase of 50 per cent in the combined output of the Atlantic Community in the decade of the Sixties [and] in the President's stated determination to achieve once again the rates of growth of 4 per cent, or better, that we experienced in the early postwar period.[23]

[22] Blass, Walter P. "Economic Planning European-Style," p. 113.
[23] Heller, Walter W. "The Commitment to Growth."

For a decade from 1933, the United States had a National Planning Board, renamed the National Resources Planning Board, which was concerned with national, regional and sectoral planning. But it did not succeed in creating co-ordinated planning machinery before it was abolished by congressional decision in 1943. The Employment Act of 1946, which established a Council of Economic Advisers in the Executive Office of the President and a Joint Economic Committee in the Congress, requires the President to send Congress an Economic Report at least once a year. The Report is expected to set forth the levels of employment, production and purchasing power required to accomplish the purposes of the Act; to estimate the likely levels of employment, production and purchasing power under existing conditions; and to indicate changes in policies and legislation required to achieve the Act's goals. Although the Act has been considered by some to be a mandate for planning,[24] neither the Council of Economic Advisers nor the Joint Economic Committee has interpreted it in this way or attempted to develop a planning apparatus to achieve the Act's purposes. Many government agencies have prepared multiannual programs of their own, especially in the Department of Defense, but except for limited attempts by the U.S. Bureau of the Budget, no agency relates these programs to over-all development goals.

There are U.S. officials who would support national planning to raise the rate of U.S. domestic economic growth, reduce unemployment and co-ordinate U.S. economic policies with those of the Atlantic Community. The American Federation of Labor and the Congress of Industrial Organizations (AFL-CIO) has proposed that a national planning agency be established to evaluate national resources and needs and set priorities in the application of resources for meeting those needs.[25] Some American business leaders are also interested in the applicability of planning to American economic problems. In June 1962, the Committee for Economic Development, an organization sponsored by large American corporations, sent a group to Europe to learn how planning worked there and to seek an answer to the question the late President Kennedy had asked a month before: "What is it they are doing that perhaps we could learn from?"[26] Under authority granted by the Congress, the U.S. Bureau of Labor Statistics has been making two long-term projections of the national income in 1970 on the

[24] See, for example, Colm, Gerhard. "Economic Planning in the United States," p. 40.
[25] *New York Times*, November 20, 1963.
[26] Blass, Walter P. "Economic Planning European-Style," p. 113.

basis of alternative rates of growth of 4 and 5 per cent per annum, as opposed to the historical rate of 3 per cent. The Government expects that the study, which is being supervised by an interagency Committee on Growth headed by a member of the Council of Economic Advisers, will furnish information about what makes the U.S. economy grow and what steps Government and business will have to take to make the economy grow faster.[27]

In April 1963, President Kennedy created an Appalachian Regional Commission composed of federal and state officials to propose means for improving the rate of progress in a depressed region of 165,000 square miles covering parts of 11 eastern states and including some 16 million people. The Commission prepared a six-year plan for the region which emphasizes the opening up of isolated areas through the construction of highways and access roads. The plan also provides for the establishment of new health and education facilities, land restoration, mine reclamation and timber development. In March 1965, a Federal law was enacted authorizing the use of funds for the first two years of the six-year plan. When the Appalachia Region legislation was being discussed in the Congress prior to its enactment, legislators from other regions indicated that they would introduce legislation to promote regional planning for greater growth in their own regions. The Johnson Administration has indicated that it would support other soundly conceived plans for regional development. The outlook is, therefore, that regional planning, which started in the United States in the 1930's with the establishment of the Tennessee Valley Authority, will soon spread to other parts of the country. If this happens to a considerable extent there may be need for Federal action to coordinate planning in the various regions.

SUMMARY AND CONCLUSIONS

In summary, national development planning has now spread throughout the world, as much to the more advanced as to the less developed countries. The unprecedented economic expansion in Europe during the postwar years has made the governments of less advanced countries profoundly concerned with the problem of raising living standards in their own countries. Rightly or wrongly, the general

[27] *Washington Post,* August 18, 1963.

belief in developing countries is that national planning has contributed greatly to European prosperity. This belief is fortified by the growing emphasis on planning within the European Common Market and the adoption of development planning by almost every European country.

These events have produced a demand in the less developed nations for faster progress toward fuller development. At the same time, rapidly rising populations in less developed countries have made a high level of economic growth mandatory if annual per capita income is to increase. In Thailand, where population is growing at over 3 per cent annually, a high official considered "economic planning a matter of necessity rather than choice." [28] While in Ethiopia,

> the introduction of planning . . . was based on the conviction that progress could be accelerated only by planning. . . .[29]

A meeting of planners and planning experts in the Caribbean did not go as far as this, but it still held that

> sound planning for economic development is essential to secure orderly progress and social and economic improvement in individual countries, as well as within the Caribbean region as a whole. . . .[30]

Thus, national planning is widely believed to offer the means for overcoming obstacles to development and for ensuring systematic economic growth at high and constant rates. In the words of one observer, all Asia—he could as well have said all the world—

> today is plan-minded: among the newly self-governing nations central economic planning is widely regarded as an *open sesame* which will allow them to pass through the barrier dividing their pitifully low standard of living from the prosperity of their former rulers. . . . they feel they must make a big effort to catch up. But this, they are convinced, requires a central plan. . . .[31]

The "demonstration effect" of Russian planning in transforming the USSR from a backward nation into one with the second largest

---

[28] *Christian Science Monitor,* September 28, 1963 (citing the Deputy Minister of Development).

[29] Ethiopia. Office of the Planning Board. *Second Five-Year Development Plan 1955–1959 E.C.,* p. 1.

[30] Caribbean Organization. *Report of Joint Meeting of Planners and Planning Experts and Standing Advisory Committee of the Caribbean Plan,* p. 8.

[31] P.E.P. *Planning in Pakistan,* p. 87.

industrial sector in the world in only four decades has been important in popularizing planning. More recently, the successes ascribed to French planning have inspired many countries to start planning. The trend was encouraged further by foreign aid programs and international institutions engaged in the lending.

The expanding interest of less developed countries in planning for economic development is reflected in recent United Nations resolutions calling for international action to strengthen national planning activity and the considerable number of international conferences and institutes devoted to economic development and development planning. The United Nations Commissions for Asia, Africa and Latin America have published manuals on techniques of planning and programing, and all have either established or are in process of establishing economic development institutes to advise and train planners in their regions. The Economic Development Institute of the World Bank, which was the first in the field, has expanded its activities with courses related to development planning in English, French and Spanish, and with courses in project evaluation.

The world-wide acceptance of planning as a means of achieving national developmental objectives has made academic the doctrinal debate about whether a country should plan. For most countries, the question now is how to plan. There are still those who equate planning with socialism or with central controls harmful to freedom and private enterprise, but these are a dwindling band! Arthur Lewis' assertion that "we are all planners now" [32] may have been premature when first published in 1949, but it is not likely to be seriously disputed today.

[32] Lewis, W. Arthur. *Principles of Economic Planning*, p. 14.

Chapter IV

Stages of Development Planning

. . . if there existed a universal mind that projected itself into the scientific fancy of Laplace; a mind that could register simultaneously all the processes of nature and society, that could measure the dynamic of their motion, that could forecast the results of their interaction, such a mind, of course could *a priori* draw up a faultless and an exhaustive economic plan, beginning with the number of hectares of wheat and down to the last button for a vest. In truth, the bureaucracy often conceives that just such a mind is at its disposal.—Leon Trotsky.

INTRODUCTION

DEVELOPMENT PLANNING takes many forms. It is not the same for all countries, nor is it the same for one country at different times. The nature of a country's development planning is influenced by many elements, like the availability of natural resources, skilled manpower, and the levels of technical, administrative and managerial competence. But two factors, more than any others, condition the form and role of a country's planning: its institutional framework and its stage of development. Despite some similarities, development planning in highly socialized economies therefore differs substantially from planning in mixed economies, and the planning in both socialized and mixed economies at early stages of their development differs greatly from their planning at later stages.

National development planning as it has existed in the Soviet Union, as well as in countries of Eastern Europe, has been a detailed, pervasive and highly centralized administrative system of resource allocation and production based on the quantitative reconciliation of needs and available supplies through a system of "balances,"[1] reaching

[1] These balances are prepared in physical and monetary terms for (1) machines, (2) materials and (3) manpower.

down to every plant and collective farm. In contrast with mixed-economy countries, markets, prices and profits are supposed to play only a minor part in regulating the balance of supply and demand.

In the mixed economies, development planning almost always starts on a piecemeal basis with the formulation of public investment projects one by one without a common perspective or unifying framework. Under both systems, however, the forms of national development planning evolve as development proceeds and planners gain more experience. But while planning in the socialized economies tends to become less detailed and less centralized, development planning in the mixed economies tends to become more detailed, more comprehensive and more centralized.[2]

THE SOCIALIZED COUNTRIES

Evolution of Central Planning

In the classic type of centralized planning, the state controls, through regulations and directives, the level of savings, the amount and composition of output and investment, and the structure of prices. Central control over production in agricultural co-operatives or privately owned farms and over consumer expenditures is maintained through a system of price regulation and credit management. For other economic branches, central planning authorities issue elaborately detailed directives and instructions to enterprises specifying what and how much they have to produce, where they are to obtain their raw materials and supplies and how much they are to pay for them, how much labor is to be employed and what its compensation is to be, how costs are to be determined, what prices are to be charged for output and where it is to be delivered, what investments are to be made and so forth.

Governmental authorities and economists in socialized countries contend that central planning was essential for their countries at early stages of development to transform the social and economic structure and to develop capital goods industries. They feel it was also needed to conserve scarce resources and to assure their allocation to strategic national goals and priority projects. They believe that in backward economies in early stages of development, decentralized investment

[2] Mason, Edward S. "Some Aspects of the Strategy of Development Planning—Centralization vs. Decentralization," p. 4.

decisions lead to haphazard, piecemeal development which do not accord with national objectives. Thus, Dr. Oskar Lange, the well-known Polish economist, has argued that in the socialized countries,

> the necessity of centralised planning arose from two considerations. One was the need to mobilise and canalise all the resources to the industrialisation process. Consequently no leakage of resources for non-essential purposes could be tolerated and all the resources were centrally and tightly managed and administered.

> The other reason was as follows. Development of industries in backward countries meets with the difficulty of lack of experienced managerial personnel. . . . But when competent managerial personnel is lacking one has to depend on the centre from where all the actions will be dictated. In this way the centralised system of management of the economy was born. Historical evidences have shown that such management proved useful.[3]

It is true that when economies are simple, as they are at first in most less developed countries, the greatest needs are clear and feasible alternatives for allocating resources are few. Central planners then find it possible to channel investments into interrelated projects which are effective in getting development started and in accelerating the rate of output. By shifting underemployed labor from agriculture to industry, standardizing products, concentrating on a few basic sectors, and relegating agriculture and consumer goods industries to subordinate positions in the scale of priorities, it has in fact been possible to increase for a period the rate of output in socialized countries through highly centralized planning and control.

As development proceeded however, economic interrelationships became more complex. The number of industrial, construction and other establishments multiplied. Possible choices for employing resources increased, making it progressively more difficult to plan everything from the center. Planners found it harder to take account of frequent changes in the economy and to predict results. The gap between their intentions and events widened. Since management rewards in a centralized planning system are based on production rather than profit, enterprises tended to give greater attention to fulfilling production quotas than to operating at lowest cost. Because a

[3] Lange, Oskar. "Economic Planning and Management in the Socialist Economy of Poland," pp. 157–158.

factory's production quota was likely to be raised if it overfulfilled its quota, a plant manager had an incentive to do no more than fulfill his quota. The system therefore tended to keep production lower than the potential. Supply difficulties compounded the manager's problem. Since fulfillment of a factory's quota depended on the availability of its raw material and other supplies, each manager spent much time ensuring that his plant was well supplied. This often resulted in excessive hoarding of raw materials and supplies. Since deliveries of quotas were more important than the salability of the goods produced, quality gave way to quantity. If goods produced did not sell, large inventories of finished goods accumulated while factories continued without abatement to produce more of the goods already in surplus. Enterprises had no incentive to produce what people wanted or to deliver their output where it was needed most. Consequently, frequent complaints were heard of poorly made products and simultaneous gluts and scarcities of the same commodity in different parts of a country. Serious planning miscalculations resulted in overproduction in some sectors and shortages in others. This was especially true of consumers' goods. Large stocks of unsold clothing, shoes, cloth and other commodities accumulated in the shops while other products like refrigerators, furniture and cars were quickly taken up by eager buyers who wanted more than there was to buy.

In initial stages of development, when the primary aim was to reduce consumption to the levels of output of the few kinds of consumer goods allowed to appear in a sellers' market, prices could be fixed centrally without serious repercussions arising from errors; but as consumers were given a greater choice as the variety and quantity of goods increased, they frequently rejected what was offered for sale at prices shown. When this happened or when other events did not develop as expected in the plan, it took too much time to get a decision to change prices or production. In Poland, as in other socialized countries,

> before the centre was informed, before the information went from office to office and before the administrator could make up his mind as to what to do about it all and the order went back, the situation was completely changed.[4]

Moreover, having central controls over almost every aspect of enterprise operations tended to stifle initiative and creativity, lower

[4] *Ibid.*, p. 164.

productivity and reduce the quality and quantity of output; yet, paradoxically, increasing numbers of enterprises and greater complexity of the economy were making planners lose control over enterprises and local administration. Misallocations of materials and other mistakes multiplied. Output targets for heavy industry were usually fulfilled, but production in light industry and especially in agriculture, generally were below plan targets. In turn, the fall in agricultural output led to serious problems for the supply of materials to industry and foodstuffs to populations.[5]

Evidence that something had gone wrong with the planning system manifested itself in substantial shortfalls in plan targets, as with Yugoslavia's First Five-Year Plan, Poland's Five-Year Plan for 1961–65 and the USSR's Sixth Five-Year Plan for 1956–60. Shortfalls made necessary important revisions in many plan targets, as with East Germany's Plan for 1959–65 and the USSR's Seven-Year Plan for 1959–65; or even the complete abandonment of a plan during execution, as with Czechoslovakia's Third Five-Year Plan for 1961–65, Mainland China's Second Five-Year Plan or the USSR's Sixth Five-Year Plan for 1956–60.

The inability to carry out plans was customarily followed by a period of stocktaking and government admission that something had gone wrong with the planning process. Thus, in Czechoslovakia, the Premier attacked the "ineffectiveness of the national economy," the

> low standards of management and planning, and the systematic failure to fulfill targets in certain important branches of the economy.[6]

Such "self-criticism" produced a realization that quality, variety and efficiency were as important as higher output in building a modern economy, a search for more rational ways of allocating resources and a recognition of the importance of incentives in improving efficiency in socialized enterprises. Eventually, steps were taken, at first hesitantly, then resolutely, to decentralize some economic decision-making. In Yugoslav, Polish and Czech agriculture, it also led to a reversal of earlier attempts to collectivize peasant farms when it became evident that the price of collectivization was too high and that collectivization was unnecessary for achieving national production objectives.

Yugoslavia was the first centrally planned country to introduce

[5] Spulber, Nicolas. "Planning and Development," p. 90.
[6] *Washington Post*, September 26, 1963 (quoting Premier Josef Lenart).

decentralizing innovations. Since the early 1950's, its planning system has been gradually transformed from a close copy of the Soviet model into one in which socialized enterprises operate increasingly within a market framework. While the USSR, Mainland China and Eastern European countries have not gone as far as Yugoslavia, they are nevertheless moving away significantly from centralized and detailed control over plan execution. Each of these countries, except Albania, is either seriously considering, or already experimenting with, methods for assessing the performance of socialized enterprises on the basis of their ability to increase "profits," i.e., net revenue, instead of their ability to fulfill centrally imposed quotas in terms of volume of output. These methods differ from country to country in detail, but they have one purpose in common: they all seek to find a working principle by which an enterprise will be able to recognize by itself what is socially desirable for it to produce and will then be motivated from within, instead of by directives from without, to produce it.[7] In essence, the devices adopted seek to achieve this objective by making the profitability of a factory depend on the extent to which it can satisfy the demand for goods. In the words of Yevsei G. Liberman, a Soviet economist who has taken a leading part in advocating decentralized management of the Russian economy,

> What is useful for the state must also be useful for the factory, and vice versa, what is useful for the factory must also be useful for the state.[8]

Simple conceptually, this precept nevertheless implies far-reaching changes in the management of socialized economies. In effect, it requires the substitution of market forces for central planners as prime regulators of production. It also requires that prices be largely determined by the market.

All proposals for decentralization, in Mainland China and Eastern European countries as well as in the USSR, have concentrated on the execution of plans. No one has suggested that the centralized preparation of plans be abandoned. Despite the similarities between the policies they propose and those found in market economies, those who advocate decentralization of plan execution do not consider their proposals antithetical to centralized preparation of plans. Quite the contrary. They contend that by liberating planners from the need to

---

[7] Holesovsky, Vaclav. "Czechoslovakia's Economic Debate," p. 15.
[8] "Experiment 52," *East Europe,* p. 27.

manage plan implementation they make it possible for them to give full time to the preparation of plans. Thus, Professor Yevsei G. Liberman of the Kharkov Institute of Engineering Economics writes that decentralized implementation of Soviet plans is

> quite compatible with the principle of central planning of the basic proportions and rates of development of the economy as a whole, and of individual branches and of geographic areas. It does not weaken central planning, but rather strengthens it, as it frees the planning bodies of detailed control, permitting them to concentrate on planning. . . .[9]

Nor do the advocates of profits as a measure of enterprise efficiency consider this proposal an implied abandonment of socialism since they view profits merely as a means of fulfilling plans. Again, according to Professor Liberman, in the Soviet Union as in other socialized countries,

> a factory's profit cannot be appropriated by its heads or by the collective as a whole. Large investments out of the profit are made only under the central plans, but with consideration given to the factory's proposals. A certain share of the profit goes for incentive premiums to the personnel. But these premiums are a form of socialist remuneration according to labor performed; they do not create owners of private capital.[10]

The Pattern of Decentralization

The innovations undertaken by Yugoslavia decisively established a new pattern of socialized planning. Although central control over the amount and general direction of investment was retained, many decision-making powers were delegated to nonpolitical authorities under a more or less self-adjusting system of automatic economic controls. These changes gradually eliminated most detailed planning measures and controls over the economy. Under the prevailing Yugoslav system, socialized enterprises, managed through workers' councils elected by the workers themselves, are permitted to make significant decisions about what they make, from whom they buy, and to whom

[9] Liberman, Yevsei G. Letter to *Economist*, October 31, 1964, p. 453.
[10] *Ibid.*

they sell, the prices they pay or set, the number of employees engaged, the wages paid, etc. There is no guaranteed market for what enterprises produce and they must compete with other enterprises for buyers, as they must for skilled workers, technicians, raw materials and invest- ment capital. Restricted only by general regulations which do not differ fundamentally from those found in mixed economies, enterprises are allowed considerable latitude to allocate their profits to wages or investment. Moreover, the Yugoslav Government considers its present form of plan implementation only a phase in a constantly evolving system which will continue to decentralize further as development continues.

In other socialized countries, however, especially in the USSR, in- novations have been slower in coming. Decisions to make profound changes in the management of their economies could not be taken lightly in countries where every branch and sector had become intricately intertwined with others in a pattern determined by central- ized controls. To greatly reduce controls over enterprises which have been subject to detailed direction from the center posed serious questions. With less control, might there not be interruptions or breakdowns in the flow of essential commodities with potentially dire results for an economy? What would prevent managers and workers released from controls from consuming profits which should be in- vested in order to secure planned levels of national growth? Might not enterprises which were free to raise prices create a price inflation? Was it possible to avoid the hazards of reduced controls by introducing procedural reforms in the existing system which would allow central planners to respond with the necessary flexibility and speed to the expanding demands of the economy?

Because of the uncertainties, the decisions to change the system have been preceded by prolonged controversy and debate. The discussions in the USSR have been particularly prolonged and revealing of the issues. On one side have been a conservative group of officials and economists who fought to retain central controls as essential to the socialized system. In January 1965, academician N. Fedorenko, a leader of the conservative school, wrote in *Pravda:*

> We should never forget that centralized, unified planning is one of the greatest achievements of the Socialist system. Centralized planning must not be weakened but improved.[11]

[11] As quoted in *Bangkok Post,* January 18, 1965.

Fedorenko and others have advocated the retention of central controls through the introduction of mathematical methods involving "inter-branch balances" (i.e., input-output analysis), cybernetics and the use of a nation-wide network of computers which they have contended could quickly produce the answers to the economic questions posed by an increasingly complex Soviet economy.

On the other side have been a large and influential group of economists who have held that the basic problem was not one of improving the internal balance of plans but of relating resources to final demand in a more effective and economically rational manner.[12] This group has made a series of proposals to this end. One proposal, by Professor Vasily S. Nemchinov, who headed a high-level study group in the Soviet Academy of Sciences, advocated replacement of detailed production plans for enterprises by a system of contracts based on competitive bidding by enterprises.[13] Another, made by Professor Vadim A. Trapeznikov, Director of the Institute of Automation and Telemechanic, advocated that (1) the USSR emulate Western systems of tax exemptions on corporate income invested in research and development as a way of stimulating technical progress; (2) heavy fines be levied on suppliers for delayed deliveries of goods as a way of reducing the delays which frequently slow down the flow of Soviet production; (3) enterprises be charged interest on their capital to encourage efficient utilization of equipment and to accelerate the turnover of operating capital frequently frozen in excess inventories; (4) profits be used as the key indicator of enterprise performance; (5) a system of flexible prices be introduced to reward plants producing new, better quality or essential goods by allowing them to set higher prices at first to compensate them for higher initial costs of introducing such goods; and (6) enterprise managers be given greater freedom to make decisions through a reduction in the number of "economic" indicators (e.g., wage fund, administrative expenditures, size of inventories, number of administrative staff, etc.), each of which may not be exceeded.[14] Still another noted economist, V. Yagodkin, called for reform of the existing bonus system which, based on the fulfillment and

[12] Holesovsky, Vaclav. "Czechoslovakia's Economic Debate," pp. 17–18.
[13] *New York Times*, April 11, 1964 (based on an article in *Kommunist*—the ideological journal of the Communist Party of the Soviet Union).
[14] Trapeznikov, Vadim A. "For Flexible Economic Management of Enterprises," pp. 3–7. Also, *New York Times*, August 18, 1964, and the *Christian Science Monitor*, August 20, 1964.

overfulfillment of production plans, encouraged plants to seek low-output plans which they could easily fulfill. He proposed, instead, that bonuses be paid for quality of output, prompt delivery of orders, and higher profit earnings.[15] The proposals of Professor Yevsei G. Liberman aroused the most discussion. He suggested that enterprises be encouraged to produce more and better products at lower cost by allowing them to apply their profits to the improvement of their own machinery and equipment, as well as to increased bonus payments for workers. To accomplish this, he proposed a series of ways of reducing central planners' control over factory operations and of giving enterprises greater freedom to determine their own production, the number of workers employed and the wages paid.[16]

Although resistant at first and wavering for a time, Soviet authorities appear to have decided that they have more to gain than to lose by experimenting with decentralized implementation of plans, at least for commodities produced for public consumption. Some steps toward decentralization of plan implementation had been taken as early as 1957, with the formulation of 103 territorial economic councils (*sovnarkhozy*) and 18 major economic regional bodies for coordinating the *sovnarkhozy*. Thereafter, decentralization moves developed more slowly, but the setting of some targets and the making of other planning decisions, formerly prerogatives of the center, were transferred to the republics, regions, territories or enterprises. At the end of 1962, the Government approved the creation of production committees in plants. These committees, which are elected by the workers, participate in the discussions affecting the establishment and execution of enterprise plans, the setting of work quotas and the placement of personnel in the plants. Managers of enterprises are supposed to report to the committees and consult them on production matters.[17] Under the terms of a decree issued in March 1964, collective and state farms have been given greater independence, especially in determining the kind and amount of crops to be planted, the number of cattle to keep, and so on.[18]

    [15] *New York Times*, November 24, 1964.
    [16] Other Soviet economists, among whom Professors L. V. Kantorovich and V. V. Novozhilov are best known, also made proposals for decentralizing plan implementation and for changing the role of planning, especially through the introduction of mathematical concepts.
    [17] Bor, Mikhail Zakharovich. "The Organization and Practice of National Economic Planning in the Union of Soviet Socialist Republics," p. 110.
    [18] *Washington Post*, March 24, 1964.

More recently, in January 1965, after some experimentation with several pilot plants, the Soviet Government announced that beginning April 1, 1965, 400 textile, leather, garment and footwear plants, constituting 25 per cent of the country's garment and shoe industries, will gradually change over from the system of centrally imposed production quotas to one in which the production of each plant will be determined by orders placed by their customers. The managers of these plants have been authorized to prepare production plans, determine the number of workers and office employees, and the size of the wage bill on the basis of purchases made by its customers. They are also given leeway to pay bonuses and other rewards for improved quality and speed of output and for other actions which increase enterprise profits. Prices are to be set contractually between buyers and sellers at levels which authorities hope will move the goods produced. They also hope that the greater voice which managers have in setting prices for their goods, as well as elimination of the need to meet production quotas, will encourage factories to introduce innovations in the kinds of goods they produce.

It was subsequently announced that four food processing enterprises in Moscow, Leningrad and Kiev are to convert to the new system in the fourth quarter of 1965. There have also been some indications that centralized planning controls over the machine-building industry are to be relaxed. But at the same time, the Government has taken steps to recentralize control over defense and space (called heavy and medium machinery) industries. In March 1965, a decree removed these industries from the jurisdiction of the *sovnarkhozy* and put them under the direction of reconstituted central ministries, thereby reverting to the general situation which prevailed before 1957. There are also other signs of recentralization. The number of *sovnarkhozy* has been reduced to less than half, their control over some other industrial activities like construction and power generation has also been eliminated and the Ministry of Agriculture appears to be regaining the control it lost three years ago over farming. In the USSR, therefore, conflicting trends are apparent, with decentralization in consumer goods industries advancing simultaneously with recentralization in other branches of the economy.

In Mainland China, events followed a pattern which, while generally similar to the Soviet one, resulted in greater decentralization than in the Soviet Union. The Government soon found it too difficult to plan from Peking every phase of the economy in so vast a country. The difficulties were aggravated by the large labor surplus and the low level of per capita income in agriculture, and the great number of small enterprises using disparate and primitive technology in industry.[19] Almost immediately after gaining control of the Mainland in 1949, the new Government instituted a system of central planning in the Soviet fashion. Although impressive progress was made under the First Five-Year Plan, the waste and economic cost was high. Plans were handed down to enterprises too late and were changed too frequently. Industrial enterprises used expensive capital instead of cheaper labor to meet their output targets. As in the USSR, plant managers were interested solely in meeting their production quotas, with much the same results. Central planning controls broke down and enterprises were often able to circumvent directives from above.

Dissatisfaction with the wasteful procedures under the First Five-Year Plan led, in 1957, to far-reaching decentralization measures. While policy decisions remained centralized, a considerable amount of economic power over enterprises was transferred to greatly strengthened regional and local authorities. They acquired a voice in fixing targets, the allocation of materials, setting of prices and in financial matters affecting enterprises in their regions, and they shared in enterprise profits. Despite "creeping recentralization" after 1961, following the failure of the Great Leap Forward, the essential features of the 1957 decentralization measures remain in effect.[20]

Among the Soviet-bloc countries, Poland was the first to emulate Yugoslavia's decentralization of plan execution through the use of workers' self-management. Between mid-1956 and April 1958, enterprises were increasingly empowered to make a variety of decisions which had formerly been made at the center. Enterprise managers shared decision-making prerogatives with workers' councils. By the end of 1958, however, when Poland's economy encountered difficulties, the trend toward decentralization was reversed. But although the power of enterprises to make their own decisions has been reduced considerably below what it was in 1956–58, especially for workers' councils, some decisions formerly made by central planners are still made by enterprises. Since January 1963, 30 enterprises producing for export have been working experimentally with almost complete autonomy. There are also signs that large-scale decentralization may

[19] Perkins, Dwight H. "Centralization Versus Decentralization in Mainland China and the Soviet Union," p. 70.
[20] *Ibid.*, pp. 54–61.

again be tried.[21] Polish economists are again writing and discussing the disadvantages of centralization and the advantages of decentralization in the situation which now confronts the country. Thus, Oskar Lange has pointed out that

> the centralised system of management of the economy was found to be inflexible. It caused a certain bureaucratic inflexibility of the economy resulting from the fact that all decisions were taken by men at the top. The new task of raising the standard of living and of satisfying the increasing consumers' demand requires a system of management more flexible than that of the preceding period.[22]

To obtain a more flexible system, says Dr. Lange, requires, firstly, separation of plan implementation from plan formulation and, secondly, replacement of administrative direction of the economy with a system of economic incentives which stimulate plan implementation. In brief, this means that plan formulation must remain centralized while current management of the economy is decentralized.[23] An indication that Polish authorities were thinking along similar lines was given in 1964, at meetings of the Polish Communist Party, where officials discussed without apparent disagreement proposals for giving greater independence to enterprises and enhanced power to workers' self-governing bodies.[24]

Hungary is also experimenting with workers' management of enterprise. It was the first country in the Soviet bloc to apply an interest charge on all fixed and working capital of industrial and construction enterprises in an attempt to improve the efficient use of their equipment and operating funds.[25] A similar step is being contemplated in East Germany. Following the Soviet example, in which the USSR delegated some planning authority to 103 *sovnarkhozy*, East Germany established some 80 *Vereinigungen Volkseigener Betriebe,* as associations of socialized enterprises, and delegated some operational authority to them. In July 1963, the Government also adopted proposals which, if fully implemented, will result in far-reaching price reforms, increased reliance on economic incentives to increase output, and

[21] Shaffer, Harry G. "New Tasks for the Enterprise Director?" pp. 11–13.
[22] Lange, Oskar. "Economic Planning and Management in the Socialist Economy of Poland," p. 158.
[23] *Ibid.*
[24] Shaffer, Harry G. "New Tasks for the Enterprise Director?" p. 13.
[25] *Ibid.*, p. 14. Yugoslavia has had such charges since the early 1950's.

decentralization of plan implementation.[26] Bulgaria started on the road
to decentralization in 1963 with an experimental "new system of
planning" involving 52 enterprises, chosen from each of the main
industrial branches of the economy. Under the careful scrutiny of the
State Planning Commission, these enterprises are being permitted to
deal directly with those who buy their products. While prices are still
fixed by the planners, profits have become the main stimulus of the
enterprises in the experiment. At the end of each quarter, profits above
a certain level are distributed among workers as additions to their
basic salaries. Workers in the enterprises concerned participate with
enterprise managers through production committees in the preparation
of production plans, assigning workers to jobs and deciding for what
purposes profits will be spent.[27] Unlike almost all other Eastern
European countries, Rumania has made only a bare beginning in
delegating to enterprise managers the right to make decisions affecting
enterprise activities. But, then, Rumania has had little incentive thus
far to change its system of centralized management since its rate of
growth has been high—much higher than in any other Soviet-bloc
country.

In contrast, the virtual stagnation of Czechoslovakia's economy
made drastic changes in the system of administrative management of
the economy in that country a matter of great urgency. Between 1958
and 1961, a series of reforms had been introduced which sought to find
some way out of difficulties into which the economy had run without
discarding the essential principles of the Soviet centralized planning
system.[28] But the attempt failed and increases in output virtually came
to a halt. After a prolonged and frequently bitter debate, the Czech
authorities approved a series of reforms at the end of 1964 and the
beginning of 1965 which promise to transform Czechoslovakia from
one of the most dogmatic practitioners of command planning to the
pacemaker—after Yugoslavia—of decentralization in Eastern Europe,
far ahead of Poland, Hungary, East Germany, Bulgaria and the
USSR.[29]

The State Planning Commission will no longer issue instructions to
factories. Instead, it will only produce over-all plans which indicate
major trends for development of the economy and give general

[26] *Ibid.*, pp. 18–19.
[27] "Experiment 52," *East Europe*, p. 27.
[28] Montias, John M. *Evolution of the Czech Economic Model, 1949–1961*, p. 115.
[29] *Statist*, January 15, 1965, p. 152.

guidelines for investment, use of credit, price policy, etc. Vertical trusts composed of enterprises producing one kind of commodity at different stages of production, e.g., raw materials, components and finished products, and horizontal trusts made up of plants producing the same kind of commodities will largely direct their own affairs. They will negotiate directly with suppliers of their materials and buyers of what they produce and set prices of the goods they sell. They will be allowed to increase or reduce their work forces, fix wages for their workers above prescribed minima and benefit or suffer from profits or losses incurred in competition with domestic and foreign producers. Workers will be given incentives in the form of shares in enterprise profits. But first, receipts from sales will have to be used to pay for materials, power, transport and depreciation, and to lay aside sums for the payment of interest on capital and loans, taxes and necessary investment. Only what remains will be available for wages, allowances and bonuses. Enterprises will have to pay income taxes to the Government and interest on capital employed, and take account of depreciation. While investment in basic development projects will continue to be centrally planned, enterprises will be able to modernize or rationalize production facilities by reinvesting their own profits or by drawing on bank credits. Subsidies to enterprises from the State budget will be eliminated, even if this means that some factories will have to shut down. Depreciation policies will be directed toward encouraging the abandonment of outmoded techniques and price policies toward rewarding technical innovations and higher quality production. Prices are to reflect production costs and, with some reservations, the relation between supply and demand. While prices for power, basic production materials and essential consumer goods will still be fixed by the Government, some prices will be allowed to fluctuate within a broad range and the prices of other goods will depend entirely on agreements between suppliers and consumers. The structure of external trade is to be adapted to the internal changes by giving enterprises more of a voice in production for export. In some cases, enterprises and trusts will be able to participate directly in export and import trade. But hereafter, enterprises using imported raw materials will have to allow for their real costs in varying aspects of production.[30] The new system of planning and management of the

---

[30] *New York Times*, November 6, 1964; *Statist*, January 15, 1965, p. 152; *Economist*, November 28, 1964, p. 955, and January 23, 1965, p. 306.

economy, which was tested in 1965 in a few transportation and trade enterprises, 110 industrial plants and a larger number of local industries and producer co-operatives, is scheduled to go into full effect from the beginning of 1966.

For the time being, therefore, the reformists in the socialized countries who favor decentralization of plan implementation appear to have won the day. But the contest between them and those who oppose decentralization is not over. The success of decentralization depends on the co-operation of many people who are concerned about their own position.[31] Even Oskar Lange, a staunch defender of the present tendency toward decentralization of plan implementation in Eastern Europe has said:

> I am not at all sure whether this tendency is a permanent one. Further development of productive forces might necessitate a return towards centralization of management. . . .[32]

Nevertheless, the outlook is that the tendency toward decentralization of plan implementation will continue and even accelerate, although not without some halts and even retreats from time to time when the advance appears too rapid or the risk too great. At least some of those who had advocated retention of centralized controls over plan implementation seem to have become reconciled to the new order. One such advocate in the USSR, Academician Nikolai P. Fedorenko, recently indicated his belief that the problems raised by decentralized plan execution through the use of incentives and centralized plan formulation employing computers were not only soluble but dependent on each other:

> These two problems, the use of economic levers and stimuli on one hand and the organization of optimal planning on the other hand, are intimately related. They must not be torn apart or opposed to each other. They are two inseparable aspects of the process of further developing and strengthening democratic centralism [i.e., relative freedom under central control] in the management of the national economy.[33]

---

[31] One argument which advocates of reform have advanced is that decentralization would result, as it has in Yugoslavia, in substantial reductions in the number of central planning personnel and administrators.

[32] Lange, Oskar. "Economic Planning and Management in the Socialist Economy of Poland," p. 164.

[33] *New York Times,* January 18, 1965 (quoting Nikolai P. Fedorenko in *Pravda*).

According to reports, an ambitious blueprint has been adopted for initiating automation of plan formulation. The blueprint envisages covering the whole country with a network for channeling information required for planning. The core of the network would be formed by 50 key computer stations, each with a computing capacity of one to one-and-a-half million operations per second. The stations would be in direct connection with each other and with the USSR *Gosplan,* and with enterprises through a series of substations. The stations would collect data, digest them and distribute them to all levels of the economy. Such data as prices and rates of interest would be issued for use by enterprises and local authorities. While the blueprint is impressive, it is by no means excessive for a system of planning which, according to estimates, involves a programing problem with some 50 million unknowns and 5 million constants. But before the blueprint can be realized, the Soviet Union will have to greatly improve its computer technology. According to informed opinion, the Soviet Union appears to be well behind leading western countries in the availability and use of advanced computational equipment.

As part of the search for new methods and techniques, Russian economists and planners are turning to sophisticated mathematical and econometric concepts, described by a newly coined word, "planometrics." The use of planometrics represents a complete reversal of the former official attitude, which considered mathematical and econometric planning techniques to be inimical to Marxian theory. The drafting of the 1966–70 plan embodied the new approach. For the first time in Soviet history mathematical procedures and models were used to construct plan variants and to check strategic choices.[34]

THE MIXED ECONOMIES

Three Stages of Planning

The Project-by-Project Approach. In the mixed economies, development planning almost always starts on a piecemeal basis with the formulation of public investment projects little related to each other or to a unifying concept. Except for being listed in the budget, often with omissions, these projects may never appear in a single document; or they may be combined to form *ad hoc* development plans or pro-

---

[34] Zauberman, Alfred. "New Phase Opens in Soviet Planning," p. 13.

grams for the public sector which makes little or no reference to the private sector. They are, nonetheless, little more than collections of unrelated projects. The Ten-Year Plan of Development and Welfare for Nigeria prepared in 1945 and the revised Five-Year Plan which followed it, like others formulated in the British colonies to guide the allocation of CD&W funds, were examples of such plans. India's First Five-Year Plan for 1951–56 and Pakistan's first development plan, the Six Year Development Programme for 1951–57, were largely collections of projects in the public sector already under way. Many countries, either without formal development plans or with plans which are largely disregarded when annual budgets are prepared, continue to "plan" in this way.

The project-by-project approach has serious shortcomings. Sometimes accompanied by economic policies and measures intended to promote development, the approach is nevertheless characteristic of governments without a clearly defined development philosophy or a long-term outlook. There may be references to raising living standards, extending social services, stimulating exports or substituting for imports, but no real attempt is made to relate policy to investment or to stated objectives. Indeed, economic policies and measures are frequently at variance with objectives. A reliable estimate of investment resources does not exist and the Government does not have complete information on the magnitude or composition of current and prospective public investment. Nor is an effort made to establish priorities for projects on the basis of uniform economic, technical and administrative criteria, or to evaluate the feasibility of the program as a whole in relation to available funds, raw materials and other supplies, technicians, skilled manpower and management.

The project-by-project approach frequently results in the frittering away of public investment resources on too many small, unrelated projects or on a few unduly large ones. It may lead to over-investment in some sectors, where one ministry, department or agency is more efficient than others in carrying out projects. Since full financing in national and foreign currencies is not assured for each project at the start, completion of projects is frequently delayed when funds run out. Poorly prepared projects also cause great delays. These imbalances may be overcome in time, but in the short run they are wasteful and can create serious inflation, balance of payments and other problems. The example of Turkey, one of many, is illustrative. During the 1950's, public investment in that country proceeded on a project-by-project basis and output in some sectors reached high levels. But the lack of intersectoral co-ordination created serious imbalances and the failure to relate investment expenditures to resources released inflationary forces which ultimately had a depressing effect on the economy.

Inadequate from many points of view, the piecemeal, project-by-project approach has nevertheless provided many countries at the beginning of their development with means for laying a foundation for their development. Thus, although Iran's Second Seven-Year Plan was little more than a list of projects, whose execution was attended by waste and duplication, a great deal was accomplished. A high level of investment was maintained, several thousand miles of roads were built, the railroad and port systems were greatly expanded, airports and dams were constructed, and the basis was laid through preinvestment studies and the preparation of projects for further development. In some countries, where government officials or leaders are indifferent or incapable, where political instability causes frequent changes in the leadership of government or operating agencies, there may not be any workable alternative to the project-by-project approach. For some countries, at a certain period of their history, therefore, it may be necessary to postpone for a time attempts to accelerate development planning through more advanced techniques.

Integrated Public Investment Planning. But whenever possible, it is desirable to replace the project-by-project approach with integrated public investment planning, a more advanced planning procedure which is free of many defects of the project-by-project approach. The preparation of a well-prepared investment plan of this type begins with estimates of available public investment resources, in local currency and foreign exchange, taking account of the possibilities of increasing them through taxation, noninflationary domestic borrowing, and external loans and aid. Then, these resources, domestic and foreign, are divided among a selected group of sectors subject to public investment and finally among projects in each sector which have been ranked in order of priority. Priorities are determined on the basis of realistic estimates of costs and benefits, the relationship of each project to others completed, under way or contemplated, administrative and technical readiness to proceed with construction, as well as other pertinent criteria. Insofar as possible, projects are selected with a view toward increasing the sum of the benefits to be derived from a given total of investment. Thus, a project for a road which opens previously inaccessible farming areas may be made into a better investment by land reclamation or irrigation projects and by projects for processing and storing the crops produced in the region. From an examination of the available projects, it may be, and usually is, necessary to shift resources from one sector to another to provide funds for available high priority projects. Ultimately, therefore, an integrated public investment plan starts with individual projects which are combined into sector programs and then into an investment plan for the public sector.

An integrated public investment plan may be annual or multiannual, but whenever possible, it should be based on sector programs with a perspective of five or ten years or even more for some sectors like agriculture. This implies that at an earlier point, surveys of electric power, transport, agriculture or other critical sectors have been completed. Where such surveys are lacking, the plan gives high priority to making them. The public investment plan then becomes the basis for determining the items and amounts of public capital and current expenditures included in the national budget each year. In integrated public sector planning, government action in the private sector is mostly limited to the adoption of clearly desirable measures designed to improve the climate for private investment and to influence the general direction of private investment to conform to the plan's development objectives. But there is no attempt to relate projects and sector programs to a set of over-all production or income targets.

It would be hard to find many countries with investment plans which met all the requirements for a properly integrated public investment plan. In the less developed countries, public investment plans fall somewhere between the project-by-project approach and the integrated public investment plan, with most plans closer to the former than to the latter.

Comprehensive Planning. Comprehensive planning, also referred to as aggregative, global or over-all planning, covering an entire economy, is the most advanced form of development planning. It begins with the projection of a specific rate of increase in income or production over the planning period as the prime target. This rate is usually determined by relating the amount of savings or investment to the proposed increase in income or output by a "capital-output ratio" or "capital coefficient" which gives the units of capital outlay required to increase income or output by one unit. The formulation of a comprehensive plan then involves the construction of a growth model for the period of the plan which estimates the effect of the assumed rate of growth on such aggregates as public and private consumption, savings, investment, imports and exports, employment, and the demand and supply implications involved in producing the national product, by economic sectors and, sometimes, by regions. A variety of economic, statistical and mathematical calculations are made to relate inputs of labor, raw materials, land and capital equipment and the resulting outputs. Similar calculations show the relationship between income generated and expended for consumption, investment, government services, exports, etc. The results are tested to determine their compatibility with the targets, their consistency with each other and whether they are within reach of available resources.

Comprehensive planning includes both the formulation of an integrated public investment plan and a plan for the private sector [35] which have been reconciled with each other and with the over-all targets. This is accomplished by two procedures which move from the general to the particular and back again to the general. The first has been variously described as "forward planning," "planning from above" or "planning from-the-top-down" to emphasize the fact that it starts with the aggregate plan and targets and "disaggregates," i.e., divides these into interrelated plans and subtargets for each economic sector or region. The second procedure, the reconciliation of the individual public and private investment projects and programs with the aggregative planning model, has been described as "backward planning," "planning from below," or "planning from-the-bottom-up," to stress the fact that the actual public and private investment projects and programs proposed by various sponsors must be built up into sector programs or regional plans which are consistent with the comprehensive aggregative plan.

In the preparation of a comprehensive plan in most countries, planning from-the-top-down generally has preceded planning from-the-bottom-up. But good planning requires that planning from-the-bottom-up should start at least as early as planning from-the-top-down to make it possible for the two to converge and mesh. When properly carried out, this procedure is an exercise in successive approximation through trial and error at the end of which each project,

[35] In mixed economies, the program for the private sector is largely based on private investment programs and governmental policies designed to influence them.

sector program and regional plan has been made consistent with the plan's aggregative targets and vice versa.

Comprehensive planning is conceptually superior to partial planning because it permits estimates to be made of the level of savings, investment, imports, exports and other economic variables required to achieve a desired rate of growth in real per capita income. It is impossible to make such estimates within the context of a public investment plan because it covers only a part of the economy. In partial planning, there is also no way of making over-all judgments about the comparative advantage of public and private projects based on alternative costs of labor, capital and natural resources. This means that an evaluation of the relative roles of the public and private sectors and an economically appropriate division of resources between them can be made only within the framework of comprehensive planning. Without such a division, there is a risk that the demands for resources may exceed the supply, leading to scarcities, bottlenecks and imbalances which can impede development.

Because of the limitations of public investment plans, much of the discussion about planning has assumed that all countries should plan comprehensively. Although the Economic Commission for Asia and the Far East (ECAFE) found in 1961 that the capital-output ratios "in almost all countries of the region are not accurately known" and that "the exact increase in income . . . cannot be deduced from a given investment programme" without the capital-output ratio,[36] a group of eminent ECAFE experts, headed by Professor Jan Tinbergen, had recommended two years earlier that even countries like Nepal, Afghanistan, Burma and Thailand should try to plan through comprehensive growth models.[37] According to the Colombo Plan Bureau,

> economic growth through comprehensive national planning is the generally accepted policy of Colombo Plan countries, which include these [previously enumerated] countries, as well as others like Bhutan, Ceylon, Indonesia and Korea, which are also in early stages of development.[38]

The United Nations Economic Commission for Latin America

[36] UN. ECAFE. "Economic Development and Planning in Asia and the Far East," *Economic Bulletin for Asia and the Far East*, December 1961, p. 3.

[37] UN. ECAFE. *Programming Techniques for Economic Development with Special Reference to Asia and the Far East*, p. 75.

[38] "Program of National Plans," *Colombo Plan*, p. 1.

(ECLA) has for many years been a vigorous advocate of comprehensive planning in its region. As part of its effort to get countries in Latin America to plan comprehensively, ECLA began in 1953 to prepare for illustrative purposes aggregate and sectoral projections based on assumed rates of growth for a series of Latin American countries. These projections were designed to show the most desirable development of the national product and its composition. The projections were criticized as being unrealistic and there is no evidence that they influenced the internal policy of any country for which they were prepared. In the opinion of Professor Albert O. Hirschman, a well-known student of Latin American development,

> ECLA's detailed projections where all economic sectors are made to mesh harmoniously are in a sense the 20th century equivalent of Latin America's [idealistic] 19th century constitutions—and are as far removed from the real world.[39]

Nonetheless, ECLA's efforts eventually bore fruit. It was a prime mover in getting the "Declaration of Punta del Este," which launched the Alliance for Progress in August 1961, to include a provision that

> each of the countries of Latin America will formulate a comprehensive and well-conceived program for the development of its economy.

The United Nations Economic Commission for Africa (ECA) also advocates comprehensive planning for African countries although, according to an ECA report,

> all of them have in common that the statistical information required for comprehensive planning is inadequate and that the number of qualified people who could formulate and execute plans is still severely limited.[40]

Among African countries, Ethiopia, Morocco, Senegal, Tanganyika, the UAR and Upper Volta have either prepared or are preparing comprehensive plans based on growth models.

---

[39] Hirschman, Albert O. "Ideologies of Economic Development in Latin America," p. 22.

[40] UN. ECA. *Report of the Working Party on Economic and Social Development* (*Draft*), pp. 4–5.

Premature Comprehensive Planning

There is much to recommend comprehensive planning for a country which is ready for it. Some countries like Israel and Mexico, with considerable experience in preparing and executing projects and sector programs, a reasonably good statistical basis for planning and a trained and experienced cadre of technicians and administrators, have reached a stage of development in which they could profit by replacing partial with comprehensive planning. But where reliable statistics and trained economists and technicians are in short supply, where experience with planning is lacking, where administrative organization and procedure are inefficient or where the importance of getting development started soon is essential, attempts to move from the project-by-project approach directly into comprehensive planning have usually been self-defeating. Experience shows that the more complex the kind of planning, the more difficult it is to carry out. Without having first learned how to prepare and execute an integrated public investment plan and the projects which compose it, and to build up the institutional arrangements required to do these things, it has generally proved impossible for less developed countries to take on simultaneously the more difficult task of planning comprehensively for both public and private sectors.

Attempts to cure the planning inefficiencies of the project-by-project approach by bypassing the integrated public investment plan stage and moving directly into comprehensive planning put too great a burden on the limited capacities of planners and administrators in less developed countries and cause the planning process to become less, not more, efficient. Yet those who believe in comprehensive planning for all countries at all times frequently prescribe comprehensive planning for countries which have clearly demonstrated their inability to cope with the problems of partial planning. This happened in Nepal after the meager results of the First Five-Year Plan became apparent. According to the Permanent Secretary of Nepal's Ministry of Finance, the failure to achieve plan targets was due to a

> lack of efficiency and promptness in the administrative machinery concerned with planning, shortage of skills and technical and trained personnel, over-emphasis on foreign aid, lack of proper publicity to generate public enthusiasm, and lack of basic informa-

tion about the different sectors of the economy . . . [which] . . . makes it almost impossible even to guess the total production of the country.[41]

Because the Government's "administrative structure was too anti-quated to implement the Plan," actual development expenditures amounted to only 35 per cent of budgeted amounts.[42] Nevertheless, planners prepared and issued a draft Second Plan based on a growth model which called for more than a ninefold increase in investment expenditures and a 6 per cent annual increase in national income, compared to an imputed annual increase of only 1.6 per cent in incomes during the First Plan period.

Those who consider comprehensive planning the appropriate way to deal with bad partial planning might find it instructive to review the evidence of past experience.

Experience Favors Staged Approach

The meager results obtained from efforts over several years to turn out a usable national comprehensive development plan based on an econometric model, caused the Director of Venezuela's Central Office of Coordination and Planning to conjecture that

> the question must be asked whether integrated planning of the national economy makes sense for oil-rich Venezuela, or whether planning activity is not being carried on as an imitation of trends in other countries.[43]

When Burma, Ceylon, Bolivia, Ghana, Ethiopia, Indonesia, Morocco and the Philippines, among other countries in early stages of develop-ment, sought to emulate planning procedures in countries at a later development stage by replacing their *ad hoc* approach with compre-hensive planning, they found the shift to be premature and most abandoned their comprehensive plans before the end of their planning periods. It was premature in the sense that they were unable either to influence appreciably the course and quantity of private investment or to achieve public investment goals in accordance with their plans. In other countries, like Upper Volta and Nepal, governments refused to

[41] Pant, Y. P. "Nepal's Economic Development: A Study in Planning Experience," p. 1726.

[42] Pant, Y. P. "Nepal's Planned Development," p. 478.

[43] Hurtado, Hector. "Planning for the 70's," p. 11.

adopt comprehensive plans prepared by planners because they were considered to be too sophisticated or ambitious to be realized.

Countries with an understanding of the complexities of comprehensive planning tend to start with partial planning. Thus, despite the availability of one of the most efficient government administrations and civil service systems in the world, the United Kingdom found it desirable in planning output during World War II to limit the scope of its planning effort:

> Indeed planning and co-ordination was successful during the war only in so far as it was recognized that it had to be rough and ready; any attempt to operate a 'perfect' system would have made even limited co-ordination impossible. And yet it is one of the ironies of planning that the more ambitious the system of co-ordination constructed, the less likely was it to be successful; and the more limited and successful it was, the less useful its results.[44]

The establishment of machinery for comprehensive planning in the United Kingdom in 1961 was preceded by the preparation and publication of sectoral programs for coal in 1950, electricity and gas in 1954, and railways, steel and nuclear power in 1955.

The experience of countries which have provided the "models" for emulation also does not support the view that all countries should start with comprehensive planning. First attempts at national development planning by countries with the longest planning experience generally covered only a part of the economy. Thus, both India's and Pakistan's first development plans concentrated on public investment and largely ignored the private sector. Even in the industrialized countries, whether with mixed or socialized economies, partial planning generally preceded comprehensive planning. The first French Modernization and Equipment Plan of 1947–1952/53 covered only six basic sectors: coal, electricity, steel, cement, farm machinery and transportation.[45] In the USSR, comprehensive planning also came after partial planning. The Goelro (Government Commission for Electrification) 10 to 20-year electrification program of 1920, other sectoral programs for food, metals, textiles and rubber in 1921–22, and the industrial program of 1924, all preceded the First Five-Year Plan which started in 1929.

[44] Devons, Ely. "Economic Planning in War and Peace," p. 19.

[45] The Plan was originally scheduled to terminate in 1951. When it was extended to 1952/53, two additional sectors—fuels and fertilizers—were added.

Czechoslovakia, the most industrialized of the Eastern European bloc, started in the postwar period by formulating sectoral programs for power, textile, clothing and raw materials, all of which were considered crucial for its economy. Similarly, other Eastern European countries started planning partially for a few sectors and industries. Planning for the entire economy in Mainland China began only with the Second Five-Year Plan. The First Five-Year Plan concentrated on large-scale industry at the national level and was little concerned with agriculture, and medium and small-scale industry.[46]

Comprehensive planning, covering both public and private sectors, has generally come in later stages of a country's development. In India, Pakistan[47] and France, for example, comprehensive planning was not attempted until their second plans, in Iran not until its third plan and in the Sudan not until its fourth plan. In the USSR, the First Five-Year Plan for 1928–33 set targets for 50 industrial branches compared with 120 industrial targets set in the Second Five-Year Plan for 1933–37. In the countries of Asia, the region with the most planning experience,

> the first plans were almost invariably a summation of individual projects in the public sector, many of which were already being implemented. . . . Even in those first plans where income and employment targets were given, the functional relationship between the investment programme as a whole and the expected increase in national income and employment were hardly more than a guess, because of lack of accurate information on the capital/output ratio. . . .[48]

The decision to postpone comprehensive planning was generally calculated and was taken because planners were convinced that better results could be obtained at first from partial planning. Thus, the Indian Planning Board, appointed in 1946 by the Interim Cabinet to recommend planning procedures and machinery for independent India, took the firm position that

> it must be frankly recognized that we do not at present possess in India either sufficient knowledge and statistical information, or

[46] Perkins, Dwight H. "Centralization Versus Decentralization in Mainland China and the Soviet Union," pp. 65–67.

[47] Pakistan's so-called First Five Year Plan followed its first development plan, the Six Year Development Programme.

[48] UN. ECAFE. "Economic Development and Planning in Asia and the Far East," *Economic Bulletin for Asia and the Far East*, December 1961, p. 2.

sufficiently extensive control over economic activity to be able either to frame or execute plans whose combined and cumulative effect will be to increase per capita income by a predetermined amount.[49]

The Board therefore decided against the preparation of a comprehensive plan and recommended that despite the possible lack of meticulousness, it was better to have a partial plan than to spend more time on preparing a comprehensive plan.[50] Experience proved this position to have been justified. For although India's First Five-Year Plan was a partial plan, good results were obtained from it.

Faced with scarcities of data, trained economists, manpower, equipment and raw materials after World War II, the relatively advanced French planners also took a similar approach in preparing their first plan. Their decision to start with partial instead of comprehensive planning was

> not because of any mistrust of econometric techniques, but because of the lack of adequate statistics, the impossibility of building an input-output table quickly enough and the scarcity of trained economists. To define the targets of the plan in terms of growth of the GNP and of income, with reference to a given level of capital formation and with a breakdown in any number of sectors covering the entire economy, would have involved much guess-work and many hazardous estimates. It was felt that, failing a certain level of statistical information and knowledge about correlations and coefficients, the wisest course was to make an incomplete plan rather than a deceptively complete one. In other words, the very real danger of pursuing inconsistent targets, or at least of allocating resources in an irrational manner, was considered a minor danger compared with that of losing a great deal of time trying to build an over-all growth model based on a short series of inaccurate statistics.[51]

It took courage and restraint for the planners "to think small" and take a partial approach to planning when the country's needs were disturbingly great. As Pierre Massé, General Commissioner of the *Commissariat Général du Plan,* has indicated, reaction to this position was not universally favorable. But it produced good results.

[49] Ghosh, O. K. *Problems of Economic Planning in India,* p. 49.
[50] *Ibid.*
[51] Lemerle, Paul. "Planning for Economic Development in France," p. 50.

Because of the shortage of means . . . , a hard choice had to be made. The choice decided upon in France, in favor of what were called the *basic sectors,* was not understood by all; the First Plan was criticized, for example, for neglecting housing and the textile industry. Experience proved, however, that through the concentration of our limited resources on these sectors, decisive progress was made in expanding the national potential.[52]

Planners in the Mexican Investment Commission, established in 1955 to co-ordinate public investment, also strongly advocated beginning with partial planning. They were profoundly skeptical of the thesis that planning in less developed countries should start from over-all targets and move downward to the project level. In a lecture to students at the University of Mexico, a high official of the Investment Commission stated his preference unequivocally:

If planning and programming take as a point of departure a convenient total of investment in order to maintain a certain development rate and . . . divide the total between public and private investment, then among big sectors of economic activity and then in even more detail, the formulation of an investment program in our country should be carried out in exactly the opposite manner: from each project to a group of projects of a given economic activity; thence to a total volume of public investment, and then link it to private investment. . . .[53]

The Mexican planners felt that problems of resource allocation and investment criteria in a country at the beginning of its development could usually be reduced to a few simple questions capable of being answered without prolonged theoretical exercises. Irrigation, power, petroleum and transportation were clearly the sectors of highest priority for Mexican public investment, as they had been for 20 years. During those 20 years, public investment in these sectors had consistently accounted for about three-fourths of total public investment. Because priorities were obvious in most cases, fairly constant investment ratios also had prevailed among most sectors and subsectors of the economy, and even among individual government departments and autonomous agencies. Although minor shifts had occurred in some years, there was little likelihood that sectoral priorities would change sufficiently in the immediate future to necessitate basic reallocations of

[52] Massé, Pierre, "French Economic Planning," p. 4.
[53] Romero Kolbeck, Gustavo. "La Inversion del Sector Publico."

investment resources. Moreover, as in most other less developed countries, a large proportion of public investment funds available each year—in Mexico as much as 80 per cent—was committed to projects already under construction. The immediate task, as seen in the Investment Commission, was to try to increase yields by rationalizing such investments (e.g., by making certain that a road from a new port to the hinterland was ready for use when the port project was completed) and by co-ordinating new projects with those already under way.[54]

The Mexicans recognized that their "rough-and-ready" approach was limited. They pointed out, however, that while Mexico was operating successfully with a limited system of integrated public investment planning, less developed countries which were attempting to plan with a comprehensive system were not doing nearly as well. They were unimpressed with the contention, frequently heard in Latin American planning circles, that even though a country did not achieve the targets in its comprehensive plan, it was nevertheless better than a partial plan for educating political leaders in planning. They pointed out that where leadership was changing frequently, the lesson was not learned. Moreover, it was likely to be easier and faster to educate inexperienced political leaders at first with a simpler integrated public investment plan than with a more sophisticated comprehensive plan based on an esoteric model. They reasoned that in the long run a country could grow faster, and its planners and officials learn more, by starting with successful partial planning than with less successful comprehensive planning. They therefore considered econometric model-building to be a largely fictitious exercise which was likely to divert attention from immediate development needs. And they considered those who advocated the construction of such models for countries in early stages of development to be bad planners in practice and those who sought to increase yields quickly through rationalization of current public investment to be the best planners.[55]

Experience of International Financing Institutions. International institutions which finance development favor a planned approach to development. But the gaps in the number and quality of projects in developing countries, as well as the widespread inability of countries to execute them, have made them conscious of the need in countries in early stages of development for plans which these countries are

[54] *Ibid.*
[55] *Ibid.*

capable of implementing. This has led them to advocate that countries start planning with integrated public investment plans. A view which is typical in the World Bank was recently voiced by one of its officials:

> Shortages of trained talent similarly threaten the implementation of development plans. . . .

> Where these limitations exist, two principal choices are presented. One alternative is to ignore the limitations or pretend they do not exist. For the absent or insufficient data, assumptions may be substituted—assumptions concerning a desirable growth rate, and further assumptions concerning the magnitude and availability of the capital and manpower required to produce that rate of growth. . . . The resulting plan is likely to be an impressive but essentially fanciful document, with a misleading appearance of precision which may have regrettable, even disastrous, consequences for the economy if taken seriously.

> The second of the alternatives is to devise a much more modest plan which takes account of the practical limitations of the data, managerial capacities and skilled manpower available and which, rather than prescribing an aggregate over-all model for the entire economy, focuses on a general strategy of development and on an investment program for the public sector based on a series of specific projects. Having seen the planning process from the Bank's side, I would without hesitation urge this second course for most countries with whose economies I am familiar.[56]

The Charter of Chile's publicly owned development corporation, the *Corporación de Fomento de la Producción* (CORFO), established in 1939, provided that it should formulate a national plan. Because of a lack of basic economic data and trained planners, CORFO postponed preparing a national plan. Instead, it concentrated on sectoral programing. In 1954, CORFO prepared an integrated program for Chile's agricultural and transportation sectors. It did not prepare a comprehensive plan until 1960. Among those who had criticized CORFO for failing to prepare a national development plan earlier was Felipe Herrera, formerly Chile's Minister of Finance and Manager of the Central Bank of Chile from 1953 to 1958. Speaking as President of the Inter-American Development Bank, however, Dr. Herrera told an

---

[56] Demuth, Richard H. (Director of the Development Services Department of the World Bank) *Planning, Projects and People*, pp. 6–7.

audience at the University of Chile in May 1963 why he had changed
his mind:

> Many years ago I criticized Chile's Corporación de Fomento on the
> grounds that it had failed to comply with the mandate of formulat-
> ing a 'general plan' for the development of production. Like the
> inexperienced person I then was, I reproached the CORFO for not
> having complied with what I thought should have been its first
> obligation.
>
> As I look back now I can say that fortunately this agency did not
> try from the very start to prepare a national plan for the develop-
> ment of production, which in the best of cases might have been
> very well presented but which might have been only a masquerade
> of a plan. In 1939 or 1940, Chile was in no way equipped
> technically nor did it have the other prerequisites for development
> that were necessary to enable it to work out the plan which is now
> in force, twenty years later.
>
> I believe that the wise and sensible course was the one that was
> followed, with that pragmatic judgment with which so many
> decisive problems in this country have been faced. . . . Develop-
> ment by sectors was started, with priorities for the basic
> ones . . . as experience was acquired, a realistic picture of the
> development plan, of possible goals that could be attained, of the
> actual amount of investment required, began to take shape. In
> short, CORFO kept its feet on the ground, reconciling aspirations
> with actual possibilities.[57]

A study made by the Columbia University School of Law in co-
operation with the University of Oregon supports this conclusion. In
Chile, states the study,

> sectoral planning proceeded vigorously before comprehensive
> planning was undertaken, with impressive concrete results, and
> the foundations for comprehensive planning were laid over a
> period of a considerable number of years devoted to macro-
> economic analysis. The sectoral planning was based on fairly
> obvious 'a priori' priorities determined for such activities as elec-
> tric power and integrated steel production, and specific projects
> and enterprises were established to carry out the sectoral plans,
> which have accounted for a large part of the external financing
> received by Chile. There is no evidence that the later development

[57] Herrera, Felipe. "The Financing of Latin American Integration," pp. 9–10.

of a comprehensive plan invalidated in any fundamental way the earlier judgments arrived at in the sectoral planning. Sectoral planning, if properly carried out, after all does involve consideration of interrelationships of the particular sector with the rest of the economy, which is not very different from what is done in comprehensive planning approaches.[58]

DIFFICULTIES OF COMPREHENSIVE PLANNING

The Capital-Output Ratio. Comprehensive plans based on growth models generally rest on two assumptions. The first is that the rate of investment is the prime determinant of the rate of growth, the second is that the capital-output ratio or capital coefficient remains fairly stable over long periods.[59] These assumptions have been challenged as oversimplifications of the growth process and as exaggerations of the role of capital in stimulating development. Thus, the United Nations Economic Commission for Africa (ECA) has pointed out:

> It is one of the weaknesses of development programming generally and one based on aggregative investment targets specifically, that it may concentrate attention too much on tangible investment as the only method of raising income.[60]

It is, of course, possible to increase output and incomes without investment by making fuller use of existing capacities, improving maintenance and repair practices, reducing waste, providing incentives, improving skills, crop rotation and agrarian reform in agriculture, etc. In the development of a country, the prime mover is the human factor. Where human beings are well organized and motivated, and willing to work together, lack of capital, while a handicap, is a handicap which can be overcome, as the experience of many countries demonstrates.[61] This view finds support in a study by the Economic Commission for Europe (ECE) which concluded that in the postwar

[58] Columbia University School of Law. *Public International Development Financing in Chile,* p. 123.

[59] UN. ECAFE. *Programming Techniques for Economic Development with Special Reference to Asia and the Far East,* p. 11.

[60] UN. ECA. *Problems Concerning Techniques of Development Programming in African Countries,* p. 32.

[61] Staley, Eugene. *Political Implications of Economic Development and Pitfalls to be Avoided,* p. 2.

growth of Western European countries, inputs of capital accounted for only a part—often a small part—of the growth while the "human factor" played a very important role.[62] In contrast, the history of oil rich countries like Iran, Iraq, Saudi Arabia and Venezuela shows that investment of capital alone does not assure development. It cannot be true, therefore, that higher investment necessarily produces faster growth.

If development has a low place in a country's scale of values, an increase in the amount of investment may yield the same or even lower results. The economic policies pursued by a government are much more important to economic development than its investment expenditures. According to Professor Arthur Lewis, this was clearly demonstrated in Ghana:

> Ghana's experience under the First Development Plan proves my proposition that policy is more important than expenditures. Very large sums of money were spent by the Government, but since the industrial, agricultural, mining, and housing policies were inappropriate, very little increase in productive capacity resulted from these large expenditures. There was a remarkable increase in public facilities, such as roads, schools, electric power, water supplies, and so on, but remarkably little increase in the output of commodities. Considering also how much was wasted by overloading the building industry, one can say without hesitation that the country would have made more progress if it had spent less and had better economic policies.[63]

Even if investment were the major determinant of growth, poor statistics in most less developed countries would make their capital-output ratios suspect and models built on them of doubtful value. For example, David E. Bell, first head of the field staff of the Harvard Advisory Group in Pakistan, found "few data on which to judge the relationship between investment and output in Pakistan"[64] and "the relationship between investment and output . . . a very doubtful datum."[65]

It is also known that the capital-output ratios for a country may vary greatly over several years. This is especially true in less developed

[62] UN. ECE. *A Study of Determinants of Growth in Europe During the Nineteen-Fifties,* p. 2.

[63] Lewis, W. Arthur. "On Assessing a Development Plan," p. 4.

[64] Bell, David E. "Planning for Development in Pakistan," p. 10.

[65] *Ibid.,* p. 8.

countries with substantial investment programs. In such countries, a shift of even a small amount of investment from one sector to another or even from one set of projects to another may result in an appreciable change in the capital-output ratio. Moreover, one of the major purposes of development policy in less advanced countries is to bring about structural changes in the economy which, if realized, is certain to alter capital-output relationships. The estimations of capital-output ratios therefore cannot depend on past experience as much as on future changes in the economy and, even more, on government policy. Consequently, capital-output ratios for a few years in the past are unreliable guides for determining the level of investment needed in the future to obtain a specific rate of growth or, to put it in economists' language, the average capital-output ratio is not a dependable indication of the marginal or incremental capital-output ratio.

When such historical ratios have been used to construct growth models, they have often proved to be misleading. Indian planning experience furnishes an instructive example of this. On the basis of highly favorable returns during the First Five-Year Plan period, optimistic capital-output ratios were used in building the growth model for the Second Five-Year Plan. These ratios proved to be unrealistic. When expected improvements in productivity in agriculture and industry failed to materialize, output was disappointingly low. The Philippine experience also provides an example of the dangers of projecting capital-output ratios based, as in the Indian case, on a short period when conditions were unusually favorable.

The use of an over-all capital-output ratio for a country's economy to estimate the amount of capital required for sectors of that economy or for individual projects has also been criticized as unscientific, as has indiscriminate application of capital-output ratios of one country to another. Unsatisfactory results obtained from these procedures prompted a group of experts of the Economic Commission for Asia and the Far East who favored the extension of comprehensive planning to write, nevertheless:

> We feel that capital-output ratios should be used with greater caution in estimating capital requirements than has been the practice hitherto; that if so used their calculation should be much more carefully done; that they should be used only if it is possible to make separate projections for the main sectors of the economy and for the large individual capital using projects; and that the greatest care should be exercised both in extrapolating past trends

in the ratios and in applying ratios derived from one country's past experience to another country's future development.[66]

Growth Models. While comprehensive planning may be theoretically more desirable than partial planning, it is technically much more difficult than partial planning. Comprehensive planning is also more difficult in a mixed, market-type economy than in a socialized, command economy because it must make judgments about demand under conditions of changing prices and incomes, something which can be largely ignored in socialized countries which treat consumer demand as a residuum. The task of devising a workable comprehensive growth model is also made more difficult by the necessity for building into it the effects of technological innovation. This is not easy to do in the current era of rapid technological change. In India, for example, the planners did not foresee the striking development in petro-chemical technology which reduced the viability of the chemical projects based on coal tar distillates and coke-oven products included in the Indian plan. As a result, these projects have had to be discarded, thereby reducing the prospects for realizing aggregative targets in the Third Plan.[67]

The more detailed or complex the comprehensive model, the greater the amount of information required; the more it relies on mathematical deductions or decisions to determine the best among alternative targets, the more accurate and detailed the basic data must be. But even if the model is limited in scope and is prepared largely by pragmatic instead of mathematical methods, comprehensive planning requires a large amount of dependable data for past periods from which trends can be extrapolated.[68]

Mathematical models can provide useful information, but not as much as some advocates suggest:

> The mathematical mode of reasoning, which has become very popular in economics, has a distinctive advantage over the literary one, in that it is able to take full account of the interdependence of a large number of variables and to specify the relationships in quantitative terms, so that a better insight in the orders of

[66] UN. ECAFE. *Problems of Long-Term Economic Projections with Special Reference to Economic Planning in Asia and the Far East,* p. 103.

[67] See *Economic Weekly,* Vol. XV, No. 27, July 6, 1963, p. 1056.

[68] Colm, Gerhard and Geiger, Theodore. "Country Programming as a Guide to Development," pp. 15–16.

magnitude of the phenomena involved is gained and the operational significance of the model is enhanced. But its importance
should not be exaggerated, for it is not an alternative to common
sense, and it can never entirely replace the non-mathematical
method of approach. Social reality is much more complicated than
the mathematical model, which is only an idealized and abstract
picture of it—a simplification of economic life, like a map of a
landscape, for convenient understanding and systematic study. To
regard the model as a cut-and-dried solution of the growth
problem, is to ignore the manifoldness of real economic life, which
cannot be caught in a mathematical web alone.[69]

Techniques used to construct a model may be theoretically valid, yet
yield nonsensical results. This is well illustrated by an experimental
multisector aggregative investment planning model which *Nacional
Financiera*, Mexico's official development bank, constructed in 1961
using a linear programing matrix with 1,900 coefficients. The results
produced by the model indicated that if borrowing abroad between
1960 and 1970 were permitted to increase moderately over the 1960
level so that by 1970 the total was only $245 million instead of $172
million, the rate of Mexico's growth could be greatly accelerated
between 1960 and 1970 from 5.5 per cent per annum to 8 per cent. In
absolute amounts, this meant that

a comparatively small increase in foreign funds [which in 1970
reached an upper limit of only $73 million] would help make it
possible to achieve a difference in 1970 GNP of virtually $5 billion
[$23.2 billion instead of $18.4 billion].[70]

A foreign adviser who worked with the group which prepared the
model, writing about the results obtained, has indicated frankly that
one would do well to be skeptical that so small an increase in foreign
loans could make so large a difference in Mexico's growth:

Results of this type are illustrative, but cannot be taken too
literally. Any one of the 1,900 coefficients in the linear programming matrix could be in serious error. . . .[71]

[69] Adhin, J. H. *Development Planning in Surinam in Historical Perspective*, p.
176.

[70] Manne, Alan S. "Key Sectors of the Mexican Economy, 1960–1970," p. 388.

[71] *Ibid.*, p. 394. Although the model was considered experimental and the results
untrustworthy, the author permitted himself to draw firm conclusions (p. 390) based
on the results produced by the model about the role of foreign loans and aid in
Mexico's future development.

As a laboratory exercise which may eventually be perfected into a usable technique for planning, the construction of such models constitutes a step in that direction. But the process is likely to be a long one and, given the state of the art and the inadequacy of the data, its practical application to planning lies far in the future. Meanwhile, these experimental activities necessarily divert scarce talent from more immediate and urgent planning tasks. This aspect of model-building was recently discussed at the 1964 ECAFE Conference of Asian Economic Planners. At that meeting, the construction of complex planning models was much criticized as inappropriate to the needs of most developing countries. One delegate, with considerable experience in development planning in Asia and elsewhere, said that he saw

> considerable danger in building overly sophisticated models, even for projection purposes. . . . What is needed are simple, straightforward formulations that can be used to measure past performance and to guide policy formulation for the future. We need methods that can be readily broken down to the policy level if we, in fact, are to give guidance to the decision-maker in the planning process.[72]

Planning models can be no better than the data on which they are based. To the extent that available information is a good measure of what is going on, models can be accurate representations of reality. But when otherwise good technique is applied to faulty information, the models must themselves depart from reality:

> The weakness of econometric, mathematical models . . . is *not* due to the fact that they are mathematical or that a numerical application is made . . . the crucial problem lies with the accuracy of the data. If they are reliable, it will not be very difficult to evolve suitable models. . . . Without reliable data our confidence must remain low. 'Intuition' and 'experience' and the like, unless they can be brought into sharp focus, are not substitutes. Either we have knowledge (of a certain type and quality) or we do not.[73]

"Up-and-Down" Procedure. Besides the difficulties encountered in building a suitable model, comprehensive planning requires that planning be carried out from "the top down" and from "the bottom up" simultaneously. This is not easy to do. It

[72] UN. ECAFE. [Conference of Asian Economic Planners, etc.] *Statement by Dr. Douglas S. Paauw, Member of U.S. Delegation on Agenda Item 4*, p. 3.
[73] Morgenstern, Oskar. *On the Accuracy of Economic Observations*, pp. 114–115.

means that the size of the different programmes in different sectors and areas should correspond to what a balanced plan would require. This already implies that the projects which are complementary from a technical point of view are either jointly included or jointly excluded from a programme; to include only one of them obviously means waste. Thus, programmes in the field of energy and in the field of roads should both be geared to the desired or expected increase in general production in a region.[74]

French and Japanese planning, and among the developing countries, Yugoslav, Indian and Pakistani planning, come closest to using both the planning "from-the-top-down" and "from-the-bottom-up" procedures. However, both Indian and Pakistani planning have frequently been criticized for their failure to plan adequately "from-the-bottom-up." For example, in India,

> in 1955/56 the second plan planners, after fumbling a bit, simply stopped short of attempting to make explicit linkages between their aggregative plan and the specific investment (or project) choices along the route that conventional development theory seemed to indicate.[75]

As in India, most countries which attempt to plan comprehensively, particularly the less advanced ones, concentrate largely on the first procedure and neglect the second.

The Problem of Projects

Advocates of comprehensive planning in all countries regardless of their stage of development do not seem to understand that in most less developed countries the basic weakness is not the absence of a comprehensive approach to development planning, but a shortage of soundly conceived projects. This is even true of developing countries, like Pakistan, which have had a long planning history. Thus, Dr. Mahbub ul Haq, an official of Pakistan's Planning Commission, wrote some ten years after the establishment of Pakistan's central planning agency:

> The fundamental weakness of the First and Second Plans has been that the planning was not built in depth; whereas an effort was made to develop consistent, aggregative planning frameworks, not

[74] U.N. ECAFE. *Programming Techniques for Economic Development with Special Reference to Asia and the Far East,* p. 34.
[75] Lewis, John P. "India," pp. 99–100.

énough effort went into filling these frameworks with well-conceived, well-engineered projects and programmes. This has had the double disadvantage of making planning somewhat theoretical and vague at the project level and creating difficulties in the way of offering an adequate portfolio of projects for purposes of foreign aid commitments.[76]

Most countries run into great difficulties, not in formulating over-all plans, but in preparing and carrying out projects and in operating them efficiently when completed. Guatemala inaugurated a public investment plan in 1960. But one year later, the Organization of American States reported that

> various ministries . . . are finding it difficult to present a sufficient number of fully developed projects.[77]

A shortage of projects which became apparent after the drafting of Chile's ten-year comprehensive development plan has impeded that plan's implementation. After the Five-Year Integrated Socio-Economic Program for the Philippines for the period 1962–66 was prepared, it became apparent that there were few projects ready to give effect to the Program. The Caribbean Organization reported in 1962 that in Surinam, which had a Ten-Year Development Plan in operation from 1955,

> the major problems encountered so far have arisen from lack of knowledge and experience in planning and project evaluation in the Ministries responsible for preparing projects.[78]

In Bolivia, a group of planners, largely composed of foreigners, prepared a national comprehensive development plan for 1962–71 which envisaged exceptionally high average annual increases of 9.2 per cent in the Gross National Product during the first five years and 8.3 per cent annually in the entire ten years of the plan period. But after working for a year and a half on the plan's preparation, the planners found themselves in the unenviable position of conceding that

[76] Haq, Mahbub ul. *Strategy of Economic Planning: A Case Study of Pakistan*, p. 21.
[77] OAS. Inter-American Economic and Social Council, etc. *Present State of Economic Development Planning in Latin America*, p. 29.
[78] Caribbean Organization. *Report of Joint Meeting of Planners and Planning Experts and Standing Advisory Committee of the Caribbean Plan*, p. 41.

the principal deficiency that will be noted in the formulation of the present Plan is the small number of specific investment projects, studied in all their details, which have been included [in the Plan]. It is a most urgent task that the pre-investment studies whose economic justification is given at length in the different sections of the Plan are now completed, including the pertinent engineering studies, so that their execution may now proceed with the speed that the imperative conditions require.[79]

Moroccan planners found themselves in the same predicament as the Bolivians with regard to their comprehensive First Five-Year Plan. After its completion it was found that there was an insufficiency of well-prepared projects with which to carry out the Plan.[80]

When the Alliance for Progress with its promise of increased development funds was inaugurated in August 1961, those who believed that the lack of investment resources had been the main deterrent to economic progress in Latin America expected a quick increase in the region's rate of growth. But the Alliance got off to a very slow start. Investigation by a group of experts disclosed that although

much [investment] credit has been granted during the last several years . . . only an insignificant amount of it has been used, and only a small fraction has even been committed.[81]

In seeking reasons for the delay in utilizing available investment funds, the Latin American Seminar on Planning, jointly organized in February 1962 by the Organization of American States, the Economic Commission for Latin American and the Inter-American Development Bank to discuss planning problems under the Alliance Program, concluded:

The shortage of specific investment projects worked out in full detail partly accounted for the fact that the principles of the Alliance for Progress had not yet been applied as generally, or as intensively, as might have been wished . . . [and further] . . . the lack of specific public and private investment projects was one of the greatest obstacles to immediate action being taken on the required scale and as promptly as necessary.[82]

[79] Bolivia. Junta Nacional de Planeamiento. *Plan Nacional de Desarrollo Económico y Social, 1962–1971: Resumen*, p. 24.
[80] Waterston, Albert. *Planning in Morocco*, p. 49.
[81] OAS. Inter-American Economic and Social Council, etc. [*Report of the Panel of Experts to the Inter-American Economic and Social Council*], p. 25.
[82] UN. ECLA. *Report of the Latin American Seminar on Planning*, pp. 5 and 19.

The Pan American Union, which acts as the General Secretariat of the Organization of American States, was even more direct. In a report prepared for the First Meeting of the Inter-American Economic and Social Council, it stated unequivocally that

> the most immediate obstacle to the attainment of increased rates of investment as called for in the Charter of Punta del Este, is an acute shortage of fully worked out development projects.[83]

The shortage of projects is by no means limited to Latin America. The problem is world-wide. In his statement to the Second Conference of Asian Economic Planners, held in Bangkok from October 19–26, 1964, the U.S. representative pointed out that

> the value of the national plan is dependent on its component sector and project plans. . . . The lack of sufficient soundly conceived projects today constitutes a major obstacle to the implementation of major development plans, and we in AID [the U.S. Agency for International Development], as well as our colleagues in the Export-Import Bank of the United States, the DAC [Development Assistance Committee] countries, and the international lending agencies such as the World Bank are all very conscious of this problem.[84]

The World Bank is indeed conscious of the problem and, in one of a series of steps it is taking to deal with it has established two offices in Africa to help African countries prepare projects and programs, initially in agriculture and transportation.

The delayed recognition of the need for well-prepared projects in sufficient number to implement plans, exemplified in the Bolivian, Chilean, Guatemalan, Moroccan and Philippine cases, as well as in the Alliance for Progress Program, is a common occurrence in less developed countries engaged in comprehensive planning. In part, this is because planners, who are mostly trained as economists, are better versed in the broader "macro-economics" of model-building than they are in the "micro-economics" of project preparation and evaluation. In part, it is because in the short run no real choice of projects exists since most investment resources have already been committed for projects already started which governments will not abandon regardless of their

[83] OAS. Inter-American Economic and Social Council, Special Committee I, etc. *Programming for Development: Five Urgent Problems*, p. 5.

[84] US. AID. *Report of the United States Delegation to the Second Session of the United Nations Conference of Asian Economic Planners*, p. 3.

priority; and in the longer run, because in most less developed countries, operating agencies, departments and ministries do not know how to prepare sound projects and cannot furnish planners with the necessary data to permit projects to be integrated with the comprehensive plan through the planning "from-the-bottom-up" procedure already described.

This is hardly surprising in view of the shortcomings of administrative organization and the lack of technicians in most less developed countries. A comprehensive plan can be, and often is, completed in less developed countries by a few technicians, especially when assisted by foreign experts, without much recourse to the governmental machinery. But it is usually impossible for a government to prepare and carry out numerous projects without heavy reliance on its administrative apparatus. The government may obtain foreign technicians and contractors to help, but because of the character, volume, and continuing nature of project preparation and execution, great reliance must be placed on the government services. In Nepal, for example, as in many less developed countries, the Government found that

> the problem of economic development is more 'organizational' than anything else. In the way of mobilising resources—both domestically and internationally—framing and implementing various schemes, organisation may prove a bottleneck. The Government has therefore accepted that energetic and proper execution, phase by phase, of long term plans is not possible unless the organisation is powerful and supreme.[85]

But since administrative reform to improve project preparation and execution generally takes a long time to carry out, problems of project preparation in most developing countries are intrinsically more difficult, and take longer to resolve, than those encountered in the formulation of either comprehensive or partial plans. This does not mean that the preparation of a comprehensive development plan is easy. It does mean that while the technical aspects of preparing a comprehensive plan often present knotty economic problems, the programing, organizational and procedural aspects of preparing and carrying out projects to implement a development plan present serious problems not only in economics, but also in psychology, sociology and public administration.

[85] Pant, Y. P. "The Process of Planning in Nepal," p. 6.

Comprehensive planning has the capacity of exciting a planner's imagination because it can encompass an entire economy in a single model in which all potential problems can receive an objectively optimum resolution. Since the aggregates in a growth model can be computed without projects, there is a tendency for planners to become fascinated with the intricacies of planning methodology and the internal consistency of their aggregates, and to lose sight of the need for reconciling investment projects and programs with their models. But the heart of any development plan consists of projects. Regardless of the kind of planning, there can be no effective implementation without them. Unless projects are integrated with the comprehensive plan, the model bears little resemblance to actual public and private investment patterns. This is why in many countries,

> total, integrated economic planning can and often does co-exist quite amicably with, and may serve to cover up, unregenerated total improvisation in the actual undertaking and carrying out of investment projects.[86]

As has been indicated, the preparation of a comprehensive plan begins "at the top" with an aggregative analysis and ends, often much later, with the integration of projects with the aggregative plan, while the preparation of a public investment plan starts "at the bottom" with individual projects which are combined into sector programs and then into an investment plan for the public sector. This procedural difference has important effects because in comprehensive planning, as has been seen, the difficulties of the planning "from-the-bottom-up," i.e., the integration of projects with development plans, have tended to fixate planners' attention on the broader or "macro" aspects of plan formulation, while in planning for the public sector, concern with projects makes planners get involved in projects and their implementation from the start. This attribute of public investment programs was acknowledged by the previously cited group of ECAFE experts headed by Dr. Tinbergen. Although they favored comprehensive planning for all Asian countries, they pointed out that

> it must be recognized that, despite the limitations inherent in such an approach, these partial plans serve some useful purposes. They help to focus public attention on planning and development; they

[86] Hirschman, Albert O. "Economics and Investment Planning: Reflections Based on Experience in Colombia," p. 39.

provide a useful framework of priorities for financial policy and budgeting; and they emphasize problems of implementation at an early stage. . . .[87]

The question therefore arises whether it would not be better for countries in early stages of development to start, as most of the countries with the longest and most successful experience with planning started, with partial planning. As long ago as 1951, a United Nations committee foresaw that

> nothing will be more disheartening and, in the long run, more disastrous than the failure to execute a fine plan or the abandonment of half-finished projects. If the choice is apt to be between waiting for a complete and perfect plan on the one hand, and making a concrete start on the basis of an incomplete plan on the other, the latter may under certain circumstances be preferable.[88]

Ten years later, the Economic Commission for Asia and the Far East, after reviewing the results of planning in Asia, came to a similar conclusion for several of the less developed nations of its region. It concluded that, because of

> their stages of development, it may be practicable for them to begin with a plan containing mainly a number of technically feasible and economically justifiable individual projects, without too much emphasis on aggregate income, employment targets and inter-industry coordination. . . . The important thing for these countries is to start in the right direction . . . development policies suitable to their economic system and needs should be designed and included in their first plans to guide, foster and stimulate economic activity in the private sector. The absence of income (and employment) targets would mean that the nation would be unable to grasp in a nutshell what the plan was meant to achieve; yet it would not necessarily deprive the plan of its operational value if the projects included are well conceived and development policies well designed.[89]

[87] UN. ECAFE. *Programming Techniques for Economic Development with Special Reference to Asia and the Far East*, p. 34.

[88] UN. TAA. *Standards and Techniques of Public Administration with Special Reference to Technical Assistance for Under-developed Countries*, p. 27.

[89] UN. ECAFE. "Economic Development and Planning in Asia and the Far East," *Economic Bulletin for Asia and the Far East*, December 1961, p. 2.

Planning of this kind has many gaps and imperfections. However, since planning is a continuous process, which implies that even the best plan is likely to need revision by the time it is published, refinement can begin immediately after the plan's preparation has been completed. Meanwhile, a country can have, in a period which should take no more than a few months, in most cases, an improved frame of reference for its investment decisions.

Countries like Mexico and Israel, as well as Puerto Rico, have been able to establish and maintain high rates of growth over extended periods with no more formal planning arrangements than a public investment plan co-ordinated through their budgets, accompanied by policies and a few measures which established a favorable climate for private investors and influenced them to react in accord with government development objectives. The empirical evidence therefore suggests that countries with reasonably integrated public investment plans and sound budgetary procedures can dispense, at least for a time, with comprehensive planning without seriously impairing their rate of growth.

In most less developed countries at the start of their development, it is easy to identify the critical sectors and the highest priority projects in those sectors, and to co-ordinate them in a public investment program produced pragmatically in five or six months. In these countries, agriculture, transportation and power are generally the most important economic sectors. In countries where water is scarce, irrigation is also important. There may be another sector with an obviously high priority in other countries. Liberia, for example, may have to develop transport and other facilities linked with the exploitation of its large iron ore deposits.

In each important sector, there are usually obvious projects of high priority. The danger in most less developed countries is not that their governments are less aware than outsiders of the high priority projects; it is rather that in seeking to promote development, governments often seek to advance more projects than available resources allow. As a result, progress on all projects is slowed. Progress is also impeded by disorganized competition in some countries among more or less autonomous public or semipublic agencies and local, state and central governments for foreign exchange, local currency and other scarce resources essential for carrying out investment projects and programs.

Rationalizing Current Public Investment

Many governments, including those of many countries which are attempting comprehensive planning, do not possess reasonably complete information of the magnitude and composition of current and proposed public investment. Since investments by autonomous or semiautonomous public agencies which use government funds are frequently carried out more or less independently of government budgets, governments have even less information about these investments or about the extent to which these agencies are committing the country's credit or foreign exchange resources by borrowing abroad, than they have about their own investment activities. Often, also, little is known about the investments and loan commitments of provincial and local governments.

In countries where adequate information on public investment is lacking, consideration should therefore be given to beginning the formulation of an integrated public investment program by rationalizing the size and composition of current public investment. As a first step in this process, an "inventory" should be taken of all public investment projects and programs being prepared for execution as well as those actually in process of execution. Since many countries also do not have reliable estimates of their budgetary surpluses on current account available for public investment, projections should also be made of estimated public investment resources available from domestic public savings and external contributions and loans. If the inventory reveals, as is likely, that more investment is being attempted or contemplated than can be supported by available financial and other resources, priorities have to be set for projects and programs by applying to them general economic, financial, technical and administrative criteria. These criteria should include, for each project and program, evaluations of (a) economic and financial costs and expected returns; (b) the reliability of cost estimates and methods of financing, including the adequacy of financial contributions by the sponsoring agency or beneficiaries of a project or program; (c) foreign exchange requirements and expected foreign exchange savings or earnings; and (d) readiness to proceed with a project or program on the contemplated scale (e.g., availability of a site, adequacy of engineering, marketing and other studies, status of bids and construction contracts, training programs for management and staffs for completed projects, and so forth).

In some cases, funds may be earmarked by law for specific projects, work on some projects of low priority may be too far advanced to stop or there may be no alternative to starting a new project in order to make a previously started or finished project effective.[90] In such cases, it may not be feasible to apply the criteria. But where it is possible to do so, application of general criteria should permit substantial reductions in the number of projects. The arbitrariness with which judgments have to be made on the priority of projects which survive these tests, as among sectors, in order to bring the total volume of investment down to the level of resources depends, ultimately, on the priority which the government assigns each sector. From the review and evaluation of the inventory, a public investment plan can emerge with a pattern of capital expenditures phased over time which provides for the elimination of bottlenecks and the productive use of available public resources.

It is instructive to review the different ways in which this "inventory approach" was used in Mexico and Colombia as a basis for preparing integrated public investment plans in these countries. Soon after its establishment in 1954, the Mexican Investment Commission took an inventory of public investment projects in process of execution. For each project, information was obtained concerning its location, starting and probable completion dates, estimated cost, amount already invested, proposed future investment sources of financing, benefits expected and other data which made possible an assessment of the project. Data furnished by sponsoring departments and autonomous agencies were supplemented with information obtained by the Commission's staff on field trips to project sites.

A series of criteria was set up to determine the priority of each project: (1) the extent of the project's productivity as measured by the ratio of expected yield to estimated cost; (2) the expected social benefit; (3) the degree to which the project was related to other projects, either completed or under way; and (4) the amount of employment which the project was expected to generate after its completion.

The inventory was kept up to date. Sufficiently in advance of each

[90] Thus, a farm-to-market road might be essential to provide access to an adequate supply of milk for a processing plant nearly or already completed or a warehouse to store goods in transit might be necessary to a newly constructed port.

fiscal year, the Commission examined the programs which all operating offices in the public sector submitted. Projects in each program were studied from the point of view of the Commission's economic and social criteria and the degree of their co-ordination with other investments. Technical aspects were not reviewed since these were considered to be the concern of the operating organization responsible for the project. Before starting the review process, the Commission's analysts visited the locations of the proposed projects of those in progress to obtain first-hand information about the projects, the benefits to be expected, the need for additional works before benefits could be obtained, the status of the projects and the problems involved in their execution, as well as the need to co-ordinate construction with other projects.[91]

Much Mexican public investment was in projects whose benefits could be measured in monetary terms. For these, it was easy to fix economic priorities. For others, e.g., small and large irrigation projects, certain maritime, colonization and industrial projects, and agricultural investment in pest control, salt control and improvement in soils, it was possible to make reasonable approximations of their economic importance. But for some, like schools, hospitals and water and sewage works, as well as certain railroad and highway projects, where the benefits were intangible or otherwise not always measurable in money, decisions had to be made on the basis of considered judgment based on an analysis of probable benefits.[92]

In applying its criteria, the Commission generally gave expected economic and social benefits the greatest weight. But, on occasion, it had to give precedence to other criteria. Some works with low cost-benefit ratios had to be continued because large sums had already been expended on them and construction had proceeded so far that it was more economic to complete than to stop construction or because it was otherwise inexpedient to halt operations. Investments with low yields also were approved because they were located in economically and socially depressed regions. In other cases, projects went forward to meet the needs of a local or national emergency and, in still other cases, the form of financing made it desirable to proceed.

On the basis of its evaluation of proposed investment programs submitted by the operating entities, and information furnished by the Ministry of Finance and autonomous agencies concerning financial re-

[91] Salinas Lozano, Raul. "Comision de Inversiones," p. 16.
[92] *Ibid.*, p. 15.

sources available for federal investments, the Investment Commission drew up each year a preliminary integrated public investment plan which divided available funds among the sponsoring departments and autonomous agencies and by project, in accordance with the priorities established by the Commission. After the preliminary plan had been reviewed by the President of the Republic and put into final form by the Commission, it became the basis for budgetary allocations by the Ministry of Finance.

About the same time that the Investment Commission was making its inventory of Mexican public investment, a similar inventory was being undertaken in Colombia, where available data on the magnitude and composition of public investment were also inadequate. A World Bank mission, in co-operation with Colombia's National Planning Committee, took the inventory and used it to prepare an integrated public investment plan for 1956. A questionnaire, sent to a total of 71 public and semipublic entities which received contributions for investment from the national budget, requested the following information for every project sponsored by each entity: (1) an estimate of the time required to complete the project and, where available, starting and completion dates for construction; (2) who was to do the work (e.g., public staffs or private contractors or engineers and whether the last two were domestic or foreign); (3) an estimate of the cost in local currency and foreign exchange divided into annual amounts; and (4) arrangements made or contemplated for financing the project. A translation of the questionnaire (originally in Spanish) is in Appendix I.

Answers to the questionnaire were received from 51 of the most important ministries and public and semipublic entities. This information was supplemented with data obtained from (a) personal interviews with officials of operating ministries and agencies, (b) sectoral surveys previously completed in agriculture and electric power, (c) a World Bank regional survey of the important Cauca Valley and (d) a series of World Bank internal reports on Colombian transport, power, agriculture and other economic sectors, as well as on Colombia's financial, fiscal and economic capacity to absorb investment capital, prepared by World Bank staff members during the preceding six years. Although the response to the questionnaire was incomplete, it was possible with the help of the supplementary information to estimate virtually all the planned public investment activity in Colombia.

Since the combined investment programs of ministries and public agencies for 1956 exceeded available public investment resources by almost 60 per cent, a series of tests had to be applied to reduce the total proposed investment to the level of financial resources. Projects to be started in 1956 were examined first to determine whether their techni-cal feasibility had been established. Application of this test eliminated a number of projects, especially in electric power. The administrative readiness of the sponsoring entity to execute the project on the contemplated scale and to operate it upon completion was next examined. Application of this test resulted in reductions in the size of projects (e.g., in housing) or their elimination (e.g., certain municipal works in small communities which had inadequate staffs). The third test involved a consideration of whether proposed projects were appropriate for the Government to undertake under the conditions prevailing in Colombia and in the light of the traditional relationship between the Government and the private sector. Application of this test resulted, for example, in the elimination of a large project for construction of a cement plant by a government agency.

Application of the three tests brought about a reduction of contem-plated investment in 1956 to an amount only 10 per cent above available public investment resources. Remaining projects were then submitted to additional tests in order to bring the total down to the level of available resources. These tests were more difficult to apply than the first three because they required information which was not always easy to obtain. Projects were examined in appropriate cases to determine whether policies and procedures existed to secure economi-cally sound and equitable sharing-of-costs of the projects among governmental entities, or between public entities and private groups benefited. It was found, for example, that many communities were making an insufficient contribution to projects they were sponsoring and that they were relying unduly on contributions from the National Government. In many cases, especially those involving municipal improvements, no system of assessing private beneficiaries in propor-tion to their benefits gained from the proposed projects could be discerned. Where projects involved the production of goods and services to be sold on the market, attempts were made to judge whether there was an adequate market demand and whether the expected costs of production were reasonable. The scale of certain power projects was reduced on the basis of this examination and other projects were eliminated because more economical methods of producing power to meet demand were available. Because of the existence of a sectoral survey for electric power, this test could be applied to power projects with reasonable assurance that the data used were reliable. In other sectors, the test rested on less satisfactory information. In the case of telephones, for example, the lack of data did not permit a careful study of each project from the point of view of the test. Instead, forecasts which had been made by autonomous agencies operating in this field had to be accepted. Finally, some judgments had to be made, often somewhat arbitrarily, on the relative priority of projects and programs as between sectors. In applying these judgments, those preparing the public investment plan were guided by the belief that Colombia's development required large expenditures for transportation, electric power and agriculture. Hence, soundly conceived projects in these three sectors were placed first. In view of the National Government's announced objective at the time to accelerate investment in water-works, precedence was also given to investments in this sector.

In preparing the public investment plan for 1956, assumptions had to be made about investments in later years. Some projects to be started in 1956 required additional resources in following years, while other projects to be started in following years required funds in 1956 for preparatory work. These factors were considered when the 1956 plan was being prepared by setting up tentative investment schedules for the 1957–60 period as implied by the investment plan for 1956. Thus, in making provision in 1956 for preliminary engineering studies for the expansion of Paz del Rio, the government steel mill, the public investment plan was in effect recognizing that heavy investments would have to be made for this purpose in later years. In turn, the prospect of future large investments in Paz del Rio required caution in initiating programs in 1956 which would call for large continuing expenditures. Those preparing the 1956 plan, therefore, decided against expansion of the housing program for 1956, not only because it appeared to be of low priority in 1956, but also because, if the program had been permitted to expand in 1956, it would have been extremely difficult to cut back in succeeding years.

While the results obtained from the exercise were far from perfect, they represented a great improvement over the haphazard way in which public investment had been proceeding. By reducing the amount of proposed investment to the level of resources on the basis of economic and other general criteria devised to improve the quality of public investment, an investment plan emerged which not only was designed to keep government expenditures in line with expected revenues, but was directed toward executing projects and programs which promised to yield the greatest benefits.

As will be seen in the next chapter, the methods used in Mexico and Colombia to rationalize current public investment on the basis of an inventory of such investment may also be used to prepare a first annual operating plan for a medium-term plan period. Argentina made such an attempt in connection with its five-year development plan for 1964–69.[93]

However, a word of caution about the use of the "inventory procedure" is in order. Unless the inventory is limited to development projects which are under active consideration or in process of construction and, what is even more important, the taking of the inventory is followed by its rationalization through the application of appropriate tests to the projects and programs in process, the exercise is without value. In the Dominican Republic, Uruguay and Peru, for example, tripartite groups under the Alliance for Progress produced inventories of public investment projects which listed many projects which had never been seriously considered (in Peru, nondevelopmental projects like prisons were also included) and no attempt was made to rationalize the inventories to produce an integrated investment plan related to available resources.

SUMMARY AND CONCLUSIONS

To summarize, the kind of planning a country does is largely determined by the combined effect of its social, economic and political structure and its stage of development. Because of differences in structure and stage, the scope of national development planning at any time can and does range from the limited and piecemeal, project-by-project approach found in mixed economies in early phases of development to the comprehensive, centralized planning found in socialized economies. Over time, changes in a country's stage of development bring changes in its form of planning. For the socialized economies, this has generally involved a gradual shift toward decentralization of plan implementation and, for the mixed economies, a movement toward

---

[93] Translations of the general instructions and forms used by the Argentine National Development Council in connection with this effort are included in Appendix II. In addition to these, special forms and instructions to meet the specific needs of some autonomous agencies were also used.

greater centralization of both plan formulation and implementation.

The question, "Should a country with a mixed economy plan?" has given way to two others: "How much planning?" and "What kind of planning?" To the first, an imposing array of experts reply: "Comprehensive planning," and to the second: "Econometric model building." The experts have theory and time on their side. In the long run, comprehensive planning based on growth models may give better results than partial planning. Comprehensive planning's view of an economy as a whole and its emphasis on internal consistency allow economic comparisons and judgments to be made which are not generally possible in partial planning.

But this does not mean that comprehensive planning meets the pressing need for immediate action which exists now in most less developed countries. Indeed, a reading of the record suggests that less developed countries have fared better in practice, in both the short and long run, by first learning how to prepare and carry out integrated public investment plans than by going from *ad hoc* project preparation and execution directly into comprehensive planning. There is, of course, no way of comparing in the same place and time period the relative results obtainable from comprehensive and partial planning. There is, therefore, no way of proving conclusively that one variety of planning is better than another for a country in the early stages of development. But the weight of evidence and logic favors partial planning.

It is now widely recognized that most less developed countries lack an adequate supply of well-prepared projects ready for financing, as well as the administrative capacity to carry them out. But a few countries which, like Mexico and Israel, have learned how to formulate soundly conceived projects and to co-ordinate their execution through their budgets have demonstrated that it is possible for them to grow at a more rapid pace with partial planning than most other countries have with comprehensive plans. The economies of other countries, like India's and Iran's, grew more rapidly at first with partial planning than they did later with comprehensive planning. The experience in these countries suggests that comprehensive planning is not always better than partial planning.

Countries which have planned longest and most successfully began with partial planning. France, India and Pakistan, among others, all started in this way and went on to global planning at a later time. Yugoslavia began with a detailed, comprehensive five-year plan, but soon beat a hasty retreat. Even in the USSR, the fountainhead of comprehensive planning, establishment of a totally planned economy was a gradual process which progressed only as the public sector was strengthened and planning methods were perfected.

Decisions to start with partial planning were based on practical considerations, like the lack of planning experience, the shortage of economists and trustworthy statistics, or the need to impart vigor quickly to stagnant economies. In these circumstances, theories usually gave way to necessity. The Commissioner General of France's *Commissariat Général du Plan* has pointed out that despite

> heated doctrinal debates, one cannot help being struck by the fact that in France *practical* planning preceded the *theory* by a long time.[94]

It is possible, as some have suggested, that the reasons which prompted France, India, Pakistan and other countries to start with partial planning may no longer be relevant, because more is known about planning technique than formerly. But the indications are otherwise. Comprehensive planning remains considerably more difficult than partial planning for the public portion of an economy. And a less developed country with a large subsistence sector, a poorly functioning market economy, untrustworthy statistics, an inadequate administrative organization and an inefficient civil service is still unlikely to overcome the complexities involved in formulating a realistic comprehensive plan and implementing it.

It is not enough to say, as some who favor comprehensive planning have said, that the need for development is so great that short-cuts to comprehensive planning must be found. The need is always great. But what is most needed in countries at the start of their development is the initial stimulus to their economies which public investment, usually by additions to the social and economic infrastructure, can provide, even at the risk of some imbalance. If that stimulus can be administered, as it frequently has been, with partial planning, comprehensive planning may be safely postponed until a country gains the experience and institutions needed for more advanced planning. The important lesson of the Mexican, Israeli and Puerto Rican experience is that it is possible for a country in the early stages of its development to grow rapidly over extended periods on the basis of partial planning largely limited to the

---

[94] Massé, Pierre. "French Methods of Planning," p. 1.

public sector. Conversely, when less developed countries borrow their ideas at too high a level and engage prematurely in comprehensive planning, they are likely to end up with less than they might have achieved with partial planning.

In Africa, as well as in other regions, it has been discovered that

> the planner was not often left with much choice . . . where planning was just beginning and most available investment funds were already committed to projects with long gestation periods. . . . Under such circumstances the use of highly mathematical techniques like linear programming and input-output tables was hardly possible.[95]

Indeed, the practical choice in less developed countries is often reduced to partial planning or no planning at all.

This has been the experience of the Alliance for Progress. Every Latin American country was originally expected to prepare a ten-year comprehensive plan in order to qualify for aid under the Program. But it soon became evident that most Latin American countries were unable or unwilling to prepare such plans, and that the few which were willing to formulate plans, would need much time before their plans were prepared. The Bolivian comprehensive plan has never been viable and almost nothing has been done to implement the Colombian ten-year comprehensive plan. Instead a Four-Year Public Investment Plan has become the basis for co-ordinating public capital disbursements. Only Chile, Ecuador and Venezuela still have comprehensive plans, but they have had little influence on private investment. The emphasis within the Alliance for Progress has now shifted from long-term comprehensive planning to short-term public investment planning. The Alliance's Committee of Nine has approved a two-year public investment plan for Honduras and has recommended that Bolivia and other countries prepare similar plans.

Experience in Latin America and elsewhere shows that if planners attempt too much by insisting on comprehensive planning, the preparatory stage is likely to go on indefinitely without tangible results. It may also lead to disillusionment with planning. With almost prophetic vision, Dr. Oskar Lange cautioned the Ceylonese planners who were preparing a national ten-year comprehensive plan against waiting the two years he estimated it would take to prepare the plan:

[95] UN. ECA. *Report of the Meeting of the Expert Group on Comprehensive Development Planning*, p. 11.

The country can hardly afford such a loss of opportunity through lack of action. Furthermore, inactivity during the period of preparation of the development plan would undermine the nation's faith in the efficacy of economic planning. This might create a stage of apathy and even scepticism towards economic planning which later would make it difficult to mobilize the support of the people when the plan is ready. It also would make it difficult to enlist the full active effort of the people in carrying the plan into practice. It might even be used as an argument for discrediting economic planning.[96]

Those who would bypass integrated public investment planning and make a great leap forward with comprehensive planning are not likely to arrive at their destination sooner. It may well take them longer. *Festina lente*, hasten slowly, is the best advice one can give them. Although fruitless detours can be avoided by reading the signs left by those who have traversed the same path, the journey must be expected to take time.

The system of national planning should therefore be permitted to evolve gradually, firstly, as soon as possible, from the project-by-project approach to a second stage in which the country learns how to prepare and implement a co-ordinated public investment plan preferably accompanied by sectoral surveys and programs; and ultimately, when improvements in information, administration and experience permit, to full-scale comprehensive planning. The kind of planning which is right at a later stage is wrong at an earlier one. As Professor Galbraith has pointed out,

> we could make no more serious mistake than to imagine that the kind of planning that is done by India or Pakistan is essential for nations in all stages of development. In earlier stages it is neither necessary or possible.[97]

The most urgent need in most less developed countries is the speedy formulation of an immediate action plan for advancing development. The rationalization of current public investment through the application of general economic, technical and administrative criteria to an inventory of current public investment offers one effective way of meeting this need. It has been found possible to rationalize the pattern of current public investment by the methods outlined in this chapter in

[96] Lange, Oskar. "The Tasks of Economic Planning in Ceylon," p. 80.
[97] Galbraith, John K. *Economic Development in Perspective*, p. 16.

a period of a few months. This technique has been used successfully in Mexico and Colombia. From the rationalization of the inventory through the use of appropriate economic and other general criteria, priorities for projects can be determined and total public investment can be reconciled with resources to produce what is, in effect, an integrated short-term public investment plan.

Chapter V

Development Plans

*No hay que hacer planes a corto plazo si
no hay que en corto plazo hacer planes.*[1]

PLANNING WITHOUT PLANS

LESS DEVELOPED countries know that they have a better chance of attracting foreign financial assistance if they have development plans. In introducing Ghana's Second Development Plan, the Prime Minister frankly expressed the hope

> that international institutions and Governments which may be interested in our country will study this plan carefully and consider whether there are any individual projects with which they can help.[2]

Indeed, Ghana's more recent Seven-Year Plan, as well as Nigeria's Six-Year National Development Plan and Tanganyika's Five-Year Plan, was prepared with the assumption that 50 per cent of the proposed investments in the Plan would be financed from abroad. More recently, Latin American countries have been preparing plans as a means of qualifying for aid under the Alliance for Progress. For example, Brazil's *Plano Trienal*, which was produced under forced draft in two and a half months, was created largely for the purpose of getting foreign aid.[3]

When a country has the capacity and the intention to carry out a development plan, the use of a realistic plan to obtain foreign resources to supplement domestic investment is generally both appropriate and desirable to help bring about a higher rate of economic growth. If

---

[1] "What is needed is not so much short-term plans as plans prepared in a short time." Statement by a Bolivian delegate to the Latin American Seminar on Planning in Mar del Plata, Argentina, May 1963.

[2] Ghana. *Second Development Plan, 1959–64*, pp. iii–iv.

[3] Daland, Robert T. "Chapter V. The Future and Brazilian Planning," pp. 32–33.

outside financial help can be obtained, it furnishes additional hope that the country will attain its planning objectives. Moreover, the availability of foreign loans and assistance for well-prepared projects and programs has had a beneficial effect in stimulating recipient countries to coordinate and otherwise improve their investment activities through better planning. For example, a study completed by the Columbia University School of Law correctly attributes Colombia's progress in sectoral programing for transportation and electric power largely to the availability of foreign financing for projects in these sectors:

> Probably the greatest impetus to such sectoral planning has come from the prospect of obtaining international financing to help carry out the programs. . . . The prospects for improvement in future Colombian economic planning may thus be very much brightened by the closer links that have recently been established with external financing agencies.[4]

But the rapid spread of planning and pressure from aid-giving countries and agencies in recent years have also converted some countries to planning almost solely because it is fashionable and because possession of a national development plan often makes it easier to obtain foreign grants or loans. There are countries where comprehensive plans have been prepared in a few weeks in an office in the capital without the planners having consulted with operating ministries and agencies. For instance, Brazil's *Plano Trienal* was prepared in this way in a period of ten weeks, while the first draft of Ghana's Seven-Year Plan, also prepared with minimal participation of operating organizations in the Government, took five weeks. In Somalia and Dahomey, among other countries, development plans were prepared by foreign advisers or consultants with little participation by those who would be responsible for their execution and with little relation to the fragile administrative structure in the country concerned.

In many countries,

> a development programme can be used as a means of window-dressing, and is often so used. The Government omits from the

[4] Columbia University School of Law. *Public International Development Financing in Colombia*, p. 144.

plan things which it intends to do but prefers not to talk about, such as some prestige expenditures; and it puts into the plan things which will impress some readers, but which it does not intend to do.[5]

Some plans are formulated on a grandiose scale with little relation to economic reality. It is hard to take a plan seriously if, as in the case of a plan recently drafted in one African country, it is necessary to double the already high level of taxation in order to achieve the plan's targets or, as in the case of another, it involves a fivefold increase in past levels of expenditure. In several new countries, large sums have been spent on extravagant office buildings and schools or on lavishly appointed showpiece palaces instead of on productive projects.[6] In laying down precepts for assessing a development plan, Professor Arthur Lewis noted that even in the more sensible of the less developed countries there is a weakness for prestige manifest in their planning which

> shows itself not so much in the objects of expenditure, which are desirable in themselves, but in doing on a lavish and magnificent scale what could be done much more cheaply, and especially in lavish expenditure on airports, model towns, and improving public buildings. . . . I would give high marks [he said,] to a development programme in which only 10 per cent of the expenditure was in nonsense of this kind whereas a programme in which the figure reached 30 per cent would seem to be well below par.[7]

A plan is a means, not an end. Yet in many countries, planning and other officials behave as though completion of the plan's formulation is the end, not the beginning, of the planning process. The plan is then apt to be forgotten after its completion while ministries, departments and agencies continue to operate much as they did before. In some countries development plans have followed one another in rapid and unproductive succession. The literature on Philippine economic planning mentions many plans—some 20 in all—over a period of 35 years, including no less than 14 in the postwar period (see Appendix III). Almost all were little more than suggestions, proposals, opinions or platitudes designed to influence public policy. Some made use of

[5] Lewis, W. Arthur. "On Assessing a Development Plan," p. 10.
[6] One Presidential palace was reported to have been constructed with Italian marble brought in by air. See, Hapgood, David. "Africa's New Elite," p. 44.
[7] Lewis, W. Arthur. "On Assessing a Development Plan," pp. 9–10.

advanced planning techniques and refined criteria for determining investment priorities. None had much effect on the country's development. The 1961 ECAFE annual survey states that in the Philippines,

> economic planning has tended to be more an intellectual excercise or a call to action than a specific blueprint to be implemented.[8]

Beginning in 1942, Brazil had one plan after another, none of which was ever implemented. Other countries, like Burma, Indonesia and Madagascar, have also produced series of plans which have been largely ignored after their publication (see Appendix III). The existence of a development plan in any country therefore gives no assurance that its government has either the will or ability to carry it out.

Just as there is more to planning than the preparation of a plan, so planning does not necessarily require a formal development plan. As will be seen later, what constitutes a plan has been the subject of controversy. But the important question is not what is a plan and what is not. In any country, it is rather whether the planning process is firmly established as a matter of government policy. The document, whether a list of policies, a budget, a partial or a comprehensive plan, is far less important than the planning process.

Nepal furnishes an illuminating example of the distinction between plans and the planning process. Following the poor results obtained from its partial First Five-Year Plan, it became evident that the country did not have the financial, organizational and technical resources needed to proceed with the ambitious comprehensive Second Five-Year Plan which the planners had proposed. The Government therefore decided, instead, to devote one year to the consolidation and improvement of previously approved projects and to a close study of the problems of project implementation before proceeding with a three-year public investment plan. In announcing the Government's decision, the Vice-Chairman of the National Planning Council aptly described the fine difference between planning and a plan in this way:

> In the past we have had a Plan without much planning. . . . During this current year, in order to achieve effective planning in the future, we shall, as it were, be planning without a Plan. What we are going to attempt to do is to make our Development Program consistent with national priorities and objectives. We will ration-

[8] UN. ECAFE. *Economic Survey of Asia and the Far East 1961*, p. 80.

alize our planning procedures by introducing interproject coordination so that planning may become more effective. And, finally, we will attempt to place development financing on a more stable and lasting basis, so that our excessive dependence on foreign aid may some day soon be brought to an end.[9]

If planning involves the formulation of a rational program of action for achieving development objectives, this is planning; and if vigorously pursued, this course could advance Nepal's development at least as much as the preparation of a more formal plan. As a matter of fact, reports from Nepal indicate that the course embarked upon has produced results.

Development planning, then, is not the same thing as a development plan. Those who confuse the two mistake a product of the planning process for the process itself.[10] Planning as a process is an indispensable precondition for the formulation of effective development policies and measures. Whether or not the bases and rationale for these policies and measures should be set forth in a paper plan is a separate matter.[11] The preparation of a document which embodies the results of development planning has advantages because it provides a systematic approach to attempts to co-ordinate development decisions and to improve on previously unco-ordinated decisions.[12] Moreover, plans have been found to be useful devices for initiating or stimulating the development process. But these advantages do not mean that a plan is a sufficient or even a necessary condition for insuring rapid development:

> It is a mistake to suppose that nothing ever gets decided or 'planned' until there is a programme. Just as it is nonsense to equate planning with the publication of a quinquennial programme, so it is nonsense to think that a programme settles everything and that no sensible decisions can be taken without one.[13]

[9] Nepal. National Planning Council, Ministry of National Guidance. *Policy Statement on Planning and Development*, p. 10.

[10] Gross, Bertram M. "When is a Plan not a Plan," p. 11.

[11] UN. ECA. *Problems Concerning Techniques of Development Programming in African Countries*, p. 18.

[12] Cairncross, A. K. "Programmes as Instruments of Coordination," p. 90.

[13] *Ibid.*

THE VARIETY OF PLANS

Uncertainty attends the question of what is, and what is not, a development plan. Is a general strategy, composed only of fiscal, monetary, wage, price, foreign trade or other policies, a development plan? Is an annual or multiannual capital or investment budget, whether separate from or combined with a current expenditure budget, a development plan? Is it proper to label a public investment program, whether integrated or not and whether or not accompanied by policies for promoting development of the private sector, a development plan?

The question need not be asked about a comprehensive development plan because everyone agrees that it is a development plan. But must all development programs be comprehensive before they can qualify as development plans? There is no complete agreement about this, although there is a more or less general consensus that mere comprehensiveness is not enough. Thus, a plan which only forecasts global economic trends and recommends the adoption of some government policies may be a plan, but it does not constitute a development plan. Such a plan, like the one in the Netherlands, is appropriate in planning for economic stability in a mature market economy with a dynamic private sector. It is unlikely to be an adequate instrument for promoting the economic advancement of a less developed country because it relies heavily on market forces which generally operate ineffectively in such countries. When such plans were discussed at the First Annual Meeting of the Inter-American Economic and Social Council in Mexico City, they were properly ruled out as development plans under the Alliance Program because

> economic theory and most recent practical experience have shown that the monetary, fiscal, and commercial policies, in themselves alone, do not supply a sufficient basis for determining the quantity, the distribution and the timing of public investments, or the incentives and restrictions needed to orient the private sector's contribution to the development effort. . . .[14]

[14] OAS. Inter-American Economic and Social Council, etc. *Report of the Panel of Experts to the Inter-American Economic and Social Council,* p. 23.

There is perhaps somewhat more doubt about the status of a capital or investment budget. There are those who feel that a capital budget is a plan. But this is a minority view and is generally held in advanced countries which do not have conventional development plans. After all, if a budget were a development plan, it would only be necessary to improve budgetary practices sufficiently in less developed countries to make them development plans. But this would not meet the need. For while, as will be seen later, it is impossible for a country to plan effectively without good budgetary practices and procedures, budgets have certain inherent deficiencies which greatly diminish their usefulness as instruments for promoting development. It would be possible to rid budgets of these defects, but in the course of doing so they would not remain budgets. This would be unfortunate since budgets are essential adjuncts to development plans.

Capital budgets cannot easily serve as development plans for a number of reasons. On the one hand, they include nondevelopment expenditures like those for the construction of prisons, and on the other, they frequently exclude "capital-like" outlays like disbursements for agricultural research and extension services, vocational training and health, which may make a great impact on development. Projects and programs incorporated in capital budgets are rarely selected on the basis of their relative costs and benefits, and the budget-making period is usually too short, as well as an inappropriate time, for making adequate appraisals of development projects and programs. Only limited attempts are generally made to relate projects and programs included in capital budgets; and the main requirement for internal consistency is simply that the sum of the parts should equal the total. Also, capital budgets are mainly financial documents and do not usually take into account real resources. Finally, capital budgets are almost exclusively concerned with the public part of an economy. They are not, by themselves, suitable instruments of co-ordination with the private sector. For example, they do not include the policies and measures required to get the private sector to behave in a manner consistent with a government's development objectives.

Multiannual capital budgets have advantages over annual capital budgets because they permit governments to take a longer, and hence more flexible, view of their development effort. It is therefore possible for government ministries and agencies to set priorities among projects and to revise them occasionally, instead of being pinned down to the rigidities inherent in annual budgets. Multiannual capital budgets also enable governments to consider financing problems against a wider background of possibilities and to improve the phasing of projects and programs to be completed over the period of years involved. Despite these advantages over annual capital budgets, multiannual capital budgets nevertheless suffer from most of the deficiencies characteristic of all capital budgets. It would therefore be stretching the concept too much to classify capital budgets like Puerto Rico's Six-Year or Four-Year Financial Programs or the Philippines' Five-Year Fiscal Plan as development plans.

The deficiencies of capital budgets have not prevented some countries from using them as substitutes for development plans. This can be done, but it is not the best way to stimulate growth, especially in later stages of development when the returns from alternative investment opportunities are not likely to be as apparent as they usually are at the beginning of the development process. However, a capital budget is most effective when it is used, not in lieu of a development plan, but in conjunction with one.

In contrast to capital budgets, public investment programs, although covering only a part of an economy, are generally considered to be development plans. But a program for a sector is generally considered to be less than a development plan. Public investment plans may range from enumerations of poorly co-ordinated government investment projects, with private investment largely ignored,[15] to integrated public investment plans which include forecasts of global economic activity, and policies and instruments for stimulating the private sector to act in accordance with a government's development objectives. Most national development plans are public investment plans. Where a public investment plan exists in addition to the budget, it should, if only as a practical matter, be accepted as a development plan, since it embodies professed national aspirations, such as they are, for promoting national development.

There are dissenters from this view. Some planners and experts consider only comprehensive plans with over-all growth targets to be development plans. Thus, the authors of Nigeria's comprehensive National Development Plan for 1962–1968 took the position that Nigeria's previous ten-year and five-year public investment plans

---

[15] The early plans prepared in 1950 and 1951 by the Colombo Plan countries and many of the British CD&W territorial ten-year plans were generally of this variety.

were not 'plans' in the true sense of the word. More accurately they constituted a series of projects which had not been co-ordinated or related to any overall target.[16]

But most planners and experts, although perhaps favoring comprehensive plans, accept national or regional public investment programs as development plans. Thus, when confronted with the practical problem of setting a minimum standard for a national or regional development plan under the Alliance for Progress after it had become clear that most Latin American countries were not going to produce comprehensive plans soon, the Committee of Nine, the Alliance authority concerned, agreed that a general development strategy

> could be a sufficient basis for obtaining external cooperation under the Alliance, if it were complemented by a few specific investment projects that met the conditions of that strategy. . . .[17]

Degree of Detail. National development plans vary greatly in degree of comprehensiveness and detail. Among public investment plans, some encompass almost all government development outlays. Others include only a part of the investments made by a government. Iran's Second Seven-Year Plan covered only public investments under the control of the Plan Organization, the central development and planning body, which added up to only about one-half the total investments made in the public sector. The remainder was made by ministries and public agencies. Tanganyika's Three-Year Plan for 1961/62–1963/64 included only those public investments which were in the capital budget, thereby excluding about one-third of total public investments largely made in conjunction with private and British Government funds. In contrast to such "partial" public investment plans, other partial plans cover some public and some private investments. Thus, Portugal's Second Development Plan contained a list of high priority investments in both the public and private sectors for which the Government was prepared to help mobilize funds. The public investments in the Plan accounted for less than one-half of the Government's investments and the private investments in the Plan for a much smaller proportion of total private investments.

There are also wide variations in the comprehensiveness and detail

[16] Nigeria. Federal Ministry of Economic Development. *National Development Plan, 1962–1968,* p. 6.

[17] OAS. Inter-American Economic and Social Council, etc. *Report of the Panel of Experts to the Inter-American Economic and Social Council,* p. 23.

of "comprehensive" plans. In the socialized economies of Eastern Europe, plans have had to be prepared in great detail in order to provide a basis for the mandatory quotas and instructions issued to each socialized enterprise and collective farm for implementing the plan. Through the system of "financial and material balances" based on the production potential of the economy, the plan has endeavored to balance inputs and outputs of raw materials, supplies and manpower and to take account of money incomes, labor productivity, costs, prices, etc.[18] The balances have been used to reconcile the planned output in each sector with available resources and the global plan. The global plan in a socialized country has been typically divided into sectoral and regional plans which not only had to dovetail into, but also add up to, the totals in the global plan. The plans of ministries, enterprises and other socialized economic units have had, in turn, to tie into the sectoral, regional and global plans. The complexity of this task often has led to serious errors and dislocations. It also helps account for the great interest in electronic computers for planning purposes in the USSR.

In most of the socialized countries, subordinate plans in the socialized sectors of the economy have had to conform to the targets, quotas, norms, rules and regulations laid down in the global plan. In Yugoslavia, however, republic, district, communal and enterprise plans are not under any legal requirement to fulfill any target in the global plan. Republics, districts, communes and enterprises tend to be guided by the global plan. But they may, and frequently do, choose not to follow the global plan when they have enough investment resources of their own to carry out projects not provided for in the global plan.

Because Yugoslav plans set aggregative targets which are carried out by means of generalized credit, banking, investment and similar instruments of economic policy instead of by instructions to regional and other economic units, their plans have tended to be much less detailed than those of other Eastern European countries. In fact, in terms of bulk, current Yugoslav national plans are among the smallest in the world, their pages generally numbering less than fifty. As the list of plans in Appendix III indicates, many national plans are voluminous. Pakistan's First Five Year Plan was a work of over 650 large

[18] Cuba also now plans on the Soviet model with hundreds of balances to equate supply and demand for about 100 basic articles.

pages with about 500,000 words; Chile's Ten-Year Plan consisted of 6 volumes divided into 20 books, totaling several thousand pages; and Indonesia's Eight-Year Plan is a monumental product composed of 4,638 pages, divided into 8 parts, 17 volumes and 1,945 paragraphs to commemorate August 17, 1945, the date Indonesia proclaimed its independence. (Unfortunately, there are indications that an inverse correlation exists between the bulk of a development plan and the success achieved in attaining its targets.)

In general, comprehensive plans in mixed economies rely, to a greater extent than comprehensive plans in socialized economies, on broad aggregates, conceived as indicators rather than binding targets, for such variables as income, output, savings, investment and foreign trade. This makes it possible to base the plan on a simple growth model composed of as few as two sectors, e.g., consumer goods and capital goods or agricultural and nonagricultural production. It is also possible to have a plan with a much more elaborate model of 20 or more sectors, prepared with the aid of high speed computers. A plan may vary greatly in complexity; it may be based on static or dynamic assumptions; it may utilize pragmatic techniques, input-output analysis or more advanced methods like linear or curvilinear programing. Some countries, like Ecuador, Turkey, the UAR and Venezuela, have used mathematical models in the course of preparing their plans. But most mixed-economy countries with comprehensive plans employ less complex methods in formulating their plans than econometricians would like. Nor does the preparation of an econometric model as a part of a procedure for formulating a plan necessarily signify that the plan will be based on the model. Thus, the draft plan-frame for India's Second Five-Year Plan, mostly prepared in the Indian Statistical Institute, proposed an advanced mathematical model for the Plan. The model had little to do with Indian realities and the Second Plan was in fact prepared by largely pragmatic methods. An econometric model was also prepared by Gerhard Tintner and Oswaldo Dávila in connection with the formulation of Ecuador's ten-year plan for 1964–73.[19] But the plan as it emerged gave little evidence that it had been influenced by the model. Even the relatively advanced French planners have found that they must modify their econometric models to take account of

---

[19] Tintner, Gerhard and Dávila, Oswaldo. "Un Modelo Econométrico para el Ecuador."

the contrast between the elaborate and accurate algebra of the
programming methods and the blurred picture of what remains
uncertain. . . .[20]

The absence of reliable data, as well as other deficiencies, accounts for
the fact that econometric models based on input-output matrices are
rarely used in national planning [21] in less developed countries. In
Africa,

> the bulk of the region's plans are inventories of urgent measures to
> be approached by the private and public sectors, particularly the
> latter. . . . They rarely attempt to build an input-output model
> that would permit testing the coherence and viability of the
> plan.[22]

In Jan Tinbergen's *Central Planning,* which summarizes responses
received to a questionnaire sent to central planning agencies, Professor
Tinbergen reported that trial and error methods were much more
common in national planning than the use of models. In its review of
the book, the *Economist* found it noteworthy that

> even such a simple method of establishing economic relationships
> as multiple correlation analysis is apparently used very rarely.
> Thus despite the proliferation of literature on high-powered plan-
> ning techniques, . . . planning in practice is fairly humdrum in
> most countries.
> A major cause of this, duly mentioned, is the shortage of detailed
> statistics. This is so even in the United Kingdom, where the latest
> official input-output table is a decade out of date and is in terms of
> an obsolete classification of industries. Yet in most respects this
> country is statistically better off than the average.[23]

[20] Massé, Pierre. "French Methods of Planning," p. 13.

[21] Besides the shortage of dependable statistics and other information, important
limitations of these models include the lack of interdependency of economic sectors
and other parts of a less-developed economy and the rapidity with which technical
coefficients used in models change in a developing economy. It is theoretically
possible to compensate for the last deficiency by forecasting the shape of future
technical coefficients. Apart from the problem of the margin of error which such
forecasts may produce, the time and effort involved in making the forecasts points
up what is probably the greatest deficiency of using such models in less developed
countries, to wit, the lack of adequately trained technicians to deal competently
with the concepts and procedures involved (UN. ECA. *Report of the Meeting of the
Expert Group on Comprehensive Development Planning,* pp. 22–23).

[22] UN. ECA. *Outlines and Selected Indicators of African Development Plans,*
pp. vi–vii.

[23] *Economist,* January 9, 1965, p. 126.

The degree to which comprehensive development plans of countries with mixed economies are divided into detailed sectoral programs varies greatly among countries and among sectors in a country. It may also vary in the same country over time, depending on the stage of development. Generally, the sectors of the plan in which public investment predominates are worked out in greater detail than those in which private investment prevails. In the plans of most mixed economies, this means that the sectors concerned with the provision of basic facilities receive the greatest attention. But where a government considers a branch of agriculture or industry to be of prime importance, it may also be planned in detail. In India, for example, basic and heavy industry, especially iron and steel and machine building, receives considerable attention in that country's plans because the Government believes heavy industry to be critically important to the country's development. But even in the public investment part, sectoral programing in the plans of countries with mixed economies is almost always less detailed than in the plans of countries with socialized economies.

The preparation of sectoral programs may take place concurrently with the preparation of an aggregative plan, in which case initial sectoral targets of output and resource requirements are adjusted to the aggregate targets through a process of successive approximations. But in many countries, the preparation of sectoral programs has preceded the formulation of comprehensive plans. Some sector programs have been prepared with the expectation that they would eventually be incorporated in an aggregative plan. But others have been formulated because the sectors involved were lagging or were considered to be important for development in countries which have had no immediate intention of planning comprehensively. Thus, the Netherlands has prepared sectoral programs for housing, education and roads without any intention of incorporating them in an over-all development plan. Even without over-all plans, well-prepared sectoral programs which project demand and resource requirements for a period of years have been found to be very useful in allocating investment resources in countries without development plans. In Colombia, for example, sectoral plans for transportation and electric power made it possible for that country to budget investment expenditures in these sectors on a rational basis without a plan and made it easier, later, to prepare a development plan. Mexico has been able to maintain a high rate of growth over an extended period of years without a national development plan partly because of the generally good quality of its sectoral programing, especially in the important fields of electric power, petroleum, transportation, irrigation and education,[24] as well as in such industrial branches as chemicals and automobiles. However, when sectoral programs are prepared outside the framework of a comprehensive plan they need to be tested by qualitative and such quantitative means as are available to determine that they are not inconsistent with a country's priority needs and resources.

Unlike comprehensive plans in socialized countries, the plans of mixed economies are almost never divided into a series of regional plans, co-ordinated with each other and with the aggregate plan. Federal governments like Nigeria's or those with separated regions, like Pakistan's, are generally the only exceptions. Some over-all plans provide for one or two regional plans. But in most over-all plans such mention as is made of regional plans is usually little more than lip service to a widely held, but apparently postponable, ideal.

Like sectoral programs, regional plans are often formulated with a view to being incorporated eventually in a national plan, as in the case of the plan for the Magdalena Valley and the North of Colombia. But regional plans for backward regions have also been prepared in countries which, at the time, had no immediate intention of planning nationally. Like national plans, regional plans may be divided into sectoral plans. And like them also, the sectors in which public investment is concentrated are likely to be programed in greater detail than those in which private entrepreneurs account for most investment.

As a rule, the plans in mixed economies are binding on the public sector where the government has direct control, but not on the private sector where persuasion is mainly relied upon to influence the size and composition of private investment. But there are many variants in this general pattern. The French plan is the prototype of such development plans for the more advanced countries, as well as for some of the less advanced, which have adopted its system of planning. In France, the Government proposes, discusses and selects a rate of growth for the plan period. The planners work out the implications of the growth target on the future development of the economy. The Government states what actions it proposes to take with respect to public investment and the policies it will follow to help achieve the proposed rate of

---

[24] Mexico's Eleven-Year Plan (1959–70) for education is an unusually well-conceived and well-organized sectoral program which is being carried out as scheduled.

growth. In preparing the plan, government officials, acting in concert with representatives of industry and labor, set sectoral and other targets which "indicate" the planned course of investment and the main actions needed to achieve the targets. While each enterprise is free to act as it chooses, it is influenced in its actions not only by government investment decisions for nationalized industries and infrastructure, which account for more than half of total investment, and by extensive official credit and financial controls over industry, but also by a tradition which approves and encourages group action by business firms. The French plans have been called mandatory in the public sector and "indicative" in the private sector. But this is not quite accurate since the Government has considerable means at its disposal, which it uses when necessary to influence the private sector. But a more precise definition is difficult to come by. The best that the Director General of the French *Commissariat Général du Plan* has been able to offer is that

> French planning can be said to be less than mandatory and more than indicative. It can reasonably be defined as active planning . . . ,[25]

which presumably implies that the Government will take whatever action is required to implement the plan.

Japan's plan, even more than France's, relies on suasion to attain development targets. The main purpose of the plan is to provide guidance to the Government and the private sector. There is no control over the private sector and little control over the public sector. The plan provides only forecasts of the economy on which private enterprises may base their plans. For the public sector, the plan describes in some detail the measures to be adopted to achieve targets. But actual public investments are determined in annual budgets which are likely to be influenced as much by the prevailing economic situation as by the plan. Because of loose controls and the wide fluctuations in public investments, some Japanese economists have contended that Japan does not have a planned economy.[26] However, Japanese planners reply

[25] Massé, Pierre. "Planning in France," p. 17.

[26] For example, Tsuru, Shigeto. "Formal Planning Divorced from Action: Japan," p. 146, stated, ". . . the Plan for Doubling National Income (1) is not a *plan* for doubling national income, but limits itself to set out certain policy objectives, within the capabilities of the central government, on the assumption that the private sector has its own dynamism of income-doubling in ten years; and (2) *appears* to have a co-ordinated plan so far as the public sector is concerned, but, in fact, is being administered largely by respective Ministries as if no overall plan had existed."

that the plan was devised to be flexible and that it assumes fluctuations in the course of fulfilling targets.

India's plans lay down broad targets, the achievement of which depends, in the public sector, on the various departments and public enterprises of the central and state governments and on local authorities, and in the private sector, on private enterprises and farms. Because of the autonomy enjoyed by state governments, local authorities and, to some extent, by public enterprises, India's plans are not binding on either the private or public sector, except for programs sponsored by the central Government. Indeed, Indian economists have complained that the Government's power to regulate economic activity is even less than it is in some Western European countries with unplanned economies.[27] In Pakistan, the plans are generally obligatory, in fact if not in theory, on the provincial governments as well as on the central Government, but not on the private sector.

THE FORMAL STATUS OF PLANS

The national development plans of all socialized countries, including Cuba, are approved, either by their legislatures or other authorities, and have the force of law.[28] The plan targets are legally binding on all executing agencies and the laws generally provide sanctions for nonperformance. Yugoslav plans constitute an exception. Although the plans and the regulations promulgated under them are supposed to be mandatory, no person, enterprise or other entity is legally accountable for not fulfilling any plan target. The practical significance of the Yugoslav contention that the country's plans are mandatory is therefore unclear. It may be only a carry-over from the time when Yugoslav plans, like those in other socialized countries, were really obligatory; or it may be that the Government wishes to show that it looks upon its plans as serious expressions of intent.

Many countries with mixed economies also provide for the enactment of their plans as laws even though they are generally binding only on the administrative units under direct control of the central government authorities. Chile, Indonesia, Portugal, the Sudan, Taiwan and the UAR are examples of countries where development plans are

[27] Gadgil, D. R. *Planning and Economic Policy in India*, p. xii.
[28] In some countries, e.g., Poland, long-term plans are required by the Constitution to be enacted by Parliament, but annual plans are adopted by the Council of Ministers.

statutes. Cambodia, Ceylon, France, India, Iran, Italy, Korea, Norway and Turkey are also examples of countries where plans have been submitted for legislative approval prior to their becoming effective. In Eire, the Government approves the plan before sending it to Parliament, and legislative approval of the plan is considered unnecessary. In Ethiopia, plans have the same standing as government administrative orders. But Greece, Jamaica and Pakistan are examples of countries which do not submit their plans to their legislatures. The plans in these countries are considered to be an expression of the government's economic policy.

There has been some debate in countries with mixed economies about the desirability of enacting a national development plan into law. It is contended that enacting a plan into law raises its status in the eyes of political leaders, civil servants and the public, thereby enhancing its chances for fulfillment. It has also been suggested that where governments change frequently, later governments are more likely to implement the plan if it has been enacted into law than if it has only been approved by a previous government as its economic policy. In Jordan, for example, where the legislature lasts four years and the executive branch has changed four or five times during the same period, some staff members of Jordan's Development Board wanted the Five-Year Plan made into the law of the land in order to help bring about a measure of continuity in the country's development policy. Their advice was not followed because it was feared that the plan as a law would be difficult to change. There was ground for fear. A plan may lose needed flexibility in return for gaining status as a statute. In Indonesia, for example, when the Provincial Peoples Congress approved the Eight-Year Plan, it decreed that the pattern of development laid down in the plan could not be altered. There is also the possibility that a legislature which is asked to approve a plan may disrupt its internal consistency with amendments. This happened in Senegal.

The system used in France provides for parliamentary approval but avoids rigid restraints on the plan or amendments. The plan itself is not enacted into law, but is attached as an annex to a brief, one-page parliamentary act which approves the appended plan as the framework for investment during the period of the plan and as the instrument for guiding economic development and social progress. The same effect is obtained in Portugal, where the legislature only approves the broad outlines of the plan. The Government is then free to make such changes as it considers necessary, and even to revise it without further legislative approval.

But experience shows that the formal status of a plan is not a critical factor in its execution. It is noteworthy, for example, that the first three French plans were never presented to Parliament for approval. Yet the French governments of the time were not dissuaded by the lack of parliamentary approval from vigorously pursuing the development objectives in the plans. Nor is there good ground for believing that governments which have made their plans into statutes are more devoted to their fulfillment than those which have not. Ultimately, it is not the plan's legal status but the commitment of a country's government and people to a plan that determines the way it is implemented.

THE DURATION OF PLANS

Development plans are almost always prepared for a fixed period, but they vary as much in duration as they do in type. For example, Laos and Rumania had development plans for only half a year. Czechoslovakia, Turkey and Yugoslavia have or have had a one-year development plan. Zambia has had one of 18 months, while Albania, Bulgaria, Burma, Costa Rica, Honduras and Morocco have or have had two-year plans. The Congo (Brazzaville), Gabon, Guinea, Hungary, Korea, Mali, Poland, Tanganyika and both North and South Viet Nam have or have had three-year plans, and Kenya had a three-and-a-half-year development plan in 1954–57. Many countries have four-year plans, although the most typical plan is one for five years. But Iran has one for five-and-one-half years. Nigeria has, while Poland had, six-year plans. Eire, Panama and the USSR, Iran, the UAR and Syria have or have had seven-year development plans. Burma used to have an eight-year plan and Indonesia has one. Liberia is unique with a nine-year plan, but the list of countries with ten-year plans is long. Finally, most of the socialized countries and an increasing number of countries with mixed economies employ longer-term plans of 15, 20, 25 years or more. The reader who is interested in national development plans issued by countries and dependent territories will find an extended list of these in Appendix III.

Short-Term Plans

Several factors account for differences in the duration of national development plans. Some arise from internal administrative or political requirements; others largely represent the result of outside influences.

Thus, Laos' Emergency Plan for the first semester of 1963 was an attempt at a more modest effort when it became apparent that even the country's one-year development plan would not be carried out. Sometimes, in periods of transition or uncertainty, conditions do not permit a country to look ahead for more than six months or a year. The choice in such instances is either to plan in the short run or not at all. For example, after Yugoslavia had broken with the Soviet bloc in 1948, the Government felt that the domestic and foreign situation did not permit planning for more than a year at a time. Between 1952 and 1956, therefore, Yugoslavia relied, with considerable success, on one-year development plans. In the early postwar years, Rumania prepared a plan for six months, followed by three one-year plans up to 1950.[29] Between 1954 and 1956, Hungary also drew up annual plans. More recently, with the collapse of Czechoslovakia's Third Five-Year Plan, that country introduced a one-year plan for 1963, while laying the groundwork for the preparation of a longer-term plan. Through the interim use of one-year plans, planners have found that they can gain experience as well as time to prepare longer-term plans. These reasons prompted Turkey to employ a one-year plan in 1962 while preparing its five-year plan. Immediately after independence, Algeria found it most convenient to have two annual "equipment" plans for 1963 and 1964. Zambia has made use of an interim plan for 18 months from January 1965 to June 1966, when a five-year plan is scheduled to begin.

Some countries, which have found it premature or otherwise inconvenient to plan for more than a short period, have chosen a two-year instead of a one-year planning period. Czechoslovakia's first comprehensive planning effort covered only 1947 and 1948 because it was felt that the planners lacked experience and that the country was not ready to plan for a longer period. East Germany also employed a two-year plan for 1949–50 because it needed time to prepare for a longer-term plan. Similarly, Burma's first attempt at comprehensive planning was for a two-year period. In spite of many shortcomings, this plan shaped the country's basic agricultural and industrial policy for a number of years.[30] France made use of a two-year interim plan in 1960–61 when dislocations following its currency devaluation greatly reduced the rate of growth and made it difficult to plan ahead for the usual four-year period. Various African countries, frequently upon be-

[29] Spulber, Nicolas. "Planning and Development," p. 88.
[30] Walinsky, Louis J. *Economic Development in Burma, 1951–1960*, p. 64.

coming independent, resorted to two-year interim plans to permit their emergent governments to carry out priority projects and to lay the groundwork for more detailed and sounder development plans.[31] Thus, a two-year period was chosen for Morocco's Biennial Investment Plan for 1958–59 to give its planners time to gather data and prepare a five-year plan. Nigeria had an interim two-year plan in 1954–55 between five-year plans. Other African countries which have found two-year interim plans useful include Chad, Gabon, Ghana, Ivory Coast, Tanzania, Tunisia and Upper Volta. Because of poor experience and uncertainties with its plans in recent years, Czechoslovakia set targets only for 1964 and 1965 as a first step toward preparing a five-year plan for 1966–70. Honduras' Biennial Plan for Public Investment was the first of what is expected to be a series of two-year plans to be prepared by Latin American countries under the Alliance for Progress Program. It is hoped that these plans will be the beginning of longer-term national planning efforts to be carried forward during the period of the biennial plans.[32]

Annual and biennial plans provide some countries at the beginning of their planning experience, or in periods of emergency or other uncertainty, with an opportunity to plan they might not otherwise have had. But such short-term plans can only play a limited part in influencing development since they do not provide adequate opportunity for examining alternatives or mobilizing resources and cannot be used effectively to bring about basic structural changes. Their chief value lies in the possibilities they present for rationalizing existing programs and production and for establishing favorable conditions for further development. Because of the limitations of short-term plans, most countries prefer and use medium-term plans.[33]

Medium-Term Plans

Political requirements frequently dictate the length of the period of medium-term plans. A five-year plan period is convenient in India

---

[31] UN. ECA. *Outlines and Selected Indicators of African Development Plans,* p. iv.

[32] OAS. PAU. *Alliance for Progress, A Weekly Report on Activities and Public Opinion,* p. 51.

[33] Most authorities classify plans with periods ranging from three to seven years as medium-term plans. In practice, however, such plans frequently extend up to ten years. But a ten-year plan may be a medium-term plan in one country (e.g., the Sudan) and a long-term plan in another (e.g., Tunisia).

because it coincides with the term of office in central and state governments. In Mexico, the termination date of plans is fixed by the date when the President leaves office. Since the presidential term is six years, plans cannot be for a longer period, but they may be for a shorter time, depending on when, in the presidential term, they were prepared. Thus, the Three-Year Immediate Plan was prepared midway in the presidential term and, in the Mexican situation, must end when the President turns over his office to his successor.[34] Planners' attempts to extend it for a year, as a guide to the next government, did not succeed. Since 1954, Norway's plan period has covered its parliamentary four-year period. In Burma, also, a three-year plan was converted into a four-year plan to coincide with the term of Parliament, and when Syria joined the UAR, its seven-year plan was changed and extended to ten years to make it coincide with Egypt's plan.

When nations plan in accordance with international regional agreements, the duration of the plans may be governed by regional rather than national considerations. During the era of the Marshall Plan, for example, the four-year period became standard among the Western European countries which participated in the program. The first plans prepared by the Colombo Plan countries were all for the six-year period, 1951–57. The United Nations' (UN) and the Organization for Economic Co-operation and Development's (OECD) Decade of Development for the 1960's has prompted some countries to terminate their current plans at the end of 1969. In Eastern Europe a five-year period, to start in 1970, has been chosen for the plans in the region to facilitate economic collaboration among member countries of the Council for Mutual Economic Assistance (COMECON). Under the Alliance for Progress, Latin American countries are expected to prepare ten-year and two-year plans.

As is evident from the foregoing, the question of what constitutes the ideal planning period is undecided. It is likely to remain so. The situation in each country must govern the selection of an appropriate planning period. Since conditions differ among countries, the periods of national plans differ. Furthermore, changing circumstances in a country may bring changes in the duration of plans. For every country like India, which has not altered its plan period (except for the abortive Six-Year Plan prepared for the Colombo Plan), many have

---

[34] A similar reason accounted for the duration of Brazil's Three-Year Plan. This Plan was produced after two years of the President's five-year term had elapsed.

shifted from one period to another. Burma, for example, has had in succession a two-year, an eight-year, a three-year and a four-year plan; Colombia has ten-year and four-year plans; Yugoslavia started with a five-year plan, shifted to one-year plans, then to five-year plans and is now preparing a seven-year plan (see Appendix III).

Despite the seeming lack of uniformity among and within nations about the duration of their plans, some useful generalizations emerge from their experience. That experience indicates that, as a practical matter, it is desirable to fix a period for a development plan which is short enough to permit reasonably accurate projections and estimates to be made and long enough to cover the lead time or gestation period of a sufficient number of major projects [35] to give a reasonably adequate indication of their effect in carrying out plan objectives. If a plan is for too short a period, it not only does not provide enough time to prepare and carry out major projects, but is likely to be little more than a statement of investment commitments already made. If the plan is for too long a period, it will be of little value because targets in later years obviously depend on unforeseeable domestic and international events as well as on accomplishments in the earlier years of the plan period. Countries which depend on export earnings of commodities whose prices are set in world markets find it particularly difficult to plan ahead for long periods. This point was made in a meeting of African planners where

> many of the participants mentioned the difficulty of maintaining development programmes—especially long-term programmes—in the face of fluctuating export proceeds and export prices for major commodities; it was [therefore] agreed that such fluctuations made necessary shorter terms of planning and more frequent revision of programmes.[36]

Consequently, the longer the term of a plan, the more uncertain and questionable the projections and the less the degree of precision possible. There is also a danger that technological innovations will upset forecasts which extend too far into the future. A long-term plan has the psychological advantage of targets often impressively higher than those for shorter-term plans. This advantage can be overrated,

[35] I.e., the time needed to prepare and construct the projects and put them into operation.
[36] UN. ECA. *Meeting of Experts on Techniques of Development Programming in Africa, 30 November to 5 December 1959, Executive Secretary's Report*, p. 7.

however, since the further away the target date, the easier it is for governments to postpone facing the unpleasant tasks which must be performed to convert the targets into realities. It is also harder to mobilize public interest and support for plan targets for a year which is far in the future.

The five-year plan period originally adopted in the Soviet Union, which has been widely and sometimes unthinkingly copied by other countries, was appropriate to the Soviet Union in its early stages of development. In what was a predominantly agricultural country, it was short enough to estimate output and other targets and long enough to permit annual crop fluctuations to be evened out. But as industry became more important, the five-year period became too short to cover the gestation period for basic investment projects in power, transportation, mining and industry. This led to the eventual adoption of a seven-year plan, as well as one for 20 years.

Few countries adopt plans at the start of their planning experience which turn out to have been too short; on the contrary, most tend to choose planning periods which are too long. This becomes clear from the historical record because (1) many plans with periods of six years or more are generally so vague for the last years of the period that they are little more than aspirations, (2) many turn out to have been so inaccurate for the later years of the plan period that they cannot easily be revised and must be replaced by other plans before the end of the planning period, and (3) there is a general tendency for countries in early stages of development to replace plans with others of shorter duration. As an illustration of the first of these three points, there is so little detail supporting the aggregates for the last five years of Chile's ten-year plan that they hardly qualify as targets. Further, the UAR and Syrian ten-year plans were so vague in the last half of the plan period that they were divided into two five-year plans. In Thailand, even a six-year plan was found to cover too long a planning period and it had to be divided into two three-year subplans.

With regard to the second point, that many plans turn out to be too inaccurate in later years to be revised, many of the CD&W ten-year plans were replaced by other plans before they expired. This was true, for example, in Ghana, Jamaica, Kenya, Nigeria and the Sudan. It is even true for the more developed countries. For example, Japan moved from a five-year to a ten-year planning period for 1961–70. Although the planned rate of growth was attained in each of the first three years of the plan period, the ten-year plan was replaced by a five-year plan for 1964–68 because the high rate of growth introduced serious problems which could not be handled by a revision of the ten-year plan. Because of these problems, it was also considered undesirable to try to plan ahead for more than five years.[37] Italy also had a ten-year plan, but divided it into two five-year subplans.

Finally, there are many examples of the general tendency among countries in early stages of development to reduce their planning periods. While Jamaica was one of the few countries in formerly British territories which retained the ten-year period, Ghana, Kenya, Nigeria and Sierra Leone reduced their planning period: Ghana, Nigeria and Sierra Leone to five years and Kenya to three and one-half years.[38] Among former French territories, Dahomey replaced a proposed ten-year plan with a four-year plan for 1962–65 and Gabon abandoned its five-year plan for 1959–64 for a three-year plan for 1963–65. The Belgian Congo's ten-year plan for 1949–59 was divided into three periods, each of approximately three years, for implementing the plan. By 1959, most development plans being implemented in Africa were for a period of three to five years.[39] In explaining why the ten-year plan had been replaced with one for three and one-half years, Kenya's Government stated:

> The number of amendments that had to be made in the old ten-year plan . . . demonstrates that a planning period of more than five years is unrealistic. In the rapidly changing circumstances at present facing the Colony an even shorter period for the present plan was indicated.[40]

Malaya reduced its plan period from ten to six years to meet the requirements of the Colombo Plan. Many other countries have shortened their planning periods as a result of experience. Bolivia reduced the period of its plan from ten to two years; Burma, from eight to four; Ceylon, from ten to three; Chile, from ten to five; Colombia, from ten to

[37] The problems included an unforeseen deterioration in the balance of payments, increases in prices of consumer goods and increased disparity in the incomes of rural as against urban populations, individuals in high and low income levels and large and small business enterprises.

[38] When Kenya's ten-year plan was replaced, it was estimated that it would require two and one-half years to complete the plan. Another year was added to make a three and one-half year plan.

[39] UN. Department of Economic and Social Affairs. *Economic Survey of Africa Since 1950*, p. 239.

[40] Colony and Protectorate of Kenya. *Development Programme, 1954–57*, p. 52.

four; Iran, from seven to five and one-half;[41] Morocco and Nepal, from five to three years. And Portugal, which has had two six-year plans, has followed them with a three-year plan. At the First Annual Conference of the OAS Inter-American Economic and Social Council in Mexico City, delegates from Latin American countries which had formerly accepted the obligation of drawing up ten-year development plans voiced strong opposition to long-term planning and advocated the adoption of plans limited to three years.[42] As a result of decisions taken at this Conference, the Alliance for Progress Committee of Nine decided to concentrate on short-term plans. "It seems advisable to emphasize," explained the Committee,

> that in view of the technical resources existing in the Latin American countries, of the statistical and economic information available, of the uncertainty of foreign markets, and of the lack of a sufficient number of projects, there is no practical value in formulating programs of eight to ten years or more. . . .[43]

A few countries have extended their planning period. Yugoslavia increased the length of its planning period from five to seven years for 1964–70, partly to add the last two years of its discarded five-year plan to the new plan and partly because it was felt that a five-year period was not long enough to cover the gestation periods of its hydroelectrical and metallurgical programs.[44] The USSR increased its planning period from five to seven years after it scrapped its sixth five-year plan. But because of an alarming retardation in the growth rate, the seven-year plan had to be superseded in its sixth year by a new two-year plan. Malawi felt three years was too short a period for effective planning and increased it to five years,[45] while Eire increased

[41] The half-year was added to shift the start of the plan period from September to March when both the Iranian calendar and fiscal year begin.

[42] *Washington Post*, October 11, 1962.

[43] OAS. Inter-American Economic and Social Council, etc. *Report of the Panel of Experts to the Inter-American Economic and Social Council*, p. 24.

[44] However, the actual planning period will be much shorter. Because of controversy over its provisions, the plan had not yet been adopted in January 1965 nor were there indications when it would be adopted. There were reports instead that the authorities would use a one-year plan for 1965, pending resolutions of differences concerning the Seven-Year Plan.

[45] Nevertheless, Malawi's planners have been quoted as stating that ". . . the detailed phasing of projects cannot be planned with any accuracy for any long period in advance." (UN. ECA. *Outlines and Selected Indicators of African Development Plans*, p. 74.)

its planning period from five to seven years in 1964–70 to have the last year of its own planning period coincide with the end of the UN's and OECD's "Decade of Development." Partly for the same reason, France also increased its planning period from four to five years for the Fifth Plan (1966–70). In part, however, the change was made because it has taken almost four years to prepare the four-year plans, and a longer interval between periods of plan preparation seemed desirable.

In most less developed countries, there are usually special reasons for their moving against the general trend. Thus, Indonesia went from a five- to an eight-year period because the planners felt that administrative, organizational and other inadequacies would prevent execution of their ambitious plan in a shorter period. But to facilitate execution, the plan period was divided into a first stage of three years for carrying out basic projects, and a second stage of five years for implementing the remaining programs in the plan. In the Sudan, the current plan was originally scheduled to cover five years. It was extended, first to seven and then to ten years, because the plan could not be carried out in less time.[46] It was politically easier to increase the period of the plan than to eliminate projects. In the UAR, the original five-year period of the Second Plan was extended to seven years when it became obvious that the desired income target could not be achieved in the original period. In Jordan, the period of the plan was extended from five to eight years after the Government announced that this was the time needed to make Jordan independent of foreign assistance. Ghana not only has moved against the general trend in lengthening its plan period from five to seven years by increasing it with the remaining two years of the last Five-Year Plan which was scrapped in the third year; it has also gone against the logic of its demonstrated need for a shorter planning period as revealed in its inability to carry out a five-year plan. It remains to be seen whether physical and administrative limitations, as well as uncertainties involved in some of the long-term projections, will permit the Indonesian, Sudanese, Jordanian and Ghanian plans to run their course without major overhaul. The period of Ecuador's first comprehensive plan was also originally five years, but it was increased to ten because of Alliance for Progress requirements. As in Chile's case, however, the second half of the plan period was prepared in lesser detail than the

---

[46] It was found impossible to carry out the large Roseires Dam project as well as other projects considered essential in a five-year period.

first half. All of these exceptions tend to underscore the general trend to shorter plan periods.

Long-Term Plans

When a country is in an early stage of development, it usually finds it possible and preferable to start planning with a short-term plan of one or two years or, more commonly, a medium-term plan of three to ten years. Immediate development objectives in such a country are clear and urgent and there is generally no feasible alternative to concentrating on their realization. In most countries, political leaders prefer to concentrate on immediate problems and solutions and it is difficult to get them to look ahead for more than a few years. The possibility of preparing a long-term plan, in addition to one for a shorter period, is therefore not given serious consideration. Moreover, planners usually have all they can do to turn out a short- or medium-term plan.

But as development proceeds, it is invariably found that an increasing number of projects and programs cannot be fitted into short or medium-term plans. This is especially true of plans for five years or less, but it can also be true of plans for six to ten years. Some countries try to get around this problem by preparing projections for critical sectors which extend beyond their plan periods. Thus, when Yugoslavia had one-year plans it prepared a ten-year agricultural program which it used as a basis for programing the agricultural component in its annual plans. More recently, ten-year sectoral projections have been prepared for electric power to link projects and programs which extended beyond Yugoslavia's five-year plan period. Mexico also employs longer-term sectoral programs, such as its eleven-year program for education, in addition to its three-year plan.

Other countries which can plan in detail for only three, four or five years, double their planning periods and fill in the last half of their plans in outline. This permits them to take account of programs which extend beyond the three- to five-year period which is adequate for most projects and programs in the plan. The UAR's first comprehensive plan for ten years is such a plan. As we have seen, Chile's and Ecuador's ten-year plans are also worked out in detail only in the first five years of their plan periods. And Thailand's six-year plan, as originally prepared, was really a three-year detailed plan with a sketchy outline for the second three years of the plan period. Tunisia's Ten-Year Perspective Plan for

1962–71 is somewhat different. It was first worked out in detail only for the first three years, 1962–64, and then for a second phase for the four years, 1965–68, divided into two two-year periods. The plan for the last three years of the ten-year period remains in outline.

While sectoral projections can be useful to supplement medium-term plans in early stages of development, they are too limited to give effect to most basic planning objectives like achieving self-sustaining growth, making substantial improvements in the standard of living, evening out regional inequalities or making fundamental changes in the relationship between the contribution of agriculture and industry to national output. These objectives involve basic structural modifications to the economy which cannot be encompassed in a sectoral projection or, for that matter, in a medium-term planning period. To realize basic planning objectives generally requires a broad perspective of the general direction in which the economy is likely to move over a long time. Moreover, as a country develops, the number of possible courses of action increases. It is then no longer possible to make rational medium-term decisions without first deciding on a longer-term strategy.

Consider, for example, the situation which might confront a largely agricultural country with a rapidly rising population. Before committing investment resources to short- and medium-term objectives, it would be useful for such a country to know the extent to which agriculture could be expected to absorb the foreseeable rise in the labor force in 15 or 20 years. In the light of this appraisal, it would be possible to estimate the scale of expansion required in nonagricultural sectors to absorb any excess in the estimated labor force. Where industrialization was required for this purpose, it would be necessary to determine the type of industrial complex suitable to the country. If the domestic market is likely to remain too small to support the industries chosen, or if imported industrial raw materials were needed, it would be desirable to determine what export industries were most likely to furnish the most employment and provide the foreign exchange required to pay for needed imports. It would also be helpful to compare relative foreign exchange and employment advantages of import-saving industries over export industries. And so on. Once a set of long-term goals was chosen, it would be necessary to determine the amounts of savings and investment capital and the number of skilled workers, technicians and engineers which would be required to achieve the long-term objectives and targets. The time needed to provide necessary resources and facilities would have to be estimated. It may take only a year or two to establish plants for producing consumer goods, but 10 or 15 years to get capital goods plants into operation. To train needed engineers and other technicians may take 20 or 25 years; and to build up a supply of scientists for basic and applied research may take a generation or more.[47]

Appraisals which attempt to look far into the future have advantages as prognoses. Since they are, in effect, long-term growth models in outline with only a few general targets based on only rough approximations of the likely supply of, and the demand for, physical resources, there is no need for detailed or elaborate calculations. Yet they can give a good enough idea of priorities to enable planners to concentrate on the most promising sectors in preparing medium-term plans. They can also indicate long enough in advance in what areas preinvestment and other surveys will be required before specific projects and programs can be formulated. In Yugoslavia, for instance, such projections indicated that a shortage of technicians would constitute a serious bottleneck to long-term development. If the problem was to be avoided, new training facilities would have to be created. This led the authorities to make substantially heavier increases for additional education facilities immediately.

What constitutes a desirable period for such appraisals varies with countries and their stage of development. It must be much longer than that of the current medium-term plan since the primary purpose of the appraisal is to give perspective to the medium-term plan. In some fields, like population, labor or education, it may be necessary to look ahead for 25 to 30 years to provide useful information. But for most other sectors, projections so far into the future become too imprecise to be of much value. The longer the term of these "perspective" appraisals or plans, the more difficult it becomes to forecast the effects of technological change on production, price variations on consumption or income distribution on savings.[48] India, for instance, found that its first perspective plan for 30 years, drawn up in connection with its First Five-Year Plan, was much too long. For its Second Plan, it prepared a perspective plan of 15 years, with projections for 20 years for some sectors. For its Third Plan it relied on 15-year projections and for its Fourth Plan it has again used a 15-year perspective, but with more

[47] Mahalanobis, P. C. *Perspective Planning in India*, p. 10.
[48] UN. ECAFE. *Problems of Long-Term Economic Projections with Special Reference to Economic Planning in Asia and the Far East*, p. 3.

concrete projections extending for only 10 years. Pakistan also has reduced the span of its perspective plan from 30 years for its Second Five-Year Plan to 20 years for its Third Plan period. In contrast, France is increasing its perspective from 15 years for its Fourth Plan to 20 years for its Fifth Plan. In a study made for the ECAFE, a group of experts advised countries in the ECAFE region to prepare perspective plans for a period covering two or three of their medium-term plans, in effect, for 15 to 20 years.

Most of the socialized countries employ perspective plans. The USSR has a 20-year perspective plan for 1961–80 which assumes a considerable increase in automated production. It lays down a series of targets, including an increase of 520 to 540 per cent in industrial output, 120 to 140 per cent in grain production and 250 to 279 per cent in meat production, "to give the USSR world leadership in *per capita* output." [49] Perspective plans are also being used increasingly in conjunction with medium-term plans in countries with mixed economies. Pakistan has prepared a Twenty-Year Perspective Plan for 1965–85, providing for the trebling of the 1962 level of per capita income, as well as full employment. In connection with the formulation of its Third Five-Year Plan for 1965–70, Ghana developed a perspective plan for 21 years within which to fit the next three seven-year development plans for the country. Ghana's perspective plan assumed that with the present and prospective size of its home market, and the rate of increase of the labor force, the possibility of a continued expansion of industrial employment is conditional upon Ghana's early integration into some sort of Inter-African trading arrangement which would permit Ghana to become an exporter of relatively sophisticated industrial products. The first seven-year development plan is considered as a first step in achieving this objective. Cameroun has a Twenty-Year Perspective Plan for 1960–80 which it used for drafting its First Five-Year Plan; Senegal prepared its Four-Year Development Plan for 1961–64 within a 16-year perspective which estimates a doubling of the standard of living in the fourth four-year plan; Turkey used a 15-year perspective, within which it hopes to prepare three five-year plans, the first of which is for the 1963–67 period; and Venezuela's 1963–66 Plan was part of an over-all 15-year perspective plan.

In contrast to the fixed perspective periods used by such countries as

[49] Bor, Mikhail Zakharovich. "The Organization and Practice of National Economic Planning in the Union of Soviet Socialist Republics," p. 102.

Senegal and Turkey, some countries prefer a "moving" perspective which moves forward and may vary in length with each medium-term plan. Thus, India set up perspective periods from 1951 to 1981 for its First Plan and from 1956 to 1971 (to 1976 for some sectors) for its Second Plan. It fitted its Third Plan into a perspective period from 1961 to 1976 and is using two periods, one from 1966 to 1976 and another from 1966 to 1981, for its Fourth Plan. France has also changed the 1961–75 perspective period used for formulating the Fourth Plan to 1966–85 for its Fifth Plan. Since the whole point of a perspective plan is to look as far ahead as possible beyond the termination date of a current medium-term plan, it is of course preferable to have the period of the perspective plan move forward with each medium-term plan. Otherwise, the perspective plan period progressively diminishes in length, and, hence, in its ability to shed light on longer-term trends.

Plan Continuity and Flexibility

Where both perspective and shorter-term plans are employed, real or apparent conflicts may arise between long- and shorter-run objectives. For example, when objectives are to industrialize in accordance with advanced technological standards and to increase employment opportunities, it may be possible to attain both objectives in the long run, but not in the short run. The investment program followed in the short run may therefore seem to favor the first objective at the expense of the second. Similarly, policy measures conducive to attaining a high growth rate may, in the short term, seem incompatible with those needed to reduce income or regional inequalities. In such cases, practical questions arise concerning the precedence of long- and short-term objectives. In the socialized countries, the objectives in the perspective plan determine medium-term objectives. In the scheme of a planned economy, therefore, it is the perspective plan which plays the leading part. If any conflict arises between the objectives of the two, the longer-term objectives take precedence. But in countries with mixed economies, the medium-term plan is the mainstay of development planning. While the medium-term plan is often formally binding to some extent, the perspective plan almost never is. It is often considered to be only a forecast based on a series of assumptions concerning domestic and international development. In theory, each medium-term plan is expected to be so formulated as to reach the goals in the long-term plan. But in practice, concessions are made to shorter-run objectives. In fact, in India, the perspective plan was revised on at least one occasion to make it consistent with the five-year plan instead of the reverse.[50]

Yet, the concept of a long-range perspective for planning is valuable, if for no other reason than that it points up the fact that development is inherently a long-time task requiring persistent application. Even though it may be convenient to divide that task into one-, three-, five-, seven-year or other periods, none of these can be considered a discrete period in a nation's life separated from the past and future. It is, in fact, organically a part of, and joined to, what has preceded and what will succeed it.[51] Planning, like the time needed for development, must be seen to be a continuous long-range process. It should not end, as in fact it frequently ends, with the formulation and promulgation of a plan. Every medium-term plan inherits unfinished work from the past and turns over work to be completed in the next period. A second plan takes up where a first plan left off. Projects begun in the first plan continue to be executed in the second. One plan glides into the other and the dividing line is not easily discernible.[52]

Nevertheless, the problem of linking one medium-term plan with another has not yet been solved in most countries. The transition between plans is often inefficient. As one reason, the time allowed for drafting medium-term plans is frequently too short. Consequently, new plans may not be ready in time to allow a smooth continuance of development activity from the old to the new plan. As another reason, new projects are not spaced to avoid bunching. In most countries new projects are prepared at the beginning of the plan period, which results in concentrating their completion in the latter part of the plan period. There may therefore be a rush at the end of the old plan period to fulfill targets, followed by a slowing down after the introduction of the new plan. India's experience, typical of that in other countries, has been that

> in the earlier years of a plan there was a slackening, and effort was made to make up the lag in the last year. Thus there was a gap between one plan and another.[53]

[50] Lewis, John P. "India," p. 96.
[51] Hussain, Z. "Organisation and Responsibilities of the Pakistan Planning Board," p. 28.
[52] *Economic Weekly*, Vol. XIII, No. 14, April 8, 1961, p. 564.
[53] Bhagat, B. R. (Minister of State for Planning). *Economic Times*, November 10, 1963.

The problem of achieving planning continuity is also exacerbated as a plan loses perspective with the passage of time and it becomes progressively more difficult to include projects and programs whose time of execution exceeds the remaining years of the plan period. Indeed, toward the end of a plan period most of the decisions which have to be made relate more to the next than to the current plan.

The failure to preserve planning continuity has had serious consequences for the socialized economies since enterprises in these countries must plan their activities on instructions from the appropriate authorities. But frequent delays in the completion of national and republican plans have repeatedly prevented enterprises from preparing their own plans in time. In a report to the Seventh Session of the Supreme Soviet of the USSR, the Premier referred to this problem:

> It is a grave shortcoming of our planning that we start planning anew, as it were, when passing from one year to the next and from one five-year period to another. When a year ends some of our enterprises and building projects do not have the plan for the coming year until the very last moment, even at the very end of the year. There is an uninterrupted process of action in life, while the plans break off, as it were, on a definite date. Planning must be so organized as to have the basic provisions of the coming year's plan available during the current year and the basic provisions of the coming five-year plan, or at least of its opening years, available in the current five-year period.[54]

The need for plan continuity is unavoidable in every kind of economy because it never happens that every project and program in a plan is carried out exactly as foreseen. Deviations are virtually certain, if not because of altered circumstances having nothing to do with the plan then because of the forces released through the plan's implementation. Thus, every target in a plan, however realistic it may have been when established, must be subject to change during a plan period. When unforeseen events jeopardize the implementation of a plan, new measures may be adopted in an attempt to maintain plan targets. But if the price of retaining the targets becomes too high, they must be adjusted. Or, what amounts to the same thing, the period of the plan may have to be extended in order to allow more time in which to achieve the original targets. In this way, the second development plan for the French territories, originally scheduled to end in 1957, was extended for two years to 1959.

[54] Khiliuk, F. "Some Questions on Improving the Organization of Planning," p. 25.

Changes in plans can be made necessary by a variety of causes. The statistics of most countries being what they are, planners are frequently forced to plan on the basis of inadequate and erroneous information, the effects of which may show up later. For instance, Pakistan's Second Five Year Plan was originally drafted on the assumption that the country's population would increase during the plan period at the rate of 1.6 to 1.8 per cent annually. When a census revealed that the population was likely to grow at a much higher rate, it became necessary to raise investment targets substantially if the planned annual increase of 2 per cent in per capita incomes was to be maintained. In many countries, revisions in investment targets have also had to be made during the course of plan implementation because, when the plan was drafted, it was not possible to incorporate accurate cost estimates for projects and programs. A plan may also have to be revised because implementation lags behind schedule.

Sometimes, unforeseen domestic or foreign developments outdate the assumptions on which plan targets were set. These developments may take many forms. Thus, a plan may have to be revised because of a natural disaster, as with Chile's plan after the earthquakes of May 1960; the need to increase defense expenditures because of the danger of external military intervention, as with India's Second Five-Year Plan after the border clash with China in 1962; a change in government, as with Tanganyika's plan after independence; the introduction of a stabilization program, as with France's Third Plan; the effect of vagaries of weather on agricultural output, as with the USSR's Seven-Year Plan; changes in the flow of foreign aid or other resources, as with Afghanistan's and North Borneo's First Five-Year Plans; [55] a decline in the price of an important export, as with Burma's Eight-Year Plan when the export price of rice declined after the Korean War; [56] a change in international association, as with Greece's Five-Year Plan after Greece joined the European Economic Community; [57] a plan having been so successful that it produced too many pressures on an economy, as with Japan's Ten-Year Plan.

Since it is impossible to foresee all eventualities, it is impossible to

[55] The change in the size of resources may be an increase instead of a decrease. In both Afghanistan and North Borneo, plans had to be revised because of enlarged resources.

[56] The plans of countries which depend heavily on primary exports are especially likely to require revision because of unforeseen changes in export prices.

[57] The first French Plan was revised by extending the last year of the Plan from 1951 to 1953 to have it coincide with the end of the Marshall Plan in France.

plan so as to eliminate the necessity for revising plans. And since it is virtually certain that targets or other parts of a plan will have to be modified during implementation if it is to remain realistic, the plan must be sufficiently flexible to allow such revisions to be made. This implies that a development plan can only be a framework of programs and policies and never an inviolable blueprint for the future. It must be sufficiently detailed to provide guidance for action, but it cannot be so detailed that it loses the flexibility needed to adjust to changing conditions. An inflexible plan is based on the assumption that no new facts will emerge during the plan period,

> no exceptional successes or failures in administration will occur, no extraordinary natural events will upset calculations, no other nations will act in unpredictable or unpredicted ways. Intelligent planning must make allowance for the possibility, indeed the probability, that things of this nature will happen and therefore plans must be made subject to revision in the light of experience.[58]

Revisions, then, are normal; failure to revise a plan during the entire course of its execution is frequently an indication of a government's lack of understanding of, if not lack of interest in, the planning process. It follows, therefore, that repeated revisions of a plan are not necessarily an indication of poor planning. They may be, but they may also be a sign of good planning if they are attempts to adjust targets to changing circumstances which the planners could not have been expected to foresee. A plan must always be subject to amendment if it is to be kept up to date.

> The idea that you need only prepare a plan once every five years is complete nonsense. A fixed plan is not only worthless but dangerous: all planning that makes contact with the real world is replanning. . . . This cannot be achieved by treating programmes like the phoenix, as if they should take wing every five years or so from their own ashes; it can be achieved only if they are kept continuously alive by amendment. . . .[59]

However, appropriate controls should be set up to assure that adjustments to a plan take place only after careful and systematic

[58] Pakistan. Planning Commission. *Outline of the Second Five-Year Plan* (1960–65), p. iii.
[59] Cairncross, A. K. "Programmes as Instruments of Coordination," p. 89.

evaluation; if this is not done, the door is opened to haphazard changes based on transient whim or a vacillating approach toward realizing plan objectives. Nor should it be necessary, except in a major emergency, to make wholesale revisions in a plan. It is pointless to have a plan if it is modified so frequently without good reason that the results at the end of the plan period bear little relationship to the original plan. As Nigeria's Minister of Economic Development pointed out in an address to the House of Representatives:

> It is very easy . . . to begin with a plan and end with confusion. If we allow projects to be taken out or inserted at will, without careful analysis of the relationships of changes in one part of the plan or program to other parts, we shall certainly end with a meaningless jumble of projects.[60]

In many countries, sponsors of projects and programs make frequent modifications or additions which reflect lack of foresight or understanding of plan objectives. For example, in Pakistan during the second plan period, almost every department sought approval for projects which had not been envisaged in the plan, or tried otherwise to amend its original proposals. These actions made it necessary for the planners to make repeated adjustments in sector programs to make room for new projects, thereby delaying execution of the plan. According to Iran's Plan Organization, during Iran's second plan period there were

> too many haphazard and ill-considered changes in the program [which] resulted in poor balance in many areas and in serious financial and administrative difficulties.[61]

Attempts have been made to build flexibility into a plan. In the case of Italy's Vanoni Plan, for instance, construction and forestation were established as "regulatory" sectors. If activity in other sectors accelerated or slowed down unduly, compensatory adjustments were to be made in the rate of investment in the construction and forestation sectors. In Yugoslav plans, reserves of money and commodities have been set aside and used to intervene in the market to counteract contingent or unforeseen events which might otherwise make it neces-

[60] Speech by the Nigerian Minister of Economic Development to the House of Representatives on the Nigerian Development Plan, 1962–68.
[61] Iran. Plan Organization. *Review of the Second Seven Year Plan Program of Iran*, p. 15.

sary to change targets. In countries with reasonably good market economies, the market itself may also help mitigate planning errors and delays by equalizing demand and supply through price changes.

Such methods, either singly or in combination, may be helpful, but they are rarely sufficient by themselves to eliminate the need for periodic revision of plans. Ideally, flexibility is assured if planners keep a plan under constant review and make modifications and improvements as and when events dictate. In Yugoslavia, for example, the plan is under continual surveillance and changes in instruments of economic policy have been made as frequently as every few months to adjust economic activity to requirements for achieving plan targets. The dependence of the Netherlands on the course of international trade makes it desirable for the Central Planning Bureau to review its annual plan at quarterly intervals to permit remedial action to be taken in time.

For most countries in early stages of development, however, ceaseless vigil over plans and events requires a greater effort than they are able or willing to expend. This is one reason why planning experts advise countries to adopt rolling plans, which at least provide for annual review of plans.

Rolling Plans

In a rolling plan, the plan is revised at the end of each year and, as the first year of the plan is dropped, estimates, targets and projects for another year are added to the last year. Thus, a four-year plan for the calendar years 1966–69 would be revised at the end of 1966 and a new plan issued for 1967–70. A similar procedure would be followed at the end of every year thereafter. In effect, therefore, the plan would be renewed at the end of each year and the number of years would remain the same as the plan "rolled" forward in time. Some advocates of the rolling plan advise rolling plans forward even more frequently than once a year, while others believe once every two or three years is sufficient. But the principle in either case is the same as in the annual roll-over.

The "rolling" system originated in budgeting procedures of business firms, and in municipal and other governments.[62] Puerto Rico has

[62] Thus, the Ford Motor Company in the United States and the Phillips Company in the Netherlands have used such plans. The City of Amersfoort in the Netherlands has a five-year rolling plan.

pioneered in the use of the rolling technique in connection with its Six-Year Financial Programs and the Philippines includes a Five-Year Fiscal Program in its annual budgets (see Appendix III).

Several countries have tried, or announced their intention to try, to use rolling plans. The USSR has indicated that it expects to use a rolling plan in connection with its five-year plans. The Union of South Africa expects to roll its Six-Year Economic Development Programme forward annually. And the Netherlands proposes to use moving five-year periods for the industrial and economic forecasts it is preparing to begin in 1966. But use of the rolling technique for development plans has been discussed more than it has been acted upon. Venezuela has revised its Four-Year Plan twice at two-year intervals, but it is not yet clear whether these changes reflect adoption of the rolling plan principle or attempts to devise a viable plan. Burma considered making its Four-Year Plan a rolling plan but nothing came of it. The Philippines have a Five-Year Plan for the 1963–67 period which was intended to be a rolling plan, but nothing has been done to give effect to the intention. In connection with the Three-Year Plan recently prepared in Mexico, attempts were made to introduce a rolling plan to carry forward planning from one presidential administration to another, but the pressures against this proved to be too strong.

There are, of course, reasons why rolling plans have not been generally adopted by developing countries. Firstly, the concept of planning as a continuous process, while receiving lip service from many, is not fully understood or accepted by most planners. Secondly, even where planners comprehend and accept the importance of continuous planning, their planning offices are generally not up to the task of revising and extending their plans each year. Thirdly, the rolling plan is a technician's device. It does not have the same psychological appeal as a brand new plan for securing public interest and participation. Nor, from the point of view of political leaders, does it offer the same opportunities for making political capital as a new plan. In some countries, a new plan serves as the election manifesto of the ruling party which takes credit for what the new plan is expected to do.[63] Finally, when targets are changed every year, as they may be with a rolling plan, there is the risk that entrepreneurs and the general public will become uncertain about plan goals and purposes and fail to react as the planners wish.

The first and second difficulties can be overcome as planners develop

---

[63] "Dhanam" in *Economic Times*, November 19, 1963.

more experience and build up planning staffs and organizations. The third and final problem can be resolved, at least as far as maintaining planning continuity is concerned, with an unpublished rolling plan. As each year passes the planners add a year to maintain the planning period constant. When the old plan nears expiration, the rolling plan can be made public as a new medium-term plan. This procedure can be repeated indefinitely.

Adoption of a rolling plan involves much more than a mechanical extension of a plan. It requires a rethinking and an appropriate revision of the whole plan each year as an essential part of the process of setting targets for an additional year. The need for such review and revision applies to all plans. But the virtue of a rolling plan is that it has built into it a procedure for regular review and revision. However, rolling plans have proved to be too difficult for most less developed countries to manage. A simpler way of bringing a medium-term plan up to date is the annual plan when it is used as a device for making a medium-term plan operational.

Annual Plans

Earlier in this chapter, the use of annual plans as interim or emergency plans was discussed. But annual plans are used mostly as recurrent instruments for detailing exactly what must be done to convert existing medium-term plans into programs for action. Thus, an annual plan deals with current development activities without losing sight of longer-term goals. Most medium-term plans indicate total investment and investment by sectors for the entire plan period and the targets to be achieved at the end of the plan period. There is usually no indication of the amounts to be spent and the production to be attained in the intermediate years. Because of this, medium-term plans are not operational plans. In order for them to become effective guides to action, output and expenditures (both in domestic and foreign currencies) must be determined for each year of the plan period. This is accomplished most effectively by the formulation of annual plans. The size and composition of each annual plan is determined, on the one hand, by the financial and other resources available at the time and, on the other, by the readiness to proceed with new projects and the progress made with projects started in previous periods. Neither the resources which will become available nor the status of projects can be foreseen far in advance with the necessary accuracy for operational purposes because they depend on future actions and development. Attempts may, and should be, made to phase projects and programs over the period of a medium-term plan, but actual expenditures will depend on what has gone before.

Annual investment and production targets are sometimes included in a medium-term plan, with the prime purpose usually to give a general notion of the approximate rate at which investment and output are to develop during the plan period. Thus, the First Five-Year Plan for Upper Volta included annual investment targets because it was considered important to emphasize that there could be a very low level of investment at the beginning of the plan period and a progressive acceleration in later years. But even where medium-term plans give yearly breakdowns and targets, a practice which is more common in Soviet-type plans than in those of mixed economies, the plans need to be reviewed at least once a year since it is usually impracticable to program investments accurately in operational detail for more than a year ahead. Unless a medium-term plan shows precisely what needs to be done in the first year of the plan, it must be accompanied by an annual plan for that first year. This rarely happens, mostly because planning agencies are not adequately equipped to prepare a medium-term and annual plan simultaneously.

The regular preparation of annual operational plans is also exceptional among developing countries with medium-term plans. This is especially true in countries where the medium-term plan is prepared largely by foreign experts who, departing after the medium-term plan is drawn up, leave no one behind who is qualified to maintain the continuity of the planning process. For example, the First Five-Year Plan for Upper Volta was formulated by foreign experts who made no provision for the preparation of annual operational plans although it was probable that the plan could not be implemented without them. Moreover, the embryonic planning group in Upper Volta was unlikely to be able to prepare annual plans without outside assistance.

In most developing countries which employ annual operational plans, such plans are recent innovations, usually started two, three or more years after the introduction of a medium-term plan. The failure to introduce annual plans which "phase" or break down resources and targets into annual components from the start of a medium-term plan can have serious consequences. In India, for instance, during the Second Plan period,

the whole five-year allocation of foreign exchange for private investment was made available at once. When, to everyone's dismay, private investors used up the bulk of this ration in the first two years of the plan period, the result was the foreign exchange crisis of 1957 and 1958 and a subsequent foreign exchange stringency that continued to impede not only further expansion but also current production in many industries during the balance of the plan period.[64]

In contrast with perspective plans, which are less detailed than medium-term plans, annual plans are more detailed. A typical annual operational plan starts with an account of the progress of the medium-term plan in the previous year. A comparison is made between planned and actual development to date and the reasons for deviations from targets are analyzed. The more important projects and programs to be carried out during the current year, along with estimates of costs and available resources, are described. Included in this description are investments and other preliminary actions to be undertaken in the current year whose benefits are expected to accrue in later years. Consideration is also given to the action to be taken in the current year to correct deficiencies and to make up for shortfalls in previous years in order to reach targets by the end of the medium-term period. The most important section of an annual plan, although the one usually most neglected, describes the specific monetary, credit, wage, fiscal and other measures to be adopted during the year to achieve the annual targets. In Yugoslav annual plans, in contrast with those of most other countries with annual plans, detailed descriptions of the instruments of economic policy consume a considerable portion of the annual plan document. Because many annual plans omit adequate treatment of the measures to be adopted to realize annual targets, they largely fail to provide the guidance required to implement medium-term plans.

Since an annual plan must try to adjust for previous shortfalls or overfulfillment of targets, it is likely to differ in some respects from original estimates in the medium-term plan. It may also deviate from the medium-term plan because of changed domestic or foreign circumstances. An annual plan is thus a convenient device for revising a medium-term plan.

The extent to which annual plans are used to modify and adjust a medium-term plan differs greatly as between socialized and mixed-economy countries. In the USSR and the Eastern European countries, annual plans, variously labeled "implementation," "practical," "current" or "working" plans, are viewed purely as instruments for carrying

[64] Lewis, John P. "India," p. 99.

out a medium-term plan. As such, they cannot alter the basic concepts or targets in the medium-term plan. In Soviet-type planning annual plans are considered to be particularly important because they provide a framework and lay down practical rules to be followed by republics, local authorities, ministries and enterprises in the preparation of their own annual plans and, in the case of enterprises, of quarterly and monthly plans. In the mixed economies, annual plans are not circumscribed by these requirements. Consequently, modifications and substitutions in the original list of projects and in their estimates of expenditure sometimes result in marked departures from the original estimates in the medium-term plan.

Where a medium-term development plan exists or is in course of preparation, the rationalization of current public investment through the application of general criteria to an inventory of projects and programs in process of execution, as described in the preceding chapter, offers what may well be the most effective method of preparing a first annual operational plan for the medium-term plan period. Since current public investment is frequently inconsistent with the objectives of a new medium-term plan, the rationalization of an inventory of current public investment provides a convenient way of bringing current investment into line with plan objectives. Rationalization of current public investment on the basis of an inventory not only requires that low priority investment be reduced, if not eliminated; it also requires that gaps in investment be filled with new projects and programs where these are necessary to get fuller benefits from projects and programs already in course of execution. The annual plan produced from this process must also include detailed descriptions of both the administrative measures to be employed in carrying out the public sector program and the instruments of economic policy to be used to stimulate private investment to conform with plan objectives. Planners intent on turning out a medium-term development plan usually miss the opportunity to get immediate benefits from their planning efforts through the preparation of a first annual operating plan obtained from a rationalized inventory of public investment projects.

PLAN OBJECTIVES

A precise definition of development objectives is at least as important for a country's economic advancement as its kind of planning, and even as important as the existence of a plan. A clear definition of national purposes is logically the first component of a development plan since it is a precondition for the establishment of a coherent strategy for allocating investment resources among competing demands. Without a definition of national development objectives which elucidates the relative emphasis to be given to each objective, plan targets and projects are likely to be chosen arbitrarily and policies and measures adopted to implement a plan are likely to be contradictory.

A country's basic development objectives are the prime determinants of the character and direction of the national planning effort. The nature of these objectives depends on national preferences grounded in the country's scale of political, social and economic values, as well as on its stage of development. Socialized countries will choose objectives unlike those in mixed economies, democratic nations will have objectives, as well as means for giving them effect, which differ from those of authoritarian lands, and the less developed countries will have different development objectives than the more developed.

Development objectives may be economic, like bringing about an increase in real incomes; they may be political, like the advancement of military security or the improvement of a country's national prestige and influence; or they may be social, like the achievement of increases in housing, education or health facilities. In many cases, objectives represent a combination of economic, political and social factors. Planners perform a useful function if they outline the different ways in which development can proceed with alternative priorities for various objectives. But the final choice of the objectives and their priorities cannot be left to the planners, whose technical training gives them no special competence for this task. Because national objectives involve political and social, as well as economic, considerations, they should be selected only by a country's political authorities, hopefully after consultation with all interested groups.

Although there may be a variety of other basic objectives, the ultimate objective of national development in most countries is to raise the level of living of all the people in the country through expanded output and use of consumer goods and services for education, health and cultural activities. For almost all less developed countries, this requires an acceleration in the rate of economic growth to provide higher per capita incomes. It is no surprise, therefore, to find this requirement emphasized as a prime objective in almost every national development plan. Iceland's Four-Year Plan for 1963–66 is an exception. It seeks to bring about a more rational rather than a faster expansion in the economy's growth rate. Malta's Five-Year Development Plan is another exception. Its major objective is merely to maintain full employment by establishing new industries to counterbalance the immediate decline in employment induced by lower British military expenditures in its area. Ceylon's Ten-Year Plan, Taiwan's three Four-Year Plans and Singapore's Four-Year Plan are also exceptions. They have or have had as their major objective the achievement of higher levels of employment. This objective, which reflects the pressure of population in these countries, represents a decision by their governments that, for the time being, the creation of jobs is more important than all other objectives, including an increase in per capita income.

Where a government defines its objectives clearly in the initial step of plan formulation, a sound foundation is laid for the planners to prepare a development plan which conforms to the country's purposes. A clear statement of objectives has also been found to be helpful in stimulating and directing development in countries without formal plans. But in most countries, governments are unable or unready to define clearly their development objectives. Sometimes this is due to a confusion of basic with secondary objectives or with what are essentially operational constraints on the orderly implementation of a development plan. Thus, one Thai plan listed nine objectives.[65] One was to raise the annual rate of growth of the national income from 4 to 5 per cent; some were to increase the output of particular crops and industries by fixed percentages; others set specific dates for the completion of individual projects like the Bhumipol Dam and the Chumporn-Nakorn Srithamaraj Highway; while still others referred to equilibrium of the trade balance and preservation of a stabilized currency, which were really not development objectives but conditions under which sound economic progress should proceed. It is also common to find in plans indiscriminate listing of qualitative and usually longer-range objectives, like the achievement of a reduction in inequalities of income distribution or a diversified economy, with quantitative and usually shorter-run objectives, like an increase in agricultural or industrial output by fixed percentages.

Incongruous mixing of primary and secondary, long- and short-term, and qualitative and quantitative objectives with aims which are

[65] *Royal Thai Government Gazette,* October 28, 1960.

not really objectives, but are essentially means for achieving the basic objectives of a development plan, is generally an indication that the authorities and the planners are uncertain about what they expect from their plan. This uncertainty in those who formulate the plan is bound to be reflected in those who must carry it out. In Surinam, for example, where objectives being considered for its revised plan ran the gamut from the provision of more precise planning information, a satisfactory infrastructure and a favorable balance of payments to increased incomes and full employment, difficulties were encountered because

> in some cases, Ministries are not yet sufficiently clear on the real objectives of the Plan and are thus not competent to undertake proper comparative evaluations of projects.[66]

During Iran's Second Plan period, the Planning Organization found that there was a need for

> much better understanding than currently exists of program objectives. This comes out most clearly, perhaps, in the agricultural sector. One of the country's major agricultural objectives should be to bring about rapid improvement of income and productivity of the peasant cultivator. However, while there are a number of projects that seek to serve this end, such as fertilizer, seed improvement, pest control, cooperatives, and agricultural credit, none of them is formulated in such clear terms as to provide a basis for agreed action by the agencies concerned. The result is a dispersion and fragmentation of responsibility in one of the key areas of economic development. . . . Without clear objectives and careful programming each agency pushes forward independently with its own favorite projects.[67]

The Economic Commission for Asia and the Far East reported in 1961 that

> a review of the development plans of countries of the region has revealed a rather long list of objectives often vaguely stated and sometimes mutually contradictory. . . . There is no doubt need for clarification.[68]

---

[66] Caribbean Organization. *Report of Joint Meeting of Planners and Planning Experts and Standing Advisory Committee of the Caribbean Plan,* p. 41.

[67] Iran. Plan Organization. *Review of the Second Seven Year Plan Program of Iran,* p. 16.

[68] UN. ECAFE. "Economic Development and Planning in Asia and the Far East," *Economic Bulletin for Asia and the Far East,* December 1961, pp. 2–3.

The same situation prevails in many African countries. In Morocco, for example, the planners had to settle for minor objectives for the First Five-Year Plan because the authorities were unprepared to make necessary decisions about major ones. The besetting problem in that country, as in some others, was the lack of basic agreement among political leaders about what the national interest required and the consequent absence of a consistent development policy.[69] In Latin America, also, there has been a

> reluctance observable at times on the part of the authorities to make a precise definition of the aims pursued by a development policy and to express them in terms of clear guidelines. . . .[70]

It is not hard to find the reasons for official hesitation to define development objectives with reasonable precision. In countries with low per capita income unevenly distributed among different regions and classes, with populations in dire need of jobs and social services, it is all too easy for the authorities to succumb to the temptation to list in a development plan objectives—as though they embodied occult curative powers—for overcoming all the economic ills of the country. It is common to find national development plans, like Pakistan's First Five Year Plan, which called for the achievement of the greatest possible increase in the national income and, at the same time, increased health, education, housing and other social welfare services, a higher standard of living, increased exports, a more rapid rate of progress in the less developed areas of the country than in other regions, as well as a more equitable distribution of income and property.

Although each of these objectives may have been desirable by itself, in combination they were contradictory. The objectives in India's First and Second Five-Year Plans were similarly incompatible. They included a large increase in national income in order to raise the level of living, rapid industrialization with emphasis on basic and heavy industries, a large increase in employment opportunities, as well as a reduction in inequalities in income and wealth. It was impossible to attain all these objectives simultaneously. A large increase in the level of living was bound to limit the increase in national income by shifting resources from investment to consumption; concentration on basic and heavy industries, which use less labor than light industry, was certain

---

[69] Waterston, Albert. *Planning in Morocco*, p. 49.
[70] UN. ECLA. *Report of the Latin American Seminar on Planning*, p. 5.

to restrict the number of new jobs; reduction in inequalities of income and wealth was possible only over the long run and, in any event, if realized might well have reduced the amount of funds available for investment in income producing programs.

Political authorities often hesitate to come to grips with the basic issues which must be decided if development objectives are clearly stated and appropriate measures are adopted to implement them. The Report of the Latin American Seminar previously mentioned noted that in Latin American countries, for example, a consistent set of basic objectives for development would require decisions on

> the structural reforms . . . needed if countries . . . [are] . . . to emerge from situations that . . . [are] . . . an anachronism, hampering development and preventing income from being more equitably distributed.[71]

In lieu of facing up to difficult decisions, political authorities frequently prefer to list objectives which, although mutually inconsistent, will include something for everybody. One may therefore find among the objectives of a plan conflicting economic objectives, e.g., development of capital-intensive industries and increased employment opportunities; conflicting economic and social objectives, e.g., a rapid rate of increase in national income and a high level of investment in social welfare; or incompatible long-term and short-term objectives, e.g., the achievement of a diversified economy and an increase in the output of the country's major export commodity. Conflicting objectives may be included in a plan if their priorities are indicated or understood. But if the authorities fail to indicate the order of priority, they in effect let the planners fare as best they can with the preparation of the plan. This was the planners' position in the case of Pakistan's First Five Year Plan, when the Government gave the Planning Commission no instructions on how to resolve the conflicts among the plan's objectives.[72] Indeed, in the absence of action by the Government itself, the plan's objectives were actually selected by the planners on the basis of general directives and were later approved by the Prime Minister without much consideration or consultation with others in the Government.[73]

The failure to reconcile incompatible objectives in a plan makes it difficult to formulate policies which are appropriate for the plan's

---

[71] *Ibid.*
[72] Bell, David E. "Planning for Development in Pakistan," p. 6.
[73] Waterston, Albert. *Planning in Pakistan,* pp. 43–44.

implementation. For example, Jamaica's National Plan for 1957–67 was prepared on the basis of two essentially conflicting objectives: the achievement of rapid growth through industrialization and the creation of the greatest number of jobs. Since apparently little effort was made to resolve the inconsistency between objectives, policies advocated to implement the Plan were also inconsistent:

> The question of using labour-intensive or capital-intensive methods of production is a case in point. It appears that as yet Jamaican planners have made no clear cut choice as to which of these forces shall predominate. Population pressures seem to be somewhat more influential at present, but the development goal has by no means been abandoned. One result of this indecision is that in many cases confusion prevails and contradictory actions are advocated.[74]

If the conflict between two objectives remains unresolved when the plan is being formulated, they may cancel each other out during the plan's implementation, in which case neither one is realized, or one may give way to the other.

In practice, the "real" objectives of planning and their priorities emerge during the period of plan implementation in the form of official actions. High-sounding phrases in the plan about rapid growth are then shown to be less important than high levels of public or private consumption. In Yugoslavia, Pakistan and elsewhere, objectives for equalizing disparities in the prosperity and growth of different regions have given way to the more compelling objective for achieving a higher national rate of growth. And in India, employment, welfare and improvement in income distribution objectives have received in practice a lower priority than they were accorded in the plans.[75] What matters for results is not the rhetoric embodying objectives, but the policies and measures adopted to achieve them.

PLAN TARGETS

A country's national development objectives are carried out through a variety of economic and social policies. In addition to fiscal and monetary policies, a government may have wage, price, industrial,

---

[74] Peck, H. Austin. "Economic Planning in Jamaica: A Critique," p. 154.
[75] Singh, Tarlok. *Planning Process*, p. 30.

agricultural, educational and other policies for promoting development. Thus, a government may pursue a fiscal policy of balancing its budget instead of one of deficit financing, or a "loose" instead of a "tight" money policy, set minimum wages, engage in and encourage or discourage private investment in certain industries, and so on. These policies may be implemented through economic and social instruments or measures formulated to achieve development objectives. Governments have access to a large number of instruments for giving effect to development policies. Some of those commonly employed include taxes, public expenditures, central bank discount rates, reserve requirements for banks, quantitative and qualitative credit controls, price controls, rationing, subsidies, currency regulations, licensing of imports and exports, customs duties and exchange controls. Some instruments, like credit and tax regulations, operate indirectly to induce people to act in accordance with a government's objectives; others, like price controls and licensing regulations, operate directly to prevent people from behaving in a manner which is inconsistent with development objectives. Both indirect and direct instruments are most effective if they are designed specifically to carry out a particular objective.

To the extent that objectives can be made concrete, they act as guideposts for the preparation of effective policy instruments. The most effective way of giving objectives concrete meaning is by quantifying them, whenever possible, thereby transforming them into targets. When an objective of a plan is not merely to increase per capita income, but to increase it at a definite rate, say 2 per cent annually, the objective has been transformed into a target. Besides making it possible to devise appropriate policy instruments for achieving plan objectives, targets perform other important functions. They may be used to set limits on output for some crops or industries, as well as to increase output for others. They provide planners with valuable guides for judging whether the measures adopted to achieve objectives are adequate for the purpose or whether they require adjustment or replacement. They are useful in helping to determine the amount of raw materials, manpower, training facilities, funds in national currency and foreign exchange and other resources which must be allocated to various sectors in order to obtain the desired results. Finally, by making an objective concrete, say by indicating precisely how much the national product is to be increased, a target makes it easier to enlist the effort of the public, the private sector and the legislative and other public officials for specific tasks calculated to reach target levels.

The formulation of a comprehensive plan involves the conversion of development objectives into a set of consistent targets. Even qualitative objectives, like the achievement of a more diversified economy or a more equal distribution of wealth and income, which are not directly susceptible to quantification, may be reflected indirectly in investment targets, targets for the production of new commodities, acreage targets for reforming the pattern of land tenure and so forth. Besides income targets, a plan may have production, investment, savings, employment, export, import and other targets. Targets may be set for regions, as well as for a country as a whole; they may be over-all, sectoral or may apply to individual industries, projects or commodities; they may be set in physical units of output or input, as well as in units of value.

Some plans limit themselves to a few aggregative targets, but many favor long lists of targets. Thus, Yugoslavia's First Five-Year Plan fixed extraordinarily detailed production targets for about 600 commodity groups for the nation, as well as for each of its six constituent republics. Perhaps reflecting the influence of the Yugoslav advisers who helped prepare Ethiopia's Second Five-Year Development Plan, that plan established targets for 23 categories of activities with a division of investment into relatively small sums. In addition, it gave targets for such things as the number of iron plows, harrows, rollers, carts and drills to be used by farmers and the output of a long list of articles which even included the number of pairs of leather shoes, canvas shoes and rubber shoes, and even the number of matches. Indonesia's Eight-Year Plan also laid down a large number of physical targets. The 1949 development plan for Sierra Leone included production targets for palm kernels, palm oil, kola nuts, piassava, ginger, cocoa, benniseed, coffee and groundnuts. Except for the one for coffee, none of the targets was reached.[76]

The inclusion of a large number of targets in a plan introduces rigidities into the planning process which may impede the growth of an economy.[77] Experience shows that the greater the number of targets in a plan, the greater the number of co-ordinated measures needed to achieve them, the more frequent the need for the plan's revision and the more difficult the realization of the targets. Less developed coun-

---

[76] UN. ECA. *Problems Concerning Techniques of Development Programming in African Countries,* pp. 48–49.

[77] *Ibid.* (quoting, Jack, D. T. "Economic Survey of Sierra Leone," p. 73).

tries would therefore do well to limit the number of targets in their plans to a few essential ones and concentrate their scarce resources on achieving them.

A target differs from a forecast or a projection. A forecast, say of an annual increase of 2 per cent in per capita income, is an estimate of what will happen on the basis of existing policies or policy changes which are expected to take place. A projection is a tool of analysis for clarifying the implication of certain assumptions or to check the consistency of the assumptions themselves. Thus, a projection of an annual increase of 2 per cent in per capita incomes for a specified period may be made to bring out the likely repercussions of such a growth rate. It may show, for example, the level of savings, investment, production and the additional number of skilled workers required to maintain the projected rate in growth.

Many countries prepare short- or long-term projections of one kind or another. Since 1958, for example, the Bank of Israel has prepared an annual National Budget consisting of a series of projections and forecasts for the forthcoming year. The British National Economic Development Council made five-year projections of the British economy and longer-term projections are being made in the U.S. Government. Such projections may be prepared with a view toward convincing others of the desirability of planning or they may provide guidance for establishing development policies, but there is no intention of implementing them. In contrast, a target implies that means will be adopted to achieve it.

> A target should not be a statement of what we should like to see achieved. . . . Neither is it the figure of what will be achieved if no action is taken. A target is the figure it is proposed to achieve as a result of the action that is contemplated.[78]

Without policies and instruments, a target becomes, at best, a forecast or a projection and, at worst, the product of a mathematical ritual of no practical importance.

> To draw up and publish a list of targets is not to plan; the real planning comes when the government takes action to realise these targets.[79]

[78] Lewis, W. Arthur. *Principles of Economic Planning*, pp. 108–109.
[79] *Ibid.*, p. 111.

Where a "plan" is prepared with targets but without accompanying instruments of policy to achieve the targets, it might be more appropriate to call the plan a forecast or a projection. Thus, the Economic Commission for Europe, in referring to the long-term "plan" for 1950–70 which the Netherlands Central Planning Bureau drew up in 1955, quite properly stated that

> since this document refrained from any discussion of or recommendations on policy measures, it is more appropriate to regard it as a forecast or an exploration of future possibilities of economic growth.[80]

In the case of the Netherlands, the planners did not specify the instruments of policy needed to implement their "plan" because they had not drawn it up with implementation in view.[81] But in some countries, plans which are prepared to be implemented turn out to be little more than projections since the planners do not specify the policies and the instruments needed to achieve the targets in their plans. A former member of the Philippines National Economic Council, the central planning agency, has called attention to this situation in his country:

> There is the general problem that targets are not always implemented. Just to give an example, the National Economic Council at the time of President Magsaysay had a five-year program. This program was approved by the President in a speech, but the targets were not implemented. Why was this so? Because, while there were many production targets, there were no economic policies adjusted to the targets.[82]

Another example among many was Brazil's Program of Targets for 1957–61. The Program set 30 specific targets in the power, transport, food, basic industries and education sectors. The Brazilian Development Council, which set the targets on the basis of sectoral estimates and projections prepared with the aid of a group of ECLA technicians, referred to the Program of Targets as a development program, although, in the almost complete absence of instruments of policy for

---

[80] UN. ECE. "Long-term Planning in Western Europe," p. 59.

[81] This is also true of the five-year forecasts for industry and the economy which the Netherlands Central Planning Bureau is preparing for the period 1966–70.

[82] Araneta, Salvador. "The Planning, Approval and Implementation of Economic Policy," p. 133.

achieving the targets, it was in fact little more than a forecast or projection.

Few developing countries have learned how to formulate appropriate policies and instruments and to coordinate them properly for carrying out their development targets. In summing up conditions in the Philippines, a high official of the National Economic Council made a statement in 1959 which is also applicable to many other countries:

> At this stage it is doubtful if we have both the technical skill and the political inclination to formulate economic policies that are comprehensive, sound, far-reaching in effect, consistent, realistic and free from unduly harmful effects. Evaluated on these basic requirements it is unlikely that many of the economic policies that we have approved would pass for satisfactory.[83]

A similar situation prevails in Latin America. The participants of the already mentioned Latin American Seminar on Planning

> expressed concern at the lack of co-ordination in economic policy and the makeshift fashion in which it was changed, often in response to purely adventitious problems.[84]

Few governments have understood that development targets and the policies and measures for bringing about their realization are inseparable. In Pakistan, for example, which has a longer history of planning than most countries, only within the last few years has the Government come to understand the integrality of planning with economic and financial policy. In that country, government entities have adopted policies without any consistent attempt to relate them to the objectives of the nation's development plans. Consequently, economic policy has often conflicted with plan objectives. Agricultural price policy has hampered the achievement of agricultural targets and administrative controls have often impeded the development of industry along lines laid down in development plans.

In contrast, Yugoslavia, more than most developing countries, has acquired considerable skill in adapting instruments of economic policy to the achievement of specific targets in its plans. Whereas in most plans, one rarely finds more than passing reference to the instruments of policy for achieving plan targets, large parts of Yugoslav annual

[83] Macaspac, Isidro (Acting Director, Office of National Planning). "A Rejoinder," p. 180.

[84] UN. ECLA. *Report of the Latin American Seminar on Planning*, p. 25.

operational plans are given over to detailed enumeration of specific instruments devised to give effect to plan targets. These instruments, which are essentially like those employed in most countries with mixed economies, have evolved through a process of purposeful experimentation to levels of effectiveness well above those in most developing countries. Through a generalized system of taxation, interest and other charges on socialized enterprises which rewards efficiency and profitability and stimulates initiative in a market-type economy by allocating public investment and foreign exchange funds in accordance with plan objectives, by influencing the supply and direction of credit through the banking system, and to a diminishing extent, by price controls and restrictions on foreign exchange and trade, the Government has achieved considerable success in realizing the targets in its development plans. Yugoslavia's success in utilizing taxation and other indirect means to channel the use of national resources has aroused the interest of other Eastern European countries in these instruments of economic policy. As already indicated, most of these countries have either adopted some of these devices or are considering their adoption.

The Size of a Plan. One of the first questions which confronts planners concerns the proper size of a plan. For a comprehensive plan, this necessarily involves setting a growth target for the plan period.[85] There is no simple formula for fixing the size of a country's development plan since it is a function of the community's willingness to accept current sacrifices for future benefits. Three main approaches have been used for determining the size of a plan. One is to have the country's requirements determine it; another is to have the country's resources fix it; the third is to set it somewhere between the two points where the requirements and resources approaches would have left it.

Since the needs of less developed nations are almost limitless, the requirements approach hardly presents a practical solution to the problem. The resources approach is both more feasible and more realistic. It involves estimating the amount of domestic and foreign financial resources which a country is willing and able to invest, and the distribution of these resources among the various sectors of the economy in such a way as to bring about the most desired results. In fixing a growth target on the basis of available resources, the size of the

---

[85] The size of a plan can also be stated in terms of proposed development investments.

plan is not only limited by the amount of domestic and foreign capital which can be obtained, but by the supply of technical and skilled personnel, the number and character of entrepreneurs and managers, and the government's administrative capacity. Consideration must also be given to the effects of contemplated capital investments on recurrent budgetary expenditures. New hospitals will need doctors, nurses and supplies, and new schools will need teachers and supplies. Such investments not only require assured current revenues to cover the cost of salaries and supplies; they require training programs established many years before the completion of welfare projects to educate and train doctors, teachers, nurses and other professional and skilled personnel in adequate numbers. A development plan is too large if the debt service on investment capital borrowed for the programs plus the cost of supporting completed projects add up to more than future current revenues will be able to support.

Sometimes, it is not the size of the plan which is at fault but excessive investments in social projects, like schools and hospitals. Such investments may eventually increase a country's development potentialities, but in the short run their support places a heavy charge on future revenues and reduces the amount of funds available for investment in projects which produce increased income more quickly. In such cases, the maintenance of future financial solvency may make it necessary to shift some social investments to more immediately productive projects. The failure to maintain a proper balance between savings and investment, to keep consumption within prescribed limits, or to give priority to productive investments carries penalties in the form of inflation or slow and misdirected growth of the economy.

Some countries, usually those with relatively adequate supplies of investment capital, have fixed the size and growth targets of their development plans solely on the basis of their available resources. For example, the targets in Malaya's Second Five-Year Plan were determined on the basis of the country's resources and capacities.[86] But the planned annual rate of increase in Malaya's per capita income during the Second Plan period was only 0.8 per cent. This illustrates the main drawback of the resources approach. It is likely to yield a rate of growth which is lower than most governments are now prepared to accept. Indeed, the ECAFE has cautioned that

[86] UN. ECAFE. "Economic Development and Planning in Asia and the Far East," *Economic Bulletin for Asia and the Far East,* December 1961, p. 3.

a modest target, carefully tailored to probable resources, may result in a growth rate barely sufficient to meet the needs of an expanding population.[87]

In practice, therefore, planners in most less developed countries base the size and targets of their plans on something more than available resources. Typically, the planners who prepared Pakistan's First Five Year Plan eschewed the requirements approach as unrealistic and likely to lead to serious inflation or the imposition of stringent controls. But they were not willing to settle for the low growth targets to which the resources approach would have committed them. They reasoned instead that

> if targets are selected with some regard to the resources likely to be available, and if at the same time resource availability is estimated with the objective of stretching capabilities to their limit, these [i.e., the resources and the requirements] approaches are not inconsistent.[88]

In preparing the Plan, therefore, they based the size and targets of the Plan on an estimate of available resources which assumed that every effort would be made to increase them.

The difficulty with this approach is that it frequently results in the establishment of plan targets which are beyond a country's capacity to fulfill. It may be true, as Professor Arthur Lewis has said, that

> there are more under-developed countries whose plans are too small than there are countries whose plans are too large.[89]

But there are also far too many countries whose plans are too large in relation to available savings and other resources or their absorptive capacity. Thus, Morocco's Five-Year Plan called for annual increases averaging 6.2 per cent when they had increased by an average of only 1.5 per cent in the previous eight years. The targets in Guinea's three-year development plan for 1960–63 were even more extreme. That plan called for *annual* increases in Gross Domestic Product of no less than 16 per cent as well as increases of 70 per cent in industrial output and 60 per cent in capital formation.[90] It is perhaps unnecessary

[87] *Ibid.*

[88] Pakistan. National Planning Board. *First Five Year Plan, 1955–1960,* pp. 73–74.

[89] Lewis, W. Arthur. "On Assessing a Development Plan," p. 7.

[90] UN. ECA. *Outlines and Selected Indicators of African Development Plans,* p. 28.

to say that these targets were not achieved. It is one thing for Japan, a country with a high rate of savings and a disciplined economy, to fulfill its plan targets to double the national income in ten years; but it is quite another matter for the United Arab Republic, a poor country with an undeveloped economy, to achieve the same target. To double its national income in a decade, the UAR would require a threefold increase in the rate of savings to raise it to 20 per cent of Gross National Product, an increase which can hardly be attained without greater hardship than the country is probably ready to undergo. Nor are the prospects promising for achieving the targets in Ghana's First Seven-Year Plan when its financing depends on doubling the already high level of taxation. Ghana's planners themselves have doubts about the country's ability to carry out the Plan's primary investment targets, which total £476 million. They have accordingly prepared a lower set of investment targets, totaling £436 million, which can be substituted for the first if, as they expect, circumstances require the slowing down of investments, especially in the public sector. This approach has much merit and could be adopted with benefit by planners in other countries when there is reason to believe that sights have been set too high.

It is hard to see how the targets in Indonesia's Eight-Year National Development Plan can be reached. The Plan envisages investment amounting to about 12 per cent of the national income. This is not an unusually high rate, but it will not be easy to achieve with the current low level of taxation [91] and the quality of fiscal administration. Moreover, production targets in the Plan call for what appear to be unduly high increases in output in a number of fields, including a tripling of electric power, a quadrupling of cement and a quintupling of petroleum. Some competent authorities consider that Indian planners may also be overreaching themselves in proposing a doubling of past growth rates for the Fourth Plan period. Thus, Professor Edward S. Mason has pointed out that

> in India over the 13-year period beginning with the First Plan, the increase in G.N.P. at constant prices has averaged a little less than 3½ percent per annum. In preparation for the Fourth Plan beginning in 1965 the Perspective Planning Division of the Planning Commission worked out a consistent set of input-output estimates

[91] Van der Kroef, Justus M. "Indonesia's New Development Plan," pp. 28–30. Professor Robert Anspach estimated that in 1957 Indonesians paid 12 per cent of their per capita income in taxes, compared to 16 per cent in Thailand, 22 per cent in Ceylon and 24 per cent in Burma.

based on the assumption of a 7 percent growth rate. . . . One can only admire the technical virtuosity of this enterprise. At the same time, it is difficult to suppress doubts concerning the usefulness of such an exercise. . . .[92]

In some countries, plan targets are so patently overambitious that the plan is never put into effect and is usually abandoned and replaced by another, more realistic one. This was true of Bolivia's Ten-Year Plan and Nepal's Second Five-Year Plan. It was also true of Upper Volta's Five-Year Plan for 1963–67, prepared with the aid of foreign advisers, which was replaced by a two-year public investment plan for 1963–64; and this was virtually what happened with Sierra Leone's Ten-Year Plan, which is to be replaced by a Five-Year Plan.

The plans of the socialized economies also frequently aim too high. The output targets in the USSR's Five-Year Plan for 1956–60 were so overambitious in relation to investment that the Plan had to be replaced in mid-term by another.[93] The Seven-Year Plan which ended in 1965 also encountered serious difficulties because of the inability of resources to meet all the demands being made upon them. Investment projects were cut back and new projects and programs were postponed. As an example of the new critical realism which prevails in Czechoslovakia since the decentralization reforms, the Central Committee of the Communist Party in that country denounced a draft of the Five-Year Plan for 1966–70 because the Committee felt it proposed investment in excess of available resources and ordered that a new plan be prepared which would be within the country's capacity.[94] In Yugoslavia, also, the abandonment of its overly ambitious Five-Year Plan for 1961–65 led to a reconsideration of the necessary relationship between plan targets and available resources. In explaining the approach to Yugoslavia's proposed Seven-Year Plan, a high Yugoslav planning official wrote that

> experience has shown that, in Yugoslav conditions, over-burdened plans are not advisable, and that the best solution is likely to be found in a realistic and a less ambitious plan, which would provide for the most rational utilization of the conditions of production, which would be well-balanced, and which would allow for comparatively large reserves.[95]

[92] Mason, Edward S. *On the Appropriate Size of a Development Program,* p. 6.
[93] Nove, Alec. "The Industrial Planning System: Reforms in Prospect," p. 114.
[94] *New York Times,* February 15, 1965.
[95] Sirotkovic, Jakov. "Drafting of the Seven-Year Plan," p. 20.

Attempts have been made to set minimum growth targets which would be generally applicable to less developed countries. Professor Arthur Lewis has suggested an annual rate of growth per head somewhat in excess of 2 per cent.[96] The Charter of the Alliance for Progress fixed as a goal for each Latin American country an average annual per capita rate of growth of not less than 2.5 per cent during the ten-year Alliance period. But such generalizations are of little value when setting growth targets for specific countries. Between 1950 and 1959 only about four Latin American countries were able to maintain or exceed the levels of growth proposed in the Alliance Charter. Most Latin American countries had much lower rates of growth and in two countries per capita income declined.

History does not offer much encouragement for the belief that growth rates can be increased abruptly without a dramatic change in technology, a great improvement in economic administration and, most important of all because it makes these and other changes likely, a considerable increase in governments' committment to the development of their countries. Where the growth rate has been declining, stagnating or increasing very slowly, an economy cannot be made viable except by slow and painful adjustments. In these circumstances, to establish substantially higher growth targets than a country has shown itself capable of achieving can do more harm than good. It may lead to inflation, balance of payments difficulties, political crises and disillusionment with planning. Korea furnishes a good example. The ambitious 7.1 per cent annual growth target in that country's Five-Year Plan for 1962–66, which the planners felt impelled to set for psychological reasons, led to an investment program of low and high priority projects which greatly exceeded the country's financial and administrative capacities and was largely responsible for the price inflation from 1961 to 1963. This put a heavy strain on the Government's financial and administrative apparatus. The country was exposed to strong inflationary pressures and the Government found it impossible to establish a consistent set of policies and measures to carry out all the programs.

In Bolivia, the improbability that the country could achieve the average annual per capita increase of about 5.7 per cent, proposed by foreign advisers after an average annual decline of about 1.7 per cent

[96] Lewis, W. Arthur. "Sponsored Growth: A Challenge to Democracy," pp. 107–108.

in 1950–59, led to considerable disillusionment and the discarding of the Bolivian Ten-Year Plan. The Government of Nepal also chose not to have any plan for awhile rather than proceed with a Second Five-Year Plan in which the planners proposed an unlikely increase in annual output four times above the level which had prevailed in the preceding five-year period. Morocco's Five-Year Plan, which provided for annual increases in investments of over 6 per cent when increases in the previous eight years had averaged only 1.5 per cent, was virtually abandoned after two years. And in Burma, much of the widespread cynicism about planning has been attributed to the overambitious plan targets recommended by Burma's foreign advisers.

Planners often manifest a predilection for ambitious targets. They tend to take to heart the dictum: "Make no little plans. They have no magic to stir men's blood." [97] Thus, Pakistan's planners justified the high targets they set in their First Five Year Plan on the ground that,

> unless the country aims at something which appears to be slightly outside its reach, it may end up by doing less than was possible.[98]

ECAFE also considers it desirable to fix targets at a higher level than resources allow because

> an ambitious target may enlist greater enthusiasm among the people and make it possible for the government to strive harder. . . .[99]

Although these appear to be worthy attitudes, they involve a fundamental misunderstanding about the roles which targets and planners play in the planning process. When planners set plan targets with a view to stimulating development efforts rather than on the basis of a realistic estimate of the prospects for achieving the targets, they greatly increase the difficulties of implementing the plan. If a target is a higher figure than resources allow, instruments of policy adopted for achieving the target are likely to have harmful side effects. As Professor Lewis has pointed out,

> it is very important that this figure be estimated without illusions as to what is possible. . . . If the targets are fanciful, the whole

---

[97] A statement attributed to Daniel Burnham, a noted American architect.

[98] Pakistan. National Planning Board. *First Five Year Plan, 1955–1960*, p. 74.

[99] UN. ECAFE. "Economic Development and Planning in Asia and the Far East," *Economic Bulletin for Asia and the Far East*, December 1961, p. 3.

plan will be fanciful. . . . Planners who promise more than they can perform throw everything out of gear, so that the economy might just as well not be planned at all.[100]

Planners have no business determining the targets of a plan. This is the responsibility of the political authorities because the targets determine the scale of the development effort which a country must be prepared to mount. When planners usurp this prerogative or permit themselves to be placed in a position where they must fix the targets, it is safe to predict that nothing much will come of the plan. Unless the heads of government are prepared to accept full responsibility for setting the level of the development effort, they are unlikely to take the steps needed to achieve the plan's targets.

Alternatives for Decision-Makers. The proper function of planners is to help political leaders make informed decisions about targets. Ideally, planners should prepare a series of targets based on alternative assumptions of effort within the range of the possibilities. It then becomes the duty and responsibility of the political heads of government to indicate which target will become the measure of the development effort. The alternatives should specify explicitly what measures the government must adopt to achieve each target and the presentation should be formulated in terms calculated to stimulate intelligent public discussion of the major issues involved. As M. Pierre Massé, Director General of the Commissariat Général du Plan has stated:

> I believe it is the duty of the planner to present elements which shall be clear, which shall be precise and which shall be feasible and compatible with the plan. They must be clear, so that the man in the street can understand the choices put before him. They must be precise, so that there shall be no misunderstandings in taking the decisions. And they must be feasible and compatible, because once the Plan is formulated, it is naturally much too difficult to introduce fundamental changes.[101]

Planners can perform a useful service in many countries if they prepare targets which show the authorities the alternative levels of growth likely if the government (1) chooses to rely only on existing policies and measures, (2) is willing to take a moderate amount of additional action to reach higher levels of development (in most cases,

---

[100] Lewis, W. Arthur. *Principles of Economic Planning*, p. 109.
[101] Massé, Pierre. "Planning in France," p. 21.

this is all that can be reasonably expected!), or (3) is prepared to take drastic action required to realize more fully the potentialities for economic growth. Such a statement of the alternatives would provide the decision-makers with the information they need and place the onus of choice where it belongs.

In France, Yugoslavia and the Union of South Africa, as well as in some other countries, planners have presented policy-makers with alternative growth targets and their implications and asked them to choose among them.[102] In preparing the Fourth Plan, for example, the French Commissariat Général du Plan gave the French Social and Economic Council three alternatives for average annual growth rates of 3, 4.5 and 6 per cent, respectively. After discussion, the 6 per cent variable was discarded as too ambitious because it left no margin of safety for the balance of payments, while the 3 per cent target was considered too low. The remaining variable, at first increased to 5.0 per cent and later to 5.5 per cent, was eventually selected by the authorities as the growth target most suitable for the ensuing plan period.

As a preliminary to preparing the Seven-Year Plan for 1964–70, Yugoslav planners made two projections which the Yugoslav Federal Assembly was asked to consider. The first variant provided for an annual increase of 8.4 per cent in gross national income, 10.2 per cent in industry, 5.3 per cent in agriculture, 9.0 per cent in the standard of living and an annual average increase of 6.3 per cent in investments. The second variant provided for somewhat higher rates of growth than the first, with an annual global growth rate of 8.9 per cent, an industrial growth rate of 10.7 per cent and a rate of growth of 5.6 per cent for agriculture. However, the annual rise in the standard of living would be lower than in the first variant, 8.5 per cent, although investments would have to be increased greatly, to 9.5 per cent.[103]

In preparing South Africa's first development plan, which covers the 1964–69 period, the planners examined the implications of three different annual growth rates. The Government eventually decided that the lowest rate considered, 4.5 per cent, would be below what could be achieved, while 6 per cent, the highest rate, would put an intolerable strain on the balance of payments and the labor supply. It chose the intermediate rate of 5.5 per cent which it considered neither too easy nor too difficult to realize.[104]

[102] The United Arab Republic discussed four variant models for its Second Five-Year Plan.

[103] "Economic News," *Review of International Affairs,* p. 24.

[104] "Paths to Plenty," *Financial Mail,* p. 863.

In India, another approach was followed for the Fourth Plan. Instead of considering alternative targets, the Planning Commission prepared a paper outlining the implications involved in three different levels of investment outlays: Rs 21,000 crores, Rs 22,500 crores and Rs 24,000 crores.[105] The paper was considered by the Cabinet, which made a choice and the Planning Commission was instructed to prepare a memorandum for consideration by the Cabinet on the basis of the choice made.[106]

French planners have recently introduced a refinement in political decision-making affecting their plan which is well worth describing, if only because it is based on a clear understanding of the respective roles of planners and political decision-makers in the planning process, and the overriding importance of government policy in determining development targets. Their experience with the Fourth Plan led French planners to conclude that the system by which a growth target was chosen from among several alternatives did not go far enough in supplying policy-makers with an adequate understanding of the consequences of their choice. For the Fifth Plan, therefore, the Commissariat Général du Plan prepared only one growth projection for the plan period based on the trend in recent years. The only changes introduced were those necessary to avoid disequilibria. The effects of certain hazards over which the Government had little control were considered. These included a downturn in the level of world business activity, changes in France's terms of trade, inflation in Europe and a change in global productivity trends. The effects of varying government policies on a series of economic questions under current consideration were then estimated. These included the possibility of substantial changes in weekly working hours, a farm policy which could accelerate the flow of agricultural labor to other parts of the economy, stronger incentives for productive investment, differing patterns of growth in social security benefits, a more efficient "incomes" policy and varying levels of government revenues and expenditures. On the basis of government decisions on the alternative policies it proposed to follow in these and other fields, the planners endeavored to determine the combined impact of these policies on the rate of growth envisaged in their projections and to make the necessary adjustments in constructing the Fifth Plan.

The French approach has the advantage of greatly broadening the

---

[105] Rs. 1 crore = 10 million rupees.
[106] *Hindu Weekly Review*, October 5, 1964, p. 2.

range of intelligent decision-making for the authorities. It may well foreshadow a new trend which other countries may soon wish to follow. In the USSR, attempts are also being made to give the authorities more data from which to select the "optimal" plan. According to reports, Soviet planners submitted to policy-makers a "menu" of 20 broad alternatives to choose from for the next five-year plan for 1966–70.[107]

A set of targets may also be prepared to demonstrate the growth possibilities inherent in different assumptions about the level of foreign aid which a country might receive. This was done in Pakistan in 1958. A difference of opinion arose between the Ministry of Finance and the Planning Commission. When the Ministry of Finance proposed levels of foreign assistance and taxation which were lower than the Planning Commission considered adequate, the Commission prepared a memorandum showing the rates of growth implied in the Ministry's and its own proposals. On the basis of the evidence in the memorandum and the public discussions it aroused, the authorities chose the higher targets proposed by the Commission, but with a sober understanding of the greater domestic effort required to obtain increased foreign aid.

Where a country is largely dependent for its export earnings on prices set in international markets, planners would do well to prepare several development targets based on alternative levels of export earnings. Because of the uncertainties inherent in a primary export economy, it is important for the planners to prepare a plan which promises no more through its targets than available export earnings will permit. For the planners to do otherwise is to risk the possibility that they "will be haunted at some later date by a conclusive record of 'targets unattained.'" [108] This was well illustrated in Burma, where rice accounted for about 75 per cent of export earnings and over 20 per cent of Gross Domestic Product in the immediate postwar period. A major reason for the shortfalls in Burma's Eight-Year Plan for 1952–59, and the ensuing disillusionment with planners and foreign planning experts, was the overoptimistic forecast of proceeds from rice exports on which the Plan's targets were based. The price assumptions for rice had already been put in question by events at the time the Plan was presented to the Government. Had a "shelf" of alternative targets

---

[107] Zauberman, Alfred. "New Phase Opens in Soviet Planning," p. 13.
[108] Krause, Walter. "Observations on National Economic Planning," p. 175.

based on lower prices of rice been prepared, they could have been substituted for the plan targets which had been made unrealistic by the fall in rice export prices before the Government accepted the Plan.

SUMMARY AND CONCLUSIONS

In many countries, the preparation of a development plan appears to be viewed as the final instead of the initial step in the planning process. Just as there is more to the planning process than the preparation of a plan, so the planning process does not depend on the existence of a development plan. There are those who confuse the two. But history shows that it is possible for a country to have a plan without any real attempt at planning, and for another to have planning without the existence of a paper plan.

There is some difference of opinion about what constitutes a development plan. But the general consensus is that public investment plans are included in the definition. However, a forecast of global trends with a set of recommended policies or a capital budget is usually excluded. There are many varieties of partial and comprehensive development plans. Those in use in the socialized countries usually are worked out in much greater detail than those in mixed economies. The use of detailed sectoral and regional breakdowns is much more prevalent in the plans of socialized economies than in those of mixed economies. In the socialized economies, also, plans are generally considered obligatory on all socialized sectors, but in the mixed economies, plans are usually binding only on the public sector, if at all, but never on the private sector. As part of the process of formalizing their plans, socialized economies give their plans the force of law. Although the plans of some mixed economies have a similar status, this has little significance in practice, since no one is held responsible for nonperformance.

There are great variations in the duration of plans. In general, most countries have shown a preference for planning periods of shorter duration, generally ranging between three and five years. Where planning experience has accumulated, countries usually supplement such medium-term plans with perspective plans to provide an improved framework for medium-term planning.

For convenience, plans generally refer to a fixed time period. But because planning is a continuous process, there is a problem of linking one plan with another. Thus far, this problem has not been resolved in most countries and the transition between plans is often inefficient. Because of unforeseen and unpredictable events, it is also impossible to plan in such a way as to avoid the need for periodic revision of medium-term plans. Plans must therefore be reviewed regularly and revised when events make this desirable. The rolling plan advocated by many planning experts for preserving plan continuity and flexibility has many technical advantages. It also has several important drawbacks which explain why it has almost never been adopted by countries which plan.

One's view of the future determines current action. That is why a perspective plan is needed for effective medium-term planning, a medium-term plan is needed for appropriate annual operational planning, and an annual plan is required to decide on immediate measures for promoting development. Perspective plans have recently been coming into vogue to supplement medium-term plans. But annual plans, which also offer a simpler alternative to the rolling plan for providing continuity and flexibility for medium-term plans, are still the exception instead of the rule. Annual plans, which are more detailed than medium-term plans, have been found to be extremely useful, if not essential, instruments for carrying out long- and medium-term targets. Because they are drafted each year, they provide planners with an opportunity to review medium-term targets and modify original estimates to adjust for under- or over-fulfillment of targets.

A clear definition of national objectives is essential to planning. Without such a definition, plan targets are likely to be arbitrarily chosen. Where a government defines its objectives precisely, a sound basis exists for preparing a development plan. But most governments are unable or unwilling to define their development objectives. This leads to a confusion of objectives which generally indicates uncertainty about what authorities and planners expect from their plan. The failure to reconcile incompatible plan objectives makes it difficult to formulate policies and measures for implementing a plan.

Targets are quantified objectives. The fewer their number, the better. Experience shows that the greater the number of targets, the harder it is to achieve them. A target is only as good as the measures adopted to attain it. A target without instruments of economic policy suited to it is more appropriately called a projection or a forecast.

Few developing countries, however, have learned that a target and the policies and measures for realizing it are inseparable.

In determining the size of a plan, a country's requirements hardly represent a practical approach to the problem, since the needs of less developed countries are practically limitless. It is much more realistic to base the size of the plan on the availability of resources. But this approach often yields a rate of growth which most governments consider too low. In practice, therefore, most planners base the size of their plans on something more than available resources.

Attempts have been made to set minimum growth rates generally applicable to less developed countries. But such generalizations are likely to be too low for some countries and too high for others. Planners, who attempt to set targets which are either unrealistically high or unrealistically low, base their actions on the wrong conception of the roles which targets and planners play in the planning process. If a target is out of line with resources, measures adopted for achieving the target are likely to have harmful side effects. Moreover, planners should not set targets. They should provide a series of alternatives to the political authorities who, in the last analysis, must assume the responsibility for selecting the appropriate targets and the policies and measures for implementing them. Unless the heads of government accept this responsibility, there is little likelihood that the plan's targets will be achieved.

Chapter VI

Basic Data for Planning

Planning is mainly based on the examination of past
trends and their extrapolation into the future.[1]

RELATIONSHIP BETWEEN DATA AND PLANNING

ALTHOUGH SOME good statistical and other data may be found in almost
every country, planning in most less developed countries is severely
handicapped by widespread lack of information. Nearly every published report of a World Bank survey or other mission has commented
on the absence, inaccuracy or other inadequacy of country data for
development planning. In Libya, there is a "lack of reliable and
up-to-date information about what is going on in the economy." [2]
Resource and output data are scarce in agriculture and

> information about production in other sectors of the economy is
> even more scanty. There is no regular compilation of statistics of
> industrial production, records of road traffic are maintained only
> on the most haphazard basis, and very little is known about the
> movements of trade within the country.[3]

In Mexico, "in most fields, the official statistics are incomplete or
inaccurate, or both, and in some instances discrepancies in a single
field have proved baffling." [4] Most of the statistics available for planning in Morocco are defective and many estimates are little more than
rough guesses. Much of the information needed does not exist.[5] The
Bank's survey mission to Syria reported "that the lack of reliable
information on many aspects of the economy made its task considerably more difficult." [6] As in Libya, little was known about agricul-

---

[1] Devons, Ely. *Planning in Practice,* p. 133.
[2] IBRD. *Economic Development of Libya,* p. 89.
[3] *Ibid.*
[4] IBRD. *Economic Development of Mexico,* p. x.
[5] Waterston, Albert. *Planning in Morocco,* p. 31.
[6] IBRD. *Economic Development of Syria,* pp. 30–31.

tural output and land use and "in industry the inadequacy of data is even more marked than in agriculture."[7] In Spain, data were often incomplete or otherwise inaccurate,[8] in Thailand "much of the required statistical data is lacking or in need of qualitative improvement"[9] and "the statistical and other data available in Venezuela are not all that could be desired."[10]

United Nations regional agencies, as well as other regional organizations, have frequently called attention to the shortage of dependable planning data in their areas. In most ECAFE countries, "the quality and scope of statistical information available are as yet hardly sufficient to make long-term projections with the minimum degree of confidence required."[11] In most Latin American countries, "there are great gaps, breaks in continuity and time-lags in data,"[12] in many African countries, "no reliable statistical data on national income, consumption or employment are available . . . ,"[13] while in the Caribbean region "many of the countries were unable to provide the basic statistical data required for the annual review" of their development plans and programs.[14]

As these quotations testify, the formulation of national economic policy and, consequently, all development planning, depend mainly on what has gone before. But implementation of plans also depends on up-to-date indicators to help gauge progress and maintain planning flexibility. The existence of facts about past and current activity is therefore essential for successful development planning; without them there can be no effective planning. Qualitative information (e.g., the nature of available skills and managerial ability or the responsiveness of people to economic incentives), as well as quantitative data (in the form of statistical series or other numerical representation), are needed. All countries also need basic resource information to plan effectively.

---

[7] *Ibid.*

[8] IBRD. *Economic Development of Spain*, pp. 77–79.

[9] IBRD. *A Public Development Program for Thailand*, p. 216.

[10] IBRD. *Economic Development of Venezuela*, p. 16.

[11] UN. ECAFE. *Problems of Long-Term Economic Projections with Special Reference to Economic Planning in Asia and the Far East*, p. 104.

[12] UN. ECLA. *Report of the Latin American Seminar on Planning*, p. 45.

[13] UN. Department of Economic and Social Affairs. *Economic Survey of Africa Since 1950*, p. 243.

[14] *Newsletter of the Caribbean Organization*, Vol. III, Nos. 2, 3, 4, October, November, December 1963, p. 15.

Data Needed for Planning

The specific kinds of statistical and other information required, and the detail in which it must be accumulated, depend to a great extent on the type of planning. In the mixed economies, for example, comprehensive planning requires more statistics than partial planning, just as mathematical planning involving input-output, linear programing and similar techniques requires more quantitative data than planning with pragmatic techniques. But since the market, not the government, is the main determinant of production in a mixed economy, market and family expenditure data are indispensable to planners for determining consumer preferences and for estimating demand. Unlike Soviet-style planning, where over-all targets are divided and subdivided until a plan for each economic unit emerges, planning in mixed economies generally rests on more general, or aggregative, data at the over-all and sectoral levels.

In countries which plan on the Soviet model, statistical information and other data are used not only as guidelines in the preparation of plans but also as operational controls to assure that in each area and at each economic level action is taken in accordance with the plans laid down at the center. Since the center controls both production and distribution, and the market is largely inoperative, comprehensive and detailed supply and resource data must be obtained for the preparation of the innumerable materials, financial, manpower and other balances which underlie Soviet-style plans. The central authorities must also collect and analyze detailed data on the capacity and operations of each enterprise and other socialized economic units. These data are needed both for working out the balances and for issuing appropriate directives to each enterprise and other economic units for implementing plans. However, since in such planning the government concentrates most of its efforts on producers' goods, there has been little attention given to market surveys or family expenditure studies to indicate consumer preferences.

The collection, tabulation and evaluation of statistics in the USSR and in other Eastern European countries is a big and important business which employs large forces. It is in fact so big that it has at times threatened to become unmanageable. The advent of the computer and the application of mathematical techniques to data have opened up analytical possibilities which have not been available heretofore. But much remains to be done before these possibilities can be realized. The amount of data needed and the processing require-ments almost stagger the imagination. One Soviet writer has pointed out, for example, that

> there are several hundred million primary norms just in the sphere of material production. To form them into groups and reduce them to tens of thousands would require billions of computing opera-tions, which could hardly be done without the help of electronic computing technique. That is why a problem of exceptional importance . . . is the creation . . . of a rational system of gath-ering, storing and shaping economic information by employing modern means of computing techniques.[15]

Yugoslavia provides an interesting example of the statistical require-ments of a country in transition from Soviet-type to mixed-economy-type planning. It still formulates its plans by means of balances and, consequently, collects the comprehensive and detailed data required for such planning. But since its plans are no longer implemented by central directives to each enterprise, but largely by market forces, it also relies increasingly on the kind of aggregative data and estimates of market demand used in mixed-economy planning.

Types of Data. There is general agreement that information about natural and human resources is a primary requirement for develop-ment planning. Planning for enlarging the scope or output of agri-culture requires knowledge about the nature of soils and the current and potential uses of land. For the development of mining or petro-leum industries, data on the incidence, extent and location of mineral deposits are necessary. For planning irrigation or other waterworks, hydroelectric power projects and the development of river basins, facts about the supply, and the rate and periodicity of water flows are needed. Since people are the source of both manpower and market demand, realistic planning for over-all increases in output depends, firstly, on information about the nature and growth of population, the size, composition and sectoral employment of the labor force, and the prevalence of skills; and, secondly, on data about family expenditures at different income levels and circumstances (e.g., rural and urban) needed to estimate potential demand.

[15] Kovalev, N. I. "The Problems in Introducing Mathematics and Electronic Computers in Planning," p. 59.

A description of the economy, including its interrelationships and movements, is always useful and sometimes indispensable for effective planning. The best description takes the form of estimates over time of the Gross National Product (GNP) by sectoral origin. These estimates indicate the over-all rate of growth of income and output and reveal the relative importance of, as well as similarities and differences of movements in, agriculture, manufacturing, mining, commerce, government and other economic sectors. In countries with regional variations, estimates of the main magnitudes for each region are also useful.

Price and wage data are needed to assess costs and benefits of projects and programs, determine the existence and extent of inflationary pressures in the economy, indicate where capacity and manpower bottlenecks may arise and shed light on money incomes and expenditures. *Fiscal data,* including estimates of revenues and proceeds of foreign and domestic loans and grants, help to determine the feasibility and timing of public expenditures for investment and recurrent expenditures associated with a plan. And information about *funds available to finance private investment* is necessary to plan for the private sector. *Estimates of capital formation* over time, by sector and by means of financing, provide an indication of past relationships between investment and output, the direction in which the economy is expanding and the relative importance of the various sources of saving. *International trade and payments data* are essential for an appraisal of the balance of payments position and its movements. They may also help in estimating capital formation and fiscal receipts. To estimate future movements in export proceeds and in the demand for imports, information about *the physical volume of various exports and imports,* and their prices, is necessary.

Data are also required for *each project and program* in a plan which will enable estimates to be made of costs, in national currency and foreign exchange, and physical requirements for raw materials, machinery, equipment, supplies and manpower, by types of skills. For projects involving the expansion of production for export or for the substitution of imports, information is needed about *world market conditions* and their outlook, as well as *costs of production abroad.*

The data required for planning must cast light on the existing state of the economy as well as the direction and speed of its development in the recent past. The usefulness of available data depends on its accuracy, coverage, form and timeliness. If existing statistics are filled with error, if the coverage is limited or varies over time, if the form in which they are presented restricts or prevents comparisons with other data, or if they refer to a time long ago, they may be worthless or misleading. The use to which statistical data can be put also depends largely on a proper appreciation of their quality and deficiencies. In the hands of one who can recognize and take account of their limitations, incomplete, old, poorly devised or even inaccurate statistics can sometimes be made to yield useful information. But the proper interpretation of statistics is difficult and even good data can be misused.

The Lack of Good Data. There is general agreement that the need for basic data is not being met in less developed countries. In countries where agriculture is the most important sector, often little is known about land resources. In most countries, only a beginning has been made in classifying soils through topographic and soil surveys. The lack of data impedes reorganization of land-use patterns in many countries. In Turkey, for example, the State Planning Organization has stated that a well-prepared and well-planned land reform program is essential for "the development of the most important sector in the economic structure." [16] But it is impossible to proceed because

> there is not sufficient information on which to base the decisions which must be taken in order to enter upon such a reform. There is no adequate information concerning distribution of land owner-ship, the relationship between ownership and operation, appropriate farm sizes according to regions and according to the types of crop and the most suitable varieties of crop. [17]

Nor do many countries have reasonably adequate knowledge of their other physical and manpower resources, not only for planning, but even for making basic policy decisions. In every developing country there are serious lacunae in historical statistical series. Even in India,

> there still are surprising gaps in national income estimates when one considers that national income accounting and national in-come oriented economic planning both are ten years old. . . . The country still has no official historical series on final demand. Even the available estimates of investments are exceptionally weak and sketchy. . . . [nor are reliable estimates of depreciation avail-

[16] Turkey. State Planning Organization. *Program for the Year 1962*, p. 118.
[17] *Ibid.*

able]. . . . There are many other serious deficiencies in the current economic series. The between-census manpower data are generally very weak. . . .[18]

But economic statistics in India are much better than in most less developed countries. In other countries, there are only a negligible number of statistical series, and in some the absence of data even makes it impossible to make a reasonably good estimate of total output. For the First Plan period in Nepal, for instance, the extent to which agricultural production went up in that predominantly agricultural country, or whether the increase was sufficient to offset the rate of population growth, was difficult to tell.[19]

Even when data are available, their coverage is usually spotty, or they are not comparable over time or with other related statistics; errors are often large, or the way in which estimates were obtained makes them questionable. In Libya, for instance, one World Bank mission found that "many of the [statistical] estimates will not stand up to examination," [20] while another Bank mission to Iraq

> found a widespread and usually justifiable distrust of published statistics, especially agricultural statistics, which sometimes led those who had some use for statistical data to try to collect their own.[21]

In inaugurating a National Statistical Council in April 1962, the outspoken Deputy Chairman of Pakistan's Planning Commission forcefully described the condition of Pakistan's statistics after 14 years of planning in this way:

> The number of statistical series is insufficient, the time length of these series is often too short and the degree of accuracy of available data is often low. We have no reliable statistics of saving and investment, no knowledge of the proportions of various distributive shares in the national income, no reliable figures of unemployment and under-employment, no data on productivity of labour and capital. Our agricultural statistics are highly questionable. We do not know much about the output of our small-scale and cottage industry. There are no statistics on construction. We

[18] Lewis, John P. "India," p. 104.
[19] Pant, Y. P. "Nepal's Economic Development: A Study in Planning Experience," p. 1726.
[20] IBRD. *Economic Development of Libya*, p. 89.
[21] IBRD. *Economic Development of Iraq*, p. 114.

have only a very vague idea of our national income and output per head. . . .[22]

These are not isolated examples. Indeed, as one well-qualified economist has remarked, only partly in jest, many statistics in less developed countries appear to have been fabricated out of the "weighted averages of your guess, my guess, and our neighbour's guess." [23]

Population data, of primary importance in planning, are frequently found to be inaccurate, sometimes by as much as one-third. For example, Nigerian census figures for 1963 show a population of more than 55 million instead of a previously presumed population of 44 million, a discrepancy of about 25 per cent. A 1960 census in Ghana indicated a population of 6.7 million instead of 5.1 million and a 1963 census in the Rhodesias and Nyasaland revealed a population of 11.4 million instead of a previously assumed population of 8.8 million.[24] But it is sometimes uncertain whether the latest census figures are more reliable than previous estimates. Thus, in Nigeria, where earlier figures were considered to be an understatement, the governments of two of the four regions rejected the 1963 census figures. According to the Premier of Eastern Nigeria, the population census disclosed

inflation . . . of such astronomical proportion that the figures obtained, taken as a whole, are worse than useless; [25]

while the Premier of the Mid-West Region described the census figures as "the most stupendous joke of the year." [26]

Some countries have underestimated the size of their populations, but others have preferred to overstate them for prestige or political reasons. The rates of population growth are sometimes underestimated to an extent which invalidates planning. Many a plan's targets have come to grief because of this. In India and Pakistan, for example, discovery that the rates of population growth used in the Second Five-Year Plans of these countries had seriously underestimated the true position made it clear that what was thought to have been an increase in the per capita rate of growth was no increase at all.

Nor are the socialized economies immune from such miscalculations. A case in point was the widely publicized and admitted inaccuracies in

[22] *Dawn*, April 14, 1963.
[23] Mitra, Ashok. "Underdeveloped Statistics," p. 315.
[24] *Washington Post*, February 27, 1964.
[25] *Times*, February 29, 1964.
[26] *Times*, March 2, 1964.

production and other data in China in 1958–59 which were officially attributed to the inexperience of statistical personnel. The blame for the failure of Czechoslovakia's last Five-Year Plan has been officially laid on incorrect statistics which led to overestimations of the country's potentialities for expanding output. In the Soviet Union, also,

> planning agencies do not have at their disposal the appropriate (in volume and reliability) data on necessary norms. The reported information of the Central Statistical Administration of the USSR, besides being somewhat limited, is supplied with great delay, which detracts from its value for the planned guidance of the national economy.[27]

While some countries do not have even one set of authoritative figures for some items others, because of a lack of co-ordination, produce two or more sets of the same kind of data. Thus, in Spain, there has been more than one cost-of-living index and several industrial production indices. Two sets of national income statistics have been produced, one by the National Economic Council, another by the Ministry of Finance. The national accounts issued by the Ministry have appeared three years after the event and bear scarcely any relation to the national income figures issued by the National Economic Council.[28] In Argentina, the Central Bank and the National Development Council have both published competing series on Gross National Product. In India, the Ministry of Food and Agriculture has issued two mutually incompatible sets of data showing total output and yield per acre for each of the principal crops. Besides, estimates of capital formation published by the Indian Ministry of Finance have been altogether different from estimates issued by the Indian Central Statistical Organization.[29]

Indian statisticians have demonstrated considerable ability and ingenuity, but their statistical exercises are

> still very much in the nature of disjointed efforts. No serious attempt is apparently being made to coordinate statistical activities at different levels, and it is surprising that parallel government offices produce figures without checking with one another.[30]

[27] Kovalev, N. I. "The Problems in Introducing Mathematics and Electronic Computers in Planning," p. 59.
[28] IBRD. *Economic Development of Spain*, pp. 77–79.
[29] Mitra, Ashok. "Underdeveloped Statistics," p. 317.
[30] *Ibid.*

The co-ordination of statistical data is made more difficult in India because, in addition to the central Government, the states issue data. The estimates of income issued by the states are often not comparable with each other or with those issued by the Central Statistical Organization. The need for co-ordination is also great in many other countries, not only to eliminate duplication and improve comparability, but also to bring about a freer flow of information within their governments. In many countries, one can find a ministry, department or government office hoarding data it has collected as its private "stock in trade," unwilling to make the information available to other branches of the government. In Mexico, for example, difficulties in obtaining statistical data are at least partly explainable

> by the disquieting propensity of certain public officials to treat any statistical information as their private property on the plausible assumption that in the bureaucratic world he who knows more holds more power.[31]

And in Nigeria,

> because government information was used to serve the advantage of the party in control, any proliferation of government intelligence undermined its political and economic utility.[32]

But as often as not, information can be found lying around unused in government departments or agencies while other government offices which could make good use of the data are not even aware of their existence. For example, a World Bank survey mission to Tanganyika reported that in that country the use of statistics

> is in fact lagging considerably behind availability. Government departments and provincial administrations appeared quite frequently to be ignorant of statistical series of relevance to them and to make insufficient use of such series.[33]

Even a central statistical body may not be aware of the existence or extent of data dispersed in various parts of the government. Thus, in Spain,

> statistics are collected by some government agencies without reference to INE [the national statistical agency]. Sometimes the

[31] Wionczek, Miguel S. "Incomplete Formal Planning: Mexico," p. 179.
[32] Clark, Peter Bentley. "Economic Planning for a Country in Transition: Nigeria," pp. 262–263.
[33] IBRD. *Economic Development of Tanganyika*, p. 345.

statistics are not distributed at all and sometimes they are distributed within the Government without informing INE.[34]

Similar conditions have been reported in Iraq, Mexico, Morocco and the UAR, among many other countries.

THE QUESTION OF PRIORITIES

A country which seeks to improve its statistics for planning quickly encounters the question of priorities. Because of the shortage of qualified statisticians available to improve the accuracy, coverage, form and timeliness of statistical series, a balance must be struck among these often competitive attributes which will yield the greatest return. Since much of the value of statistical series used in planning lies in the relationship between one set of figures and another, it would be desirable to make them consistent. One way of doing this is to incorporate the available data in an integrated system of national accounts. Such a system is ideally suited to show interrelationships between different parts of the economy. Without a system of national accounting, it is often impossible to establish these connections because different systems of classifying data have been used by the agencies which collected the data.

However, because of deficiencies in basic data, it is frequently impossible to prepare estimates of national accounts with accuracy. The question then arises whether it is preferable to concentrate first on expanding and improving basic demographic, economic and social statistical series until enough good information has been accumulated to construct a reasonably accurate set of national accounts; or, alternatively, to "make do" with whatever data are available and prepare a set of partial accounts which takes account of deficiencies in the data. Here is where the experts disagree.

The first approach has been advocated by the United Nations Statistical Commission. While recognizing the value of a system of national accounts for development planning, the Commission has given first priority to the improvement and expansion of basic data on population, labor, agriculture, forestry, fishing, mining, manufacturing, construction, production of gas and electricity, wholesale and retail trade, transportation, education, health, external trade, money, bank-

[34] IBRD. *Economic Development of Spain*, p. 77.

ing, finance, prices, government, personal income and expenditure, and housing.[35]

In contrast, others have given higher priority to the preparation of national accounts estimates. Thus, Gerhard Colm and Theodore Geiger are in full accord that every effort should be made to develop the statistical series described in the United Nations' list. But they see the United Nations Statistical Commission's view as

> a counsel of perfection in the statistical field that is quite unrealistic not only for underdeveloped countries but for the developed countries as well.[36]

Colm and Geiger concede that in some countries national accounts fabricated without reliable statistics have done "little good and much harm," [37] but they believe it possible for countries with inadequate statistics to prepare reasonably good "aggregate estimates of income, production, consumption, investment, savings and international trade" [38] by steering a middle course

> between a frustrating statistical perfectionism, on the one hand, and imaginary statistics produced by wishful thinking, on the other.[39]

The view of the United Nations Statistical Commission is the one most generally held by statisticians; the view presented by Colm and Geiger, by economists and planners. This is perhaps an oversimplification, but it is a useful one. The proper preparation of a census of population, agriculture or industry takes time and the results may not be known for two or three years. The improvement of individual series of statistical data is an even longer-term task. To the statistician, however, these "micro-economic" estimates constitute the basic components of a nation's statistical system. Since national income estimates can be no better than the original data, even though subjected to a variety of sophisticated mathematical adjustments, he tends to view the activities of the planner-economists, who mostly prepare national

[35] UN. Statistical Commission. *Basic Statistics for Economic and Social Development,* and UN. Statistical Commission. *Report of the Commission to the Economic and Social Council on its 10th Session, held in New York from 28 April to 15 May, 1958,* p. 20.
[36] Colm, Gerhard and Geiger, Theodore. "Country Programming as a Guide to Development," p. 64.
[37] *Ibid.*
[38] *Ibid.*
[39] *Ibid.*

income estimates, as futile attempts to overcome deficiencies in the data by short cuts they think will save time. He sees them as

> always in a hurry for data, especially when plans are being drawn up . . . [unable or unwilling to recognize] . . . that many statistical data are worked out only after prolonged effort.[40]

The statistician is also keenly aware that the preparation of "micro-economic" statistics is devoid of glamour because results do not often lend themselves to the formation of government policy. In contrast, the aggregative, or "macro-economic," estimates of national income, capital formation, savings, consumption and the like are frequently fraught with social and economic implications for the formation of government policy and for planning a country's development. Their importance has also been enhanced as a status symbol in many less developed countries because their use is associated with the more advanced nations. Consequently, the planner-economists are generally closer than the statisticians to the decision-makers in government and are therefore in a more favorable position to influence the course of a country's statistical policy.

Besides the "statistician's view" represented by the United Nations Statistical Commission, examples of the "economist's view" can also be found in the United Nations. Thus, the Economic Commission for Latin America has put the greatest stress on national accounts and related statistics in contrast to basic statistical series.[41] And in practice, it has been this view which has prevailed in the less developed countries, in many of which the preparation of a national income or product series has been elevated to the level of an economic rite.

> For reasons of prestige, many of these nations have felt compelled to concentrate their statistical activities to compilation of such global estimates as those of national income, capital formation, and savings. When an expert, under the auspices of the UN, has gone out to a country on a short-term assignment, pressure has been brought upon him to help the local statisticians in assembling glamorous macro-economic estimates. Fashion has thus pushed aside necessity. As a result, development of basic statistics, such as data on production, prices, population movements, growth and

[40] UN. ECA. *Memorandum on Statistical Development*, p. 2.
[41] See, for example, UN. ECLA. *Use of National Accounts for Economic Analysis and Development Planning*, p. 3.

distribution of labor force, variation in money supply, etc., has been on the whole neglected.[42]

Unfortunately, regardless of whether basic statistical series or national income estimates are given preference, the results are likely to be partial or unreliable. The question then facing the planner is whether the available data, although inadequate, should be used to start to plan immediately or whether planning should be postponed until improved information in sufficient quantity is obtained. There are considerable risks in using poor data. The planner is warned that

> 'bad' statistics are possibly worse than no statistics, when viewed in terms of the role statistics can play in planning. It would be a grave error to formulate a plan that is heavily dependent on statistical series when these statistics admittedly are of poor quality.[43]

This is also the view of the Economic Commission for Asia and the Far East:

> Planning on the basis of inaccurate data may be worse than no planning at all, since such data may not only point to wrong solutions to problems but also create a false sense of complacency and lead to serious bottlenecks and rigidities.[44]

For some planners, therefore, the answer to the question of priorities is to postpone planning and concentrate first on collecting and analyzing data needed to formulate a plan. In Ethiopia, for example, up to 12 Yugoslav experts and an Ethiopian staff worked for a year on this preparatory task before starting to formulate Ethiopia's First Five-Year Plan. The preparation of "pre-planning" surveys required about a year and a half in Nigeria, and similar studies in Senegal, conducted with the aid of French foreign technical assistance, took two years to complete. Nicaragua's National Planning Office, which was established early in 1962, was for a long time entirely absorbed in preparing an over-all historical "diagnosis" of the Nicaraguan economy as it was in 1945–60. Only after this task was completed was the Planning Office prepared to turn to the job of formulating a development plan. In order

[42] Mitra, Ashok. "Underdeveloped Statistics," p. 315.
[43] Krause, Walter. *Economic Development: The Underdeveloped World and the American Interest,* p. 208.
[44] UN. ECAFE. "Economic Development and Planning in Asia and the Far East," *Economic Bulletin for Asia and the Far East,* November 1955, p. 69.

to provide a firmer informational basis for future planning in Latin American countries, tripartite groups of foreign experts sponsored by ECLA, OAS and the IDB have been gathering and collating statistics and making national income studies in some countries. After working for more than a year, a tripartite team of experts with a staff totaling 70 persons began publishing in May 1963 a detailed "diagnosis" of the Uruguayan economy, which is eventually to comprise 15 volumes and thousands of pages. The report contains a description of basic economic problems in Uruguay, a statistical description of the various sectors of the economy, a first attempt to prepare national income estimates and a comprehensive list of public investment projects, many of which are in an embryonic stage. During a six-month period in 1963, another tripartite group of 16 experts, aided by a staff of 50 in the Peruvian central planning office, prepared a seven-volume "diagnosis" of the Peruvian economy which ran to about 1,500 pages. The report is mainly a compilation of statistical information and a detailed description of all aspects of the Peruvian economy.

By adding to the small fund of knowledge about the economies concerned, such studies are of great potential value. But since they require the concentration of scarce planning expertise on laying the informational groundwork for planning in the future, they frequently have the effect of diverting official attention and effort from all planning activities. It is sometimes forgotten how high the "opportunity cost" of collecting data can be because of the need to use scarce technicians who could be used elsewhere. For example, concentration on statistical research completely occupied planners in Nicaragua, Uruguay and Peru while their diagnostic studies were being prepared, with the result that no planning was undertaken.

Planning with Inadequate Data

But most planners are not prepared to delay all planning activities until inadequacies in data are overcome. They take the ECAFE position that

> in view of the generally limited financial resources available for planning and the scarcity of trained personnel, it would be wise to avoid devoting too many resources to the collection of new data as a preliminary to planning.[45]

[45] *Ibid.*, p. 63.

The accumulation of reliable statistics in quantity is a task which takes a long time. Most planners feel that "development planning cannot await the building of a comprehensive system of statistics."[46] Or as one writer put it,

> it does not make good sense to delay action on grounds that 'one *cannot* plan without good statistics.' If good statistics are regarded as an absolute prerequisite, the day when serious economic planning will commence in numerous countries is not yet in sight.[47]

The Economic Commission for Africa (ECA) feels at least as strongly about this question. To its rhetorical question: "Must the preparation of the plan, then, await the completion of the most important statistical survey?"[48] it replies,

> This would be absurd; for it would mean a loss of valuable time for many valuable projects that are known to be useful even if their influence on the general economy of the country cannot be measured.[49]

ECA points to Somalia's Five-Year Plan for 1963–67 as an instructive example for those who assert that the preparation of a development plan is a pointless exercise in countries where basic indicators are absent. In the words of Somalia's planners:

> The methodology of planning for the Somali Republic does not follow the usual pattern based on the GDP [Gross Domestic Product] approach, for the simple reason that information about GDP is not available. Certain other necessary data are either not available at all, or if available, are unreliable and incomplete. This is true of population, birth and death rates, age distribution, immigration and emigration, labour force, employment and unemployment, wages and salaries, areas under different crops, agricultural production, yields of different crops, agricultural holdings, livestock products, livestock trade, forestry, fisheries, small scale and handicraft industries, building construction, electricity, etc.[50]

[46] United Nations Center for Industrial Development. *Organizational Aspects of Planning*, p. 18.

[47] Krause, Walter. *Economic Development: The Underdeveloped World and the American Interest*, p. 208.

[48] UN. ECA. *Memorandum on Statistical Development*, p. 2.

[49] *Ibid.*

[50] UN. ECA. *Outlines and Selected Indicators of African Development Plans*, pp. 79–80.

Despite these truly formidable informational gaps, Somalia's planners found it possible to formulate a development plan which, although deficient, constituted as valid an effort as those of most other countries at the start of their planning experience in attempting to improve living standards by raising incomes, output and employment.

Planners who concur with the ECA point of view recognize that good statistical data are important for planning, but they believe that where, as in most countries, such data are not available, "recourse has to be taken to statistics of the second-best, and make do with rough and ready indicators. . . ."[51] Even inaccurate or incomplete data can disclose bottlenecks or gaps in an economy, and a plan which employs such data judiciously can still promote development.

> It should . . . be remembered that it is not the ultimate test of a good development programme that the data contained in it should be accurate. . . . Rather, the test of a good development programme is that it should lead to measures which make growth more rapid, and make total investment more efficient, than would otherwise have been the case.[52]

Of course, care must be exercised in interpreting inadequate statistics, but most planners would agree with Arthur Lewis that "it is better to rely on figures and hunch rather than upon hunch alone."[53]

A little economic detective work can be rewarding. By comparing different statistical series within the planning country or the data of that country with those of comparable countries, or by studying earlier data for more advanced countries, the planner may be able to fill statistical gaps in his information or discover and eliminate errors in estimates. Thus, if production data are inconsistent with consumption statistics, it may be possible to track down sources of error by referring to available data within the country for incomes, imports and exports;[54] the likely yield from a unit of investment may be estimated by reference to investment yields in countries of similar size and situation; or consumer expenditure studies in advanced countries may

---

[51] Mitra, Ashok. "Underdeveloped Statistics," p. 316.
[52] UN. ECA. *Problems Concerning Techniques of Development Programming in African Countries,* p. 16.
[53] Lewis, W. Arthur. *Theory of Economic Growth,* pp. 389–390.
[54] Where regional income figures are difficult to collect, some idea of regional relationships can be obtained in certain African countries by examining the district sales records of the large tobacco and shoe manufacturers. Useful indication of changes in income over time can be seen from the changing sales of such consumer goods.

furnish leads about the way changing incomes are likely to be spent in a less developed country. Finally, even in the absence of statistics, it is

> often possible to find officials, experts and other personnel who were sufficiently well acquainted with the country, its problems and the relevant aspects of such problems to be able to make a reasonably accurate contribution to an analysis of the situation.[55]

The planner who must resort to guesses must, of course, be on guard because

> the danger for those drawing up development programmes is that they become prisoners of their own guesses, i.e., having once put the best figure down they may assume that this figure is a fact, when it may be a guess.[56]

Nevertheless, "it is surprising how much can be learned if the right sort of questions are asked." [57]

But while the planner can improve on existing statistical and other information, he should not try to make poor data provide a foundation for a plan which only good data can provide. As has been indicated, this is precisely what planners in Bolivia, Burma, Indonesia, Morocco, Nepal and other countries in early stages of development have done by introducing comprehensive planning before adequate supporting statistical and other information were available. Experience has shown this to be a mistake. Ambitious comprehensive plans which were prepared without sufficient data to guide action have resulted in bottlenecks which prevented completion of the plans. Lack of facts has resulted in shortages of goods to meet increased effective demand, and ignorance because of the absence of good data has allowed balance of payments difficulties to arise and plague some countries. When comprehensive planning is attempted without adequate data, the remarks of Professor Tress are particularly relevant:

> Complex planning, without statistical data, knowledge of vital inter-relationships or adequate intellectual grasp is bound whatever the circumstances . . . , eventually to lead to error, to the

[55] UN. ECA. *Report of the Latin American Seminar on Planning*, p. 8.
[56] UN. ECA. *Comprehensive Development Planning*, pp. 15–16.
[57] UN. ECA. *Problems Concerning Techniques of Development Programming in African Countries*, pp. 15–16.

creation of numerous bottlenecks and hence to a serious waste of resources.[58]

But this does not mean, as some think, that all planning needs to be postponed until statistics have been improved to a point where comprehensive planning become feasible. It only means that, where data are lacking or inaccurate, it is possible to start planning immediately on the limited scale permitted by the existing data.

All planning, whether comprehensive or partial, requires some basic resource data and statistics. So do individual projects and programs. There are pitfalls to the establishment of industry without market and other data. A lumbering industry established by sponsors who do not have knowledge of forestry resources, the type of tree best suited for timber and climate, the years of growth to maturity and other technical and economic factors, is not likely to be successful. The creation of a paper mill without data on raw materials, water supply and the demand for the kind of paper to be produced, can be costly. In Pakistan, for example, a new paper mill miscalculated the market and produced enough blotters in a short while to take care of Pakistan's demand for several decades. There is no point in establishing industries based on local raw materials if geological or other surveys have not been made to discover the extent of availability of these resources. In some countries, cement works have been placed on uneconomic sites because of the absence of resource data. There are countries where sugar industries have been set up without knowledge of the suitability of the soils for sugar production, the amount of rainfall or water supplies. A well-known example of the bad effects which lack of information may produce was the attempt to grow groundnuts in Tanganyika in 1947 without sufficient knowledge of resources. This led, among other things, to the establishment of farms where it was impossible to drink the local water.

But partial planning, in the form of an integrated public investment plan or a sectoral program requires fewer data than comprehensive planning, whether mathematical or pragmatic. Moreover, the data need not be as precise for partial as for comprehensive planning. The kind of data needed for the former are less rigorous, and rough and ready indicators may often be used.[59] While basic soil, land use, mineral,

---

[58] Tress, R. C. "The Practice of Economic Planning," p. 212.
[59] UN. ECAFE. "Economic Development and Planning in Asia and the Far East," *Economic Bulletin for Asia and the Far East*, December 1961, p. 2.

water and other resource surveys are useful for partial as well as comprehensive planning, in most countries at early stages of development the need for specific projects and their scope is so obvious that decision to proceed with them does not depend on the completion of detailed surveys. Most of the statistical and other information needed to carry out the projects in a public investment project are to be found in government offices, and additional data are obtainable from foreign technicians or engineering and other concerns which have had experience in carrying out similar projects in other countries.

IMPROVING PLANNING DATA

As has been seen, many countries do not have accurate information in sufficient detail to make sound decisions on economic policy. The advent of development planning in these countries has greatly increased the need for reliable statistical and other information. Although this has led to some improvements in statistical systems, surprisingly little has been done in most countries in the last 10 or 15 years to overcome obvious deficiencies in their basic data. This could not have been because of a lack of technical assistance. Many countries have had the benefit of expert advice on how to improve their statistics and other data from foreign technicians furnished by the United Nations and the more advanced countries engaged in bilateral aid programs. Nor could it be because of a lack of interest in the subject on the part of international organizations. The type of information needed for planning has been described in many documents and has been the subject of extensive discussion in many international conferences. Principles have been enunciated, lists of required data have been drawn up and resolutions adopted advocating that governments take steps to improve their data.[60] The 1961 Conference of Asian Economic Planners made a typical recommendation, repeating a plea other conferences and groups have made many times before:

urgent action should be taken by all the countries in the region to improve the quality of available statistical and other information,

[60] See, for example, UN. Statistical Commission. *Basic List of Statistics for Economic and Social Development;* UN. ECA. *Report of the First Conference of African Statisticians;* UN. ECAFE. *Report of the Seminar on Basic Statistics for Economic and Social Development;* and UN. ECLA. *Use of National Accounts for Economic Analysis and Development Planning.*

to enlarge its coverage and to ensure its systematic use both in planning and in reporting on plan fulfillment.[61]

But there is no evidence that this recommendation had any greater effect than previous recommendations in increasing government efforts to improve and expand statistical and other informational data. Several reasons appear to account for the general failure of governments to take action. With some experts insisting that planning data must take the form of national income estimates, and others equally insistent that such aggregates are less important for most less developed countries than the accumulation of basic statistical series, there has been understandably some uncertainty in less developed countries about what action is appropriate. But a more important factor, perhaps, has been the discovery, by experience in most countries, that it is possible to plan in the rudimentary way most governments plan, without making the ambitious revisions and expansions in national statistical systems called for by the experts. This appears to be true even in India, which has one of the more advanced comprehensive planning systems among less developed countries.

The usual proposals by experts for enlarging the scope and improving the accuracy of statistical and other data look to the building up of advanced statistical systems which are capable of producing information needed for comprehensive planning. Many experts consider the lack of data as a major stumbling block to comprehensive planning. But it appears more likely that in most countries, it is government unwillingness or lack of readiness to engage in comprehensive planning which mainly accounts for the lack of reliable planning data. The need for improved data in greater quantity may therefore not be as critical as outside experts sometimes think. Rudimentary public administration and planning have in general been able to get by with rudimentary statistics.

Most international agencies concerned with economic development or statistics, or conferences sponsored by them, have issued prescriptions for improving data needed for planning in less developed countries. Not only has there been, in large part, a failure to co-ordinate these proposals among these agencies; there has sometimes been a failure to co-ordinate the proposals made by the same agency at different times. The Final Report of the Fourth Inter-American Statisti-

---

[61] UN. ECAFE. "Economic Development and Planning in Asia and the Far East," *Economic Bulletin for Asia and the Far East,* December 1961, p. 78.

cal Conference of the Pan American Union listed criticisms which planners in less developed countries had made against international agencies because of these proposals. Besides the lack of co-ordination within and among the agencies concerned, mention was made of

> the pressure they [the international agencies] sometimes brought to bear in favor of the production of statistics that answer to their interests rather than statistics that are more useful to the countries themselves . . . and the lack of continuity in the activities which they encourage.[62]

To make matters worse, many planning experts have a tendency to use the more developed countries as a model. This has induced

> some statistical services to carry out investigations under the influence of the programs developed by more advanced countries even though there was no real demand for the information sought.[63]

Thus, the preparation of national income estimates, when given first priority, can take precedence over the production of information which is much more important. For example, Burmese national income estimates released in 1951 were used in 1952–53 as a basis for preparing Burma's Eight-Year Plan. When income from rice exports, a prime determinant of the country's national income, fell sharply in 1954–55, it became evident that it would have been better for planning purposes if the time and effort spent in producing the national income estimates had been used instead to make market and foreign trade studies for rice.[64] Those who insist that effective planning in less developed countries must be based on estimates of national product sometimes forget that many of the main effects of development are on variables which are excluded from the national product but are nonetheless of great importance.[65]

Scarce professional talent can also be misused in the collection of data for, and the preparation of, input-output matrices, a favorite instrument of planning experts from the more advanced countries.

[62] OAS. Fourth Inter-American Statistical Conference. *Final Report,* p. 10.

[63] OAS. Fourth Inter-American Statistical Conference. *Factors Affecting the Statistical Development of America,* p. 29.

[64] UN. ECAFE. "Economic Development and Planning in Asia and the Far East," *Economic Bulletin for Asia and the Far East,* November 1955, p. 64.

[65] Seers, Dudley. "The Role of National Income Estimates in the Statistical Policy of an Under Developed Area," p. 168.

Input-output analysis undoubtedly has considerable potentialities for planning, but most less developed countries are not yet able to employ the technique effectively. Yet, quite a few less developed countries have constructed input-output tables of their economies, although it would be hard to find one which has made effective use of them for planning purposes. The testimony of one planning expert with experience in less developed countries could be confirmed by others:

> I have been exposed to [input-output] matrices in the United States, India and Puerto Rico. In each case I was working in the field to which they had been presumably dedicated. Upon investigation I found that in no instance were they used for making development planning decisions.[66]

There is thus a great difference between the limited immediate needs for planning data in most less developed countries and the ambitious, seemingly insatiable, programs sometimes advocated by the experts. Because of this, few government authorities in less developed countries have seriously entertained any thought of executing the sometimes grandiose and costly proposals for statistical betterment which foreign advisers make. Instead, attempts to improve data are usually haphazard and piecemeal. It is a classic example of the perfect being the enemy of the good.

In most less developed countries, there is little official appreciation of the need for data. The collection and tabulation of statistics therefore remain a neglected function of government. Most less developed countries have only elementary statistical services and their statistical organizations are almost invariably weak and ineffective. The complaint of Turkey's State Planning Office that Turkey's Central Statistical Office

> under present conditions is unable to perform the functions expected of it,[67]

is typical of similar complaints made in other countries. There is a commonly held belief in less developed countries that statistical work requires little or no professional knowledge. The gathering, classification and evaluation of statistics are often regarded as

---

[66] Mayne, Alvin. "Designing and Administering a Regional Economic Development Plan with Specific Reference to Puerto Rico," p. 142.

[67] Turkey. State Planning Organization. *Program for the Year 1962*, pp. 179–180.

inferior, degrading and routine work on which the most inefficient clerical staff could best be employed [when], in fact, this sort of work demands a high degree of skill. . . .[68]

Many persons engaged in statistical work are inadequately trained. What a World Bank survey mission found in Thailand in 1959 describes the general situation in many countries:

> In . . . the Central Statistical Office (CSO), there is no single individual trained specifically for the career of statistician. Those in supervisory positions in the CSO have received only incidental statistical training. . . . The remainder of the CSO staff of some 50 persons, except for two or three with some mathematical competence, are simply clerks assigned to statistical work.[69]

Even when trained statisticians are available, they are likely to find salaries and working conditions unattractive in government statistical services. There is usually a shortage of funds for statistical work which reflects government failure to recognize the importance of basic data. Spain is one example among many. In that country, economic censuses for industry and agriculture, authorized by a law approved in 1957, had not yet been carried out by 1963 because of the Government's failure to make the necessary money and machines available to the National Statistical Institute (INE). The report of the World Bank survey mission to that country concluded that

> the trouble is certainly not a dearth of talented Spanish statisticians. But the INE is not in a position to offer them a career. This is an outstanding case . . . of the present system of remuneration of public servants. As a consequence, most of the best talent is working either whole-time or part-time in the universities, in other branches of the Government or for private firms; some have gone abroad.[70]

Analogous conditions obtain in Latin American countries:

> Aside from the lack of financial resources, there are, for example, other factors which are often felt with greater impact, such as the absence of conditions that would make it possible to utilize the services of increasing numbers of trained statistical workers and to keep them on the job, the lack of coordination between units operating in the statistical field, and the lack of interest on the part

[68] Devons, Ely. *Planning in Practice*, p. 134.
[69] IBRD. *A Public Development Program for Thailand*, p. 216.
[70] IBRD. *Economic Development of Spain*, p. 78.

of the higher governmental agencies to which these units pertain within the national administration.[71]

Any serious attempt to increase the basic stock of reliable planning data in most less developed countries must therefore include provision for strengthening the financial position and status of government statistical agencies and the quality and standing of their staffs. It is also essential to build up organizations which can make surveys of land, forest, water, energy and mineral resources to fill basic gaps in planning information. The establishment, strengthening and perfecting of such institutions, and the training and creation of staffs to administer and operate them, is a slow process. To carry out the required censuses, studies and surveys and to obtain usable results from them may take years. Since it is very costly to create and maintain such bodies, their establishment and expansion have to be phased in accordance with the availability of budgetary funds.

Blueprints for Statistical Betterment

The character of the statistical apparatus and the organizations for making natural resource studies, as well as the speed with which they are established, enlarged and staffed, depends on the kind of planning information required. While the planner should adapt his planning techniques at first to the state of the existing statistical apparatus,

> the statistical apparatus should, over a longer period, be adapted to more advanced planning techniques.[72]

To accomplish this, it would be useful to include in each national development plan a program or blueprint for expanding and improving the statistical and other data needed only to formulate and implement the next plan. The statistician or other fact-finder must always be ahead of the planner if he is to provide the planner with information when it is required. Rarely is it possible to collect information which can greatly influence present planning decisions. Usually, information collected now can only influence future decisions. To permit statisticians to provide data for future planning needs in an organized way requires a decision by planners about the kind of planning they intend to do in the future.

[71] OAS. Fourth Inter-American Statistical Conference. *Final Report,* p. 9.
[72] UN. ECA. *Memorandum on Statistical Development,* p. 3.

It is, of course, possible to draw up a statistical program or blueprint which goes beyond the needs of the next plan. Since 1947, for example, the Inter-American Institute of the Pan American Union has been trying to persuade Latin American countries to adopt a much more ambitious program for improving statistical services. The Final Report of the Fourth Inter-American Statistical Conference, sponsored by the Institute, itself states that the all-embracing list of the Institute's statistical aims

> suffices to show that what has been attempted in the American region has constituted a program which, because of its scope, is without precedent even in regions with more tradition and experience in the field of statistics.[73]

The fact is, however, that the Institute's program has not been adopted in its essentials by any Latin American country. It has been found, outside as well as within Latin America, that it is extremely difficult to get government support for such ambitious and costly statistical improvement programs.

A blueprint for statistical betterment related specifically to the next plan would be much more modest than most proposals to overhaul the statistical apparatus and practices prevailing in less developed countries. It is likely to be much easier to achieve, given the scarcity of statistical and technical staffs and the uncertain interest of governments in most less developed countries in the collection of data. A blueprint which would limit the acquisition of data primarily to essentials for the next plan would make it easier to set up priorities for data and to weed out unnecessary items. Few planners ever feel they have all the information they need. They would therefore have to exercise restraint in setting up the blueprint. Thus, while there might be instances when items which take a long time to gestate would have to be included in the blueprint to permit planning advances after the next plan period, they would be exceptional.

Any blueprint for improving statistics for planning purposes should be included as a project or program in the current development plan to allow appropriate financial, personnel and other resources to be allocated for its implementation and to make certain that the data to be produced meet planning needs.[74] Unless planners and producers of the

[73] OAS. Fourth Inter-American Statistical Conference. *Final Report*, p. 6.
[74] Provision would also have to be made for betterment of non-planning information.

data co-operate closely in this endeavor, the data may be found, like the list of basic statistics for planning produced by the First Conference of African Statisticians, to have been

> constructed for the producer of statistics and not for the convenience of the user.[75]

Attempts have been made on an international basis to prescribe a uniform system for collecting data for all countries. As has been seen, some experts consider the establishment of basic statistical series in less developed countries more important than the preparation of national income estimates; others believe the reverse to be true. Regardless of the substantive content of the prescription, it is doubtful whether a single prescription for all countries is practicable. It has not produced appreciable results despite persistent effort. It is equally doubtful whether one prescription is feasible even for all countries in the same region. The Economic Commission for Africa has pointed out, for example, that the basic list of planning statistics produced by the First Conference of African Statisticians was inadequate, among other reasons, because it failed to

> distinguish among the very different situations prevailing in African countries, some of which have a statistical development going back more than fifty years, while others have just created a central statistical service.[76]

There seems to be no better way of improving the stock of planning information for any country than by fitting its program for informational improvement to its own particular needs at the particular stage of development which it has reached. This does not mean that each country's requirements for planning data are fundamentally different from those of all other countries. It means only that a blueprint for improving a country's statistical and other data is likely to come closer to meeting the country's urgent and essential informational needs, if it is fitted to the kind of planning the country is *going* to attempt, than if it is prepared on the basis of the kind of planning someone outside the government thinks the country *ought* to attempt. Since most countries engage in simple forms of planning, a blueprint adapted to such planning will call for a limited amount of simple data which can be put

[75] UN. ECA. *Memorandum on Statistical Development*, p. 6.
[76] *Ibid.*

to use quickly. It would therefore have a better chance of being carried out than a larger, more complex program, like those generally proposed by advocates of comprehensive planning for all countries and for which there is no immediate use in many lands.

In an era when international regional co-operation is becoming increasingly important, international statistical groups and conferences have urged developing countries to adopt statistical classification systems which permit international comparisons of country data. But if each informational improvement program is to be tailored to the specific requirements of a country, it may be necessary to sacrifice international comparability if it is against the interests of a country. Thus, where hoes are important in a country's agriculture, as in some African countries, it will not do for the country's planning purposes to adopt a broader definition for agricultural implements advocated by an international agency which may result in concealing the number of hoes imported. Or in a country where, say, cedar and graphite exist, it may be desirable to separate out even so small a classification as pencils from larger import classifications recommended by an international group of statistical experts, to provide market information for a would-be investor in a pencil manufacturing plant utilizing the indigenous raw materials.

The type of information required will therefore differ from one country to another even if the different countries are at the same level of development. If planners' activities in the short run are to be limited to one or two sectors, statisticians and other fact-finders might well largely limit themselves at first to the collection or improvement of information in those sectors. If the planners intend to work on a public investment plan providing a basic infrastructure, information for appraising the possible direction of transport, power, water supplies and related development should get the highest priority. If the public investment plan includes agriculture, basic resource information on soils, land use and other data will be required. And if the plan comprehends the private sector, market research and other information to guide and encourage private investors should be gathered and made available. Although hard and fast rules cannot be made, there is a strong probability that for most developing countries the approach described would result in concentrating scarce statistical and other fact-finding personnel on the improvement of basic statistical and resource data in early planning stages, and the development of national income and other aggregative estimates in later planning stages.[77] In some less developed countries in an early development stage, it may be desirable to make aggregative estimates. But for most countries,

> a line must be drawn beyond which ambitious and, for the present, futile efforts to concoct aggregative figures should be discouraged. For each such country efforts must be made to work out a rough and ready allocation of statistical resources which, while not ruling out global estimations altogether, should assign adequate importance to strengthening basic data.[78]

SUMMARY AND CONCLUSIONS

In summary, planning depends on the existence of qualitative and quantitative facts about resources and economic and social activity. All countries need information about basic resources to plan effectively, but the kind of statistical information needed, and its detail, depends on the type of planning.

The usefulness of available data depends on its accuracy, coverage, form and timeliness. If existing statistics are full of mistakes, the coverage is limited or changes frequently, the form of the data restricts or precludes comparisons with other data, or the data are out-of-date, they may do more harm than good.

Planning in most less developed countries is severely handicapped by the lack of dependable data in sufficient quantity. While some countries lack data, others, because of a lack of co-ordination, produce two or more sets of similar data. There is need to co-ordinate statistical activities in many countries, not only to eliminate duplication, but also to improve comparability and a freer flow of information within governments.

A country which seeks to improve its statistics for planning must set priorities. It must decide, for example, whether to build up its basic

[77] The speed with which reliable data may be accumulated in many fields can be accelerated through the use of aerial photography. Aerial photography has proven feasible for the discovery and analysis of mineral deposits; the exploration of forest resources; the mapping of soil types; and hydrological surveys. But it is also possible that it could be put to use in developing countries (in conjunction with sampling surveys) for estimating population, numbers of grazing animals, the kinds and quantities of growing crops, land use patterns, etc. (National Planning Association. "Aerial Photography and Development Planning.")

[78] Mitra, Ashok. "Underdeveloped Statistics," p. 315.

data first or whether it is more desirable to prepare aggregative national accounts estimates, even though the data on which they are based are inadequate. Some experts advocate the first course; others the second. There is also the question whether the available data, although inadequate, should be used to start planning immediately or whether planning should be postponed until improved information is obtained. Some planners prefer to postpone planning for a year or two until they accumulate more reliable information. But this causes great delays in meeting a country's problems through planning and most planners feel that it is preferable to start planning as soon as possible even if there is need to use statistics that are second-best.

This approach makes sense provided the planner does not try to support a complex plan with poor data. But this is exactly what many planners have tried to do by introducing comprehensive planning before necessary supporting information was available. All planning requires data. But partial planning requires fewer and less precise data than comprehensive planning.

Although some countries have improved their statistical systems, surprisingly little has been done to remedy known deficiencies. One explanation for the widespread failure of governments to act may be the frequently conflicting recommendations made by the experts. Another, and perhaps more significant explanation for inaction, may be the realization in many countries that it is possible to plan without making the basic reforms in statistics which most international experts consider a *sine qua non* for effective planning. Experts tend to blame the lack of data for the lack of comprehensive plans. But the greater likelihood is that most countries are not prepared to adopt grandiose and costly programs for providing data for comprehensive planning because they are not yet ready, for other reasons, to plan comprehensively.

There is a great divergence between the limited needs for planning data in most less developed countries and the ambitious programs sometimes advocated by international statistical or planning experts. Since there is little appreciation of the importance of data in the governments of most of these countries, there is little genuine interest in carrying out the experts' recommendations. Instead, most countries make *ad hoc* and piecemeal attempts to improve planning data. Statistical services are generally rudimentary, neglected and without adequate funds. Statisticians in government service are not given appropriate status and are underpaid.

There is great need in most countries, regardless of the kind of planning they attempt, to improve both the quantity and quality of planning data. But it might be the wiser course to take a more modest and realistic approach than the usual one, and include in each development plan a program for expanding and improving the statistical and other data only to the extent it is needed to formulate and implement the next plan. By making provision for the blueprint in the current development plan, attention can be drawn to the need for tying in statistical improvement with planning and for providing resources in the plan to carry out the betterment program. By relating the blueprint specifically to the next plan, it is possible to concentrate on essentials only and to weed out unnecessary items. Since it is not feasible to prescribe a uniform system of data collection for all countries, blueprints should be fitted to the specific needs of each country.

Chapter VII

The Budget's Role in Planning

> . . . planning without regard for the realities
> of annual budget implementation becomes an
> academic exercise of little operational value.[1]

THE RELATIONSHIP BETWEEN PLAN AND BUDGET

SINCE ANNUAL budgets are the principal means by which governments authorize and control most of their expenditures, most outlays provided for in the public sector portion of a development plan must be incorporated into these budgets if the plan is to be carried out. From a practical point of view, therefore, the conversion of a public development plan into a series of annual budgets is likely to be the most important stage in the planning process. It is by examining the link between a plan and a budget that one can tell whether or not a government means to carry out a plan. If an operating organization can obtain a budgetary allocation for one of its projects or programs only if it has been approved as part of a development plan, we may assume that a government is in earnest about carrying out a plan. If, however, significant exceptions are permitted, doubts arise about a government's intentions to implement a plan. A government's budget is therefore a key element in converting a development plan into a program for action.

Where the relationship between a plan and a budget is close, the budget is, as far as it goes, the financial counterpart of the public sector plan. To perform this role adequately, the budget must provide not only for planned capital expenditures but also for associated current expenditures, as well as for revenue and other domestic financial resources which, in combination with available external financial resources, will support the required outlays. As indicated in Chapter V, the ideal connecting link between a plan—more specifically a medium-

[1] Herman, Robert S. "Two Aspects of Budgeting," p. 319.

term plan—and an annual budget is an annual plan. By identifying what must be done and the resources and measures needed to do them in the coming year, an annual plan reduces the multiannual tasks and targets of a medium-term plan to the quantities required for incorporation in an annual budget and, in this way, greatly simplifies the task of "translating" the relevant portions of a medium-term plan into an annual budget.

An annual plan reaches, or should reach, its conclusions after consideration of the totality of resources available to a country. These include physical factors, like natural resources, manpower and existing productive capacities, as well as financial resources in domestic currency and foreign exchange. The annual plan apportions these physical and financial resources among the various sector programs and, frequently, among projects included in the plan; and it sets savings, investment, export, import, output and other targets which involve the utilization of these resources in a way which is consistent with the institutional, administrative and managerial setup in a country.[2] An annual plan for the public sector includes the programs of autonomous and semiautonomous agencies, state, regional and local bodies, as well as those of ministries and departments. If the plan is comprehensive it must also provide a framework for development in the private sector.

[2] The foreign exchange availabilities and requirements to carry out a development plan are generally incorporated in a foreign exchange budget. There should be a foreign exchange budget for the entire period of a medium-term plan since the amount of foreign exchange available to a country is an important determinant of the size and composition of its plan. To fix the extent of foreign exchange needed for a medium-term plan, planners must estimate the foreign exchange required for imported capital goods, raw materials, components and services for planned projects and programs. The gap between total foreign exchange requirements and foreign exchange availabilities must equal the gap between planned investment and domestic savings. One is the counterpart of the other in a consistent plan. (UN. ECAFE. "Problems and Techniques of Foreign Exchange," pp. 38–39.)

A detailed foreign exchange budget must be prepared annually in conjunction with an annual development plan and an annual budget. An annual foreign exchange budget shows both the sources and uses of foreign exchange. The sources side indicates the amount of accumulated foreign reserves, the amounts expected to be earned from exports of specific goods and services, receipts from foreign loans and grants, etc., by country and currency. The uses side allocates foreign exchange among competing demands in accordance with criteria laid down in a development plan. These include allocations of foreign exchange between the private and public sectors and between consumption and investment goods. Details will include payments for imports of goods and services, interest and principal payments on public and private foreign debt, reserves needed to be carried forward, etc., by country and type of currency.

Finally, an annual plan incorporates those instruments of economic policy and organizational and institutional measures required to mobilize resources and achieve plan objectives.

An annual plan is therefore broader in scope than a conventional administrative budget, which is almost always limited to the domestic funds required for general government activities, usually the only part of the public sector which is covered by the government budget. An annual plan takes a broader view than a budget in another sense. It is likely to be expressed in more general terms than a budget. An annual plan is mostly concerned in broad outline with objectives, priorities for the use of resources and expected outputs from proposed inputs of physical, human and financial resources. While an annual plan should indicate how financial and other resources are to be allocated among projects and programs, a budget must be concerned much more specifically with receipts from various taxes and other sources, the availability and commitment of funds, cost estimates for projects and programs, the administrative feasibility of individual projects and programs, and the canons of financial custodianship and control.

It is possible for a budget to substitute for an annual plan, and vice versa. In Malaya, for instance, annual budgets are prepared without an annual plan on the basis of recommendations of the Economic Planning Unit (EPU), which is guided generally by the terms of Malaya's Five-Year Plan. But since the EPU's recommendations for allocating capital expenditures and for reconciling these allocations with current expenditures generally form the basis for the budget, plan and budget are more completely related to each other than in most other countries. In contrast, Yugoslavia's annual development plans embody investments in the economy which are never incorporated in annual budgets. This is because annual budgets in that country are largely limited to "nonproductive" administrative expenditures for carrying on the ordinary business of government. In Yugoslavia, therefore, it is the annual development plan rather than the budget which directly determines how public financial resources are allocated from a General Investment Fund and a series of decentralized investment funds.

But for most countries, especially less developed countries, annual plans and budgets, and their co-ordination, are virtually *sine qua non* for putting medium-term plans into effect. The task of implementing a medium-term plan, without first phasing it in annual plans, appears to be well beyond the capacity of most less developed countries. In this

respect, Malaya is an exception rather than an example.[3] Yugoslavia is
even more exceptional since practically every other country includes a
large part of its public development expenditures in its budgets.

In countries with Soviet-type economies, budgets based on annual
plans are an integral part of the planning process. With retained profits
of enterprises, they are in fact the principal source of investment funds
for implementing annual development plans. But financial budgets are
subordinate to development plans. In these countries, finance is

> conceived as an instrument of proper implementation of a devel-
> opment plan and not as an independent factor limiting the rate of
> economic development. The only limits to economic development
> are set by nature and the given historic heritage of society. They
> consist of limitations in natural resources, human skills and organ-
> ising power. To allow finance to act as a limit would introduce a
> man made limit on economic development which has no justifica-
> tion in the state of available natural and human resources.

> However, finance is an important instrument for assuring a smooth
> course of economic development, for avoiding disturbances. Fi-
> nance is an instrument by which the needed physical resources are
> made available for the plan and by which they are directed to their
> proper allocation. Furthermore, finance is an accounting device
> which shows whether the total requirement of physical resources
> balances with the available quantity. Such balance is necessary to
> avoid bottlenecks and inflationary disturbances in the course of
> realisation of the plan of economic development. Consequently,
> the plan of economic development must be balanced both in terms
> of physical and of financial requirements and availabilities.[4]

This concept of the role of a budget is clearly reflected in the
budgets of countries which plan on the Soviet model. In the USSR,
itself,

> the crucial budget figures . . . do not have an independent exist-
> ence, but are built up at each stage on the draft or final figures of
> the national economic plan.[5]

Similarly, the Czechoslovak budget is thought of as mirroring

---

[3] Even in Malaya, however, the absence of annual development plans has made
it necessary to revise medium-term plan totals to bring them into line with budgetary expenditures.

[4] Lange, Oskar. "The Tasks of Economic Planning in Ceylon," p. 78.

[5] Davies, R. W. *Development of the Soviet Budgetary System*, pp. 186–187.

the material proportions of the comprehensive plan. Hence, a close connexion between plan and budget is unavoidable and necessary; [6]

while in Hungary, the budget is carefully

drawn up in close conformity with the guide-lines and targets of the economic plans. Thus, the financial plan [i.e., the budget] of the economy is built upon the fundamental indicators of the economic plan and comprises their financial aspects. [7]

Consistency with an annual plan is therefore a prime requisite of a well-prepared budget in Soviet-type economies. A deficit in the budget

indicates that the production, consumption and accumulation targets and the quantitative and qualitative indicators of the economic plan are not properly co-ordinated. [8]

Discrepancies arise between budgets and plans, especially when an annual plan has been revised at the last moment. But on the whole, consistency is achieved.

In contrast, there is only a tenuous relationship between plans and budgets in most mixed-economy countries. For example, the annual Income and Expenditure Budget in Honduras was supposed to be drawn on the basis of co-ordinated action by the Honduran Bureau of the Budget and the National Economic Council, the country's central planning agency. But the Council did not see the (1962) budget until after it had been approved by the President and only a few days before it was to be submitted to the Congress. As a result, there were

serious and irreconcilable discrepancies between the plans drawn up and the appropriations recommended to Congress in the draft Budget. [9]

In Guatemala,

inclusion of a project in the plan did not ensure that the necessary funds would be appropriated. Further, even if funds were appro-

[6] Vergner, Zdenek. "Economic Planning in Czechoslovakia," p. 8.
[7] Hungary. "The Main Features of National Economic Planning in Hungary," p. 22.
[8] Bor, Mikhail Zakharovich. "The Organization and Practice of National Economic Planning in the Union of Soviet Socialist Republics," p. 165.
[9] Collett and Clapp, Inc. *Organización y Administración de la Función de Planeación*, p. 15.

priated, the implementing agencies retained substantial leeway to
use the funds for projects not forming part of the development
programs.[10]

And in Burma,

> there was no financial framework for the plan as a whole and no
> attempt was made to fit the plan into the Government budget.[11]

Investments made under Surinam's Ten-Year Plan are controlled by
the Planning Bureau. Outlays for implementing the Plan are not
incorporated in the budget which the Ministry of Finance prepares.
But there are substantial amounts included in the Ministry's budget for
development outside the Ten-Year Plan over which the Planning
Bureau has no control.

Where, as in Pakistan and India, budgets are prepared on the basis
of annual plans, this is a recent innovation. Even in France, the Fourth
Plan was the first to be included in the budget when the Ministry of
Finance finally consented to give up some of its traditional independence and include some plan items in the budget for 1962.[12]

Many problems other than the traditional independence of a Ministry of Finance impede the integration of plans and budgets. One of the
most important problems is the failure of most less developed countries
with medium-term plans to prepare annual development plans. In the
absence of annual plans, many less developed countries with medium-
term plans resort to annual budgets to co-ordinate their development
efforts. In Tanganyika, for example, a World Bank survey mission
reported that despite the issuance in the postwar period of a somewhat
confusing sequence of development plans, in practice, planning has
been largely carried on through annual budgets.[13] But since medium-
term plans do not indicate clearly the action to be taken annually to
fulfill plan targets, what is included in budgets may fall short of what is
required by a plan.[14]

Where annual plans are prepared, they often do not relate proposed
expenditures to physical targets. Many annual plans are little more

---

[10] OAS. Department of Economic Affairs. *Planning Organization and Implementation in Guatemala*, p. 33.
[11] Burma. Ministry of National Planning. *Second Four-Year Plan for the Union
of Burma* (1961–62 to 1964–65), p. 1.
[12] Wickham, S. "French Planning: Retrospect and Prospect," p. 343.
[13] IBRD. *Economic Development of Tanganyika*, p. 340.
[14] UN. TAO. *Report of the Inter-Regional Workshop on Problems of Budget
Classification and Management in Developing Countries*, p. 15.

than lists of projects with amounts to be included in a budget. In some countries, it is impossible to fit plans into budgets because annual plans are drawn up on a calendar year basis while annual budgets are prepared for a different fiscal period. Where this situation exists, the period used for plans and budgets must be made to coincide before plans and budgets can be integrated. Recently, Ghana, Guatemala, Italy, and Trinidad and Tobago, among other countries, provided for changing their fiscal years to the calendar year to integrate their budgetary and planning periods.

Where the periods of a plan and a budget coincide, the timetable for preparing the annual plan may not have been synchronized with the one for preparing the budget, with the result that the plan is not ready in time to be incorporated in the budget. If an annual plan is to provide guidelines for a budget, its preparation should begin before work on the budget starts. But work on a plan cannot begin too far ahead because the results of the current year's plan, on which the coming year's plan should be based, will not be known until late in the current year and because a plan prepared long in advance is likely to be out of date by the time its period begins. Moreover, the formulation of an annual plan cannot proceed very far without reasonably reliable budgetary estimates of the coming year's receipts, current expenditures, and surplus on current account available for public investment. This is because the size of an annual plan is usually influenced greatly by the balance available after nondevelopment requirements are met. Basic budgetary figures for the coming year are also needed because they help detect current economic trends and because the annual plan for the coming year must evaluate the probable effect of that year's budget on the economy. This is because a budget influences economic activity. Decisions on how much of total financial needs are to be covered by taxation and how much by domestic borrowing, drawing down cash balances, external loans and foreign grant aid will affect the levels of supply and demand for resources for the entire economy; and the proposed level and composition of taxes and budgetary spending will affect private savings and investment incentives.[15]

Planning and budgeting thus constitute a two-way process in which the data of each feed the other. It is therefore unavoidable that much of the work of preparing an annual plan and a budget must proceed simultaneously and with the close collaboration of planning and

---

[15] *Ibid.*, p. 19.

budget officials. In federal governments, such as in India and Pakistan, annual plans and budgets must also be prepared by each political subdivision and dovetailed with both the annual plan and budget of the federal government. This requires the establishment of a time-table with deadlines for the submission of new projects and programs by political subdivisions, as well as the provision of data on other aspects of their plans.

For foreign exchange allocations to be co-ordinated with the domestic currency component of financing required for projects, it is also essential that the preparation of an annual foreign exchange budget be synchronized with the preparation of an annual government budget and that both be presented for simultaneous consideration and approval by the appropriate authorities. Unless this is done, shortages of foreign exchange are likely to develop which will delay the execution of projects.

Delays in preparing a budget can also seriously hinder the integration of plans and budgets. It frequently happens that budgets are not ready at the start of a fiscal year. Thus, in Syria, budgets for the financial year beginning January 1 were supposed to be ready by the end of the preceding December. But a World Bank survey mission found that budget preparation often fell behind this schedule.[16] Until a budgetary reform was instituted in 1964, most of the Italian Parliament's time each year was consumed in approving 19 separate ministry budgets. They were supposed to be enacted into law by July 1, the start of the financial year, but the task was never completed before the end of October.[17]

INADEQUACIES OF CONVENTIONAL BUDGETS

Even when a budget is ready on time, it often is not an effective instrument for allocating financial resources in accordance with a plan. In many countries it is an incomplete statement of government receipts and expenditures, with significant exclusions; in some countries there are a multitude of segregated funds which complicate and restrict the usefulness of a budget; and in other countries formalistic controls take the place of efficient budget management. In a study which the Public Administration Service of Chicago, Illinois, completed for the U.S.

[16] IBRD. *Economic Development of Syria*, pp. 264–265.
[17] *Financial Times*, January 28, 1964.

Agency for International Development in 1962, legalistic restrictions were found to hamstring budgetary administration in the governments of many countries:

> Generally it will be found that the handling of individual fiscal transactions is controlled in minute and inflexible detail. Often there is much concern over how documents are authenticated, processed, and filed, how transactions are classified, and how accounts are maintained. At the same time, large areas of governmental expenditure are under little or no control, slight relationship exists between expenditure estimates and results, and many procedural requirements are met by *pro forma* and 'after the fact' actions.[18]

The same study also discovered many other shortcomings in budgets which greatly impeded their use as instruments for carrying out development plans. In fact,

> in some countries there is no central budget administration worthy of the name. Expenditure estimates are compiled on some historical basis, and programs and projects are initiated without any idea of when and how they may be completed or how they are related to one another. The annual budget represents a totaling up of departmental estimates of receipts and expenditures that are generally unrelated to governmental programs or foreign exchange resources or monetary policy.[19]

These countries may be extreme cases. Some countries have established the basic elements of a budgeting system and have introduced methods and techniques which are increasing the usefulness of their budgets for development purposes, but the study concludes that,

> in many countries, . . . budget administration is so inadequate as to make impossible the implementation of any reasonable development plan.[20]

Budgetary Fragmentation

The conventional administrative budget commonly used by governments does not encompass all public sector activities. Some exclusions result from political organization. The conventional budget does not,

[18] US. AID. *Modernizing Government Budget Administration*, p. 35.
[19] *Ibid.*, p. 24.
[20] *Ibid.*, p. 35.

for instance, include public sector transactions carried out by states or other political subdivisions, even when the national budget makes large contributions to their activities. Nor should a national budget include the expenditures and receipts of state and local governments which have a degree of independence.[21] But since budgetary transactions for development at subordinate levels of government may be substantial, especially in countries with a federal constitution, their exclusion from a central government's budget reduces the budget's comprehensiveness and may thereby reduce its capacity to implement public sector programs.

Other exclusions from national budgets are less understandable or defensible. A World Bank survey mission to Syria found, for example, that in that country

> the ordinary budget gives an incomplete and misleading impression of the fiscal position of the government because it does not cover certain extraordinary defense expenditures and receipts and transfers of funds between the Treasury and independent agencies.[22]

It is the failure to include transfers or other transactions of public or quasi-public agencies in the conventional administrative budgets commonly used in less developed countries which constitutes the most serious omission in these budgets.[23] When public and semipublic agencies, whose transactions are outside the budget, account for substantial proportions of public income and expenditure, the usefulness of the budget for allocating financial resources in accordance with a plan is greatly diminished. In Ecuador, for instance, 65 per cent of the public revenue was administered by over 700 public and semipublic agencies whose transactions were not recorded in the government budget,[24] while in Mexico about half of all public investment was

[21] As will be seen later, conventional budgets may not even include data on intergovernmental transfers between a central government and subordinate political governments.

[22] IBRD. *Economic Development of Syria*, p. 266.

[23] The extent to which data on autonomous and semiautonomous agencies are included or excluded in a national budget is largely the result of historical accident or tradition. In many countries, information on the transactions of these agencies is limited to budget transfers to agencies on current or capital account or net transfers from agencies to government.

[24] Ecuador. National Board of Economic Planning and Coordination. "Chapter IV. The Organization for the Plan for Economic Development and the Administrative Reform," p. 15.

financed by such agencies with extrabudgetary resources.[25] In Venezuela, also, 50 per cent of public investment outlays have been carried out by public and semipublic agencies, states and municipalities. Neither their transactions nor budgetary transfers to and from the autonomous agencies have been included in the national budget although a substantial part of their investment has been financed by National Government transfers.

The absence of information about transfers between a budget and public or semipublic agencies generally implies a lack of adequate government control over their activities. In Thailand, for instance, a World Bank survey mission reported inadequate financial controls over

> the 80 or more quasi-independent government organizations which are engaged in various commercial, industrial and financial activities. The scale of financial transactions of many of these is very large . . . , [yet] for the majority of these organizations supervision does not go beyond a routine audit of accounts.[26]

In many countries, semipublic or public enterprises circumvent national development plans and invest in low-priority projects and programs outside plans which they finance with loans from banks or with expensive, short-term foreign suppliers' credits. These activities may not only lead to a diversion of resources needed to implement national development plans but may also jeopardize a country's credit standing and balance of payments position.

While the omission of items which should be included in a budget is the more common weakness, some budgets are impaired by the inclusion of unnecessary or largely meaningless receipts and expenditures which reflect mainly the transfer of funds between accounts. For example, one Middle Eastern country has four types of budgets. Interrelationships among these budgets are not always clear; transfers from one budget to another are not easily distinguished from actual expenditures or revenues of the public sector; neither is it always clear whether certain receipts are revenues or only counterparts of increased government indebtedness. These and other procedural inadequacies make it almost impossible to obtain an over-all view of the financial position of the public sector.

[25] Beginning with the 1965 budget, transactions of about 20 semiautonomous agencies which in 1965 were expected to spend slightly more than the rest of the Mexican Government were included in the National Budget.

[26] IBRD. *A Public Development Program for Thailand,* p. 200.

The usefulness of a budget as an instrument for implementing a development plan may also be impaired by excessive "earmarking" of tax receipts or other revenues for specific purposes. Some earmarking, like a payroll tax to finance social security payments, gasoline taxes to finance road construction, or toll revenues from a bridge to retire indebtedness incurred to finance its construction, is economically and politically justifiable because it ties a government service to a tax or payment which made the service possible. There are other examples for which a case could be made for setting revenues aside in a special fund to be used for a designated purpose. Earmarking of taxes may make people less reluctant to pay increased taxes when they know that the proceeds from a tax will be used for a purpose from which they will benefit. Moreover, when taxes are increased and earmarked to pay for more or better government services approved by a legislature, there is increased assurance (if the tax is large enough) that the additional services will not require inflationary financing.

But when a substantial proportion of total budgetary revenues is segregated into special funds earmarked for specific use, a budget loses flexibility for development because it becomes difficult if not impossible to allocate financial resources in accordance with priorities called for by a plan. Earmarking of revenues is common in Latin America and is growing in Asia and Africa:

> In one Latin American country in 1961 income from 291 out of 330 taxes was wholly or partly earmarked for subordinate authorities or marginal entities, leaving only 39 to the national government for general use.[27]

In Costa Rica, at least 60 per cent of total current revenues have been allocated in the form of fixed percentages of budget estimates to the University, the judiciary and to a series of specific purposes like housing. It has been estimated that in another Latin American country

> 80 percent of the central Government's expenditure is predetermined and cannot be altered by those responsible for preparing the budget.[28]

Fragmentation of a budget into a series of separate funds or accounts because of earmarking of receipts and expenditures or

[27] US. AID. *Modernizing Government Budget Administration*, p. 25.
[28] UN. ECLA. *Fiscal Budget as an Instrument in the Programming of Economic Development*, p. 70.

because of a proliferation of more or less autonomous agencies whose transactions are extrabudgetary, generally results in unduly complex budgeting and accounting systems. It also makes it difficult for a government to follow a coherent budgetary policy and to determine how much money is available for development and other expenditures.[29] In Ecuador, for instance, more than 600 separate, earmarked taxes have been included in the budget. For most of these taxes separate accounts have had to be kept. This greatly complicates budget management.

Consequences of Staff Inadequacies

Largely because of a lack of qualified staff and poor organization, budget agencies in most less developed countries are little more than bookkeeping offices. Budget personnel frequently lack the stature and prestige needed to review the submissions of operating organizations. Even where budget staffs have the necessary competence and standing, the short time usually allowed for a budget to be prepared does not permit adequate review and analysis. All too often a budget is only the sum of the budget requests of operating ministries, departments and agencies, put together without adequate examination or screening. The Organization of American States has reported that in Latin American countries, budget offices have seldom-challenged authority to reshape budget requests, but that this authority is not enforced to a very considerable extent

> and many budget offices are often concerned with little more than adding up the requests for funds of individual ministries. There is remarkably little pruning of expenditures; and what cutting off takes place is often overcompensated for by politically inspired last-minute requests for special-interest expenditures.[30]

Deficiencies in Budget Procedures

In a report which is typical of those for other countries, the World Bank survey mission which visited Thailand in 1958 found that

> the procedure for preparing the annual budget is deficient. Government departments request appropriations with only vague

---

[29] Herman, Robert S. "Two Aspects of Budgeting," p. 322.

[30] OAS. Inter-American Economic and Social Council, etc. *Programming for Development: Five Urgent Problems*, p. 5.

justification and in amounts that are consciously set beyond any expectation of achievement . . . the Ministry of Finance lacks personnel with the necessary competence and detailed knowledge of departmental requirements to evaluate adequately the reasonableness and priority of requests. In these circumstances it is almost axiomatic that requests for appropriations will be cut; but the nature and extent of cutting involves substantial elements of arbitrary judgment and political pressure. Hence some appropriations may be unrealistically low and in important cases almost certain to be exceeded, while others may be well in excess of any reasonable justification. The result has invariably been the enactment of total appropriations substantially beyond the available non-inflationary sources of financing.[31]

This method of operation has not been limited to Thailand. The budgeting procedure followed by Pakistan's Ministry of Finance, particularly during the period of the First Five Year Plan, was similar. The Ministry incorporated into the budget estimates, submitted by ministries and departments, which it knew were unsound or projects which it knew were not ready. After the budget had been approved, however, the Ministry scrutinized all proposals before it allowed any expenditures to be made. This only compounded the problem. Since a project's inclusion in the budget and an allotment for it gave no assurance that the Ministry of Finance would later approve expenditures to carry it out, operating organizations made little effort to submit accurate budget estimates when the budget was being prepared and generally made excessive demands for funds. This in turn led to indiscriminate budget cutting by the Ministry of Finance and the substitution of bargaining and haggling between the Ministry and the operating organizations in lieu of rational consideration of projects.[32] In Burma,

> review of the current budget was made difficult by the inadequate submissions of the operating ministries and departments and by the lack of Finance Ministry staff appreciative of the need for and capable of adequate substantive review. Knowledge that even after budgetary approval the agencies concerned would still be required to obtain financial sanctions for all but routine expendi-

[31] IBRD. *A Public Development Program for Thailand*, pp. 201–202. In Thailand, the story has a happy ending. Subsequent to the mission's visit, the Government introduced budgetary reforms which greatly improved the situation described in the mission's report.

[32] Waterston, Albert. *Planning in Pakistan*, pp. 51–52.

tures, and the possibility of rectifying errors at mid-year, led to disinterest on the part of both the Ministry of Finance and the submitting agencies in the quality of current budget submissions.[33]

In Ecuador, also, the budget as submitted to the Congress was largely a conglomeration of ministry and other proposals compiled by the budget authority without any attempt at review. The budget office understated expenditures and overstated revenues to give the budget the appearance of being balanced. The real "budget-making" occurred after the Congress had approved the budget and had adjourned. Then, a series of executive decrees were issued which transferred money from one budget purpose to another. In one year (1957), the President signed more than 400 such decrees.

Other countries also make unrealistic estimates of revenues and expenditures. While some budget offices, like Ecuador's, tend to overstate revenues and understate expenditures in order to bring budgets into nominal balance, more often they tend to do the opposite. A budgetary authority may underestimate receipts to restrain demands of operating organizations or to provide a reserve for new projects and program changes. For instance, in Burma,

> typically, the Finance Ministry would underestimate prospective revenues and overstate requirements for current government expenditures, thus tending to minimize resources available for public capital investment.[34]

Sometimes, as when a country depends greatly on agriculture or foreign trade, it may be difficult to predict receipts and expenditures. Rapid price inflation may also interpose serious difficulties in the way of accurate forecasting of receipts or expenditures.[35] In these events, wide discrepancies between estimated and actual receipts and expenditures may be unavoidable. But deviations from estimates are also frequently due to poor or misguided techniques. Whatever the reason, however, in many countries emergency, supplementary, or other extraordinary appropriations often have to be made to fill gaps or correct

[33] Walinsky, Louis J. "Burma," p. 42.

[34] *Ibid.*, p. 43.

[35] In Brazil, for example, budget estimates made during periods of inflation could not be taken seriously because everyone expected the estimates to be obsolete before long. The Government could have tried to make realistic guesses about the degree of inflation to be expected during the year, but it hesitated to do so for obvious reasons.

miscalculations which become evident after a basic budget has been authorized. These additional authorizations may reach sizable proportions of total budgetary outlays. Continued and unco-ordinated use of such special appropriations reduces the effectiveness of expenditure controls and the usefulness of budgets for carrying out development plans.

Paradoxically, laxness in major budgetary matters is often accompanied by excessively rigid and formalistic controls over details of budget execution.[36] In many countries, unduly detailed systems of expenditure control are often a substitute for good budget practice. Requirements for the preaudit of expenditures by a budget authority or a general accounting office before authorized funds are disbursed, as well as involved rules which ministries, departments or agencies are expected to apply, result in cumbersome procedures which place great stress on legal niceties but put little emphasis on prudent economic use of resources.[37] These controls and procedures, which are usually more apparent than real and almost invariably have the effect of impeding the implementation of plans, are discussed in greater detail in the next chapter.

Poor Accounting

Out-of-date, complex, confusing or otherwise inadequate accounting systems widely used in less developed countries, as well as poor accounting practices, also diminish the effectiveness of national budgets, either as instruments of financial control or as means for giving effect to development plans. As one of many examples which could be cited, a World Bank survey mission found archaic accounting methods employed in Libya. In that country, there was considerable laxity in the control of public expenditures, long delay in closing accounts, as well as a general lack of information about how much money was being spent and on what it was being spent.[38]

In many countries, accounting systems and procedures used in operating ministries, departments and agencies seriously interfere with proper budgetary control. In Pakistan, for instance, three different systems of accounting have been employed in operating organizations. All have defects, some of which are serious. Accounts often are not

[36] US. AID. *Modernizing Government Budget Administration*, pp. 25–26.
[37] IBRD. *Economic Development of Syria*, p. 266.
[38] IBRD. *Economic Development of Libya*, p. 93.

maintained to keep pace with the execution of projects and programs. Because expenditures are not entered to appropriate accounts as they occur, large sums remain in suspense accounts which have become convenient repositories for disbursements of unidentified purpose. In many cases, as in Libya, accounts remain unclosed for long periods after completion of projects and programs. Consequently, it is often impossible to determine the capital costs or recurrent requirements of a project or program. If a project is a plant which is to produce and sell commodities or services, it is difficult to estimate costs of production and to fix selling prices for the output which will bring an appropriate return on investment.[39]

A clear distinction must be made between budgetary estimates and actual receipts or expenditures. Budgets necessarily are first presented as estimates, and actual receipts and expenditures frequently differ substantially from original or even revised estimates. It is the actual transactions rather than the estimates which are, of course, most important for planning, as well as for management and budgetary review. But reliable "actuals" generally become available only after a budget audit has been completed at the end of a fiscal period. Because of this, it is of the utmost importance for a budgetary audit to be completed as soon as possible after the close of a fiscal period. But delays of one or two years are frequent, with the result that planners too often must prepare annual and medium-term plans on the basis of guesses and assumptions instead of facts about budgetary performance.

Classification Systems

The system used to classify accounts and the form in which they are presented in conventional budgets may also make it difficult or impossible to obtain information needed for development planning purposes. Among other things, accounts may be so detailed and voluminous that it becomes difficult or impossible to group them into categories related to specific projects, programs or activities; or they may be insufficiently itemized for this purpose. Thus, the World Bank survey mission to Nicaragua reported that

in its present form the budget is essentially a list of salaries to be paid by the government. . . . No uniform principle governs the

[39] Waterston, Albert. *Planning in Pakistan*, p. 16.

detail given on non-salary expenditures. In some cases they are
given in superabundant detail, while in others relatively large
items, mainly for the purchase of goods and services, are not
broken down.

In spite of its bulk and detail, the budget is of extremely limited
analytical value. Total expenditures are not broken down between salary, capital, and other categories of expenditures. It is
impossible to appraise from the budget either the actual cost of the
various functions of government or the profitability of the various
quasi-business activities of the government.[40]

For a budget to be a reasonably efficient instrument for plan execution it must have a classification system which (a) permits allocations and expenditures to be related to specific projects, programs
and other purposes in a plan; (b) distinguishes between capital and
current expenditures and receipts, and shows the extent of public
savings (in the form of a surplus on current account) available for
investment; and (c) distinguishes between development and nondevelopment expenditures on both capital and current account. The
classification system employed in conventional administrative budgets
does not meet these requirements. It was designed primarily as a
framework for making appropriations to government ministries and
departments, facilitate internal management and control, insure accountability, usually to a legislature, and help execute government
policies under conditions which antedate postwar development planning. It virtually precludes an assessment of the full cost of most
government functions or services.

A conventional budget is divided into separate sections for each
ministry, department or agency. Under each spending organization,
expenditures are classified according to "object accounts," e.g., wages
and salaries, travel allowances, purchases of specified materials and
equipment, etc. Within a spending organization, expenditures for each
of these "object accounts" may be lumped together under a single
"head." This may be done for administrative convenience, to insure
centralized control or for other reasons, although the expenditures
relate to different functions, programs, projects or activities. Thus, a
partial or no breakdown of wages and salaries by purpose, program or
project may be available in the budget of a ministry of public works
whose responsibilities include the construction and maintenance of

[40] IBRD. *Economic Development of Nicaragua*, pp. 395–396.

highways, ports, railways and air transport facilities. It may therefore be difficult if not impossible to determine the costs allocable to each of these fields or to individual projects or programs within each field. In Afghanistan, typically, "object" budgeting has resulted in

> a serious lack of data respecting development projects. While the development activities are planned on a project-by-project basis, and the Ministry of Planning tries to follow the execution of the plan on a project-by-project basis, annual appropriations to the agencies and the agencies' own records of expenditures are maintained according to objects of expenditure rather than projects or program.[41]

It may be equally difficult or impossible to separate expenditures on capital account from those on current account (e.g., new construction as against maintenance); or for development as opposed to nondevelopment purposes (e.g., work on a highway as opposed to work on a stadium or monument), either on capital or on current account.

Similarly, where expenditures on the same program, project or activity are made by more than one government organization, each with its own set of not always comparable object accounts, it becomes difficult or impossible to determine the total expended on the program, project or activity. Thus, it would not be easy where budget accounts are maintained on an object basis to get the total expenditures on an agricultural program where a ministry of public works cleared land for the project, a ministry of education provided training and a ministry of agriculture furnished expertise, seed and implements. The problem would become even more complex if autonomous or semiautonomous public agencies, whose transactions were not included in the budget, contributed to the program. Not only would the budgetary classification systems, and the rules and standards of the agencies probably differ from each other and the ones used by the ministries; the relevant information would probably not be available in one place to make aggregation or comparison possible.

Still another complication arises when expenditures are undertaken for the same program, project or activity by governments at different levels, each with its unique set of undifferentiated object accounts. An example of this would be expenditures on an educational program financed partly by a central government and partly by a state or local

[41] United Nations Conference on the Application of Science and Technology, etc. *Planning Machinery in Afghanistan*, p. 6.

government.[42] In this case, also the total spent on the program or project would probably be difficult to come by.

Limitations of classification and lack of comprehensiveness in conventional budgets not only make it hard for a government to know the magnitude and composition of its public investment, as well as the quantity and kind of capital produced; they also make it hard for governments to acquire information on the financial resources available for current as against capital expenditures. In some countries, budget authorities do not always clearly distinguish tax receipts from sales of goods and services, dividends from state enterprises or other receipts. Sometimes, receipts from several sources are lumped together in a miscellaneous or other catchall account so that receipts from each source are unknown; sometimes, the price of goods and services includes a tax component; sometimes receipts from one source are improperly credited to another. These problems are frequently encountered in Latin American countries, but they are by no means limited to them. In Afghanistan, for example,

> there were no very clear definitions of . . . receipt sources, which made comparisons from one year to the next and from estimates to actuals very difficult.[43]

A reliable breakdown of receipts from at least the major types of taxes and other revenues is needed for estimating annual budgetary receipts since individual tax and other revenues are affected differently by changes in production, income, employment, foreign trade or other economic variables.[44] Without this information, projections of multi-annual budgetary receipts required for planning purposes are especially difficult to make.

Nor do conventional budgets sometimes distinguish sufficiently among resources available to a government for capital investment. It then may become uncertain whether public investment is financed from current receipts; drawings on accumulated balances; borrowings from a central bank, a commercial banking system or the public; loans or grants from autonomous agencies, foreign governments or international agencies; or foreign supplier's credits. Lack of clarity or uni-

---

[42] OAS. Inter-American Economic and Social Council, etc. *Development Planning and Budgeting*, pp. 4–5.

[43] United Nations Conference on the Application of Science and Technology, etc. *Planning Machinery in Afghanistan*, p. 5.

[44] OAS. Inter-American Economic and Social Council, etc. *Development Planning and Budgeting*, p. 8.

formity in defining transactions leads to the confusion of capital with current transactions. For example, in Ecuador, payments on the public debt which should be treated as capital transfers, are classified as ordinary expenditures. Moreover,

> the classification of revenue is not clear either. Some of the revenue, which should finance investments, is considered among the sources of the Current Budget while obviously ordinary revenue backs up capital expenditures.[45]

Finally, because the conventional budget does not usually distinguish in sufficient detail between current and capital receipts and current and capital outlays, it is an inadequate tool for economic analysis. It is therefore difficult to assess the impact of budgetary transactions on such economic variables as public savings and public investment.

BUDGETARY REFORM

The many shortcomings of conventional administrative budgets as instruments of financial management, greatly aggravated by the requirements of development planning, have given rise to widespread demands for budgetary reforms. If a budget were only a document for giving effect to a country's development plans, problems of budgetary reform and modernization, while difficult, would be much easier to resolve than they are. But since a budget is, or should be, an instrument through which a government carries out the full range of its activities, a budget has many functions. Besides being a device for implementing development plans, a budget must be a means for financial control and management of government operations; it must provide data required to make basic decisions on fiscal and economic policy; it must be a suitable vehicle for carrying out the decisions which are made; and it must be designed to provide for accountability to a national legislature or other body and to the public. Thus, in addition to the need for making budgets better for the purpose of implementing plans, the need for improving budgets is

[45] Ecuador. National Board of Economic Planning and Coordination. "Chapter IV. The Organization for the Plan for Economic Development and the Administrative Reform," pp. 35–36.

frequently made synonymous with such objectives as strengthening administrative processes, achieving more effective or more stringent fiscal controls, securing efficiency and economy, effecting better utilization of resources, controlling inflation or improving economic conditions, or simply broadening the awareness and understanding of budget content.[46]

Not surprisingly, therefore, a wide variety of proposals has been advanced for improving budgets. Some are merely intended to make conventional budgets more informative and more effective as instruments of management and control through improvements in the practices and methods by which they are prepared and executed. These proposals concentrate on such matters as improving the timetable for budget preparation; extending the period covered by a budget to provide information on receipts and expenditures for more than one fiscal year; [47] improved budgetary and accounting practices in spending agencies and better screening of their budgetary requests; reduced budgetary fragmentation arising from earmarking of revenues and expenditures or exclusion of transactions of autonomous and semiautonomous agencies; reduced supplementary and other special appropriations; uniform accounting systems and adherence to established accounting precepts and practices; clarity and uniformity in defining development and nondevelopment budgetary transactions, especially with regard to capital as compared with current account; and the replacement of formalistic and restrictive rules, regulations and procedures with more efficient and effective financial controls. Of these examples, further discussion of two, i.e., the comprehensiveness of a

[46] US. AID. *Modernizing Government Budget Administration*, p. 24.

[47] Among other things, multiannual budgets provide much more useful information for planning than do annual budgets. There has been an increasing trend recently toward multiannual budgetary projections. For example, Puerto Rico has a six-year budget and now prepares a four-year budget. In Israel, five-year expenditure projections for individual ministries have been prepared each year since 1959. This is sometimes also done in the United States, particularly in the Department of Defense. The United Kingdom is making expenditure surveys for five years ahead to ensure that the size and composition of public expenditures conform with the expected availability of financial resources. In 1963, a White Paper was issued giving figures from the latest Survey (Great Britain. Chancellor of the Exchequer. *Public Expenditure in 1963–64 and 1967–68*). Other European countries are also making multiannual projections of expenditures and receipts to obtain better budgetary control over expenditures. (UN. TAO. *Report of the Inter-Regional Workshop on Problems of Budget Classification and Management in Developing Countries*, p. 31.)

budget and the close relationship between capital and current transactions, is desirable.

Budgetary Comprehensiveness

There is universal agreement that a consolidated set of figures
encompassing all financial transactions in the public sector is a useful
tool for both development planning and formulation of financial
policy. This set of figures should include pertinent transactions of
quasi-autonomous and autonomous public agencies usually outside a
government budget, as well as those of governments at national and
subordinate levels. To reveal the full extent of income available to the
public sector, as well as the amount and kinds of public subsidies, it is
especially important that a consolidated table of public financial
transactions show intergovernmental transfers, as well as transfers
between government on the one hand, and autonomous and semiautonomous agencies on the other.[48]

There is less agreement about where the consolidated figures should
be prepared and who should do it. One view is that all public sector
transactions should be included in the budget of a national government. Thus, the Economic Commission for Latin America has contended that

> specialists in budgetary problems have long been stressing the
> need to conceive of the public budget as a single unit, in the sense
> that it must embody absolutely all the income and expenditure
> of the public sector. This emphasis is dictated by the conviction
> that the budget statement should be the instrument wherewith to
> judge the direction and cohesion of Government policy.[49]

In contrast, others think it would be impractical in most countries to
require that all transactions conducted by every semiautonomous and
autonomous agency or at every government level be recorded in a
single budget document. For instance, a paper prepared by the United

[48] To avoid double counting in making up a consolidated set of figures, these
transfers have to be adjusted to arrive at net payments among them. Thus, it is
necessary to eliminate ("wash out" or "net out") grants which local governments
receive from a national government and the amounts which agencies charge for
goods or services supplied to other government units, although these transactions
must be fully detailed in the accounts of each agency and government unit.

[49] UN. ECLA. *Fiscal Budget as an Instrument in the Programming of Economic
Development*, p. 29.

Nations recognized that it might not be feasible to include all transactions of public enterprises in one budget for the public sector as a whole.[50] It would probably be equally unfeasible in some countries, especially those with federal governments, to arrange for the inclusion of the transactions of political subdivisions in a national budget. Most authorities would probably agree that the best approach for getting the information needed for planning would be to prepare a consolidated table in which gross receipts and expenditures in the public sector are combined with intergovernmental, interagency and governmental-agency transfers, with the budgets of each government and agency annexed as appendices.

For planning purposes, it matters little whether the combination of public sector transactions takes the form of a budget prepared by a budget authority or a consolidated table prepared by a central planning agency or other government office. What is important is that where the budget of a central government incompletely reflects development activities in the public sector, a government body can and regularly does assemble and consolidate all the relevant information in one document.

Complementarity of Capital and Current Expenditures

As important for development planning as the consolidation of all public sector transactions is the relationship of capital and current expenditures. Capital expenditures for development always require increases in current expenditures, but there is a widespread failure among planners and budgeters to recognize their complementarity. In Burma, it proved very difficult for foreign advisers to the Government

> to ascertain and make the Finance Ministry sensitive to those components in current budget submissions which require priority consideration because of their essentiality to capital projects and programs. Indeed this problem was never satisfactorily solved.[51]

Planners and budgeters tend to concentrate on capital expenditures. Thus foreign economic advisers who helped Nigeria prepare its Six-Year Development Plan found that

[50] UN. Inter-Regional Workshop on Problems of Budget Classification, etc. *Relationship Between Planning and Government Budgeting in Developing Countries,* [Part I], p. 11.
[51] Walinsky, Louis J. "Burma," p. 43.

none of the [regional and federal] governments . . . was able to make a head-by-head [i.e., object-by-object] budgetary estimate of its future recurrent costs. Instead, officials turned mainly to the contemplation of new capital expenditures. . . . The danger that rising recurrent expenditure would encroach seriously on the pace of the development program was given little weight.[52]

Every capital investment requires current expenditures of some kind. Sometimes, current expenditures must precede or coincide with capital outlays for the purpose of conducting preliminary experiments (as in agriculture) or to train operating personnel for the completed projects; today's capital expenditure leads to tomorrow's current expenditure for maintaining and operating the facilities created by the capital expenditure.[53] Over five years the recurrent expenditure on a school is likely to be more than twice the capital cost.[54] Even if a hospital is obtained as a gift, the recurrent budget must provide money for paying its staff.[55] In Upper Volta, road construction equipment obtained through foreign aid produced considerable problems because expenditures on fuel, spare parts, maintenance and personnel increased the size of the budget by 12 per cent.[56] A careful comparison of current and capital cost requirements for a project or program can also reveal that increases in capital outlay are desirable. For example, in Iran, the annual cost of maintaining gravel roads was found to be so high in comparison with the cost of paving and maintaining them as asphalt roads that it led planners to recommend increased capital outlays for paving gravel roads in order to reduce recurrent expenditures for maintenance.

Failure to give adequate consideration to current cost requirements stemming from capital outlays may lead to increased current expenditures which cut into investment resources and threaten a whole plan. What a World Bank survey mission to Ceylon found in the early 1950's is just as true today in other countries. In Ceylon, lack of information on the relationship between public capital investment and costs of

[52] Clark, Peter Bentley. "Economic Planning for a Country in Transition: Nigeria," p. 275.
[53] UN. ECA. *Problems Concerning Techniques of Development Programming in African Countries,* p. 4.
[54] Lewis, W. Arthur. "Planning Public Expenditure," p. 11.
[55] Stolper, Wolfgang F. "The Development of Nigeria," p. 174.
[56] United Nations Meeting of Experts on Administrative Aspects of National Development Planning. *Administrative Aspects of Planning in Developing Countries,* p. 70.

operation made execution of a development plan a hazardous financial undertaking:

> The danger is that current expenditures may be driven up to a level where they absorb the government's revenue completely, leaving no surplus for further capital development. Estimates for 1951–52 already foreshadow this danger, since they provide for an increase of almost 100 per cent in capital investment. This large volume of new investments—if it were carried out—would undoubtedly require a higher level of current expenditure in 1952–53; but, so far as we know, no attempt has been made to draw up detailed estimates in this respect.[57]

If current funds for maintenance and operation are not made available, full use cannot be made of the facilities created by capital expenditures. For instance, in their review of the results obtained from the Second Five-Year Plan, Iran's planners indicated what happened in their country when current expenditures were not co-ordinated with capital outlays:

> The agriculture and irrigation programs have suffered greatly from this lack of coordination between investment and operating requirements. We see appropriations for animal husbandry stations that are not given the necessary operating budget for personnel and investigations. We see irrigation systems constructed with no provision for operating and maintenance expenses. Perhaps most wasteful of all is the present system of sending students abroad for scientific training and then failing to provide adequate salary and other employment conditions upon their return.[58]

Is a Divided Budget Desirable for Planning?

Because there is need to establish an effective relationship between capital and current expenditures, it is important that each type of expenditure be clearly identified and consistently defined. Some authorities go further. They advocate that budgetary estimates of receipts and expenditures be divided into a completely separate capital (sometimes also referred to as "extraordinary," "nonrecurrent," "investment" or "development") budget and current (sometimes also referred

[57] IBRD. *Economic Development of Ceylon*, pp. 186–187.
[58] Iran. Plan Organization. *Review of the Second Seven Year Plan Program of Iran*, p. 32.

to as "operating," "recurrent" or "ordinary") budget. This divided, dual or double budget, with its separate capital and current components, is considered especially desirable where large additions to budgetary expenditures for investment are contemplated.[59] In these cases, there is a danger that a government will resort to inflationary financing if it cannot finance the increased capital requirements from current receipts. Those who favor a divided budget, as well as others, feel that all current expenditures should be fully financed from current receipts. If current receipts are insufficient to cover current expenses, taxes or other revenues should be increased. In contrast, when the surplus on current account is inadequate, proponents of the divided budget believe that the loan financing of capital expenditures is justifiable as long as investments financed by loans yield a return which is higher than the cost of the loans. If loans are not available in required amounts to finance proposed capital expenditures and the surplus on current account cannot fill the gap, or if the increased level of recurrent expenditures made necessary by the higher investment cannot be financed from current receipts, proposed capital expenditures should be reduced accordingly.[60]

[59] The discussion which follows assumes that only capital items are included in capital budgets and only current items are included in ordinary budgets. This is an oversimplification. Governments follow a great variety of practices in preparing so-called capital budgets. In Western Europe, for example, only the Netherlands has a divided budget of the classical capital-current type. Sweden's capital budget includes only items which produce revenue. This relegates expenditures for road construction to the current budget (UN. Inter-Regional Workshop on Problems of Budget Classification, etc. *Relationship Between Planning and Government in Developing Countries* [Part I], p. 9). In Ghana, the capital budget (called the Development Budget) includes some current expenditures, while in Nigeria, the capital budget (also called the Development Budget) contains only capital and other nonrecurrent items.

[60] It is accepted practice for a private business concern to finance its capital requirements by borrowing. Those who advocate that governments adopt a double budget frequently consider it equally desirable that governments finance their capital outlays in the same way. In fact, one budget authority has written:

Double budgets, almost without exception, have had their origin in attempts to justify loan finance, so that the extraordinary portion, or the nonrecurring portion, or the capital portion could be identified to serve as a rationalization, sound or unsound as the case may be, for government borrowing. (Burkhead, Jesse. *Government Budgeting*, p. 182.)

The idea of separating capital from current estimates and expenditures in a government capital budget first gained acceptance in some countries during the depression of the 1930's, when governments greatly increased outlays on public works to provide employment. In Sweden, for instance, where a capital budget was introduced to overcome the traditional notion that it was fiscally irresponsible

Advocates of a divided budget hold that where estimates of current expenditures are separated from those of capital outlays, it becomes easier to finance each in a noninflationary manner. This, they say, is because the separation enables those concerned to maintain a close watch on the size of current expenditures (including the servicing of public debt), whether caused by increased investment, growing population or increases in the cost of government services. If recurrent expenditures concentrated in a separate budget rise above current receipts, it quickly becomes apparent that compensatory action is required. They hold that a dual budget also permits capital outlays to be handled with the flexibility they require. It is not always possible at the beginning of a fiscal period to know precisely how much capital financing will be required or obtained during the fiscal period because projects and programs may not be ready, agreements for foreign loans or aid may not have been concluded, or progress made in the construction of projects begun in previous periods may not be known. It has also been contended that a separate capital budget makes it easier to insure that loans and grants are utilized only for capital expenditures and are not diverted to current outlays. Summing up the advantages which they saw in a divided budget, several participants in a Workshop on Budgetary Classification and Management conducted by the Economic Commission for Latin America held that

> separate identification of capital programmes facilitates the formulation of fiscal policy and leads to clearer decisions on current expenditure and the treatment of capital expenditure, thus expediting the means of financing with respect to the contracting of loans and to increases in domestic taxation.[61]

But there are also cogent arguments against the use of a divided budget. For while a divided budget may facilitate the solution of some

---

for a budget not to be balanced every year by current receipts, the use of a capital budget permitted a public investment plan to be financed by borrowing:

> By greatly widening the scope of the loan budget the Government procured funds for realizing the plan, and the intention was that these loans should be repaid when times had improved and production had again reached a more normal level. If calculated over the trade cycle in its entirety the budget would by this means be put in equilibrium; on the other hand, it meant the abandonment of the principle that each individual year's budget should be made to balance in conformity with traditional practice. . . . (Montgomery, Arthur. *How Sweden Overcame the Depression, 1930–1933*, p. 49.)

[61] UN. TAO. *Report of the Workshop on Budgetary Classification and Management in South America*, p. 27.

problems in some countries, it can introduce problems in other countries which are not easy to resolve. One problem involves a confusion of concepts. In many countries, a capital budget is considered to be the same as a development budget, and an ordinary budget the same as a nondevelopment budget. This is wrong.

It is wrong because not all capital expenditure is developmental, nor is all developmental expenditure capital. Expenditure on splendid public buildings is capital expenditure but not necessarily developmental. . . . The salaries of agricultural extension workers are developmental, but they are recurrent expenditures, not capital expenditures.[62]

Those who oppose the use of a separate capital budget contend that

it tends to consider asset formation from a narrowly physical point of view to the detriment of other expenditures . . . which contribute to the asset formation of the nation. The emphasis on physical assets, it is argued, may prevent sufficient investment in human resources which are equally important for development.[63]

Current outlays for such programs as the expansion and development of health and educational services, research, vocational training, and agricultural experimentation and extension work may contribute greatly toward raising productivity although they do not lead to direct additions to a nation's capital stock. In fact, recent research indicates that the rate-of-return on investments in the health and education of human beings may be at least as large as that on physical capital.[64] What is even more important, unless such expenditures, which are generally of a recurrent nature, also expand, mere physical asset creation by itself is unlikely to raise national output appreciably.

It therefore appears illogical when those who favor a divided budget contend that it is all right to finance capital outlays with loans, whether or not they aid a country's development, but inappropriate to do so for current expenditures which promote development. Moreover, the argument that it is justifiable to finance capital outlays by borrowing is

---

[62] UN. ECA. *Problems Concerning Techniques of Development Programming in African Countries,* p. 85.

[63] UN. Inter-Regional Workshop on Problems of Budget Classification, etc. *Relationship Between Planning and Government Budgeting in Developing Countries* [Part I], p. 10.

[64] Aukrust, Odd. "Factors of Economic Development: A Review of Recent Research," p. 41. The author also cites a survey of recent research in this field in "Investment in Human Beings," p. 2.

not without danger in many less developed countries, even when it can be shown that these outlays advance development. This approach may lead to reduced efforts by a government to finance capital outlays through feasible and desirable increases in taxation. Especially in the absence of real savings and capital markets, conditions which are common in many less developed countries, it can also lead to undue inflationary domestic borrowing, usually from a central bank, to finance public investment. Or it may help persuade a government to engage in excessive borrowing abroad which can overburden a country with debt and lead to impairment of its future rate of development.

Finally, experience in some less developed countries has demonstrated that a divided budget may lead to practices which make it especially difficult to co-ordinate capital and current expenditures. In these countries, a capital budget may be prepared by a central planning agency and a current budget by a ministry of finance without co-ordination. Before 1964 in Malaya, for example, the recurrent budget was prepared in April by the Ministry of Finance and the Development Budget was prepared in October, largely by the Economic Planning Unit (the central planning agency), with the result that the effects of investment on recurrent expenditures were not always considered.[65] When Burma's Ministry of Planning prepared the capital budget and the Ministry of Finance prepared the current budget there was also inadequate co-ordination between the two agencies.[66] And in Iran, where the Plan Organization prepared the capital budget and the Ministry of Finance prepared the current budget, the Plan Organization reported that, although the separate capital budget may have helped the investment process,

> it has led to a dangerous neglect of the future financial requirements for making good use of the new facilities. It is true of course that the development program has gone forward in an atmosphere where careful program planning and budgeting are not yet part of government tradition. It is therefore not surprising that there has been little or no coordination between investment decisions and the effect these would have on the annual budgets of the ministries or other agencies that would be responsible for projects upon completion.[67]

[65] United Nations Meeting of Experts on Administrative Aspects of National Development Planning. *Administration of Planning in Malaya*, p. 21.

[66] United Nations Conference on the Application of Science and Technology, etc. *Organization of Planning Machinery: Lessons from Burmese Experience*, pp. 10–11.

[67] Iran. Plan Organization. *Review of the Second Seven Year Plan Program of Iran*, p. 31.

Because of the serious problems encountered when a divided budget has been adopted, especially in countries where "careful program planning and budgeting are not yet part of government tradition,"

> many countries are increasingly swinging around to the idea that it is really the over-all deficit or surplus that is relevant, and not the current or capital deficit or surplus.[68]

The World Bank survey mission to Tanganyika took a similar position. The mission concluded that because

> the feasible level of expenditures on projects and activities of the most direct relevance to development is influenced by the amounts which it is considered necessary to spend on other things of less direct relevance to the developmental process . . . , meaningful planning of government development activities involves planning of the budget as a whole.[69]

When a country starts to plan, it is important that its budgetary system permit capital transactions to be identified and separated from current transactions. This information is needed to determine the extent to which a surplus on current account can be mobilized from domestic public savings for investment. But because capital expenditures may be nondevelopmental and current expenditures may be developmental, it is at least as important for effective integration of a plan and budget that development transactions, whether capital or current, be identified and separated from nondevelopment transactions. Where a development plan exists, development expenditures in a budget are tantamount to the capital and current expenditures required by the plan, while nondevelopment (sometimes referred to as "nonplan") expenditures are outside it. More important for planning, therefore, than the choice between a unitary or divided budget is the choice of a system of classification which permits budgetary transactions to be identified and classified in two ways, firstly, as development or nondevelopment outlays, and secondly, as capital or current outlays. Such classification systems are in use in the budgets of some countries.

Functional classification permits budgetary transactions to be identified or separated by general purpose or function (e.g., agriculture, health, education or highways). Each general head can then be divided into several subheads. Outlays for education, for instance, may

[68] UN. Inter-Regional Workshop on Problems of Budget Classification, etc. *Relationship Between Planning and Government Budgeting in Developing Countries* [Part I], p. 9.
[69] IBRD. *Economic Development of Tanganyika,* p. 341.

be divided into expenditures for primary, secondary and higher education. Classification of budgetary transactions along functional lines makes it possible to distinguish development from nondevelopment estimates and expenditures. It also enables all expenditures in a specific field to be grouped under one heading, e.g., agriculture, regardless of the ministry or other government entity making the expenditure, thereby making it possible to aggregate a government's total effort in each field. Functional classification is especially useful to insure comparability of budgetary data over time where responsibility for a function, e.g., agriculture, may be shifted from one entity to another or where government entities themselves are undergoing change.[70]

In contrast to functional classification, economic classification permits government transactions to be divided into current expenditures and receipts, capital outlays and receipts, and transfers made and received on both capital and current account. These main headings may then be divided into subheadings.[71] The distinction between capital and current transactions is particularly important for planning purposes since it makes it possible to determine the extent to which a government is able to develop a surplus on current account to apply to capital formation. By identifying economically significant items in a budget, economic classification also makes it easier to include government transactions in a country's national income and product accounts. Economic classification of a budget therefore constitutes a useful tool for analyzing the impact of a government budget on a national economy and, hence, provides data for determining public policy.

Functional and economic classifications can be reconciled and combined into a compatible cross-classification system which distinguishes between development and nondevelopment transactions on current or capital account.[72] The value of an economic-functional cross-classifica-

---

[70] UN. TAO. *Report of the Workshop on Problems of Budget Reclassification and Management in Africa*, p. 19.

[71] Thus, economic classification makes it possible to distinguish among such receipt and expenditure items as wage and salary payments to government employees; purchases and sales of property, goods and services; income from property; intergovernmental and other transfer payments and receipts; and interest and principal payments on public debt. The importance of such a breakdown arises from the fact that different kinds of expenditure have a varying impact on an economy and on the shares of each economic sector.

[72] The United Nations has issued two publications as guides to the preparation of economic and functional classification systems: UN. Department of Economic and Social Affairs. *A Manual for Economic and Functional Classification of Gov-*

tion system is, of course, greatly increased if it is adopted by all levels of government in a country and by semiautonomous and autonomous agencies.

Whether or not a budget making use of the combined functional-economic classification system is presented as a unitary or divided budget is a matter of convenience. For planning purposes, it is important only that the form of budget adopted by a government facilitates the identification of development, nondevelopment, capital and current items, and their co-ordination with each other and with an existing development plan. It is conceivable that in some countries a divided budget will be most effective for these purposes and that, in other countries, a unitary budget will be preferred.[73]

Program and Performance Budgeting

But some budget specialists are convinced that mere reclassification of government transactions from the usual object-oriented classification to a functional-economic system, although a step in the right direction, is not enough. They believe that the conventional administrative budget is completely outmoded and propose its replacement by an entirely new approach to budget formulation and execution which they consider to be best suited to the needs of a modern government. The system of "program" and "performance" budgeting which they advocate stresses a government's ends and the progress made in achieving them rather than the means by which those ends are achieved. This method of budgeting focuses

> attention upon the general character and relative importance of the work to be done, or upon the service to be rendered, rather than upon the things to be acquired such as personal services, supplies, equipment, and so on. These latter objects are, after all, only the means to an end. The all-important thing in budgeting is the work or service to be accomplished, and what that work or service will cost.

Under performance budgeting, attention is centered on the func-

---

ernment Transactions, and UN. Statistical Office. *A System of National Accounts and Supporting Tables.*

[73] For a discussion of criteria and problems associated with the use of dual budgets, see Goode, Richard and Birnbaum, Eugene A. "Government Capital Budgets," pp. 23–45.

tion or activity—on the accomplishment of the purpose—instead of on lists of employees or authorizations of purchases.[74]

This is why this form of budgeting is alternatively called "program" budgeting (to emphasize its concern with programs instead of objects of expenditure), or "performance" budgeting (to emphasize its concern with accomplishments instead of means). In program and performance budgeting, both the government entities and the objects of expenditure are secondary. What is primary is that the data are detailed under specific programs in terms of workloads, units of work and unit costs.[75]

But program and performance budgeting is much more than an improved system of classifying or presenting a budget. Whereas traditional budgetary procedures emphasize only the financial aspects of expenditures when a budget is formulated, executed or audited, the distinguishing feature of program and performance budgeting is that it seeks, whenever possible, to measure the results achieved in physical or real, as well as in financial, terms. Thus, at the start of a budgetary period a program and performance budget may show estimates of miles of roads to be leveled or paved, the number of teachers to be trained, additional number of students to attend schools, acres of land to be cultivated, irrigated or cleared, as well as the expected cost of each function, program, project or activity.[76] After the budgeting

[74] Yoingco, Angel Q. "Performance Budgeting for the Philippine Government," p. 230, citing the report of the U.S. (Hoover) Commission on Organization of the Executive Branch of the Government on Budgeting and Accounting Systems of the Federal Government (February 1949).

[75] *Ibid.*

[76] The classification system used in program and performance budgeting generally comprises functions, programs, projects and activities. A program is a subdivision of a function. Current and capital expenditure programs are separately identified and are subdivided into projects or activities. Thus, where agriculture is the function, production of fertilizers is a program, construction of a fertilizer plant is a project and agricultural research is an activity. This system can easily be related to workload data, use of human and material resources and to financial outlays. (UN. Inter-Regional Workshop on Problems of Budget Classification, etc. *Relationship Between Planning and Government Budgeting in Developing Countries* [Part I], p. 15.)

Some authorities believe that a distinction should be made between program budgeting and performance budgeting. They consider the term "program budgeting" appropriate whenever expenditures are separated in accordance with the classification system described in the previous paragraph. They contend that the term "performance budgeting" is applicable only when, in addition to the use of program budgetary classification, an attempt is made to measure physical output in terms of output per employee, unit cost or by some other standard of

period has passed, a program and performance budget can show the actual achievement in each of these fields obtained from actual budgeting expenditures. When reporting and accounting systems are based on such breakdowns, they provide data on work accomplished and its cost, thereby enabling direct comparisons to be made with plan expenditure estimates originally approved in a budget.[77]

A conventional budget with object headings is therefore a much more limited instrument than a performance budget for planning and other purposes. It does not supply physical measurements or comparisons. Even as a financial instrument it is inadequate for planning because it does not relate what is bought with what is done. For since the object heading shows *what* government buys but not *why*, it does not reveal the nature of government programs or accomplishment under those programs.[78] A budget which does not relate expenditures to specific programs and projects cannot easily be linked to a development plan which is couched in terms of programs and projects. This explains some of the difficulties encountered when attempts are made to implement a development plan through a budget classified by object. In contrast, as those who favor program budgeting quite correctly point out, program budgeting is "attuned to planning" because it has taken over

> some of the main characteristics of a plan. The basic features of a plan are the use of programmes or projects as operational units, the emphasis on their physical inputs and results or benefits and on their cost in relation to benefits. Cost-benefit analysis plays an important role in the selection of projects. These are also the attributes of a programme budget.[79]

---

measurement. There is much to be said for this point of view. But because most writers in the budgetary field use program budgeting and performance budgeting in conjunction with each other or interchangeably, it proved to be simpler to use these terms in the same way in this chapter.

[77] UN. Department of Economic and Social Affairs. "Some Problems of Financial Administration in African Countries," p. 104. Performance budgeting cannot quantify all benefits received from expenditures. For example, it would be difficult to measure the benefits derived from outlays on maintenance of public parks or the performance of a ministry of finance. Nor can performance budgeting measure the *quality* of benefits received from expenditures. Thus, it would be difficult to measure objectively qualitative improvements in education obtained from expenditures which were not reflected in increases in quantity.

[78] Burkhead, Jesse. *Government Budgeting*, p. 133.

[79] UN. Inter-Regional Workshop on Problems of Budget Classification, etc. *Relationship Between Planning and Government Budgeting in Developing Countries* [Part I], p. 12.

Some budget authorities consider program budgeting to be only a means for bringing

> budgeting and development planning closer together by providing a common language which is useful to both. . . . [80]

But others believe that a program budget *is* a development plan because

> the programme budget makes it possible to determine exactly what the Government has to do to meet its development aims and targets. It translates the direct participation of the Government in the programme into terms of specific decisions and becomes the operative instrument for short-term governmental action. In this sense, it may be said that the programme budget is a veritable short-term plan, since it relates to the Government's direct sphere of action for the attainment of medium- and long-term objectives.[81]

According to one group of specialists, a program budget differs in one important respect from a plan in that it

> centers attention on direct and immediate outputs of project execution and not on indirect or total, including inadvertent, benefits although such benefits may have been intended. For example, on a road construction project a performance budget would give information on miles of road constructed but not on its effects, among others, on the increases in marketable surpluses of different commodities. Such information on total benefits may be found in the plan or assessed by the planning agency.[82]

Nevertheless, those who promote program budgeting generally believe that a budget authority should go beyond ensuring that the required funds are made available for implementing a plan and that the most economical means are employed in the process. They consider that, in addition, a budget authority should advise a government whether the most effective combination of programs is being employed to achieve its development objectives and assist it in appraising alternative proposals for expenditure as well as tax programs.[83] As a proponent of this approach says:

[80] Herman, Robert S. "Two Aspects of Budgeting," p. 325.

[81] UN. ECLA. *Experience of the Advisory Groups and the Practical Problems of Economic Development*, p. 41.

[82] UN. Inter-Regional Workshop on Problems of Budget Classification, etc. *Relationship Between Planning and Government Budgeting in Developing Countries* [Part I], p. 13.

[83] Johnson, A. W. "Planning and Budgeting," pp. 148–149.

All of this begins to sound very much like planning as most people in government think of it. This is scarcely surprising, for the culmination of the budgetary process is a document which outlines the programmes and the resources required to implement the programmes which the government believes to be the most effective for implementing its policies.[84]

There can be no doubt about the usefulness of the data which program budgeting seeks to develop. They are substantially like those which central planning agencies try to get operating organizations to produce and to supply in reports on the progress of program and project execution. Such information is essential for formulating well-conceived plans. The assignment of physical output targets and the use of unit costs for each program, project and activity provides norms and yardsticks for efficient and timely implementation of plans. They also provide a basis for instilling in the personnel of operating organizations a greater sense of cost-consciousness and responsibility for adhering to work schedules.

Planners and budgeters are therefore likely to agree on the necessity for physical as well as financial accounting and reporting for programs, projects and activities. They may, however, part company on the question of who should be responsible for collecting and evaluating these data. Whether a budget office or a central planning agency should perform these tasks is, of course, a political decision. But it is important that duplication of effort be avoided. The scarcity of talent in less developed countries would make such duplication too costly.

Because of the great scarcity of trained accountants, economists and planners in these countries, a question also arises whether current efforts to improve budgets which place primary emphasis on the introduction of program and performance budgeting constitute the best use of available technicians. In recent years, the United Nations and its regional economic commissions, as well as budget specialists from the United States (which first applied program and performance techniques to its 1951 Federal Budget), have made considerable efforts to get less developed countries to adopt program budgeting.[85]

---

[84] *Ibid.* This point of view is, of course, in sharp contrast with Oskar Lange's, as described earlier in the chapter. It is interesting to speculate whether the divergence is due mainly to differences inherent in planning for a socialized as against a mixed-economy country or differences in the attitude of a planner as against a budgeter.

[85] The Economic Commission for Asia and the Far East and the Economic Commission for Latin America have each conducted three workshops on budget reclassification in their regions to spread knowledge of program budgeting tech-

Largely as a result of these efforts, some less developed countries have adopted or have taken steps to adopt program budgeting. The best-known example of the application of program budgeting techniques in a developing country is the Philippines, where the new techniques were initiated partially in the 1956 budget and more fully in the 1957 budget. Latin America has been particularly receptive to the new budgetary form. Reforms instituted in the early 1960's in the budgets of countries in the region, including Bolivia, Colombia, El Salvador, Honduras, Paraguay and Peru, and those still in progress in Argentina, Chile, Columbia, Ecuador and Venezuela and in other Central American countries, reflect a desire to use program budgeting techniques. In Africa, program budgeting has been mainly attempted in Ghana and the United Arab Republic. Israel has used program budgeting procedures for capital outlays for several years and for current operations since 1961. Program budgeting has also been introduced to some extent in Iran and Thailand,[86] and a start has been made in the Republic of Viet Nam.[87]

But the results obtained thus far indicate that it takes a long time before less developed countries can make effective use of these techniques. As one budget authority has pointed out, those who would have countries adopt program budgeting often overlook that

> its installation requires much work and study over a fairly long period of time. The effectiveness of this approach to budgeting depends upon the manner in which it is applied and used. Standards can be set only after considerable analysis and under-standing of programmes, and these standards must be subject to continuous review and re-evaluation. Data must be constantly refined, policies re-considered in the light of new development,

---

niques. The Economic Commission for Africa has conducted one workshop in its region. In September 1964, the United Nations also held an interregional workshop on budget classification. In addition, the Fiscal and Financial Branch of the Department of Economic and Social Affairs has produced for the United Nations Economic Commission for Latin America, *A Manual for Programme and Performance Budgeting (Draft)*, which sets guidelines for the installation of program and performance budgets. Technicians provided by the US. AID. Mission in the Philippines played a major part in introducing program budgeting in that country.

[86] UN. TAO. *Report of the Inter-Regional Workshop on Problems of Budget Classification and Management in Developing Countries*, p. 10.

[87] UN. TAO. *Report of the Third Workshop on Problems of Budget Reclassification and Management in the ECAFE Region*, p. 10.

and the applicability of unit costs continuously tested on the basis of changing conditions.[88]

Few budget offices are adequately equipped with staffs qualified to perform these difficult and continuing tasks. In fact, in some countries, budget agencies and ministries of finance have not even had the capacity to change the budget presentation from an object to a functional or economic classification. In Peru, for example, it was the central planning agency which performed this task.

Needless to stress, attempts by outsiders to initiate new approaches to budgeting have only rarely had an appreciable and lasting effect on the budgetary procedures of budget offices. Even when a budget office actively participated in the introduction of program budgeting techniques, the results have almost always been incipient and inchoate. Thus, Ecuador's planners reported on the attempt to introduce a program budget in their country:

> It must be admitted that . . . the traditional form has not been changed. It is not yet feasible to obtain data on the achievements of the different programs which form part of the budget. Therefore it is not yet possible . . . that the agencies responsible for the execution of the budget can take measures to avoid waste and immorality.[89]

These results, in other developing countries which have sought to introduce program budgets as in Ecuador, are unavoidable as long as spending ministries and agencies lack organization, staff and information about projects and programs to formulate their own budgetary requirements on a reliable basis, maintain adequate accounts and prepare reasonably accurate and timely reports on the progress of their work. What Paul H. Appleby said about India in the period between 1954 and 1956 has as much import for other developing countries, many of which have a long way to go before they reach the Indian level of development:

> Expenditure control in the proper terms which relate outgo to program objectives can only be closely and usefully achieved in the program agencies. It is only when these agencies have had experience in this superior kind of financial management that they

[88] Herman, Robert S. "Two Aspects of Budgeting." p. 330.
[89] Ecuador. National Board of Economic Planning and Coordination. "Chapter IV. The Organization for the Plan for Economic Development and the Administrative Reform," p. 110.

begin to be able to make budget submissions of a proper sort. It is only after the ministries are thus doing an improved job of budgeting that the Ministry of Finance can produce the kind of budget appropriate to its responsibility.[90]

In recognition of this fact, program budgeting has been introduced in a few countries by authorities who were willing to start on a modest scale in an agency or two. This was done, for example, in 1959 in the Republic of China for the budget of the Shihmen Development Commission, an entity mainly concerned with construction and operation of irrigation, flood control, water supply and power generating facilities.[91] But it is generally much more difficult to introduce budgetary innovations in operating organizations than in a central budget office. Those who favor the use of program budgets therefore tend to postpone tackling operating organizations and begin instead by introducing program budgeting in a central budget office. They hope that they can then gradually get operating ministries and agencies to accept the new system. This approach was reflected in the advice given by the Workshop on Budgetary Administration in Central America and Panama, held in September 1963. The Workshop felt that countries introducing program budgeting

> should do so on as broad a basis as possible, and try to cover in the first year the whole of the central administration, with a view to extending the system in subsequent years to autonomous agencies and enterprises.[92]

But experience in the United States, the Philippines and other countries where this general approach has been tried demonstrate that program budgeting cannot be grafted onto a government's administrative structure from above.[93] The obstacles to installing the new system in ministries, departments and agencies, which are found to be too difficult to surmount at first, generally remain insurmountable; and without operating organizations capable of providing accurate budget-

[90] Appleby, Paul H. *Re-Examination of India's Administrative System with Special Reference to Administration of Government's Industrial and Commercial Enterprises,* p. 31.

[91] UN. TAO. *Report of the Third Workshop on Problems of Budget Reclassification and Management in the ECAFE Region,* p. 10.

[92] UN. Inter-Regional Workshop on Problems of Budget Classification, etc. *Review of Developments in the Budget Field,* p. 93.

[93] UN. ECLA. *Fiscal Budget as an Instrument in the Programming of Economic Development,* p. 67.

ary estimates and measurements of progress, most program budgeting procedures carried out by central budget offices are largely shadow without substance.[94]

The incomplete implementation of program and performance budgeting in countries where it has been tried is partly due to its complexity. It attempts to do much more than conventional budgeting. It also requires that a government break with traditional concepts and methods of budget management. As those in the United Nations who favor program budgeting recognize,

> the establishment of a budget of this type implies radical altera-tions in the structure and operation of governmental machinery, and, what is more, a metamorphosis of the behaviour patterns and mental attitude of public officials. . . . Hence, in order to intro-duce the system, an invisible and powerful enemy must first be overcome—established custom.[95]

How difficult it is to overcome custom is well illustrated in the Philippines. Eight years after performance budgeting was introduced in that country, the Commissioner of the Budget reported that

> there has been a noticeable lack of enthusiasm on the part of Congress to adopt it fully. . . . [With some exceptions], the appropriations for the departments, bureaus and other agencies of the National Government continue to be enacted on the line item basis. . . .[96]

Performance budgeting has also been slow in spreading after its introduction in most countries because of the scarcity of superior personnel, an effective public administration and efficient procedures within operating organizations, as well as in a central budget office. To a degree unknown in object budgeting, success in performance budgeting depends on the prevailing standards of measurement, the level of personnel and public administration and the organizational efficiency of a government. The strength and weaknesses of these determine the strength and weaknesses of performance budgeting.[97] Hence, although performance budgeting is conceptually superior than

---

[94] Parsons, Malcolm B. "Performance Budgeting in the Philippines," p. 175.

[95] UN. ECLA. *Fiscal Budget as an Instrument in the Programming of Economic Development*, p. 67.

[96] UN. Inter-Regional Workshop on Problems of Budget Classification, etc. *Budgetary Developments in the Philippines Since the Early 1950's*, p. 26.

[97] Parsons, Malcolm B. "Performance Budgeting in the Philippines," pp. 178–179.

other budgetary systems, it is rarely much more effective because little is done to remedy underlying personnel, organization and procedural inadequacies which exist in all governments. This was well illustrated in the Philippines. As one foreign technician closely associated with the effort to initiate performance budgeting in that country pointed out,

> no serious attempt was made to come to grips with excessive organizational rigidity stemming from legislative prescription of even minor structural details. In most instances, the implementation of an approved plan merely substitutes an equally inflexible new structure. This will be a serious handicap in the administration of a budget having for its rationale the transferability of resources to activities of greatest need and priority.[98]

Small wonder, then, that the record of success has not been up to promise. Small wonder that performance budgeting frequently encounters misgivings and even opposition in countries where it is introduced.[99] In these circumstances it is perhaps unfortunate that many countries have been made to feel that better budgeting and performance budgeting are synonymous. Performance budgeting has sometimes been represented as the remedy for most fiscal ills.[100] But the truth is that even at best, the adoption of performance budgeting cannot solve all budgetary problems. And where, as in most less developed countries, the situation is not propitious, innovation of performance budgeting may produce only the appearance, not the reality, of improvement. While the educational value of an effort to install performance budgeting may be applauded, it may have been carried out at a high "opportunity cost" by absorbing the time of scarce technicians who might have been put to better use elsewhere.[101] It may also have had the effect of obscuring inability or unwillingness to undertake needed reforms or other action elsewhere.[102]

Order of Priority

Experience shows that there is no one budget system which meets the planning and other needs of all countries. The kind of budget

[98] Zimmerman, Virgil B. "Comments on 'Performance Budgeting in the Philippines,'" p. 45.

[99] UN. TAO. *Report of the Inter-Regional Workshop on Problems of Budget Classification and Management in Developing Countries*, p. 22.

[100] Waldby, Odell. "Chapter 5, Performance Budgeting," p. 228.

[101] This is equally true of attempts to adopt performance budgeting on a step-by-step basis, as proponents of this system of budgeting have advocated.

[102] Parsons, Malcolm B. "Performance Budgeting in the Philippines," p. 179.

which a country requires is determined not only by the objectives of the budgetary process but also by its institutional structure and stage of development. Thus, although the introduction of program and performance budgeting may be desirable for one country, it is by no means the only reform, or even the most immediate reform, needed in the budgeting of most countries engaged in development planning.

Attractive though they are in theory, performance budgeting techniques which require unit cost measurements of all government functions, programs, projects and activities are much too advanced for application in most less developed countries. In these countries, the foundations on which this kind of budgeting system must be erected are largely lacking. There is a shortage of accounting and administrative skills; there are gaps in government organization; there is sometimes an inadequate sense of personal responsibility for the conduct of government affairs.[103] In this environment it is not possible to build a budgeting system of considerable complexity without first improving established budgetary practices and strengthening existing staff and organization in central budget offices, operating ministries, departments and agencies. This was the general position taken by the participants of a Seminar on Urgent Administrative Problems of African Governments conducted by the Economic Commission for Africa in February and March 1963, when they decided that the time was not ripe for most African countries to adopt performance budgeting. Although the Workshop considered the prevailing circumstances not to be propitious for undertaking major reforms in financial administration in African countries, it felt that it was, nevertheless,

> possible and desirable, if the overriding objective of planned economic development is to be effectively pursued, to conceive of certain goals of improvement in the systems of financial administration. . . . Such goals could be envisaged, firstly, in developing appropriate information on the public sector transactions and, secondly, in improving the efficiency of budget management technique and procedures.[104]

Much could be done to improve existing budgets, in most less developed countries outside as well as inside Africa, if effect could be given to these goals. Because all budgetary systems are limited by deficiencies of discipline in formulating and executing a budget, the

[103] Burkhead, Jesse. *Government Budgeting,* pp. 455, 480.
[104] UN. Department of Economic and Social Affairs. "Some Problems of Financial Administration in African Countries," p. 99.

achievement of these goals is a precondition to effective budgeting, including program and performance budgeting. Since there can be no authoritative budgetary model which fits all countries, modernization of budgetary systems and procedures must be planned to meet the needs of each country. Hasty implementation of ambitious budget reforms have shown themselves to be self-defeating.

For planning purposes, therefore, it is essential that a high order of priority be given to reforms for improving budgetary presentation, management and control. Among these would be the adoption of a simple functional-economic classification to distinguish between development and nondevelopment, on capital and current account; [105] improvement of methods and procedures for formulating and executing budgets; [106] establishment of viable budgetary units in operating ministries, departments and agencies; and the strengthening of existing central budget offices and budget units in operating entities through the establishment of training programs for their staffs and the supply of appropriate technical assistance.

If it were possible to do these things and install a workable system of performance budgeting, too, there would be no problem of priorities. But given the shortage of manpower in most less developed countries, there is need to concentrate mostly on improvements of current methods and procedures which can greatly enhance a budget's value for planning in reasonably short periods of time. Since, in addition, these improvements are basic prerequisites for effectively carrying out major reforms like program and performance budgeting, there is much to be said for beginning with them.

SUMMARY AND CONCLUSIONS

A government budget is a key element in giving effect to a development plan. The ideal connecting link between a medium-term plan and

---

[105] Less need is likely, however, for a detailed economic breakdown whose main justification is that it facilitates the preparation of statistical estimates for the government sector in the national accounts of a country.

[106] These have already been discussed. They would include alignment of an annual plan with a budget, preparation of a consolidated table of government accounts, elimination of practices which unduly fragmentize budgets, elimination of rigid and restrictive systems of expenditure control, reduction in the number of special budgetary appropriations, improved accounting systems and practices, preparation of medium-term projections of revenues and expenditures and so forth.

an annual budget is an annual plan. An annual plan is generally broader in scope than a conventional administrative budget.

In Soviet-type countries budgets are, in fact, the financial counterparts of development plans. In contrast, there is only a tenuous relationship between plans and budgets in most mixed-economy countries. Where budgets are prepared on the basis of annual plans, this is generally a recent innovation. And where annual plans are prepared, they are often little more than lists of projects with amounts to be included in a budget.

Sometimes, it is impossible to co-ordinate annual plans and budgets because the periods of plan and budget do not coincide. Delays in the preparation of either hinder the integration of plans and budgets. Because planning and budgeting constitute a two-way process in which the data of each feed the other, it is unavoidable that much of the work of preparing an annual plan and budget should proceed simultaneously and with the close collaboration of planning and budget officials.

The conventional national administrative budget in common use in most countries normally does not include all transactions of the public sector. Thus, it does not usually include transactions at subordinate levels of government or those of autonomous and semiautonomous agencies. These omissions can greatly diminish the value of a budget for allocating public resources in accordance with a plan's objectives. The usefulness of a budget is also often impaired by excessive earmarking of tax receipts or other revenues for specific purposes. Finally, considerable constraints on the allocation of budgetary resources are imposed where budgetary commitments to ongoing projects and programs are already so great that little is left for new projects and programs.

Fragmentation of a budget into a series of separate funds or accounts because of earmarking of receipts and expenditures or because of a proliferation of more or less autonomous agencies whose transactions are extrabudgetary generally produces unduly complex budgeting and accounting systems; it also makes it difficult for a government to follow a consistent budgetary policy and to determine how much money is available for development and other expenditures.

Conventional budgets also suffer from a series of other major defects. Lack of qualified staff and poor organization convert budget agencies into mere bookkeeping offices in most less developed countries. Procedures followed in formulating budgets are loose and haphazard. In many countries, real "budget-making" takes place when operating agencies seek to spend budgetary allocations. At that time, indiscriminate budget-cutting may occur with little relevance to the real issues involved. Some budget authorities habitually overstate revenues and understate expenditures in order to bring them into balance; more often, however, budget authorities understate receipts to restrain demands of operating organizations or to provide a reserve for new ventures. Such misguided procedures make it necessary for many countries to resort repeatedly to supplementary or extraordinary appropriations, thus reducing the effectiveness of expenditure controls and the usefulness of budgets for implementing plans.

Laxness in major budgetary preparation is often accompanied by unduly rigid and formalistic controls over budget execution. Inadequate accounting systems and practices, widely used in less developed countries, also diminish the effectiveness of budgets as means for giving effect to development plans. Delays of one or two years in auditing accounts often make it necessary for planners to prepare their plans on the basis of guesswork instead of facts about budgetary performance.

The system used to classify accounts in conventional budgets may also make it difficult or impossible to obtain information needed for planning. The so-called "object" classification system used in these budgets was designed primarily with accountability and management control in mind. It virtually precludes an assessment of the true cost of most government functions, programs, projects and activities needed for planning purposes. And it makes it difficult or impossible to separate capital from current, or development from nondevelopment expenditures.

Limitations in classification also make it difficult for governments to acquire information on the financial resources available for current as against capital expenditures. This not only hinders current budget operations but makes it difficult to make projections of multiannual budgetary receipts required for planning purposes.

If a budget were only a document for giving effect to a country's development plans, problems of budgetary reform and modernization would be easier to resolve than they are. But a budget is an instrument through which a government attempts to carry out the full range of its activities, and this accounts for the wide variety of proposals which have been put forward to improve budgets. Some are only intended to make conventional budgets more informative and more effective as instruments of management and control through improvements in the current practices, methods and procedures by which they arc prepared and executed. Everyone agrees, for example, that there is need for a consolidated set of figures encompassing all financial transactions in the public sector. Similarly, there is general agreement that it is essential that planners and budgeters give more attention to the complementarity of capital and current outlays. Because of the need to ensure an effective relationship between capital and current expenditures, some authorities recommend the establishment of a divided budget with separate capital and current components. Advocates of a divided budget contend that where estimates of current expenditures are separated from those of capital outlays, the differing treatment which each type of expenditure requires is facilitated. They believe that separation of capital from current requirements makes it more readily apparent when one or the other must be reduced if noninflationary financing is not available.

Those who oppose divided budgets feel it is not enough merely to identify capital and current expenditures since some capital expenditures are nondevelopmental and some current expenditures are developmental. They also point out that when a capital budget is separated from a current budget, it leads in some countries to the very lack of co-ordination between the two which advocates of a divided budget contend a divided budget ensures. Finally, a divided budget may induce governments in countries with inadequate savings to rely unduly on inflationary domestic borrowing or on excessive foreign borrowing to finance development plans.

Fortunately, there is a way out of the apparent impasse. A combined functional-economic classification is available which permits budgetary transactions to be broken down into capital and current, as well as development and nondevelopment, expenditures. Whether or not a budget making use of a functional-economic classification is presented as a unitary or divided budget becomes, then, a matter of convenience.

But some budget specialists are convinced that mere reclassification of government transactions, although generally desirable, does not go far enough. They believe the conventional administrative budget must be replaced by an entirely new system, alternatively or synonymously called program and performance budgeting. This form of budgeting attempts to classify budgetary transactions on the basis of government functions, programs, projects and activities and to measure results achieved in physical, as well as in financial, terms. Some of the more enthusiastic sponsors of program and performance budgeting visualize it as essentially a public sector development plan.

There can be no doubt about the usefulness of the data which program and performance budgeting seeks to develop. Such information is essential for formulating and implementing soundly conceived plans. A question arises, however, whether current efforts to improve budgets which place primary emphasis on the introduction of program and performance budgeting procedures constitute the best use of scarce technicians. Results obtained thus far in countries which have sought to apply these techniques indicate that it will take a long time to make effective use of them, due to the complexity of the method, the necessary break with traditional concepts and practices, and the elimination of underlying personnel, organizational and procedural inadequacies.

In some circles, better budgeting is equated with this form of budgeting. But experience shows that there is no one budget system which meets the needs of every country at every stage of its development. Although program and performance budgeting may be desirable and feasible for one country, it is by no means the only reform, or even the most immediate reform, needed by most less developed countries which plan. For planning purposes much more could be gained if highest priority were given to improving current budgetary presentation, management and control instead of to a radical reform like the installation of program and performance budgeting.

Chapter VIII

Administrative Obstacles to Planning

> . . . no great improvements in the lot of
> mankind are possible, until a great change
> takes place in the fundamental constitution
> of their modes of thought.—John Stuart Mill

THE ADMINISTRATIVE PROBLEM

FEW GOVERNMENTS of less developed countries can cope with the
range, variety and complexity of administrative problems which development planning brings. In the Philippines, the Five-Year Integrated
Socio-Economic Program for 1962–66 has gotten off to a slow start and
is likely to take much longer to execute than originally envisaged
because the administrative apparatus is not up to the task of carrying
out a development effort on the scale required by the Program. In Iran,
administrative problems have restricted the speed with which the
Third Plan has moved forward. In India, the late Prime Minister Nehru
stressed the need for a complete revitalization of the country's administration and attributed the Government's failure to implement plans to
the many weaknesses in the administrative machinery.[1] In Ethiopia
and Nepal, in Turkey and Nigeria, indeed, in one country after
another, it has been discovered that a major limitation in implementing
projects and programs, and in operating them upon completion, is not
financial resources, but administrative capacity.

The administrative systems of governments in almost all less developed countries with mixed economies are anachronistic. Established
long ago to meet conditions which differ greatly from those prevailing
today, they have not been adapted sufficiently to greatly changed
circumstances. Countries which were colonial areas until recently,
inherited government administrations established in their territories
primarily to preserve law and order, collect taxes and provide basic

---

[1] *Statesman Overseas Weekly,* September 7, 1963.

government services. These things they did well and, if a cadre of expatriates or trained nationals was available after independence, they still do with reasonable efficiency. In these countries, deficiencies in public administration arise largely because government machinery which worked well enough in colonial societies no longer is able to operate effectively in independent societies which seek to accelerate greatly their development.

Countries which have been independent for a long time also inherited administrative systems designed in another and more static era for a purpose other than development in a dynamic age. But in contrast with the newly independent countries, most traditionally independent nations failed to build up efficient government administrations, even for collecting taxes, preserving law and order or providing basic services. Although taxes are generally low and exemptions large in Latin America, for instance, Dr. Alberto Lleras Camargo has noted that "there are many extremely well-to-do and even very rich people who pay no taxes." [2] He continues:

> To indicate how outlandish this situation is, it is enough to say that not a single Latin American, whether of high standing or of the underworld, has ever been imprisoned for not paying his taxes or for sending in a fraudulent income tax report. In all that vast area it is unthinkable that deceiving or defrauding the state in this matter of taxes should be considered a crime, and what is more, the law does not consider it as such. As a result, tax evasion is widespread.[3]

The situation is often not very different with regard to other legal violations. Thus, a World Bank survey mission to Iraq reported widespread violations of existing labor laws which the Government's inadequately staffed Labor Department was in no position to enforce. Out of 1,228 enterprises, only 136 were found to be complying with the law.[4] In Colombia, a report prepared by the inadequately equipped national police complained about the lack of enforceable laws against crime and about the judiciary which,

---

[2] Lleras Camargo, Alberto. "The Alliance for Progress: Aims, Distortions, Obstacles," p. 33.

[3] *Ibid.* Since Dr. Lleras wrote the statement quoted, the Government of Chile has imprisoned three persons for violating existing tax laws and other cases are pending. But as far as can be determined, the Chilean action is unique in Latin America.

[4] IBRD. *Economic Development of Iraq,* p. 42.

swamped with the accumulation of cases and documents, weakened by the irresponsibility of many of its members, has not been effective.[5]

In many countries which have been politically independent for a long time, as well as in some newly independent countries, government services which are essential to development are frequently in varying states of disarray and insufficiency: highways and railroads are not maintained, publicly owned and operated telephone and telegraph systems are undependable, schools have severe shortages of teachers, textbooks and even pencils and paper, and hospitals have few doctors and nurses.

The primary administrative task in most ex-colonial territories is to reorient government machinery to meet the demands of accelerated development. The complexities of this task are considerable. But the task is perhaps even more complicated in most countries which have been politically independent for a long time. Administrative structures must not only be modernized to meet the needs of developmental planning; they must also be made to function with tolerable efficiency in providing the usual government services, collecting taxes and preserving law and order.

Development planning puts a special premium on co-operation within government. Ideally, a plan should be prepared with the co-operation and participation of every interested party, both within and outside government. However, a comprehensive or partial development plan can be, and often is, formulated by a few technicians, sometimes assisted by foreign experts, without much recourse to governmental administrative machinery. But it is impossible to implement a plan in this way. A government must usually rely heavily on its administrative apparatus to prepare and carry out projects and programs. It may obtain foreign technicians and contractors to help, but because of the character, volume and continuing nature of project and program preparation, execution and operation, it must, as it should, place great reliance on its administrative machine. It is at this point that the condition of a country's public administration is usually seen to limit development policy and planning.

Of course, administrative inadequacy is not a peculiarity of the less developed countries. It is also to be found in the most advanced countries. But it is a much more urgent problem in the less developed

[5] *New York Times,* December 23, 1963.

countries than in the more advanced countries because it impedes development. It was not as great a problem when the advanced countries were developing because *laissez faire* generally prevented government administrative systems from getting as involved in the early development of the advanced countries as they now are in the development of the less advanced countries.[6] In addition, poor countries can afford administrative inefficiency even less than the richer ones. Defective tax systems and lax collection may reduce the amount of funds available for development investment, outmoded budgetary procedures result in the misallocation of scarce resources, and archaic and time-wasting administrative practices slow down the disbursement of available funds for development projects and programs.

BACKWARD PERSONNEL PRACTICES

In many countries, government personnel practices impede development planning. Government employment frequently depends on personal or political influence. Competence or the lack of it is often unimportant. Government offices are generally overstaffed at lower levels with untrained clerks and flunkeys, while vacancies for professionally trained personnel at upper levels cannot be filled. Kuwait, for example, has 53,000 employees, excluding the Armed Forces, to serve a total population of 350,000.[7] Yet there is a great scarcity of talent at administrative levels. Other less developed countries, less affluent than Kuwait, also support a bureaucratic burden which is disproportionate to their needs and, in many cases, to their financial resources. In Senegal, for instance, two-thirds of budget expenditures are for salaries

[6] Some writers have made the point that even under *laissez faire*, governments often gave considerable aid to the private sector during early periods of the development of what are now industrialized countries. But such help rarely involved the direct intervention of governmental administrative systems in development activities. In the heyday of *laissez faire*, government administration in what are now the developed countries was probably more deficient than it is today in less developed countries. As Professor Lewis has pointed out (Lewis, W. Arthur. *Principles of Economic Planning*, p. 121), the argument in favor of *laissez faire* was essentially based on the assumed inadequacy of government administration: ". . . eighteenth century writers, who saw the mess that was made by weak, incompetent and corrupt governments, . . . sought therefore to confine the activities of government within the narrowest practicable limits, so as to minimize the damage that they might do."

[7] Shehab, Fakhri. "Kuwait: A Super-Affluent Society," p. 466.

paid to 35,000 government workers serving a nation of 3 million. As a result, the 1965 budget of about $144 million was expected to show a deficit of $20 million.[8]

In Iran, the High Council for Administration estimated that from a total of 260,000 government employees, 60,000 were superfluous.[9] World Bank survey missions have frequently reported personnel practices which impose serious strains on efficiency in public administration. The mission to Iraq reported that

> many government offices appear to be overstaffed, while others cannot obtain extra personnel for essential increases in services. Officials are frequently shifted from one position to another without regard for their qualifications and experience. Often government officials both in the provinces and in the capital do not enjoy sufficient continuity in office to enable them to become really useful. Promotion appears to be based almost entirely on seniority and other considerations rather than on merit. Morale among government servants is generally low [and] many civil servants are compelled to supplement their salaries by engaging in business or accepting other employment with resulting neglect of their official duties.[10]

In Syria, also, government salaries are very low and many government employees

> eke out a living by taking outside jobs. Some find it difficult to resist the temptation to use their official position as an opportunity for illicit gain. . . . In many cases, they are not placed in positions for which their training and education have especially suited them.[11]

Inadequate pay is an important cause of slackness and poor work in Thailand's civil service. Comparable jobs in private business pay two or three times as much as in the Government. Many of the ablest people shun government employment and many others leave the civil service as soon as possible.[12] The Government finances training programs for many Thais abroad, but many of the foreign-trained staff are

[8] *Christian Science Monitor*, January 25, 1965, p. 12.
[9] Olsen, P. Bjørn and Rasmussen, P. Nørregaard. "An Attempt at Planning in a Traditional State: Iran," pp. 229–230.
[10] IBRD. *Economic Development of Iraq*, p. 78.
[11] IBRD. *Economic Development of Syria*, p. 194.
[12] IBRD. *A Public Development Program for Thailand*, p. 226.

given positions upon their return for which they are not suited.[13] This aggravates the shortage of competent technical, administrative and managerial talent in the country. In Jordan, where political and private influence may result in the engagement of unqualified personnel or in determining promotions, many Jordanians who have studied abroad stay in government service only a short time.[14] And in Turkey,

> inefficiency and waste seem to be common. . . . Recruitment often has had no relation to need with the result that many government offices are over-staffed. . . . The inefficient are protected by rigid personnel laws and regulations designed to protect personnel rather than to promote efficient administration. Advancement is not based on merit.[15]

Low pay and poor personnel practices are also common in Latin America. While in most countries in the region, a small number of government employees at the top, operating with inadequate help, carry the main burdens of government administration, there is usually a large surplus of poorly trained functionaries at lower levels. Many of these owe their jobs to

> the widespread custom of appointing to office the relatives of new presidents, ministers, and other officials, together with a prohibition on the discharge of officials appointed by previous administrations. This is one way of avoiding serious unemployment, but . . . it exacts a toll in the form of low labor productivity.[16]

In many Latin American countries, there is usually little prestige in working for the government and capable individuals frequently avoid it. Many employees regard their jobs as sinecures. Prescribed hours of work are not followed and much time is wasted in gossip and extraneous activity. Morale is low. High severance pay and regulations make it difficult to get rid of the incompetent.

Some personnel problems found in the traditionally independent countries (e.g., low salaries, poor placement and promotional policies, frequent and irrational transfer of personnel) are also problems in newly independent countries. But the latter also have some special problems. In many African countries, for example, there is an under-

---

[13] *Ibid.*, pp. 220–222.
[14] IBRD. *Economic Development of Jordan,* p. 431.
[15] IBRD. *Economy of Turkey,* p. 199.
[16] Rijken van Olst, Henri. "Economic Development and Cooperation in Latin America," p. 245.

standable tendency for governments to employ their own nationals instead of expatriates. But since there are not enough nationals with education and experience, "Africanization" of government staffs has greatly reduced the number of officials in ministries and agencies who are qualified to prepare and carry out development plans and programs. In some newly independent African countries, African junior officials were promoted to high posts and "frozen" into the civil service system. When better trained Africans return after schooling abroad, they often find it difficult to obtain suitable positions in government because the best jobs have been pre-empted by more poorly prepared officials who stayed at home. Civil service regulations inherited from the colonial period persist although they are often incongruous after independence. Thus, one country gives tropical allowances to its own nationals in the civil service because such allowances were formerly given to civil servants who came from the home territory of the metropolitan power.

When independence came to India and Pakistan, each inherited a disciplined civil service which was probably better trained and superior to civil services in most other emerging countries for the administration of justice, the maintenance of internal order and the collection of taxes. Their great contribution was to keep traditional governmental services going after independence. But by their very commitment to tradition and routine, these civil service systems, arising from a common colonial tradition, demonstrated their inability to operate with the verve and initiative required to carry out development plans. While official policy favored development, there were in many parts of both governments an unavowed attitude which regarded development activity as being of secondary importance. This manifested itself, among other things, in lower pay and less advantageous conditions of service for personnel serving in some development departments and in the fact that junior officials were often assigned to deal with these departments.

Each civil service system, to which recruits are added in carefully controlled numbers, consists of an elite cadre of "generalists" or general administrators whose influence far exceeds its size.[17] The generalists, sometimes at junior levels, have often been in position to pass on technical matters about which they know little. The technicians' lower salaries, promotional opportunities and status, as well as

[17] Burma, Ceylon and Malaya also inherited similar civil service systems.

their frequent exclusion from the formulation of policy, have kept many technicians from seeking government employment. Yet, increasingly government development activity has become more technical, making it difficult for an administrator with only general knowledge to operate effectively. It has therefore become increasingly apparent that the generalist tradition is in need of revision to meet the requirements of developing societies. Some changes have already been made to improve the position of technicians, but much more needs to be done before each system can operate with tolerable effectiveness. Meanwhile, the difficulty of recruiting technicians remains a serious obstacle to development.

DILATORY PROCEDURES

Every country has had some experience with investment projects and programs before it begins to plan its development. But an organized effort at national development planning differs radically from these earlier efforts because it introduces new and unfamiliar entrepreneurial and managerial tasks on an unprecedented scale. Time, which was not very important before, becomes vital. Management is challenged to do all the things needed to marshal resources and reach targets on a fixed schedule.[18] The number of government functions increases greatly. The fulfillment of these functions not only requires the reorientation or modernization of public administrations steeped in old traditions, but their rapid expansion. Autonomous agencies multiply. The number of ministries increases. In Jordan, to cite one example, ministries increased from 5 in 1947 to 15 in 1955. The number of government employees rises. Existing government offices increase in size and the number of their branches grow. Yet the same old administrative procedures—legacies of the past which have been outmoded and made unwieldy by changed circumstances—continue to be followed because of dogmatic adherence to precedent. New procedural practices arise because of the increasing size and scope of administrative structures. But many of these are also inappropriate for development purposes because, as Sir Oliver Franks has pointed out,

---

[18] UN. Seminar on Industrial Programming. *India's Experience in Industrial Planning*, p. 45.

large-scale organization compels men to take many decisions at a point remote from the places where their decisions will take effect. They work on paper. The in-tray and out-tray symbolize the situation. It is easy not to see beyond the paper and hard to preserve a lively awareness of the real issues, human and material, on which the decisions are made.[19]

From remoteness born of large-scale organization, from adherence to the past, as well as from caution carried to extreme lengths, arise bureaucratic inertia and "red tape," or as the French call the same thing, *paperasserie*. No subject, however trivial, can be considered until it has been put in writing. But this penchant for putting things in writing does not always lead to appropriate administrative action. Nor does it necessarily lead to the compiling of dependable records. In many countries, disorganized filing systems, antiquated office procedures and the lack of trained stenographers and competent clerks preclude good record-keeping.

In many ex-colonial countries, a system of rigid hierarchical routing of correspondence and other communications delays decision-making. In what is now South Viet Nam, for instance,

when a case calls for an opinion or concurrence from an opposite number in a different service, the file on it ordinarily must ascend to the director of the originating service, who then sends it to the director of the second service for reference down to the appropriate officer. The file is eventually returned along the same circuitous route. Lateral short-cuts are the exception . . . the telephone is seldom used to secure quick agreement by related services on matters of joint concern. . . .[20]

In India and Pakistan, documents and files must also follow a prescribed series of steps through administrative layers. Papers received in a government office are first routed to subordinate clerical personnel for recording and checking against preceding action. They then are routed to all interested officials, sometimes on the same level, sometimes upward through multiple layers in the administrative hierarchy. Each officer adds his comments, often in considerable detail, in this "noting process." Decisions are made only at or near the top. But

[19] Franks, Oliver. *Central Planning and Control in War and Peace*, p. 28.
[20] Sharp, Walter R. "Some Observations on Public Administration in Indo-China," p. 47.

much of the time of high officials is taken up merely with the review of papers and files received from subordinates and in passing them on to still higher officers. In decrying the wastefulness of this process, Pakistan's Planning Board pointed out that

> often there seems to be a disposition to shift the file from one office to another, or from one ministry to another. The resultant delays are sometimes unbelievably long.[21]

Many attempts have been made to shorten these delays, either by reducing the number of administrative layers or by the setting of deadlines. But thus far, only peripheral improvements have been achieved.

Because of a general reluctance to take responsibility, administrative procedures which diffuse responsibility are favored. A World Bank survey mission found that in Turkey

> group responsibility is often substituted for individual responsibility. Documents must be signed and countersigned by several persons at the expense of much delay and confusion. . . . Lower ranking civil servants feel that safety lies in letting a group or the man above take all decisions. These tendencies are reinforced by the present government regulations which impose on officials personal financial responsibility for errors, including those of subordinates.[22]

It is possible that these regulations discourage carelessness, abuses and dishonesty; what is certain is that they deter initiative and the effective action required to carry out development plans.[23]

In India and Pakistan, the difficulties and delays of "decision-making by committee" have been compounded by the methods of operation of the generalists who dominate the administrative machinery of their countries. The generalists are expected to administer every kind of program. But since they recognize their limitations and "have been

---

[21] Pakistan. National Planning Board. *First Five Year Plan, 1955–1960*, p. 118.

[22] IBRD. *Economy of Turkey*, p. 196.

[23] The tendency for committees to multiply is not a problem only for less developed countries. U.S. President Johnson has been conducting a campaign to reduce the number of inter-agency committees in the U.S. Government. He has found that in many instances they waste the time of busy officials, delay action and produce undesirable and weak compromises. But the President has not had much success. During the fiscal year which ended June 30, 1964, 163 inter-agency committees were abolished but 203 new committees came into existence, increasing the total to 560 (*Washington Post,* March 5, 1965).

reared in an administrative system that abhors the making of mistakes," [24] they frequently rely on group action.

> The result is a jungle of unnecessary committees. Intelligent and cautious generalist administrators, charged with deciding technical issues about which they are not adequately informed defer to the collective wisdom of a committee of their peers, most of them equally intelligent, cautious, and ignorant of the matters at hand. The committee typically appoints a subcommittee of the same sort, which typically convenes an advisory committee likely to include a number of distinguished industrialists and academicians. While the latter may be generally conversant with the subject at hand they seldom have the incisive knowledge of it possessed in some fields by half a dozen (often younger, but experienced) specialists in the country whom no one gets around to consulting.[25]

This method of operations has had a dampening effect on the planning process.

> Indian planning has tended to be too cautious, too afraid of making mistakes, too little animated with an uncompromising determination to activate idle resources. It still looks too much like what it is—the progeny of an administrative system dedicated to the prevention of wrongdoing rather than to the marshalling and energizing of 'rightdoing.' [26]

But if individual civil servants at middle and lower levels are unwilling to exercise such discretion as they have to make decisions, there is also unwillingness at higher levels to delegate authority to subordinates to deal with even minor matters. In situations where lack of trust is common, where competence is frequently limited to a thin upper layer of civil servants and where there is a long-established administrative tradition of centralized authority, decision-making tends to be concentrated in the hands of a few top officials. These officials frequently become so overburdened with miscellaneous and routine matters that they have little time to give to policy and other important decisions. A World Bank survey mission to Nicaragua found that in the case of the Minister of Finance,

> from 60% to 80% of his office time is spent in signing checks and in receiving private citizens who come to discuss various matters, not

[24] Lewis, John P. "India," p. 105.
[25] *Ibid.*
[26] Lewis, John P. *Quiet Crisis in India*, pp. 135–136.

always directly related to taxation or fiscal administration.[27]

The failure to delegate authority also leads to wasteful delays at lower administrative levels, to a failure to use available staff effectively and to a failure to develop staff capabilities through use. Since practically every project requires the concurrence of many persons, each of whom can block it, disputes are common. Because authority is concentrated at the top levels, ministers and other high

> administrators become embroiled in continual inter-agency conflicts while subordinates piddle away their time waiting for requisite approvals.[28]

Many of these disputes, despite their minor character, eventually end up in the Council of Ministers, where a great deal of time is taken up with them. Cabinet meetings are also frequently occupied with a host of other trivial operational matters which reduce the time available for important policy decisions. A World Bank survey mission to Thailand reported that

> ministers have been known to refuse to decide matters that are clearly within their jurisdiction, preferring instead to pass them on to the Cabinet for collective resolution. The result is an inordinate volume of work for that body, including a large proportion of petty matters with which it should not be bothered—such as civil service promotions, foreign leave for subordinate officers and other issues that should in many instances be decided by heads of departments.[29]

The time which ministers and other high officials have for important matters is also frequently reduced by the multiple positions they hold. It is not unusual in Ethiopia for a Minister or Assistant Minister to be a member of as many as 10 or 15 boards of directors of government corporations, bureaus and other agencies. Ministers who hold many auxiliary posts must attend meetings which keep them away from their offices for long periods. The World Bank survey mission to Colombia concluded that if the Ministers in that country attended meetings of all the councils and boards of which they were members, they would have

[27] IBRD. *Economic Development of Nicaragua*, p. 390.
[28] Riggs, Frederick W. "Public Administration: A Neglected Factor in Economic Development," p. 76.
[29] IBRD. *A Public Development Program for Thailand*, p. 225.

little time to administer their Ministries or to operate as a cabinet.[30] In many countries, ministers are also required to leave their offices for long periods to attend innumerable ceremonies and to make tours related to their duties or for political or other purposes. When they are away, the work of their ministries usually slows down. What a World Bank survey mission found in Colombia is typical of most other Latin American countries:

> The number of officials who have the right and privilege of direct access to the President is staggering. The demands on his time arising from relatively trivial matters are such as to leave him little time for the most important matters of state.[31]

As a result, heads of government, as one Latin American President remarked to a visitor, become little more than public relations officers.

Far from objecting to the trivia which consume much of their time and energy, and which prevent them from concentrating on important business, many high administrators consider these things appropriate matters for their attention. For instance, although

> the chief administrators of Turkey are overwhelmed with routine and trivial obligations that impair their capacity to give administrative direction or leadership to their agencies, . . . many officials would not know how to justify their existence if they did not sign innumerable papers, receive an endless stream of petitioners and make decisions more appropriate to their subordinates two or three levels removed.[32]

The associated problems of overcentralization of decision-making and failure to delegate authority extend beyond ministries, departments and agencies in the capitals of less developed countries into field offices. The World Bank survey mission to Venezuela found that,

> despite the federal principles underlying Venezuelan constitutional arrangements, power is very much centralized in the national government located in Caracas. . . . Ministries and agencies of the national government are overly centralized; their field offices and operations are heavily dependent on the national

[30] IBRD. *Basis of a Development Program for Colombia*, p. 345.
[31] *Ibid.*
[32] Caldwell, Lynton K. "Turkish Administration and the Politics of Expediency," pp. 131–132.

offices; they are . . . often compelled to refer to Caracas for decision on the most minor problems. This overcentralization leads to a burdensome bureaucracy, a lack of flexibility, and therefore to a diminution in administrative efficiency.[33]

It is exceptional when regional, state or local authorities are able to make any but the most unimportant decision on development matters without referring them back to the center of government, where the action files are moved with exasperating slowness up the hierarchical ladder to the top administrative rungs. This leads, in many ministries, to

> an intolerable congestion of business in the office of the minister and his immediate subordinates, and many decisions essential to the rapid implementation of a programme of national development are interminably delayed.[34]

In India, for example,

> it still takes weeks, if not months, to obtain an answer to references to certain organisations in the Central Government; the position in State Governments continues to be, if anything, worse. State Governments as well as public sector enterprises have to send their officers to Delhi repeatedly to obtain answers to their references! [35]

The socialized countries also have their administrative problems. Centralized planning involves much paper work which, in turn, requires large administrative staffs in government and enterprises. It is estimated that over ten million specialized officials in the Soviet Union are engaged in collecting and processing economic data, according to one Russian authority, by 17th-century methods. As a result, central planning agencies are deluged in avalanches of paper.[36] Regional and local bodies issue directives for enterprises and collective farms to carry out. Enterprises are required to submit monthly reports on production, employment and productivity as well as estimates of future output and resource requirements to their regional economic

---

[33] IBRD. *Economic Development of Venezuela*, pp. 9–10.
[34] UN. Department of Economic and Social Affairs. *A Handbook of Public Administration, Current Concepts and Practices with Special Reference to Developing Countries*, p. 7.
[35] Patel, H. M. "Some Administrative Problems," p. 301.
[36] Smolenski, Leon. "What Next in Soviet Planning?" p. 607.

councils. Buyer is separated from seller by many layers of agencies and organizations. In the Soviet Union,

> for example, documents concerning distribution of tires pass through 32 echelons, ball bearings through 20 agencies. . . . The prohibitive amount of paperwork involved may be gathered from the well-publicized experience of the Moscow automobile plant named after Likhachev. The documentation required for it to obtain its annual supply of ball bearings from the adjacent GPZ factory weighs over 400 pounds and is handled by 14 agencies.[37]

Since co-ordination is all important in a system of centralized planning and is difficult to achieve, bottlenecks are common. For example,

> a building site in Kuibyshev held up through failure to deliver machinery, which in turn is held up by failures to deliver components to the machinery manufacturers in Saratov, which failure is then traced up the line until it is discovered that the Cherepovets steelworks had been expected to deliver steel from a workshop which had not yet been completed. . . .[38]

Reluctance to take responsibility, failure to delegate authority and the concentration of power in Moscow over enterprises in all parts of the country have been responsible for bureaucratic delays in settling production and other questions. Attempts to decentralize in 1957

> replaced centralized industrial structures with a system nationally territorial, but in fact based on a multiplicity of central agencies . . . but unable to delegate any effective power. . . . These agencies can scarcely do anything which does not impinge on other organizations. The task of keeping them in harmony is of such a nature that new organizations are set up to co-ordinate and to be co-ordinated.[39]

Bureaucracy in socialized countries dislikes change as much as it does in countries with mixed economies. Attempts by Soviet political leaders to bring about a partial shift in investment resources from heavy industry to chemicals met with widespread bureaucratic resistance. Indeed, Soviet officials have complained that the schedule for developing the chemical industry has lagged "because of bureaucratic inertia." [40]

[37] *Ibid.*, pp. 605–606.
[38] Nove, Alec. *Soviet Economy, An Introduction*, p. 202.
[39] *Ibid.*, p. 205.
[40] *New York Times*, February 16, 1964.

Administrative problems also hamstring economic activity in other socialized countries. Thus, in a broadcast in February 1964, the Czechoslovakian Prime Minister complained that "People administer too much";[41] and a Communist Party Secretary, addressing the Party Central Committee, announced:

> A state of affairs where everybody is responsible for everything and everybody does everything—and which masks profound irresponsibility—can no longer be tolerated.[42]

But in Czechoslovakia, as in other socialized countries, it is hard to get rid of incompetence in Government because most government employees are faithful party members on whose loyalty the regime counts. Cuba, the youngest of the socialized States, has already encountered the "bureaucratism" which characterizes all countries with centralized management of their economies. The Government blames the mounting red tape on functionaries who, it says, like to head sprawling administrative empires "with plenty of departments, sections, offices and . . . secretaries." To counteract the trend toward more paper work and administrative red tape, a network of regional and local "commissions for the fight against bureaucratism" is being set up.[43]

ARCHAIC ACCOUNTING AND FINANCIAL CONTROLS

In many less developed countries, the methods of allocating investment funds and the systems of financial accountability and control also have had the effect of unduly delaying development programs. In fact, measures adopted to prevent misuse of government funds or arbitrary action by public officials have frequently proved to be so time-consuming that many countries have been unable, on this account alone, to disburse available investment funds. Ministries of finance generally are able to exercise great control over development activities. But in seeking to protect public funds, they are prone to be more concerned with reducing expenditures than with stimulating development. In Turkey,

> the Ministry of Finance enjoys preeminence among the ministries second only to the Prime Minister. As the principal agency of the

[41] *Economist,* February 15, 1964, p. 610.
[42] *Ibid.*
[43] *New York Times,* March 28, 1965.

government for budgeting, taxation and fiscal control, it occupies a position of greater strength than other ministries. Nevertheless it has not assumed leadership in national economic planning and has been content with the exercise of largely negative controls.[44]

Ever since the start of India's First Five-Year Plan, the Ministry of Finance's system of expenditure control has been the subject of discussion and debate, and its restrictive effects have been recognized and deplored. Yet the problem remains unresolved after some 15 years. It is widely believed that

> probably the most important source of delay in the execution of projects in India is the procedure involved in obtaining appropriation of funds from the Ministry of Finance. The procedure involves detailed scrutiny of each item of proposed expenditure by the officials of the Ministry of Finance before incurring any liability. The enormous increase in scope of expenditure under development planning makes it impossible to comply with this practice without causing inordinate delays.[45]

Pakistan's experience is similar. In order to reduce expenditures to the level of expected resources and to curb irregularities, the Ministry of Finance in that country had evolved a complicated system for approving expenditures after budgetary allotments had been made, consisting of a series of multiple checks which required a great deal of useless paper work. This system permitted the Ministry to probe deeply into every detail of each proposal which frequently went beyond financial considerations. The expenditure approval system created an illusion of tight central control, with the Ministry of Finance casting itself in the role of sole guardian of the Treasury. In fact, the system did not constitute effective control because decisions on expenditures were actually taken in the operating ministries and agencies. But it resulted in considerable delays which, according to Pakistan's central planning agency, made it take

> about a year for the average provincial scheme requiring central review to emerge from the sanctioning machinery.[46]

[44] Caldwell, Lynton K. "Turkish Administration and the Politics of Expediency," p. 136.
[45] U.N. Seminar on Industrial Programming. *India's Experience in Industrial Planning*, pp. 48–49.
[46] Pakistan. National Planning Board. *First Five Year Plan, 1955–1960*, p. 95.

Outmoded auditing and accounting procedures employed by some less developed countries are another common cause of undue delays in carrying out development plans. In several Latin American countries, including Colombia, Chile, Ecuador, Peru and Venezuela, a system of accounting and auditing controls is carried out by a Comptroller General's Office (*Contraloría*).[47] The *Contraloría* system was established in the 1920's and 1930's as a direct or indirect consequence of the recommendations of the so-called Kemmerer Missions to Latin America, composed of groups of experts from the United States headed by Professor Kemmerer of Princeton University. There is reason to believe that the *Contraloría* system was inappropriate when it was introduced, but there is little doubt that it is unsuitable now.[48]

Under the *Contraloría* system, all proposed expenditures must be pre-audited by the *Contraloría*, whose approval is a legal prerequisite to payment. Most *Contralorías* also maintain centralized accounts for their governments and perform post-audits, in violation of the well established principle of financial administration that those responsible for post-auditing accounts should not have been involved in either the approval of expenditures or the preparation of the accounts which they post-audit.

By shifting responsibility for maintaining accounts from operating departments and agencies in the Executive branch of the Government, where it belongs, to the Comptroller General, who generally owes his appointment to the legislature, the pre-audit and the attendant centralized accounting systems have had the effect of reducing financial responsibility of operating officials. There is a tendency among such officials to propose expenditures on the basis of what the *Contraloría* is likely to approve rather than on the basis of need. Moreover, since they are not required to account for expenditures, officials tend to spend whatever the *Contraloría* approves. Since the rules and regulations promulgated by *Contralorías* are frequently archaic, controls are not always consonant with the public interest. The inordinate amount of paper work usually involved in getting the *Contraloría's* approval also frequently prevents operating officials from giving sufficient attention to the preparation and execution of development projects and programs.

Complicated and time-consuming financial accountability checks frequently used in many countries outside Latin America also are

[47] UN. Department of Economic and Social Affairs. *Public Administration in Venezuela, 1958–1961*, p. 109.
[48] Munoz Amato, Pedro. *Introducción a la Administración Pública*, pp. 198–202.

outmoded. The system used in Turkey does not have the intended effect.

> Turkey's administration has over-elaborated the machinery of accountability and control to the extent of impeding the public business and discouraging initiative—but it is by no means certain that the machinery is adequate to its purposes. For example, the regulations of the Court of Accounts have been applied in a rigid and unimaginative manner and have contributed little to really effective financial control.[49]

A reasonable number of checks and balances, as well as "red-tape" within limits, is essential to the proper examination and co-ordination of investment proposals. If they are to be considered with care, a certain amount of time must be taken up with the task. But the necessity for each check and the time to be spent on it must be determined in the light of a realistic assessment of the cost in money and time. When the administrative apparatus becomes so clogged with checks and rechecks that the flow of public business is almost halted by bottlenecks at many points on every level, the safeguards may cost more than they are worth. Moreover, many financial checks are applied so mechanistically that it takes little sophistication for operating officials to get around them. On their part, financial officials sometimes evade their responsibility for effective financial control by adhering rigidly to a series of formalistic procedures which provide little protection against inefficiency or corruption. But it is difficult to get people to change old and familiar ways. After many years of effort to modernize Indian procedures, the late Prime Minister Nehru found it necessary to say:

> Government officials even today spend hundreds and thousands of rupees to save four annas.[50] This outlook is old and they must change. Many of them do not take quick decisions but delay the files for days and months. This costs the Government each day Rs. ten lakhs.[51]

LACK OF CO-ORDINATION

Centralized decision-making and expenditure controls are sometimes defended as being essential for proper co-ordination of develop-

---

[49] Caldwell, Lynton K. *"Turkish Administration and the Politics of Expediency,"* p. 136.

[50] One-fourth of a rupee.

[51] One million rupees. *Hindu Weekly Review,* December 23, 1963, p. 13.

ment activities. But, as Pakistan's central planning agency pointed out, the kind of overcentralization which existed in Pakistan at the time of the First Five Year Plan and which is common in most less developed countries,

> is an ineffective and in fact a spurious form of co-ordination. It exhibits itself in time-consuming, energy-wasting, and patience-exhausting checks and counter-checks, references and cross-references, conferences and consultations, often at the wrong levels and about unimportant matters. Co-ordination in the true sense of unified administrative leadership at vital points is generally lacking.[52]

Evidence to support this conclusion can be found in almost any developing country. Because true co-ordination is lacking, approved projects frequently fail to get local currency or foreign exchange needed to order raw materials or equipment, or to get approval to engage personnel in time to meet construction schedules. The highway department does not plan its road construction program to meet the needs of agricultural programs being set up by the ministry of agriculture, industrial undertakings being planned by the ministry of industry or port programs being sponsored by the authority in charge of port construction.[53] In Jamaica, the Department of Housing was planning to construct a housing project on the same land which the Ministry of Agriculture was preparing to flood for an irrigation project. In Madagascar, the Ministry charged with repaving a highway after the Ministry of Telecommunications had placed telephone cables underground, repaved the highway before the Ministry of Telecommunications had laid the cables. Many other examples of this kind can be cited since incidents which reveal lack of co-ordination among government ministries and agencies constantly recur in many countries.

Co-ordination of development activities is made difficult in many countries because responsibility for different aspects of a project or program are divided, often incongruously, among many ministries and agencies. In Iran, according to the Plan Organization,

> the planning and execution of each major program within the Plan involves more than one public agency. The divided responsibility

---

[52] Pakistan. National Planning Board. *First Five Year Plan, 1955–1960*, p. 94.
[53] See, for example, Stone, Donald C. "Government Machinery Necessary for Development," p. 57.

and often independent policy pursued by these agencies have led in many instances to confusion, waste and duplication. This has been true to some degree in every field—communications, industry, social affairs, and agriculture.[54]

This excessive fragmentation or duplication of functions makes it hard to get all government entities concerned to do what is needed to carry out projects and programs in accordance with a coherent policy. Waste and duplication are the frequent results. The existence of two government agencies in Spain engaged in irrigation work led to overlapping of functions and contributed to the accumulation of a large number of partially completed projects.[55] In Turkey,

> extensive confusion and an acute lack of coordination are uppermost among electrification problems. Numerous organisations perform identical tasks independent of one another. Due to such duplications, electrification work is conducted in an unplanned and uncoordinated fashion. This in turn gives rise to excess capacity in certain regions and shortage of supply in others. Moreover, scattered and uncoordinated efforts lead to unnecessary and undesirable conflicts, duplication and wastage of resources and manpower among various agencies and organisations.[56]

A similar complaint was made by Thailand's planners:

> There are at present no less than six semiautonomous Authorities concerned with the planning, generation and distribution of electric power. This multiplicity of separate agencies not only inflates overhead expenses but results in imperfect coordination and lack of uniformity in regard to standards, procedures, equipment and technical practices.[57]

In Morocco, the progress of a sugar beet project was long delayed because the three agencies involved were unable to agree on their respective roles. A project for a chemical complex was discussed for several years with little to show.[58] Lack of co-ordination among organizations engaged in parallel activities has equally serious repercussions in the USSR. According to one Soviet official,

[54] Iran. Plan Organization. *Review of the Second Seven Year Program of Iran,* p. 16.

[55] IBRD. *Economic Development of Spain,* p. 280.

[56] Turkey. State Planning Organization. *Program for the Year 1962,* p. 44.

[57] Thailand. National Economic Development Board. *National Economic Development Plan 1961–1966, Second Phase: 1964–1966,* p. 105.

[58] Waterston, Albert. *Planning in Morocco,* pp. 40–41.

a substantial shortcoming in the organization of material-technical supply is parallelism in the work of organizations of the State Planning Committee of the USSR, the state planning committees of the Union Republics and economic councils. Thus, in the Russian Federation, the Ukraine, Kazakhstan and Uzbekistan, in addition to the material-technical supply bodies of the economic councils, offices and points have been set up under the state planning committees of the Union Republics. All this leads to a situation in which, despite adequate total resources of various raw materials, supplies and equipment, some plants and construction sites experience a shortage while superfluous stocks are available in other areas.[59]

It is hard enough to co-ordinate development activities of government ministries, departments and agencies in the capital city; it is even harder to co-ordinate them as between the central government, on the one hand, and the provincial and local governments or field offices, on the other. Civil servants generally prefer to live and work in the relatively more attractive conditions of the capital. Few travel far from home or travel frequently enough to become familiar with problems as they exist in the hinterland. There is a lack of reliable information about the needs and progress of development outside the capital and the larger centers of population. Poor communications between central authorities and those in the provinces, districts and villages or other local areas also work to reduce the flow of information from the central government to officials in outlying areas. In Latin America,

> the great ethnic and geographic distances which separate the inhabited provinces of some of these countries from their capitals, not to speak of the educational abyss which lies between them, make the solution of the administrative problems even more difficult. In no part of the world are regional and local separateness and cultural autonomy more notable than in most of Latin America and, paradoxically, in very few places is complete centralization of administrative operations more prevalent.[60]

Administrative interconnections generally become more tenuous and less certain the further one goes from the capital. In India,

[59] Miroshnichenko, B. "Some Problems of National Economic Planning at the Present Stage," p. 16.
[60] Emmerich, Herbert. "Administrative Roadblocks to Co-ordinated Development," p. 346.

such measures as the government is taking to promote rural advance tend to peter out the nearer they approach the actual village level. The pyramid of Indian bureaucracy, immensely efficient at the top, crumbles at the point of impact with the masses, particularly in the agricultural sector.[61]

INADEQUATE ORGANIZATION

The lack of effective administrative organization for agriculture is especially notable in most less developed countries, and the establishment of a new, independent administrative agency has often been a favored panacea for dealing with it. A group of officials sent by the Indian Government to various states in 1963 to review the progress of agricultural programs, reported

> 'unsatisfactory administrative and organisation' arrangement was by far the most important single factor responsible for poor results in agriculture. This automatically led the Agriculture Ministry to set up a Working Group 'to review the existing arrangements and suggest concrete measures for bringing about adequate co-ordination within the entire administrative and organisational structure.' [62]

The problem of administrative organization has often been turned over to such special working groups and their deliberations have often led to the creation of new agencies. This has led to a proliferation of government agencies and even greater need for co-ordination. A World Bank survey mission to Spain found that the central problem in the field of agricultural development was inadequate co-ordination, both in Madrid and in the field, arising essentially from the establishment of a large number of autonomous and semiautonomous agencies.[63] Another World Bank survey mission to Colombia found that the pronounced tendency in that country's Government toward the creation of a new agency for every new function had unduly diffused governmental powers and made it hard to plan effectively.

> Numerous agencies are involved in almost every field of activity, often with little coordination. In the field of agriculture alone,

[61] *Economic Weekly,* Vol. XV, No. 44, November 2, 1963, p. 1811.
[62] *Ibid.*
[63] IBRD. *Economic Development of Spain,* pp. 308–311.

there are twenty or more agencies, corporations or boards, in addition to the Ministry, whose activities affect agriculture in one way or another. Under such a setup, it is difficult to plan a coordinated program for agriculture as a whole, to determine the proper degree of emphasis on different parts of the program, establish priorities and provide for a rational allocation of available funds.[64]

In some countries, administrative reform follows a pattern of frequent and haphazard changes in organization, often superficial in nature, which also makes it difficult to carry out plans. In Pakistan, for instance, there have been cases where projects have been transferred from one agency to a second and then to a third within the space of a few months. Where new agencies have been created, they sometimes did not have enough people to carry out projects entrusted to them. In many agencies, top officials have been changed so often that they have not had a chance to familiarize themselves with their jobs before they are transferred. In other cases, they have been transferred to posts where they have had no opportunity to use specialized knowledge acquired in previous posts. One reason for the problem is the rigid concept of seniority which prevails in the civil service. If one official is promoted, mechanical application of the rules requires the upward movement of every other official in the hierarchy below him. This system of frequent rotation may have helped broaden the outlook of generalists when one administrative job was not basically different from another. But today, when specialized experience takes time to acquire, frequent transfers or transfers to positions where there is no opportunity to use scarce skills, tend to aggravate the acute shortage of experienced managerial leadership. Moreover, because of frequent shifts in or lack of staff, it has not been unusual to find projects languishing or even abandoned.[65]

There is much to be said in favor of creating autonomous public corporations or authorities when they offer clear advantages over regular government ministries and departments in preparing, executing and operating development projects and programs. Such advantages are generally evident when projects differ in important respects from activities normally carried on by governments, as in the case of economic projects, especially if their operation involves the sale of a commodity to the public. They may also exist in the case of regional

[64] IBRD. *Basis of a Development Program for Colombia,* p. 344.
[65] Waterston, Albert. *Planning in Pakistan,* p. 118.

development, where in the interest of efficiency, it is desirable to consolidate all work on projects which cut across the jurisdiction of several government departments. But where autonomous agencies are established to perform public services normally conducted by regular government offices in an effort to escape existing administrative deficiencies or onerous financial and accounting controls, they are likely to create more problems than they solve.

For one thing, proliferation of autonomous bodies may undermine the effectiveness of established ministries. In Colombia, for example, the continual sloughing off of responsibilities from the Ministry of Agriculture in that country as the number of autonomous agencies handling agricultural matters increased, eventually reduced the Ministry to little more than an organization on paper. Similar problems have accompanied the increase in the number of autonomous agencies in other countries. Thus,

> the proliferation of autonomous entities, as it has occurred in El Salvador, favors irresponsibility in the conduct of public programs, makes it extremely difficult to secure the coordinated planning and administration of public works and services, fosters paralleling and duplicating programs with the attendant inefficient use of limited public resources, and contributes substantially to overburdening ministers and other top officials of the Government.[66]

The increasing use made of autonomous public enterprises for development purposes has also raised a number of administrative problems which have in most countries been only incompletely resolved. One serious problem has been the difficulty, because of scarcity and other reasons, of selecting suitable personnel to manage public enterprises. Some public enterprises have not been as effective as they could have been because their top management, by training and experience, has been more qualified to handle traditional government functions than the technical business tasks of public enterprise. But the big problem has been how to reconcile the requirements for a coordinated development policy for the public sector with the autonomy needed for efficient management of the enterprise. On the one hand, some of these public agencies have been granted such complete autonomy that governments are prevented from including activities of public agencies in plans for developing the public sector. On the other

---

[66] Public Administration Service. *A Program of Administrative Improvements for the Government of the Republic of El Salvador*, p. 11.

hand, autonomous agencies have been hamstrung by political interference with their internal management, by burdensome and restrictive government procedures and by their inability to obtain necessary
financial and other clearances to carry out their mandates.

MALADMINISTRATION AND THE PRIVATE SECTOR

To get a permit to graze his cattle on government land, a villager in
one country normally is required to go eight times to four offices
located in two different cities.[67] To obtain approval for a business
transaction frequently requires a businessman to fill out numerous
forms,[68] to visit several government offices and to wait outside offices
for long periods, sometimes for many days. According to Mr. G. L.
Bansal, of the Federation of the Indian Chambers of Commerce and
Industry (FICCI),

> for an Indian businessman to build himself a plant these days, even
> with private capital, he must deal with his own state government
> first and then go to New Delhi to the Ministry of Industries, then
> the Ministry of Finance and finally the Planning Commission—all
> before being granted the necessary permit.[69]

Foreign investors must go through an even greater number of steps
to obtain the Government's approval. Under procedural formalities
existing in early 1965, they must obtain:

(a) An industrial license under the Industries Development
and Regulation Act of 1951.
(b) Approval from the capital goods and the foreign agreements
committees.
(c) Approval for the issue of any capital stock under the Capital
Issue Act of 1947.
(d) A license to import capital equipment and machinery under
the Imports and Exports Act of 1947.
(e) An approval from the Reserve Bank under the Foreign Exchange Regulation Act of 1947.

[67] U.N. Department of Economic and Social Affairs. *A Handbook of Public
Administration, Current Concepts and Practices with Special Reference to Developing Countries,* p. 26.
[68] Ram, Bharat. "Government and the Private Sector," p. 423, mentions a study
which found that "there were nearly 312 forms and returns prescribed by various
Government agencies for the textile industry."
[69] *Washington Post,* September 16, 1963.

(f) A certificate of incorporation under the Indian Companies Act of 1956.[70]

Little wonder, then, that

the formidable array of forms to be executed and officials to be consulted greatly discourages both the domestic investor and the foreign investor or collaborator.[71]

Indian government regulations require that official decision on applications for industrial licenses must be taken within a period of three months. But a committee established by the Government, which made a study of eight applications for industrial licenses, chosen at random, found that in six of the eight cases, the time taken for action ranged from 150 to 396 days.[72] Another leading spokesman for private business in India and a former head of FICCI, Mr. G. D. Birla, addressed a letter to the Prime Minister in which he indicated why he thought Indian businessmen had to contend with administrative delays:

The indecision in the administration is most frustrating. I can understand where there is a controversy. But where the Government has agreed on certain principles, even then the final decision is not taken. The officers, I fear, are afraid to take decisions because when you take decisions you make some mistakes for which blame may be apportioned later. The safest position, therefore, for the services to avoid mistakes is not to act. This, I fear, is happening in India at present. By this delay we have lost hundreds of crores in foreign exchange and in production.[73]

Foreign investors also manifest considerable frustration. One foreign business executive operating in India reported that

bureaucratic red tape and delays are particularly irritating, to the point that in certain cases we have foregone opportunities rather than fight through the procedural battle.[74]

The interminable delays in getting government approval of transactions in the private sector, the necessity for businessmen and others to scurry from one government office to another, and to wait outside offices for a long time in order to complete their business, create

[70] Negandi, Anant R. "GOI's Decision-Making Apparatus," p. 131.
[71] *Ibid.*
[72] *Economic Times*, January 14, 1964.
[73] *Economic Times*, October 27, 1963. A crore equals 10 million.
[74] Negandi, Anant R. "GOI's Decision-Making Apparatus," p. 133.

dissatisfactions among citizens, which reflects itself in widespread public criticism of government administration. Civil servants are often charged with arrogance and aloofness in dealing with the common people. Typical of these criticisms is the one in the Karachi newspaper, *Dawn*:

> There should be greater contact with the masses than in the past. The policy of aloofness in official dealings should be discarded. And it should not be considered beneath the dignity of a civil servant to pay frequent visits to remote and inaccessible areas within their jurisdiction for examination, study and discussion of the problems of the day. There should be more field work and less of desk notings.[75]

Businessmen feel, as one well-known Indian industrialist has said, that the implementation of regulatory policies and measures which affect the private sector is

> left in the hands of civil servants who, because of their different training, background and outlook, frequently fail to understand or appreciate the *practical* difficulties of the businessman. Indeed, it would not be an exaggeration to say that they sometimes do not even understand each other's language.[76]

Delayed granting of permits and licenses to import, to establish enterprises, to obtain needed transportation facilities, or to carry out other business ventures develop pressures which induce favoritism, nepotism, bribery and other abuses. The system of *bakshish*—i.e., extralegal fees which businessmen pay civil servants to speed administrative action—has been defended as the lubricant that makes the administrative machinery operate quickly.[77] Some inducement must be offered hesitant administrators if they are to take the risk of side-stepping the rigid administrative systems for the sake of speedier action.

> By injecting a new element of personal motivation, the illegal fees paid by businessmen to local administrators often provide the

---

[75] *Dawn*, April 24, 1963. It is interesting that in the USSR, also, "Centralized Bureaucracy is criticized as being separated from life, as giving directions without knowledge of local conditions." Hulička, Karel. "Political and Economic Aspects of Planning of the National Economy in the USSR and the Soviet Bloc," p. 261.

[76] Bansal, G. L. "Liaison Between Government and the Private Sector," pp. 32–33.

[77] Weiner, Myron. *Politics of Scarcity*, p. 120.

necessary incentive to speed decisions. Many economic activities would be paralyzed were it not for the flexibility which *bakshish* contributes to the complex, rigid administrative system.[78]

But if graft quickens decisions, the manner in which it is done and the results obtained cannot fail to introduce serious difficulties in the development process. In some countries, charges of corrupt practices in the conduct of public business compete with countercharges of bribery of public servants by businessmen who seek special treatment for themselves. Besides its undesirability on ethical grounds, graft is economically undesirable because it frequently results in increasing the cost of development by persuading public administrators to select less than the best available choice among development alternatives.

> Corruption is a blight which affects the administration adversely in many directions. Such a weakening of the administration has a direct effect on the efficiency of Plan implementation. The appointment of the less efficient, the selection of the more costly contractor, or the award of an industrial licence to the less competent party, in each case because of a bribe—these and many other 'distortions' have affected the progress of the Plan considerably.[79]

Nevertheless, it is not corruption which increases development costs most. As Professor Arthur Lewis told a group of economists in Ghana:

> We hear much about corruption in under-developed countries but the harm done by bribery or by theft seldom exceeds hundreds of thousands of pounds a year, and though morally deplorable, is quite small when compared with the harm which is done by appointing people to big jobs which they are not competent to do properly.[80]

The cost of corruption is also smaller than the cost of time-consuming administrative procedures and official circumlocutions which delay necessary action unduly. When civil servants, in attempting to protect the public interest, take a rigid approach to government business, the cure may be worse than the disease.

> Too much precaution to avoid an error and too much pains to do a thing well can run up costs, delay action and create annoyance for

[78] *Ibid.*, p. 235.
[79] "Dhanam," in *Economic Times*, November 5, 1963.
[80] Lewis, W. Arthur. "On Assessing a Development Plan," pp. 5–6.

the general public comparable if not equal to that which results from incompetence, indifference and dishonesty.[81]

DEALING WITH ADMINISTRATIVE OBSTACLES

The Difficulties of Reform

Every country which starts to plan its development seriously has recognized the urgent need for improving its administrative apparatus. Every well-prepared plan mentions basic administrative reforms which are essential to its implementation. Pakistan's First Five Year Plan devoted a whole chapter to needed reforms. Each of India's three five-year plans contained recommendations for reforming or expanding administration in the Central Government and in the districts, and no doubt the Fourth Five-Year Plan will have more recommendations on the subject. "In order for Turkey to prepare and implement plans," stated that country's *Draft Program for 1962* on its very first page, "it is necessary to undertake a task of administrative reorganization." "Experience shows," wrote the former head of the UAR's central planning agency,

> that far-reaching improvements in public administration are required if the goals of economic and social development are to be reached.[82]

In Latin America, Africa and Asia, conferences of planners have recorded their conviction that administrative reform is essential to successful development planning. Typically, delegates at the 1961 Conference of Asian Planners

> emphasised that deficiencies in the administrative machinery constituted a major obstacle to the effective implementation of development plans. The reform of the administrative structure, its strengthening and reorganization . . . had to be carried out urgently if the administration as a whole of each country was to be fully geared to the enormous obligations which planned development placed upon it.[83]

[81] Hyneman, Charles S. *Bureaucracy in a Democracy*, p. 524.
[82] Abdel-Rahman, I. H. and Ramzi, M. *Organizational and Administrative Aspects of Development Planning*, p. 33.
[83] UN. ECAFE. "Economic Development and Planning in Asia and the Far East," *Economic Bulletin for Asia and the Far East*, December 1961, p. 80.

Attempts to raise the standards of public administration in countries with extended planning experience go back a long time. For instance, a committee established in 1946 by Iran's Central Bank to formulate a development plan for the country produced a report which called attention to the need for administrative reform. Since then, many reports have been written in Iran in the same vein. Between 1956 and 1961 alone, foreign experts produced for the Iranian Government over 150 papers on a variety of public administration problems requiring action.[84] In the Philippines, a Government Survey and Reorganization Commission produced a series of plans for reorganization, but

> in the main, the commission's proposals have been idealistic, formulary schemes for improving executive direction, coordination, and control. . . . [The Philippine Congress approved many of these proposals but in practice] there is often a marked discrepancy between what actually transpires in administration and what the Statutes and administrative orders prescribe.[85]

Since Pakistan's independence, foreign and domestic experts on public administration have submitted several extensive reports to the Government which called for a variety of fundamental administrative reforms in the Central and Provincial Governments. India probably holds the record for the number of comprehensive reports on administrative reform:

> Sometime during his tenure of office every Home Minister feels that the time has arrived for him to give attention to the problem of administrative reform. The result is usually the appointment of a commission or a committee to make yet another thorough investigation of the problem as a whole. The knowledge that the subject has in fact been thoroughly investigated any number of times before—the precise figure is apparently 16 since independence, that is to say, an average of a report a year—rarely proves a deterrent.[86]

In each report, the nature of the problem and the appropriate solutions are detailed by experts. There is, therefore, no dearth of knowledge of why there are administrative delays, wastefulness and inefficiency or what needs to be done to correct the deficiencies. The

[84] The titles are listed in Harwood, Wilson R. *Advice to the Plan Organization of Iran, 1956–61.*
[85] Parsons, Malcolm B. "Performance Budgeting in the Philippines," p. 177.
[86] *Economic Times*, November 27, 1963.

problem is how to get it done. It has proved easy to "solve" administrative problems by redrawing organization charts, showing unequivocal chains of command and logically deployed personnel, and indicating who makes decisions on whose advice and gives orders for execution to whom. It has also become evident that there are usually several ways of solving an organizational or other administrative problem. Experts from different countries have produced differing formulas for correcting specific administrative deficiencies, each based on a particular national experience, all of which appeared to be equally workable. The precise formula adopted has shown itself to be less important than achieving the desired result. But the desired result has generally been elusive.

Periodic reshuffling of government departments or the establishment of new agencies have frequently brought little or no improvement. The reorganized or newly created organization has been found not to be immune from the administrative maladies that afflicted its bureaucratic predecessors. It is true that every government administration can be improved by streamlining and that faulty structure can frustrate the best administrators. But the crucial administrative task has been not so much in finding a correct organization as in devising effective working relationships among those whose responsibility it is to make decisions. It is in this area that the least progress has been made in adapting administration to the needs of development planning. Despite some successes, attempts to reform public administration in less developed countries often appear to be a losing battle. A member of India's Planning Commission frankly conceded in 1963, after many years of effort to improve administration in that country, that

> experience in the past two years has tended to strengthen the view that in its structure, methods of functioning and capacity to meet the requirements of rapid development, the administration has not been able to catch up, and the distance may be increasing rather than diminishing.[87]

Unfortunately, this also describes the situation in most other less developed countries.

Many reasons, some simple and others complex, have been advanced to explain why public administration in less developed countries has proved to be difficult to improve and "why there is often a big gap

[87] Singh, Tarlok. "Administrative Assumptions in the Five-Year Plan," p. 336.

between knowing and doing." [88] Increased size of administrative machinery once a government embarks on development planning, scarcity of trained and experienced personnel, lack of political stability and maturity, pressures from vested interests, the force of deeply rooted traditions, as well as underlying cultural, social and psychological values, have each been mentioned as accounting, in varying degree, for the tenacity of old administrative institutions and methods. One author suggests that

> the problems of administration in developing nations arise mainly as a result of the conflict between tradition and modernization. On the one hand, administration is still based on the earlier bureaucratic pattern and has to function in a traditional society; on the other hand, excessive reverence for traditional administrative forms and procedures and failure to rationalise and reform the administration leads to much frustration. [89]

Whatever factors govern in a particular country, they impart to public administration

> a certain persistency, a built-in resistance to change and a capacity for evasion which would break the heart of any would-be reformer. This is the reason why so many attempts made in the past to remodel administrative procedures have all come to nought. . . . At bottom, it is a question of the official's attitude to work and performance and his feeling for public good that is decisive. Thus, the key problem is really how to bring about a change for the better in the fundamental attitudes of our public servants. [90]

Many, perhaps most, planners and public administration experts take the position that administrative improvement is a pre-condition to sustained development. But another view is that good administration is a consequence of development, especially development of an industrial base, which then provides the great impetus needed to improve patterns of administration. [91] There is, finally, the position that administrative reform is neither cause nor effect but a concomitant of development. Thus, Professor Albert O. Hirschman has sought to demonstrate

---

[88] Hartog, Floor. "Economic Development and Cooperation in Africa," p. 198.
[89] Bhalerao, C. N. "Substantive Forces in Indian Administration," p. 1681.
[90] *Economic Times*, August 1, 1963.
[91] Mello e Souza, Nelson. "Public Administration and Economic Development," p. 163.

that a society can begin to develop by neutralizing or even by making beneficial use of such well-entrenched obstacles to change as bad administration.[92] There are, therefore, differences among experts about whether administrative improvement must precede, follow or accompany development. But there is no disagreement that improvement takes a long time to achieve.

Although the difficulties of improving administration are clear, planners often appear to ignore them in preparing plans. In one African country, for example, the ten technicians plus some clerks and stenographers who constituted the staff of the central planning agency were scattered in two separate buildings, with the personnel in one of the buildings distributed on two floors. It is understandable why the head of the agency felt frustrated when he could not get an administrative decision on his repeated requests to consolidate his staff in one location, despite his strenuous efforts to this end over a three-year period. Yet, the planning agency he headed was producing plans during this time whose successful implementation depended on fundamental improvements in the government's administrative machinery in the immediate future. Africa is not alone. A report of the Pan American Union concluded that in Latin America

> most economic and social development plans are made upon an unrealistic basis. . . . Usually lacking is an evaluation of the operative capacity of the administrative machine to accomplish that part of the over-all development plan that is the responsibility of the public sector.[93]

Because so many planners and public administration experts believe that administrative reform is a prerequisite to development, many plans are drawn up which depend for their implementation on basic changes in administration during the few years of a medium-term plan. These plans sometimes call for a comprehensive reorganization of the executive branch of government to conform with practices in advanced countries as though this were both needed and feasible. This is a naïve approach to the problem because it is neither likely to happen nor desirable that it should.

A lesson of experience is that, even under the most favorable

[92] Hirschman, Albert O. *Journeys Toward Progress: Studies of Economic Policy-Making in Latin America*, p. 6.
[93] OAS. Department of Economic Affairs. *Rio Organization and Methods Workshop, Development Administration Program, Public Administration Unit*, p. 21.

circumstances, administrative reform only comes gradually as development proceeds and not through a wholesale recasting of organizations and procedures carried out in a short period:

'Administrative reform,' like planning, instead of being the sporadic result of efforts confined to one period of government, must be a continuous process of adapting techniques, legislation and structure to the country's growth. Thus administrative reform and programming are not only directed to the same ends, but since both must be continuous processes, they will be carried on side by side.[94]

Proposals for revising administrative systems in less developed countries are often made by foreign experts who are guided by principles which work well in advanced countries. The application of these principles may require major innovations or the grafting on of institutional forms which are alien to the traditions of the country receiving advice. In many cases, therefore, less developed countries either refuse to adopt the proposals or, if they adopt them, find that they do not work well because they are not accepted. Experience indicates that

adaptations and the introduction of changes are accomplished more readily where the established and traditional institutions are used and radical reforms in administrative structure and procedures are not insisted on as a primary objective.[95]

Everyone involved in government operations is only too well aware that ineffective administration seriously limits implementation of plans, but there is often a lack of communication between planners and public administration experts about what should be done about it. The practitioners in each field tend to adopt parochial views about the importance of their own specialities. Those in public administration have not been development-minded.[96] They sometimes think of public administration as a separate matter from development—something in and of itself. On the one hand, reports by public administration experts, with their urgent recommendations for revising administration from top to bottom, have an unspecific eloquence with which it is hard

---

[94] UN. TAA. *Introduction to Public Administration in Development Policy, Preliminary survey of the experience of several Latin American countries,* p. 45.
[95] *Ibid.,* p. 3.
[96] Spitz, A. A. and Weidner, E. W. *Development Administration, An Annotated Bibliography,* pp. vii–viii.

to find fault, but which often seems wide of the mark to planners. As two public administration specialists have pointed out:

> As a whole, public administration writers remain intrigued by civil service, budgeting, O and M,[97] and bureaucracy, but not with the development objectives that may be achieved by them.[98]

On the other hand, planners and other officials are often unable or unwilling to give administrative reform the high priority it deserves. After studying on-the-spot administrative impediments to development in Colombia, India, Indonesia, Iran, Nigeria, the Philippines, Sudan, Thailand and the United Arab Republic, among other countries, Dr. Donald C. Stone, Dean of the University of Pittsburgh's Graduate School of Public and International Affairs, an authority on public administration in developing countries, concluded:

> Most persons charged with planning and other development responsibilities in individual countries, as well as persons made available under technical assistance programs, do not have adequate knowledge or adaptability in designing and installing organizations, institutions, and procedures suitable for the particular country.[99]

Thus, planners rarely attempt to integrate a systematic program for improving or expanding administrative machinery with their development plans. Instead,

> planners talk eloquently of goals and objectives, but administrative implementation tends to be neglected in favor of resounding policy directives which carry no executive bite.[100]

Planners have an obligation to go beyond a mere listing of administrative shortcomings which impede development and recommending that they be corrected. They must include in their plans specific measures for creating an administrative system which can produce and carry out development plans. When planning or other experts

> discover an 'obstacle' such as poor public administration, . . . their job does not consist in merely advising its removal; they ought to explore also how, by moving the economy forward else-

[97] Organization and Management.
[98] Spitz, A. A. and Weidner, E. W. *Development Administration, An Annotated Bibliography,* pp. vii–viii.
[99] Stone, Donald C. "Government Machinery Necessary for Development," p. 53.
[100] Fainsod, Merle. "The Structure of Development Administration," p. 1.

where, additional pressure (economic and political) could be brought on the obstacle to give way.[101]

But since good planning demands a proper skepticism about the possibilities for over-all administrative reform in a short period, planners must help set more limited but more practicable goals for eliminating specific obstacles to development. And they must recommend how pressure can be brought to bear on them to make the obstacles give way.

The Nuclei Approach

It may be that the trouble with most efforts to improve administration has been that too much was attempted at once. In any event, little has been accomplished by a comprehensive approach to administrative reform. While haphazard, piecemeal improvements are also of little value, a more limited approach directly oriented to development efforts may prove to be more successful. For example, instead of insisting on an "all or nothing" basis, on drastic, across-the-board changes in personnel practices, administrative procedures and organization, it might be better to select a few large or otherwise important projects or programs and concentrate on improving administration and organization to the extent required to facilitate the preparation, execution and operation of these projects or programs. These projects or programs might be in an economic sector or a geographic region. Administrative reform might be centered in a ministry or department; a regional organization; or another kind of autonomous or semiautonomous corporation or agency. The establishment of such "nuclei" of administrative reform would, it is true, provide only modest improvement immediately.[102] But it would create springboards for more sweeping reforms later.

It would be desirable, of course, to relate these nuclei of reform to a comprehensive program for improving public administration. For this purpose, as well as to provide a basis for wider reforms, it would be useful to have such a program, at least in broad outline, for every country which planned its development. The "nuclei approach" would

---

[101] Hirschman, Albert O. "Comments on 'A Framework for Analyzing Economic and Political Change,' " p. 41.

[102] However, the marginal return from the concentration of limited technical resources might well be higher than from a more even distribution of these resources.

not be an alternative to comprehensive reform, but an adjunct. The comprehensive and nuclei approaches would constitute two variables in a co-ordinated approach to administrative betterment. The extent to which each variable was employed in any country would be determined by the prevailing conditions. Wherever over-all reform was feasible, there might be little need for nuclei of reform. In some circumstances, both comprehensive reforms and the nuclei approach might yield the best results. But where comprehensive reform was unlikely, the nuclei approach might be the only practicable alternative. In all countries, attempts could be made at appropriate times to introduce over-all reforms based on the comprehensive program for improving public administration. These efforts would surely be aided by the existence of nuclei where reforms consonant with the program had already been instituted.

The ability to select viable nuclei would be an important determinant of the success of this approach. The ideal nucleus is a project or program in an economic or social sector or in a geographic area where there is a recognized need for economic or social development backed by a powerful group or entity which stays powerful and interested long enough to allow reforms to be institutionalized. More is, therefore, needed than the presence of a strong administrator in an organization, or a vested interest promoting a project or even an urgent need for administrative or other reform. It is not enough to select as a nucleus a program or a place where there is a demonstrated need for action (e.g., for improving education, whether national or regional), even if sponsored by vested interests (e.g., teachers), if they are not sufficiently powerful to exert sufficient pressure on the political authorities. Conversely, the mere existence of a capable administrator in an organization or a powerful pressure group sponsoring a program or project where there is no imperative need for action is not enough to constitute the organization, program or project as a nucleus because the expenditure in time, effort and money cannot be justified on economic or social grounds. Where an otherwise worthwhile project or program lacks capable personnel or powerful sponsors, an attempt must be made to get them. This may not be as difficult as it seems if there is, in fact, a recognized need for action in the field concerned. Thus, if an influential government official, the business community or an organization which is prepared to aid in financing will back a project or program, the chance of establishing a viable nucleus of administrative reform is, of course, much improved.

Given the instability and lack of commitment to development of some governments which makes the nuclei approach worth trying, there is much to be said for enlisting the support of groups outside government for worthwhile projects and programs around which nuclei of administrative reform can be erected. The World Bank has co-operated with borrowing countries to establish nuclei of administrative reform in connection with Bank loans for specific projects. In Colombia, for instance, reforms instituted in the Highway Department of the Ministry of Public Works when a loan for highways was under discussion provided for reorganizing the Highway Department, improving disbursement and administrative procedures, higher remuneration for engineers who were needed to fill long-standing vacancies, elimination of incompetent personnel, etc. The Bank's willingness to support these reforms with a development loan made it easier for highway officials in the Ministry to obtain the Government's approval for the needed changes. This experience and similar ones elsewhere suggest that the establishment of such nuclei might be facilitated if an international financing agency participated in the effort.

If the "nuclei approach" works as it should, improved administration should result in reducing both the financial cost and the time of execution of the most important projects. The actual number of nuclei which could be expected to operate effectively at the same time would depend on what opportunities existed for introducing improved administration at various points in a government. These opportunities are not likely to be many. Since the nuclei approach could not be used for most projects and programs in a plan, it would be prudent to assume that the cost of most projects and programs would be increased and their time of execution would be lengthened because of administrative inadequacies. Rising standards in administration might bring some reductions in costs and times of completion, but experience indicates that not too much improvement can be expected within the period of a medium-term plan.

Measuring Administrative Capacity

A realistic evaluation of the possibilities for reform is essential if reliable estimates are to be made of the cost of, and the time needed for, achieving plan targets under prevailing administrative conditions. Failure to appreciate fully the high cost of inefficient organization and administration and the time required to eliminate inefficiencies are major reasons for underestimation of the cost of, and the time needed for, reaching plan targets. Yet, most plans continue to be prepared without relevance to administrative capacity.

It should not be very difficult to produce reasonable estimates of the cost of administrative inefficiency, in terms of money and time. Wherever development projects have been carried out, it is possible to determine for each economic sector or branch, the extent to which average costs and time of completion have exceeded original estimates. Several elements generally are involved, but experience shows that poor administration is the major and most persistent reason for increased costs and delayed execution of development projects and programs. On the basis of previous performance, as well as any other pertinent quantitative or qualitative data which may be available, factors could be computed by which all project estimates in each sector or branch could be increased to take account of administrative friction.[103] Thus, if experience and other information revealed that average costs for housing exceeded original estimates by 75 per cent and the time of execution by 50 per cent, appropriate increases would be made in original estimates submitted by the sponsors of housing projects. This approach is, admittedly, crude and it has pitfalls.[104] But its use entails fewer risks than those which arise when plans are formulated without reference to administrative limitations. It also has the virtue of simplicity.

Any procedure which took adequate account of the effects of poor administration on the cost of projects and their period of execution would result in reducing estimated growth rates. This might not be a bad thing. For if planners could show political leaders, before the beginning of each planning period, how much administrative inefficiency costs in terms of reduced growth, there is some prospect that political leaders would be stimulated to take more forceful measures to improve administration.

---

[103] It will be found, for example, that the gap between estimated and actual costs and construction time will generally be much greater for transportation than for electric power projects.

[104] For instance, it is possible that the sponsors of projects may themselves increase estimates on the basis of experience before submitting them for review. In that event, addition of cost and time factors during the review process would result in overestimating cost and time lags. This is less probable, however, than that they may submit lower estimates when they learn that their estimates are likely to be increased during review. But proper review procedures could take care of either eventuality.

Until improvement is clearly foreseeable, however, planners would be well advised to draw up plans which take account of the administrative realities. Complex forms of planning should be avoided when the quality of administration is unable to support such planning. The difficulties of co-ordination increase rapidly as the scope of planning widens. As Professor Arthur Lewis has aptly cautioned:

> no administration should be loaded with tasks more numerous or more delicate than it can handle; the quantity and forms of planning should be limited strictly within the capacity of the machine.[105]

SUMMARY AND CONCLUSIONS

To summarize, the administrative systems of government in almost all less developed countries with mixed economies are outmoded. Countries which have recently become independent generally have administrative machines which are suitable enough for carrying out police, judicial and revenue collecting functions of government, but are not effective in performing functions required in dynamically developing societies. Countries which have a long tradition of independence also have administrative machines which cannot meet the demands of accelerated development. But, in addition, most of these countries do not even have efficient administrations for carrying out the usual government services, collecting taxes and preserving law and order.

An organized attempt to plan a country's development introduces new and unfamiliar entrepreneurial and managerial tasks on an unprecedented scale. Few countries can cope with the administrative problems which development planning brings. These problems are so complex that in most less developed countries the limitation in implementing plans is not financial resources, but administrative capacity. Political influence in recruitment and promotions, overstaffing at lower levels and understaffing at upper levels, misuse of trained staffs and low pay are important factors accounting for low morale, incompetence, slackness and waste. Rigid personnel regulations protect the inefficient and scare away the well trained and competent. Large-scale organization, procedures made convincing by years of repetition

[105] Lewis, W. Arthur. *Principles of Economic Planning*, p. 122.

and cautiousness give rise to "red tape" and "the deadening hand of bureaucracy." Excessive amounts of paperwork, files passing through too many hands, a general reluctance to take responsibility on one hand and failure to delegate authority on the other lead to overcentralization and delays in decision-making.

In many less developed countries, archaic financial and accounting controls have also led to considerable delays in carrying out development plans. Measures adopted to prevent abuses or arbitrary official action have had the effect of preventing the disbursement of available development funds. Some checks, of course, are essential, but when they result in the creation of many bottlenecks, they may cost more than they save.

Centralized decision-making and expenditure controls are sometimes defended as being necessary for the co-ordination of development activities. But the facts reveal that co-ordination in the sense of unified administrative leadership is generally lacking. Co-ordination is made difficult, and waste and jurisdictional disputes are accentuated, by excessive fragmentation of functions and by diffusion of responsibility for executing projects and programs. Co-ordination among the various ministries, departments and agencies is hard to get. It is even harder to get as between the central government and regional, provincial and local governments and field offices.

There is a notable tendency in many countries to try to overcome administrative deficiencies, especially in agriculture, by creating new organizations. This solution often results in increasing the difficulties in the way of achieving proper co-ordination. In some cases, there are clear advantages in establishing autonomous public organizations. But when such entities are set up to carry out regular government functions mainly to escape administrative deficiencies, they are likely to create more problems than they solve. The biggest problem is how to reconcile the autonomy they need for managerial efficiency with the need for a co-ordinated development policy in the public sector.

Government regulations often interfere with efficient operation of public enterprises. They also have the same effect on enterprises in the private sector. Government approval for various business purposes is often obtained only after long delays. This encourages favoritism, graft and other abuses. Besides the ethical objections to corruption, it increases the cost of development because it is likely to lead to the selection of less than the best available choices among development alternatives. Nevertheless, the increase in the cost of development from corruption is frequently less than the increased cost from poor personnel policies, time-consuming administrative procedures and inadequate organization.

Every country which starts to plan seriously has recognized that it must improve its administrative machinery. Many reports on the subject have been written in many countries. There is, therefore, no lack of knowledge about what is wrong and what needs to be done. As one influential Indian newspaper has said:

> It is too late in the day to say anything especially novel about administrative reform. . . . There have been so many reports, so many investigations, the whole ground has been covered with such thoroughness . . . that the problem today is not one of enlightenment but of implementation.[106]

There are differences among experts about whether administrative improvement must precede, follow or accompany development, but there is general agreement that reform takes a long time to achieve. Nevertheless, many plans are drawn up which depend for their implementation on basic changes in administration in a few years along lines followed in advanced countries. This is neither possible nor desirable. It must be recognized that each country must adapt its own institutions for development purposes, rather than exchange them for a new set that is alien to its own tradition. It must also be understood that this takes time to accomplish.

Planners should go beyond announcing administrative shortcomings which impede development and recommending their correction. They must consider it a part of their task to help establish an administrative system which can carry out development plans. It might be more practicable, however, if planners set a more limited goal than comprehensive reform carried out in a short time. Thus, a wise course could be to select a few important projects and programs and concentrate administrative improvements around them, in the hope that these "nuclei" would later become springboards for wider reform. For other projects and programs, it would be well to recognize that poor administration results in higher costs and longer periods of execution. As a rule of thumb, a realistic approach is to increase original cost and time of completion estimates submitted by sponsors of projects and programs by quantitative factors which take account of the effects of adminis-

---

[106] *Economic Times,* October 1, 1963.

trative inadequacies. Until administrative improvements are clearly foreseeable, planners must prepare plans which take account of administrative capacity. This means, among other things, that complex forms of planning must be avoided when a country's administration is not ready for them.

Chapter IX

The Implementation of Plans

War is easy; it is waging it that
is difficult.—Napoleon Bonaparte

PROMISE AND PERFORMANCE

WITHOUT QUESTION planning has helped promote growth in less developed countries. The visible evidence in many countries of the results of planned expansion of transport, communications, ports, power, industry, irrigation, and community facilities is too plain to be argued away. Nor have the benefits of planning been limited to construction and increases in physical capacities. The process by which development is planned, whether implemented well or poorly, often forces the introduction of new attitudes and procedures which are essential to improved administration and decision-making in a country and its government.

But even when the intangible values of planning are taken into account, an examination of postwar planning history reveals that there have been many more failures than successes in the implementation of development plans. By far the great majority of countries have failed to realize even modest income and output targets in their plans except for short periods. What is even more disturbing, the situation seems to be worsening instead of improving as countries continue to plan. Thus the United Nations has reported that

the actual growth in income and output of the developing countries during the first part of the nineteen sixties has generally not been sufficient to offer assurance that the target of the Development Decade will be reached. For the developing countries as a whole, the annual rate of growth in gross domestic product over the first four years of the present decade amounted to 4 per cent. Instead of the acceleration that was hoped for, this denoted a deceleration over the pace of advance recorded in the nineteen fifties. . . . Expressed in *per capita* terms, output during recent

293

years has been increasing annually by only 1.5 per cent; this is to be compared with an annual rate of increase of over 2 per cent between 1955 and 1960 and of nearly 3 per cent between 1950 and 1955.[1]

In Asia, where countries have had more experience with planning than those of any other region, ECAFE found that

> the rates of economic growth generally recorded in the . . . region in the early sixties had, in fact, fallen short not only of the planned targets but also of the growth rates of the 1950's. The conclusion derived from the secretariat's long-term economic projections was both significant and alarming; unless fundamental changes and improvements in economic structure and policy were made in time, the region as a whole would most probably not be able to grow faster than at an annual rate of 4.2 per cent, . . . [compared with the considerably higher rate of 6.4 per cent at which national planning authorities in the region were aiming] for the period up to 1980.[1a]

With the exception of Japan, Pakistan, Thailand and Taiwan, growth rates during recent years have been disappointing in most Asian countries. Thus, the first four years of Indonesia's Eight-Year Development Plan produced little. The Plan provides that proceeds from eight large so-called B-projects (in the oil, timber, fisheries, copra, rubber, tin and aluminum branches of the economy) are to supply most of 240 billion rupiahs needed to finance 335 so-called A-projects (in the food, clothing, industrial, communications, distribution and other branches of the economy). Since none of the eight B-projects had been realized at the Plan's half-way mark, only 200 of the 335 A-projects could be begun and far fewer completed.

The widening gap between promise and performance is also well illustrated in India. In that country, national income increased by 3.4 per cent annually during the period of the First Five-Year Plan (compared with a target of about 2 per cent); 3.7 per cent during the period of the Second Five-Year Plan (compared with a target of 5 per cent); and only 3.1 per cent during the first three years of the Third Five-Year Plan (compared with a target of 5.4 per cent). Moreover, per capita income during the first three years of the Third-Plan period

[1] UN. Department of Economic and Social Affairs. "Chapter 1, Problems and Policies in the Development Decade," p. 8.

[1a] UN. ECAFE. *Draft Report of the Conference of Asian Economic Planners,* pp. 2–3.

rose only by about 1 per cent (compared with an annual target of 3 per cent). For the Third Five-Year Plan period as a whole, the Planning Commission estimated a shortfall of 20 per cent in the target for the Gross National Product.[2]

But the bleakness of the vista is by no means limited to Asia. In Africa, few plan targets are achieved. For example, in Morocco none of the targets in the Five-Year Plan for 1960–64 was realized and the Plan itself was virtually scrapped in 1962. The targets of Nigeria's Six-Year Plan are not being realized. Other African countries, including Dahomey, Gabon, Sierra Leone and Upper Volta, have abandoned or replaced their plans before they were scheduled to end. Some have had to extend the periods of their plans when it proved impossible to implement them in the time originally set. As this book was going to press, the UAR announced that it would be necessary to extend the period of its Second Five-Year Plan to seven years in order to reach plan targets. In Latin America, also, significant deviations of actual from planned development are common. Thus, there is little prospect that Venezuela will achieve the 8 per cent annual growth rate called for by its 1963–66 Plan; Colombia's four-year development plan appears to have fallen far short of its targets, and Chile and Ecuador are encountering difficulties in carrying out their ten-year plans.

Nor is the inability to implement plans a problem only for countries with mixed economies. Although plan targets of countries which are members of the Council of Economic Mutual Assistance (COMECON) have been kept at fairly constant levels, growth rates have been declining. Among COMECON's eight active members—the Soviet Union, Poland, Czechoslovakia, East Germany, Hungary, Rumania, Bulgaria and Mongolia—annual growth rates have fallen from 13.3 per cent in 1951–55 to 10.4 per cent in 1955–56 and to 8.6 per cent in 1961–63.[3] Even Yugoslavia, which has been more successful than most developing countries in fulfilling plan targets, ran into difficulties in 1961 and 1962 and had to abandon its Five-Year Plan. Nevertheless, the plan implementation record of the socialized countries, especially that of Yugoslavia and more recently Rumania, is far better than the record of most mixed-economy countries.

Any attempt to judge the success or failure of a development plan raises questions about the validity of the criteria used to make the

[2] *Economic Times*, October 11, 1964.

[3] *New York Times*, March 11, 1965 (reporting on an article in *International Affairs*, published in Moscow).

judgment. There are those who contend that the proper test of a plan is not whether it achieved targets, but whether it was instrumental in getting development projects and programs started, advanced or completed, or in getting policies and measures adopted when these things would not have been done without the plan. They feel, therefore, that a plan has not failed if it has achieved results in one or more sectors and not in others. Moreover, they consider the procedure by which a plan is formulated a sufficient good in itself to justify a plan because it stimulates planners and others to think in terms of co-ordinating a nation's development efforts for a longer period than was customary. Those who feel this way tend to believe that almost any plan is better than no plan.

There is no denying that most if not all plans produce some worthwhile results. In this sense, no plan can be said to have failed in all aspects and almost any plan can be considered to be a step—however short—toward promoting development. But aside from the inherent difficulty of determining whether certain things were done because of a plan which would not have been done without it, the proposed standard is inadequate because it compares a plan with no plan at all. This approach may be justifiable for a first plan, although in the light of what is known about planning it is debatable that it is even then; but it can hardly be accepted as a test for later plans. It is demanding too little to ask whether a plan merely improved results somewhat over no plan, especially when performance has been palpably poorer than it might have been under prevailing conditions. A more realistic measure of plan implementation is the extent to which reasonable plan targets have been achieved. The record reveals that among less developed countries only a very few have succeeded in more or less consistently achieving reasonable plan targets over a period of a decade or more.[4]

---

[4] By "reasonable" targets is meant those which competent planners determine are within the capacity of a country's resources and other capabilities. This excludes the plans of some countries whose targets are so patently overambitious that there is little chance from the outset that they will be attained. It is thus appropriate to ask whether plan targets were fixed on the basis of realistic evaluations of the likely level of resources, the efficiency of the public administration and government leaders' will to advance development; and whether, given the plan targets and existing circumstances, it would have been possible through appropriate action within the reach of the political authorities to achieve the targets. Because the first approach discussed above reflects satisfaction with little, it can lead to resignation if not complacency; because the second approach is postulated on the supposition that something has gone wrong when reasonable targets are not

Sectoral Shortfalls

Countries which fail to meet reasonable plan targets almost always have the greatest shortfalls in agriculture. For instance, not more than 83 per cent of the production target for agriculture is expected to be achieved during India's Third Five-Year Plan period as against 90 per cent of the target for industry. While many of Spain's four-year development plan targets were easily reached and even exceeded in the first year of the Plan, agricultural production declined by 3 per cent.[5] At the end of Pakistan's First Five Year Plan, it was found that the greatest successes had been scored in the industrial sector; in agriculture, only about half the planned investment had been carried out with large shortfalls in output. Similar relationships are generally found in other countries.

Since agriculture's contribution to the Gross Domestic Product of most less developed countries is high—e.g., it ranges from 34 to 56 per cent in the developing countries in the ECAFE region—the failure of agriculture to attain targets is often the main factor accounting for lower than planned growth rates. Thus, ECAFE reported that it is the poor performance of the agricultural sector which largely explains the failure of most economies of the region to grow as rapidly as desired.[6] Not only does a lagging agricultural sector reduce output directly; it

---

achieved, it can lead to a search for the factors which resulted in the shortfalls and to the accumulation of information based on experience which can be put to good use later.

If targets in a plan are not so unrealistically high that they are beyond reach or so low that they are too easily fulfilled, they constitute as good a measuring device as one is likely to find for determining the success or failure of plan implementation. That is why they are almost universally used for the purpose. Nevertheless, they have shortcomings. For example, although shortfalls from realistic plan targets must be considered failures, whatever the cause, fulfillment or overfulfillment does not necessarily signify success in implementing plans. The plan may have had little or nothing to do with the results. Thus, output in the Philippines, particularly in the private sector, has increased to the level of targets in various Philippine plans. But since the plans have never been adequately implemented or even adopted by the Government in most cases, the plans have not appreciably influenced the rate of growth. Perhaps it might be said of these plans that they were good forecasts but it can hardly be claimed that plan targets have been "fulfilled" or that Philippine development plans have been successfully carried out.

[5] *Financial Times*, February 24, 1965.

[6] UN. ECAFE. "Economic Development and Planning in Asia and the Far East," *Economic Bulletin for Asia and the Far East*, December 1964, p. 21.

also exerts a depressing influence on other economic sectors. In the ECAFE countries,

> lack of agricultural raw materials has tended to reduce the volume of current production in certain industries. Balance of payments difficulties, arising from increased imports and/or decreased exports of agricultural products (especially foodstuffs), have reduced the foreign exchange funds available for financing imports of both industrial raw materials and capital goods, thus adversely influencing both the current and future level of industrial activity.[7]

The socialized countries have also been brought to the realization that they must allocate a greater proportion of investment funds to agriculture than they have in the past if their economies are to expand more rapidly. For example, the First Secretary of Poland's Communist Party has stated that the failure to earmark more resources for farming accounts for the fact that

> agricultural production has turned out to be a bottleneck in our national economy and the main cause of the troubles we are now facing both on domestic and foreign markets.[8]

In the mixed economies, performance in realizing industrial targets is almost always better in the private than in the public sector. However, while the private sector may fulfill more of its targets in a plan than the public sector, increases in private investment and output are likely to occur in industrial branches whose growth was not envisioned in development plans. As a typical case, in the first two years of India's Third Five-Year Plan, total investments by private entrepreneurs apparently kept pace with Plan expectations, but there were nevertheless serious shortfalls from planned investment in the machine tool, cement, fertilizer and metallurgical branches of the private industrial sector. Consequently, the actual composition of private investment is turning out in India, as it often does in other countries, to be substantially different from what is called for in the Plan. Nevertheless, in many countries which have expanded output and income, it is the growth of the private sector—often in ways inimical to plan provisions—which accounts for most of the increase. This has been true, for example, in Pakistan, the Philippines and Thailand, among other countries.

[7] *Ibid.*, p. 4.
[8] *New York Times,* December 15, 1963.

MANIFESTATIONS OF FAILURE

Failure to carry out development plans may manifest itself in a variety of ways. Sometimes, there is an overemphasis on financial targets to the detriment of physical targets; sometimes, a country demonstrates a chronic inability to invest in soundly conceived targets. There are almost always extended delays in the execution of projects and programs, and higher than expected costs. Frequently, also, inferior construction and the selection of low-yield projects aggravate difficulties. Finally, after projects are completed, there may be an inability to make full use of new facilities.

Overemphasis on Financial Targets

Because some governments consider investment virtually synonymous with development, they have emphasized the fulfillment of the financial investment targets in their plans rather than the physical output targets which the investments are aimed at achieving. They have sometimes seemed to act as though the attainment of production targets follows automatically, or with minor additional effort, the realization of financial investment targets. Thus, the Indian Planning Commission has been criticized for talking and behaving as though the primary goal of the development effort was to reach a certain level of investment rather than a certain level of production:

> This is, however, to mistake the means for the objective: the fundamental *objective* of the plan is to attain the higher levels of output, and it is these levels of future output which have to be kept in balance as between one product and another, if the plan is to be a coherent one. The capital expenditures are a very important means of helping to attain these outputs, but they are not an objective in themselves; if some other method of raising output could be discovered during the plan period (e.g., by the use of better seeds instead of costly irrigation schemes) then the essence of the plan would be fulfilled, even if the capital expenditure were far below the original figures.[9]

The orientation toward achieving financial targets has frequently led, in other countries as well as in India, to the neglect of physical

[9] Reddaway, W. B. "Importance of Time Lags for Economic Planning," p. 227.

planning and programing. Thus, Burma's Ministry of National Planning reported that, in Burma,

> executing agencies have their operations so exceedingly oriented toward financial planning that the physical aspects of project implementation are relegated to a minor position.[10]

In governments which measure plan achievements primarily on the basis of how quickly instead of on how well money is spent, the spending rate is likely to be higher than the ability to evaluate and prepare soundly conceived projects and programs. Not surprisingly, therefore, financial targets in these cases are often fulfilled or overfulfilled, while physical output targets record serious shortfalls. For instance, in India, mounting plan outlays have not always been accompanied or followed by the realization of physical targets. In Nepal, also, preoccupation with investment

> led to the expenditure targets being attained in some programmes though the physical targets in most cases remained beyond any immediate grasp.[11]

Underspending

Although Nepal sought to increase investment, it was unable to put all the funds it had available to effective use. During the First Plan period in 1957–61, the Government was able to spend only a third of original planned expenditures.[12] Although performance improved, only two-thirds of budgeted development funds were spent in the period of the Three-Year Plan in 1962/63–1964/65.

Such lack of "absorptive capacity," which essentially reflects an inability to invest in soundly conceived development programs and projects that can be carried out well and operated economically upon completion, is a common characteristic of less developed countries.[13] In

---

[10] Burma. Ministry of National Planning. *Second Four-Year Plan for the Union of Burma* (1961/62 to 1964/65), p. 88.

[11] Pant, Y. P. "Nepal's Planned Development," p. 475.

[12] Shah, Rishikesh. *On Planning and Development*, p. 13.

[13] But it can also be found in more advanced countries. According to France's *Cour des Comptes,* administrative bottlenecks in the French Government accounted for the fact that, in 1960, 44 per cent of the money voted for navigable waterways, 62 per cent for flood control, 42 per cent for fishing ports and 78 per cent for administrative buildings remained unspent (*Washington Post,* May 30, 1963).

Asia, Africa and Latin America, many countries have found it impossible to invest all their available funds in well-prepared projects and programs. Criticism has been heard in India's Parliament "every year regarding overbudgeting and lapses," i.e., the inability of expenditures to reach the level of budgetary allocations.[14] In Iraq, Syria and other countries in the region, underspending has been frequent. Morocco has had to carry forward large unspent sums from one anuual budget to the next. So have Ghana and Nigeria. Tunisia and other African countries have been able to spend only a part of foreign funds made available to them, while in Latin America, also, "domestic appropriations and available foreign financing often are not spent within the original timetable." [15]

Some countries find it difficult to spend both domestic and foreign financial resources; others find it much more difficult to spend domestic than foreign funds. For example, Burma found it relatively easy to commit and spend foreign exchange because it required little more of operating organizations than the calling for tenders and the awarding of contracts for imports.

> Their outlays tended to lag, rather, on the domestic side where more action on their own part was called for. Thus the Telecommunications Department accumulated vast stores of communications equipment from abroad considerably in advance of completion of the buildings in which the equipment was to be installed. Much spoilage resulted, and it was necessary later, after underground cables for the new dial telephone system in Rangoon had been laid, to rip them up and replace them.[16]

However, many countries find it hard to make productive use of foreign resources available to them. Thus, donor nations and international lending agencies frequently find that recipient or borrowing countries are unable to draw down proceeds of grants and loans without long delays. In a study which the World Bank made of 255 of its loans to member countries with original closing dates [17] prior to

[14] UN. Inter-Regional Workshop on Problems of Budget Classification, etc., *Relationship Between Planning and Government Budgeting in Developing Countries* [Part II], p. 16.

[15] OAS. Inter-American Economic and Social Council, Special Committee I, etc. *Programming for Development: Five Urgent Problems*, p. 9.

[16] Walinsky, Louis J. "Burma," pp. 42–43.

[17] The closing date is the last date on which loan proceeds may be withdrawn by a borrower.

June 30, 1963, it found that 60 per cent of the loans required one or
more extensions and 20 per cent required three or more extensions. The
study also disclosed a marked slowing down in the annual speed with
which the loans were being drawn down by borrowers during 1961–63
as compared with 1957–60. What makes these results especially noteworthy is that they refer to loans which were made in many cases for
projects in relatively advanced stages of preparation and readiness to
proceed with execution.

Repeated shortfalls in spending available development funds are a
certain indication that something is wrong with the way plans are
formulated or implemented or both. Aside from random causes, like
the illness of a project manager or consultant or failure to obtain
foreign deliveries on time, a variety of reasons may account for the
"inability to spend." To begin with, many operating ministries, departments and agencies are unable to assess with reasonable precision their
capacity to disburse funds effectively. When they prepare budgetary
estimates they tend to be unduly optimistic about how much they can
invest well. This can lead to highly inflated budgetary estimates. For
instance, Iraq proposed to spend twice as much in the 1964/65 fiscal
year as it had spent the year before. Since there was a scarcity of
well-prepared projects and limited construction capacity besides, it
was almost inevitable that there would be shortfalls. According to
Syria's Ministry of Planning, inability to utilize budgeted funds in that
country was also due to "the appropriation of relatively large amounts
to projects whose studies were not completed." [18]

The head of Pakistan's Planning Board attributed slow disbursement
of budgetary investment allocations in his country to "poor phasing of
projects or the failure to adhere to time schedules"; [19] and in East
Pakistan, chronic underspending was attributed to a lack of administrative organization, an absence of effective programs and projects, and
a lack of technicians and other human resources. [20] According to
one Finance Minister in Ceylon, disbursements of budgeted investment funds in his country were not made when expected mainly
because of

[18] Syrian Arab Republic. Ministry of Planning. *Annual Report on the Economic
and Social Development Plan, 1960/1961*, p. 13.
[19] Hussain, Z. "Organization and Responsibilities of the Pakistan Planning Board,"
p. 28.
[20] UN. ECAFE. "Some Social Aspects of Development Planning in the ECAFE
Region," p. 13.

the lack of trained staff, the inadequacy of existing organizations to meet the increased demands of development and the dilatory effects of certain existing financial regulations.[21]

In Morocco, large proportions of the funds allocated to projects were not utilized because many ministries and agencies were unable to meet the construction schedules laid down for projects,[22] while Tunisia found it difficult to use U.S. credits because it was unaccustomed to U.S. specifications and working methods.[23] Foreign loan funds to Colombia have gone unused for long periods because autonomous or semiautonomous entities have been unable, usually because of inflation and failure to get government approval for compensatory price increases for the services they sell, to assemble enough pesos to pay local expenses for projects whose foreign exchange costs are to be financed by a loan from abroad.[24]

Underspending can increase development costs, reduce investment and growth rates, and distort the planned pattern of investment. Besides indirect losses on idle funds, a borrower may lose money directly from delayed use of loan proceeds because commitment or other interest charges generally must be paid on loans even before the proceeds are used. When disposable funds are only partly spent, resources which might have been used for other projects and programs are immobilized, thereby reducing the rate of investment and, frequently, the rate of growth and development. Inability to use proceeds of foreign and international loans or grants over extended periods may result in their lapsing. Since such loans and grants are generally tied to a specific project or program, the proceeds usually cannot be transferred to others. When a government attempts to use unspent domestic investment funds by transferring them from operating organizations which cannot spend their appropriations to those which can, the resulting shift may alter the planned composition of investment. Even without such transfers, underspending tends to distort planned investment since the rate of underspending usually varies among operating organizations. For example, the Moroccan Ministry of Agriculture used as little as 30 per cent of its annual budgetary investment allotments,

[21] Snodgrass, Donald R. *Ceylon: An Export Economy in Transition*, pp. 36–37. (Quoting Felix R. Dias Bandaranaike. *Budget and Economic Growth*. Presented to Parliament on July 27, 1961, p. 10.)

[22] Waterston, Albert. *Planning in Morocco*, pp. 43–44.

[23] *Financial Times*, November 26, 1963.

[24] *New York Times*, November 17, 1963.

while the Ministry of Public Works spent 75 or 80 per cent of the funds made available to it.[25] In most countries of Latin America, also,

> the Ministry of Public Works has been the most proficient at project preparation and execution. Having more experience with construction projects than other operating ministries, it has generally been able to spend an average of 70 to 80 percent of the appropriations granted it. In contrast, those ministries now faced with the tasks of investments in health, community development, and others, often find it difficult to spend as much as half of their investment appropriations.[26]

Since planned public investment patterns rarely coincide with the relative spending capacity of operating organizations, uneven rates of spending frequently play havoc with plan targets and planned composition of investment.

Delays in Execution

When financial outlays lag behind targets, projects and programs generally take longer to complete than was expected. Long delays in executing projects are frequent, in socialized as well as in mixed-economy countries. Thus, average construction time of high-priority plants in Poland took two years longer than had been foreseen in the Six-Year Plan.[27] Ex-Premier Khrushchev complained that while chemical plants usually are built in two years in Western countries, in the USSR,

> because of shortcomings in the organization of construction we build some plants in four or five years.[28]

Similar lags are common in other countries. In Ghana, Syria and Chile, among many other countries in their respective regions, projects have taken longer to finish than was expected. The World Bank survey mission to Spain reported that

> in several sectors, many projects are begun with limited funds so that all of them take a long time to complete. . . . The average

[25] Waterston, Albert. *Planning in Morocco*, p. 43.
[26] OAS. Inter-American Economic and Social Council, Special Committee I, etc. *Programming for Development: Five Urgent Problems*, pp. 9–10.
[27] Montias, John M. *Central Planning in Poland*, p. 66.
[28] *Washington Post*, August 13, 1964, quoting the then Premier.

time for completion appears to be about three years, which it should be possible to cut in half.[29]

According to Iran's central planning agency, the Plan Organization,

a majority of Plan Organization's industrial projects have taken significantly longer to execute than originally scheduled.[30]

The Mid-Term Appraisal of the Third Five-Year Plan by India's Planning Commission made it clear that many important projects scheduled to be completed by the end of the plan period in 1965–66 would have to be carried over into the fourth plan period. Another Indian study indicated that three-fourths of the private projects surveyed experienced unforeseen construction delays which averaged eight months above their expected period of gestation.[31] Delays were even longer in the public sector. For steel plants, installation of various units lagged from 13 to 18 months, and for heavy electrical plants, from one to two years. Similar delays occurred in the completion of fertilizer, machine tool, alloy and tool steel, and other projects.[32] In fact, few projects progressed on schedule; completion on time was a rarity.[33]

The costs of delays in carrying out projects and programs are higher than less developed countries can afford. If interest during construction is included, every extension of the period of execution adds to the cost.[34] But interest is only part of the cost to an economy; there are also the annual losses in production foregone and income unearned. Delays in completing a project which is to supply a commodity for export can reduce foreign exchange earnings substantially. It has been estimated, for example, that a delay of one year in starting Kiriburu iron ore exports to Japan from Vizagapatam in India was equivalent to a loss of about $20 million in foreign exchange. The cost to a country of delays in completing an import-substitution project can also be great. Thus, India paid out considerable amounts of foreign exchange which might have been saved, and lost potential farm output besides, when

[29] IBRD. *Economic Development of Spain*, p. 62.

[30] Iran. Plan Organization. *Review of the Second Seven Year Plan Program of Iran*, p. 72.

[31] *Economic Times*, November 11, 1963.

[32] *Economic Times*, December 25, 1964.

[33] *Economic Times*, October 26, 1963.

[34] Where capital can earn (or as economists say, when the opportunity cost of capital is) 10 to 12 per cent, as is true in many developing countries, the cost of completing a project in 5 or 6 years instead of 3, may add 25 to 35 per cent to the economic cost of a project.

fertilizer plants were not completed as scheduled. Because of the delay, foreign exchange had to be used to import fertilizers. Since foreign exchange was scarce, only limited amounts of fertilizer could be imported and this resulted in limiting increases in agricultural output.[35]

In countries where prices are rising, extension of scheduled construction periods also raises costs above what they would be if projects were executed in time. There are other ways in which costs may increase, either directly or indirectly, because of long delays in carrying out projects. Thus, even before a project is completed, maintenance of, or repairs to, insufficiently protected parts finished early may be required. Changes in technology or in the market for a product may occur which alter the value of a project as originally designed. In Spain, for example,

> a conspicuous case of this is the new railway lines which have been and are still being built. Some of them, when first conceived, may very well have had a function, but with increasing use of the automobile and the airplane, the need is rather to reduce the number of rail lines than to add to it.[36]

High Costs

Because of delays in executing projects, as well as for other reasons, actual costs of projects often turn out to be substantially higher than originally estimated. During Pakistan's First Five Year Plan period, for instance, final costs in some cases were as much as 260 per cent above those predicted in original project reports, with the average about 160 per cent.[37] According to a high official of Pakistan's Planning Commission, cost increases for important projects in the Second Five Year Plan period have ranged from between two to nine times above original cost estimates.[38] Iran's planners reported that

> it is the rule rather than the exception that . . . [industrial and mining] projects have cost significantly more than their original

---

[35] Patel, H. M. "Some Administrative Problems," pp. 299–300.

[36] IBRD. *Economic Development of Spain*, p. 62.

[37] Bell, David E. "Allocating Development Resources: Some Observations Based on Pakistan Experience," pp. 96–97.

[38] Haq, Mahbub ul. *Strategy of Economic Planning: A Case Study of Pakistan*, p. 193.

estimates. In other words, we have bought less for our money than we thought we would.[39]

The same situation prevails in many if not most other countries. According to Prof. Arthur Lewis, one-time Economic Adviser to the Government of Ghana, in that country,

> projects cost twice as much as they should, contractors make enormous profits, works are badly designed or badly built, and everything takes much longer to achieve than was expected.[40]

In Greece, large public works often cost too much, besides being badly designed and delayed in construction; [41] while in the United Arab Republic, expenditures for projects have constantly exceeded original cost estimates.[42] Cost estimates for the three Indian publicly owned steel plants, their townships, ore mines and quarries were typically wide of the mark. The Second Plan first provided 4,250 million rupees to finance their construction, but estimates had to be increased, first to 5,590 million and then to 6,200 million rupees.[43] The foreign exchange for the plants, which was initially estimated at about 2,290 million rupees, had to be raised to 3,020 million rupees.[44] At the end of the first two years of India's Third Five-Year Plan, estimates indicated that, in the public sector, costs had risen above original estimates by 23 per cent for industrial projects, by 27 per cent for transport and communications projects and by 38 per cent for minerals projects.[45] In the private sector, they were 25 per cent higher.[46]

Besides being costlier than expected, public sector projects often cost much more than similar ventures in the private sector. During Pakistan's First Five Year Plan period, for example, the cost of industrial projects was frequently "higher than the costs of execution of similar projects in the private sector." [47] According to Iran's Plan

[39] Iran. Plan Organization. *Review of the Second Seven Year Plan Program of Iran,* p. 71.

[40] Lewis, W. Arthur. "On Assessing a Development Plan," p. 5.

[41] Columbia University School of Law. *Public International Development Financing in Greece,* p. 112.

[42] Wheelock, Keith. *Nasser's New Egypt: A Critical Analysis,* p. 172.

[43] India. Planning Commission. *Third Five-Year Plan,* p. 454.

[44] UN. Seminar on Industrial Programming. *India's Experience in Industrial Planning,* p. 39.

[45] *Economic Weekly,* Vol. XV, No. 50, December 14, 1963, p. 2048.

[46] *Economic Times,* December 25, 1964.

[47] Pakistan. Planning Commission. *Report of the Panel of Economists on the Second Five Year Plan* (1960–65), p. 26.

Organization, publicly owned plants in that country were often more expensive to build than private ones:

> A comparison of the investment costs of the Plan Organization and private projects in the textile, cement and oil extraction industries shows that it costs the country much more to build these plants under public than under private entrepreneurship.[48]

In India, also, iron ore mines have cost much more than similar enterprises in the private sector. As a consequence, costs of production are often uncompetitive.

In many countries, public sector projects have proved to be unprofitable for long periods after completion and have had to be heavily subsidized by their government, thereby reducing the amount of funds available for development. This was true in Iraq, for example, where out of five large government owned cement, textile and sugar plants operating in the early 1960's, three showed losses. At the same time smaller, privately owned plants operating in the same sectors were producing substantial profits.

Inferior Construction

Besides delays in completing projects and higher than expected costs, projects are often shoddily built. Vaguely defined or otherwise inadequate or inappropriate specifications, poor siting, the use of defective or other improper materials, poor workmanship, construction under adverse weather or other conditions, or inadequate quality control and supervision of contractors may result in the construction of works or facilities which either cannot perform as expected or soon deteriorate. Thus, in one Latin American country welded seams of pipe for the pressure penstock and inverted syphons connecting canals on a hydroelectric project developed so many leaks that the pipe appeared to be part of an irrigation scheme instead of a system for funneling water to electrical equipment. In Cambodia, a road originally estimated to cost $15 million and completed for $30 million deteriorated so much in two years that repairs costing $2.7 million had to be made.[49] Because of defective concrete work in the construction of the Rourkela

[48] Iran. Plan Organization. *Review of the Second Seven Year Plan Program of Iran,* p. 72.
[49] *Washington Post,* June 7, 1961.

steel plant in India, additional work at an estimated cost of 800,000 rupees ($160,000) had to be carried out.[50]

Low Yields

In many countries, also, considerable amounts of capital are invested in large projects with little prospect of more than negligible returns. The World Bank survey mission to Spain suggested that some irrigation projects under way in that country were unlikely to yield results commensurate with their cost.[51] During the period of Pakistan's First Five Year Plan, officials tended to overemphasize big projects and to ignore small ones which were crucial for increasing agricultural production. In part, this could be attributed to the preference of foreign lending and donor agencies for large projects, since one large project is simpler to finance than a series of smaller ones. But the tendency of officials to concentrate on large projects went beyond the requirements of foreign aid and lending agencies.[52]

Unused Capacity

Inadequate utilization of completed projects is another important reason for disappointing results obtained from development plans. Time may cure this problem, but a country's economy may in the meantime derive little benefit from investment, or worse, may be subjected to difficult strains. Thus, overinvestment in industry to the neglect of agriculture has caused considerable pressure on the balance of payments of some countries. In the Philippines it was estimated that, because of overexpansion, existing industrial plants in 1957 were operating at a level of only about 50 per cent of rated capacity. But to raise operations to only 70 per cent of capacity would have strained the balance of payments because it would have required a substantial increase in foreign exchange for raw material imports from 55 to 73 per cent of total merchandise imports. At the end of the fourth year of Pakistan's First Five Year Plan, many of Pakistan's large-scale industrial plants were also operating at an average of 50 per cent of capacity. In Pakistan, too, increases in plant operations would have required

---

[50] *Economic Times*, December 25, 1964.
[51] IBRD. *Economic Development of Spain*, p. 63.
[52] Waterston, Albert. *Planning in Pakistan*, pp. 61–62.

considerable increased expenditures of scarce foreign exchange. Idle industrial capacity in India and Taiwan has also been substantial at times. Because of these conditions in countries in Asia, the ECAFE quite understandably considered that

> the question is whether fuller utilization of existing plants should not be given priority over installation of new industrial undertakings, or whether agriculture should not be allowed to catch up with industry.[53]

While incorrect assessment of the market can lead to overinvestment and unused capacity, there are many instances where underutilization of existing plants is due to inadequate provision for required complementary investment. In some cases, no provision has been made for related facilities or works; in others, where provision has been made, the complementary works may not be completed in time. In either event, there is a period during which little or no benefit accrues from a project. In Spain, for example, benefits from irrigation projects have been delayed because one agency with funds completed its part, while another agency with less money was unable to carry out its part of a project in time.[54] And

> in this category also fall[s] . . . a costly housing project far out of Tehran destined for government employees where out of the 1,000 apartments completed to date not one has been occupied. . . . There is no road leading to the site, there are no shops, and there is no water. Neither is there a school.[55]

In some countries, projects handled by one ministry have been completed before a program or project for the supply of raw materials handled by another ministry. Thus, a ramie plant initiated by Indonesia's Ministry of Industry was completed three years before the complementary project to expand ramie cultivation was begun by the Ministry of Agriculture. Meanwhile, since domestic production of ramie was sufficient to keep the factory operating for only six days a year, more expensive raw material had to be imported. Similarly, production in a government coal mine, in which new equipment had been installed, had to be cut back because inadequate provision had

[53] UN. ECAFE. "Economic Development and Planning in Asia and the Far East," *Economic Bulletin for Asia and the Far East,* December 1961, p. 12.

[54] IBRD. *Economic Development of Spain,* pp. 62–63.

[55] Olsen, P. Bjørn and Rasmussen, P. Nørregaard. "An Attempt at Planning in a Traditional State: Iran," p. 234.

been made by the government railroad to haul the coal.[56] The Plan Organization reported that in Iran's publicly owned jute, olive oil, vegetable oil and sugar processing plants, inadequate attention was paid to the need to supply the plants with agricultural raw materials. As a result, there was "a serious problem of getting adequate quantities of acceptable raw materials to operate the plants at high operating rates"; [57] in Nigeria, a canning plant built by the Northern Nigerian Government had to close down because of inadequate supplies of vegetables and fruits; and in Iraq, a government sugar factory constructed to use locally grown sugar beets has had to process imported raw sugar because of the unavailability of domestic supplies, and a publicly owned cigarette factory, built to provide an outlet for domestic tobacco, has had to process imported tobacco because it could not find the right type and quality of tobacco in the country.

In India, also, phasing was imperfect in the public sector. According to the official Committee on Plan Projects:

> Storage capacities of head works of water supply schemes have been expanded without a corresponding increase in the treatment plant, conveying mains or in the distribution system. Buildings in residential colonies are put up much in advance of the services with the result that they remain unoccupied for a long time resulting in loss of revenue and the added consequence of damage to structure by way of pilfering or breakage. Projects are delayed for want of completion of small items which though insignificant from a financial point of view may yet have a halting influence on the project as a whole. Bearings for bridges, sewerage, pumps, etc., can be quoted as examples of this category.[58]

In India's heavy industry, while cement capacity was completed long before it was needed, steel capacity lagged badly.[59] The three publicly owned steel plants in India have been at the core of planned industrial development in that country. Yet in 1961–62, steel output in the three plants was only equal to 48 per cent of their combined capacity. Although 90 per cent of the Bhilai plant's capacity was being utilized,

[56] UN. ECAFE. *Economic Survey of Asia and the Far East, 1961,* p. 113 [citing, Indonesia. State Planning Bureau. *Report on the Execution of the Five-Year (1956–1960) Development Plan,* pp. 188, 208].

[57] Iran. Plan Organization. *Review of the Second Seven Year Plan Program of Iran,* p. 72.

[58] Vedagiri, T. S. "Planning and Programming of Projects Since Independence," p. 21.

[59] Lewis, John P. "India," p. 99.

capacity utilization was 45 per cent in the Durgapur plant and only 29 per cent in the Rourkela plant. In the same year, the privately owned plants at Jamshedpur and Burnpur were producing at 87 per cent of their combined capacity.[60] Since 1961/62, steel ouput in the three plants has continued to be below target. According to the United Nations,

> the continuing gap between output and capacity cannot be explained only by teething troubles of the new plants. Inadequate preparations for the capacity utilization by advance action on raw materials, transport and other services and training of technical and managerial personnel have led to the under-utilization of the capacity. It was not realised that it takes somewhat longer to develop mines and quarries and to establish fully serviceable traffic links than to construct the steel plant proper. . . . Out of the five coal washeries projected in the Second Plan to serve public and private steel plants, only two were ready before the end of the Second Plan period and neither of them achieved rated output capacity. Due to the inadequacy of preparatory studies, a few raw materials reckoned upon from nearby sources of supply were found to be unsuitable. . . . This led to lengthening of transport lead from other sources and added to the strain on . . . railway transport.
>
> . . . The shortage of trained personnel . . . primarily resulted from under-estimation of the requirement. The requirements of senior engineers for the higher supervisory posts and for plants maintenance was estimated at 120. The estimate has been revised to 350. The estimate of junior engineers has been revised from 1,200 to 1,750 while that of skilled workers and operatives has been increased by 2,000 to 19,000.[61]

The failure of one government agency to train personnel needed for completed projects undertaken by another also helps account for much unused capacity. In Iran, as in other countries, schools and hospitals which were built at considerable expense could not operate effectively because teachers and nurses had not been trained by the appropriate agencies for the purpose.[62]

---

[60] UN. Seminar on Industrial Programming. *India's Experience in Industrial Planning,* p. 37.

[61] *Ibid.,* pp. 38–39.

[62] Olsen, P. Bjørn and Rasmussen, P. Nørregaard. "An Attempt at Planning in a Traditional State: Iran," pp. 233–234.

But more often, under-utilization is due to bad planning by the sponsoring agency. For instance, in Spain, where investment in ports has concentrated on construction of quays and breakwaters, wharves have not been utilized adequately for lack of cranes. A comparatively small expenditure for cranes and other equipment would have saved much time in loading and unloading ships and greatly increased the use obtained from ports and, thus, the returns from the investment.[63] In Pakistan, benefits from irrigation and multipurpose projects under the jurisdiction of East Pakistan's Water and Power Development Authority were delayed because officials concentrated most of their attention on the engineering aspects of the projects to the neglect of their agricultural aspects. Thus, when dams and subsidiary canals had been completed, it was often found that feeder canals to farms which were to use the water had not been built and that other preparatory work had not been carried out.

In some countries, inadequate amounts of working capital have prevented public sector plants from operating at high levels. The Iranian Plan Organization, for example,

> found that in estimating the capital requirements for particular projects much too small an allowance has been made for the liquid capital needed to operate the plant after it is built.[64]

While in India,

> lack of foreign exchange for spare parts and raw materials accounted for much under-utilization of existing industrial capacity.[65]

But much more than lack of funds, scarcities of experienced and competent plant managers and other managerial personnel are responsible for unused capacity. Thus, India has a serious shortage of managers in the higher echelons of private industry and commerce, as well as in public sector undertakings. According to the report of an official committee, 20,000 managers were required during the third plan period, but only 12,000 were trained. Consequently, it will be necessary during the fourth plan period to make up the shortfall by

[63] IBRD. *Economic Development of Spain*, p. 63.

[64] Iran. Plan Organization. *Review of the Second Seven Year Plan Program of Iran*, p. 73.

[65] UN. Seminar on Industrial Programming. *India's Experience in Industrial Planning*, p. 41.

training 35,000 managers for industry, commerce, construction and transportation.[66] Some governments are unable to mobilize managers for their enterprises even when they are available because they pay as little as one-fifth or even one-tenth as much as similar private plants for supervisory staff. As a result, government plants in these countries, e.g., Iraq, are unable to obtain experienced management officials who know how to organize procurement, production and sales activities adequately to permit full use of plant capacity.

WHY IMPLEMENTATION LAGS

Many factors, usually in combination, account for a country's lack of attention to physical as well as financial targets, underspending, abnormal delays in executing projects, higher than expected costs, shoddy construction, selection of low yield projects, underuse of completed facilities and, consequently, failure to fulfill plan targets. The catalog of causes of poor plan implementation is long. Some causes are the result of circumstances over which a country has little control. In this category are civil disturbances and political upsets, droughts, excessive rainfall or floods and other natural calamities which interfere with construction or output, and unforeseeable declines in world prices of export commodities which reduce local currency and foreign exchange resources. Sometimes, a country is only able to influence events partially, if at all, as when foreign or international donors and lenders take longer than was expected to make available foreign exchange resources for projects which they had agreed to help finance. Rising foreign and domestic prices and labor costs frequently make planners' estimates wrong, especially when their effect is intensified by undue delays in executing projects.[67] But the lack of success in implementing plans is in large part attributable to poor planning.

Dispersal of Resources

Thus, unduly ambitious plan targets, as well as poor financial controls, account for many failures to carry out projects and achieve

[66] *Economic Times*, February 6, 1965.

[67] Rising prices can affect adversely projects in the private sector as well as those in the public sector. In addition, increased taxes can raise costs and delay completion of private investment projects.

plan targets. In some countries, projects are started without sufficient funds or with the overcommitment of available financial resources. A development effort which may have started with a core of much-needed projects may be augmented greatly with many less essential and dubious schemes which obscure plan objectives and make public investment appear to be moving in all directions at one time. This has happened in Korea during the execution of the Five-Year Economic Development Plan for 1962–66. The OAS has reported that in Latin American countries there is a prevailing tendency

> to scatter investment funds in small amounts among an excessively large number of individual projects. This habit is born of a marked reluctance to withstand political pressure for public works. The practice has the unfortunate result of retarding unnecessarily a large number of projects . . . and [bringing about] . . . a dispersion of resources on many . . . projects from which little fruit can be derived over the short run.[68]

This problem also has had serious effects in the USSR. In 1963, the head of the Soviet State Committee for Construction Affairs severely reprimanded local authorities who permitted construction to begin simultaneously on an excessively large number of projects. The newspaper, *Pravda*, revealed that in the four years ending in 1963, the number of unfinished projects had risen from 160,000 to 195,000. In addition, the value of uncompleted buildings and uninstalled machinery had also risen. As a result, a large part of recent Soviet investment had failed to contribute to current growth.[69]

When funds run out, construction on projects stops all along the line and no new projects, however promising, can be started for a long time. One example from Iran is typical of similar situations in other countries. According to the planners themselves, the

> Plan Organization has started projects before it had all the necessary money to finance them. Consequently, the resource reductions of the past year have forced a cancelling of projects not yet started and [the] cutting back [of] others. [As a result of the shortage of funds] there is no room whatsoever for thinking of starting new construction projects for another three and one-half years. This is a pity, for no plan can foresee *all* possible projects at the start, and

[68] OAS. Inter-American Economic and Social Council, Special Committee I, etc. *Programming for Development: Five Urgent Problems*, pp. 10–11.
[69] *New York Times*, July 14, 1963.

some funds should be reserved in all sectors for adding new
projects as time goes by.[70]

In the USSR, enterprises and economic organizations had so overspent
and overcommitted themselves that Ex-Premier Khrushchev found it
desirable to suggest to the 22nd Communist Party Congress that a
moratorium on all new capital construction be imposed for a year.[71]
More recently, the Hungarian Government had to counteract the
spread of its investment resources over too many projects by ordering a
reduction of one-third in large investment projects.[72]

When governments are forced to cut down on the number of
projects in process of execution in this way, it is very difficult to do so
without upsetting the smooth implementation of the plan. Where they
do not reduce the number of projects to conform to the level of
resources, budgetary deficits may cause inflationary pressures to develop, as well as pressures on the balance of payments. In either event,
achievement of targets is likely to be more difficult.

Lack of Discipline

Another major reason for lags in implementation is the widespread
failure of governments to maintain the discipline implicit in their plans.
In many countries plans govern actual developments to a much smaller
degree than one would suppose from a reading of progress reports.
What is planned and what is done often bear no discernible relation to
each other. This was true, for example in colonial Nigeria, where
development plans had only a limited effect in determining what
developments in fact occurred.[73] It has also been true of other parts of
Africa. Thus, most of the important economic expansion of colonial
East Africa occurred independently of the development plans in the
area and "owes nothing to them."[74]

Most countries make only a token effort at co-ordinating fiscal, price,
monetary, credit and other economic and financial policies with the
requirements implied in their plans. Plans are prepared by a planning
agency in one corner of a government and policy is made by various

[70] Iran. Plan Organization. *Review of the Second Seven Year Plan Program
of Iran,* pp. 73–74.
[71] Goldman, Marshall I. "Economic Controversy in the Soviet Union," p. 500.
[72] *New York Times,* January 10, 1965.
[73] Schatz, Sayre P. "The Influence of Planning on Development: The Nigerian
Experience," pp. 460–462.
[74] Great Britain. *East African Royal Commission, 1953–1955, Report,* p. 95.

bodies in other corners. There is usually little communication among them. In the Philippines, for example,

> the policies and programs of the government's departments and agencies, up to the 1960's, bore no relation to the provisions of the country's development plans. The Budget Commission prepared fiscal programs with priorities that differed from those included in the plans. The Central Bank ignored the plans in controlling credit and in allocating foreign exchange. The Development Bank adopted its own lending program. The other departments and agencies proceeded as if the plans did not exist.[75]

If, as in Venezuela, an import licensing system exists, there is little evidence that licenses are issued in accordance with national development plans. In most developing countries, if projects and programs are carried out, they are unlikely to follow the priorities implicit in national plans.

Well-established criteria and procedures for including public sector projects and programs in a plan are the exception instead of the rule; if procedures have been established, they are more often "honor'd in the breach than the observance." The selection of highway, power, port and other projects is more often than not based on political decisions taken with little reference to the economic merits of the projects or the available alternatives. Political leaders, accustomed to look on public works as political plums or as means of providing employment in favored constituencies, do not easily understand and accept the concept of public works as infrastructure for development. In Iraq,

> Nuri-al-Sa'id, frequent Prime Minister (and even when not in office, the key figure in Iraqi politics), thought of development in terms of constructing more and more physical works which could be 'turned over' to the people in elaborate dedication ceremonies. He failed to realize that these physical structures provided only some of the tools for progress and did not in themselves constitute development.[76]

The maintenance of traditional ways of behavior frequently means that plans are not taken seriously and that they have little chance of being carried out. In Burma, for instance, casual decisions made by political leaders, especially the Prime Minister, disrupted efforts to implement

---

[75] Wilcox, Clair. *Planning and Execution of Economic Development in Southeast Asia,* p. 10.
[76] Tesdell, Loren. "Planning for Technical Assistance: Iraq and Jordan," p. 394.

plans.[77] At the last moment in the annual programing process, the Prime Minister occasionally superimposed new projects on those already included in the plan which

> put intolerable strains on the program and required the planners either to scramble for new resources or to rephase other essential projects already incorporated in the program—and sometimes to lose control over program outcomes.[78]

In most countries, the central planning agency is politically weaker than the operating ministries, departments and agencies. Operating organizations usually get their way regardless of allocations in a plan. In some Latin American countries, co-ordination of ministry programs is made especially difficult because individual ministers sometimes operate like potentates who do not feel bound by cabinet decisions. This has also been true in some African and Asian countries. For example, in Senegal, operating ministries acted as they wished with the result that the priorities outlined in the Plan were upset.[79] In Ceylon, also, there was little unity in the Cabinet and each ministry put forward projects which often were unrelated to plans.

In some countries, one ministry, department or agency may be more effective than others in preparing and carrying out projects. In these cases, the criterion for allocating funds tends to be based on the operating organizations' efficiency rather than on actual needs. This happened in Malaya. The Road Department was able to build highways so rapidly that it outran operating organizations in other sectors. As a consequence, the Plan was not followed. During the first Plan period in Pakistan, almost every ministry and department sought and sometimes obtained approval of projects which had not been envisaged in the Plan. Organizations which could submit a large number of projects had an advantage over those which could not. Politically powerful agencies received backing for their projects despite opposition of the central planning agency. While the Planning Commission is widely accepted today and tries to allocate resources for projects objectively, according to a high planning official,

> the process by which the competing claims of various departments are finally resolved and accommodated in the Plan is by no

---

[77] Hagen, Everett (ed). *Planning Economic Development,* p. 24.
[78] Walinsky, Louis J. "Burma," p. 44.
[79] Chaigneau, Yves (Conseiller Technique au Secretariat d'Etat au Plan et au Développement). *Réflexions Sur La Planification au Sénégal,* p. 18.

means a perfect one and it is still weighted in favour of the more
aggressive and well-organised departments which may not always
be the more deserving ones.[80]

In Burma, also, high priority projects were held back because departments and ministries concerned lacked enthusiasm or capability.

> Programs for manufacturing industry and electric power, on the
> other hand, went forward on an accelerated and enlarged scale,
> and in a rather undisciplined way, because of the drive and power
> status of the responsible minister who was able to obtain not only
> larger allocations but also a greater degree of freedom in their use
> than had been provided in the plan.[81]

In many countries, reductions in requests for funds by operating
organizations are more likely to be made by the budgetary authority
than the planning agency. Such reductions often are not in line with
what an existing plan requires. In practice, therefore, there is frequently little connection between plans and budgets. For example,
during the period of Morocco's first Five-Year Plan for 1960–64, the
capital budget was supposed to include only projects which came
within the purview of the Plan. Nevertheless, projects were included
which had no discernible relationship to it. If the highest dignitary in
the country unexpectedly promised a community a new road or
facility, the project was simply added to the budget.[82] Nor were
semipublic agencies like the National Development Board or the Office
for Industrial Research and Participation, both of which financed
development projects, noticeably restrained by the Plan.[83] Experience
shows that autonomous or semiautonomous agencies are particularly
difficult to subject to the discipline of a plan.

Because plans seem to have little influence on government decisions
in some countries, the point is sometimes made that these countries can
hardly be said to be planning. When the Chairman of the National
Economic Council in the Philippines resigned, his report to the
President opened with the statement that, in the Philippines,

> it is meaningless, at this stage, to talk of national planning. It is
> meaningless because neither the Philippine government nor any of

[80] Haq, Mahbub ul (Chief of the Perspective Planning Section in the Planning
Commission). *Planning Agencies*, p. 4.
[81] Walinsky, Louis J. "Burma," pp. 37–38.
[82] Waterston, Albert. *Planning in Pakistan*, p. 43.
[83] *Ibid.*

its agencies is in any position to draw up a meaningful national plan. The whole public administration system . . . militates . . . against *implementing* a plan. The 'five year plans' we have had during the whole post-war period were not really plans but merely statements of general aspirations. . . . There has really been no national economic planning in this country. The government organization is not capable of it.[84]

This is apparently also the consensus among most students of Philippine planning.[85]

Similar comments have been made for other countries. Even India has not escaped them. Because the Government has not always manifested a sense of urgency in taking measures needed to execute plans and to counteract activities and events which impede implementation, some Indian economists have taken the position that India does not really plan. Thus, one well-known Indian economist wrote:

> It is my contention that, in spite of all claims to the contrary, planning as such does not operate in India today. There are only schemes of public expenditure or of aid to private or co-operative enterprise. There is no co-ordinated conscious effort to lead development along predefined lines. As a consequence, development proceeds largely as if in a *laissez faire* regime. . . .[86]

If this be a case in which a point is carried too far, it at least focuses attention on the well-known fact that even in India, discipline in implementing plans is frequently weak.

Inadequate Preparatory Work on Projects

By far the greatest number of failures to carry out public sector projects and programs are reasonable cost and in reasonable periods of time are traceable to inadequate project selection and preparation. Few less developed countries are fully aware of the necessity for selecting soundly conceived projects with potentially high yields, defining their scope with clarity, estimating their national currency and foreign

[84] Roxas, Sixto K. *Organizing the Government for Economic Development Administration*, p. 1.

[85] Golay, Frank. *Environment of Philippine Economic Planning*, p. 1; also Higgins, Benjamin. *Economic Development, Principles, Problems, and Policies*, pp. 746–747.

[86] Gadgil, D. R. *Planning and Economic Policy in India*, p. 140.

exchange requirements with a sufficient degree of accuracy, and laying down realistic schedules for their execution; fewer yet have the administrative capacity and the political will to cope with these needs and, especially, to carry out plan projects and programs in accordance with carefully developed programs of action.

The process by which good projects are selected and properly prepared follows well-defined lines. Ideally, the choice of projects for inclusion in a plan is preceded by sector studies. A sector study is an analysis of an economic sector which outlines the basis for a co-ordinated development program for the sector and makes a prelimi-nary identification of the nature, size and scope of the most promising projects within the terms of the sector analysis. Thus, a sector study for electric power might seek to identify the regions in a country which have the greatest need for electric power, the desirable relationships between thermal and hydroelectric power facilities, and the projects which appear to be most worthy of further investigation. A transporta-tion sector study might assess the relative development needed in air, sea, river, railroad and highway facilities, including the need for ports, the relationship between trunk and feeder roads, etc., and indicate which potentially desirable projects in each branch required further study. A sector study for industry might indicate the relative merits of developing light as against heavy industries, given the nature of a country's natural and other resources and possibilities, and it would indicate which projects in branches recommended for development were worth further investigation. And a sector study for agriculture would seek to identify the relative prospects of development in forestry, animal husbandry and cropping for domestic consumption or export and make suggestions for further study in one or more of these branches and for projects to process their production. Good sector studies take time to arrange and complete. They are rarely carried out in less than a year or a year and a half. They are also costly.

When a potentially desirable project has been identified, whether by a sector study or otherwise, a feasibility study needs to be made to determine whether it is practicable and justified. A feasibility study involves a detailed examination of the economic, technical, financial, commercial and organizational aspects of a project. It aims to produce all the information required to determine whether and how a project can be carried out in accordance with sound principles and at a cost which is lower than the contribution it can be expected to make to a country's development.

Feasibility studies vary according to the sector and problems involved. Thus, a pipeline is being considered for moving petroleum products between the Terai area and Katmandu in Nepal. Normally, pipelines have too large a capacity to be economic or practicable where the movement of material is as small as it will be in Nepal. But there exists a possibility that a small diameter line can be constructed which would be economic if it were constructed through the mountains instead of over them. A feasibility study could determine both the technical and economic practicability of the proposed pipeline. Another kind of feasibility study would be required if a proposed project were a plant to produce a commodity or a service. Such a study would require careful investigation of the likely market demand for the plant's production, the best location for the plant and its proper size, the availability and prices of required raw materials, the number and kind of workers needed and their availability, manpower training requirements, costs of production, reasonably firm estimates of the plant's construction time and costs, etc.[87] If the establishment or expan-

----

[87] A financial appraisal of a project's costs and benefits is generally made in terms of market prices to determine if it is self-liquidating and if it is likely to yield an appropriate return to its sponsors. Although it may be used to assess the financial profitability of public sector projects, it is more generally applicable to privately sponsored projects since private entrepreneurs usually have no alternative to market prices. But a financial appraisal of costs may be an inadequate measure of the real economic costs and benefits of a project to a country as a whole. Thus, if some market prices are subsidized (as when a government can borrow at interest rates below market rates) or inflated (as when the prices of imported machinery, equipment or materials are increased by duties), prevailing prices may be artificially out of line with each other and with world prices. If many people are unemployed and there are no alternative opportunities for employing them, prevailing wage levels may also exaggerate the "true" value of labor for a project from the point of view of a country's economy.

If the true or economic cost of a project is to be determined in situations where market prices are out of line (the economist might say where prevailing prices do not equilibrate supply and demand), it may be necessary to "adjust" the prevailing prices by estimating the extent to which they deviate from "equilibrium" prices. The adjusted prices, variously known as "shadow" or "accounting" prices, are then substituted for prevailing prices and used to determine real costs and benefits to an economy and to compare the project under consideration with other projects on a comparable basis. With the use of "shadow-pricing" techniques it may be found that a project which promises to produce a financial profit on the basis of market prices is nevertheless likely to yield a much lower rate of return than alternative projects, thereby making a shift in investment resource allocation desirable. A government may therefore wish to subject proposed private investment projects, especially if they require considerable foreign exchange or other scarce resources, to economic analysis before approving the project, if approval is resion of port facilities are under consideration, a feasibility study might start with a traffic forecast for exports and imports. Since in most less developed countries, exports comprise a few bulky items and imports consist of a larger variety of commodities, different ways of handling the two will have to be studied. To forecast the movement of exports through the port, estimates may have to be made of production and likely sales abroad for domestic commodities. Thus, in Nigeria, Ghana or the Ivory Coast, the outlook for cocoa would have to be considered. In Nigeria or Senegal, the future of groundnuts production would have to be studied. On the basis of such forecasts, requirements for docks, sheds and warehouses would have to be calculated. Cost and revenue projections for a port handling the estimated traffic would then be determined, the organizational aspects of the project surveyed, etc.[88]

Such studies, when carefully made on the basis of realistic assumptions, can yield sound judgments on the feasibility and desirability of a proposed investment in terms of benefits to its sponsors and to the economy of a country.[89] Without a careful feasibility study it is usually impossible to ascertain what benefits are likely to be obtained for money invested and how one project compares with alternative projects. While good feasibility studies cannot eliminate all investment risks or provide an infallible guide to the selection of desirable

---

quired; it is, of course, desirable to apply "shadow-pricing" techniques to public investment proposals.

Shadow-pricing technique is particularly useful for analyzing alternative investments on a comparable basis. By substituting shadow prices for actual prices for all investment opportunities, planners can determine the "opportunity costs" for investing resources in different ways. Shadow-pricing technique can also permit valid comparisons to be made of a public sector project with a private sector project to determine which would be more desirable from the point of view of an entire economy.

Because the extent of differences between market prices and shadow prices, as well as the state of shadow-pricing technique, is surrounded by considerable uncertainties, it is not always easy or possible to obtain reliable shadow prices to substitute for prevailing ones. In some cases, only crude estimates of shadow prices can be made. These considerations sometimes restrict the use of shadow-pricing as a practical matter.

[88] UN. ECA. *Comprehensive Development Planning*, p. 20.

[89] Care must be taken in selecting a suitable firm without vested interests in a proposed project to make the study. In Iran, for example, preliminary studies were in many cases found to be based more on hope than on realistic assumptions; this is especially likely to be the case where the study of a plant's desirability is made by a foreign firm interested in selling machinery as well as advice. (Iran. Plan Organization. *Review of the Second Seven Year Plan Program of Iran*, p. 71.)

projects, they are particularly useful in identifying especially bad projects and especially attractive ones, identifying the crucial variables in a project and setting standards for controlling construction and operating costs.[90]

Feasibility studies, like sector studies, are often time-consuming and costly. Thus, the feasibility study for the steel plant at Bokaro, India (which involved the use of 150 technicians, engineering surveys by five subcontractors and the use of data supplied by 33 firms), took a year to complete and cost $686,344. Moreover, it was estimated that the work of verifying the assumptions in the study concerning the availability and cost of raw materials which the plant would require would be a considerable additional undertaking in terms of personnel, time and money and that it would take two years or more to find satisfactory long-term solutions to basic raw material problems.[91] The Bokaro plant is an exceptionally large project which is expected to cost over $1.5 billion. But feasibility studies for much smaller projects may take more time to complete than the feasibility study for the Bokaro plant. Thus, it may take five years to determine whether enough water flows in a river to provide adequate quantities for a hydroelectric power project costing only a small fraction of what the Bokaro plant will require.

Once the feasibility of a project has been determined, preliminary and then detailed engineering and other preparatory work can begin. This includes the design of the project on a specific location; the preparation of working drawings for construction; the phasing of component elements to insure that they are ready when needed; [92] the preparation of detailed specifications, lists of quantities of materials required, unit or other detailed cost estimates; financial requirements

---

[90] *Ibid.*

[91] *New York Times*, April 28, 1963.

[92] Even for a relatively simple project, phasing involves the setting up of time schedules for acquiring land, staffing, providing housing and communications for the project, procuring stores, materials and equipment, securing spare parts and installing workshop facilities for repairs and maintenance of machinery used in construction, etc. For a complex, integrated project like the Bokaro steel plant, phasing requires that *timely* provision be made for adequate rail transport both during construction and operational phases, ample supplies of water and power, expansion of coal mining and coal washing facilities, the establishment of quarries and other mineral sources, the construction of adequate highways, a new town site for workers and managerial staff, training facilities (it is estimated that 8,200 Indians out of a total of 20,000 men needed for the entire plant, will have to undergo training before production gets under way), etc.

and returns during construction and for a period after operations begin (including their timing in the form of a "cash flow" chart or table), etc. The time needed for preliminary and detailed engineering studies varies, but they often take a year or more to complete. In preparing a highway program, for example, it is not uncommon for two or more years to elapse between a sector study and the detailed engineering of the roads included in the program. It is taking about three years to complete the engineering work on the 435-mile Darien Gap section of the Inter-American Highway through the rain forests of Panama and Colombia, at an estimated cost of well over $3 million. In the case of hydroelectric projects, it may take five to ten years or more to complete the necessary feasibility and engineering studies. Thus, the time involved in carrying out careful sector, feasibility and engineering studies for a project may well exceed the time needed for construction.

It is partly because procedures used to choose and prepare good projects take a long time to complete that there is a great dearth of such projects ready for execution in most less developed countries. Foreign and international lending and donor agencies, which generally are unwilling to commit funds for projects which are not based on sound preinvestment and other studies, are frequently hard put to find enough well-prepared projects to help finance in less developed countries. This may even be true where, as in Malaya, there are many projects being carried out, if they were not studied adequately before execution.

In some countries, shortages of technicians or funds make it difficult to carry out preparatory studies; but these are no longer insurmountable impediments since international and foreign lending and donor agencies are increasingly making available funds and technical assistance for preinvestment studies and surveys.[93]

In many less developed countries, requisite feasibility and other

[93] Thus, Mr. George D. Woods, President of the World Bank, has indicated that because

there is very little value in planning unless it is solidly based upon knowledge of the resources available and of the technical and economic feasibility of particular projects [the Bank had decided to offer more help to under developed countries] in organizing and financing feasibility studies either of promising projects or of the development of specific sectors of the economy. (*New York Times*, March 8, 1963, reporting on Mr Woods' Address to the UN. Economic and Social Council.)

studies are not carried out largely because the need for them is not fully appreciated. In some countries, one encounters a strongly held belief that time and money spent on preinvestment and careful technical, economic and financial studies are wasteful because they seemingly delay, and increase the cost of, the execution of projects.[94] According to Afghanistan's Minister of Planning, lack of technicians and the time factor were both involved in his Government's decision to proceed without preinvestment and other studies.

> There was the lack of personnel qualified to make engineering studies to determine costs and economic benefits of proposed projects. Much the same was true with respect to surveys of natural resources such as water, minerals, gas and oil. Such preinvestment studies are time consuming, and the Government felt a strong urge to get started with development.[95]

According to the Planning Commission of Pakistan, preparatory work on public sector projects in that country also was frequently lacking and "impatience and enthusiasm frequently took the place of prudence and engineering judgment." [96]

Because of the lack of good feasibility and other studies for projects, actual costs, benefits and construction time often deviate substantially from original estimates. In the absence of reliable data which carefully prepared studies produce, sponsors of public sector projects tend to overestimate the benefits and underestimate the costs and time needed to complete projects, with the result that projects almost always look much better on paper than they are in reality. Sometimes, overestimation of benefits and underestimation of costs and construction time are the consequence of ignorance; sometimes, it is because sponsors seek to persuade budget or other authorities to approve the start of their projects. Experience has taught many sponsors of public investment projects that once construction has begun, it is generally easier to obtain allocations to keep a project going than it was to get the first allocation, even if costs greatly exceed original estimates. In some

[94] The World Bank has often encountered this attitude among would-be borrowers. A government official in one country complained that if he acquiesced to all requests for preinvestment and other studies which the Bank wanted his government to carry out, "all the good projects would be delayed and all the bad ones would go forward unhindered."

[95] United Nations Conference on the Application of Science and Technology, etc. *Planning Machinery in Afghanistan,* p. 4.

[96] Pakistan. Planning Commission. *Second Five Year Plan, 1960–1965,* p. 201.

cases, estimates turn out to be wrong because they are based on the assumption that materials and equipment for a project will be paid for in cash when there is little likelihood of this. Thus, India's Third Five-Year Plan estimated foreign exchange requirements for projects on the assumption that machinery and equipment would be obtained from the cheapest sources of supply for cash, although the planners foresaw that the estimates would not stand up if projects were financed by countries whose equipment and other prices were higher than cash prices.[97]

Iran's Plan Organization found that the absence of soundly prepared preinvestment studies almost always opened the door to "letting personal prejudices and interests determine the selection of projects." [98] Because preliminary investigations and surveys essential to the formulation of well-conceived projects were rarely carried out for projects in Pakistan's Second Five Year Plan, operating departments and agencies generally presented projects for approval which had been prepared hurriedly on the basis of their financial implications without much information about the physical or management problems which were likely to be encountered. The financial data submitted were often only rough cost estimates based on untested assumptions or on price schedules which were already or would soon be outdated. Often only guesses were included for the cost of land, materials, machinery or construction. Cost-benefit ratios were frequently unrealistic.[99] Describing the way projects were selected and the results obtained, a high official of Pakistan's Planning Commission wrote that the procedures followed reduced

> project formulation and planning to a state of mockery. In retrospect, many projects would not have been undertaken if their true

[97] India. Planning Commission. *Third Five-Year Plan*, p. 460. While more realistic costing procedures can greatly reduce discrepancies between estimated and actual costs, there will always be some unforeseeable events which will increase costs. Some of these eventualities can be covered by the provision of reasonable contingency allowances; others cannot. Thus, if a project is to be partially financed with tied foreign loans or grants, it may be difficult to estimate the cost since it depends ultimately on which country helps finance the project. Prices charged by aid-giving countries may vary by as much as 50 per cent. Time needed to carry out a project also depends on when financing becomes available.

[98] Iran. Plan Organization. *Review of the Second Seven Year Plan Program of Iran*, p. 71. The Iranian steel project was cited by the planners "as an example of a major project that should have had a thorough and independent feasibility study many years ago."

[99] Waterston, Albert. *Planning in Pakistan*, pp. 114–115.

costs and benefits had been known before their commencement.[100]

It is after inadequately prepared projects have been approved and begin to run into difficulties, which greatly increase costs and delay execution, that the value of careful preinvestment and engineering studies becomes apparent to officials in developing countries. It then becomes apparent that a well-prepared project has merits beyond its value for attracting external financial assistance. For example, the Cuban Government sought to save time by purchasing a series of ready-made, "package" or "turnkey" plants to manufacture products which were being imported in quantity. Preinvestment studies were not made to determine the economic desirability of the plants. Many of the plants turned out to be poor investments, not least because the foreign exchange requirements for imported raw materials, supplies, spare parts and equipment put an even greater strain on the balance of payments than the imported manufactures had. Commenting on this experience, the Cuban Minister of Industry conceded that because his Government was

> racing against time and worked without a sound plan, we started building factories and committed grave mistakes because we had failed to conduct adequate studies. . . .[101]

In Iran, the Plan Organization reported,

> the result of bad planning is bad plants. A very serious result of bad plants is the demoralization of the engineers and administrators who are assigned to them. This is already a problem of some recently completed projects. . . . Men with good training hate to be assigned to 'a horse they know can never win.' [102]

Moreover, bad planning also was responsible for raising costs of plant construction.

> Although domestic price inflation has accounted for some of these cost over-runs, the major cause has been faulty planning and an almost complete absence of financial and administrative controls

---

[100] Haq, Mahbub ul. *Strategy of Economic Planning: A Case Study of Pakistan,* p. 193.

[101] *New York Times,* March 26, 1965.

[102] Iran. Plan Organization. *Review of the Second Seven Year Plan Program of Iran,* p. 71.

during the construction period. Much 'tighter' planning before projects are approved could have saved large sums of money.[103]

In India, failure to carry out project studies which provided accurate and detailed cost estimates resulted in serious underestimations of foreign exchange requirements during the period of the Second Plan. Indeed, directly and indirectly, the lack of preinvestment and other studies was largely responsible for foreign exchange shortages.

> The errors in estimation of foreign exchange requirements result-
> ing from the inadequate preparation of industrial projects, inade-
> quate scrutiny of projects from the viewpoint of maintenance
> imports and defective formulation of interdepartmental projects
> and failure to synchronise their execution over time are the
> principal factors responsible for aggravating the foreign exchange
> shortage difficulties in India.[104]

In Pakistan, especially in agriculture, projects were retarded unduly because of problems encountered in acquiring land which the sponsoring agency assumed would be available as soon as funds were obtained. In some cases, no specific site for a project had been selected. After the project was approved, it was found that land was either unobtainable or more expensive than expected. Or because of shortages of water, inadequacies of soil, lack of communications or necessary technical personnel, execution of the projects was impossible or much delayed, and required basic revisions or much higher costs. Inadequate procurement machinery also caused execution of many projects to lag. Delays usually increased costs, which in turn made it necessary for various government bodies to re-examine and re-approve the projects. Such revisions and reviews sometimes delayed the project's progress as much as the physical limitations.[105]

In some countries, it is not uncommon to find that engineering plans for a project are being prepared only as construction moves forward, and in some cases, there is not even a complete set of engineering plans after the completion of the project. Even when a project has been well engineered and surveyed, occasional changes in specifications after construction begins are sometimes made necessary by unforeseen problems. But when construction starts before thorough engineer-

---

[103] *Ibid.*

[104] UN. Seminar on Industrial Programming. *India's Experience in Industrial Planning*, p. 43.

[105] Waterston, Albert. *Planning in Pakistan*, pp. 114–115.

ing and other studies have been completed, alterations, extensions
and additions to a project may be so frequent that the project which
finally emerges is often substantially different from what was visualized when it was begun. In such cases, delays of two or three years and
doubling or tripling of original cost estimates are not unusual.

Lack of Engineering Supervision

A sponsor who has not seen fit to expend the time and money to
prepare preinvestment and engineering studies for a project is even
less likely to engage engineering consultants, at a charge which may
approximate 5 per cent of the total cost of construction, to supervise
the project's execution. In some cases, even if engineering and other
studies have been carried out for a project, sponsors have been known
to balk at engaging engineering or other technical consultants to
supervise execution of the project.

But the engagement of a reputable and experienced firm of engineers or other qualified technicians to supervise the execution of a
project is a characteristic of a well-organized operation. Such firms,
which usually specialize in engineering design and consulting and do
not engage in construction work, exist in most advanced countries and,
increasingly, in developing countries. The consultant's prime responsibility is to protect the interests of the project's sponsors and to insure
that contractors and others carry out the project in accordance with
approved design and specifications at the lowest possible cost and in
the shortest possible time consistent with quality considerations. The
consultant firm provides the project's sponsor with a variety of services.
It may prepare tenders for bids, analyze bids received, advise on the
selection of experienced contractors, help set up work procedures,
provide field supervisory personnel, render progress reports on the
project, recommend solutions to problems which arise, and act as the
sponsor's adviser on all other technical aspects of the project.

If experienced engineering supervision is not available during the
construction phase of a project, the likelihood is that the project will
move from one crisis to another. Construction contracts may be
awarded to the lowest bidders although they lack the experience,
equipment or financial resources to perform the work. When this
happens, as it did for one public sector project in India, the project
suffers. In the Indian case, for example, two contractors who were not
qualified to carry out projects of the size involved were selected

because their bid was much below other bids. The Management Group which subsequently reported on the project stated that "many of the later project delays could be traced to this initial decision." [106] As the Management Group pointed out:

> Extremely low bids need to be carefully scrutinized, as well as the ability of the low bidder to execute satisfactorily a contract of the size and nature proposed.[107]

These are tasks which supervisory engineers, but few government agencies by themselves, are qualified by experience to carry out. Inadequate supervision may also result in a lowering of construction standards and the use of inferior materials; or the need for a sponsoring agency to deal on a day-to-day basis with many contractors which may cause undue delays.[108] Since most operating organizations in less developed countries which sponsor projects are more accustomed to dealing with routine situations than with irregular and unforeseen events, delays become chronic and costs mount.

Administrative and Procedural Delays

Even without such problems, procedural and administrative delays constitute one of the commonest contributing causes for the failure to implement plans. In many governments, extraordinary lapses of time occur before a problem or a need for action is recognized, between the time it is recognized and a decision is made what to do about it, and finally, between the time a decision is made and it is carried out.[109]

A great deal of time is often spent in discussing preliminary matters. Much time may be absorbed in settling the question of whether a project should be carried out in the public or the private sector; if the former, which foreign or international agency's collaboration and what

[106] Management Group. Committee on Plan Projects. "Management Planning in Public Enterprises," pp. 398–399.

[107] *Ibid.*, p. 389.

[108] For example, Iran's planners reported that delays in executing industrial projects were caused, among other reasons, by the Plan Organization's

> inexperience and lack of equipment of many building contractors chosen to do the work, the over-centralization of Plan Organization's control procedures so that almost no questions are settled at the site but . . . [had to] be referred to Tehran, . . . and administrative delays within the Plan Organization . . . (Iran. Plan Organization. *Review of the Second Seven Year Program of Iran*, p. 72).

[109] Morgan, Theodore. *Economic Planning—Points of Success and Failure*, p. 14.

terms should be sought, if the latter, under what conditions.[110] Procrastination is much in evidence. In Iraq, for example, some projects first studied almost ten years ago have been repeatedly studied since then without a decision having been taken whether or not to proceed with them. Procrastination in the public sector manifests itself in innumerable ways, including delays in starting technical, financial, economic, and other studies needed to make decisions about the feasibility of a project; selecting one project from among several alternatives; deciding on whether construction is to be handled by a government agency, a private contractor or some other body; scrutinizing and evaluating bids; deciding on forms of contracts; entering into contractual relations with engineers and construction contractors; placing orders for materials and equipment; dealing with contractors (e.g., making payments for work done and approving deviations from original specifications); training personnel; selecting a site; starting procedures to acquire land or rights of ways; and getting necessary approvals from government units.[111] The principal ways in which governmental administrative and procedural delays usually hamper private industrial developments are through lags in the processing of import and other licenses and in approving releases of foreign exchange to private investors for machinery, equipment, materials and spare parts. These and other administrative problems seriously impede private investment in many less developed countries.

RELATING PLAN FORMULATION TO IMPLEMENTATION

The Problem Posed

With many factors accounting for the inability of most countries to achieve targets in their plans, a question arises whether one factor—more than any other—is responsible for this inability. Until very recently, it was thought that the key element in the planning process was the formulation of an economically consistent plan. While the importance of a well-prepared plan based on clearly defined development objectives is indisputable, it was not generally realized, as it is

---

[110] Reddaway, W. B. "Importance of Time Lags for Economic Planning," pp. 231, 233.

[111] An example of the last item is the publicly owned coal washing plant at Kargali in India, which was delayed ten months because of lags in getting permission from the State Government to construct roads, the foundation and drainage system for the project (*Economic Times,* December 25, 1964).

not yet realized in some places, that a consistent plan does not insure implementation any more than an inconsistent one. When the plans they had prepared were not implemented, planners trained as economists assumed, and still assume in some circles, that the failure to achieve targets was mainly attributable to errors in computing and allocating resources or to errors in basic data. Such errors were not difficult to find. Targets had sometimes been set too high, financial availabilities, especially foreign exchange, and other resources had been overestimated, capital-output ratios were too low, the level and rate of growth of population had been underestimated, resource allocations among sectors had been faulty, and so forth.

Conscious of the inadequacies of the data with which they had to work and some of the techniques used to formulate plans, planning experts and practitioners re-doubled their efforts to get governments to improve basic statistics, while they sought to refine their concepts, sharpen their tools of analysis, broaden the coverage of plan formulation to include manpower and other aspects formerly ignored, and introduce more sophisticated and advanced econometric techniques. Adjustments were made in planning models, input-output matrices were prepared, and experimental attempts were sponsored to introduce simulation technique, operations research and shadow pricing, and to substitute curvilinear for linear programing in the construction of planning models.

Formulation vs. Implementation

But even as plan formulation methodology advanced, implementation remained inadequate and even worsened. This eventually led some to conclude that the major problem in planning for less developed countries was not plan formulation, but implementation. Thus, the ECAFE, which has been in the forefront of institutions promoting the use of econometric techniques for projections and plan formulation, nevertheless came to the unhappy conclusion that, although in many Asian countries,

> plans are prepared with a great amount of care so as to make them as comprehensive, realistic, specific and consistent as possible, their implementation is often partial, slow and inefficient. This may lead to results worse than those expected to follow in the absence of any plan.[112]

[112] UN. ECAFE. "Economic Development and Planning in Asia and the Far East," *Economic Bulletin for Asia and the Far East*, December 1961, pp. 30–31.

The failure to implement plans is a popular subject of discussion among those interested in Indian planning. Thus, Professor D. R. Gadgil, in a generally critical account, found little to criticize in India's Second Five-Year Plan; instead he directed most of his comments to the failure to implement the Plan.[113] Barbara Ward wrote that

> it is not unfair to say that from the beginning Indian planning has been stronger on formulation than on implementation—or, less pompously put, on thinking things out rather than getting things done.[114]

India's respected *Economic Weekly* contended that

> the drafting of the Plan has become an end in itself. In the maze of words, the task of implementing the Plan most efficiently has often been lost sight of. . . . There is still no sense of urgency; [115]

while in a well-known comment, the late Prime Minister Nehru agreed that

> we in the Planning Commission and others concerned have grown more experienced and more expert in planning. But the real question is not planning, but implementing the Plan. That is the real question before the country. I fear we are not quite so expert at implementation as at planning. . . .[116]

Similar sentiments have been heard in other parts of the world. In Ethiopia, where the First Five-Year Plan was kept secret for half of the Plan period and, even when released, was never accepted as a program of action by the agencies which were supposed to carry it out, an economist in the University College of Addis Ababa distinguished between two types of planning:

> In a discussion of planning in Ethiopia it is essential to draw a distinction between planning as an advice and planning as a programme of action. The plan may be divorced from implementation. This was to a large extent the case in Ethiopia.[117]

[113] Gadgil, D. R. *Planning and Economic Policy in India*, p. 51.
[114] Ward, Barbara. *Plan Under Pressure: An Observer's View*, p. 31. John P. Lewis had much the same view:

> The Indians are better talkers than doers, better planners than executors. . . . Too often the execution is half-hearted, inept, or bogged down in cross-purposes. (Lewis, John P. *Quiet Crisis in India*, p. 5.)

[115] *Economic Weekly*, Vol. XIII, Nos. 27, 28, 29, July 1961, p. 1023.
[116] Nehru, Jawaharlal. "Annual Address by the Prime Minister," p. 435.
[117] Gulilat, Taye. "Approach to Economic Planning in Ethiopia," pp. 130–131.

But Ethiopia is not the only African country where plan formulation has been divorced from implementation. An ECA planners' group which considered the problem concluded that,

> in some African countries there is not enough political and economic stress put on implementation of plans. Thus planning becomes limited to setting the targets and not much effort is made towards carrying the plans out. Preparing the plan becomes art for art's sake with very few practical results.[118]

The gradual awakening to the realization that plans do not implement themselves, and that specific measures must be adopted if plans are to be converted from expressions of aspiration to programs of action, has led to considerable discussion about what role the planner should play in implementation. Many persons—among them planners and planning experts—hold the view that a planner's training and predilection as an economist equip him only to prepare integrated plans which economize on the use of scarce resources in a way calculated to yield the highest possible returns from investment within limits prescribed by plan objectives. They feel that he has no special competence to deal with the question of how plans are to be implemented because this aspect of planning largely involves administrative, institutional and political factors.

Whether consciously or not, those who maintain this position see or imply a major difference or even a clear-cut separation between plan formulation and implementation. They consider a plan to be a product of a few specialists in a central planning agency who have need for only limited recourse to other government organizations. (They have experience on their side because, in fact, most plans *are* prepared by a few technicians operating in virtual isolation from the rest of government.) They point out that, in contrast, implementation of a plan necessarily involves the preparation and execution of projects by many people dispersed throughout a government and the private sector of an economy. Thus, one foreign planning expert in Ghana wrote that

> the techniques of planning [i.e., plan formulation], which are developing by leaps and bounds, . . . can be applied and adopted comparatively easily. Their application and adaptation in every country involves only a small and exclusive group of experts. Project-planning [i.e., the preparation and execution of

[118] UN. ECA. *Report of the Meeting of the Expert Group on Comprehensive Development Planning*, p. 5.

projects] requires many more engineers and economists. . . . Implementation is different from the plan, for the latter is made only once while the former is going on day by day, hour by hour, in the most varied fields.[119]

The word "planning" is often used, as it was used by the author of the preceding quotation, to refer to the formulation of plans, but not to their implementation. The conceptual separation of "planning" from "implementation" is more than a matter of semantics: it is symbolic of an attitude which prevails widely among planners. Nevertheless, experience shows that nothing is more conducive to bad planning than the separation of plan formulation from provision for, and follow up on, its implementation. Nothing can be more parochial than restricting the planning function to the mere manufacture of plans without reference to what is needed for their implementation. Planning cannot leave off where plan formulation ends and action to execute a plan begins. As we have seen, every target must be accompanied by policies and measures which have been devised specifically to fulfill it—otherwise, it becomes only a forecast or a projection. But more than this, policies and measures adopted to achieve targets must undergo constant review, and targets or instruments of policy may have to be adjusted in the light of experience gained during the period of execution. Planning may begin with the formulation of a plan as a guide to implementation, but implementation becomes, at a later stage, a guide to revision of the original plan. The whole process is organic and continuous, with plan preparation blending into implementation, then into revision of the plan, and again into implementation and the formulation of the next plan, *ad infinitum*.[120]

It is, then, undesirable to separate conceptually the preparatory and executory phases when referring to planning. Planning must encompass both the preparation and execution of plans.[121] This means that such activities as the preparation and execution of sectoral surveys, feasibility and other preinvestment studies; the preparation and execution of projects and programs in the public sector; the formulation and

[119] Bognar, J. "The Importance of Devising Effective Machinery for the Implementation of Development Plans," p. 78.

[120] The term "feedback" has been borrowed from cybernetics to describe this process.

[121] As will be seen later, those who implement a plan may be, and generally should be, different from those who formulate it. But those who formulate plans must respond promptly to events during implementation by adjusting the plan appropriately.

application of policies and measures for stimulating and guiding private investment; reporting and evaluating plan progress, and more, are all part of what is meant by planning:

> The final element of a well-conceived development plan is the provision for its implementation. This includes the organization of the planning function and its administrative relationships with the chief executive, the policy-making and operating departments of the government, and the legislature; the assignment of responsibilities of carrying out its component programs; the relationship of the plan to the national budget; the roles of the fiscal and monetary authorities; the provisions for progress reporting and evaluation; and the selection and training of planning personnel.[122]

Where plan formulation is viewed as an exclusive or isolated element divorced in practice if not in theory from plan implementation, as it has in fact been viewed in many countries, one finds that planners pay little attention in their plans to the choice of means to be employed to achieve plan targets. This is why most plans almost always provide detailed information only about *what* is to be achieved, but not about *how* to go about securing development objectives or targets,[123] or about *who* in government or elsewhere should be responsible for carrying out the required tasks. The case of Nigeria's National Economic Plan for 1962–68 is illustrative of the widely held belief that a plan comes first and that measures to implement it can be postponed until after the plan has been accepted and put into effect. Policy changes needed to achieve the planned allocation of resources and to implement targets were not included in the Plan; instead, they were left to be initiated at a later time by the various ministries concerned with the various programs.[124] Even in the case of India's Third Plan,

> the most glaring defect . . . is the almost complete absence in it of provision for techniques with which the Plan would be implemented.[125]

Many planners consider their job is finished when they have prepared a plan and that it is up to others to work out the detailed policies

[122] Colm, Gerhard and Geiger, Theodore. "Country Programming as a Guide to Development," p. 51.
[123] Kannappan, Subbiah. "Planning Pitfalls in India," p. 319.
[124] Clark, Peter Bentley. "Economic Planning for a Country in Transition: Nigeria," p. 284.
[125] Gadgil, D. R. *Planning and Economic Policy in India*, p. 51.

and measures needed to implement the plan. Even among those who recognize that they have an obligation to suggest policies and measures, few think in specific terms of what is required to achieve the targets in their plans. The organic link between the targets in a plan and the policy or other measures required to achieve them is a concept which many planners and political authorities find difficult to grasp; this is equally true of the idea that a target is not really a target unless and until specific economic and financial policies and administrative and organizational measures are adopted to implement them. The need to provide incentives to stimulate private entrepreneurs to behave as envisaged in a plan is little understood; nor is there adequate appreciation that before a plan's targets can be attained, consumption may have to be curbed, the rate of domestic savings may have to be increased by taxation, or credit may have to be reduced or redirected.

The failure of most planners to indicate precisely what must be done to execute their plans has tended to intensify the belief that the problems of plan formulation are different and separable from those of implementation. Thus, a former head of the Philippine National Economic Council wrote as follows about the dichotomy between plan formulation and implementation in his country:

> In the past, efforts to establish economic planning in the Philippines were overly obsessed with the writing of economic plans rather than with the establishment of a meaningful planning process. Assistance from outside economic consultants served often merely to emphasize this obsession. It is normal for economists to be more interested in the internal content of an economic plan than in the planning process as such. It is the plan as a document which embodies the problems that are interesting to economic theory—the form of the planning model, the handling of the variables, given assumptions, projection techniques, target and policy variables, parameters of behavior, etc. It is in the formal preparation of plans that the particular expertise of economists is most useful.
>
> The establishment of a planning process is an exercise of quite a different character. Here the problem is not one of producing an internally consistent and analytically elegant document. The task is to spread a planning habit, establish rational economic calculation as the common norm for decision-making, and have this

accepted by those responsible for making decisions. It is a problem of organization and management.[126]

There can be little doubt that the prevailing separation of plan formulation from implementation has been exacerbated by the concentration of planners' attention on economic factors to the virtual exclusion of organizational and management factors which predominate when a plan is being implemented. Professional planners and planning experts appear to be divided into two main groups: one tends to believe that better planning depends on further improvements in their imperfect planning instruments (as witness the preoccupation with model building, simulation and input-output technique), while the second tends to feel that the shortcomings of the planning process reflect the inadequacies of the administrative and political environment within which plans must be carried out more than any deficiency of planning technique. But whatever their position, planners are little likely to concern themselves with the problems of public administration and politics.

Importance of Administration and Politics

Public administration is crucial to planning for two reasons: firstly, because the successful implementation of a plan is largely a matter of proper organization and administration, and secondly, because in most less developed countries the possibilities for economic growth, based on available real and financial resources, greatly exceed the organizational and managerial capacity to attain these possibilities. When, therefore, planners fix plan targets solely on the basis of economic potentialities and fail to take appropriate account of organizational, managerial and administrative limitations, plan targets are likely to be set at unrealistically high levels; and if, in addition, the planner ignores the restriction which political instability or a government's lack of commitment to development imposes on economic potentialities, the targets in his plans generally turn out to be beyond reach. For the fact is that in most less developed countries the greatest obstacles to implementation are administrative and, more especially, political rather than economic.

[126] Roxas, Sixto K. *Lessons from Philippine Experience in Development Planning*, pp. 47–48.

Importance of Political Support. Examination of the available evidence makes it clear that in countries with development plans, lack of adequate government support for the plans is the prime reason why most are never carried out successfully. The Report of the Conference of Asian Economic Planners, which met in Bangkok in October 1964, listed many factors which caused actual performance to deviate from targets in the plans of countries in the ECAFE region. But it singled out one factor as the most important:

> Above all, if Governments have not made planning an article of faith and pursued planning objectives wholeheartedly it is not surprising that actual performances have not sometimes measured up to expectation.[127]

History demonstrates that where a country's government is reasonably stable and its political leaders give a high priority to development, the country generally develops even when there is no formal plan. Conversely, in the absence of political stability, and firm and continuing government support, development plans, no matter how well devised, have little chance of being carried out successfully. The cardinal lesson to be learned from the planning experience of developing countries is that sustained governmental commitment is a *sine qua non* for development. For example, Pakistan's planning experience gives dramatic evidence of the overriding importance of governmental support. Although the planners of Pakistan's First Five Year Plan produced a development plan with targets well within the limits set by available economic and financial resources, the Plan could not get very far without the help of the Government. Given that support from a strong and stable leadership, the Second Five Year Plan promises to overfulfill its main targets and objectives.

The experience has been similar in other periods and countries. In the 19th century, Japan, with fewer resources than Burma, China, India or Indonesia (it had only skilled manpower and waterpower), nevertheless became the most industrialized country in Asia. In large part, development was made possible because of sustained effort supported by a determined government. In the 20th century, the histories of such diverse countries as Mexico, Israel, Yugoslavia, the USSR and China (Mainland and Taiwan) give ample evidence of the

---

[127] UN. ECAFE. *Draft Report of the Conference of Asian Economic Planners,* p. 6.

importance of firm and continuing support from a stable government for the development of a country.

Although political leaders in many countries talk a great deal about their great concern with the development of their countries, only a few follow up on their words with appropriate action. In some countries, government leaders adopt measures to stimulate development, but too often these are piecemeal, inadequate and poorly administered. The extent to which a government with a plan pursues policy and other measures which planners tell them are essential for the implementation of the plan usually provides a reliable index of that government's commitment to development planning. The evidence reveals that, on the basis of this index, many governments fall short.

One hears much about the need to find ways and means to imbue the people of this or that country with an understanding of their country's plan and to evoke their desire to participate in the planning effort. But another problem precedes this one: How can political leaders be made to become more deeply committed to the economic development of their countries? In many countries, political leaders give other matters higher priority than they give to development. Among these are nationalism, internal politics, defense, territorial expansion, the formation of international alliances or power blocs, and short-run economic problems. It may be that at a given time in a country's history, one or more of these may be more important for a country's welfare and future than its development. But it must be recognized that the relegation of development to a subordinate place in the scale of values of a country's political leaders cannot help but depress development efforts and, hence, the results of development planning.

Importance of Economic Incentives. Experience shows that until the political leadership of a nation becomes deeply committed to development, the people are unlikely to show much interest in national planning objectives. If a country's leaders make development one of their central concerns, experience shows that the people can be interested. But except temporarily, e.g., during or immediately after a war or other catastrophe or upheaval, people are not likely to become concerned with development objectives solely because of appeals to their patriotism, devotion to abstract ideals or altruism. Direct government controls over economic activity, or threats of imprisonment or other punishment, are even less effective.

The evidence teaches that the best long-term method of eliciting behavior which conforms to planning objectives is to make it profitable for people to act in ways required to achieve those objectives. Where governments have replaced restrictive administrative controls on the private sector by well-devised and adequate economic incentives, the results in increased economic activity have usually been too clearly linked to the change in approach to be misunderstood. In Pakistan, for example, government officials as well as competent outside observers agree that administrative restraints seriously hampered industrial growth during the First Plan period; they also agree in attributing the high rate of industrial progress during the Second Plan period largely to the reduction of government controls over imports and foreign exchange and the introduction of a system of tax incentives and bonuses which encouraged businessmen to expand plant capacities and output. In Pakistan's agriculture, also, the use of incentive prices played an important part in increasing production. As we have seen, Yugoslavia has had extraordinary success in the use of economic incentives. Since the early 1950's, when it replaced centralized controls based on the Soviet model with decentralized management of the economy, Yugoslavia has evolved a system of incentives in which workers and enterprises are paid largely in accordance with their output. These incentives have proved to be so effective in raising production that other Eastern European countries, notably Czechoslovakia, but also Poland and Hungary and even the USSR, are adopting major elements of the Yugoslav system.

The importance of having a vigorous, adaptable and capable entrepreneurial class can hardly be overestimated. This is true for countries with all kinds of political and economic systems, for the task of organizing a country's productive forces toward achieving the most effective use of resources and the highest rates of development must largely fall to entrepreneurs, whether they operate primarily as private businessmen, government officials or enterprise managers.[128] While it takes time to develop a viable and enlightened entrepreneurial class, experience shows that the process can be greatly speeded if a government is sufficiently committed to development to override dogma and provide adequate economic incentives to attract the right individuals.

The Necessity for Political Commitment. In the public sector, as in the private sector, then, it is the attitude of a country's political leaders

[128] UN. ECAFE. "Economic Development and Planning in Asia and the Far East," *Economic Bulletin for Asia and the Far East,* December 1964, p. 23.

toward development which primarily determines the success or failure of plans. In carrying out public investment plans, the level of administrative efficiency is important. But the extent of a political leadership's commitment to the plans is crucial since, as Woodrow Wilson pointed out, "politics sets the tasks for administration." [129] Even for government leaders wholeheartedly committed to the task, it is no easy matter to reform the ways of an inefficient administrative and organizational government structure, nor can it be accomplished in a few years. But such commitment is a necessary condition for reform. With it, reform is possible; without it, it is not. Here again, Pakistan's experience provides important lessons. When Pakistan's political leaders were too immersed in political issues to give the lead, fundamental administrative and organizational reforms which the First Plan required for its successful implementation were not forthcoming. Mere talk, of which there was a great deal by government leaders, about the importance of development did not significantly change the attitudes and performance of a civil service oriented toward the maintenance of law and order and tax collection, or bring about essential organizational reforms. But when a new Government in 1958 created the proper atmosphere by giving strong and unfailing support to the Second Plan, and used its powers to adopt policies and measures to give effect to the Plan's objectives, conflicts of interest among officials were resolved, administrative bottlenecks were broken, intractable problems were overcome, and the civil service responded to the will of the Government. The lesson is clear: good administration and activity below depend heavily on firm and constant commitment of the political leadership above.[130]

Measuring Inept Administration and Political Commitment

The planner may not be able to do much about a government's administrative inefficiency and its lack of political commitment or will to develop. But if in preparing his plans he ignores these critical factors, which together constitute the main limitations on the ability of most less developed countries to realize their economic possibilities, he does so at his peril; for in ignoring them he does in fact separate his

---

[129] Riggs, Frederick W. "Relearning an Old Lesson: The Political Context of Development Administration," p. 71.
[130] Waterston, Albert. *Planning in Pakistan*, p. 4.

activities and the plans he formulates from the real world outside a
central planning agency.

Yet, as previously indicated, most national development plans have
been formulated on the basis of what planners considered feasible,
given available resources or, alternatively, what they considered minimal, given the rate of population growth or the level of unemployment.
The plans they have prepared have therefore been primarily concerned with a country's economic possibilities or needs and have been
little related to its administrative capacity to carry out the plans or to
its will to develop. But economic potentiality or need is not enough to
insure implementation of development plans. A country's development
largely depends on how much its people and government want it and
how much they are willing to pay for it. Unless a plan takes adequate
account of a country's administrative and managerial capacity, and its
will to develop, as well as its economic potential, the plan is not really
so much a plan as it is a hortatory instrument of propaganda. It can
hardly be surprising then that most plan targets are never achieved.
Because targets are set on the basis of what is possible or desirable
instead of what is likely, they usually are set so unrealistically high—
not in terms of potential or need, but in terms of administrative
capacity and will to develop—that they never have much chance of
being fulfilled.

A good plan is realistic and a realistic plan does not set unattainable
targets. Hence, a plan cannot be considered good if its targets are
attainable only in the unlikely event that a government, which has
previously shown little inclination or capacity to do so, introduces
major land, administrative and other reforms. Yet, planners frequently
base their targets on such unfounded suppositions. Thus, the growth
targets in Pakistan's First Five Year Plan were probably well within the
economic capacity of the country if the Governments in power at the
time had made reasonable efforts to carry out the land reforms, make
the fundamental administrative, organizational, procedural and other
changes, and train the large numbers of technicians and managers
which the planners indicated were needed to implement the Plan. The
Governments did not do so, nor was there ever a strong likelihood that
they would. The evidence indicates that the planners were unduly optimistic about what could be accomplished in Pakistan in a period when
coalition governments were following each other with such rapidity
that all public business was seriously impeded.[131]

[131] *Ibid.,* p. 68.

Nor can a plan be considered good when the fulfillment of its targets requires a government in a less developed country to introduce many organizational and administrative innovations and to do so early in a plan period in order to make the necessary impact on the plan's implementation. For example, Ethiopia's Second Five-Year Development Plan for 1963–67 proposes that many new organizations be created to improve administrative and organizational efficiency, presumably to insure implementation of the Plan.[132] Among these are a new investment bank, an agricultural development agency, a foreign trade corporation, a water resource agency, an agency to deal with land reform, and many other agricultural, forestry and fishery organizations. Since the proposed organizations were still on paper when the Plan was issued, they were likely to require most of the Plan period before they became accepted and approved by the competent authorities, not to mention the creation, staffing and carrying out of their responsibilities in an effective manner. They cannot be expected, therefore, to contribute much to the fulfillment of the targets in the current Plan.

If planners are to set realistic targets in their plans, they must somehow find means to measure quantitatively administrative inadequacy and the lack of political will to develop. These measurements are essential if planners are to "discount" the overly optimistic results usually obtained by the formulation of plans solely on the basis of economic potentialities. It is, of course, no easy matter to obtain these measurements; but it is not impossible. For example, a simple method was described earlier in Chapter VIII for quantifying the cost of administrative inefficiency, in terms of money and time, on the basis of the historical gaps between original estimates and actual performance for projects and programs in each sector. Such data are easily obtainable wherever projects and programs have been carried out. Indeed, the data are likely to be easier to get and more reliable than most of the statistics used in preparing the economic aspects of a plan. These data could be used to adjust cost and time of construction estimates furnished by sponsors of projects and programs where their previous estimates have been shown to be overoptimistic, thereby providing planners with more dependable estimates of what projects are likely to be completed during a plan period and what their cost will be. The

[132] It is not clearly stated whether the successful implementation of the Ethiopian Plan depends on the establishment of the proposed institutions. This is typical of the vagueness with which planners generally prescribe for the implementation of their plans.

prudent use of such data can go a long way toward closing the gap between promise and performance, by reducing inflated estimates of the promise.

In connection with the formulation of the Fifth Plan, French planners introduced a refinement in political decision-making which lends itself, with appropriate modification, to the indirect measurement of a government's "will to develop." The French procedure is described in the section on plan targets in Chapter V. It will be recalled that it involved having the French Government decide *before* the draft plan was prepared what measures it proposed to take on specific basic policy issues. Thus, the draft plan which the planners produced was based on *known* government policies.

The same approach can be employed in less developed countries. If planners set up for each major policy area feasible alternatives from which political authorities can make a choice before a plan is drafted, planners can determine the combined impact of these choices on the rate of growth [133] and construct their plan accordingly. In the process of selecting the alternatives which suit them most, the political authorities will be supplying concrete and specific information about the extent to which they are prepared to adopt policies and other measures for furthering development which, collectively, will constitute a veritable measure of their "will to develop." Thus, if planners provide political authorities with, say, three levels of possible tax revenues (e.g., one based on current taxes, a second based on a moderate rise in specified taxes and a third based on specified substantial increases in the level of taxation), the selection made by the political authorities will not only provide the planners with an important datum for drafting their plan but will also provide them with an indirect indication of how far the authorities are willing to support development objectives with concrete measures in the tax field. A similar approach can be used to determine the level of domestic and foreign borrowing; the distribution of government receipts between development and nondevelopment expenditures, economic and social welfare projects, and advanced and backward regions; the level and direction of credit to be extended to industry and agriculture for specific purposes; monetary policy; the extent to which a government is prepared to provide increased incentives for productive investment in the

---

[133] Following the French example, planners can calculate a preliminary rate of growth for the period of their proposed plan by projecting the trend in the years immediately preceding the proposed plan period.

private sector; the government's wage or "incomes"; and so forth.

The alternatives which the planners prepare must be capable of being implemented. Thus, it means little if the political authorities agree to a substantial rise in taxes if the tax authority is inefficient and incapable of handling the increased workload. If there is uncertainty on this score, planners have to get expert advice on whether the tax office can be strengthened in time to take on the additional tasks involved. In addition, the administrative and organizational changes needed to give effect to each alternative have to be spelled out for the political authorities so that they fully appreciate the cost and effort which each alternative involves.

Since the level of a political leadership's "will to develop," even when generally high, is likely to vary from one policy area to another, planners would be well advised to narrow the area of decision-making and prepare alternatives for decision-makers in as many relevant areas as possible. However, it should be understood that the political "will to develop" encompasses more than political commitment to development. A government, although firmly committed to development, may consider it necessary or desirable for political or social reasons to divert substantial resources from productive economic projects to education, health, housing or other social welfare programs even if this would result in reduced rates of growth, at least in the short run; or, also for reasons of politics or social justice it may deem it necessary or desirable (e.g., as in Pakistan and Yugoslavia) to allocate investment resources in a way which will help equalize the distribution of incomes among regions instead of in the most efficient way. This, too, could reduce or postpone benefits during a plan period. Thus, the reasons why a political authority may not be prepared to support the most effective policy for immediate growth may vary, and may not even be known. Nevertheless, the procedure outlined here for measuring the political "will to develop" would provide planners with the effects of a government's policy decisions, whatever their motivation, and permit them to formulate a plan based on a government's known policies for the proposed plan period.

The procedures recommended here are not as radical as they may seem. In practice, planners make such alternative calculations and selections in preparing their plans.[134] The only changes proposed here

---

[134] Implicit in every plan are assumptions and policy decisions of many kinds. But because they are implicit rather than explicit, political authorities often fail

are that political authorities, not the planners, choose the main assumptions and policies on which a plan is based, that the political authorities be involved in the planning process much earlier than is usual, and that they make decisions about policy and other measures *before*, not *after*, a plan is drafted. If political authorities are not prepared to do this, or if they are unwilling or unable to make changes in policy required to accelerate the rate of development, it will become evident that they are not yet ready for comprehensive planning. In that event, planners would be well-advised to shift to some form of partial planning more suited to prevailing conditions.

The suggestions made for building into development plans the quantitative effects of political and administrative limitations are intended to show what can be done to make plans reflect problems which are almost certain to be encountered during implementation. Other ways can undoubtedly be found for accomplishing the same purpose. More important than the specific method is the need for broadening the scope of quantitative technique to encompass political and administrative factors, as well as the economic factor in the formulation of plans. The point emphasized here is that it is not enough for planners to refine techniques of economic analysis and ignore techniques for measuring the effects of administrative inadequacy and lack of political commitment to development.

If the three basic elements which enter into the planning process—economic potential, administrative capacity and political will to develop—are all taken into account in plan formulation, plan targets are bound to be more in line with a country's real capacity to achieve its economic potentialities.[135] Since these plan targets are likely to be lower than those set in most plans (which, however, are almost never realized), development plans would focus attention squarely on the

---

to appreciate the policy and administrative implications of the plans they adopt. Sometimes, planners include in their plan a list, usually general in nature, of the policy and administrative changes required to achieve plan targets. But as previously pointed out, government leaders usually have great difficulty relating specific policies with specific targets. Consequently, policy, organizational and administrative changes are usually postponed or forgotten after a plan has been prepared and adopted.

[135] Because a realistic evaluation of a country's administrative and political capacity to implement plans would probably result in higher cost and longer gestation estimates for projects and programs, estimated capital-output ratios are likely to be higher than if the estimates were based on the usual criteria. In effect, this would reduce the estimated amount of growth obtainable from a given outlay of resources.

administrative and political problems which limit plan implementation in most countries, and on the high cost they exact in reduced rates of development. If a plan accurately indicates how little can be accomplished to achieve economic potentialities because of existing administrative frictions and political inaction, some governments may be moved to come to grips with the real obstacles to plan implementation. Hopefully, this could lead eventually to the adoption of appropriate measures to improve economic policy and public administration and, more immediately, to a redistribution of development resources more in line with the practical possibilities for implementation.

There are further benefits to be obtained. By narrowing the area of decision-making the planner would be improving the process by which decisions are made in many countries. In spelling out in detail the feasible alternatives in each policy area and pointing out the effect of each decision on the size of the plan and the level of its targets, the planner would be helping decision-makers acquire a better understanding of the planning process. By requiring political leaders to give explicit consideration to the difficult choices imposed upon them by the desire to develop, the planner would be educating them to the need to think in the specific and selective terms essential to the achievement of plan objectives. By getting political authorities to participate in plan formulation at an early stage, the planner could get decision-makers started on needed policy changes and administrative reforms long before a plan period begins. Too frequently, discussion of policy and administrative changes required to implement a plan begins only after the plan has gone into effect. Moreover, by requiring policy-makers to indicate *before* a plan was drafted what policies and measures they were prepared to adopt, planners would be able to draw up a plan "to order" on the basis of the choices made, thereby making the political leaders fully responsible for the plan. This is as it should be.[136] Finally, by basing their plans on what political leaders had indicated they were prepared to do in the fields of policy and administration, instead of on what planners think should, or hope will, be done, plan formulation could exert an influence on the course of events. Plan formulation would then become in fact, what it is in

---

[136] There is, of course, no assurance that political leaders would adopt the measures and policies they indicate they will adopt. In that case, the onus is theirs and the planner does not share responsibility for the failure to implement the plan, as he does when he formulates his plans on the basis of policies which political leaders have not approved.

theory, a rational and efficient way of mobilizing and organizing productive resources for development, and the separation which now exists in most countries between plan formulation and implementation would tend to disappear.

IMPROVING IMPLEMENTATION

Improving the Conditions of Implementation

It would be useful and an improvement over current practice, then, for plan formulation to take account of political and administrative limitations on economic potentialities. But planning would have little justification if it only brought the targets of a plan down to levels which more accurately reflected the actual capacity of a country to attain them. A prime purpose of planning must be to improve implementation to make it possible to accelerate the rate of development.

However, the difficulties of improving implementation should not be underestimated. Shortfalls in achieving plan objectives and targets have brought home to many planners and government authorities the need to pay much more attention to improving plan implementation. But even where governments have tried to do this, results have generally not been good. For example, the Report on India's Third Five-Year Plan stated that

> the greatest stress in the Plan has to be on implementation, on speed and thoroughness in seeking practical results, and on creating conditions for the maximum production and employment and the development of human resources.[137]

In conformity with this declaration, the Government formulated specific measures for strengthening development administration and informed Parliament that

> the vigorous and punctual implementation of the Plan today forms the core of administrative activity.[138]

Yet despite the Government's resolve and the measures taken, the gap between plan targets and actual performance was greater in the Third

---

[137] UN. Inter-Regional Workshop on Problems of Budget Classification, etc. *Relationship Between Planning and Government Budgeting in Developing Countries* [Part II], p. 3.
[138] *Ibid.*

Plan period than ever before. In other countries, too, attempts to improve plan implementation have rarely brought quick results.

In part, this is because improved implementation of plans largely depends on improvements in administrative and organizational efficiency which necessarily take time to carry out. Where governments are prepared to make superficial changes, but not the basic changes required to reform public administrations, only piecemeal improvements are possible, and these reflect themselves in similarly piecemeal advances in improved plan implementation. But even in countries with a political leadership firmly committed to development, and hence where more comprehensive reforms are possible, it must be expected that fundamental changes in public administration and organization will take place slowly.[139]

Although improvements in administration are important, they are only part of the problem. This is because the effectiveness with which a plan is implemented is to a great extent determined by the amount of preparatory work which preceded its formulation. Thus, a resolve to spend more time and effort on implementing a *current* plan is unlikely to yield much result. The time for that resolve was in the *previous* plan period. In the current plan period, with few exceptions, a government can only resolve to start action to implement the plan in the *next* plan period. It does little good for planners to prepare a macroeconomic plan with growth targets which promise much, unless preinvestment and investment studies are sufficiently advanced on a sufficient number of projects and programs to give effect to the plan's targets. Similarly, there is no point in increasing the size of a plan, as India is doing for its Fourth Plan, if preparatory work has not started

[139] Various devices exist for speeding administrative reform, but the methods used will vary, mostly on the basis of whether or not a country's political leadership is firmly committed to development. Where it is not, the "nucleus approach" outlined in Chapter VIII is probably the most practicable approach. But where a government's commitment to development is well established and a broader approach to administrative reform is feasible, consideration should be given to the establishment of a standing, high-level commission, with responsibility for supervising the organizational and administrative reforms called for in the country's development plans. The central planning agency should be represented on the commission and the commission should advise the central planning agency on administrative and organizational reforms required to implement plans. The effectiveness of the commission will largely depend on the support it receives from government. Experience shows that where such a commission has been set up without the government being prepared to support it, it had little effect. This happened in Venezuela.

long before on the increased number of projects and programs needed
to implement the larger plan.

Because it usually takes several years to identify and prepare
soundly conceived projects and programs needed to implement a plan,
it is too late for planners to become concerned about them only when a
plan is being formulated. If little has been done long before to start
sector, feasibility and engineering studies, there is not much planners
can do at the point when a plan is being formulated except to note the
lack of projects and programs needed to carry out their plan. Thus,
Thai planners indicated that for the first phase of their National
Economic Development Plan,

> the formulation of projects left much to be desired and large
> sums had to be provisionally held in reserve subject to reallocation
> after subsequent review of specific projects.[140]

The same procedure had to be followed for East Pakistan in Pakistan's
First Five Year Plan and the lump sum set aside was never fully
utilized during the plan period because of a persistent insufficiency of
projects. In Syria, also, the Five-Year Economic and Social Development Plan included many projects for which suitable studies were not
well advanced.

Even where the need for sector, feasibility and engineering studies is
recognized, at least to meet the requirements of foreign lending or
donor agencies, enough "lead time" [141] is rarely allowed to complete
studies in time for reasonably accurate cost, benefit, construction time,
and other estimates to be included in over-all plans. As a result, there
are frequently not enough projects prepared in sufficient detail to be
included in development plans. Because of this, plans often contain
only generalizations about projects and programs. For example, Ethiopia's Second Five-Year Development Plan contained the following
statement:

> In the course of the elaboration of the Plan, for understandable
> reasons the micro-location for each new industrial project could

[140] Thailand. National Economic Development Board. *National Economic Development Plan, 1961–1966, Second Phase: 1964–1966*, p. 14.

[141] "Lead time" refers to the time that elapses between the inception of a project
and its completion. A project which takes three years to construct may easily
require a lead time of six years or more to allow time for initial sector and
feasibility studies, and engineering designs to be prepared. If realistic allowances
are also made for administrative delays, lead time for a project which should take
six years may increase to as much as ten years.

not be foreseen. It will be possible to make a decision on this only on the basis of detailed studies and investigation of all the factors and conditions concerned, but new projects should be erected in all parts of the country providing the feasibility studies allow it. The location of the new industrial projects will have to be decided primarily according to the raw material and power sources, transport facilities, and the marketing and consumption analyses with the view of maximizing the returns and profitability.[142]

For a large proportion of the projects included in India's Third Five-Year Plan, reasonably precise information about their costs, benefits and other attributes was not available and only preliminary data about them could be included in the Plan.[143] In addition, as the Minister for Steel, Mines and Heavy Engineering reported, it was discovered that

> many of the Third Plan projects are not possible of implementation during the Third Plan because they are still in the preparatory stage and are nowhere near the implementation stage.[144]

Closing the "Project Gap." Just as planning on the macro-economic level is a continuous process, preparation or programing of projects on the micro-economic level must become a continuous process if the "project gap" which frustrates most plan implementation is to be closed. In the private sector, this is largely a matter of providing suitable incentives to private investors and eliminating administrative, legal and other regulations and procedures which tend to dampen the interest of domestic and foreign investors. In the public sector of most less developed countries, it requires that programing machinery be set up in operating ministries, departments and agencies, with suitably trained staffs, supplemented by outside technicians and consultants.

These are the means; the end is to accumulate enough well-designed projects and programs to meet all foreseeable needs for projects on which construction should begin in the next few years. Since it is often impossible to foretell before feasibility studies are completed whether a project is economically and technically sound, more projects need to

[142] Ethiopia. Office of the Planning Board. *Second Five-Year Development Plan, 1955–1959 E.C.*, pp. 192–193.

[143] UN. ECAFE. *Speed and Efficiency in Development Administration*, pp. 12–13; and India. Planning Commission. *Third Five-Year Plan*, p. 280.

[144] *Economic Times*, December 1, 1965, reporting on the speech by Mr. C. Subramaniam to the All-India Manufacturers Organization in Madras on November 30, 1965.

be studied than are likely to be required. The best way to meet the
continuing need for new projects is to build up and maintain a "stock"
of well-prepared projects from which a suitable variety and number
can be selected to provide a steady flow of new projects to be added to
those already in process of execution.

It must be expected that some of the projects studied will never be
carried out. Nevertheless, the money, time and effort expended to
prepare them are likely to be greatly outweighed by savings from
projects which are used. Because such projects would be ready for
execution whenever resources become available, costly delays could be
avoided. In addition, the existence of a supply of well-prepared
projects ready for execution would make it easier for a country to
secure foreign financing for its development activities.

Once a stock of projects has been accumulated, it is easy to maintain.
If annual operational plans allocate resources for starting new preinvestment and other studies each year, as well as for the continuance
of such studies in progress, a stock of projects can be replenished as
projects are removed for execution. But to build up a stock of projects,
in the first instance, is a difficult task for most less developed countries.
It requires that many feasibility studies be started at once for as many
promising projects as can be identified. The number of such projects
which can be identified can usually be greatly increased by sector
studies. It is therefore desirable, also, to start sector studies going for
the most important sectors in an economy.

In most less developed countries, the simultaneous preparation of
many sector and feasibility studies cannot be carried out without the
help of outside consulting and engineering firms; nor can the whole
operation usually be set up without outside technical assistance. There
is also a need to provide financing for the program, a large part of
which is likely to require foreign exchange. Part of these requirements
may have to come from domestic resources, but supplementary financing from abroad may also have to be arranged. But where such
financing is arranged and effective use is made of outside skills, much
can be done. For example, in Pakistan, over 100 project and program
feasibility studies, besides a number of important sector surveys, were
carried through at the same time in a specially organized "crash
program." The program was inaugurated early in the Second Plan
period to build up a stock of projects for the latter part of the Second
and, especially, for the Third Plan period. The availability of a large
number of projects "ready to go" not only has made it possible for

Pakistan to obtain increased foreign aid, but also helps account for its success in fulfilling and exceeding its plan targets.

Evaluating Plan Progress

As pointed out in Chapter V, flexibility is an essential element of development planning because changing conditions, as well as operational laxity, make deviations from original plan targets unavoidable. A central planning agency must therefore constantly review and assess progress in relation to events. It must seek to identify potential bottlenecks as early as possible, determine their causes, evaluate the extent to which deviations threaten the attainment of plan objectives and suggest measures for dealing with problems.

To perform these functions properly a central planning agency should prepare timely quarterly, semiannual and annual evaluations of plan progress. Almost none does so on a quarterly or semiannual basis and few prepare annual evaluations. Where evaluations are prepared, they often are issued long after the end of the period to which they refer. The best that most planning agencies seem able to do is to issue a mid-term report in a four- or five-year planning period and a review of performance at the end of the planning period, often long after the close of the period concerned.[145]

Reporting Systems. But the fault is not all the central planning agency's. Since implementation of a plan is decentralized in many operating organizations, evaluation of a plan's progress depends on complete, accurate and timely reports on the progress of sector programs and projects. These are almost never available for all projects and programs.

In countries where operating organizations are required to prepare progress reports on prescribed forms by specified dates, many reports do not follow the forms and reports are often late. Some operating

---

[145] For example, the Indian newspaper, *Economic Times,* reported in its issue of November 8, 1963:

> The Second Five-Year Plan ended more than two and a half years ago, but we still do not have a complete review of the Plan operations and results. The Third Plan will shortly enter the fourth year, but the progress for the first year (1961–62) of the Plan period was released only a short while ago.

Even so, the Indian Planning Commission issues progress reports more frequently than planning agencies in most other countries.

organizations submit correct and timely reports, but others exaggerate the progress made on their projects and most fail to report essential data. Information furnished is often too vague and sketchy for a central planning agency to be able to assess the progress made. Progress may be reported in percentage terms without adequate criteria for determining whether the progress made is better, worse or equal to what had been expected. Many operating agencies do not establish physical and financial criteria against which to measure progress, nor do they maintain up-to-date records on the physical or financial progress of their projects.[146] They, therefore, cannot furnish accurate and meaningful information on the status of their projects or programs.

To some extent, the inadequacy and tardiness of reports may be due to an operating organization's hesitation to reveal undue delays in execution; but they are as likely to be caused by apathy toward reporting, the importance of which is often not made apparent to reporting officers. In some cases, the general lack of enthusiasm for progress reporting is a reaction to the elaborateness of the forms used and the multiplicity of reports on the same projects which operating organizations must send to various government offices. Many of these factors have been responsible for inadequate progress reporting in Pakistan. According to a high planning official in that country,

> reports on various projects are filled in half-heartedly and too late to be of much use in the planning process. By the time the Planning Commission learns that a particular project is going to cost about two to three times as much as was originally anticipated, the project is nearly half finished and beyond the point of no return.[147]

But in many countries, even inadequate reports on the progress of projects are never sent to central planning agencies. Thus, Ecuador's National Board of Economic Planning and Coordination reported that in that country,

> since there are no systems of communication between the line agencies and the central planning office there has not been a firm basis for a periodic evaluation of the progress made in the

---

[146] In keeping with the greater interest in some countries in the financial rather than the physical aspects of a project, progress reports often contain information about money spent but little or nothing about physical progress.

[147] Haq, Mahbub ul. *Planning Agencies,* p. 6.

execution of the plans, therefore causing difficulties in making the adjustments necessary due to changing conditions.[148]

Because of the inadequacy of plan evaluation activities and the ineffectiveness of progress reporting by operating agencies, some countries have set up evaluation boards or committees to study projects which have either been completed or are being executed to see what can be learned. India, for example, has a number of evaluation bodies in the Central Government and the states. Some of their work has been useful, especially in calling attention to mistakes commonly made in executing projects, suggesting norms or better organization, and proposing methods and standards for improving the execution and management of projects. But much of their work has merely ended up in a report which,

> in addition to becoming a substitute for action, merely adds to the growing number of reports which pile up on the desks of people too busy to read them.[149]

Such "post-mortems," however good, cannot take the place of a current reporting and evaluation system because they almost always become available too late to permit needed remedial action to be taken for the projects to which they refer. This is inevitable because they are prepared by outside investigators who must probe for facts in a variety of places before they can establish their accuracy. Outside investigators cannot substitute for insiders if timely information is to be obtained on a regular schedule. For an effective current reporting system, what is needed is a two-way communication system between a central planning agency and operating organizations.

---

[148] Ecuador. National Board of Economic Planning and Coordination. "Chapter IV. The Organization for the Plan for Economic Development and the Administrative Reform," p. 7.

[149] Gross, Bertram M. *Activating National Plans*, p. 20. For example, *Economic Times* of February 16, 1965, reported that the Indian Programme Evaluation Organization (PEO) has submitted 13 reports on various projects which, according to the *Economic Times*, achieved little: "Irrespective of these reports the nation continues to spend crores [tens of millions] of rupees on these projects with disproportionately low return compared with the expenditure. The PEO has also pointed out various drawbacks in the implementation of many other schemes like minor irrigation, distribution programme for improved seeds, soil conservation and family planning. But the question arises whether the planners have taken adequate notice of these findings and whether the necessary measures have been taken to improve the situation."

A central planning agency must make explicit the kind of information it requires if operating agencies are to produce data, periodically and promptly, which can be combined quickly to evaluate a plan's progress. While this requires a uniform pattern of reporting, it does not necessarily require the same form for all projects. In fact, the size of individual forms can be reduced and their clarity increased if different forms are used for different kinds of projects. For example, power, industrial, agricultural, educational and health projects can and should be reported on different forms which nevertheless permit the combination of the physical and financial data they supply.

The shorter and simpler the reporting form, the more likely the information will be forthcoming. Project supervisors, understandably interested primarily in carrying out their projects, tend to think of progress reporting as an interference with their main activity. In these circumstances, voluminous or complex forms get short shrift and defeat their purpose. In the UAR, for instance, reporting forms were so complicated to fill out and time-consuming (e.g., the progress reporting form for construction of industrial projects was a folder of 20 pages which required data for 14 different tables) that few of the ministries bothered to complete the forms. Those that did usually provided inaccurate data and sent their reports late. Eventually, the forms had to be scrapped.

In contrast, Malaya (now a part of Malaysia) uses a form for construction projects whose simplicity and effectiveness would be hard to improve upon. The form for each project has 12 rectangles, one for each month in the year. Each rectangle is divided diagonally from bottom left to upper right into two triangles. An appropriate symbol is entered in each of the 12 upper triangles which indicates the expected progress of the project each month of the year.[150] Every month, the agency responsible for executing a project must enter the symbol recording actual performance in the appropriate lower triangle. If performance is on schedule, it is entered in black; if ahead of schedule,

[150] The following standardized symbols are employed:

A—Preliminary action (including acquisition of site).
B—Detailed planning (including the preparation of surveys, designs and specifications).
C—Purchase of equipment (or machinery, if required).
D—Tenders and awards of contract.
E—Project under construction or otherwise being executed.
F—Project completed.

it is entered in green; if behind schedule, in red. If projects are behind schedule, the report must give reasons for the delay. Anyone concerned with a project can therefore tell at a glance when it is lagging.[151]

Copies of the same form are sent to all ministries and departments interested in a project, as well as to the central planning agency. In some countries, however, requests for reports from several government agencies may require a project director to fill out a large number of different forms periodically. In Pakistan, for example, project directors have had to provide 10 to 50 different reports on a simple project each quarter to meet the demands of various government agencies. Project directors have complained that the large number of reports they must prepare periodically, plus the voluminous correspondence they give rise to, greatly reduces the time they can give to the execution of their projects.

The reporting interval needs to be fitted to the needs of different kinds of projects. The reporting period in Malaya is a month. This is satisfactory for some projects which can record appreciable progress in that time, but it is too short a period for other projects which progress more slowly. Where there is little progress on a project within a reporting period, reporting officers tend to delay reporting since they see no point in repeating the previous month's report. In most countries, an interval of three months has generally been found suitable for most projects, but it may not be possible to report progress on some slow-moving projects, like those for agricultural research, in intervals of less than six months. In contrast, for fast-moving projects like some building and road construction work, it may be desirable to have monthly or even fortnightly reports.

The time limit for the submission of progress reports must also be determined by reference to the kind of projects involved. Usually, reports should be submitted within one month after the close of a reporting period. In the case of simple projects, the time limit can be reduced to 15 days. But where information has to be gathered from several sources, this time limit is generally inadequate. This was the experience, for example, when West Pakistan had a 15-day time limit. It was found that data on the progress of education programs, each of which usually comprised a number of smaller projects in various parts

[151] Thong Yaw Hong. *Building Institutions for Preparing and Executing Development Plans, the Malaysian Experience*, pp. 16–17; and Wilcox, Clair. *Planning and Execution of Economic Development in Southeast Asia*, pp. 29–30.

of the Province, could not be collected and entered on reports in less than a month after the close of the reporting period.[152]

The setting up of a reporting system for all projects and programs may be too difficult for some countries to carry out at one time. If so, it would be preferable to establish partial progress reporting. For this purpose, priorities have to be set up for including only the most important projects in the reporting system. Such an approach was recommended by a Working Group of the Indian Planning Commission created to consider ways of improving progress reporting and evaluation in the various states of India; the suggestions of the Group illustrate the establishment of reporting priorities in one situation. The projects and programs considered of sufficiently high priority for inclusion in state reporting systems were those (a) of a pilot nature; (b) showing persistent shortfalls, lags and difficulties; (c) considered to be "impact" or "crash" projects or programs; (d) involving large outlays; (e) relying for their success on the co-operation and participation of the people and local institutions; and (f) for the benefit of backward areas.[153]

Even if a good reporting system is set up, it will not work unless the political authorities in a country support it. In Burma, for example, a reporting system was designed which met planning needs. Regular progress reports were to be supplemented with special reports where necessary, but

> when in practice it proved impossible to get the supervising authorities to pay attention to these reports, the basic objectives [of the reporting system] were abandoned.[154]

In contrast, in Malaya, the authorities' exacting and continuing demands for up-to-date, accurate and complete information make officials all along the line respond with alacrity to the requirements of the reporting system. The Cabinet periodically reviews the progress of development plans on the basis of reports received from the districts, each of which has its own plan embodied in a "red book." [155] The

---

[152] Khan, Jehanqir. *Progress Reporting—How Can We Achieve the Contemplated Objectives,* p. 5.

[153] *Economic Times,* February 16, 1965.

[154] Walinsky, Louis J. "Burma," p. 49.

[155] The book is colored bright red to make it conspicuous. It is three feet by four feet to make it difficult to mislay. It contains a basic map of the district concerned which can be placed under any of a number of map tracings in the book. One tracing shows road projects in the district plan, another schools, a third industries, a fourth

Deputy Prime Minister, who is in *de facto* charge of planning, also calls for monthly briefings, which may be convened on short notice. Because of this, every official responsible for a program is expected to keep himself fully informed at all times about the course of his program.

Reviews and briefings are carried out in a "National Operations Room," adjacent to the offices of the Deputy Prime Minister and the Economic Planning Unit. The National Operations Room contains the red books of all the districts, progress reports, wall maps and charts [156] depicting the status of development programs in each economic sector throughout the country. Each ministry in charge of a program must enter up-to-date data on the map and chart depicting its program. The Operations Room is equipped with movie and slide projectors, a lectern and a public address system with tape recorder. Ministers or department heads must give the briefings called for by the Deputy Prime Minister. Briefings are recorded and retained in the National Operations Room for reference purposes. The Deputy Prime Minister's instructions require that briefings be concise and precise, and that they refer to the wall maps, charts and progress reports.

In addition to these briefings in the capital, the Deputy Prime Minister and other officials regularly tour the states and districts. The Deputy Prime Minister makes frequently unannounced visits to each of the 70 districts at least once a year and sometimes as many as three or four times. These visits to each district permit him to discuss problems with the local people, mobilize their support and participation in implementing projects and eliminate bottlenecks on the spot. The Deputy Prime Minister, frequently accompanied by high officials concerned with the various programs, tries to make on-the-spot decisions to resolve problems and, where necessary, allocates additional funds to carry out specific tasks or works from a special fund he controls for the purpose. In every state and district he visits he is briefed on the status of the territory's projects and programs. Each state and district

waterworks, etc. When a tracing is placed over the basic map in the red book, the exact location of each project can be determined. A pocket adjoining each tracing contains written summaries of the projects in order of priority in the economic sector concerned. Each red book thus provides all the information needed for anyone to visualize a district's development projects. (Wilcox, Clair. *Planning and Execution of Economic Development in Southeast Asia*, pp. 26–27; and Thong Yaw Hong. *Building Institutions for Preparing and Executing Development Plans, the Malaysian Experience*, p. 11.)

[156] The charts contain information transferred from progress reports. Like the progress reports, entries are made in black, green or red to indicate whether projects are advancing on time, ahead of schedule or behind schedule, respectively.

has its own operations room, with its red book(s), wall maps, charts, etc. Since there is no telling when the Deputy Prime Minister or another high official may arrive without prior notice, state and local officials tend to keep the data in their operations rooms up to date, and what is more important, keep themselves informed on the progress of their projects and why any may not be progressing as expected. In this way, officials know what needs to be known and everything that is known about projects is exposed for all to see in the operations rooms instead of being locked away in a file which might not be accessible.

The use of a standardized system of records on the Malayan federal, state and district levels enables any official in the operations room at any level to see for himself the status of development projects in the territory concerned. The system reduces unnecessary paper work, correspondence and red tape because the common pattern of recording and procedures permits problems to be resolved by telephone. An official can put in a call to another and, by referring to maps and charts they both maintain in the same way, clear up any point much more quickly than by writing.[157] This has helped reduce congestion at the center of government and enabled officials concerned with development to act swiftly in response to changing circumstances.[158] The methods employed have proved to be so successful that it is proposed to extend them to all the states which comprise the Federation of Malaysia.[159]

Other countries have sought to model their reporting and plan evaluation systems on the Malayan "Operations Room" pattern. Thus, the Ministry of National Development in Thailand set up an Operations Room, and a Presidential Economic Operations Center was established in the Philippines. But while these were equipped with wall maps, charts, audio-visual aids and other trappings, they proved to be ineffective because they lacked the prime factor which accounts for the success of the Malayan evaluation and reporting system: someone in high authority to put the full force of his office behind the system on a continuing basis.

Analysis of Projects. Just as the basic technical requisite of a good evaluation system is a good reporting system, the basic technical

---

[157] Moynihan, M. J. *Ops Room Technique,* pp. 14–15.

[158] Thong Yaw Hong. *Building Institutions for Preparing and Executing Development Plans, the Malaysian Experience,* p. 19.

[159] *Ibid.*

requisite of a good reporting system is prior analysis of projects and programs which permits realistic time schedules and cost estimates to be set up as criteria against which to measure progress. The whole process—plan evaluation; progress reporting on the plan, sector program and project levels; and the analysis of the projects for the purpose of setting goals against which to measure and evaluate progress—must be seen as a series of closely interrelated steps in which prior detailed analysis of each project is the key element.

This is because the reports which operating agencies send to a central planning agency must reveal whether progress on a project or program has been slow, satisfactory or fast. Such reports are possible only if the time required to complete a project or program has first been analyzed and divided into reporting periods and a set of specific financial and physical goals have been predetermined for each period. Otherwise, it may not be possible to judge whether progress indicated for a reporting period is satisfactory.

Goals set for a project or program are likely to vary from one reporting period to another. Thus, when a project or program has just begun, it generally shows little progress in early reporting periods because most of the time is spent on preliminary work. As work gains momentum, however, progress may be expected to be faster than in previous periods. But unless a time schedule and cost estimates have been worked out for each reporting period, it is not possible to determine whether progress in any period is what it should be. For this purpose, a schedule and a cost estimate for the project as a whole are worth little, since actual progress is generally made in a series of small steps on a variety of jobs. Indeed, a reliable time schedule or cost estimate for a project or program as a whole can be estimated only by adding up how long it will take and how much it will cost to complete the many tasks which must be done before the entire project is completed.

It is therefore essential for the purposes of progress reporting that a project be divided into a series of discrete segments (e.g., selection of a site, acquisition of land, issuance of tenders, erection of a plant, purchase and installation of machinery, construction of an access highway, training personnel for the plant, etc.) for which specific time schedules and cost estimates can be set for each reporting period. The segments of the project and the goals set must be consistent with the way orders will be placed and contracts awarded. If, for instance, a plant with three major components is to be built, each by a different contractor, separate time schedules and cost estimates have to be set up for segments of each of the three components in the project. If the goals cut across contractors' areas of operation, the contractors' reports will be difficult to reconcile with the goals. A similar approach is necessary when several government organizations work on different aspects of a project or program. Such divisions of a project are in any event essential if operating organizations are to check on and maintain appropriate control over the progress of their projects and programs.[160]

When goals are set for clearly defined jobs to be performed by each contractor, government organization or project director, means are provided by the periodic reports they prepare to measure the per-

---

[160] A number of programing techniques which have recently come into wide use in the United States and the United Kingdom are being applied to development projects to separate them into basic components for facilitating both control and reporting functions. These include CPA (Critical Path Analysis), PERT (Program Evaluation Review Technique), RAMPS (Resource Allocation and Multi-Project Scheduling) and SPAR (Scheduling Program for Allocating Resources). Two of these techniques, CPA and PERT, are generally similar and are the most frequently used. To illustrate, CPA requires that, on the basis of a careful analysis, a project be divided into a "network" of individual jobs showing the sequence in which each job has to be done and the time it is expected to take. By presenting the time sequence for each job as a line or "path," a graphic presentation is made of the project from start to finish as a series of separate paths which merge eventually at or just before the finish of a project.

The path (or job) which takes the longest to complete is the limiting or "critical path" for a project. Anything which can be done to reduce the length of the critical path reduces the time needed to complete the project. Since all the "noncritical" paths require less time to complete, there is no point in trying to reduce the time it takes to complete them if it involves increased expense. Instead, every effort needs to be made to transfer unused manpower and other resources from noncritical paths to the critical path to reduce its length.

A variety of advantages are claimed for CPA (and the other techniques). It not only permits a project to be divided into component parts for reporting and control purposes; it also can provide a reliable prediction of a project's completion date. It focuses attention on the more important aspects of a project, thereby making possible improved utilization of resources and reductions in the time it takes to complete a project. Moreover, it provides a common, easily understood language for every person, government organization and contractor engaged on a project; they can, therefore, better comprehend their own relationship to the project and fit their activities into the entire operation with minimum friction. Finally, it facilitates coordination of the efforts of the various participants working on a project.

CPA and the various other techniques can also be used to assure that complementary projects are dovetailed or "phased" so that each related project is finished when needed. In this way, time and money is not wasted, either by delays in completing complementary projects or components of projects, or by completing them before they are needed.

formance of those responsible for carrying out a project. If a project is going poorly, it then becomes possible to determine whether those who are carrying it out are primarily responsible or whether inadequate results are due to factors beyond their control.

If actual costs and physical progress have not corresponded to the original goals, it is important to revise them, taking account of the experience gained. This may merely involve rescheduling work which has not been completed as originally scheduled. But if discrepancies between goals and performance are great, it may require reappraisal of an entire project to see whether it pays to go ahead with it. In some cases, it may be better to discontinue the project and take a loss rather than continue with it and lose a lot more. Where, after reappraisal, a decision is made to continue with a project, review and revision of goals may nevertheless make it apparent that prompt steps need to be taken to obtain additional financial or other resources to complete the project. It is important to recognize mistakes and problems early. Periodic review and revision of goals based on past experience help reveal errors and make it possible to foresee and deal with difficulties before they become serious.

SUMMARY AND CONCLUSIONS

Planning has done much to help promote growth in less developed countries, but there have been many more failures than successes in the implementation of development plans. In fact, very few less developed countries have succeeded in consistently achieving reasonable plan targets over an extended period. Moreover, the gap between promise and performance appears to be widening.

The greatest shortfalls are usually in agriculture. Since agriculture's contribution to the output of most less developed countries is high, the failure to achieve agricultural targets mainly accounts for lower than planned rates of growth. In the mixed economies, successes in realizing industrial growth targets have generally been greater in the private than in the public sector. It is the growth in the private sector—often in ways inimical to plan provisions—which usually accounts for most of the increases in a country's national income.

Some governments tend to overemphasize the fulfillment of investment targets to the neglect of physical targets because they believe that investment virtually insures development. Concentration on how quickly rather than on how well money is spent often leads to serious shortfalls in output targets. Because of a scarcity of well-prepared projects, many countries find it difficult to invest all the money they have available on such projects. They also experience abnormal delays in executing projects, higher than expected costs, shoddy construction of projects, selection of low yield projects and under-utilization of completed facilities which, taken together, explain why plan targets are often unfulfilled.

Causal factors, which vary greatly, are only partially within a country's control. But, in general, most of the problems which arise are attributable to poor planning. Failures are traceable to unduly ambitious targets and poor financial controls, the widespread failure of governments to maintain the discipline implicit in their plans, token efforts to co-ordinate economic and financial policies as required by plans, the absence of general criteria and procedures for selecting projects and programs in accordance with plan objectives, and, perhaps the most common reason for failure, inadequate project selection and preparation.

The great dearth of good projects ready for execution in most less developed countries is only partly due to the long time it takes to choose and prepare them. The main reason is that the need for the requisite sector, feasibility and engineering studies is not fully appreciated. Without proper studies, the actual costs, benefits and construction times often deviate substantially from original estimates, and sponsors of projects almost invariably overestimate the benefits and underestimate the costs and the time needed to complete them.

Administrative and procedural delays also constitute one of the most important reasons why plans are not implemented. In many governments, extraordinary lapses of time occur before a problem or a need for action is recognized, between the time it is recognized and a decision is made what to do about it, and finally, between the time a decision is made and it is carried out.

The failure of most planners to indicate precisely what must be done to carry out plans has tended to intensify the belief that the problems of plan formulation are separable from those of implementation. The tendency to separate plan formulation from implementation has been exacerbated by planners' preoccupation with economic factors to the exclusion of organizational, administrative and political factors. This gives rise to serious problems because in most less developed countries, the greatest obstacles to implementation are administrative and, especially, political, rather than economic.

The available evidence makes it clear that in countries with development plans, lack of adequate government support for the plans is the prime reason why most are never carried out. Conversely, the cardinal lesson that emerges from the planning experience of developing countries is that the sustained commitment of a politically stable government is a *sine qua non* for development. Where a country's political leadership makes development a central concern, the people can also be interested through the judicious use of economic incentives. And, although it is never easy to reform administrative and institutional inefficiency, commitment by political leaders is a necessary condition for reform; without it, reform is impossible.

If planners are to set realistic plan targets, they must find means to measure, quantitatively, administrative inadequacy and the lack of political "will to develop." These measurements are essential if planners are to "discount" the overly optimistic results usually obtained by the formulation of plans solely on the basis of economic potentialities alone. Administrative inefficiency can be measured by reference to previous discrepancies between original estimates and actual performance for projects in each sector. The political "will to develop" can be measured by requiring political decision-makers to select, in each of a series of relevant policy areas, one of several practicable alternatives which collectively indicate the extent to which a government is prepared to take concrete measures to further development. If these decisions precede plan formulation, planners can prepare their plans on the basis of known government policies instead of the planners' estimates of what a government might do.

If the three basic elements which enter into the planning process—economic potential, administrative capacity and political will to develop—are all taken into account in plan formulation, plan targets are bound to be more in line with a country's real capacity to achieve its economic potentialities. Since these plan targets are likely to be low, plans would focus attention on the administrative and political problems which limit plan implementation in most countries. By bringing home to government leaders the full impact of these limitations and presenting them with specific alternatives for overcoming them, planning could become in fact, what it is in theory, a rational way of mobilizing and organizing productive resources for development. The separation which now exists in most countries between plan formulation and implementation would then tend to disappear.

But planning would have little justification if it only brought the targets of a plan down to levels which more accurately reflected the

actual capacity of a country to attain them. A prime purpose of
planning must be to improve implementation to make it possible to
accelerate the rate of development. Because it takes several years to
identify and prepare soundly conceived projects and programs needed
to carry out a plan, it is too late for planners to become concerned
about them only when a plan is being formulated. Just as planning is a
continuous process, preparation of projects must be continuous. In the
public sector, this can best be accomplished by building up and
maintaining a "stock" of well-prepared projects from which to draw on.

As pointed out, planning requires periodic evaluation of plan progress. But the evaluations prepared by most central planning agencies
are not sufficiently frequent and timely. This is not entirely the central
planning agency's fault. Plan evaluation depends on accurate, complete and timely reports by operating organizations and these are
practically never available for most projects and programs in process of
execution. For an effective current reporting system to operate, a
two-way communication system must be set up between a central
planning agency and operating organizations. The planning agency
must make explicit the kind of information it requires. Forms must be
short and simple if they are not to defeat their purpose. The forms used
must be "tailored" to the needs of different kinds of projects and, as far
as feasible, one form should be used for reports to all government
agencies concerned with a project. The reporting interval and the time
limit for progress reports must also be determined by reference to the
kinds of projects involved.

Just as the basic technical requisite for a good evaluation system is a
good reporting system, the basic technical requisite of a good reporting
system is prior analysis of projects which results in the setting up of
realistic time schedules and cost estimates as criteria against which to
measure progress. For this purpose a schedule and a cost estimate for
an entire project are worth little since actual progress is generally made
in a series of small steps on a variety of jobs. It is therefore essential for
reporting purposes—and also for controlling execution—for projects to
be divided into a series of discrete segments for which specific time
schedules and cost estimates can be set for each reporting period.
When this is done in accordance with techniques which have come into
use in recent years, it is not only possible to prepare meaningful reports
which accurately depict the financial and physical progress of projects
and programs, but also to control execution in a way which insures
maximum returns from resources employed.

PART TWO

The Organization of Planning

Chapter X

Planning Machinery Priorities

> If we could first know *where* we are, and *whither*
> we are tending, we could better judge *what*
> to do, and *how* to do it.—Abraham Lincoln

INTRODUCTION

THE KIND of planning machinery a country establishes, like the kind of development planning it adopts, depends largely on its political, social and economic institutions and its stage of development. In the socialized economies, establishment of a central planning agency is an essential first step in the planning process. The economic plan in these countries is not the only instrument for setting economic policy, but it is frequently the principal and decisive one. The two primary tasks of a central planning agency in most socialized countries are to prepare plans based on government directives and to co-ordinate all major controls on wages, demand, manpower, investment, prices and other economic factors for the purpose of achieving plan targets. As indicated earlier, there is a clearly noticeable tendency in socialized countries toward the decentralization of economic decision-making as their economies develop. This involves the creation or expansion of regional or local planning bodies and the gradual devolution of an increasing amount of authority to them. In Yugoslavia, since 1952, planning bodies in republics, districts and, especially, communes have taken over many planning functions formerly exercised by the central agency. Since 1957, a similar trend has developed in the USSR, Mainland China and, more recently, in most Eastern European countries. But in every socialized country, a central planning agency continues to formulate the national development plan which planning bodies in the regions, localities and enterprises use as the main guide in preparing their own plans.

In the mixed economies in contrast with the socialized economies, a central planning agency has generally been established long after development activity has started in the form of a series of projects, an integrated public investment plan or a more comprehensive development plan. In India, for example, when a Planning Commission was established in 1950, it found a large stockpile of projects in process of execution which, after being collected, largely constituted the First Five-Year Plan. In several countries, more advanced development plans have been prepared before a central planning agency was established. Sweden and Norway, where several five-year "national budgets" were formulated by *ad hoc* commissions, have only recently established central planning agencies. And Finland, where a temporary commission prepared a five-year plan, has not yet established a central planning agency. In Taiwan, also, the establishment of a real central planning agency came long after development programing began.

WHEN A CENTRAL PLANNING AGENCY WORKS BADLY

In most countries with mixed economies, development efforts—whether reflected in projects, programs or plans—have generally been more or less co-ordinated through an annual financial budget. As we have seen, this remains the commonest way in which public investment activities are co-ordinated. This means that, in practice, it is the budget office, usually located in a ministry of finance, which is the *de facto* planning authority in most countries. The establishment of a central planning agency frequently does not alter existing practice appreciably. The ministry of finance is apt to continue determining the allocation of public funds through the budget with only limited reference to plans which a central planning agency produces.

The shortcomings of this system are obvious. Yet it must be recognized that even without a central planning agency, a country can sustain a high rate of growth when reasonably well-prepared projects are co-ordinated through a budget by a competent ministry of finance. This was, for example, true in Mexico until 1955 and in Israel until 1961, when functioning central planning agencies were first established in both countries. And since the planning agencies in both countries have not operated effectively, the allocation of public investment resources is still largely determined by their respective ministries of finance through their annual budgets. The available evidence in these and in other countries suggests that, although a central planning agency may be useful and, possibly, essential to rapid development sometimes in some countries, it is not necessary for rapid development in all countries at all times.

Nor does the addition of a central planning agency to a government administration, by itself, improve efficiency, eliminate bottlenecks or speed development appreciably in most countries. Experience indicates that where a government is administratively backward, corrupt or politically unstable (or ruled by a coalition of parties or by a military junta), or where its leaders are not genuinely committed to development planning, the establishment of a central planning agency is generally of little value in bringing about a significant improvement in the rate of development. The presence of one or more of these limiting factors in many less developed countries explains why most central planning agencies have been far less effective than they might have been. In countries where government ministries, departments and agencies have considerable autonomy, a central planning agency is also unlikely to play a significant role in development activities. This is an important reason, for example, why the central planning agencies in Mexico and Israel have had only limited influence on the course of development in their countries.

Despite the ineffectiveness of central planning agencies in most less developed countries, the prevailing assumption in planning circles is that it is desirable as a first step in the planning process for every country with a mixed economy, regardless of its stage of development or conditions in its government, to establish a central planning agency. Thus, the Latin American Planning Seminar, composed of 37 experts "with wide experience in the work of economic and social planning" [1] recommended that

> at the initial stage the minimum organization would consist only of the central nucleus . . . [i.e., the central planning agency].[2]

In practice, the creation of such an agency generally involves the grafting of the new entity to some point in the public administration in an otherwise essentially unchanged government structure. The head chosen for the new agency is then expected simultaneously to staff it, set up a working planning organization and produce a development plan, usually within a period of a few months or a year. He never succeeds in doing all these things and frequently fails conspicuously in accomplishing any of them within the assigned period.

---

[1] UN. ECLA. *Report of the Latin American Seminar on Planning*, p. 1.
[2] *Ibid.*, p. 44.

There is a widespread lack of understanding that it takes a long time to staff and build a viable central planning agency. In this connection, Pakistan's experience with its central planning agency is both pertinent and revealing. Since 1954, Pakistan has received the continuous services of a group of advisers provided by Harvard University with the aid of a Ford Foundation grant.[3] Few countries have received high caliber foreign planning assistance on as large a scale. But after more than a decade, the central planning agency was still without an adequate staff and faced serious organization problems which prevented it from effectively performing all the functions assigned to it.

Nor is there adequate appreciation that the preparation of a good development plan takes time. The time allotted for preparing a plan is consequently likely to be much too short. As a result, many plans are completed late. The publicity which attends the establishment of a central planning agency, as well as its very existence, tends to create strong pressures for the early production of a plan. What often happens in response to these pressures is that a medium-term plan is hastily formulated with incomplete data and an inadequate number of supporting projects (which are often poorly conceived and poorly prepared), mostly within the confines of a central planning agency, sometimes almost exclusively by foreigners who usually leave the country soon after the plan has been drafted. Eventually, the plan is embodied in a volume and published with much fanfare.

In a typical case, the few available trained technicians, both domestic and foreign, have been straining hard to complete the plan within an arbitrarily prescribed period and so have had little time to acquire and train a permanent staff for the planning agency and to organize it as a going concern. Thus, with the completion of the plan, the central planning agency is not equipped to prepare the annual plan needed to make the medium-term plan operational nor to do the other tasks required to make it operational. Unhappily, therefore, although it may make a readable addition to the economic literature of the country, the medium-term plan prepared in this way is almost never fulfilled. Indeed, in some countries, it is shelved soon after its completion because it is found to be too unrealistic in the prevailing circumstances.

When the planning effort turns out badly, the central planning

[3] Beginning June 1965, the World Bank has financed this technical assistance program.

agency may be abolished or replaced. More frequently, it is permitted to continue operating in virtual isolation from the rest of the government, largely ignored by government officials and political leaders.[4] Sometimes, a second agency, with vague and apparently overlapping functions is established. Or the head or members of the first planning agency are replaced several times, the character of the planning agency is altered one or more times or it is moved from one place in the administrative structure to another. In many countries, including Burma, Colombia, Korea and Nepal, frequent changes of the head of the central planning agency, or shifts in its structure or location, have reflected dissatisfaction of political authorities with the work of the agency. Frequent changes in direction, organization or administrative location of a planning agency, generally lower its standing and impair its ability to influence development.

PRIORITY FOR PROGRAMING UNITS

Because those concerned with the creation of national planning machinery have considered it essential to concentrate on the establishment of a central planning agency, they have given little attention to the creation of "programing" units in operating organizations. The establishment of such units, which are essentially planning bodies on the level of operating organizations, is important for improving the quality of project and sector program preparation, execution and reporting.[5] In fact, the need for special programing units in operating ministries and agencies has not been recognized by planners in most countries until long after the creation of a central planning agency. Pakistan's planning authorities only got around in earnest to the task of creating programing units in operating organizations seven or eight years after the founding of its central planning agency. The Iranian Plan Organization began to sponsor the creation of programing units in operating ministries in 1963, 15 years after its own establishment. And it took the Indian Planning Commission 13 years after its establishment to reach the conclusion that,

[4] In Morocco, the standing of the *Division du Plan,* the central planning agency, declined to a point where it was not even involved in the formulation of the Three-Year Plan for 1965–67. The Plan was prepared by technicians from the French *Commissariat Général du Plan* in conjunction with government officials appointed by the Government to a series of sectoral and other commissions.

[5] The role and function of programing units are discussed in the last chapter.

in order that planning of projects is done in sufficient detail, it appears necessary to set up appropriate planning units in the Ministries and design and technical organizations in major public sector undertakings. These suggestions are currently under examination in consultation with the Ministries.[6]

But most countries have not even gone as far as this. Consequently, only a few governments have organized programing units and fewer still have units which operate effectively.

As already indicated, a prime technical difficulty encountered in the execution of most public investment plans has been the absence of a sufficient number of well-prepared projects, as well as the lack of effective systems for carrying them out. Since the proper preparation of enough good projects and their combination into sector programs which take account of priorities and resources are indispensable to rapid development, whether or not a plan exists, it is clear that programing units in operating agencies are at least as important as a central planning agency for any country which seeks to speed its rate of growth. Indeed, the absence or ineffectiveness of programing units is the most important flaw in the planning apparatus of even the more experienced less developed countries. But the almost complete lack of such units in countries in earlier stages of development, practically all of which have barely begun to learn how to prepare projects and sector programs, is an especially severe handicap to effective planning. Thus, Ecuador's planners concluded that

> it can be said that the National Planning Board has not yet reached a high level of its functions due to the fact that, in order to carry out the process of national planning, it is necessary to have a central office as a nucleus, and programing offices in all the economic sectors. There is the nucleus in Ecuador for this process which is the National Planning Board; but the sectoral components which would permit this process to be fully carried out is lacking.[7]

Experience shows that in countries at the beginning of the planning process, there is little chance that aggregative plans can be carried out until the rudiments of project and sector programing are mastered.

[6] India. Planning Commission. *Third Plan Mid-Term Appraisal*, pp. 124–125.

[7] Ecuador. National Board of Economic Planning and Coordination. "Chapter IV. The Organization for the Plan for Economic Development and the Administrative Reform," p. 8.

There is therefore a reasonable probability that these countries would benefit more at first from the establishment of programing units than from the establishment of a central planning agency. It is also possible that more rapid progress toward development could be obtained from programing units in operating organizations than from a central planning agency in countries characterized by political instability, or lack of genuine commitment of political leaders to development. Such countries have shown that they are not yet ready to make effective use of a central planning agency because they will not or cannot do what is required to carry out a national development plan. Yet, there are often "islands" of relative stability or commitment in one or more ministries or government departments and agencies in these governments where programing units can do effective work in improving project and sectoral programing.

The creation of such units would tend to speed up development and could also provide an essential foundation for the formulation and execution of plans prepared by a central planning agency established at a later stage. The number of programing units created at one time in government operating organizations would depend on the availability of technicians and the opportunities for such units to do constructive work. Even if the lack of technicians or conditions in a government made it feasible to establish a unit in only one operating organization, it could have a significant "demonstration effect" on the rest of the administration.

The ideal approach, of course, is to try to establish both a central planning agency and programing units simultaneously. But the acute shortage of technicians precludes this solution in many, if not in most, less developed countries. There just are not enough trained planners and technicians, whether of local or foreign origin, available to do both jobs at the same time in most countries. Nor is it to be expected that, if a central planning agency is given first priority, it can take on as one of its first assignments the creation of programing units. As already noted, there are generally too many pressures on a newly created central planning agency to produce a development plan quickly to permit it even to organize itself as a viable entity in less than five to ten years. But even more important, as will be seen later, there are good reasons for believing that a central planning agency is not an appropriate medium for organizing programing units in operating organizations. For most less advanced countries in early stages of development, therefore, the choice comes down to whether a central planning agency or programing units in ministries, departments and agencies will do more to accelerate development in the first instance.

PRIORITY FOR IMPROVING BUDGETARY PROCEDURES

It is desirable that a central planning agency be established as soon as a government is willing and able to make a reasonably adequate effort to carry out the more advanced development plans which a central planning agency is best qualified to prepare and co-ordinate. But until then, it is likely to be easier and quicker in many countries to get better co-ordination of public investment expenditures by improving budgetary procedures of an existing budgetary authority (along lines described in Chapter VII) than to get it through planning procedures of a newly created central planning agency. Experience shows that it is undesirable to try to establish a central planning agency prematurely. The time and benefits gained by its creation are likely to be outweighed by the time and effort needed to secure its acceptance within the government.

In many countries where central planning agencies have been in existence for years, they are still unable, under conditions prevailing in their governments, to exercise the co-ordinative functions which their enabling legislation gave them. Although it is usually neither practicable nor desirable to abolish an ineffective central planning agency in countries where one already exists, the most effective way of quickly improving co-ordination of public investment in these countries may also be by improving current budgetary practices and organization. Experience shows that it is largely a waste of time to try to force upon an indifferent, reluctant or hostile public administration a theoretically more advanced form of co-ordination through a central planning agency which, at best, must take a long time before it is accepted by the rest of the government administration. It is apt to be easier to improve co-ordination through a budget office which is already fully accepted by operating organizations in a government.

The discussion in previous chapters has made the point that sound budgetary controls and practices, like effective project and sector preparation and execution, constitute a prerequisite for successful implementation of development plans. This implies, of course, that the improvement of budgetary procedures and practices, where needed, must get at least as high a priority as (1) efficient project and sector program preparation and execution, and (2) aggregative planning. Experience unfortunately shows that countries almost never have the technical resources to prepare a plan and tighten budgetary controls simultaneously. Of course, they are even less able to establish programing units, as well as improve budgetary procedures and prepare a plan at the same time. In practice, therefore, budgetary betterment, like programing units, almost always gives way to the establishment of a central planning unit and the preparation of an aggregative plan. The effects of this approach to planning are all too evident in the record of failure to implement development plans in most less developed countries.

A PLANNED APPROACH TO PLANNING ORGANIZATION

Before setting up planning machinery for a less developed country, therefore, serious consideration needs to be given to the alternatives to a central planning agency. Even if a central planning agency is decided upon, much thought needs to be given to the kind of planning which the agency will be expected to do. One might think it is obvious that the kind of central planning organization required for simple planning ought to be different from one needed for complex planning. But experience shows that it is not obvious. Many countries establish central planning agencies without giving much thought to whether the agency is going to begin by rationalizing current public investment, preparing sector programs, regional plans, an investment plan for the public sector or a comprehensive development plan; or whether it will draw up a one-year, five-year or twenty-year plan. If one may judge from the functions usually assigned to central planning agencies, there appears to be a notion, vague and undefined though it may be, that it is to do all these things and more.

A country about to establish a planning apparatus has much to learn from the experience of countries which have been planning for some time. Indeed, few countries seek to avail themselves of the experience of other countries before they establish their planning apparatus. Partly, this is because the experience of other countries is not always known; but it is also partly due to the fact that each country tends to assume that its own social, political and economic problems are unique. Of course, this is true. But it is also true that most countries have many similar problems and, experience shows, frequently make the same mistakes. Clearly, investigation is called for before a country embarks on a planning course. But if a country has much to learn from the experience of other countries, there are also dangers in the uncritical adoption by one country of the planning organization of another. For example, India's planning organization has attracted many countries. But, as Professor Galbraith has pointed out,

> the Government of India is a complex and multifarious thing which reflects the great variety of tasks undertaken by India in her stages of development. An equally complex organization would be a major misfortune for one of the newer African states with, for the foreseeable future, a far simpler range of tasks.[8]

Recent successes of the French planning system and organization have also made French planning organization particularly attractive to other countries. The French system of "indicative planning," involving the use of a large number of sectoral and general commissions which perform important tasks in the course of plan preparation, is based on cartelized industries, much of it nationalized, public investments which approximate half of total investment in the country, along with a nationalized credit system and government controls over private industrial financing, a weak trade union movement and a tradition of close co-operation between business and government. In addition, it relies on a civil service system of especial competence. Few less developed countries can lay claim to a similar set of circumstances. Yet several less developed countries with very different conditions, including Egypt, Morocco and Tanganyika, have modeled their planning organization on the French prototype.

What happens when a less developed country adopts a system of planning which is beyond its capacity has nowhere been revealed better than in Morocco. Soon after independence, the Moroccans abstracted from the French governmental structure the relatively complex French planning apparatus and transplanted it almost without change to their own country. But Morocco was not ready to make effective use of a planning system which depended on a well-co-ordinated public administration, staffed with experienced civil servants working under broadly agreed and consistent directives. Partly for this reason, planning in Morocco fell far short of potentialities.

There is much to be said, therefore, for a country about to plan its

[8] Galbraith, John K. *Economic Development in Perspective*, p. 27.

development to begin by planning its planning organization in a systematic way. To this end, it might be worthwhile for the head of government to appoint a high-level committee, with access to the best available local, foreign and international technical advisers, to determine the kind of planning machinery most suited to a country which seeks to begin to plan. In making its recommendations, the committee must take account of the country's political, economic and social circumstances, its stage of development and the scarcity of technicians, as well as the kind of planning called for in the prevailing situation. If hearings, at which qualified and interested persons could testify, were held and the committee's proposals widely circulated, the committee could become the medium for creating workable planning machinery whose creation was based on a careful consideration of all the relevant facts.

This was, in essence, what was done in India. In 1946, just before India's independence, the Interim Cabinet of the Government appointed an Advisory Planning Board to survey the planning work which had already been done and to recommend means for establishing effective planning machinery.[9] The Board produced a widely publicized report which, together with the work of other groups, led in 1950 to the establishment of the Indian Planning Commission. In contrast to this organized approach, many less developed countries have an individual or two draft a decree or other legislation informally, often *in camera*, which provides for the setting up of a central planning agency with an ill-assorted list of functions. Only rarely is there consultation with those inside or outside government most likely to be affected. Planning machinery set up in this way has usually proved to be inappropriate to the need.

SUMMARY AND CONCLUSIONS

In the socialized economies, a central planning agency is established as an essential first step in planning. But in the mixed economies, it is usually established long after development activity of one kind or another has begun. For a variety of reasons, the creation of a central planning agency has not, by itself, speeded development appreciably in most countries. Experience shows that where a government is

[9] Ghosh, O. K. *Problems of Economic Planning in India*, p. 48.

administratively backward, corrupt or politically unstable, where its leaders are not genuinely committed to planning or where ministries, departments and agencies have considerable autonomy, a central planning agency has little chance to operate effectively. Nevertheless, there is a widespread assumption among planning experts that it is desirable that a central planning agency always be set up as soon as national planning starts. It is rarely recognized how long it takes to build a viable central planning agency or to prepare a good development plan. Consequently, it frequently happens that inexperienced planners attempt simultaneously to organize and staff a new planning agency while framing a plan under forced draught. Not surprisingly, they almost always fail.

When the planning effort turns out badly, the planning agency may be abolished or replaced, continue to operate largely ignored by the rest of the government, or its director may be removed. In many countries, including Burma, Colombia, Korea and Nepal, frequent changes in the head of the central planning agency, or shifts in its structure or location, have reflected dissatisfaction of political authorities with the work of the planning agency.

Because those concerned with the creation of national planning machinery have considered it essential to concentrate on the establishment of a central planning agency, they have given little attention to the creation of "programing" units in operating organizations for improving the quality of project and sector program preparation and execution. Consequently, only a few governments have established effective programing units in operating agencies. Since the proper preparation of enough good projects and their combination into sector programs which take account of priorities and resources are indispensable to rapid development, whether or not a plan exists, it is clear that programing units in operating agencies are at least as important as a central planning agency for a country which seeks to speed its rate of growth. For countries in early stages of development, which have only barely begun to learn how to prepare projects and sector programs, they may be even more important. Experience teaches that in these countries, there is little chance that aggregative plans can be carried out until the rudiments of project and sector programing are mastered. It is also possible that more rapid development could be obtained from programing units than from a central planning agency in countries which are politically unstable or where political leaders are not genuinely committed to development. Such countries have shown that they are not yet ready to make effective use of a central planning agency because they will not or cannot do what is required to carry out a national development plan. But there are often "islands" of relative stability or commitment in one or more ministries or agencies in these governments where programing units can do effective work in improving the preparation and execution of projects and sector programs.

It would be desirable, of course, for a central planning agency and programing units to be established simultaneously. But there are not enough trained planners and technicians available to do both jobs at the same time in most countries. Nor is it to be expected that, if a central planning agency is given first priority, it can take on as one of its first assignments the creation of programing units. Planning agencies have shown themselves to be ill-suited for this task. For most less developed countries, therefore, the choice comes down to whether, at the beginning, a central planning agency or programing units will do more to accelerate development.

Until a government manifests a readiness to make a reasonably adequate effort to plan effectively, it may be easier and quicker to co-ordinate public investment by improving budgetary procedures of an existing budgetary authority than through planning procedures of a newly created central planning agency. Where a central planning agency already exists in an inhospitable environment, it may be neither feasible nor desirable to abolish it. But in these countries, also, the most immediate way of improving co-ordination of public investment may also be by improving budgetary practices.

In most mixed-economy countries, development efforts are generally co-ordinated through a budget. In practice, therefore, it is the budget office, usually located in a ministry of finance, which is the *de facto* planning authority in most countries. Although not the ideal way to advance development, it must be recognized that, even without a central planning agency, some countries have demonstrated a sustained ability to grow at a high rate when reasonably well-prepared projects are co-ordinated through a budget by a competent ministry of finance. The available evidence in Israel, Mexico, Taiwan and elsewhere suggests that although a central planning agency may be useful and, possibly, essential to rapid development sometimes in some countries, it is not necessary for rapid development in all countries at all times.

Thus, before setting up planning machinery for a less developed country, serious consideration needs to be given to the alternatives to a central planning agency. If a central planning agency is to be established, thought needs to be given to the kind of planning the agency will be doing. Less developed countries about to start organized planning activities frequently seek to reproduce planning machinery of another country. While there is much to learn from the experience of countries which have been planning for some time, there are also dangers in the uncritical adoption by one country of the planning organization of another.

Chapter XI

The Distribution of Planning Functions

If one takes care of the means, the end
will take care of itself.—Mohandas Gandhi

THE NEED FOR DEFINITION

EXPERIENCE TO date with development planning provides valuable insights into the proper functioning of planning machinery. For some activities, the central planning agency must be the key organization, but for others, different organizations are better. The effective formulation and execution of a development plan requires that almost every unit of government contribute to the process. Projects and proposals should be prepared at every level of government, from the village or municipality to the center of government and in every ministry, department or agency concerned with development. These proposals and projects should be reviewed and made a part of local, regional and national plans.

> Decisions must be reached and sanctions given for the execution of plans by operating organisations, and their work must be co-ordinated to achieve maximum results. The organisational arrangements for accomplishing these purposes will involve several elements: planning units in ministries and departments; central and provincial planning organisations for review and co-ordination; arrangements for reaching decisions and giving sanctions; and systematic procedures for co-ordinating execution, observing progress, and measuring results.[1]

There is, therefore, a need for every country which seeks to plan well to define as precisely as possible who is to do what and how, i.e., by what criteria or standards it is to be done. Few countries bother to do this. Consequently, in many countries there is a lack of clarity about the division of responsibility between planning and operating bodies

[1] Pakistan. National Planning Board. *First Five Year Plan, 1955–1960*, p. 95.

and an even greater uncertainty about the manner in which planning functions are to be performed. This is bad enough when there is only one central planning agency. But the difficulty is compounded when two or more planning agencies with overlapping functions compete. In Thailand, for example, the National Economic Development Board (NEDB), the legally constituted central planning agency, has had an ambiguous relationship with the Thai Technical and Economic Co-operation Office (TTEC). Although at one time the TTEC was presumably intended to be the part of NEDB responsible for negotiating with foreign and international lending and aid-giving countries and agencies, it in fact often operated independently with its own Program Division. Early in 1963, a super-Ministry of National Development, with a planning section of its own, was established and the TTEC was incorporated into the Ministry. Since the Ministry is charged with overseeing the execution of a substantial proportion of total public investment, some qualified persons believe that the role of the NEDB, never a very influential one, will diminish even further, while others think that the NEDB will be unaffected because it is expected to have the right to review the new Ministry's proposals as it has for other ministries. But since the Government has only poorly defined the new Ministry's relationship to the NEDB, no one knows for sure.

In the Philippines, also, duplication of planning agencies has confused development planning. The National Economic Council (NEC) is the nominal central planning agency, but at various times other planning agencies have been set up which sought to usurp, with more or less success, the NEC's planning functions. A National Planning Commission, established in 1950, proved to be abortive, but the Budget Commission created in 1957 prepared a five-year investment program which the then President of the Republic supported over the five-year plan formulated by the NEC. In 1963, a Program Implementation Agency (PIA) was established to give effect to development goals set by the NEC. With the division of authority between the two agencies only vaguely defined, PIA took over many of the NEC's functions. In the Philippines, as in Thailand, the failure of government authorities to state unambiguously the respective responsibilities of planning agencies and their relationship to the rest of the Government, as well as to support them in carrying out these responsibilities, has seriously interfered with their effectiveness. Other countries also have or have had more than one central planning agency operating simultaneously. Thus, Brazil had a Development Council and a Planning Commission (COPLAN) competing with each other, while Mexico has a planning body in the Department of the Presidency as well as an Interministry Planning Commission. As in other countries, the simultaneous existence of two planning agencies in Brazil and Mexico has raised jurisdictional questions and confused lines of authority.

RESPONSIBILITY FOR ANNUAL OPERATIONAL PLAN

Ultimate responsibility for all aspects of national development planning rests with a nation's supreme governmental authority, although many planning functions must be distributed throughout the public administration and to the private sector. But there are some responsibilities which this authority—be it a council of ministers, a cabinet, a chief executive, a head of state or a legislature—should not normally delegate. Among these are approval of plans and the setting of planning objectives and targets. The authorities must exercise these responsibilities themselves because together they determine the main directions and the scale of a nation's development effort, as well as the economic, political and social policies and measures required to achieve development goals.

In theory, the central planning agency should prepare plans based on objectives, targets and policies chosen by the political authority after careful consideration of the alternatives. In practice, the central planning agency often makes suggestions which the authority may adopt. This is true even in the USSR and in Eastern European countries, where planners' proposals are considered with those of others by each council of ministers when it prepares the over-all directives which provide the central planners with guidelines for the preparation of plans.[2] But, as was indicated in Chapter IV, in some less developed mixed-economy countries, where political authorities are not sufficiently concerned to select planning objectives and targets, the planners have taken upon themselves the task of choosing objectives and targets incorporated in a plan. When planners are able to go this far, the prospect is slim that government will do what is necessary to achieve the planners' objectives and targets.

[2] UN. Department of Economic and Social Affairs. *Planning for Economic Development, Report of the Secretary-General Transmitting the Study of a Group of Experts*, p. 90.

Where a central planning agency exists, it is almost always assigned the task of preparing and, when necessary, revising national development plans. In every country with a central planning agency, the agency which prepares the medium- and long-term plan also prepares the annual operational plan. However, there have been attempts to separate the two. From 1960 to 1964, this was tried in the Soviet Union. In 1960, its central planning agency (the USSR *Gosplan*) was split in two. One part, still called the *Gosplan,* retained responsibility for annual operational plans, while the second part, set up as a new agency—the State Scientific-Economic Council (*Gosekonomsovet*)— was made responsible for longer-term plans. The separation of annual operational planning from longer-term planning seems to have been prompted by the Government's desire to distribute the growing burden of planning centrally for an increasingly complex economy.[3] But in March 1964, *Gosekonomsovet* was abolished and both annual and longer-term plans are again being prepared by *Gosplan.*

In the late 1950's Yugoslav authorities gave some consideration to limiting its central planning agency, the Federal Planning Institute, to the preparation of longer-term plans and to turning over the preparation of annual plans to its Federal Secretariat of General Economic Affairs, an operating agency. But the idea was rejected and has not been raised again. The separation of annual planning from longer-term planning does not appear to have been seriously considered in other socialized countries. Special circumstances seem to have played a role in the USSR. In this large and complex economy, due to the abolition of industrial ministries, the central planning agency had to perform an exceptional number of executory functions. These circumstances have not been encountered in the other socialized countries. They are even less relevant to mixed-economy countries, where the main responsibility for executing plans generally resides outside the central planning agency. One of the rare attempts in a mixed economy to separate annual from long-term planning occurred

[3] When the central industrial ministries were abolished in the reforms which began in 1957, some of their functions were transferred to new regional economic councils, or *sovnarkhozy,* and others to the USSR *Gosplan,* the central planning agency. The functions acquired by the USSR *Gosplan,* especially the task of preparing and implementing allocations of essential commodities in connection with the execution of annual operational plans, greatly increased its workload. It was apparently because of the USSR *Gosplan's* increased responsibilities in the field of annual planning that the task of preparing medium- and long-term plans was turned over to *Gosekonomsovet,* the second central planning agency.

in the Philippines. The Program Implementation Agency was supposed to do annual planning, while the National Economic Council was to continue preparing longer-term plans. But, as has already been indicated, this arrangement has not worked out as expected.

Since an annual plan is the most convenient medium for adapting a longer-term plan to changed conditions, its formulation is an essential part of the continuous planning process by which a medium-term plan is revised. But because an annual plan can make basic changes in a medium-term plan, the agency which is responsible for formulating the annual plan is in fact the agency which determines the ultimate character of the medium-term plan. An annual operational plan is essentially like the medium-term plan on which it is based, expressed in greater detail. For these reasons and also because the scarcity of planning technicians makes it desirable to reduce competitive claims upon them by different agencies, annual and longer-term plans should be prepared by the same agency.

THE PLANNING AGENCY AND THE BUDGET OFFICE

The annual development or operational plan—which covers physical, human and financial resources—must be distinguished from the annual capital or public investment budget, which is concerned only with financial resources. While the first is primarily the responsibility of the central planning agency, the second is primarily the task of the budget office, ordinarily the ministry of finance. But this does not mean that the central planning agency can prepare the annual operating plan without consulting the ministry of finance, or that the latter should prepare the annual budget without consulting the central planning agency. On the contrary, there is need for the closest collaboration.

The central planning agency is responsible for making estimates of total financial resources, including nonbudgetary resources of a national government like foreign loans and aid, depreciation funds and receipts of autonomous and semiautonomous government corporations and subordinate governments. But the central planners must confer with appropriate officials in the ministry of finance to obtain estimates of national budgetary receipts and expenditures, as well as the surplus on current account which is expected to be available for public investment. While the ministry of finance has the main responsibility for making these estimates, the central planning agency should be free to propose ways of augmenting revenues and to make other suggestions for increasing development resources. As Thailand's planners pointed out, the central planning agency

> should exchange views with the Treasury on the possibility of increasing taxes, of introducing new forms and tapping new sources of public borrowing, and of reallocating appropriations between development and other kinds of expenditures. Guidance of this kind is needed as a counter to the frequent tendency to limit capital outlays to what is left over after demands for current purposes have been met.[4]

Conversely, when the annual budget is being prepared, the ministry of finance should work closely on a continuing basis with the central planners. This is essential if public investment funds are to be distributed in conformity with the annual development plan and if appropriate allocations are to be made for current expenditures (e.g., for training personnel and for additional wages and salaries) required as a result of public investments.

Where an agency is responsible for allocating foreign exchange for both public and private investment, it should also furnish the central planning agency with estimates of the available supply of exchange, and the central planners should participate in the apportionment of the available foreign exchange to various uses. If, as happened in the Philippines, the Central Bank allocates foreign exchange without reference to the priorities in a plan, there is little likelihood that the direction of development will coincide with that envisaged in the plan.

Close and continuous co-operation between budget and planning offices is therefore necessary, not only in the preparation of plans and budgets and in formulating programs for foreign aid and loans, but also in appraising the progress of development programs and projects. The central planning agency is especially dependent on the budget office for data to prepare a proper annual operational plan. The budget office, in turn, requires guidance from the central planners' operational plan if it is to prepare a budget which is consistent with the annual plan. Various ways have been worked out in different countries to regularize collaboration between budget offices and central planning agencies. One of the more effective devices, used in Burma and Pakistan among other countries, has been an interdepartmental budget committee with budgeters and planners as members, together with representatives of interested operating organizations, which make joint decisions on the inclusion of allocations in a budget.

[4] IBRD. *A Public Development Program for Thailand,* p. 211.

But if a ministry of finance chooses to ignore all or a part of the annual operational plan, it may prepare a budget which bears little resemblance to the annual plan. This often happens in countries in which the ministry of finance is powerful and the central planning agency is not. One foreign adviser in the Harvard Group which counseled the central planning agency in Pakistan described the one-time attitude of the Ministry of Finance in that country in a way which recalls the situation in many other countries:

> If the [Finance] Minister's estimates indicated that the domestic resources or the foreign exchange available for development purposes would be smaller than had been expected by the planners, he required that the development program be curtailed. . . . More might be allocated for nondevelopment uses and less for development than specified in the annual program. When this determination was made, however, the planners might not be represented; if represented, they did not have a vote. . . .[5]

Because ministries of finance in less developed countries often pay little attention to central planners' plans, some experts have advocated that the central planning agency be given authority to prepare the capital budget. Thus, the Latin American Seminar on Planning recommended:

> The preparation of the capital budget and the public investment plan, which constitutes the first step towards the effective application of the plan, should also be the responsibility of the central planning body. The government bodies responsible for fiscal and financial matters would naturally contribute their advice, since the administration of funds and the calculations of costs falls within their jurisdiction.[6]

In Malaya, an interdepartmental National Development Planning Committee—whose secretariat is the central planning agency, not the Ministry of Finance—prepares the annual capital budget. The Permanent Secretary of the Prime Minister's Office chairs the Committee. He also chaired the Committee when he was Permanent Secretary of the Ministry of Finance, but in his personal capacity rather than as an official of the Ministry. In practice, the central planning agency has had much more influence than the Ministry of Finance in preparing annual capital budgets. In Venezuela, the central planning agency prepares a capital budget, called a program budget, which is annexed

---

[5] Wilcox, Clair. "Pakistan," p. 67.
[6] UN. ECLA. *Report on Latin American Seminar on Planning*, p. 45.

to the fiscal budget prepared by the Ministry of Finance. In Costa Rica, also, the budget, as it affects development expenditures, is prepared by the Planning Office. In Iran and Korea, the current as well as the capital budget is prepared by the central planning agencies. The Ministries of Finance in both countries have been reduced to revenue collecting agencies. This may be carrying the matter to its logical conclusion, but it goes too far. Whatever its role in preparing a capital budget (and insuring that related current expenditures are provided for), a central planning agency should not get involved in current budgetary allocations which have no direct connection with development.

There is no doubt that when a central planning agency assumes responsibility for preparing the capital budget, it acquires direct control over a powerful device for implementing its plans. But by taking on this task, it almost invariably reduces the time available for planning, its main function. This has been the experience in Surinam. The Planning Bureau there not only prepares the capital budget, but also is responsible for controlling expenditures under the Ten-Year Development Plan. About three-fourths of the planning staff are occupied with the checking of bills and the authorization of payments. As a result, long-range planning activities are neglected. When a central planning agency prepares budgets and controls the payment of bills it assumes functions normally handled by a ministry of finance. As will be seen later, central planning agencies also seek other responsibilities customarily handled by operating agencies because they facilitate execution of plans. But the answer to the problem of implementing plans can hardly be for a central planning agency to take over functions which other government offices should perform; otherwise, a central planning agency could end up encompassing much of a government.

RELATION BETWEEN PLANNING AND STATISTICAL AGENCIES

The arguments above are also relevant to the placement of statistical services. Planning is so heavily dependent on statistics that close association between those who plan and those who prepare statistics is indispensable. Because of this, especially where the statistical service has been unable to supply the data needed for planning, some countries have made the central statistical office a part of the central planning agency. There are advantages in this arrangement. Planners are thereby able to insure that statistics are prepared in suitable form for planning. Where the planning agency and the statistical office are separated, the data frequently are not arranged as they should be for planning purposes or they are not supplied in time to be useful. In many countries, the status of the statistical office is low. Since planners are apt to appreciate the importance of statistics more than most others in government, they are likely to do more to improve the quality and quantity of the data if the statistical service is put under the administrative direction of the central planning agency. This was the primary reason, for example, why Ecuador's General Statistical Office was transferred to the National Planning Agency in 1963. Those concerned believed that the National Planning Agency was in a better position than the General Statistical Office to obtain funds for gathering data and for raising statisticians' salaries.

But there are also serious disadvantages in placing the statistical office in the planning agency. A central statistical service has to provide data for purposes other than planning. Statistics on health conditions and other social data may be of little direct value for planning but of great importance to government administrators. Moreover, the statistician may need much more time to do his job well than the planner feels he can allow. Nor, given the extent of his training and experience in many less developed countries, does the planner always know what the statistician should be doing. As indicated in Chapter VI, the points of view of the planner and the statistician do not always coincide. Their ideas about how to measure the effects of development plans may diverge.

Although the two points of view must be generally reconciled, there is still much to be said for giving the statistician a degree of independence from the planner to enable him to produce data whose reliability is not impugnable by the overriding interests of the planner. In considering the reasons for and against combining the statistical office with the central planning office, a World Bank survey mission to Uganda noted that amalgamation could endanger the objectivity and professional competence of the statistics. Moreover, the mission felt that there was also a real danger that either the planners' or the statisticians' function would be neglected if the two bodies were combined.[7]

Experience supports this view. In some countries where the statisti-

[7] IBRD. *Economic Development of Uganda,* p. 58.

cal office has been incorporated into the planning agency, statistics have been neglected by the planners; in others, planning has given way to statistics. Morocco is an example of the latter case. The Moroccan central planning agency became concerned mostly with statistical matters, with about four-fifths of the planning agency's staff being employed in gathering and collating basic statistical material which, although required by planners, was not directly related to planning. More important, however, was the fact that much of the time of the director and other supervisors of the central planning agency was absorbed in statistical work to the neglect of planning. This has also been true in Syria, where more than 125 of the 165 employees of the Ministry of Planning have been concerned with statistics.

In some countries, a central statistical office is located within a central planning agency but is independent of the planning section of the agency; or it is outside the planning agency but reports directly to its head. For example, the Planning Division and the Statistics Division are independent divisions of Nigeria's Federal Ministry of Economic Development, while a separate Research and Statistics Bureau reports to the Minister and Vice Minister who head Korea's Economic Planning Board. Until 1964, a Planning Department and a Statistics Department also constituted two separate components in the UAR's Ministry of Planning and Finance.[8] A Central Statistical Office and a Planning Office used to be separate parts of Thailand's National Economic Development Board (NEDB) until the Statistical Office became an independent entity in 1963.[9] Arrangements like those in Nigeria or Korea are preferable to one which makes a central statistical office an integral part of a central planning agency. They provide needed autonomy for statisticians, but make it easier to arrange closer consultation and co-ordination between planners and statisticians than is likely if a statistical office and a planning agency are completely separate.

Nevertheless, the linking of a statistical office to an agency responsible for development planning in the same ministry or board involves the risk that statistical priorities will be largely determined by planners' wants. It may not be possible to find an organizational structure

---

[8] In the latter part of 1964, the Planning Department was transferred to the Prime Minister's jurisdiction and the Statistics Department became a part of a new Mobilization and Statistics Department in the Prime Minister's Office.

[9] Although nominally under the jurisdiction of the NEDB the Central Statistical Office in fact was virtually independent of it.

which is free of defects, but it is important that priorities for statistical work be fixed on the basis of the needs of a country as a whole and that they not be distorted because the statistical service is linked with another agency with a partial sphere of interest.[10] Because the statistical function must have the broadest scope if it is to provide every legitimate need for data, the most satisfactory solution to the problem of locating the central statistical office is to establish it as an autonomous body, as free as possible from partisan pressures, including those of planners. It is noteworthy that even in the USSR, where statistical offices were incorporated in planning agencies between 1930 and 1948, they have been removed from the jurisdiction of the central planning agency and placed directly under the Council of Ministers.

It is, of course, important that there be close co-operation between the central statistical office and the users of its data. This has been obtained in some countries through a co-ordinating or steering committee, which includes as members the head of the statistical office, the chief planner and the senior officers of other interested ministries and agencies. In Uganda, for example, a Steering Committee established in 1954 had the Economic Adviser as Chairman and the permanent secretaries of ministries and the head of the East African Statistical Office as members. Through this Committee, co-ordination was achieved by balancing planning and other government requirements for data with the capacity to produce them. India's Central Statistical Organization, though administratively separate from the Planning Commission, is located in the same building as the Commission. Co-ordination is obtained through the Statistical Adviser to the Government, who is connected with the Central Statistical Organization and is also a member of the Planning Commission. A Statistics and Surveys Division in the Planning Commission is essentially a wing of the Central Statistical Organization, and is headed by its principal officer.[11]

CO-ORDINATING FOREIGN TECHNICAL SKILLS

There is also a pressing need to co-ordinate the flow of foreign technical skills into less developed countries. In these countries,

[10] United Nations Conference on the Application of Science and Technology, etc. *Organization of Statistical Services*, p. 3.
[11] Paranjape, H. K. *Planning Commission, A Descriptive Account*, p. 36.

satisfactory preparation and execution of development projects, programs and plans may depend on the availability of suitable foreign specialists and the use made of them. Yet, a haphazard and poorly conceived approach to the provision, acquisition and use of foreign skills is common. Responsibility for engaging foreign personnel or acquiring technical assistance furnished by foreign governments and international volunteer or other agencies is frequently left with each operating ministry, department or agency in a recipient country. These organizations tend to consider themselves best able to ascertain and arrange for the procurement of their own technical assistance needs. This is sometimes true; often it is not. Even if true, it is nonetheless desirable that requests for foreign technical skills in a government which is importing a substantial amount of these skills be reviewed and co-ordinated at some point.

There is, firstly, a need to bring collective demands for foreign technical assistance into line with available supply. To this end, general criteria have to be set up to determine the extent to which requests for technical skills reflect the requirements of a recipient country's economy rather than special interests or enthusiasms of the various ministries, departments and agencies making the requests. Operating organizations sometimes are carried away by their view of the importance of projects and programs they promote. This may make them overestimate their needs for technical assistance and the amount they can usefully absorb in a given period of time.[12] It is also necessary to determine the extent of the total supply, as well as alternative sources, of technical skills. Donors' scales of priorities in providing technical assistance are not always the same as those of a recipient's. A donor's program may be largely influenced by its desire to supply a recipient with certain kinds of equipment or goods—or by its foreign policy. When seen from the point of view of a recipient country, technical assistance programs of international agencies sometimes seem to be affected by too strong a belief by these agencies in

> the primacy of their own special field of activity. They have tended to view the development of recipient countries too much in the light of their own contribution to it. They have also been known to press particular projects on countries, often against the latter's best

[12] Stavrianopoulos, Alexander. *Co-ordination in the Administration of Technical Assistance: The Point of View of a Recipient Country*, p. 2.

judgment of their needs, and to compete with each other in so doing.[13]

Requests for technical assistance may involve a recipient country's relations with donor countries or other agencies and lead a government to select a particular source for reasons of national policy.[14] Or a recipient government may consider it preferable to engage foreign specialists directly instead of through foreign technical assistance.[15] Review and co-ordination can help in these matters; and in insuring that the fullest possible use will be made of domestic technical skills as an alternative to foreign technical assistance; that foreign technical assistance will be used effectively and economically; that national counterparts will be available to work with foreign experts; and that there will not be unnecessary duplication and avoidable waste in the use of technical assistance. Where co-ordination is lacking, scarce technical resources are likely to be squandered. In a typical case, a World Bank survey mission to Ceylon found that unco-ordinated requests for foreign technical assistance in that country

> resulted in duplication and overlapping, waste or poor use of specialists once obtained, sometimes procurement of the wrong type of specialist or even, occasionally, of an incompetent or completely unnecessary one.[16]

Procedures followed in awarding foreign and international scholarships and fellowships for study abroad are usually even less rational. Despite deficiencies, technical assistance requests are much more likely to reflect government objectives than are attempts by individuals to obtain foreign training for themselves. Frequently, scholarships and fellowships for training abroad are awarded on an *ad hoc* basis in inappropriate fields or in unsuitable universities or, from the point of view of national interest, to the wrong persons. This often leads to inadequate or improper training of individuals, unnecessarily long absences of key government officials from their jobs, or, where no prior commitment is made to return home for a stipulated period after

---

[13] *Ibid.*

[14] This is especially true of bilateral technical assistance.

[15] For example, a recipient country might prefer to engage foreign technical assistance directly if it believed there was a possibility or semblance of divided loyalties on the part of specialists furnished by another government or if it found donors reluctant to furnish technicians for operational jobs.

[16] IBRD, *Economic Development of Ceylon*, p. 62.

completion of foreign training, to the emigration of well-trained professionals.

When there is a lack of co-ordination, donors and recipients of technical assistance both suffer. Because of the world-wide shortage of competent technicians available to donors for use in developing countries, donor countries and agencies can ill afford the waste of this scarce resource when their technicians are not put to productive use in a recipient country. But when this happens, the worst sufferers are, naturally enough, the recipient countries. For besides direct costs for foreign technical assistance which recipient countries may have to bear, there is often a diversion, sometimes substantial, of equally scarce counterpart skills which might have been better used elsewhere. Consequently,

> the real question for the Government of a recipient country is not: 'Will this Technical Assistance project make a contribution to the country's development?' but 'Will this project make a greater contribution than another possible project involving equivalent costs in scarce resources?' [17]

Co-ordination of foreign technical assistance is a dual task. There is, firstly, the job of choosing among rival claims in behalf of the different sectors of national economic and social activity. This is implicit in the reconciliation of requests from the various government ministries, departments and agencies. There is, secondly, the task of welding together offers of technical skills from different sources into a coherent program which avoids gaps, duplications, inconsistencies and wasteful allocation of resources.[18] This twofold task requires, in addition to the co-ordination of technical assistance requests submitted by the several government organizations in a recipient country, that foreign agencies which supply technical assistance co-ordinate their activities. Such co-ordination can, in practice, be achieved best only in the country receiving the assistance, although broad guidelines can be laid down elsewhere. But experience shows that even when done in the recipient country, co-ordination by supplying agencies is unlikely to be effective unless the country itself has first co-ordinated its own agencies' technical assistance requests.

This can be best achieved by centralizing the review of requests for

[17] Stavrianopoulos, Alexander. *Co-ordination in the Administration of Technical Assistance: The Point of View of a Recipient Country*, p. 3.
[18] *Ibid.*, p. 1.

technical skills in one government organization. In some countries, however, co-ordination is divided between two or more organizations. Thus, the Nigerian Federal Ministry of Economic Development is supposed to co-ordinate requests for all technical skills required by the Federal and Regional Governments except technical assistance supplied by the United Nations Special Fund, which is handled by the Ministry of Finance.[19] In Turkey, the Ministry of Finance is responsible for administering technical assistance from the Organization for Economic Co-Operation and Development and from the United States, while the Ministry of Foreign Affairs administers technical assistance from certain other countries, the United Nations and some other international agencies. These split arrangements do not seem to work as well as when co-ordination is centralized in one organization. The arrangement in Turkey, for example, has made it difficult to co-ordinate the Government's technical assistance activities.

A special problem is encountered in federal governments where powers are divided between the center and political subdivisions. In these countries, different ways have been evolved for dealing with foreign technical assistance. In Nigeria, for example, each regional government co-ordinates its own foreign technical assistance requests. In Pakistan, on the other hand, it is the Central Government which carries out this function. Since regional authorities in federal and in some unitary governments are in a better position than authorities in the capital to determine their requirements for technical assistance, there is much to be gained by having them co-ordinate their own requirements. Nevertheless, there is also likely to be an advantage if the combined requests of each are then co-ordinated in an organization at the national level. This permits a country to review its total requirements in the light of national policy and the availabilities of domestic, as well as foreign, technical skills, and to take fuller advantage of economies of scale than each political subdivision can.

The co-ordination of foreign technical assistance and foreign training programs involves a recipient country in negotiations with foreign nations and international agencies. Some countries have therefore considered it appropriate to charge their ministries of foreign affairs with this responsibility. But these ministries have not proved to be efficient media for the purpose because they are generally poorly

---

[19] Special Fund assistance is considered different from other technical assistance because it is concerned with projects and programs in the preinvestment stage.

informed about priorities for using technical skills effectively in their own countries. A ministry of finance or a ministry of economic affairs has sometimes done well in co-ordinating foreign technical assistance activities. A ministry of finance is, however, prone to be concerned with the financial aspects of technical assistance instead of its wider implications for development. In countries with a national development plan, experience shows that a central planning agency is in the best position to determine development priorities. Because development plans generally lack comprehensiveness and are far from adequate in other respects, they are not infallible guides to productive use of technical skills. But despite their limitations they are likely to provide the best available indications in a developing country for employing technical skills most efficiently and in accordance with development priorities. When technical skills are allocated in accordance with the requirements of a development plan, it is possible to insure that all phases of the planning process, i.e., data collection, preinvestment studies, plan preparation and plan implementation, receive appropriate proportions of the available supply of technical talent.

> Basing technical assistance directly on countries' plans and programmes has manifold advantages. It saves many time-consuming enquiries on the part of those providing technical assistance as to how the assistance asked for fits into the development plans and priorities of the country. [Moreover], . . . basing technical assistance on the clearly stated plans or priorities of the developing country, is the best way and perhaps the only way of making certain that the assistance is provided only at the request of the country and does not reflect sales pressure of the providers.[20]

It is desirable, therefore, that a central planning agency be closely linked with the co-ordination of foreign technical assistance and training programs. This does not mean, however, that the planners themselves need to co-ordinate technical assistance requests or negotiate with foreign and international providers of such assistance. In fact, it is desirable that planners not be diverted from planning by these operational tasks.

In some countries where a central planning agency co-ordinates foreign technical assistance activities, one or more ministries have been

[20] Singer, H. W. *Co-ordination of Technical Assistance and Development Planning: Determination of Priorities*, pp. 13–14.

designated to negotiate with foreign or international supplying agencies. Thus, since 1962, Turkey's State Planning Organization gathers, screens and evaluates requests for technical assistance made by operating organizations. It prepares a co-ordinated technical assistance program consistent with development plans. The Ministries of Finance and Foreign Affairs are then responsible for implementing the program. While this system may work in some countries, it is needlessly complex and tends to lead to bureaucratic duplication and delays. Other countries have incorporated the technical assistance co-ordination and negotiation functions in their central planning agencies but in a separate unit from the one in which the planners work. Thus, Korea's Economic Planning Board is headed by a Minister and a Vice-Minister, assisted by two Assistant Vice-Ministers. One Assistant Vice-Minister is responsible for a Technical Management Bureau concerned with technical assistance activities, while the second supervises the Planning Bureau which prepares development plans.

It is desirable, when it can be done without diverting planners from their own work, that a unit concerned with co-ordination of technical skills be organically linked to a central planning agency to insure that they function in close co-operation. But the fact that the unit concerned with technical assistance co-ordination is within a central planning agency is not enough to insure that it will co-operate closely with the planning unit. In Thailand, for example, when the Office of Thai Technical Economic Cooperation (the unit which co-ordinated technical assistance) was nominally within the National Economic Development Board (the central planning agency), it frequently failed to inform the planners about its activities or to allocate technical assistance in accordance with priorities called for in national development plans. In contrast, Pakistan has an effective organization for co-ordinating technical assistance activities which, although outside the central planning agency, is closely allied with it. Since the operating head of the central planning agency also heads the organization which co-ordinates foreign technical assistance activities, close administrative links between planning and technical assistance co-ordination have been maintained despite the administrative separation of the entities concerned with these functions.

A central entity responsible for co-ordinating and negotiating foreign technical assistance will do well to make full use of the knowledge of those in operating ministries, departments and agencies. These organizations are likely to have more specialized knowledge of their

requirements than the agency concerned with co-ordinating and negotiating foreign technical assistance. It would be desirable, therefore,
for operating organizations to participate in negotiations for the
specific technical assistance which they require.

Many countries make use of interministry committees for co-
ordinating technical assistance activities. These committees may include representatives of the government organizations which use
foreign technical assistance, the ministry of finance, the central planning agency and, where considerations of foreign relations are important, the ministry of external affairs. They also constitute a convenient vehicle for consulting with the private sector and seeking its
advice and co-operation where this is indicated. For this purpose,
private representatives can be invited to attend meetings of the
committee as required, or a subcommittee with representatives from
the private sector can be constituted to advise the committee on
appropriate matters.

In some countries, a committee is used as a co-ordinating mechanism
in lieu of a government organization. But the available evidence
indicates that a committee, unaided by a strong supporting secretariat,
lacks the initiative, flexibility and, often, the authority needed to
prepare a co-ordinated program of technical assistance. Such a committee has shown itself equally unable to insure that the necessary
measures are taken to carry out the program.[21] However, where an
interministry co-ordinating committee has been employed as an
adjunct to a government entity charged with the co-ordination of
technical assistance, it has performed an effective advisory and educational role. This has been found to be especially so where the staff of
the co-ordinating entity acts as the committee's secretariat.

NEGOTIATING FOREIGN FINANCING

One government entity should also be assigned responsibility for
co-ordinating all foreign development financing and for getting the
greatest benefits from such funds. It should formulate, for approval by
the government, general policies to govern the use of external foreign
assistance; it should seek to insure that such assistance is compatible

---

[21] Stavrianopoulos, Alexander. *Co-ordination in the Administration of Technical
Assistance: The Point of View of a Recipient Country*, p. 6.

with planning objectives; and it should serve as a liaison with foreign lenders and donors, negotiate all external loans and aid, and maintain records relating to the status of all foreign loans and financial assistance.

In many countries these functions are performed by the ministry of finance. But since the central planning agency has to assess the total amount in foreign loans and aid needed, and is in position to judge where these funds can be used most effectively for development, it should participate in negotiations with consortia, consultative groups and other foreign or international lenders and donors when global amounts of foreign financing for development are being considered. Similarly, since the sponsoring ministry or agency is apt to know more about the details of its projects than the ministry of finance, the sponsor should participate in negotiations for the financing of its projects.

In some countries, responsibility for co-ordinating and negotiating foreign aid and loans rests with the central planning agency. This is not an arrangement to be recommended. For while it is essential that a central planning agency help determine the extent of foreign resources required and their distribution for development purposes, it need not be made responsible for actual negotiations for foreign aid and loan agreements and for co-ordinating the use of aid and loan proceeds. In fact, it should not be saddled with these responsibilities because their exercise might interfere with planning activities. The negotiation of foreign aid and loan arrangements and co-ordination of the use of aid and loan proceeds are operational tasks which other government bodies are at least as qualified to perform as a central planning agency. However, where a planning agency has been made responsible for co-ordinating and negotiating foreign aid and loans, these functions should be carried out by a unit separated from the planning unit; [22] and in this case the sponsoring ministry or agency should participate in loan negotiations for financing its projects. In addition, the ministry of finance should be consulted and kept informed about the terms of repayment of all foreign loans and other commitments.

Regardless of which agency is responsible for negotiating foreign loans and aid, there must be the closest co-operation between it, the government organizations concerned with the execution of projects and

---

[22] This is done in Korea, for example, where an Economic Cooperation Bureau charged with these functions is independent of the Planning Bureau in the Economic Planning Board.

programs for which foreign funds are to be obtained and other entities involved (be they a central planning agency, a ministry of finance or another organization). Since such co-operation is essential for effective co-ordination of foreign loan and aid activities, it is best institutionalized. For this purpose, a steering committee might be set up, with membership consisting of officials from the ministry of finance, the central planning agency and the ministry, department or agency for whose project or program a loan or aid is being sought. The steering committee should be composed of high officials with authority to speak for their organizations; and its recommendations, while not necessarily binding, should be given great weight by the agency responsible for negotiating loans and aid.

Pakistan has a system for co-ordinating foreign and international loan and aid transactions, as well as requests for foreign technical skills, which works well. All such transactions, as well as the maintenance of records of commitments and disbursements for all loans and aid, are centralized in an Economic Affairs Division, one of five divisions in the President's Secretariat. The Planning Commission is a second division in the Secretariat. Although the Economic Affairs Division functions as a separate entity, effective co-ordination between the two divisions has been established by putting the Economic Affairs Division under the Deputy Chairman, i.e., the operating head of the Planning Commission. As a result of this arrangement, relations between the two agencies are close and harmonious. The Planning Commission is responsible for preparing documents required for negotiating foreign aid, but actual negotiations are carried out by the Economic Affairs Division. The Economic Affairs Division consults with the Ministry of Finance concerning the terms on which foreign loans are to be obtained and provides the Ministry with data on actual commitments as they are made. Operating ministries, knowing that they must move through the Economic Affairs Division to obtain foreign financing for their projects, co-operate by providing data which the division requests.

There are countries where responsibility for making foreign commitments for loans and aid is not centralized in one government body, or where, because administrative discipline is weak, operating ministries and agencies engage in negotiating foreign financing for their projects on their own initiative despite official regulations prohibiting this. In these countries, ministries and agencies vie with each other for foreign funds and no one in the government knows at any time the extent to which the government's credit has been committed abroad. A frequent form of financing in these circumstances is short-term suppliers' credits. Some countries have accumulated heavy short-run obligations in this way which have put a serious strain on the balance of payments. In Latin America, for example, CIAP [23] found that one of the

> main causes for Latin America's difficult short-term debt position . . . [was] the lack of centralized control in most countries over the contracting of foreign debt.[24]

There are countries where foreign lenders and donors compete so vigorously to furnish loans and aid that economic planning is reduced to little more than an effort to co-ordinate the various assistance programs sponsored by foreigners. This is not easy to accomplish, as experience with the first plans of Afghanistan, Nepal and other countries similarly situated demonstrated. Such countries run the risk that unco-ordinated foreign sponsorship of development programs will yield disappointingly low results for the investments made.

The preferred way of centralizing control over foreign loans and aid is for a government to designate one entity as the only one authorized to negotiate all loans and aid. But the government must then be able and willing to enforce this arrangement. Experience shows that the mere establishment of rules and regulations for centralizing foreign borrowing and assistance has not sufficed to control these activities where administrative discipline is not firmly enforced. In Thailand, for example, the Thai Technical and Economic Cooperation Office (TTEC) has been the agency designated to negotiate with foreign and international lending and aid-giving countries and agencies, but operating ministries have sometimes negotiated for foreign financing of their projects without consulting the TTEC. Where administrative control cannot be enforced effectively, operating ministries and agencies which negotiate with lenders or donors should be required, by law, to obtain the approval of the ministry of finance or another designated entity before the government's credit can be legally committed.

RESPONSIBILITY FOR REGIONAL PLANS

Whether a central planning agency should be responsible for the preparation of regional plans depends on several factors. Among these

---

[23] The letters stand for the Spanish name of the Inter-American Committee of the Alliance for Progress which co-ordinates the activities of the Alliance.

[24] OAS. PAU. *Alliance for Progress, Weekly Newsletter*, p. 1.

are the character of a country's economy, the type of planning in which a country engages, the nature of its government, the country's size, the stage of development in the region concerned and the availability of technicians to staff regional planning agencies. In the socialized economies, where the national plan is divided into a series of republican (and subordinate territorial and local) plans, regional planning bodies are generally charged with the preparation of regional plans and the central planning agency with their integration into the national plan. But the character and scope of the regional plans differ greatly in different countries. In Yugoslavia, regional plans are primarily based on the national plan. But they may deviate from the national plan to the extent that projects and programs outside the national plan can be financed from the regions' own resources. This allows regional planners some independence. But in most Eastern European countries, regional and local planning bodies produce plans which deal mainly with activities of local interest, such as housing, public utilities and production to meet local requirements.[25]

In the USSR, where regional plans must adhere strictly to the requirements of the national plan, the republic, territorial and local planning bodies act largely as servicing units for the central planning agency. They do this by providing information to the central planning agency and by carrying out its orders. Thus, for each annual plan the planning body of each of the territorial economic councils or *sovnarkhozy* [26] obtains from every factory in its area the factory's estimates of what it can produce and the resources required to achieve that production. The planning body of each *sovnarkhoz* reviews, adjusts, consolidates and transmits these estimates to the *gosplan*, or planning body, in its republic. Each of the 15 republican *gosplans* reviews, modifies and aggregates the estimates received from the *sovnarkhozy* in its area on the basis of guidelines provided by the USSR *Gosplan*, estimates how much of the materials required can be supplied from within the republic and how much must be obtained from without, and transmits its estimates to the USSR *Gosplan* in Moscow.

On the basis of these and other data, the USSR *Gosplan* works out a balanced national output and supply plan. When the USSR *Gosplan*

---

[25] UN. Department of Economic and Social Affairs. *Planning for Economic Development, Report of the Secretary-General Transmitting the Study of a Group of Experts,* p. 93.

[26] Prior to 1962, there were 103 *sovnarkhozy*. In December 1962, the number was reduced through amalgamation to 47.

has prepared the draft national plan and it has been approved by the Government, the flow is reversed. Orders, subject to some later revision, are then issued to each republican *gosplan* in the form of "control figures" for basic products and resources, such as steel and cement, which also indicate the quantities of various goods each republic may expect from other republics and the quantities it must supply other republics. On the basis of these data, each republic produces a plan which includes a set of directives for each factory indicating what it must produce during the plan period. The territorial councils' planning bodies then draft the plans for their territories, including the total production program, and manpower and other balances.[27] Despite tight controls from above, territorial planning agencies allocate many materials in their own areas.[28] In fact, retail trade and much consumer goods manufacturing are handled entirely by territorial bodies. The functions of the republican *gosplans* have been greatly broadened in recent years. Before 1957, each republican *gosplan* planned mainly for republican industries producing consumer goods, building materials and timber; now it prepares plans for all industries located wholly within its boundaries.[29] The *gosplans* of all but three republics are also responsible for implementing the plans in their areas.

In the mixed-economy countries, regional plans are sometimes prepared by regional planning bodies and sometimes by a central planning agency. Where an autonomous regional development authority has been set up, it is both desirable and usual for it to prepare the plan for its area. Such plans should be integrated into a national plan by the central planning agency. Because regional aspirations are politically potent and competitive, regional plans prepared without reference to national plans pose a great threat to orderly national progress in many less developed countries. It is, therefore, important that they be formulated whenever possible as part of a national development plan.

But in most countries with mixed economies, regional planning has proceeded independently of national planning, with the result that a series of unintegrated regional plans has sometimes been produced, based on regional aspirations rather than on available resources. In

[27] Bond, Floyd A. "The Nature and Goals of Soviet Planning," p. 6.

[28] Besides being subject to control by republican and national bodies, as well as political authorities in their own territories, territorial planning bodies have been grouped into 18 major regions for co-ordination purposes.

[29] UN. Department of Economic and Social Affairs. *Planning for Economic Development, Report of the Secretary-General Transmitting the Study of a Group of Experts*, p. 91.

Colombia, for example, several competitive regional plans were pre-pared in quick succession between 1954 and 1957, some by regional planning bodies and others by the central planning agency itself. Their total investment requirements were so obviously beyond available resources that the plans could not be taken seriously for long even by their own sponsors.[30]

Most Indian states also prepare plans but inadequate co-ordination of the plans often leads to wasteful duplication and anomalies.[31] Al-though the Plan Organization of Iran has initiated most regional plan-ning in that country, regional planning efforts have not been integrated with national development plans prepared by the Plan Organization. Moreover, there has been little co-ordination between the Plan Organ-ization's investments in a region and resources allocated to the same region by other government organizations. In Khuzistan, for example, while the Plan Organization allocated almost 20 per cent of its invest-ment resources, other government entities like the Ministries of Agri-culture, Education, Health and Communication and the Agricultural Credit Bank allocated less than 1 or 2 per cent of their smaller resources for basic services needed to complement these investments.[32]

In a mixed-economy country with a federal system of government, regional plans are generally prepared by planning bodies in the politi-cal subdivisions concerned. These plans are generally limited to activi-ties for which the political subdivisions have responsibility and exclude projects and programs which the central government undertakes in the regions. The regional plans are then more or less integrated with the national plan by a central planning agency. This system has been used in India and Nigeria. In contrast, the regional components in Pakistan's First Five Year Plan and, to a somewhat lesser extent, its Second Five Year Plan, were largely prepared by the central planning agency in Karachi. But this was recognized to be undesirable in a country with two Provinces separated by more than a thousand miles. As part of a general move in Pakistan toward decentralization of government func-tions, regional plans are now expected to be prepared increasingly by the regional planning agencies in East and West Pakistan. The central

[30] The financial resources required to meet investment goals in regional plans covering about one-tenth of the country's area were greater than those available to the entire country.

[31] Chatterji, Manas. "Regional Economic Planning," p. 553.

[32] Iran. Plan Organization. *Review of the Second Seven Year Plan Program of Iran*, p. 113.

planning agency is to be mostly concerned with consolidating the regional plans into a coherent national plan.

But in many countries, regional plans continue to be prepared and executed by a central planning agency. This is especially true in countries with unitary governments, as well as with federal governments where (as in Mexico) executive power is nevertheless centralized; where the country is too small to support a series of planning agencies; where there is a shortage of planners; or where a region is too backward to initiate or carry out its own development. In some cases, for example, where a region is backward or lacks enough trained planners, there may be no alternative to having the central planning agency prepare a regional plan. But as a general principle, it is preferable to have a regional plan prepared and implemented by the people most concerned, i.e., those in the region. Where a regional plan is prepared by a central planning agency, it frequently comes to naught since the plan comes from outside the region. The experience in Colombia, Israel, Mexico and elsewhere suggests that the greatest successes in regional planning are obtained when local interest and initiative are harnessed to formulate and execute the regional plan and not when it originates in and its execution is controlled from a distant capital.

This has been found to be true even when new regions are opened up to settlement. In the Guayana Region of Venezuela, for example, where residents are almost all new settlers, the planners in the *Corporación Venezolana de Guayana* (the autonomous regional authority created by the National Government) in Caracas, the capital, are sometimes looked upon by those in the Region as outsiders seeking to impose their plans on the Region. The *Corporación* recognizes that it should have its headquarters in the Region and plans to move there when adequate housing for its staff and other facilities become available. This problem has been avoided in Israel because the Government has started the development of each new region with the construction of basic facilities for the staff of the regional authority, whose members become the first settlers of the region.

RESPONSIBILITY FOR PROJECTS AND PROGRAMS

It is generally accepted that each operating ministry, department or agency has prime responsibility for (1) formulating individual public investment projects (determining their technical feasibility, preparing engineering and other project studies, estimating costs, benefits and schedules of construction, etc.), (2) combining them into a series of related projects with fixed priorities to form an integrated program in accordance with development objectives for the segment of the economy with which the operating agency is concerned, (3) carrying out the projects and programs or supervising their execution, and (4) making periodic reviews and reports on their progress. It is logical that these responsibilities should reside with operating ministries and agencies because in most countries they are the depositories of most of the specialized, technical and administrative knowledge and have the greatest practical experience with actual problems in their fields of operation.[33]

Operating ministries and agencies also may have close contacts with the private sector because they issue licenses for new ventures, permits for importing machinery, equipment and raw materials, approve financing arrangements, or exercise other regulatory functions. In the process of carrying out their duties, these ministries and agencies not only implement a government's economic policies, but accumulate a considerable amount of information concerning private investment programs. They are therefore also apt to be in the best position to estimate private investment for the parts of the economy in which they operate.

The projects, subsector and sector programs prepared by the various operating ministries and agencies have to be integrated into the over-all plan. This is a task for a central planning agency. Ideally, the process proceeds as follows:

Early in the planning cycle, the central planning agency prepares for the appropriate government authorities an analysis in outline indicating the main policy alternatives available to give effect to the plan objectives previously selected by the authorities.

> The core of such an outline should be a table of resources, and the alternative uses of these resources, indicating in each case the contribution to the national income and foreign exchange resources, the extent to which investable resources would be available for the subsequent plan, impact on the distribution of income, expansion of employment, improvements in per capita and total consumption, etc.[34]

[33] United Nations Center for Industrial Development. *Organizational Aspects of Planning*, p. 41.
[34] *Ibid.*, p. 45.

After the authorities have chosen the specific set of policies which is to govern the development plan, the central planners can prepare instructions, within the framework of the selected objectives and policies, which set standards for the operating ministries and agencies to follow in preparing their programs; or, they may first prepare a "plan frame," i.e., a general outline of the proposed development plan, based on the accepted objectives and policies. When the authorities have approved the plan frame, it can provide a broader foundation than objectives and policies alone for the instructions which are to guide operating ministries and agencies in preparing their programs.

The main purpose of these instructions is to get the operating ministries and agencies to select and prepare projects and programs in a reasonably complete and consistent manner in accord with a fixed timetable. This is important for facilitating the task of integrating projects and programs into an internally consistent development plan, as well as for providing the operating organizations themselves with data they need to operate efficiently. In many countries, projects and programs are put together haphazardly and without a common basis. In Spain, for example, a World Bank survey mission found

> the lack of such a common basis . . . has been most marked, with different ministries often preparing plans on quite different assumptions.[35]

The instructions should call for estimates for each project of the total cost and the proposed rates of disbursements each year during construction in terms of national and foreign currencies; proposed sources of financing; the time schedule; manpower, materials, and machinery and equipment requirements; the extent to which the project is to be carried out by the operating ministry or agency itself and by contractors; the need for outside engineering or other technical assistance; the conditions and personnel required, training programs to be conducted and other steps to be taken to provide for operating the completed project; the financial and economic benefits which are to be realized from the project, including its impact on domestic production, employment and foreign trade. The instructions should also detail the criteria for assigning priorities to projects and for combining them into a unified program.

The instructions must be prepared and transmitted to the operating ministries and agencies far enough in advance to permit them to

[35] IBRD. *Economic Development of Spain*, p. 69.

prepare and submit projects and programs in time for review and incorporation into the over-all plan. For a medium-term plan, 18 months is not too much time; for an annual plan, six months should be sufficient.

The instructions to each operating ministry or agency must be accompanied by an indication of the total resources to be made available for its program. The allocation may be a fixed amount or it may be a range, with minimum and maximum amounts dependent on specified circumstances. It is important that each operating organization knows precisely the financial and other limits to which its program must conform. Otherwise, demand may outstrip available resources. This happened in India when the Second Five-Year Plan was being prepared, with unhappy results.

> The lower echelons in the planning process [i.e., ministries and states] were not given any clues as to the total resources which would be available to them and the effect was that, generally speaking, the demand on resources was something like three times the available supply. It was then necessary to cut back and eliminate projects. Not only was this bad from the standpoint of morale, but it also tended to result in decisions based on isolated projects without paying sufficient attention to the balance between government programs and the emphasis desired. The global view required from the central government and from the Planning Commission was lost sight of.[36]

When the operating ministries, departments, agencies or other entities complete their programs, they must be sent to the central planning agency. There they must be reviewed to determine whether they are consistent with each other and with the proposed rate of development and to see that the combined demand of the public and private sectors does not make excessive claims on national and foreign exchange funds, manpower and other real resources, and on the administrative capacity of the country. If, as is generally the case, some programs have to be reduced, increased or otherwise changed to reconcile conflicting claims, the adjustments must be made by the central planning agency in close collaboration with the operating organizations concerned. Where differences arise which cannot be settled by discussion between the central planning agency and operating organizations, they must be submitted to higher authority for decision. The cycle of consultations,

[36] Mayne, Alvin. *Perspective Planning in India*, p. 24.

decisions by government authorities and reworking of the draft plan (by the "planning-from-above" and "planning-from-below" techniques previously described) usually has to be repeated several times. Through a series of successively more detailed and specific approximations, the plan evolves toward its final form. When the process has been completed, the draft plan is ready to be transmitted to the government for its consideration and adoption.

The system described in the last half-dozen paragraphs, with its clear-cut division of responsibilities, may work as it is supposed to in a few developed countries. But in the less developed nations, it does not. In these countries, organizations usually do not have personnel qualified to initiate good projects and prepare them well, let alone combine them into coherent programs based on a rational analysis of costs and benefits. It may be all right to leave project preparation to operating ministries and agencies in advanced countries. But is this feasible in less developed nations? In the circumstances which actually confront them in most less developed countries, planners ask themselves:

> What can be done to avoid undue priority being given to big, showy, spectacular projects as against the scattered, inconspicuous, yet possibly very important projects? Should those responsible for formulating a development programme play a direct part in the formulation of projects, should they leave this to people in the various government departments, or should there be a combination of the two? Which is the best way for economists and technicians to cooperate in the formulation of development projects, and in measuring costs and benefits? How does one best insure that those preparing development projects in one department are aware of related projects under study in other departments, so that proper 'packages' can be formed? [37]

Under pressure to produce a development plan in a reasonable period of time, planners have generally taken the position that the political and administrative obstacles in the way of reforming operating organizations and building up their capability to prepare sound projects and programs are too difficult to overcome in the time usually available for preparing an over-all plan. When organized planning begins in most less developed countries, therefore, it is common practice for the central planning agency to take over some of the work of

[37] UN. ECA. *Problems Concerning Techniques of Development Programming in African Countries,* p. 95.

initiating, preparing, evaluating and even executing public investment projects, as well as the job of preparing private and public sector programs.

When Pakistan's First Five Year Plan was being prepared, for instance, the central planning agency considered it essential that it participate actively in the preparation, evaluation and choice of public investment projects for the Plan, because many of the projects submitted by operating ministries were not supported by a proper appraisal of their technical feasibility, real costs and benefits or the administrative and technical arrangements required for their implementation. Moreover, since there were also many important fields where no projects had been submitted, the central planners felt it necessary to fill some gaps with proposals of their own. The central planning agency realized that this was not the ideal way for it to operate. It would have preferred to leave the choice and preparation of projects to operating organizations. But others felt that the Planning Board, the central planning agency at that time, had not gone far enough. This made it necessary for the President of the Pakistan Economic Association to explain why the Board could not have gone further:

> It has been suggested in certain quarters that more schemes if needed should have been prepared by the Board. This view is based on a misunderstanding of the functions of a Central Planning Organisation and the strength and composition of its staff. If schemes were to be prepared by the Central Planning Organisation it would have to develop a substitute for the entire development organisation of the Central and Provincial Governments. It would lead to a duplication of technical and administrative staff which our personnel resources would not permit. It would end in a complete separation of the staff responsible for detailed planning from the staff engaged on execution, a separation which is possible neither in theory nor in practice.[38]

In Iran, Iraq and Jordan, this separation was avoided, but as events were to show, in a most unsatisfactory way: the central planning agencies in these countries not only initiated and prepared projects; they also carried them out without the participation of the ministries.

[38] Pakistan. Planning Board. *Report of the Special Conference of Economists of East Pakistan on the Draft Five-Year Plan and Connected Papers*, p. 7. Address delivered by Zahid Husain, President, Pakistan Economic Association, at a Special Conference held to consider the First Five Year Plan, Dacca, August 24, 1956.

They did this against the advice of their advisers.[39] Overseas Consultants, Inc., which the Iranian Government had engaged, had advised in 1949

> that existing agencies of the Government should be utilized for the execution of the Plan projects in preference to creating new Government of Plan agencies for the purpose. . . .[40]

This was also Lord Salter's advice to Iraq in 1955. He foresaw that the administrative burden would be too great for Iraq's Development Board if it tried to execute projects. And it was also the advice of the International Bank survey mission to Jordan in 1955:

> Save in exceptional circumstances the Development Board should not itself undertake the execution of development projects but should entrust them to the established Government agencies. . . .[41]

The assumption of project preparation or executive functions by a central planning agency is usually justified as a provisional expedient until the situation in the operating organizations can be improved sufficiently to permit them to perform their normal functions. But once a central planning agency assumes these responsibilities, it becomes increasingly difficult to relinquish them. As time passes, the staff of the central planning agency, often assisted by foreign technicians, becomes more expert in initiating, preparing and evaluating projects and programs, while the operating organizations remain as inept as ever. They may even worsen, as they did in Iran, because in that country the best technicians in the ministries left to join the central planning agency, the Plan Organization, where salaries, working conditions and the very functions which it took over from the ministries made it much more attractive than the ministries as a place of work. Another result of the exodus of technicians was that the ministries were less able than before to administer and maintain the completed projects which the Plan Organization turned over to them. When the Plan Organization was finally forced to relinquish responsibility for project preparation and

---

[39] Rose, E. Michael. *Some Political and Administrative Problems of Economic Development in the Middle East,* p. 7.

[40] Overseas Consultants, Inc. *Report on Seven-Year Development Plan for the Plan Organisation of the Imperial Government of Iran,* Vol. V, p. 10. Similar advice was given by other advisers: Harwood, Wilson R. *Advice to the Plan Organisation of Iran, 1956–1901,* p. 17.

[41] IBRD. *Economic Development of Jordan,* p. 429.

execution to the ministries, they were ill-equipped to assume the responsibility.

When a central planning agency takes over some responsibility for projects and programs, friction between it and operating ministries and agencies almost invariably follows. Understandably, operating organizations prefer to prepare their own projects and programs. They therefore tend to resist carrying out projects and programs prepared by an outside authority.

Training Institutes

When a central planning agency takes over responsibility for projects and programs, it may have sincere intentions of training persons in operating organizations to assume full responsibility for projects and programs eventually. But it almost never works out as expected because the central planning agency has more work than it can do when it must concern itself with projects and programs in addition to preparing aggregative plans. Indeed, the time-consuming tasks of project selection, preparation and evaluation often prevent central planning agencies from concentrating on the assessment of total resources, the selection of alternative patterns of investment, the formulation of policy proposals and the conduct of other activities which are more appropriate to a central planning agency. Thus, the central planning agency is too overburdened usually to conduct training programs outside its own confines. Moreover, since operating ministries and agencies tend to look with suspicion on a planning agency which has usurped functions they consider their own, they have not generally been amenable to training activities conducted by central planners. These reasons account for the fact that in Iran, for example, the central planning agency could make no real attempt to strengthen the ability of operating ministries to handle project preparation and execution, although it was foreseen several years in advance of the event that responsibility for these tasks would have to be turned over to the ministries.

To meet the need for training staffs in ministries and other parts of government, the United Arab Republic, Venezuela, Spain, Greece and some other countries have established semiautonomous government institutes for conducting research in planning and for training planning and programing personnel. These institutes perform a much needed and frequently neglected research and training function. Since they are oriented to operational problems, they do not duplicate the more general educational facilities in academic institutions. As semi-independent entities dedicated to development planning, but free from the suspicion with which operating organizations often view central planning agencies, they are in a much better position than a central planning agency to bring programing practices in operating ministries and agencies into line with the requirements of aggregative planning.[42] Their ability to do this can be considerably bolstered if foreign technical assistance for planning is assigned, to the extent feasible, to them (instead of to a central planning agency or to operating organizations) to be used as appropriate, perhaps interchangeably, either in a central planning agency to help prepare plans or in operating organizations to help prepare and execute projects and programs. Among other advantages, assignment of foreign technical advisers to an institute provides a degree of flexibility in making full use of foreign technicians which is not possible otherwise.

Where an institute trains the staffs of operating organizations in programing techniques, it is unnecessary for a central planning agency to get involved in project and program preparation which, on the one hand, interferes with its own planning work and, on the other hand, arouses suspicions in operating organizations that the central planning agency is seeking to meddle in operations. An institute can also serve other purposes. It can, for example, use its good offices to reconcile differences between the central planning agency and operating organizations. It can also supervise the rationalization of current investment through the taking of a public investment inventory as described in an earlier chapter. Furthermore, by combining this task with a training program for those participating in the exercise, it can provide on-the-job training for operating personnel in programing techniques. There is, therefore, much to be said for having a training institute work with planning and operating personnel from the very inception of the planning process in a country. If domestic technicians were largely concentrated in the operating organizations of government and trained in programing techniques while on the job, central planners could safely leave the preparation of projects and programs to them while they turned their attention to the preparation of over-all plans.

---

[42] This is not true, of course, where an institute takes over planning functions. This happened in Greece when the Centre of Economic Planning and Research, a quasi-government body controlled by the Minister of Co-ordination, was made responsible for preparing national plans.

For a training institute to be effective in these varied activities requires that it enjoy the confidence of the central planning agency and operating organizations. Its director would have to have access to the chief executive and command the respect of ministers and other high officials. These things imply that the institute would have to be sponsored by, and be under the direction of, the highest governmental authority. It would, in most countries, also require foreign consultants capable of acting as advisers and teachers to both the central planners and the ministries.

Interministry Project Review Committees

The "planning-from-below" process essential to good planning requires that projects and programs be reviewed to insure their consistency with plan objectives, policies and targets. This requires a central planning agency to correlate the various projects and programs, scrutinize them for consistency with each other and a national plan, and relate them to available foreign exchange and other resources. But since operating organizations in few less developed countries prepare projects well, central planning agencies in these countries correctly believe it is indispensable to review in detail the projects which operating ministries and agencies submit. But where a planning agency attempts this review, it often ends up with much the same work and frictions as if it had taken over the initiation and preparation of projects in the first place.

Because of this, a central planning agency should not itself conduct the review. Experience shows that better results are obtainable with interministry committees whose members represent all interested parties. Such committees have been employed in several countries. In Pakistan, for example, "Development Working Parties" in the Central and Provincial Governments have evolved into reasonably effective media for reviewing projects to be included in Pakistan's medium-term and annual development plans. The Central Development Working Party's emphasis on adequate technical and other preparation before a project is approved for inclusion in development plans and the annual budget has had a salutary influence on the preparation of projects and programs by sponsoring bodies. Since the Deputy Chairman (i.e., the operating head) of the central planning agency is the presiding officer of the Central Development Working Party, the planning agency is able to assure itself that projects and programs conform to plan requirements.

It is essential that these interministry review committees be provided with secretariats of their own to examine and report to committee members on projects submitted by operating organizations in accordance with appropriate criteria. In Pakistan, the central planning agency acts as the secretariat of the Central Development Working Party. As a result, the central planning agency's staff has to devote time and effort to detailed project review which should be given to broader aspects of planning.

CO-ORDINATING PLAN IMPLEMENTATION

As an Advisory Function

As indicated in Chapter IX, the periodic progress reports on individual projects and programs, which operating ministries and agencies prepare, should be combined into a consolidated report for the head of government, the cabinet, the planning committee of the cabinet (if there is such a committee), the legislature, the public or a combination of these. The report should evaluate the progress made in fulfilling plan targets, anticipate or identify deviations and bottlenecks and suggest appropriate compensatory action or, if necessary, revision of targets or the plan. To obtain complete and timely information from operating organizations on a regular schedule, appropriate reporting forms have to be devised and formal reporting procedures for operating organizations to follow have to be established. These tasks, as well as the preparation of the consolidated progress report, are generally performed by a central planning agency. There are some, it is true, who think that planners should not evaluate their own plan. They believe that planners will find it hard to be objective, and that they will tend to blame failures on operating organizations instead of on their own errors of judgment in formulating the plan. This danger may exist, but it must be risked. If the central planning agency is to prepare realistic annual plans and propose adjustments of medium-term plans in the light of experience during their implementation, it must be allowed to review and evaluate the progress of implementation.

Moreover, a central planning agency's right to review, report and make recommendations on the progress of national plans conforms with a generally accepted principle that it has as important an advisory role in plan implementation as it has in plan formulation. This role is by no means limited to giving advice only to the heads of government.

Since good planning requires co-ordinated action by almost all parts of government, the central planning agency should maintain close and continual contacts with various government ministries and agencies, as well as with private organizations, and it should advise them on the execution of their development projects and programs. It should also advise those concerned with the formulation of monetary, credit, fiscal, foreign exchange, trade, price and other financial and economic policies, and advise on the reconciliation of conflicting policies to insure that, individually and collectively, they further the achievement of development goals.

Few would deny, at least in theory, the legitimacy of these advisory functions for a central planning agency although, in practice, most planning agencies do not exercise them as frequently or as completely as effective planning requires. But since a central planning agency is naturally deeply concerned that plans it has prepared be implemented properly and is, besides, more informed than any other government body about what needs to be done, a question arises whether it is also not the best organization to supervise, control, police or expedite the execution of plans.

As an Executive Function

This question has been answered in different ways. At one extreme, the central planning agency in some countries has not been permitted to intervene operationally in any way in implementing plans. This is not always because the planning agency is weak. In Yugoslavia, for example, where the central planning agency is important in the government process, plan implementation has been virtually divorced from plan formulation since the early 1950's. The Yugoslav Federal Planning Institute has only an advisory role with regard to both plan formulation and implementation. This is also true of the French Commissariat Général du Plan. At the other extreme, as has been seen, the central planning agency in a few countries, of which Iran and Iraq are examples, has not only formulated plans, but has then carried them out.

Between these opposites are many variations. In Mexico, the staff of the central planning agency makes periodic visits to construction sites to check on the progress of projects being carried out by operating organizations. The results of these inspections are discussed with the operating organization concerned and necessary action is agreed upon, sometimes on the spot. Operating organizations are undoubtedly stimulated to take the planners' advice because they know that the central planning agency's approval is necessary before the Ministry of Finance will include an appropriation for a project in the annual budget and because the planning agency reports its findings to the President of the Republic.

The Indian Planning Commission, although considered an advisory body, has exercised a series of important executory functions, notably in the fields of public co-operation works, water supply, rural works and rural industrialization. Moreover, it has involved itself frequently in the formulation of public policies, as well as in other than development matters.[43] It has frequently prodded state governments and operating ministries and agencies in the Central Government to get things done and has gone beyond suggestion to discourage them from wasting resources on nonessentials. It has, in fact, gone so far at times that a wrong impression was created that it was the Planning Commission's responsibility to insure the implementation of development plans.[44] Because experience with the execution of the Third Plan has not been happy, individuals in the Government have indicated a desire to redefine the scope of the Planning Commission's authority and to divest it of some of its controversial policy-making and executory functions.

Central planning agencies in other countries enter into operational activities in varying degrees. For example, the Venezuelan central planning agency initiated a program for establishing seven automotive assembly plants, as well as plants for the manufacture of automotive parts, and carried out the program over a two-year period before turning it over to a ministry. In the USSR, central planning agencies are nominally advisory bodies, but in practice they have been given many executive duties. Thus, recent reorganization of Soviet planning machinery entailed a considerable increase in the executive functions of the USSR *Gosplan,* the agency in charge of annual plans. But in other socialized countries, notably in Poland and Czechoslovakia, organiza-

---

[43] Gadgil, D. R. *Planning and Economic Policy in India,* p. 107.

[44] See, for example, comment to this effect by Dr. V. K. R. V. Rao, Member of the Planning Commission, *Economic Times,* November 10, 1963. Mr. T. T. Kirshnamachari, India's Finance Minister, also has "expressed serious concern over the growing tendency on the part of the Planning Commission to indulge in executive responsibility and day-to-day decisions of the Government instead of concentrating on specialization in the techniques of planning and the vital task of improving its efficiency." (*Bank of Baroda Weekly Review,* April 24, 1964, p. 1.)

tional reforms have shown a pronounced tendency toward reducing or completely eliminating operational functions formerly exercised by central planning agencies.

Control over plan implementation requires crucial choices to be made among alternative policies, as well as the issuance of directives to operating organizations for action to be taken or avoided in order to carry out policy and other decisions. Since ministers and heads of agencies are not likely to accept directives from their equals or subordinates, supervision over plan execution must, ultimately, reside at the highest government level. This is as true in the mixed economies as in the socialized countries. In the USSR, the Council of Ministers is responsible for co-ordinating execution of the plan; in the mixed economies, it may be the chief executive, a cabinet or a top-level committee of the cabinet.

Authority to co-ordinate plan implementation, in the sense of directing operating organizations to take action, can rarely be effectively delegated to a ministry, a planning agency or other body at a lower government level. When the matter of creating an all-powerful implementation agency was being discussed in the Philippines, one former member of the National Economic Council, the central planning agency, correctly pointed out why it was impossible to separate the President from the implementation of plans:

> We must not forget that under the Constitution the executive power is vested in the President of the Philippines. But, even without having to resort to the Constitution, from the political point of view I cannot see how it would be possible in the Philippines to create a powerful Economic Council that would supervise the implementation by the President and his Cabinet of those portions of the economic policies and plans entrusted to their respective jurisdiction. Proposals, made from time to time in the Philippines, for a so-called Economic Czar, if this function is to be vested in an official other than the President, are unrealistic, even if limited to the implementation of economic plans. Only the President, and no other, could exercise the power of an Economic Czar in the Philippines, and see to it that economic policies adopted by Congress or by the Council, within the limits of an enabling act, were carried out by the different departments, offices and agencies of the Executive Departments.[45]

[45] Araneta, Salvador. "The Planning, Approval and Implementation of Economic Policy," p. 141.

The chief executive or cabinet may have a secretariat or may designate a central planning agency or other body to operate as a secretariat in issuing instructions to, or in dealing with, other parts of government. But it must be clear that the secretariat or other body is acting in behalf of the chief executive or the cabinet, not on its own prerogative. When, for instance, the Prime Minister was in direct charge of Jamaica's Central Planning Unit, instructions to operating organizations on matters concerning implementation of development plans were drafted in the planning agency, but were transmitted to operating ministries and agencies as communications of the Prime Minister—not of the Central Planning Unit. In Chile, also, the central planning agency [46] was the secretariat for an interministerial commission (*Cómite de Programación Económica y de Reconstrucción* or *CO-PERE*) established to supervise execution of the country's Ten-Year Development Plan. Responsibility for supervising and expediting the execution of development plans in Malaya rests with a Ministry of Rural Development. The Ministry has several operating departments dealing with surveying, mining, land development and the promotion of rural industry. But its most important function is to co-ordinate and expedite plan implementation. However, since the Deputy Prime Minister (who, as the country's chief planning authority, has charge of an Economic Planning Unit which formulates development plans) holds the Ministry's portfolio, the Ministry is, in effect, his secretariat for supervising execution of plans. Indeed, the Ministry's considerable effectiveness is largely due to the fact that its officials speak in the name of the Deputy Prime Minister.

Some experts feel that a central planning agency which has only advisory functions is unlikely to be effective. Thus, one expert has contended:

> The body that formulates an over-all development programme cannot be fully effective if it is merely in an advisory position without executive functions and without influence on the planning activities of individual government departments.[47]

These experts believe that a planning agency without executive functions will not even be able to get essential data for operating agencies. They have no difficulty finding examples of planning agencies without

[46] More precisely, the Planning Department of CORFO, the Government's development corporation.
[47] Meior, G. M. *Role of an Expert Advisory Group in a Young Government*, p. 10.

executive power which have been unable to get planning data through official channels and which have had to rely on personal contacts in other parts of government to get information. And they can give other examples to show that if, for instance, a planning agency allocates funds, prepares the capital budget or has power to withhold approval of projects or programs, it is apt to get the information it needs as a by-product of its authority. This state of affairs may explain, at least partially, why many planners endeavor to obtain operational responsibilities.

There is no denying that in the circumstances prevailing in many countries, a central planning agency with executive powers is apt to be in a stronger position than one with only advisory functions when it seeks the co-operation of operating organizations. But those who advocate executive powers for planning agencies on this account forget that it is the responsibility of the heads of government, not the central planning agency, to enforce the discipline of a plan. If political leaders are committed to a plan, the requests and advice of a central planning agency will be respected; if heads of government lack commitment, executive powers which a central planning agency may have will not prevent operating organizations, or the heads of government themselves, from exerting bureaucratic or political pressures to which the planning agency will usually have to yield. The history of planning is replete with examples of political projects outside existing plans which planning agencies, theoretically empowered to turn them down, reluctantly approved. There are, of course, many instances where a central planning agency has withheld its executive approval for wasteful projects which might otherwise have gone forward. But if they were important to the operating organization concerned, the planning agency's disapproval was more likely to prevail because of the support of the government leadership than because of the executive powers of the planning agency. In most countries, the crucial factor is the extent to which heads of government are willing to support a central planning agency, not whether it has executive or advisory powers.

Separate Implementing Agencies

While some who favor executive powers for a central planning agency believe that it should be responsible for implementing plans, others advocate that an autonomous body be set up for this purpose.

They contend that plan formulation, as an advisory function, is incompatible with the executive responsibilities inherent in co-ordinating implementation of plans. They feel that planners cannot have it both ways. If they get involved in operations, frictions are likely to be generated which will hamper co-operation with operating organizations needed for effective preparation of plans. They say that the job of preparing and keeping plans up to date is difficult enough and if executory supervision over plan realization is added, the job becomes too difficult for one agency to manage. Moreover, the skills required for executing plans differ greatly from those needed by planning advisers and good planners are not always good executors. Where planners get involved in daily operational activities, such as reviewing and approving projects and inspecting work under way, or even reporting on the progress of the plan, broader planning activities may be crowded out.

For a time, this view prevailed in Pakistan. It led to the establishment of an autonomous Projects Division with authority to follow up and report on the execution of projects, measure performance against estimates, identify causes of delays in implementing projects and propose appropriate corrective action. But the Projects Division did not work well. It was supposed to collaborate closely with the central planning agency, but both agencies tended to act as though their functions were unrelated to the other and neither made the necessary effort to insure constant co-operation. As a result, the central planning agency was sometimes without information which the Projects Division had on the progress of plan implementation.

The Projects Division also found it difficult to get the co-operation of operating organizations, which often saw the division's activity as an intrusion on their own fields of operation. Government dissatisfaction with the Division led to its abolition and the transfer of its staff to the central planning agency. But the method of operation remained unchanged, as did most of the problems which had led to the Projects Division's termination. Eventually, therefore, a new solution was sought. The expediting function was transferred to the East and West Pakistan Planning and Development Departments. But since experience had shown that the preparation of effective plans could not be divorced from review and evaluation of their implementation, the central planning agency took over and has since retained these responsibilities.

Because the Burmese Government believed at one time that one agency could not successfully formulate plans and supervise their implementation, Burma also separated the two functions. A Ministry of National Planning was charged with preparing plans while an Economic and Social Board was put in charge of expediting.

> In practice, however, it was found difficult to secure such a rigid separation of functions. In particular, the line of demarcation of activities of the Planning Ministry and the Economic and Social Board often became blurred so as to require a constant re-demarcation of responsibilities. It was also found that more or less the same group of people was sitting on the working committees of both the Ministry of National Planning and the Economic and Social Board, thereby impairing the original principle that those who do the planning work should not be charged with the supervision of the execution of the plans.

> Apart from the confusion on the part of other agencies of the Government as to which of the twin economic bodies, namely, the Planning Ministry or the Economic and Social Board, they should approach or deal with on certain matters, there was also a certain amount of duplication of work between the Planning Ministry and the Economic and Social Board.[48]

As a result of these difficulties, the two organizations were eventually merged into a National Planning Commission. Later, because plan implementation continued to lag, the idea of having a separate supervisory body was revived in the form of a Standing Committee for Supervision and Coordination.[49] But the Committee, which consisted of high-ranking civil servants, proved to be ineffective because its members did not have the status to intervene against politically powerful ministers who were sponsoring projects.[50]

Ghana also established separate organizations for drafting and supervising the implementation of plans. A National Planning Commission was charged with producing plans and a State Control Commission, more recently a State Planning Committee, was responsible for controlling execution. But the use of a separate body to co-ordinate plan execution was not more successful in Ghana than in other countries. In December 1963, Korea established an Office of Planning and Control under the Prime Minister to co-ordinate the formulation

[48] Thet Tun, U. *A Review of Economic Planning in Burma,* p. 50.
[49] United Nations Conference on the Application of Science and Technology, etc. *Organization of Planning Machinery: Lessons from Burmese Experience,* pp. 10–11.
[50] Walinsky, Louis J. "Burma," p. 48.

and implementation of plans and review and evaluate progress of plans and programs. It remains to be seen whether this organization will be more successful than others have been.

A special organization created to oversee plan implementation often has the effect of reducing the status of a central planning agency. This has been evident in the Philippines, where a Program Implementation Agency (PIA) was set up to expedite the execution of that country's development plan. The PIA soon became the real focal point of the Government's development activities, pushing the already weak National Economic Council (NEC) further into the background. More recently, however, the PIA lost many of its best personnel. Consequently, the outlook for the agency is less bright than at its beginning. But as long as PIA exists, it casts a shadow on NEC's standing as a central planning agency.

A similar situation has prevailed in Thailand. In that country, a Ministry of National Development was established in 1963 with powers to oversee the implementation of the major public works projects in the plan. The Ministry was formed with departments transferred from ministries which together accounted for 60 to 70 per cent of total public investment. Not only was the role and status of the central planning agency put in doubt by the creation of the new Ministry; the loss of their most important operating departments left several ministries with greatly reduced responsibilities.

In a well-ordered government, there is no need for a specially constituted entity to expedite plan implementation. The chief executive, cabinet or high-level cabinet committee is the only overseer needed. The central planning agency, through regular economic analyses and evaluations of plan progress provides information and recommendations on the basis of which the political leadership can choose between available alternatives. When decisions are made and communicated to the appropriate ministers and heads of agencies for action, these executives are held accountable for the results.

In governments which lack internal discipline, it becomes all the more important that political leaders retain responsibility for seeing to it that development plans are carried out since a subordinate body is unlikely to accomplish what the heads of government can. But it is precisely these governments which usually resort to subordinate expediting bodies. The creation of a separate autonomous body to follow up on plan implementation is often an indication that the heads of government are not themselves ready to assume responsibility for co-ordinating the implementation of their development plan. The prospects for its successful implementation are therefore reduced.

If a government considers it necessary to have a separate organization to co-ordinate development operations, the least objectionable choice is a central planning agency. If a central planning agency does the co-ordinating, it at least eliminates the need for yet another organization and obviates the problem of insuring close co-operation between the planning and implementing agencies. Since the effectiveness of a plan depends, ultimately, on the ability to implement it, fusion of the planning and supervisory functions may also lead to improved plan formulation by bringing planners closer to problems encountered in implementing plans. Furthermore, use of a planning agency to expedite plan execution involves a pragmatic recognition that in most countries, undesirable though it may be in theory, central planning agencies concern themselves to some degree in executory activities to influence implementation.

The main objections against having a planning agency oversee the implementation of plans can be overcome. If the staff in the planning agency dealing with the operational task of plan co-ordination is organized separately from the staff engaged in plan formulation, review and revision, the dangers of confusing advisory and operational responsibilities are minimized.[51] In Tunisia, for example, the development planning portion of the Secretariat of State for Planning and Finance is divided into two sections: a Planning Office, responsible for formulating plans, and an Office of Plan Control, responsible for supervising and co-ordinating plan execution.

If the planning agency carries out its co-ordinative functions in the name of the chief executive, the cabinet or a cabinet committee, it becomes as it should, a secretariat for the person or group with prime responsibility for surveillance over the execution of plans. But it is of the utmost importance that the planning agency not act on its own prerogative. As Barbara Ward pointed out in her account of the Indian situation, the extent to which one government department—in the Indian case, the Planning Commission—can prod another is limited. One wonders, she asked,

[51] It is well to recognize, however, that partly because of shortages of trained personnel and partly because planners usually like to get involved in operations, this division of responsibilities is hard to achieve and is, in fact, almost never made when a central planning agency assumes executive functions.

whether a sub-committee of the cabinet or some other high-level body reporting directly to the Prime Minister should not undertake the responsibility of seeing, month-by-month, that planned development is going forward at a coherent pace and that the various schemes and sectors hang together. Could the bottlenecks in basic industries have developed so far if a strong cabinet body had been breathing down the neck of the Minister responsible for coal mines and demanding why, month after month, his figures were below target? [52]

This is a question which, when adapted to their own circumstances, other governments which rely on subordinate expediting organizations would do well to ponder.

SUMMARY AND CONCLUSIONS

There is a need for every country which seeks to plan well to define as precisely as possible who is to do what and how, i.e., by what criteria or standards it is to be done. Few countries bother to do this. Consequently, there is often a lack of clarity about the division of responsibility between planning and operating bodies and an even greater uncertainty about the manner in which planning functions are to be performed.

Ultimate responsibility for all aspects of national development planning rest with a nation's supreme government authority, although many planning functions must be distributed throughout the public administration and to the private sector. But there are some responsibilities which this authority should not delegate. Among these are approval of plans and the setting of planning objectives and targets.

Where a central planning agency exists, it is almost always assigned the task of preparing and, when necessary, revising national development plans. In every country with a central planning agency, the agency which prepares the medium- and long-term plan also prepares the annual operational plan. Since an annual plan is the most convenient medium for adapting a long-term plan to changed conditions, its formulation is an essential part of the continuous planning process by which a medium-term plan is revised. Because an annual plan can

---

[52] Ward, Barbara. *Plan Under Pressure, An Observer's View*, p. 31.

make basic changes in a medium-term plan, the agency responsible for formulating the annual plan is in fact the agency which determines the ultimate character of the medium-term plan. For these reasons, as well as because the scarcity of planners in less developed countries makes it desirable to reduce competitive demands upon them by different agencies, annual and long-term plans should be prepared by the same agency.

An annual development or operational plan—which covers physical, human and financial resources—must be distinguished from an annual capital or public investment budget, which is concerned only with financial resources. The first is primarily the responsibility of a central planning agency; the second is primarily the task of a budget office. But there is need for the closest collaboration between the two bodies. Where an agency is responsible for allocating foreign exchange for both public and private investment it should also work in close co-operation with the central planning agency.

Because ministries of finance in less developed countries often pay little attention to central planners, some experts have advocated that the central planning agency be given authority to prepare the capital budget, thus giving it direct control over a powerful device for implementing its plans. But by taking on this task, it almost invariably reduces the time available for planning, its main function.

Because planning is heavily dependent on statistics, some countries have made the central statistical office a part of the central planning agency. There are advantages in this arrangement, not the least of which is that planners are thereby able to insure that statistics are prepared in suitable form for planning. But there are also overriding disadvantages. A central statistical service has to provide data for purposes other than planning, and there is much to be said for giving the statistician a degree of independence from the planner. Experience shows, also, that where the statistical and planning functions have been combined in a single agency, either the statistical or planning function has been neglected.

In some countries the central statistical office and the central planning agency are independent divisions or departments in the same ministry. This is better than having the central statistical office within the central planning agency. Nevertheless, it still involves a substantial risk that statistical priorities will be largely determined by planners' wants. The most satisfactory solution appears to be to establish the statistical office as an autonomous body. The close co-operation needed between the statistical office and the users of its data can then be obtained through a steering committee which includes as members the head of the statistical office, the chief planner and the senior officers of other interested ministries and agencies.

In most less developed countries there is also a great need for one government body to co-ordinate the acquisition and use of foreign technical skills. Attempts to co-ordinate relationships with external organizations rendering technical assistance through a ministry of foreign affairs have not proved successful because this ministry is generally poorly informed about development priorities. This is also true, although to a lesser extent, of co-ordination through a ministry of finance or ministry of economic affairs. Where a plan exists, it furnishes the best guide for allocating technical assistance. In countries with a plan, a central planning agency is best situated to determine development priorities. It is best to have a separate unit in or out of the central planning agency, but closely associated with the planning agency, to carry out these operational tasks.

One government body also should be assigned responsibility for co-ordinating all foreign development financing and for getting the greatest benefits from such funds. A central planning agency should help determine the extent of foreign resources required and their distribution for development purposes, but the actual negotiation of foreign aid and loan arrangements and co-ordination of the use of aid and loan proceeds are operational tasks which other government bodies are more qualified to perform. The preferred way of centralizing control over foreign loans and aid is for a government to designate one office as the only one authorized to negotiate all loans and aid. Where administrative regulations cannot be enforced effectively, operating ministries and agencies should be required, by law, to obtain the approval of a ministry of finance or another designated entity before the government's credit can be legally committed.

Whether a central planning agency should be responsible for the preparation of regional plans depends on factors such as the size and character of a country's economy, the type of planning and government, the stage of development in the region concerned and the availability of technicians to staff regional planning agencies. In the socialized countries, regional planning bodies generally prepare plans for their regions which are integrated by the central planning agency into the national plan. In the mixed economies, regional plans are sometimes prepared by a central planning agency but where an autonomous regional development authority has been established, it is both desirable and usual for it to prepare the plan for its region. However, one problem in many countries is that regional planning has proceeded independently of national planning, with the result that a series of unintegrated regional plans has sometimes been produced, based on regional aspirations instead of available resources.

It is generally accepted that operating ministries, departments and agencies have prime responsibility for preparing public investment projects, combining them into integrated sector or subsector programs, carrying out or supervising the execution of the projects and programs and making periodic reports on their progress. They are usually the depositories of most of the specialized, technical and administrative knowledge and have the greatest practical experience with actual problems in their fields of operations. These organizations are also apt to be in the best position to estimate private investment for the parts of the economy in which they operate. In practice, however, operating organizations in most less developed countries do not have enough personnel qualified to initiate good projects and prepare them well, let alone combine them into coherent programs based on a rational analysis of costs and benefits. When organized planning begins in most less developed countries, due to the pressure to get a plan in operation, it is common practice for the central planning agency to take over some of the work of initiating, preparing, evaluating and even executing public investment projects, as well as the preparation of private and public sector programs.

The assumption of project preparation, or other executive functions by a central planning agency, is usually justified as a temporary expedient until the situation in the operating organizations can be improved sufficiently to permit them to perform their normal functions. But experience shows that once a central planning agency assumes these responsibilities, it becomes increasingly difficult to relinquish them. This is because the staff of the central planning agency tends with practice to become more expert in initiating, preparing and evaluating projects, while the operating organizations, more or less deprived of practical experience, remain as inept as ever.

When a central planning agency takes over some responsibility for projects and programs, friction between it and operating organizations almost invariably develops. Operating organizations resist carrying out projects and programs initiated or prepared by outsiders. The central planning agency may intend to train persons in operating organizations to assume full responsibility for projects and programs eventually. But it almost never works out as expected, because the central planning agency has more work than it can do when it must concern itself with projects and programs in addition to preparing aggregative plans.

To meet the need for training staffs in operating organizations, some countries have established semiautonomous government institutes for conducting research in planning and for training planning and prograing personnel. Where an institute is available to train the staffs of operating organizations in programing techniques, it is unnecessary for a central planning agency to get involved in project and program preparation, which, on the one hand, interferes with its own planning work and, on the other hand, arouses suspicions in operating organizations that the central planning agency is seeking to meddle in operations.

Good planning procedure requires that projects and programs be reviewed to insure their consistence with plan objectives, policies and targets. Where a central planning agency attempts to make this review in the detail required, it often ends up with much the same work and frictions as if it had taken over the initiation and preparation of projects in the first place. Experience demonstrates that better results are obtainable with interministry committees whose members represent all interested parties.

The preparation of a consolidated report on the progress of a development plan is a task which is generally entrusted to a central planning agency. Some believe a planning agency may not be able to be objective about failures, but this is a danger that must be risked.

Some experts feel that a central planning agency which has only advisory functions is unlikely to be effective. There is no denying that, in the circumstances prevailing in many countries, a central planning agency with executive powers is apt to be in a stronger position than one with only advisory functions. But those who advocate executive powers for planning agencies on this account forget that it is the responsibility of the heads of government, not the central planning agency, to enforce the discipline of a plan.

Some who favor a central planning agency with executive powers believe that it should be responsible for implementing plans. Others, who consider it desirable to have a government agency supervise implementation, advocate that an autonomous body be set up for this purpose. But special organizations set up to supervise plan execution have not worked well. In a well-ordered government, there is no need for a special entity to expedite implementation. However, if a government considers it necessary to have a separate organization to co-ordinate development operations, the least objectionable choice is a central planning agency. If the staff in the planning agency dealing with the operational task of plan co-ordination is organized separately from the staff engaged in the advisory task of plan formulation, review and revision, the dangers of confusing operational and advisory responsibilities are minimized. If the planning agency carries out its co-ordinative functions in the name of the chief executive, it becomes as it should, a secretariat for the supreme political authority who has ultimate responsibility for surveillance over the execution of plans.

Chapter XII

The Function and Role of a Central Planning Agency

> Programming of development requires a number of different abilities and types of knowledge. . . . The way in which the large number of people necessarily involved in the process cooperate and the way their various acts succeed each other and fit into the pattern are by no means arbitrary or unimportant. It is a common misunderstanding that activities can simply start at the bottom of the pyramid of agencies and that the coordinating role of the center comes in later.[1]

FUNCTIONS OF A CENTRAL PLANNING AGENCY

As THE preceding discussion has indicated, where the heads of government accept their responsibility to co-ordinate and supervise the execution of development plans, there is little need for a central planning agency to assume executive responsibilities. A central planning agency should be an advisory body. When a planning agency assumes executive functions, it may indicate that the heads of government or the planners themselves lack a proper understanding of the role of a central planning agency; but because it involves a transfer of responsibility to the planning agency which only heads of a government should possess, it may also indicate that the heads of government are unable or unwilling to face up to the implications of a plan's objectives and targets.

From what has been said, it becomes clear that a central planning agency should be responsible for:

[1] Tinbergen, Jan and Bos, Hendrics C. *Mathematical Models of Economic Growth*, pp. 4–5.

1. The formulation and revision of long-term, medium-term and annual national development plans, including the combination and reconciliation of sector and subsector programs in these plans (as distinguished from projects and programs for a sector or, sometimes, a subsector,[2] which are properly the responsibilities of operating agencies);

2. the formulation of regional development plans in small, less developed countries where the establishment of separate regional planning bodies is unwarranted or unfeasible (but this should be considered exceptional; in most countries, regional plans should be formulated and their execution supervised by local or specially constituted regional planning bodies);

3. the preparation of annual operational plans for implementing medium-term plans [3] (but not annual—or multiannual—development budgets, which are the prerogative of budgetary authorities);

4. recommending policies, instruments of economic policy and other measures and machinery required to mobilize financial, material and human resources for implementing development plans (although responsibility for setting policy, adopting measures or establishing new machinery lies in other parts of a government);

5. periodic reporting, and evaluating of, the progress of development plans (on the basis of project, program, subsectoral or sectoral reports prepared by operating organizations and other information), identifying factors which are retarding or may retard development and suggesting means for dealing with them; and

6. co-ordinating the use, and negotiating the acquisition of, foreign technical skills (although preferably through a unit separated from, but closely linked administratively to, the planning unit in a central planning agency).

[2] Where one ministry or other agency is responsible for an entire sector, it prepares the sector program; but if two or more ministries or agencies prepare programs in the same sector, the central planning office is responsible for combining these programs into a program for the entire sector.

[3] A distinction is made here, as elsewhere in this book, between an annual plan which is intended to give effect to a medium-term plan, and one, like those referred to in Item 1 above, which is prepared without reference to a medium-term plan.

Central planning agencies usually have most of these responsibilities, although provision for co-ordination of, and negotiation for, foreign technical skills is frequently omitted. But central planning agencies are sometimes given a variety of other powers. It would be hard to find another central planning agency which has been endowed with the sweeping authority which the Korean Government gave its Economic Planning Board in 1961. Its responsibilities included (a) not only the formulation of plans, but the supervision of their implementation and the provision of policy measures required for the purpose; (b) the formulation of the national budget within the framework of the development plan; (c) the integration and modification of policies or measures initiated by any ministry or agency; (d) the conduct of economic research and the administration of governmental statistical activities; (e) the co-ordination of foreign financial and technical aid programs and the promotion of foreign investment; and (f) the preparation of the basic policy for over-all scientific and technological development; and the co-ordination of the activities of technical agencies and institutions, both public and private.

While the scope of these powers is unusually broad, other central planning agencies have also been given considerable powers. Iran's Plan Organization and Iraq's Development Board, for example, were not only authorized to prepare and carry out projects, regional programs and development plans but also were given special funds outside the budget to disburse for these purposes. Nicaragua's National Economic Council is empowered to prepare projects, sectoral and regional programs, and long-term plans. In addition, government organizations are required to obtain the Council's approval for all their investments, whether or not they are within the framework of a national development plan. In Honduras, also, all foreign loans contracted by the Government, or by private firms with the guarantee of the Government, must have the approval of the National Economic Council, Honduras' central planning agency. And in the Philippines, the National Economic Council is empowered to formulate trade, tariff and other policies and to implement foreign aid programs.

But the fact that a central planning agency is given certain powers does not mean that it is able to exercise them. Indeed, the more its powers intrude upon the spheres of responsibility of existing government organizations, the less the planning agency is likely to perform the functions assigned to it. The established bureaucracy will see to that. Where the heads of government are not genuinely committed to planning, it matters little what powers are given to the central planning agency. If the heads of government do not take planning seriously, no one else will either and the planning agency will soon be ignored by operating ministries and agencies.

But experience shows that even when the heads of government support planning it is unwise to give a central planning agency so much power over operations that it arouses the active antagonism of civil servants and political appointees. In Iran, for example, the Plan Organization (PO)—an autonomous agency which was endowed with unusually wide powers over development planning and execution— was under constant attack from ministers and other politicians from its inception. Incessant pressure led progressively to the forced resignation of its dynamic and independent Director, loss of control by the PO over its administrative budget, subordination of the PO to the Prime Minister and, finally, to the transfer of its plan implementation powers to operating ministries and agencies. In Brazil, an announcement at the end of 1962 that the President proposed to establish a ministry of development and planning as a "superministry," with powers to program and control the execution of a wide variety of projects and regional programs then under the supervision of other government bodies,[4] created enough immediate opposition from Cabinet members and others to make the President give up the idea. In fact, the hostility aroused was so great that the chief planner associated with the idea was soon returned to the regional planning agency whence he had come, and a central planning agency never was established as a going concern by the President. The dismissals of the heads of planning in Iran and Brazil are not isolated incidents of their kind. The annals of planning history are replete with cases of planners who proved to be no match for politicians when, often with the best interests of their countries at heart, they sought to take over operating responsibilities from ministries and agencies.

Even a central planning agency with only advisory powers is unlikely to be welcomed by established political and administrative interests. Despite the extraordinary increase in interest in development planning,

---

[4] According to Daland, Robert T. "Chapter IV. The Politics of the Plano Trienal," p. 7, specific fields which were to be turned over to the new Ministry, in addition to the usual powers of a planning agency, included authority over drought programs, sanitation, aid to Indians, the statistical system and the census, assistance to municipalities, regional banks and the development of territories.

it is still mistrusted by many in old-line ministries and agencies. In Nigeria, for example, ministers

> mistrusted the activities of economic planners, considering the intrusion into their ministries' affairs by outside officials as an invasion of their jurisdiction.[5]

When not suspicious or hostile, officials usually lack understanding of the purpose and role of planning. Thus, a former director of the Colombian Planning Department complained:

> I was constantly surprised during my two years as head of the Planning Department at the number of highly cultivated people who asked me the same question: 'Just what is planning?' [6]

Pakistan's experience after it established its Planning Board is typical. The Planning Board was an advisory agency without authority to make decisions. Its views, even the plan it eventually prepared, were merely recommendations which could only gain official status if and when approved by the Government. The idea of an advisory agency such as the Board was an innovation in Pakistan, where almost all governmental units were executing bodies. Not surprisingly, therefore, few persons in government, among the public, and even within the Planning Board itself, clearly understood what it was supposed to do. The Board's requests for information or for the submission of proposals frequently encountered passive resistance which handicapped and delayed its work. When it began making suggestions for changing projects submitted by the various ministries, departments and agencies, apathy sometimes gave way to open hostility.

In the governments of many less developed countries, the available supply of trained economic and technical expertise is often concentrated in the central planning agency. It is perhaps to be expected, therefore, that the planning agency will be called upon occasionally to do some tasks which are extraneous to planning. Sometimes, a central planning agency has to take on irrelevant responsibilities to obtain funds required for its operation. In Ecuador, for instance, the Government for some years did not provide funds for the Planning Board, which had to seek financing from the Central Bank, ministries and

---

[5] Clark, Peter Bentley. "Economic Planning for a Country in Transition: Nigeria," p. 263.

[6] Franco Holguin, Jorge. "Politica Económica y Planeación," p. 371.

other government agencies. In return, it had to prepare special studies little related to planning. There have also been cases where the head of a planning agency himself has volunteered to do extraneous work or complied too readily to requests for such work from a head of government in order to justify his agency's existence or to strengthen his own position.

But widespread failure of officials to appreciate the function and purposes of planning and planning agencies accounts for a great deal of the extraneous work which central planning agencies are often required to perform. For instance, because government leaders were unfamiliar with planning in Morocco, the Council of Government and the Ministry of National Economy and Finance, in which the planning agency (DECP) was located, frequently turned over odd jobs to the DECP which had little or no relationship to planning. The DECP was required to study and make recommendations on import licensing problems, an investment guarantee program and the establishment of a thermal water resort. It was made the repository of any statistical or other documents received by the Government for which no other recipient could be conveniently located. An autonomous public agency which regulated prices of imports and exports of scarce commodities was incorporated into the DECP because government officials thought its functions were related to planning.

Examples in other countries are not wanting. The Ecuadorean Government considered it appropriate for its Planning Board to administer an "Industrial Encouragement Law," while the Colombian Government had its planning office licensing exports. The Colombian Government also turned over to the central planning agency the question of whether the Government should approve the establishment of commercial bank branches (a political "hot potato" which the Central Bank did not want to handle). The Honduran National Economic Council had to act as a staff secretariat for the President of the Republic, while the Indonesian National Planning Council was responsible for assisting the President on all economic matters. In Jamaica, the Central Planning Unit did a variety of odd jobs. Among other things, it prepared programs for foreign professional groups visiting the country, provided staff to accompany them on observation trips and prepared the Government's political proposals for the Constitutional Convention which considered the establishment of a West Indies Federation.

There appears to be a belief in some countries that planning can be a part-time activity. Thus, several countries combine the planning function with finance, economic affairs or with a variety of other portfolios. The Congo (Brazzaville) has a Ministry of Planning and Supply, Mali, a Ministry of Planning and Rural Economy, and South Africa and Gabon, a Ministry of Planning and Mining. In Burma, in the early 1950's, a minister who held the portfolios of Religious Affairs and National Culture, which were his major concern, was also made Minister of National Planning. More recently, the Minister of Foreign Affairs was also Minister of Planning; while in Uruguay, a banker is the part-time director of the central planning agency (CIDE). Even in India, the Deputy Chairman of the Planning Commission at one time was Minister of Planning, Labour and Employment.

The heads of planning agencies are often expected to assume a variety of nonplanning duties as a regular matter and are frequently commandeered for special assignments. Thus, the Chairman of Pakistan's Planning Commission was also chairman of a committee which spent several months studying and recommending basic reforms in public administration. The head of the Technical (i.e., the planning) Department of Ecuador's Planning Board had to serve on a variety of committees dealing with such matters as smuggling, textile industry problems and commercial relations with other countries. In the UAR, the head of the planning agency was also a member of more than a dozen other organizations and committees. In addition to being on several committees concerned with the modification of tariffs and other matters little related to planning, the one-time director of Colombia's central planning agency was kept in the United States for about five months to help renegotiate short-term commercial bank loans to Colombian banks and to perform other duties extraneous to planning, while the head of Venezuela's Central Office of Coordination and Planning, a close confidant of the President, spent much time advising him on day-to-day economic and political problems. Responsibilities which are unrelated to planning, as well as attendance at innumerable conferences and meetings outside their countries, often require the heads of planning agencies and their chief assistants to be away from their duties for prolonged periods, diverting a great amount of their time and attention from the planning activities of their agencies.

The widespread lack of understanding of planning and its purposes in most governments inevitably produces friction. However, even where the nature of the planning function is better understood, it is futile to expect that no dissension will arise between a central planning agency and other parts of government. When a planning agency prepares a plan which necessarily requires ministries, departments and agencies to change their long-time ways of doing business, divergencies and conflicts are bound to appear. The problem of keeping individuals and organizations hewing to the line of a plan also makes differences unavoidable. But friction can be minimized by bringing operating ministries, departments and agencies into the planning process. This can be done in various ways. As we shall see later, it can be done by making key ministers members of the planning agency, as well as by establishing and maintaining close contact between the staffs of a planning agency and operating organizations. And it can also be done if, whenever possible, a planning agency uses the work of operating organizations instead of its own.

In less developed countries, where trained and experienced planners are scarce, the smaller the burden placed on a newly established central planning agency, the better its chances of being effective. The planning agency should therefore restrict itself, as much as possible, to determining the extent of development resources, assessing broad alternative courses of action required for development, formulating plans, detailing the crucial policies, measures and machinery required to implement plans, and following and evaluating progress of plan implementation. If, in addition, it is represented on important committees related to planning, and acts as the secretariat for the various committees, advisory councils or boards and panels of experts which (as will be seen later) are essential for co-ordinating economic and investment policy, it is likely to have all the work it can do. Hence, a planning agency would do well to leave to other ministries, departments and agencies as much work as possible. The number of specific jobs that must be done to prepare and carry out a development plan, and the number of individual and detailed decisions that must be made at all levels, are so great that broad delegations of power are necessary. Even in a small country and in a simple economy, the formulation of a development plan is a complex job and the task of carrying it out must necessarily be diffused among a great many agencies of governments. The larger the country and the more complex the plan, the greater the number of agencies on whose action plan implementation depends. Yet many planning agencies fail to delegate work.

Some short-term policies are important for development and central planning agencies must be concerned with them. For this purpose, appropriate liaison must be established between a central planning agency and government groups entrusted with making decisions on important short-run policy matters. In India, for example, the Planning Commission participates in activities of committees and agencies dealing with the granting of protection to industries, licensing of capital goods, issuing of permission to private enterprise to undertake investments and raise capital, and foreign aid and agreements; and in Pakistan, the Planning Commission participates in the activities of the National Economic Council, a high ministerial body which is responsible for co-ordinating economic policy with planning objectives. But many planning agencies become too involved in day-to-day policy decisions which are only loosely and indirectly connected with the problem of sustaining growth and development. These matters might well be left to a central bank, ministry of finance or other government body.

Planning agencies also frequently undertake research projects which could and should be farmed out to other government agencies or to private research firms. Planning requires much research in methodology, investment criteria and statistical methods, among other subjects, which a central planning agency is generally ill-equipped to carry out. Nevertheless, some planning agencies attempt to engage in long-term research projects in addition to planning. They thereby divert staff from planning operations. In some cases, they take on the appearance of research or study groups rather than planning agencies. As one example among many, Colombia's central planning agency during most of the 1950's largely neglected planning to concentrate on a series of research projects which other government agencies were well qualified to prepare. The central planning agency in Iceland prepares the country's national accounts. The central planning agencies in Argentina and Peru also produced national income series despite the fact that their respective central banks were already engaged in preparing similar figures.

In happy contrast, some central planning agencies have found it useful to associate themselves with universities or independent institutes which carry out research needed for planning while they concentrate on planning. One of the best known of these institutes, the Indian Statistical Institute, has for many years worked closely with the Indian Planning Commission. While the Institute's head is the Statistical Advisor to the Government, the Institute is independent of the Commission. It is, in fact, located in Calcutta and not in New Delhi, the site of the Commission. The Institute of National Planning in the UAR, which co-operates with the central planning agency in research and training, is a part of the Ministry of Finance and Planning. However, it operates independently of the planning agency in the Ministry. Although experience has shown that it is desirable to separate planning and research, Greece recently brought them together by integrating its formerly independent Economic Research Institute with the planning group in its Ministry of Coordination.

If data furnished by a central statistical office is inadequate, a planning agency should try to help the statistical office improve them instead of setting up a competing unit of its own. Where operating organizations are unable to prepare projects and sector programs, a central planning agency should help operating agencies obtain technical assistance which would permit them to do the work instead of taking over the job itself.[7] By getting other government organizations to contribute their work, and by providing assistance for this when needed, a central planning agency not only frees itself from burdens which prevent it from concentrating on subjects which are more appropriate for central planners; it also helps build up ministries, departments and agencies to do the job they should be doing, draws into the planning process organizations whose collaboration is essential to successful planning and avoids a common cause of conflict between central planning agencies and operating units. Common sense, as well

---

[7] Sometimes, an operating agency's inability to prepare projects and sector programs is due to deep-seated traditional attitudes and administrative inefficiency or inertia which cannot be overcome merely by employing outside technical assistance. In this event, personnel changes and administrative reorganization may be called for which are necessarily difficult and time consuming to carry out. When a planning agency encounters this situation it often engages technicians for its own staff to do work which operating bodies should do. Professor Everett Hagen contends that, "This remedy is the only one in some circumstances," although he agrees that "it is far from ideal because it leaves operating officials with less interest in the project than if they had explored and planned it, and it leaves the agency without the technical capacity to execute the project effectively." [Hagen, Everett (ed). *Planning Economic Development*, p. 354.]

There is, of course, the question already discussed whether a central planning agency can be expected to operate effectively where the only remedy is for it to take over the functions of operating organizations. But besides this, the proposed remedy is of dubious value. Experience shows that it frequently creates more problems than it solves because it antagonizes operating agencies. Even more important than this is the fact that, when a central planning agency takes over an operating organization's functions in order to speed the progress of a plan, it implies a choice in favor of quick results in carrying out projects without lasting benefits in the planning process over one which might delay results but bring about an improvement of programing procedures in operating organizations. Because of this, the proposed remedy is likely, in the long run, to retard rationalization of the planning process.

as experience, tells us that an operating organization will co-operate more wholeheartedly on a project or program which it has conceived and prepared than on one which was formulated and foisted upon it by another agency.

One way for a central planning agency to curb any tendency it may have to duplicate the work of, or replace, other government bodies is to keep its staff small. The French Commissariat Général du Plan, from its inception, has deliberately maintained a small staff—it has between 40 and 50 professionals—in order to make sure that it will

> call on others for help. Thus, the danger of that administrative calamity, a conflict of authority, is reduced at the very start.[8]

But this is not the only, or even the most important, reason for the Commissariat's insistence on a small staff.

> It has sometimes been thought that this position reflected the cautious attitude taken by a new agency in its dealings with older departments jealous of their functions. In fact, the Commission was prompted rather by its anxiety to perform a sufficiently broad synthesizing role and to avoid becoming absorbed in over-specialized administrative tasks.[9]

It is not, therefore, to avoid conflict with other government bodies, desirable though that is, which primarily explains the Commissariat's position. It is rather its concept of what is a proper role for a central planning agency. For the French Commissariat Général du Plan recognized from the start, and has since had it amply confirmed by experience, that if planners are to make a significant impact on the development process, they must "avoid becoming absorbed in overspe-cialized administrative tasks" and "perform a sufficiently broad synthe-sizing role."

ROLE OF A CENTRAL PLANNING AGENCY

"Let us not think," writes a planning expert, "that by setting up some agency that produces 'plans' or that even by boldly putting the word 'planning' in its name, we have established a planning process." [10] There

---

[8] Massé, Pierre. "French Economic Planning," p. 5.
[9] UN. Consultative Group on Planning for Economic Development. "The Political and Administrative Organization of the Planning System in France," p. 44.
[10] Gross, Bertram M. "When is a Plan Not a Plan?" p. 11.

is, it is true, a tendency in many countries to equate the establishment of a central planning agency with actual performance. Underlying this is the naïve notion that planning is the concern of a single agency, not the entire government. But as the Latin American Seminar on Planning pointed out, a country's development problems cannot be solved

> simply by superimposing a planning agency on the existing administrative structure. It is essential for this structure to be overhauled too so that it can satisfy planning requirements or . . . the requirements of economic development policy. It is . . . a question of . . . the rational and systematic use of all the instruments at the disposal of the State for shaping deliberately the forces of the economy.[11]

The creation of a central planning agency, in itself, does little to eliminate bottlenecks to increased output, increase productive efficiency or improve the rate of development. Planning agencies have been established in most less developed countries, but many are little more than paper organizations. They are frequently undermanned and their staffs are almost always untrained and underpaid. They are often out of touch with, and ignored by, ministers and heads of departments and agencies, and even by chief executives. In March 1963, the Organization of American States reported that

> perhaps the deficiency most common to the Latin American planning agencies at the present time is that they stand isolated from much real economic decision-making and from the implementation and evaluation of development programs.[12]

The situation is often similar in Asia and Africa. In the Philippines, where the National Economic Council has been able to exert little influence on the course of development, a former member of the Council has stated that it was

> the disregard by the President alone of policy recommendations of the Council which undermined the effectiveness of the Council.[13]

In Ceylon, Madagascar, Spain and other countries, planning offices were put in buildings far from the center of government activity, as

[11] UN. ECLA. *Report of the Latin American Seminar on Planning*, p. 126.
[12] OAS. Inter-American Economic and Social Council, Special Committee I, etc. *Programming for Development: Five Urgent Problems*, p. 2.
[13] Araneta, Salvador. "The Planning, Approval and Implementation of Economic Policy," p. 144.

though to symbolize their remoteness from the activities of other government offices.

Planners, perhaps aided by foreign technicians, sometimes produce plans largely within the confines of a central planning agency's office in virtual isolation from other government offices or the private sector. Small wonder, then, if officials and businessmen devise their own investment programs without reference to these plans. In Colombia, for example,

> to a considerable extent, the Ministries of the Government and the Presidential Cabinet have proceeded to work out individual investment programs with little regard for definition and coordination through a comprehensive national planning procedure. And the influence of planning with respect to goals for the private sector has been even less apparent. There has been virtually no attempt to involve the leaders of the private sector, who are of great importance in the operation of the economy, in the planning process. The projections and plans for the economy that have been developed to date, including the latest Ten-Year Development Plan, have been little more than abstract, mathematical exercises by small groups of technicians, usually from the foreign agencies indicated [i.e., the United Nations, especially the Economic Commission for Latin America], with little or no participation in the formulation of plans by those who would be concerned with their execution either in the public or the private sector.[14]

The success of any kind of planning, especially development planning carried out on a national scale, depends on the understanding, participation and support of those who must implement the plan. Herein lies a fundamental difference between wartime planning and development planning: in the former, the goal, to win, is clear-cut and universally accepted; in the latter, objectives are never so simple and agreement is never unanimous. A development plan, moreover, affects frequently conflicting political and economic interests of powerful groups. The planners' task becomes a matter of trying to reconcile, or at least to strike a workable balance between, a whole series of divergent interests, national and regional, executive and legislative, public and private, long-term and short-term.[15] This can best be done by making the preparation of a plan a combined operation in which every one and

---

[14] Columbia University School of Law *Public International Development Financing in Colombia*, p. 144.
[15] P.E.P. *Town Planning and the Public*, p. 16.

every group likely to be affected by it—government authorities and administrators, legislative and other representative bodies, regional and local authorities, technical and advisory bodies, the private sector and the public—is involved in the process in some appropriate way. It is in the course of preparing a plan that the various groups and interests are brought together and come to see eye to eye. The purposes of planning and the objectives of a proposed plan must be made clear to all concerned, the views and knowledge of the different groups must be considered and attempts must be made to make their activities consistent with plan objectives.

Experience shows that there is much value in this exercise. If the job is done skillfully, it leads to a plan which is respected and supported by all parties.[16] The French Commissariat Général du Plan has been so successful in reconciling divergent views by bringing together all interested parties to help formulate national development plans, that the system it employs has been widely copied. A series of so-called modernization commissions are established for each plan. Each commission has between 30 and 50 members, more in exceptional cases, who serve without pay. Members are appointed by the Government upon nomination by the Commissioner General. They are selected from civil servants in the various ministries concerned, industry and other business, and labor unions. No attempt is made to maintain fixed proportions among these groups, since the commissions seek a consensus, not the vote of a majority, for their reports. Experts, especially university professors and consumers' representatives, are co-opted as required.[17]

The commissions are advisory. They have two main responsibilities:

1. To provide as much pertinent information as possible on past activities and future prospects for their sectors as basic material to be used in preparing the plan, and

[16] *Ibid.*, p. 11.

[17] For the Fourth Plan, 24 modernization commissions were established. Twenty were "vertical" commissions, each of which dealt with a specific economic or social sector (e.g., agriculture or power); four were "horizontal" commissions, each of which was concerned with general economic or other problems (e.g., manpower or financing). Each modernization commission set up study or working groups to consider and report to it on specific problems within its terms of reference. A commission might set up as many as 50 or 60 study or working groups. The number of persons who have served on the commissions and the working groups has been increasing with each plan. In 1946, 1,000 participated in the commissions set up for the First Plan; by 1961, almost 3,200 persons participated for the Fourth Plan.

2. to recommend policies and measures which they believe would improve conditions in their sectors.

But in the process of carrying out their duties, the commissions also lay a basis for getting members and the groups with which they are associated to adjust voluntarily the activities of their own enterprises or groups to conform with plan objectives.

Some developing countries which have adopted the French system have been successful in drawing a considerable number of persons and organizations into the planning process. Thus, the UAR was able to draw into the planning process large numbers of public and private persons through the use of six consultative committees operating with more than 60 subcommittees known as Joint Committees for Planning. These groups sat from January to May 1958 to prepare sectoral and other programs for inclusion in the over-all plan. They made detailed studies which specified projects to be included in the plan and estimated capital requirements for each project, as well as their expected yield, employment effects and likely impact on the economy.

But other countries have not fared as well. In Morocco, for example, where 15 specialized commissions were set up to help in preparing the First Five-Year Plan, the commissions did not operate effectively. Although many persons representing varied interests in the economy were members of the commissions or their subcommissions, the commissions and subcommissions were largely run by technicians from the government ministries most concerned. These technicians prepared the agendas and drafted all the reports. The reports not only did not take adequate account of views which differed from those who drafted the reports but frequently did not consider the impact of proposals on the economy. Despite the participation of some 1,500 persons in the commissions, the plan which ultimately emerged was hardly a joint product of those who had attended the meetings of the commissions.

The evidence indicates that where planners fail to include in the planning process those who must execute a plan, there is little likelihood that it will be implemented. It is, of course, no easy matter for central planning agencies in most less developed countries to prepare a plan co-operatively. Technical planning problems, especially if they are of the aggregative variety, are often beyond the comprehension of political leaders and administrators, and even more so of the average businessman or man on the street. The dilemma encountered when Nigeria's comprehensive National Development Plan was being formulated illustrates the problem:

Since the interpretation of the technical analysis of the national economy was subject to controversy even for trained economists, it was unrealistic to expect government officials to digest such complex data and then determine the targets for the development plan when they did not customarily work with such material. Many of the basic difficulties in formulating the government development plans stemmed from the fact that the planners, the officials, and the ministers each conceived of economic development in different terms. Each group was unsuccessful or reluctant to translate its concepts and unit of measure into terms comprehensible to others.[18]

Many planners feel that it is up to them to prepare an "ideal" plan and up to political and administrative officials to implement it. They therefore try to bend political and administrative officials to their concepts. But as we have seen earlier, it is rather the planners who should adjust to political and administrative realities. They must try to pose for political leaders and policy-makers a variety of options and courses of action for carrying out plan objectives. But, sometimes,

> the danger exists that planning agency officials may seek to decide planning policy by virtue of *their* authority rather than through a process of discussion of the relative advantages of alternative possibilities. Even if their authority carries the day, the result will be to choke off the prospect of effective cooperation in the execution of programs.[19]

In the best circumstances, it is difficult for a new central planning agency to establish good working relations with operating organizations—most of them well entrenched by time and often headed by powerful ministers or other important political figures. Each organization has its job—defined by constitution, parliament or executive authority—and each does the programing it considers necessary to its job. But its programing and its work may be and often are (however unwittingly) inconsistent, not only with those of other government organizations but also with the policy laid down by the government. This is likely to be the case among the old ministries and agencies, long set on routine lines, especially with respect to the taking of the long economic view and rounded perspective which distinguish development planning from other kinds of economic activity. It may also be

[18] Clark, Peter Bentley. "Economic Planning for a Country in Transition: Nigeria," p. 273.
[19] Hagen, Everett (ed). *Planning Economic Development,* p. 353.

true of the newer, development-directed agencies which, fired by the enthusiasm for the programs that bring them into being, become claimants for resources for their own particular tasks, with little concern for a general development strategy.

So long as a plan drafted by a central planning agency remains largely an intellectual exercise, as it does in many countries, it can be regarded by operating ministries as requiring merely ceremonial approval. But once a plan shows signs of acquiring a measure of standing in a government as, for example, in the case of Japan's 1961–70 Plan, the ministries concerned

> awake suddenly to the need of guarding their vested interests and attempt to take advantage of the plan for extending their own interests without in any way surrendering ministerial prerogative.[20]

Ministries of finance, in particular, are soon made aware that as a central planning agency's activities broaden they necessarily impinge increasingly on budgetary and other financial functions, as well as on their control over public investment. In a *milieu* in which officials often view attempts to have them share their authority as a reflection upon their competence or integrity, ministries of finance tend to consider planning agencies as a threat to their position. This attitude is understandable where a central planning agency seeks, as it sometimes does, to take over budgetary or other functions from a ministry of finance. But even where a central planning agency has no intention to taking over such functions, legitimate differences of opinion between planners and financial authorities arise about the level of investment to be attempted in development plans. A central planning agency, influenced by the rate at which population is growing and the need to maintain or increase per capita income, may propose a rate of investment which financial and budgetary authorities may consider inflationary or a threat to foreign reserves. Where planners and fiscal authorities work in harmony, it is possible to reconcile conflicting viewpoints. Development and fiscal responsibility are then found to be complementary, not antagonistic, objectives. That this is so has been revealed in Pakistan, among other countries. At first, Pakistan's ministers of finance frequently resisted the central planning agencies' attempts to increase public development expenditures. But, as a pleased high official of Pakistan's Planning Commission reported, a marked change occurred:

[20] Tsuru, Shigeto. "Formal Planning Divorced from Action: Japan," p. 143.

Fortunately, in recent years, the Minister of Finance has been even more 'bullish' about economic development than even the Planning Commission itself. This happy situation of course is not inherent in the institutional set-up but depends largely on the goodwill of the Ministry of Finance.[21]

But if bureaucratic interests are allowed to intervene, they tend to acquire a force and logic of their own. A central planning agency and a ministry of finance may then feel impelled to contest each other's views. Since in most countries, the ministry of finance is one of the most powerful ministries, frequently the most powerful, it can and occasionally does undermine a planning agency's position. In seeking to redress this situation by appealing to heads of government, a central planning agency is at a disadvantage. For although budgetary and financial officials may employ inadequate techniques and have a short-run view, these techniques and views are well known and generally easy to understand. But planning is new in most countries and its techniques and long-run objectives are generally harder to understand. Too frequently, they are also made even more unintelligible and esoteric by being presented in unnecessarily abstract forms. As a result, planners usually find it more difficult to convince political leaders that their approach is preferable to that of budgetary and financial officials.

The weakness of a new central planning agency in "the power configuration" of an established bureaucracy then becomes apparent.[22] The old-line ministries and agencies continue to play an important part in determining the direction and amount of investment; indeed, considering that they include the budgetary authority and finance, they often play the crucial role. It helps the central planning agency if its functions, the manner in which it is to perform them and its relationships with other parts of government have been clearly defined. Inevitably, however, the dynamism of the agency will come not from any formal exposition of its powers and responsibilities but from the extent to which (a) it is supported by a strong and stable government, (b) the head and staff of the planning agency have the knowledge, experience and ability to command respect and (c) it is successful in establishing good working relationships with other government bodies.

Support by a strong and stable government is essential if a planning agency is to obtain guidelines and information needed to prepare a

---

[21] Haq, Mahbub ul. *Planning Agencies,* p. 5.
[22] Tsuru, Shigeto. "Formal Planning Divorced from Action: Japan," p. 143.

draft plan. It is also essential if a final plan is to be evolved which represents a consensus of means by which political decisions can be given effect. The whole procedure requires close and constant rapport between the planners and the chief executive. Where a legislature exists, it also requires that appropriate members of that body, preferably a committee, be brought into the planning process as early as possible. In India, relations between the Planning Commission and the Legislature are considered so important that one person of ministerial rank, the Minister of Planning, sometimes assisted by one or two Deputy Ministers, gives most of his time to dealing with Parliament on all matters connected with the Planning Commission.[23]

A central planning agency, beset by a multitude of technical and co-ordinative problems in the executive branch of government, can easily neglect establishing adequate liaison with the legislature. Even in France, where the Commissariat Général du Plan and the Government go to considerable lengths to bring every group into the planning process, members of Parliament complained during the debate on the Fourth Plan that Parliament had not had sufficient opportunity to comment on the Plan before it was too late to make any basic changes. The Government accordingly agreed that for the Fifth Plan, Parliament should be consulted at a much earlier stage and be allowed to express its views when the preliminary alternative proposals were being discussed.[24] Where a legislature has not been adequately briefed at an early stage so that its leaders understand and agree with a plan's broad objectives, the consequences may be serious. In Senegal, for instance, when that country's Plan was presented to Parliament, the discussion and proposals for changing the plan showed that members of Parliament did not understand what a development plan was and that those who did were not sympathetic to the plan's objectives. These attitudes were not without repercussions for the plan's future.[25]

Few central planning agencies have a staff of technicians and a head

---

[23] He heads an Informal Consultative Committee of Parliament for Planning consisting of about 86 legislators from both Houses, which provides a forum for detailed discussions between Committee members and the Planning Commission. The Prime Minister presides over a second and smaller group, the Prime Minister's Informal Consultative Committee for Planning, composed of 14 representatives of different political parties in Parliament. This Committee is intended to provide opposition leaders with an opportunity to participate in discussions involving plans and, in this way, make the plans more acceptable to all parties.

[24] UN. ECLA. "Planning in France," p. 30.

[25] Chaigneau, Yves. *Réflexions sur la Planification au Sénégal*, p. 17.

who have both the technical capacity and the good will needed to carry out its functions effectively. Assistance from abroad can temporarily fill gaps in technical knowledge until national personnel gain better mastery of planning techniques. But a planning agency's ability to work with other groups and organizations is a skill not obtainable from outside. Yet without this ability it cannot establish relationships with operating agencies on which much of its effectiveness depends. Operating organizations may at first regard a central planning agency with apathy if not with hostility. Much depends on the planning agency if this is to change. For in carrying out its duties, a central planning agency's attitude goes a long way toward determining the attitudes of those with whom it deals. If it is secretive or arrogant, there will be apathy or antagonism; if it is open and tentative in its suggestions, it is likely to induce co-operation and support.[26] If it pries on operating organizations or gives the impression that it wishes to do so, it will soon find itself excluded from many offices; if it consistently demonstrates a desire to work with operating bodies in settling differences, it improves the chances that its advice will be heeded.

When a plan is being prepared, operating organizations can provide useful information and experience in the fields of their competence. This is important in the preparation of a multiannual plan, but it is crucial in the preparation of an annual operational plan, since the latter requires considerably more detailed information than the former. Operating organizations are generally bound to have a much more intimate knowledge than a planning agency has of the administrative problems involved in carrying out projects and programs. Where a planning agency proceeds without consulting them, resources may be wasted and development delayed. In Jamaica, for example, after most of the funds allocated for the outright purchase of a site needed to execute a project had not been used, the planning agency's consultation with the operating organization concerned revealed that it normally takes three years to alienate land in Jamaica. Had the operating organization been consulted earlier, all the funds allocated for the purchase except the small amount actually needed to start necessary legal proceedings could have been allocated elsewhere where they could have been employed productively.

In connection with the execution of a plan, the consent and co-operation of operating organizations are also essential if they are to

[26] P.E.P. *Town Planning and the Public,* p. 11.

adhere to an agreed program and do the jobs required of them. In addition, if periodic evaluations of a plan's implementation are to be made, a central planning agency must rely on operating organizations for regular reports on the progress of projects and programs.

There is, therefore, a need for a central planning agency to establish channels of communication with operating organizations. These must be used to keep operating organizations informed of planning objectives and policies so that their work can be properly oriented. They must also provide means for an upward flow of information which will permit a planning agency always to know the progress of events. With such knowledge, changes in a plan can be made in good time and operating organizations which are deviating seriously from the plan can be brought back into line quickly. But the problem is not simply one of establishing formal channels of information and enforcement. If it were, it could be met, as many less developed countries have tried to meet it, by a continuing flow of minutes and reports and ceaseless inspections. These are likely to be needed, at least to some extent, but they do not guarantee the co-ordinated effort that good planning requires.

This is so because the major obstacle in the way of building up effective channels of communication is administrative. The governments of developing countries which try to plan have to assume a great many new tasks which strain their traditional organization and methods of administration. The general level of education may be low and the technically trained persons required for specialized tasks are few. Many of the governments faced with these problems are new and their top policy-makers and administrators are inexperienced. In this situation, administrative deficiencies become serious obstacles to the co-ordination of development activities. Because of this, some of the most effective co-ordination comes, not from formal machinery, but from regular informal contacts between individuals. It is in this way that the man concerned with the plan as a whole can best learn of the latest developments down the line which bear on the plan and the man down the line can learn of changes in policy which affect his work.

However desirable, liaison between a planning agency and operating organizations is not enough. Effective planning requires also that there be continual contact and close co-operation among operating ministries, departments and agencies. Where several government bodies are concerned with different aspects of the same economic sector, it is essential that they co-ordinate their activities to develop a common policy and approach to the development of the sector. This need is especially great in agriculture and transportation because several agencies frequently operate within each of these sectors. It is also necessary to insure co-ordination of programs of agencies dealing with sectors—like transportation, communications, power, urban facilities and some types of training—which complement programs of agencies in other sectors.[27]

Co-ordination of such programs can be advanced through the establishment of interministry working parties at the subministerial level whose members are drawn from the various government agencies concerned and from the central planning agency. These working parties, with staff from a central planning agency acting as a secretariat, have been found useful not only in co-ordinating sectoral programs but in dealing with foreign trade, monetary policy and other problems which cross ministry lines. They cannot make final decisions since this would infringe on the authority of ministers and agency heads. But if their membership is composed of the highest civil servants, they can speak with authority for their agencies and advise on courses of action which stand a good chance of being adopted. Among other advantages, they provide a useful way for each ministry or agency to learn about the problems and objectives of the others. They can thereby help reduce conflict among different agencies which arise from an unawareness of the consequence that an action taken by one agency may have on another's program.

In the formulation of India's Third Five-Year Plan, many officials who were expected later to participate in implementing the Plan were associated in the planning exercise from the beginning as members of a working group established for each important sector. Members of each group were selected from administrators and technicians in the ministries and agencies most concerned with the sector to be considered and from the staff of the Planning Commission. Of the 23 working groups, many had a number of subgroups (e.g., the Working Group on Agriculture had 20 subgroups). Each was responsible for co-ordinating activities of government ministries, departments and agencies operating in its sector and for preparing a program for the sector on the basis of provisional five-year targets furnished by the Planning Commission as guidelines. While the groups were to report to the Planning Commission, each was usually headed by the secretary of the ministry most

[27] Hagen, Everett (ed). *Planning Economic Development,* pp. 355–356.

concerned. A considerable part of the studies undertaken by each group was made by personnel in the ministries and associated agencies. The working group reports provided the basic material for a draft memorandum on the Plan which the Commission prepared. For the Fourth Plan, 45 working groups have been set up and these have established over 100 subgroups. It is also expected that steering groups may be established to co-ordinate the work of working groups operating in related fields.[28]

The mere creation of such groups, however, does not guarantee coordination or insure the production of a jointly prepared plan. Experience shows that the effectiveness of such working groups largely depends on the efforts which a central planning agency brings to bear on the enterprise. In Ghana, for example, where the National Planning Commission set up nine subcommittees to help prepare sector and other programs to be used in the preparation of the Seven-Year Plan,

> the sub-committees' work proceeded under unsatisfactory conditions. The members of the National Planning Commission had too much to do in their own spheres of activity to devote themselves wholeheartedly to this additional task. This being the case, the head of the Office of the Planning Commission . . . set about producing a detailed draft plan, which was therefore largely an individual effort.[29]

The co-ordination of diverse programs and plans may be complicated by the constitutional structure of a country. For instance, this is true in India, Nigeria and Pakistan, where the authority of the Federal Governments, although great, is limited by their Constitutions. In these countries, state or regional authorities are deeply concerned with development and must be drawn into the framework of the national planning process. The political problems inherent in a federal system have usually been found to require the creation of a special, high-level body with members representing federal and state or regional governments to co-ordinate planning policy between different levels and to give over-all development plans a national character. For example, the state plans prepared in India are reviewed and combined with the national plan by the Planning Commission in New Delhi, after consultation with representatives from state governments. But a National

[28] Paranjape, H. K. *Planning Commission, A Descriptive Account*, pp. 48–49.
[29] United Nations Meeting of Experts on Administrative Aspects of National Development Planning. *Administration of Planning in Ghana*, pp. 12–13.

Development Council, composed of the Prime Minister, the chief ministers of all the states and the members of the Planning Commission, is the body charged with co-ordinating planning policy between the states and the Central Government.[30] In addition, the Planning Commission maintains three, more recently four, Advisors on Programme Administration whose function it is to co-ordinate state plans with national plans. Each adviser is responsible for specific states to which he frequently travels, sometimes with teams of experts from central ministries. His job requires him to give the states for which he is responsible the fullest possible assistance and advice on matters affecting implementation. At the same time, he checks cost estimates of projects assisted by loans or grants from the Central Government and reports to the Planning Commission on the progress of plan implementation in the states.

In Nigeria, regional plans prepared by regional planning bodies, together with the federal plan, were integrated by the central planning agency into the National Development Plan for 1962–68. But a National Economic Council, with the premiers of the four regions, five federal ministers, four ministers from each region and the Economic Adviser to the Federal Government as members, and the Prime Minister of the Federation as Chairman, has final authority for co-ordinating regional and national development plans. It meets infrequently and most of the co-ordinating work is done by a Joint Planning Committee set up by the National Economic Council. The Joint Planning Committee is composed of civil servants from the Federal and each Regional Government, with the Economic Adviser to the Federal Government acting as Chairman.[30a] The Federal Ministry of Economic Development, i.e., the central planning agency, acts as the secretariat for both the National Economic Council and the Joint Planning Committee. In Pakistan, also, a National Economic Coun-

[30] The recommendations of the National Development Council are treated with respect by the Central Government, the states and the Planning Commission, although the Council has no constitutional or statutory authority. There is also a Standing Committee of the Council. It was originally intended that the Standing Committee would have a small membership and meet more frequently than the National Development Council. In practice, however, the Council has been meeting more frequently than its Standing Committee.

[30a] Members include the Permanent Secretaries of the Federal Ministries of Finance, Trade, Industries, and Economic Development, the Director of Research of the Central Bank, the Chief Statistician who heads the Federal Office of Statistics, and three to six officials from each of the four regions, the actual number varying with the items on the agenda.

cil (NEC) and its Executive Committee, both containing representatives from the Central and Provincial Governments, play important roles in co-ordinating provincial and national plans. Co-ordination between the Planning Commission and NEC is insured through the Secretary of the Planning Commission who also acts as Secretary of the NEC (with the Planning Commission as secretariat). And in Yugoslavia, a Committee for Social Planning, whose members include the heads of the six Republican Governments, provides guidance to the Federal Planning Institute in the preparation of first drafts of Yugoslavia's plans.

Eliciting Public Participation

A development plan, of course, affects the public as well as a government. Unless the population of a country is not sufficiently articulate to create "public opinion" with which a government needs to concern itself (a situation which is becoming ever less prevalent), or a government intends to rely entirely on force to carry out a plan (a situation which has become even less prevalent), a plan's success depends on public acceptance of its objectives. In particular, it is the response from the private sector, which in almost every mixed-economy country comprises the great bulk of producers and consumers, which determines a plan's destiny. That response will to a considerable degree be fixed by the nature of the plan itself. But the desired response can be facilitated by some kind of public participation in the discussion and formulation of the plan. Thus, a draft plan may be made public and comments thereon invited. Discussion in the press, in professional societies and in public meetings can help elicit useful suggestions and stimulate interest and enthusiasm for the plan. Sometimes, educational programs are effective. Some countries conduct educational programs through special organizations established for the purpose. The Socialist Alliance of the Working People of Yugoslavia, for example, is such an organization. In India, numerous bodies have been established, both to give advice and to disseminate information about the plan.[31] Pakistan

[31] The Indian Planning Commission has set up a variety of *ad hoc* groups to study and make recommendations on particular problems and it maintains a series of advisory and consultative committees with representatives of industry, commerce, labor and agriculture, as well as panels of experts drawn from professional groups. Among the formal groups are development councils for a number of industries established by the Ministry of Commerce and Industry. They meet two or three times a year and, in association with the Planning Commission, draw up plans for their

also set up 15 panels to associate experts, as well as representatives from different economic sectors, in the formulation of the Third Five Year Plan. The most important of these was a 24-man high-level panel with 24 members, 10 of whom belonged to the private sector, and headed by the Deputy Chairman (the operating head) of the Planning Commission. This panel was convened to discuss the sector programs in the plan for industry and commerce.[32]

Yet in many countries, surprisingly little is done to disseminate the contents of national plans. Only limited quantities of the plan document may be printed, frequently not in the prevailing vernaculars of the country. Often planners have neither the time nor the opportunity of acquainting the people of a country with their plan. In most African countries, for example, governments have neither staff nor organizations responsible for bringing business interests, trade unions or other public groups into the process of formulating development plans.[33] Except for a small number of civil servants and students, most people in a country may never have heard of their country's plan. According to the Economic Commission for Africa,

> in a certain country only 3,000 persons of various professions and trades were informed of the plan's main features, although in that country the working force is about one million persons.[34]

In Ethiopia, far fewer persons outside those immediately concerned in the Government ever saw the first Five-Year Development Plan. The plan was never published, nor was it made available to anyone outside a select circle.

---

industries. The Planning Commission also meets with various business groups including representatives of the Federation of Indian Chambers of Commerce and Industry, the Associated Chamber of Commerce of India and the All India Manufacturers Association. Experts from outside the Government are brought into the planning process by means of eight panels, as follows: (1) Economists, (2) Scientists, (3) Agriculture, (4) Land Reforms, (5) Ayurveda or indigenous system of medicine, (6) Health, (7) Education and (8) Housing and Regional Development. These panels meet two or three times a year to express their views on policies and programs referred to them by the Planning Commission. (Natarajan, B. *Plan Coordination in India*, p. 17.) Early in 1964, the Planning Commission set up a National Planning Council, composed of 18 nonofficial members including economists, scientists, social workers, trade union representatives and other experts. The Council is to meet periodically and advise the Commission (*Economic Times*, January 19, 1965).

[32] *Dawn*, March 6, 1965.
[33] UN. ECA. *Outlines and Selected Indicators of African Development Plans*, p. vii.
[34] *Ibid.*, p. vi.

In contrast, the Indian Government has made a great attempt to inform Indians about the contents of the country's Five-Year Plans. A National Advisory Committee on Public Cooperation coordinates all activities involving public participation in the planning process. A wide variety of activities are promoted. The plan document is translated into and printed in all 13 important languages of the country. Popular versions of the plan summary are produced and sold at low prices. The radio and documentary films are used. Lectures and seminars are held in various parts of the country. Educational institutions are drawn into the informational program in specific ways. For example, every college is encouraged to start a planning forum, and student excursions to projects under way are arranged. Peasants are given travel concessions to visit important projects, and organizations of various kinds are used to get the participation of women and other groups in the country.[35]

But it has proved to be no easy matter to inform the mass of people about the purposes of planning. Despite all that has been done to bring the plan to the people in India, a Study Team on Five-Year Plan Publicity appointed by the Government in 1963 concluded that

> the impact on the people of the existing programmes [for promoting understanding of the Plans and enlisting public support and cooperation in their implementation] has been tenuous, vague and diffused in content and no section of the population has been touched in a forceful manner.[36]

Another study prepared by India's National Council of Applied Economic Research has reported that more than half the urban population in the nation was completely ignorant of the Five-Year Plans.[37]

In Yugoslavia, the legislature has been used as a means of funneling information about the plan to the public, as well as for promoting public discussion and support for the plan. This is also done in India. Where a legislature does not exist or is inadequate as a sounding board for development policy, it becomes all the more important for a government to establish advisory bodies which reflect the various social and economic interests in the community. Some countries have made use of mixed commissions composed of government and private individuals to advise their governments on plans and economic policy. The Nether-

[35] Natarajan, B. *Plan Coordination in India*, p. 19.
[36] *Report of the Study Team on Five-Year Plan Publicity*, p. 224.
[37] *Economic Times*, November 16, 1964.

lands, for example, has established a Central Planning Committee consisting of 300 government officials, employers, trade unionists and economists to advise the Central Planning Bureau and the Government. Its Chairman is the Director of the Central Planning Bureau, Holland's central planning agency. France's Higher Planning Council, a similar body of 55 members which is presided over by the Prime Minister, has representatives of business and professional associations, trade unions, regional committees and the Economic and Social Council, a body which is described below. The twofold purpose of these mixed advisory bodies is to provide the private sector with a high level platform to air its views and the governments with a convenient vehicle for sounding out ideas it is considering. Both the Dutch and French advisory bodies have served a useful purpose in bringing to both the government and the private sector a better understanding of each other's problems and interests.

In 1963, Eire established a National Industrial Economic Council of 29 members representing government, industrialists and trade unions to give its views on the principles to be applied for the development of the country's economy. The Council started by examining in detail Eire's Second Plan. It published an interim report on the Plan and intends to follow up with additional reports. But an attempt by the Moroccan Government to make use of a similar mixed commission, the Superior Planning Council, ended in failure. Instead of discussing specific points in the First Five-Year Plan, as it was supposed to do, it became a political sounding board where discussions were more concerned with basic differences in the philosophies of the Government and the groups represented in the Council. After it became evident that it was without any influence on government decisions, it was permitted to expire.

The Netherlands and France have also experimented with organizations embodying the corporative principle, in which representation is determined on the basis of economic interest.[38] The Netherlands has a Social and Economic Council, on which employers, trade unions and independent experts are represented in equal numbers, while France has made increasing use of an Economic and Social Council, a body of 366 persons representing industry, agriculture, trade, services and labor. The Dutch Council meets frequently to discuss proposals,

---

[38] Yugoslavia used this approach to determine the representation of one of its Houses of Parliament.

forecasts and plans before they are considered by the Government and Parliament. The French Council has not been used as much as the one in the Netherlands, but the Government has announced that it purposes to make greater use of it. Italy has also used a National Council of Economy and Labor (CNEL) as an advisory body to consider its Five-Year Development Program before it was presented to Parliament.

Despite the attraction which French planning has for many less developed countries, they have generally not established bodies like the Economic and Social Council. This is probably because few countries have the close relationships which the French Government has with business interests and trade unions. In one Latin American country where the establishment of such a council was proposed by a French planning expert, the Government decided that it would be premature until experience and mutual confidence between the Government and the private sector had been built up. It was felt that a council convened to discuss a proposed plan in general terms might get unduly involved in controversial wage, price and other issues, thereby promoting schisms instead of better understanding between the Government and the business community. For the time being, therefore, the Government proposed to have the private sector participate in the planning process through less formal joint working parties created to discuss specific aspects of the plan which it was preparing.

It is clearly impossible to generalize about the form of a central planning agency's consultations with the private sector. In some countries *ad hoc* machinery may be preferable to permanent, formal machinery. But it should also be obvious that where permanent machinery has been established through which businessmen, farmers and workers can regularly and freely express their views, there is a better chance that a plan will reflect the realities in the private sector and induce the co-operation and support required for the plan's successful implementation. Whatever the means used to consult with the private sector, it must be adequate enough and take place sufficiently early in the planning process to give the business community a sense that it has participated in the preparation of the plan. Otherwise, it will not exert much effort to help implement the plan. The experience with Colombia's Ten-Year Plan is a good example of this. The Plan was prepared mostly *in camera* by a small group of technicians:

The major objectives had already been finally decided and the branch targets already fixed when the representatives of industry were consulted about the figures adopted for their sectors. The amendments they requested were in general taken into consideration and the branch targets were accordingly modified.

However, Colombian business circles consider that this consultation was not thorough enough and feel that it should have taken place much earlier, i.e., before the general targets were decided.

As a result, it is not surprising that the private sector, the large majority of which is hostile to the very idea of planning, is reluctant to carry out projects it had very little share in preparing.[39]

SUMMARY AND CONCLUSIONS

A central planning agency should be responsible for (1) the formulation and revision of national development plans and, in exceptional cases, regional development plans; (2) the preparation of annual operational plans; (3) recommending policies, measures and machinery required to implement plans; (4) reporting and evaluating plan implementation; and (5) co-ordinating foreign technical assistance activities or, preferably, be closely linked administratively to the unit responsible for this function.

Central planning agencies usually have most of these responsibilities and are sometimes given a wide variety of other powers. But the fact that a planning agency is given certain powers does not mean that it will be able to exercise them. Experience teaches that the more a planning agency's powers impinge upon the spheres of responsibility of existing government organizations, the more antagonism it arouses and the less it is likely to be able to perform the functions assigned to it. Even when not suspicious or hostile, officials frequently do not understand the purpose and role of planning. This largely explains why central planning agencies are often called upon to perform work extraneous to planning. There appears to be a belief in some countries that planning can be a part-time activity. The heads of planning agencies are often expected to assume a variety of non-planning activities as a regular matter and they are frequently commandeered for special assignments.

[39] United Nations Meeting of Experts on Administrative Aspects of National Development Planning. *Administration of Planning in Colombia,* p. 10.

Friction between planners and operating officials can be minimized by bringing operating officials and entities into the planning process. The smaller the burden placed on a planning agency, the better its chances of operating effectively. Hence, a planning agency does well to leave to other ministries, departments and agencies as much work as possible. Many planning agencies become too involved in short-run policy matters which are only peripherally connected with long-term development. They undertake research projects which should be farmed out to others. By getting others to contribute their work, central planning agencies not only free themselves to concentrate on planning *per se;* they also help to build up operating bodies in government to do the job they should be doing, draw into the planning process organizations whose collaboration is essential to successful planning and avoid a common cause of conflict between central planning agencies and operating units.

Experience teaches that where planners fail to include in the planning process those who must execute a plan, there is little likelihood that it will be implemented. In the best circumstances, however, it is difficult for a new planning agency to establish good working relations with operating ministries and agencies in a government. Once a planning agency acquires some standing in a government, ministries awake to the need of guarding their vested interests without surrendering prerogatives. Ministries of finance, especially, become aware that a planning agency's activities unavoidably impinge on budgeting and other financial functions. Where planners and fiscal authorities work in harmony, it is possible to reconcile their interests and points of view. But if bureaucratic interests intervene, a central planning agency and a ministry of finance frequently find themselves at loggerheads. Since in most countries, the ministry of finance is one of the most powerful ministries, it may undermine a planning agency's position. The weakness of a new central planning agency then becomes apparent. The old-line ministries and agencies, including the ministry of finance, largely ignore the planners in determining the direction and amount of investment.

Support by a strong and stable government is essential for a central planning agency if it is to operate effectively. There must be close and constant association between the planners and the chief executive. Where a legislature exists appropriate members of that body must also be brought into the planning process as early as possible. Where a legislature has not been adequately briefed at an early stage so that its leaders understand and agree with a plan's broad objectives, the consequences may be serious.

A planning agency must establish channels of communication with operating organizations both to keep operating organizations informed of planning objectives and to provide itself with information needed for plan preparation, execution and progress reporting. In less developed countries, administrative inadequacies account for most deficiencies in channels of communication. Because of this, some of the most effective co-ordination comes, not from formal arrangements, but from regular informal contacts between individuals.

Effective planning requires also that there be continual contact and close co-operation among operating ministries, departments and agencies. Where several government bodies are concerned with different aspects of the same economic sector, or where a program in one sector (e.g., transportation) complements programs in other sectors, it is essential that a consistent approach to development be assured. It has been found that co-ordination in these cases can be advanced best through interministry working parties whose members are drawn from the various government agencies concerned and from the central planning agency. The political problems inherent in a federal system usually require the establishment of a special, high-level body with members representing the federal and the state or regional governments to co-ordinate planning policy.

A plan's success also depends on public acceptance of its objectives. Planners should never forget this. In particular, it is the response from the private sector, which in almost every mixed-economy country comprises the great bulk of producers and consumers, which determines a plan's destiny. The desired response can be facilitated by some kind of public participation in the discussion and formulation of the plan.

In some countries, the legislature is also used as a means of funneling information about the plan to the public, as well as for promoting public discussion and support for the plan. Other countries have made use of mixed commissions composed of government and private individuals for the same purpose and to advise their governments on plans and economic policy. Experience shows that a wide variety of ways may be used to consult with the private sector, but whatever means is used must be adequate enough and take place sufficiently early in the planning process to give the business community a sense that it has participated in the plan's formulation.

Chapter XIII

Locating a Central Planning Agency

A central planning unit may be placed in the office of a prime minister or president, but if the president or prime minister is incapable of choosing able planners or of relating the planning unit to the ongoing operations of government, such organizational propinquity is irrelevant. . . . Every government [also] has its positive and negative ministers and ministries. Both types have essential roles to play. But the illusion that planning should be attached to negative ministries simply because such ministries have economic functions is one of the most crippling illusions of our time.[1]

INTRODUCTION

WRITERS ON planning and planners themselves often differ about the preferred administrative location for a central planning agency. One well-known writer, expressing a widely held view, insists that whatever form a central planning agency takes,

it must be a unit within or attached to the office of the chief executive.[2]

But when the Norwegian Government established a permanent planning office it contended, as many others have also, that

the planning apparatus should be situated in the Ministry of Finance which is the central organization occupied with questions of economic policy.[3]

Some authorities believe that it is generally more expedient, given the resistance to new institutions in many governments, to introduce

[1] Bailey, Stephen K. "The Place and Functioning of a Planning Agency Within the Government Organization of Developing Countries," p. 130.

[2] Hagen, Everett (ed). *Planning Economic Development*, pp. 332–333.

[3] Norway. Royal Norwegian Ministry of Finance. *Extension of Economic Planning*, p. 11.

planning offices into existing ministries, departments or agencies. They feel this is preferable to setting them up as separate entities, even though these can be shown to be theoretically more efficient and desirable.[4] They say that as part of a well-established ministry with accepted functions, a planning agency is in position to operate most effectively. This was one of the arguments advanced for putting the Norwegian planning unit in the Ministry of Finance:

> The planning division must have an important position in the administration, and in the Ministry of Finance economic planning can be coordinated with the use of essential instruments of economic policy such as taxation, appropriations, and monetary and credit measures.[5]

Similar arguments have been used for placing planning agencies in existing ministries of economic affairs or development and in other operating ministries.

Others have taken a position which is diametrically opposed to that of authorities who advocate putting central planning agencies in existing ministries. Some believe that

> the planning agency should be an independent body, preferably located in a separate Ministry of Planning.[6]

Others contend that the political and administrative situation prevailing in at least some countries is so inhospitable to planning that a central planning agency is almost inevitably doomed to ineffectiveness if it is established anywhere within the existing government structure. They would therefore free central planning agencies from the baleful effects of bad politics and unduly restrictive administrative and financial controls by placing them outside the regular government administration. This line of argument has been advanced to justify the creation of autonomous planning organizations, partially autonomous planning commissions and even for putting planning agencies in central banks.

There is, finally, a school of thought which holds that it is an illusion to believe

---

[4] UN. TAA. *Introduction to Public Administration in Development Policy, Preliminary survey of the experience of several Latin American countries,* p. 3.

[5] Norway. Royal Norwegian Ministry of Finance. *Extension of Economic Planning,* p. 11.

[6] UN. ECAFE. "Economic Development and Planning in Asia and the Far East," *Economic Bulletin for Asia and the Far East,* December 1961, p. 36.

that the precise location of a planning unit in a formal organization chart is a matter of great consequence, whereas what is important is not in which ministry or office the unit is administratively attached, but that it should have access to all ministries and agencies involved in development.[7]

As one writer expounding this line of reasoning points out, since planning is difficult and complex, it requires the mobilization of the ablest and most vigorous innovators and administrators in government and society. In the last analysis, he asserts, it is the persons involved, not a planning agency's administrative location, which determines its effectiveness:

> Without suggesting in any way that organizational structure is unrelated to the successful performance of governmental functions, it is flesh and blood rather than bones which give life and vitality to any organism—individual or institutional.[8]

If the right persons can be found and the preconditions for genuine planning can be established, the precise place for a planning agency within the government organization of developing countries is "residual." The writer suggests, therefore, that a number of possible locations exist for a central planning agency:

> In some countries the actual planning function has been placed under finance ministries; in other countries separate planning advisory councils have been successful. Planning agencies located in the structure of the office of the chief executive can be particularly successful if the chief executive, himself, is not preoccupied with other matters, and if more traditional centers of power in subordinate ministries are not so engrained as to be unduly disruptive of the planning function.[9]

THE PLANNING AGENCY AND THE CHIEF EXECUTIVE

In the light of the diversity of views on the subject, can it be said that there is one place in most if not all governments which has been found to be the most desirable location for a central planning agency? Or does

---

[7] United Nations Conference on the Application of Science and Technology, etc. *Science and Technology for Development*, p. 4.

[8] Bailey, Stephen K. "The Place and Functioning of a Planning Agency Within the Government Organization of Developing Countries," p. 130.

[9] *Ibid.*, p. 136.

"the most desirable location" differ so much from one government to the next and in the same government from one time to another that generalization becomes impossible? A case could be made from experience for the view that the best approach in less developed countries (where organization is frequently less important than the personality of a government leader) is to locate a central planning agency wherever there is someone especially qualified, interested and powerful enough to give this new and weak arm of government the best chance of surviving and progressing. Indeed, in some countries, a central planning agency would not have been established when it was if such a person had not taken the initiative and convinced his government of the need. Thus, the Dutch Central Planning Bureau owes its existence, as well as its location in the Ministry of Economic Affairs, to the fact that the Minister of Economic Affairs at the time of its establishment took the initiative to establish a planning agency in his Ministry. Similarly, planning agencies were started in the Ministries of Finance of Israel, Mexico and Singapore because the Ministers of Finance in these countries were the only Ministers in their Governments prepared to sponsor planning. Even the location of Iran's Plan Organization outside the government administration can be traced to the insistence of Iran's most prominent advocate of national planning, later the Plan Organization's first Director (who as Governor of Iran's Central Bank was outside the Government), that only a completely autonomous planning agency could work in Iran.

Nevertheless, attempts to link a planning agency to a specific individual has serious drawbacks. It may mean that the central planning agency has to move from one place in a government to another whenever its sponsor changes jobs. It happened in Israel when the Minister of Finance became Prime Minister and was replaced by another Minister of Finance who was not as interested in planning as his predecessor. This way of handling the problem may help preserve the existence of the planning agency but it can retard the institutionalization of the planning process. Granted that a sponsor's commitment and drive are important for success in planning, institutions last longer than people. If planning is to become a permanent and legitimate part of the machinery of government, it must—like finance and other traditional functions—be primarily identified with government as a whole instead of with an individual.

The alternative to moving about with a sponsor may be as undesirable as moving. If a planning agency stays where it is after a minister who is interested in planning is succeeded by one who is not, the position of the planning agency usually deteriorates. In Pakistan, for example, after the politically powerful Minister of Economic Affairs, who had been the major force behind the country's Planning Board, left the Government and was replaced by a series of ministers who did not give much attention to planning, the Board entered into a long period of decline.

The dilemma posed by both alternatives—whether a central planning agency should or should not move with its sponsor—arises only when we are dealing with governments where development and, hence, planning are not of paramount political importance. The real issue in these countries is not so much where to put a central planning agency, but whether they are ready to make effective use of one. If the continued existence of a central planning agency largely depends on the sponsorship of one individual in a government in a specific position, there is little point in debating the merit of other locations. It either stays with him or it ceases to exist as an effective entity.

Doubts about the preferred location for a central planning agency generally arise only in countries which are either not deeply committed to development planning or are new to it. Where a country gives planning high priority, its central planning agency is almost invariably closely associated with its chief executive or, in a cabinet form of government, with its council of ministers. Indeed, an almost infallible way in which to tell whether a government is in earnest about planning is to see whether the central leadership is consistently involved and concerned with the decision-making which characterizes the planning process. In the socialized countries, for example, where planning holds a commanding position, a central planning agency is always near the source of executive power. In these countries, the central planning agency reports to the council of ministers or, in Yugoslavia, to its equivalent, the Federal Executive Council. As more experience with planning accumulates and planning becomes more important in the mixed economies, there has emerged a clear tendency for these countries also to establish central planning agencies within the office of the chief executive or with the chief executive at its head. Although nominally outside the regular government administration, India's Planning Commission has from its beginning had the Prime Minister as its Chairman. Pakistan's central planning agency, originally under the supervision of its Minister of Economic Affairs, was made responsible to the Chief Executive when a new Government, much more committed to planning than its predecessors, took power in October 1958. The French Commissariat Général du Plan was originally attached to the Office of the Prime Minister. In 1954, it was placed under the Minister of Finance, but in 1962, it was again put under the Prime Minister,

> who wished thereby to indicate the importance he intended to give the Plan in the Government's economic and social policy.[10]

As already indicated, when planning begins in a country, a central planning agency may be established almost anywhere because of the fortuitous administrative position of its sponsor. It may also be located in one place or another because of tradition. In many new countries which were once British or French colonies, central planning agencies have been established in ministries of finance at the time of independence because these ministries were the centers of whatever public investment planning or "development budgeting" prevailed during the colonial period. A ministry of finance also is especially likely to be favored as the site of a central planning agency in countries which have difficulties making financial ends meet. But whether because of the location of an original sponsor or because of tradition, the trend has been to shift central planning agencies from their original position in a ministry of finance or elsewhere to the jurisdiction of the chief executive. Thus, Iran's Plan Organization, long autonomous, was made responsible to the Prime Minister. In Burma, Ethiopia, Ghana, Madagascar, Mexico, Morocco, Senegal, Sierra Leone, Singapore and other countries, the direction has been the same. There is also an increasing tendency for countries establishing planning agencies for the first time to place them under the authority of the chief executive from the beginning. For example, all but one of the nine new planning agencies established in Latin America under the stimulus of the Alliance for Progress are located close to the Presidents of their countries.

The trend could hardly be otherwise. Planning is by its nature a staff function which cuts across the responsibilities of all government ministries, departments and agencies. If properly carried out, the preparation and execution of development plans affect in some measure every important economic and social group, class and sector. Whether it is handled well or poorly, many people and powerful interests in the public and private sectors of an economy will be

---

[10] UN. Consultative Group on Planning for Economic Development. "The Political and Administrative Organization of the Planning System in France," p. 44.

disturbed by the preparation of a plan and its execution, if not by the very idea that planning is taking place. Those inside and outside government who believe themselves to be aggrieved or affronted will invariably seek to exert pressure on the most important government officials they can reach. Where a budget has been the main instrument for controlling public investment, a minister of finance is likely to assert what he considers to be his prerogatives. To reconcile differences between a minister of finance and a head of a planning agency, to deal effectively with the important issues raised by planning and to bring everyone into line with a government's development policies requires basic decisions which only the highest government authority can make and enforce. It is therefore unavoidable that the chief executive power in a country (be it prime minister, president of the republic, council of ministers, king, emperor or shah) will be the head of a central planning agency which seeks to give effect to plans, in fact if not in name.

In a handful of countries, the chief executive has successfully delegated responsibility for development planning to someone else. But this has worked well only when the chief executive has completely excluded himself from the field and has given unfailing support to someone who could act for him in virtually all circumstances. It has been done, for example, in Malaya, where the Deputy Prime Minister is in full charge of planning. In Israel, the Prime Minister was able at one time to transfer responsibility for all investment planning to his Minister of Finance, but only because the Minister was recognized by all concerned as the Prime Minister's spokesman on development matters. But in Turkey, because of a coalition Government which made it necessary at one time to divide the planning function between two Deputy Prime Ministers, the Prime Minister in practice had to make the final decisions when he arbitrated their frequent differences. In Bolivia, also, disagreements about policy made it necessary to transfer the planning agency from the Vice-Presidency to the Presidency of the Republic. In some countries, e.g., Ethiopia and Iran, the central planning agency is under the nominal jurisdiction of the prime minister. But since basic decisions are almost always made by the sovereign, most important planning problems have a way of ending up with him, too.[11] In Nepal, the Deputy Prime Minister was at one time in

---

[11] In Ethiopia, the Imperial Planning Board is actually presided over by the Emperor.

charge of planning. However, the King really made the decisions and he eventually recognized planning's affinity for the highest authority by assuming direct responsibility for planning himself as Chairman of a National Planning Council.

Nevertheless, "organizational propinquity" to the chief executive power is insufficient to insure a planning agency's effectiveness. If, as in Burma during the 1950's, a prime minister is unable or unwilling to devote himself sufficiently to development problems, the planning agency's proximity to the chief executive matters little. Colombia's

> Planning Office has acted as something of a floating appendage in the government structure, even though it has nominally always had the strategic location of being directly attached to the Office of the President, and has failed to have the influence that might have been expected *at least* on the composition of *public* investment.[12]

In Mexico, the effectiveness of the planning agency was actually reduced after it was transferred to the Presidency and it was necessary to appoint an Interministerial Planning Commission, composed of representatives of the Ministries of Finance and the Presidency, to prepare a Three-Year Plan.

There is, therefore, no assurance that a central planning agency under the authority of a chief executive will work better or even as well as one located in another administrative niche. The available evidence indicates only that where a country has a genuine and continuing concern for development, it is best to link a central planning agency with the chief executive because his power and prestige is usually essential to successful planning. But where a country is new to planning or is not yet prepared to do what is needed to plan effectively, a case can be made, at least in the short run, for establishing a planning agency wherever the most powerful sponsor happens to be located on the administrative chart. If this approach is taken, however, it must be recognized that, much more often than not, the central planning agency will not remain viable for long after its sponsor leaves. What is even more important, even if a planning agency sponsored by a strong (and often controversial) administrator produces plans and carries out some projects and programs, it is unlikely to have a lasting effect in diffusing better development procedures throughout a skeptical or hostile government bureaucracy. Perhaps a somewhat stronger case can be made,

[12] Columbia University School of Law. *Public International Development Financing in Colombia*, p. 144.

again as an interim measure, for putting or keeping a central planning agency in the spot where it has traditionally been located until more planning experience and greater acceptance of planning make it evident that the time has come to place the planning agency under the direct authority of the chief executive.

The problem, then, may be reduced to whether it is better in a specific instance to take the long or the short view. In the long run, it is clearly desirable to make the chief executive power responsible for a planning agency. Those who are prepared to postpone immediate returns for greater ones in the future can point out that if a central planning agency is to make its mark, the sooner it settles in what is to be its permanent location, the better. When a new agency is moved from one spot to another before it has had a good chance to fit into the prevailing administrative order, it can be unduly disruptive to its relationships with other entities and, sometimes, to its prestige. Those who take the long view therefore believe that planning is likely to be institutionalized sooner than otherwise if a planning agency is located from the beginning where it should be when a country is ready to plan in earnest.

On the other side are those who believe that the only sensible test of a good planning agency is whether it works well now—not some time in the future. Those who espouse this view discount the disruptive effects of moving a central planning agency later, or they consider that the greater immediate benefits obtained from locating a planning agency where it works best in the short run more than counterbalance the ill-effects associated with later changes in location. It would be difficult to prove or disprove this. But problems associated with moving a planning agency do not end here. Because personal interests tend to become vested in a planning agency as much as in most other institutions, it has not always been possible to transfer a planning agency from one place to another when the desirability for this has become clearly apparent. Thus, attempts to change the location of planning machinery in one country from a Ministry of National Planning to the Office of the Chief Executive had to be abandoned because the Minister involved successfully resisted the move which would have involved a reduction in his rank and status. In countries where the planning agency is located in a ministry of finance, attempts to move the planning agency to another spot have also frequently encountered strong opposition from the minister of finance or from his officials.

Despite these difficulties, it would be dogmatic to insist that in all countries at all times a central planning agency must be under the direction of the chief executive. Perhaps the most that can be said is that since this is the preferred relationship in the long run, anything less than a close link between a head of government and a planning agency should be a temporary compromise with expediency.

AUTONOMOUS PLANNING AGENCIES

If experience does not furnish a ready-made answer to the question of where to locate a central planning agency in every country and circumstance, it does provide significant clues about some places it would be better to avoid. Foremost among these is a location outside government. Some countries, like Finland, as well as Sweden until recently, purposely set up non-government planning agencies which produce national budgets or plans on their own responsibility. The government is then free to adopt what it likes and disregard the rest. This procedure works for a time in developed countries which are not greatly concerned with planned development. But when a country wants to get down to serious planning, it sets up a government planning agency, just as Sweden did. Indeed, a planning agency must be a government organization if it is to express government policy. A government is unlikely to pay much attention to a planning agency outside its regular administrative structure. This became evident, for example, in the United Kingdom, where the National Economic Development Council (variously known as NED or NEDC) produced projections which assumed an accelerated rate of growth. The Council's "plans" had little effect on national policy. The *Economist* complained that

> at present NED is a body whose staff produces rather vague reports which are then read and to some extent regarded by the Treasury when it is working out national economic policy, although to what extent is never very clear. . . . The need is to extend the way in which what can be called the 'NED approach to planning' is brought into national policy.[13]

But this was difficult, given the Council's location outside the Government. As the Rt. Hon. Harold Wilson, then leader of the opposition, pointed out:

[13] *Economist*, September 5, 1964, p. 890.

What NEDC's first report raises is whether, in the long run, a report by an 'outside' body, however well-staffed and expert, can ever have the necessary authority to initiate the policies, in government and in industry, which will be required. A planning organization needs to acquire its authority from the Cabinet and the economic departments if it is to be able to call, in the national interest, for the cooperation that will be required. For that cooperation, and the sacrifices entailed, will only be forthcoming if those concerned know that the Cabinet, too, is committed to the governmental decisions which are needed if the plan is to become a reality.[14]

As with Sweden, the United Kingdom also established a central planning agency within the government administration when the Government wished to begin planning in earnest. It remains to be seen to what extent Canada's Economic Council, also established outside the regular government administrative structure, will influence the Government's economic policy.

Sometimes, in the hope of divorcing development policy and execution from politics, planning machinery is set up in the form of an autonomous development board or corporation outside the normal structure of government.[15] But it is impossible for a planning agency to be both autonomous and effective. A plan which is to have a good chance of being implemented must be a joint project of those who have to carry it out and must express their co-ordinated aspirations in the context of a common goal. Moreover, the very essence of planning, indeed the very decision to begin planning, is political. There is no way of avoiding this, even if it were desirable. No chief executive and his cabinet can be expected to abdicate their authority over policies which touch the heart of all governmental activity to an agency which they do not control.

Nor can development policy be divorced from other aspects of government policy when it needs to be integrated with it. As the Iranian and Iraqi experience has demonstrated, the establishment of an "independent" planning agency can lead to its isolation from the rest of government, confusion of responsibility, unproductive rivalry and

---

[14] "Planning in a Vacuum," *New Statesman*, p. 558.

[15] Such entities may also be considered desirable for a number of other reasons. Thus, they may make it easier to get participation from persons outside government, they are not subject to burdensome government accounting and auditing controls or salary and other civil service limitations and, in general, they can conduct business with the freedom of action of a private firm.

wasteful duplication. Attempts to insulate Iran's Plan Organization from the hazards of political life only succeeded in stimulating political opposition which, over a four-year period, gradually eroded its autonomy until it came completely under the influence of the Prime Minister. In Iraq, the independence of the Development Board was even more short-lived before it gave way to pressure from the Cabinet in 1953, three years after it was founded. In Chile, the success of the *Corporación de Fomento de la Producción* (CORFO) as a development corporation has not been equaled as a central planning agency. As an autonomous entity, CORFO has indeed been removed from politics, thereby giving its management and personnel a measure of stability. But it has also been far removed from the seat of political power and decision-making. Since CORFO is itself a claimant for available development resources for its own projects and programs, ministries and other government bodies sometimes took the view, whether justified or not, that it was likely to favor its own interests above those of others in the over-all development plans it prepared. They therefore were inclined to consider the planning it did as its private affair. Consequently, as CORFO's Director General pointed out, CORFO found

> it more difficult to enlist the cooperation of all sectors for the preparation of the plan. The private sector has by and large proved cooperative, but some of the government agencies have shown themselves reluctant to give assistance.[16]

This is hardly surprising, since CORFO, operating apart from the government administrative structure much like a private firm, finds it easier to deal with businessmen than with civil servants. To help counteract CORFO's isolation from the government administration, an interministerial Economic and Reconstruction Programming Committee (COPERE) was created in 1960 to supervise execution of Chile's Ten-Year Development Plan. Through COPERE, the Government sought to impart to the biggest investors of public funds a sense of participation in the implementation of the Plan.[17]

Those who consider independence from government an essential

[16] OAS. Inter-American Economic and Social Council, etc. "Summary of Mr. Diaz's Remarks on Chile's Experience with an Autonomous Planning Agency," p. 29.

[17] COPERE's members were the Ministers of Economy, Development and Reconstruction; Finance; Public Works; and Mines and Agriculture, as well as the Vice-President and General Manager of CORFO; the Vice-President of CORVI (the public housing corporation); and the Director of the Budget.

attribute for a planning agency sometimes favor its establishment in a central bank outside the government. Central banks generally enjoy reputations for integrity, efficiency and financial soundness. They usually have good research departments, occasionally the best available. In some countries, e.g., Israel, they have issued multiannual economic projections or even, e.g., in Peru, multiannual development plans. Officials of central banks have taken the initiative in advocating the establishment of planning agencies and have been selected to head new planning agencies in Iran, Israel, Pakistan and other countries. It has therefore seemed reasonable to some who value autonomy in planning agencies to propose a central bank as an appropriate location for a planning agency. But for the reasons previously given, planning agencies in central banks are not likely to be more successful than other autonomous planning agencies. The question has remained academic despite efforts of advocates because until now governments have been unwilling to place a national planning agency in a central bank.

The main objection to attempts to insulate planning from politics through the use of an autonomous planning agency is that the attempts are based on the naïve assumption that economic development is largely determined by the sum total of public works and other projects and programs completed in a country. Of course, this is far from the truth. If all that was needed were enough completed projects, underdevelopment could be overcome, at least by the oil-rich countries, if they imported enough foreign engineers and other technicians and contractors from the developed countries to design and construct the roads, power stations, dams and industrial plants which superficially distinguish the advanced from the less advanced nations. Indeed, some countries have tried to build their major regional and other works in just this way.

But the problem is, of course, much too complex and difficult to resolve through such means. It is, for instance, a waste of money to build a dam unless a government is capable of administering it when it has been completed, unless the land use pattern permits benefits to accrue to those who farm the land and unless farmers are taught how to make effective use of the water and power which the dam makes available. To induce the decisions needed to bring such things about requires political, economic and social changes in attitudes of many people in and out of government. It is this which makes development a difficult process and one which takes time to consummate. The basic ingredient in the development of a country, therefore, is not the number of projects completed, but the gradual change of attitudes, the development of skills, the dropping of old ways and the taking on of new ones which come from the continuing participation of people in the development process. It is through the joint and repeated endeavors by which development plans are devised and carried out that these changes can be brought about and government machinery can be reoriented to act in increasingly rational ways. An autonomous agency deliberately separated from a backward government, whose attitudes and procedures must be transformed before a country can develop, is hardly a suitable mechanism for bringing about the necessary metamorphosis.

PLANNING AGENCIES IN MINISTRIES

Nor is it usually possible for a central planning agency to exert the necessary influence if it is located within a government but too low in the administrative hierarchy. A planning agency must have the high position which corresponds to its function. If it is to prepare realistic plans which conform to government policy, it requires free access to information in any ministry, department or agency whose work is related to its task and it must be in close contact with the highest political authority. It is rarely in position to achieve these objectives if it is made part of an existing ministry. In Morocco, for example, the Division of Economic Coordination and Planning (DECP) was originally situated in the Ministry of National Economy and Finance. Although this was a "super-ministry" with considerable influence in the Government, the DECP was greatly handicapped in bringing this influence to bear on others because its own position within the Ministry was subordinated, in fact if not in form, to those of the more powerful divisions of Finance, Commerce and Industry, and Industrial Production and Mines. The DECP found it hard to get the requisite attention from the Minister, whose wide range of short-run operational responsibilities left him with little time for the longer range and, hence, postponable activities of a planning agency. Within the Ministry, the DECP was largely ignored; outside the Ministry, the DECP had trouble getting other ministries and offices to comply with the government order requiring them to furnish it with statistical, financial and economic data and to co-operate with it in other essential ways.[18] The

[18] Waterston, Albert. *Planning in Morocco,* pp. 39–40.

other ministries and agencies tended to view the DECP as the planning agency of the ministry in which it was located instead of the central planning agency for the whole Government.

Similar experiences are common in other countries where planning agencies are placed in ministries of development or economic affairs.[19] In Sierra Leone, for example, an Economic Planning Unit came within the Ministry of Development, while in the Netherlands, a Central Planning Bureau is in the Ministry of Economic Affairs. In these ministries, planning, an advisory function, is combined with development operations of various kinds. Thus, when planning started in Nepal, the planning agency was made a part of a Ministry of Planning and Development which included operational departments for mining, village development, multiple purpose projects and other matters. Not only was the planning function too low in the administrative structure; the combination of planning and operations proved to be too much for the Ministry's personnel to handle. When it became apparent that the Minister and his hard-pressed staff were not paying enough attention to planning, some operating functions were transferred to other ministries. Eventually, however, the Ministry itself was replaced by a Ministry of Planning which had no operational responsibilities.

The location of a planning agency in a ministry of development or economic affairs has proved to be a good one only in special circumstances. In the Netherlands, for instance, the Central Planning Bureau in the Ministry of Economic Affairs operated effectively because several economists who recognized the advantages of planning held positions of political power when the Bureau was established and also because the first Director of the Bureau was himself an eminent economist, highly esteemed by his colleagues in the Government. When he left the Bureau, however, its status declined, in considerable part because as a subordinate office of the Ministry of Economic Affairs, its later directors did not have direct access to the Cabinet. More recently, with the need for planning becoming more apparent in Europe, the Bureau has become more important. But this has required the Bureau, despite its official connection with the Ministry of Economic Affairs, to function independently of the Ministry and for its Director to have direct contact with members of the Cabinet. In Jamaica, also, the Central Planning Unit operated effectively as a part

---

[19] Development ministries may go by other names. For example, such a ministry in Korea was called the Ministry of Reconstruction.

of the Ministry of Development when the Prime Minister held the portfolio of Development. Under this arrangement, the Central Planning Unit was for all practical purposes within the Prime Minister's Office and its Director acted in his name. However, when the Government changed, the planning agency became a subordinate unit in the Ministry of Development headed by a regular Minister, with all the disadvantages inherent in this arrangement.

At one time, Turkey located its planning agency in its Ministry of Foreign Affairs because pressure for planning, with funds for financing development, came from abroad. During the period of the Mali Federation, the Bureau du Plan was in the Ministry of Agriculture because Mali is a predominantly agricultural country; while, in 1948, Norway put its planning office in its Ministry of Commerce because that Ministry was concerned with imports at a time when limited foreign reserves made it essential to plan for their control. But it has proved to be even more undesirable to establish central planning agencies in other traditional ministries than in ministries of economic affairs or development. Not only is planning, an advisory function, an anomaly in an operating ministry; not only does it, as a segment of a ministry, generally function at too low a level to carry out its responsibilities properly; it must also endeavor somehow to spread ideas and modes of behavior which frequently seek to shatter precedent from the stultifying confines of an old-line ministry which, in most cases, accepts precedent as its main guide to action. In addition, a planning agency in a regular operating ministry finds it difficult to enlist the co-operation of other ministries and agencies because they tend to look on it as being mainly concerned with the interests of the ministry in which it is located. This, it will be recalled, happened in Morocco.

A ministry of finance is by far the commonest location among traditional ministries for a central planning agency. It is the first choice of many new countries which have, as colonies, become accustomed to a government's financial authority as the center of public economic activity and co-ordination. In many countries, where financial stability is a prime requirement, the minister of finance is often the most powerful minister next to the chief executive. It has seemed natural, therefore, to put a planning agency in the ministry which, through its control over taxation, budgetary appropriations, and monetary and credit policy, is likely to have the most influence on the execution of development plans.

The effectiveness of a planning agency located in a ministry of finance may vary greatly from one country to another. If the chief planner is subordinated to the chief civil servant in the ministry, as in Kenya and the Sudan, he is likely to have less authority than if he is the top civil servant in the ministry or reports directly to the minister in some other way. The planning agencies in France and Israel were, for practical purposes, autonomous when they were associated with the Ministries of Finance of their respective countries because they reported directly to the Minister and not to any official in the Ministry. In Tunisia, the Director of Planning in the Ministry of Planning and Finance has a higher status than the Directors of the Budget and the Treasury in the same Ministry because he also holds the rank of Undersecretary of the Ministry. In the UAR, planning had a favored status over finance when it was in the Ministry of the Treasury and Planning because the Minister (who also was a Vice-President) was Minister of Planning before he assumed the portfolio of the Ministry of Finance.

Those who believe a ministry of finance to be the best location for a planning agency can muster an imposing array of arguments in support of their position. Planning is, of course, closely associated with the raising of funds through taxation and borrowing, the preparation of budgets and the control of public expenditures. There is also need for the closest co-ordination between development plans and budgets. Where co-ordination has been imperfect, it has sometimes had disastrous effects on a country's financial standing. Since projects and programs in a plan must be examined by the budgetary authority in a ministry of finance, which has built up the necessary expertise for the job, it appears to be an unnecessary duplication to set up a separate planning agency to scrutinize the same projects again. Moreover, where skilled technicians are scarce, it may not be easy to find adequately qualified personnel. Thus, it has been held that co-ordination would be more likely and duplication less likely if the financial and planning functions were in the same ministry. Finally, since a ministry of finance has no projects of its own, it has no special interest in favoring one project or program over others, thereby making it what appears to be a natural arbiter among the various claimants for development resources.

But there are also a number of telling arguments against putting a planning agency in a ministry of finance. Firstly, in many countries, large investments made by autonomous agencies, and provincial and local entities are outside the budget and, hence, outside the control of a ministry of finance. There is no special advantage in these cases for having a planning office in a ministry of finance. However, the most important argument against this location is that a ministry of finance's approach to development differs fundamentally from that of a planning agency. A ministry of finance is necessarily and correctly concerned with controlling and conserving financial resources to insure that allocated funds are well spent and that more money is not disbursed than is available. A planning agency, while bound by the limits of available finances, must think in terms of expanding these resources to provide the basis for a rate of growth which is greater than the increase in population. Typically, these different approaches require a ministry of finance to achieve its goal by trying to keep expenditures from exceeding financial resources, while a planning agency must, to achieve its major goal, encourage the acquisition of increased resources to allow higher investment. Moreover, a ministry of finance is concerned almost solely with the husbanding of financial resources, while a planning agency must be as much concerned with the mobilization and allocation of scarce human and physical resources as with financial resources. Finally, a ministry of finance tends to concentrate on short-run objectives, while a planning agency must frequently recommend action on proposals which yield only distant and indirect returns.

A planning agency's approach to development is therefore radically different from that of a ministry of finance. It does not duplicate the work of a ministry of finance; it complements it. Both approaches are useful and necessary. Each casts a different light on development problems which can enhance understanding and improve the quality of decision-making by political authorities. As one authority put it,

> there is no point in denying that the budget function is preponderantly negative. It is on the whole rather strongly against program and expenditure expansion. This approach is desirable, because the programmatic agencies and most of the potent pressure groups are so expansive that there will be little danger that the undesirable values they represent will be overlooked or smothered by budgeteers.[20]

It is, of course, imperative for growth with stability that planning objectives be pursued within the limits of available financial (and

[20] Appleby, Paul. "Role of the Budget Division," p. 156.

other) resources. A ministry of finance has to make sure that development expenditures do not exceed available funds. But it is in position to achieve this through appropriate budgetary procedures. It is not necessary for a central planning agency to be located within a ministry of finance to accomplish this purpose. Furthermore, as experience in Morocco, Nepal, the Sudan and other countries shows, it does not follow that there will always be better co-ordination between plan and budget if a planning agency is located in a ministry of finance. In Nepal and the Sudan, the permanent undersecretaries in charge of the planning part of the Ministry of Finance were often at loggerheads with the permanent undersecretaries in charge of finance. It was largely because Morocco's Division of Economic Coordination and Planning was submerged and largely ignored by the budget and other authorities in the Ministry of National Economy and Finance that it was transferred to the jurisdiction of the Royal Cabinet.

It is true, of course, that a minister of finance must be a friend of a central planning agency if a plan is to be co-ordinated with the budget. But this does not make it necessary or desirable that he be its boss! It is, in fact, undesirable for a number of reasons, including the fact that the responsibilities of running a ministry of finance in most countries already is a full-time job for a minister. For instance, the Norwegian State Council for Organization and Method, although agreeing that Norway's planning unit should be placed in the Ministry of Finance at first, recommended that further study be given to other possibilities.

> The Ministry of Finance is already a large and heavily occupied ministry. The pressure on the higher personnel will presumably be even greater as development of economic long term planning progresses. . . . The various possibilities of affording some relief to this ministry should, however, be investigated. The advisability of collecting the work of long term planning and general economic planning which now occurs in the Ministry of Finance into a new ministry for economic planning should be gone into.[21]

The argument that a ministry of finance already has all it can do is of particular relevance in less developed countries where financial and budgetary procedures and practices are generally in need of basic overhauling and improved supervision. As a well-known Latin Ameri-

---

[21] Norway. Royal Norwegian Ministry of Finance. *Extension of Economic Planning*, p. 13.

can expert on the public administration problems of Latin America has cautioned:

> If the budget office and the general planning office were amalgam-
> ated, the ordinary day-to-day tasks of the former would tend to
> absorb the staff's attention. The functions of budget departments
> vary from country to country; but even if they did not go beyond
> the mere preparation of the budget and related studies there
> would be little time left for planning and the tendency would be to
> approach problems on a short-term basis and purely from the fiscal
> standpoint.[22]

Nor is a ministry of finance a desirable site for a planning agency in a coalition government because in such governments it is often impossible for a minister of one party to make plans for ministries headed by ministers of another party. This problem in France made it desirable to transfer the Commissariat Général du Plan from the jurisdiction of the Minister of Finance to that of the Prime Minister. But even in countries where the ministry of finance is generally acknowledged to be a strong ministry, other ministries have a way of circumventing a planning agency located in a ministry of finance when they are unwilling to abide by its determinations. In Mexico, for example, attempts by an Investment Commission set up under the auspices of the Minister of Finance to co-ordinate public investment were largely ignored by other ministries and made it desirable to transfer the Commission to the President's Office.

Because of the shortcomings of traditional ministries as sites for central planning agencies, many countries have at one time or another created new ministries concerned solely with planning. A separate planning ministry has many advantages over an old-line operating ministry as a location for a planning agency. A planning ministry has a full-time minister who can devote all his time to planning and to representing the planning agency in the cabinet and the legislature.[23] A planning ministry is therefore more likely than an autonomous planning agency, or one in a subordinate spot in a traditional ministry, to be able to promote planning, integrate it into government operations, have better access to information needed for planning and bring its points of

---

[22] UN. TAA. *Introduction to Public Administration in Development Policy, Preliminary survey of the experience of several Latin American countries,* p. 47.

[23] UN. ECAFE. "Economic Development and Planning in Asia and the Far East," *Economic Bulletin for Asia and the Far East,* December 1961, p. 36.

view to the highest levels of political authority. Despite these seeming advantages, ministries of planning have rarely had more than transient success and in most cases have had to be replaced after a short period after their establishment.

This is because a ministry of planning suffers from two serious, seemingly contradictory, drawbacks. On the one hand, it raises an essentially advisory function too high to the ministry level usually reserved for executive responsibilities. On the other hand, by making the head of planning a minister who is no more than the equal of other ministers, it makes it easy for them to out-vote him. Planning is, moreover, the concern of the whole government, not of one minister. But it is precisely because planning affects other ministries, that their ministers are not prepared to grant another minister of equal rank authority superior to their own. Attempts by a planning ministry to plan for the government or the economy as a whole have usually been considered by other ministries as encroachments upon their domains. The situation in Burma was typical:

> The Ministry of Planning was only one among many other Ministries, and the intervention of the Ministry of Planning in the activities of other Ministries was not unnaturally resented.[24]

The jurisdictional differences which arose as a consequence led to the establishment of an Economic and Social Board, with the Prime Minister as Chairman, to oversee planning activities. Greece also created a separate planning ministry, called the Ministry of Coordination. It was supposed to have a higher standing than other ministries, but the operational ministries did not accept this until a Vice Premier assumed the portfolio of the Ministry.[25] The higher status of the Ministry of Planning in Afghanistan has never been in doubt since the Prime Minister has retained for himself the portfolio of the Ministry of Planning. The available evidence, therefore, makes it clear that a ministry of planning is unlikely to be effective unless it is elevated above other ministries and put under the jurisdiction of a chief executive or his deputy. If a planning ministry is effective mostly because it is close to a chief executive or his deputy, it is well to recognize that it is in fact a staff organization rather than a ministry.

[24] Furnivall, J. S. *Governance of Modern Burma*, p. 55.
[25] In November 1964, the United Kingdom established a Ministry of Economic Affairs as its central planning agency with the Deputy Prime Minister at its head.

There is, therefore, little point in leaving it as a ministry which might, at a later time, lose its status when an ordinary minister is appointed as its head. This happened in Jamaica after a change in government.

SUMMARY AND CONCLUSIONS

Summing up, we find that the experts differ about the preferred administrative location for a central planning agency. Some authorities insist that a central planning agency must be located in the office of a chief executive, some feel that it should be a part of an existing ministry; others that it should be set up in a new ministry of planning; while still others consider it essential, at least in some countries, that a central planning agency operate as an autonomous body outside the regular government administration. There is, finally, a group which contends that a central planning agency can be located in any of these places if it can be made to work effectively.

It is questionable whether one location for a central planning agency exists which can meet the need of all countries at all times. A good case can be made for locating a central planning agency wherever a government leader is sufficiently interested and powerful enough to sponsor it effectively. But this approach has serious short-comings. If the sponsor moves to another post, the planning agency must either move with him or remain where it was established. If it moves with the sponsor, it tends to become identified with him instead of with the government, thereby delaying its institutionalization; if it stays behind, it runs the risk of declining in importance.

In countries which are deeply committed to development planning, there is little doubt about the preferred location for a central planning agency. Where a country gives planning high priority, its central planning agency is almost invariably closely associated with its chief executive or council of ministers. Where central planning agencies have been established at other points because of the location of original sponsors or tradition, there has been an increasing tendency to shift them to the jurisdiction of the chief executive.

Because of the nature of planning, the trend could hardly be otherwise. Planning affects many vested interests inside and outside government. It is inevitable that the chief executive power in a country will be drawn into the planning process to make the basic decisions required to reconcile differences and enforce decisions for carrying out development policy. In only a handful of countries has the chief executive found it possible to delegate real responsibility for planning to a subordinate.

Where to put the planning agency when a government is not yet deeply committed to planning becomes a matter of deciding whether to take the long- or short-term view. Those who take the long view contend that planning is likely to be institutionalized sooner than otherwise if it is put at the beginning under the chief executive, where it should be when the country begins to plan in earnest. Those who feel that the disruptive effects of moving a planning agency from one place to another are more than outweighed by good results obtained immediately, advocate putting a planning agency wherever it works well in the short run. It is hard to decide between these two opposing views as a general matter. Perhaps the most that can be said is that anything less than a close link between the chief executive power and a central planning agency is acceptable only as a temporary expedient.

Although experience does not provide a ready answer to the question of where to locate a central planning agency in every country and every time, it provides clues about some locations which should be avoided. Foremost among these is a location outside the regular government administration. A planning agency must be a government body if it is to express government policy.

Sometimes, with the aim of divorcing planning from political interference, planning machinery is set up in the form of an autonomous development board or corporation. But experience shows that the establishment of an independent planning agency often leads to its isolation from the rest of government, confusion of responsibility, unproductive rivalry and wasteful duplication. The main objection to attempts to insulate planning from politics through the use of an autonomous planning agency is that they are based on an assumption that development is determined by the number of projects completed instead of by changing basic attitudes, organization and practices. It is through the joint and repeated endeavors by which development plans are prepared and executed that these changes can be brought about and government machinery can be reoriented to act in increasingly rational ways. An autonomous planning agency, deliberately separated from a backward government, is hardly a suitable vehicle for bringing about the necessary changes.

Neither is a central planning agency located within a government but too low in the administrative hierarchy likely to exert the required influence. Thus, a planning agency which is a subordinate unit in a ministry usually does not have the standing in government which it must have to do its job. It has also been found to be undesirable to put the planning function in a ministry which has operational functions. Not only does a planning agency which becomes a part of an existing ministry usually function at too low a level to carry out its responsibilities properly; not only is planning, an advisory function, an anomaly in an operating ministry; it must also try somehow to spread new ideas and modes of behavior from an old-line ministry which is devoted to precedent.

A ministry of finance is the commonest location among traditional ministries for a central planning agency. Many arguments can be adduced in favor of this location, but there are as many against it. The most important argument against putting a planning office in a ministry of finance is that a planning agency's approach to development is fundamentally different from that of a ministry of finance. Rather both approaches are useful and necessary. It is true that a minister of finance must be a friend of a central planning agency if a plan is to be coordinated with the budget, but this does not make it necessary or desirable that he be its boss!

Because of the shortcomings of traditional ministries as sites for central planning agencies, some countries have established new ministries solely concerned with planning. Despite some advantages over old-line agencies, planning ministries have not proven to be successful. Basically, this is because other ministers are not willing to grant another minister of equal rank authority over their own ministries. Available evidence makes it clear that a ministry of planning is unlikely to be effective unless it is raised to a level above other ministries. If this is done the agency comes, as a practical matter, under the direction of the chief executive or his deputy.

Chapter XIV

Types of Central Planning Agencies

It is a curious thing about the study of government that the identification of its implicit processes almost always leads to the creation of formal organizations for perfecting them. What is more, such new organizations seem frequently to induce a host of problems, which formerly appeared not to exist, concerning the relationship between the newly identified process and other processes. An example of this phenomenon is the planning process.[1]

INTRODUCTION

THE PREPARATION and overseeing of national plans requires organized machinery to carry out two main sets of tasks:

1. The procedures by which a plan's goals are approved and realized. This involves the making of decisions about the level of the development effort (e.g., through the choice of investment, production and other targets to be included in a plan), policies to be followed to achieve development goals, and provision for appropriate action to attain planning ends (e.g., by the issuance of administrative orders or the adoption of other measures).

2. The process by which a plan is prepared on the basis of approved goals. This involves an examination of alternative ways in which available real and financial resources may be allocated to achieve development objectives and plan targets; detailing the measures and instruments of policy required to attain them; advising on the advantages and disadvantages of alternative courses of action; framing multiannual and annual development plans; keeping their implementation under review; and, through a system of progress reporting, advising on the need for appropriate action to achieve plan targets or to revise them.

[1] Johnson, A. W. "Planning and Budgeting," p. 145.

Because the first set of tasks requires the issuance of administrative orders to all parts of government and the adoption of policies and measures which greatly influence an economy, effective action on these matters can normally be taken only by an authority at the highest political levels. In most governments, this is the chief executive and his cabinet. The second set of tasks can be accomplished by a body of technicians who are qualified by training and experience to do the required work.

One may speak, therefore, of two tiers or levels of central planning machinery—the political and the technical. For the sake of administrative efficiency, as well as operating effectiveness, the more direct the connection between these tiers, the better; conversely, the interposition of additional tiers in the form of agencies, committees or other groups between the political tier and the technical tier complicates their relationships and increases the possibilities that their contacts with each other will be weakened. This is undesirable because effective planning requires that the technical body have access to, and the confidence of, the political body in order to be heard and to be in a position to know what is required of it. The presumption is, therefore, that the technical body should be attached directly to the political body. This is the way it is, in fact, in the USSR, where the central planning agency, the *All-Union Gosplan,* reports directly to the Council of Ministers. In a very few mixed-economy countries, also, the technical planning body reports directly to the chief executive and his full cabinet. Thus, when Jamaica's Prime Minister held the portfolio of the Ministry of Development, the draft-plan produced by the Ministry's Central Planning Unit went directly from the Unit to the Cabinet.

But this is not the only or necessarily the best way. In most mixed economies, where planning does not occupy the preponderant position it holds in the socialized economies, a chief executive and his cabinet are generally so heavily burdened with a wide range of foreign affairs, defense and internal political problems that they are unlikely to be able to devote to development planning the time required. Sometimes, the chief executive tries to lighten his workload by delegating some planning duties to someone else. As we have seen, this was done in Malaya (where the Deputy Prime Minister was given responsibility for planning) and Israel (where the Minister of Finance relieved the Prime Minister of planning duties).

But in most countries, a committee, agency or other body is set up to care for planning tasks which the chief executive and his cabinet feel they cannot or should not handle. This can be a good thing because some ministers have little interest in planning and because a cabinet is usually too large and unwieldy to give adequate consideration to many planning problems, especially in the earliest stages of discussion. A group or entity which has the necessary prestige and confidence of a chief executive and his cabinet can provide general guidance on planning matters to government offices and supervise all planning activities including those of a technical planning body. It can screen and refine planning objectives, targets, policies and other proposals prepared by a technical planning body and other government offices before they are presented with its recommendations to a chief executive and his cabinet for final determination. It can thereby greatly lighten their duties, improve the bases for planning decisions and expedite planning procedures.

Nevertheless, the introduction of another organization between a cabinet and a technical planning agency creates new administrative problems, if only by raising questions about the status of the new organization vis-a-vis the technical agency and other parts of government. The form and composition of the new organization can also produce serious problems. It may take the form of a division of a ministry of development or finance, or a ministry of planning which reports directly to a chief executive or cabinet or, instead, to one or more intermediary groups. Or it may be a group composed of members of the cabinet, or of a mixed group of cabinet, legislative, regional or other government representatives, or one of politicians and technicians, or of representatives of the public and private sectors or, finally, of combinations of these. Some groups make a clear distinction between themselves on the political or decision-making tier and the planning group on the technical tier, while others seek to combine the two into a single organization which reports directly to a chief executive or a cabinet. To the bewildering array of forms must be added an equally bewildering array of names. Appendix IV lists the names (and the addresses) of most central planning agencies. Groups which are generally similar in composition and function in different countries vary greatly in the names by which they go.[2] Finally, within the same

---

[2] Thus, a planning committee of the cabinet, largely if not entirely composed of ministers, has been called an Economic and Social Board in Burma, an Economic Committee of the Cabinet in Malaya, a Development Committee in Kenya, an Economic Development Commission in Tanganyika, a National Economic Council in Honduras, an Inter-Ministerial Economic Committee in Israel, a Cabinet Com-

country, a planning body with one name may follow planning bodies with other names in rapid and confusing succession.[3]

CABINET COMMITTEES

Despite the wide variation in the form, composition and name of planning agencies, there has been a clearly discernible trend in recent years in less developed countries toward the establishment of a committee of the cabinet as an intermediary group between a cabinet and a technical planning agency. Among other countries, Ceylon, Colombia, Ethiopia, France, Guatemala, Iraq, Kenya, Liberia, Libya, Malaya, Nepal, Paraguay, Saudi Arabia, Tanganyika and the United Arab Republic have created such committees.

The members of these committees are generally the ministers in a cabinet most concerned with development policy. The exact composition varies from country to country, but it frequently includes the ministers of finance, economic affairs or development (if one exists), agriculture, industry, transportation and communication, and public

---

mittee for National Planning in the United Arab Republic and a Supreme Planning Board in Saudi Arabia. In addition to planning committees of a cabinet, there are other planning bodies on a variety of levels with an equally wide range of names. Thus, there are Planning Commissions in India and Pakistan, Commissariats for the Plan in France, the Malagasy Republic, Senegal and Spain, a National Economic Development Board in Thailand, a General Directorate of Planning in Viet Nam, a National Planning Office in Hungary, an Economic Planning Agency in Japan, a Higher Inspectorate of the Development Plan in Portugal, a Central Planning Organization in Turkey, a Federal Planning Institute in Yugoslavia and a State Planning Commission (*Gosplan*) in the USSR. (Treves, Giuseppino. *Government Organization for Economic Development*, p. 55.)

[3] For example, in Burma, the first planning organization was a National Planning Board, established in 1947. It was renamed the Economic Planning Board in 1948, but the name was later changed back to National Planning Board. In 1948, an Economic Council, under the chairmanship of the Minister of Industry and Mines, was created to screen development proposals before final Cabinet consideration. Earlier the same year, a Ministry of National Planning had also been established. Subsequently, an Economic Planning Commission and a Social Planning Commission were attached to the Ministry. In 1952, an Economic and Social Board was set up to supervise execution of projects and to advise on development policies. In 1957, the Ministry of National Planning and the Economic and Social Board were merged in a National Planning Commission. In the latest move, the nature and composition of this Commission were changed in 1961. In Ceylon, Ghana, Indonesia and the Philippines as well, many planning agencies have also followed one another or been added to the existing supply.

works.[4] In countries with special problems or interests, other ministers are included. Thus, since oil is of particular importance in Libya and Saudi Arabia, each of these countries includes its minister concerned with petroleum on its cabinet planning committee. In countries where an autonomous central bank controls the supply of money and credit, it has also been found desirable, because of the importance of monetary and credit policy for development, to include the head of the bank as a member of the committee.[5]

A planning committee of a cabinet composed of ministers who are most concerned with development and headed by a country's chief executive is in a strong position to make decisions which the cabinet will accept and to facilitate co-ordination of the most important sector programs in a development plan. This was true, for example, when Burma had an Economic and Social Board. Recommendations made by the Board were generally approved by the Government.[6]

Although this experience is typical in countries with such committees, some countries believe it is undesirable to have the most important claimants for development resources become judges of the way these resources are distributed. They feel that a committee of ministers with the greatest stake in development has a serious weakness because it places undue stress on compromise and because it is likely to have difficulties dealing with issues which are not questions with simple answers but complicated alternatives. They believe, therefore, that it is better to establish a cabinet planning committee with so-called "neutral" ministers who do not have an important claim on investment resources. They consider such a group to be best able to assess objectively the respective merits of the various proposals put forward by the interested ministries. This system has been attempted in the Sudan. The cabinet planning committee in that country, called the Economic Council, includes such "neutral" ministers as the Minister of Information and Labor, the Minister of Foreign Affairs and the Min-

---

[4] In countries where the public works ministry is merely a central construction unit for executing projects and programs already accepted, it is unnecessary and undesirable to include the minister of public works on the committee, since he has little to do with development policy. Nevertheless, he is sometimes included, as in Singapore.

[5] In countries like Turkey, where the central bank is not independent of the ministry of finance, the minister of finance can represent the central bank.

[6] Nelson, Joan Marie. *Central Planning for National Development and the Role of Foreign Advisors: The Case of Burma*, p. 191 [Citing, Economic and Social Board, *Annual Report for 1955–56*, Appendix II, pp. 5–6].

ister of Cabinet Affairs, besides the Minister of Commerce, Industry and Supply and the Minister of Finance and Economics (in which the Planning Secretariat is located), the Prime Minister and the President of the Supreme Council of the Armed Forces.

A committee with neutral ministers is not to be recommended. The basic interests of neutral ministers lie outside the area of development policy. If they have no strong opinions about resource allocation, they can easily be swayed by those in charge of development ministries; if they have strong views they may not be able to obtain the support of their colleagues who head development ministries and have responsibility for carrying out projects and programs. In the latter case, most problems are likely to end up in the full cabinet. It is true that a cabinet planning committee composed of the ministers who have vested interests in development may have to fashion compromise solutions acceptable to them all. It is also likely that the compromises will not appear to be ideal from the point of view of the technician. In working out final allocations of resources, each minister will probably not obtain all he wants and will usually have to settle for less in the light of the requirements of others. But in the political context in which governments operate in the real world, the results are likely to reflect the basic policies and objectives of the government in power.

It has sometimes been found in setting up a committee of the cabinet that too many ministers wish to be associated with it. Although a committee may have been established originally with only five or six members, other ministers may join its deliberations one by one until almost the whole cabinet is in attendance. In Ceylon, for example, provision is made for 15 members on the Sub-Committee of the Cabinet. Where a committee of a cabinet reaches this size it is just as well to have a meeting of the full cabinet. Experience shows that a committee of about six or seven members can operate effectively and that one of over eight is likely to have meetings where the depth of discussion is limited and its quality diluted. The best way of getting around the problem of ministers who wish to be associated with a cabinet planning committee but who have no major responsibilities for development policy is for the committee to invite them to join its meetings when subjects of direct concern to their ministries are being discussed. In this way, each minister is given an opportunity to be heard whenever his interests are involved. At the same time, the committee has an opportunity to acquaint him with factors which affect his programs.

If it is pointless to have a committee of a cabinet unless attendance at its meetings is normally substantially smaller than at cabinet meetings, it is also important that the ministers themselves, not their subordinates, attend committee meetings. Wherever one minister starts sending a deputy to a committee's meetings, other ministers soon follow suit. Then, what began as a high-level political decision-making body is likely to become a discussion group of civil servants without power to make basic decisions. Experience shows that in countries with a civil service tradition, a subministerial committee composed of civil servants of high rank can assist a cabinet planning committee by reviewing, commenting upon and criticizing proposals. Because it provides officials in one ministry with an opportunity to acquaint themselves with the problems of other ministries, it is also a useful vehicle for educating them to take a broad view of development problems. Consequently, where it is employed, as in the case of Tanganyika's Coordinating Committee of Permanent Secretaries and Tunisia's Interdepartmental Planning Council, to review proposals before they go to a cabinet planning committee or to secure co-operation among ministries on the working level, it can perform a useful function. However, because a committee of civil servants has "a built-in drive toward lowest denominator solutions"[7] which too often produces "watered down versions,"[8] it is a poor instrument of innovation. Because of this limitation, it is no substitute for a cabinet planning committee. This is evident, for instance, in Jordan. In that country, the Development Board, largely composed of undersecretaries from various operating ministries, does not have the necessary authority to develop planning policy. As a result, the Council of Ministers must perform this task.

Where a cabinet planning committee exists, it is especially important that the chief executive of the government be the chairman and that he attend meetings whenever major matters come before the committee for decision. For example, the fact that Prime Minister Nehru made it a practice to preside over India's Planning Commission whenever important policy questions were up for determination, greatly enhanced the Commission's prestige and effectiveness. In some countries, the chief executive has found it possible and desirable to appoint a high official to act as vice-chairman when ordinary business comes before the

[7] United States Senate. Committee on Government Operations, Subcommittee on National Policy Machinery. *Organizing for National Security*, pp. 4–5.
[8] *Ibid.*

committee. In Ceylon and Saudi Arabia, for example, the Ministers of Finance are Vice-Chairmen of their respective cabinet planning committees. The UAR has used a variant of this form. The Cabinet, with the President of the Republic as presiding officer, has been constituted a Higher Council of Planning to issue general planning directives and approve the plan in its final form. There is also a Cabinet Committee for National Planning composed of the approximately ten ministers most concerned with development problems. The Committee is permanently headed by the Minister of National Planning who also holds the portfolio of finance and is, in addition, a Vice-President of the UAR.

Some argue against a cabinet planning committee composed of a chief executive and ministers on the ground that they are already so busy that they have no time to attend meetings of a cabinet planning committee. The answer to this argument is that if development of a country is not considered important enough to get the attention of top political authorities, the country is unlikely to develop rapidly. Planning cannot be regarded as another onerous burden added to those carried by an already overworked chief executive and his cabinet. It is, rather, a means by which they can execute their responsibilities for overseeing and co-ordinating development operations.

MIXED COMMITTEES

A planning committee composed exclusively or almost exclusively of ministers who dominate development policy in their government can maintain a close relationship with a cabinet and serve as its direct agent in planning matters. Despite these advantages, some countries have chosen to forego them or have sought to obtain them and others besides by setting up a planning group which combines ministers with others from outside a cabinet. With rare exceptions, such planning groups have been less effective than cabinet planning committees in obtaining the co-operation of their governments. This is because ministers, and others who are responsible for carrying out projects and programs, find it easier to ignore or resist recommendations which would limit their freedom of action when they are made by a planning group whose executive strength has been diluted by outsiders than when they are made by a prime minister and cabinet ministers most concerned with development policy.

Sometimes, the advantages of a cabinet planning committee are needlessly sacrificed to attain an advantage which could have been obtained as easily in some other way. For example, Burma, which had had relatively good experience with a cabinet planning committee,[9] subsequently replaced it with a planning body which also gave representation to states in the Union. The 16-member National Planning Commission which was established included ministers from both the Central Government and the states, as well as other individuals. In addition to producing too large a body to manage effectively, this arrangement put the state representatives in the wrong place. A more desirable solution would have been to retain a cabinet planning committee because of its special advantages and to set up a separate group with state ministers to advise the cabinet planning committee or the Cabinet itself on planning matters affecting the states. Experience in India, Pakistan and Nigeria indicates that in countries with a federal form of government, adequate voice can be given to states or regions through separate advisory co-ordinating groups without increasing the size or changing the nature of a planning group concerned with national planning policy.

The inclusion of foreigners as members of a national planning agency concerned with policy matters, as in the case of the Development Boards in Iraq and Jordan, has also inhibited close relationships between planning agency and Cabinet. Nor have attempts to combine representatives of the executive and legislative departments of a government in a planning agency on the policy level had much success. Here, too, experience shows that the best results can be obtained from separate advisory committees with legislative representatives and representatives of the central planning agency or government.

Colombia had a National Planning and Economic Policy Council, presided over by the President of the Republic, with four councilors as members. Two councilors were appointed by the President and two were selected by the National Congress. The Council, joined by four Ministers (Finance, Public Works, Agriculture and Development), the Manager of the Central Bank and the Manager of the Coffee Federation (which is important in Colombia), the Director of the Planning Department (the planning secretariat), as well as other invited ministers or heads of agencies, generally met as a group to consider planning policy and programs. With 12 or more participants at each meeting, the

[9] The Economic and Social Board.

group proved to be too large to function properly. The Council soon degenerated into a "debating society" in which the four ministers habitually resisted what they considered were infringements on their prerogatives. The legislative members came into conflict with members of the executive branch and particularly with the Director of the Planning Department, who was eventually forced to resign. The failure of the Council eventually resulted in its abolition and replacement by a cabinet planning committee. Iran's Plan Organization was provided with a Board of Control chosen from members of Parliament, but it was never permitted to carry out the functions assigned to it. In the Philippines, four representatives of Congress, two from each House, have been *ex officio* members of the National Economic Council. The presence of members of Congress has inhibited the President from making full use of the Council. Agreement among members of the Council and between the Council and the Executive is made more difficult because the congressional members include representatives of the opposition as well as the government party. The four congressional members on the Council were supposed to facilitate the approval by Congress of the economic policies and programs which the Council recommended.

> Actually, however, this has not materialized. In fact, on several occasions members of Congress have expressly had recorded in the minutes of the Council that they were refraining from participating in the deliberations of the Council and not expressing their views on policy matters, precisely in order not to feel themselves bound to any commitment on the subject. . . . The last two economic plans of the Council, . . . both subscribed to without any dissent by the four members of Congress, contain important definite policy recommendations concerning the problem of exchange controls. Yet these recommendations of the Council, as far as I know, have not been sponsored in Congress by any of the Congressional members serving in the Council.[10]

In addition to members of Congress, the Council contains three members "at large" drawn from outside the Government. Other countries have included representatives of the general public or the private sector in their planning bodies on the policy level, some without government representatives, others in conjunction with ministers or

[10] Araneta, Salvador. "The Planning, Approval and Implementation of Economic Policy," pp. 135–136.

heads of government agencies. Thus, prior to 1958, a Planning Board composed solely of three distinguished private citizens functioned in Colombia. More commonly, private individuals serve jointly with ministers and sometimes a head of government on quasi-government commissions. The Philippines, as well as Ceylon, Ecuador, Guatemala, Honduras, India, Iraq, Jordan, Sweden, Thailand, Uganda and the United Kingdom, among other countries, have or have had planning agencies which include or included both government and non-government members.

Those who favor the inclusion of non-government representatives in the membership of planning bodies on the policy level, generally do so because they believe that this broadens the planning base by giving a direct voice to those outside government whose interests are affected by development plans. While some consider it desirable for a planning agency to have members who represent industry, agriculture or business, others advocate the addition of distinguished and respected citizens who represent no vested interest and, presumably, can thereby bring an objective point of view to a planning body.[11]

In practice, planning groups on the policy level composed in whole or in part of non-government members have almost never been effective. In Iran's Plan Organization (PO), for instance, a High Council of seven members drawn from outside the Government which was supposed to supply policy guidance for the PO was largely bypassed. In Ceylon, the Government did not convene its National Planning Council for long periods because the Government was reluctant to disclose confidential information to the Council's non-government members. In Guatemala, Ecuador and Honduras, ministers who were members of mixed planning bodies often did not attend meetings. They and their countries' chief executives usually paid little attention to the plans and proposals prepared by these planning bodies. In Ghana, where a National Planning Commission with mixed membership operates,

> the Cabinet Ministers appear so little inclined to accept the Commission's authority that it is intended to appoint as its Vice-Chairman a Minister who will be politically responsible for planning.[12]

[11] In Iraq, it was believed that the presence of non-government members would provide the Planning Board with a stabilizing influence and insulate it from political change. In 1953, out of nine members, six were from outside the Government.

[12] United Nations Meeting of Experts on Administrative Aspects of National Development Planning. *Administration of Planning in Ghana*, p. 5.

Even in India, where the first Prime Minister's interest in the Planning Commission was a cohesive force, minister-members of the Commission absented themselves for long periods from the Commission's deliberations, leaving the field to its non-government members. The ministers took the position that it was unnecessary for them to attend because they could review planning proposals and express their views when the proposals were considered by the Cabinet. When ministers boycott or ignore planning bodies with mixed membership, members from outside government are indeed made to feel that they are outsiders. This happened in Uganda, where an ineffective Development Council with mixed membership eventually had to be abolished.

> [The] failure of the Council to act as a high-level co-ordinating body is good evidence of the very great difficulty of operating a combined official and unofficial committee. After all, the purpose of Government is to govern and though it may take advice from unofficial people outside the government machine it can never be overridden by it. In these circumstances there is very great danger of the unofficial members feeling themselves to be serving no very useful purpose.[13]

It will be interesting to see what happens in Iraq, where a new Supreme Planning Council was set up in May 1964. The Council, under the chairmanship of the Prime Minister, has as members three ministers (the Ministers of Planning, Economy and Finance), the Governor of the Central Bank and four private full-time members. The Minister and Under-Secretary of Planning and the four full-time members form a Steering Committee of the Council which will do the actual work. The Steering Committee is, at least theoretically, administered by the members from outside the Cabinet. Kuwait also has a central planning agency with a mixed membership. But the Planning Board in that country has seven ministers against four members from the private sector. Lebanon's Planning and Development Council is headed by the Minister of Planning as Chairman and is composed of the Director-General of the Ministry as Vice-Chairman and eight experts in the fields of economics and other social sciences, resources and regional development. But the Council acts, in effect, as an organ of the Ministry of Planning. The Council of Ministers is the only policy-making group on planning matters.

[13] Walker, David. *Balanced Social and Economic Development in Uganda: A Case Study,* p. 85.

The record reveals that governments generally hesitate to entrust policy-making functions to outsiders who bear no public responsibility for governing. Ministers and other political leaders tend to hold the view that since they are responsible to their country for the success or failure of economic development plans they, and not outsiders, should have authority to formulate development policy. Although a government can accept or reject a planning body's recommendations and development plans, ministers seem to fear that if outsiders are members of a planning policy body they may "capture" it. They believe there is then a danger that the outsider will have an unduly partisan influence on planning and may use it to further his personal ends. Because of this attitude, which is widespread, it is best not to have outsiders on a government planning policy body. While political leaders in most countries recognize that a wise government will call on industrial, business, agricultural and other community interests for advice and suggestions, it is preferable to obtain these by setting up outsiders in separate advisory groups to the government instead of making them the equals of ministers in a planning agency on the policy level.

Attempts by some countries to combine in a planning agency on the policy level representatives of several interests have generally resulted in compounding the defects found in mixed groups with only two kinds of members. They have also produced excessively large and unwieldy planning groups. In Tunisia, for example, inclusion of ministers and other executive department officials, members of the National Assembly and the Economic and Social Council, as well as representatives of workers', students', women's, farmers' and businessmen's organizations in the National Planning Council, raised the number of members of that planning body to over fifteen. Other countries, among them Ceylon, Sweden and the Philippines, have or have had planning agencies of approximately the same size, while Burma has had one with 18 members. The National Economic Development Board, established in the United Kingdom in 1962, included a total of 20 members, composed of ministers, chairmen of nationalized industries, industrialists, trade union leaders and college professors; while Ghana's National Planning Commission had 25 members drawn from public and private spheres of activity. Canada's Economic Council has 28 members: a full-time chairman, two full-time directors and 25 other members who are intended to represent different parts of the country and the economy. Italy's Planning Commission consists of 31 members of whom 13 are "experts" and the rest represent various economic interests; Korea's Economic Planning Board has seven ministers and about 25 other representatives; and Thailand's National Economic Development Board (NEDB) has 45 government and non-government representatives besides the Prime Minister, who is the Chairman, two Deputy Prime Ministers, who are Deputy Chairmen, and the Secretary General of the NEDB, who is an *ex officio* member of the Board and its Secretary. But the unchallenged record for size belongs to Indonesia's National Development Council, which had a membership variously reported to be from 74 to 83 persons drawn from regional and functional groups in the population.

NUMBER OF PLANNING TIERS

Most countries have been satisfied with one tier, in the form of a cabinet planning committee or one of mixed composition, between the cabinet and the technical planning level. Some have felt the need for a second tier. Thus, in Thailand there is the National Economic Development Board (NEDB) and the NEDB Executive Committee between Cabinet and Planning Office, while in Malaya, the National Development Planning Committee operates between the Cabinet and the Economic Committee of the Cabinet, on the one hand, and the Economic Planning Unit (i.e., the technical planning body) on the other. A few have even interposed three tiers between the Cabinet and the technical planning level. For instance, in what seems to be a superfluity of steps, planning proposals and plans in the Sudan move upward from an Economic Planning Secretariat in the Ministry of Finance to a second level, the National Technical Planning Committee (NTPC), a group of 17 permanent under-secretaries from various ministries, departments and boards. The responsibilities of the NTPC are to assess the country's resources, prepare draft development plans, recommend priorities for projects and the stages in which plans are to be carried out, and follow up the progress in implementing plans. The NTPC reports to a Development Committee, on a third level, under the chairmanship of the Minister of Finance and consisting of the ministers most concerned with development. The Committee's responsibilities are to consider the recommendations of the NTPC and report to an Economic Council, on a fourth level, composed in part of "neutral" ministers. The Council's responsibilities are to formulate economic policy, and approve plans and annual budgets. These must go upward again to the Council of Ministers, on a fifth level, to obtain final approval. The five levels through which planning decisions must proceed might constitute a greater problem than they do if the NTPC were not the key group. In practice, once a matter has cleared through this Committee, the approvals of the Development Committee and the Economic Council are generally given routinely.

In sharp contrast with this approach, some countries have tried to combine into one planning agency both the policy and the technical planning functions. Under this arrangement, technicians and politicians are joined in a single agency immediately below a cabinet or council of ministers. Thus, the High Planning Council in Turkey's State Planning Organization is headed by the Prime Minister and has three ministers selected by the Cabinet,[14] the Under-Secretary in charge of the planning secretariat and his three department heads. The Indian Planning Commission also is a mixed body of ministers and technicians. Its membership has varied from 7 to 11 members. The Prime Minister is Chairman and the Ministers of Finance and Planning are *ex officio* members. Between 1951 and 1956 there were three ministers who were members. The number was thereafter increased to four and, more recently, to five. There are usually three to seven other members, some from outside the Government. All but one of these have been full-time members.[15]

The main rationale for planning agencies with both technical and political representation is based on two assumptions, both of which have already been mentioned. The first is that it is desirable for a central planning agency to be independent of government. The second is that government has an obligation for maintaining its authority over the planning process. These conflicting purposes are not believed to be

[14] The ministers were not specified in the law setting up the State Planning Organization because Turkey was being governed at the time by a coalition Government and it was necessary to assure representation on the High Planning Council for each of the three parties in the coalition. It was correctly expected that ministers selected would reflect political alignments rather than planning requirements. Thus, the Minister of Finance, who next to the Prime Minister is the most important Minister in Turkey, was not selected as one of the first group of the three ministers to serve on the Council.

[15] Paranjape, H. K. *Planning Commission, A Descriptive Account*, pp. 17–19. In mid-1964, the Planning Commission consisted of the Prime Minister, who was the Chairman, a full-time Deputy Chairman, the Ministers of Planning, Finance and Home Affairs (formerly Deputy Chairman of the Commission) and six full-time members.

necessarily incompatible.[16] Indeed, they are considered to be reconciled in a planning agency with both technical and political representatives. At the same time, these agencies are supposed also to have the additional advantage of bringing about a confrontation of political and technical views within the planning agency

> to create a balance between the political and technical authorities, or rather to secure co-operation between politicians and technicians in the formulation and adoption of political decisions.[17]

Ministers and planning technicians in the planning agency are each supposed to contribute toward achieving this balance. The technicians supply the facts as they find them, letting the chips fall where they may, while the ministers provide their views based on political experience, thereby insuring that the final result adequately reflects both the technical and political aspects.

A cabinet planning committee composed only of ministers who control most public investment expenditures automatically provides in its membership direct liaison with the most important spending ministries for the purpose of co-ordinating planning activities. Adequate liaison with the technical planning body is obtained if the technical body acts as the secretariat of the cabinet planning committee, and if the person in charge of the technical planning body is appointed as the cabinet planning committee's secretary. But the presence of technicians (who are sometimes from outside the government) in a planning policy body makes it more difficult to insure liaison and co-ordination with other parts of government. In Turkey, where the technical members of the High Planning Council are the civil servants who run the technical planning body, the problem is minimal. The civil servants provide liaison with the technical planning body and the minister members link the Council with the Cabinet. Although it is an autonomous body, a somewhat similar arrangement is supposed to operate with Jordan's Development Board, because of the presence of ministers and civil servants as well as non-government representatives as members of the Board. In Iraq the Minister of Development, who was also a member of the mixed Development Board and whose Ministry contained the planning secretariat, used to provide such liaison as was possible at the

[16] See, for example, Salter, James Arthur. *Development of Iraq, A Plan of Action,* p. 98.

[17] Turkey. State Planning Organization. *Planning in Turkey, Summary of the First Five-Year Plan,* p. 5.

time to both the planning secretariat and the rest of the Government through his membership in the Cabinet. But among planning agencies with both technical and ministerial members, India has the most elaborate liaison system. The Government has gone to great lengths to counteract both the presence of outsiders as members of the Planning Commission and the Commission's location outside the mainstream of government administration.[18]

As with other planning agencies on the policy level with mixed membership, planning agencies with both political and technical members have been found to be wanting. In practice, attempts to merge the technical and political points of view in one agency "in order to balance them" have largely failed. Experience shows that a planning agency cannot be both autonomous and politically directed at the same time. The two purposes are, in fact, irreconcilable. It is unrealistic to suppose that technical factors can be put on an equal basis with political factors in the planning process. As one Indian economist put it,

> it has to be recognized that the preparation of a plan is itself, at least in part, a political process. A certain amount of exercise of

[18] A series of close links has been established between the Commission and the central ministries. Thus, the Prime Minister is Chairman of the Commission. Several ministers are members. The Secretary to the Cabinet, who as the highest civil servant in the administration and as Chairman of the Committee of Secretaries to the various ministries co-ordinates the work of all other government secretaries, is Secretary to the Commission. He is assisted by an Additional Secretary who devotes full time to the Commission's work. Finally, the Chief Economic Adviser to the Ministry of Finance has until recently been Economic Adviser to the Commission. Besides, by convention, members of the Commission who are not members of the Cabinet are usually invited to attend meetings of the Cabinet or its committees when proposals related to their respective fields of work are being considered. Important development proposals made by ministries are first considered by the Planning Commission before they are sent to the Cabinet. Similarly, whenever the Commission considers any matter which concerns other ministries, representatives of those ministries are associated with its work. Co-ordination between the Commission and Parliament is the responsibility of the Minister for Planning, who for a time was also Deputy Chairman of the Commission and, in effect, its operating head. Liaison with the states is obtained through the National Development Council, whose membership includes the Prime Minister of India, the chief ministers of all the states and the members of the Planning Commission. In addition three, more recently four, high-level Advisers on Programme Administration in the Commission, who operate as "touring ambassadors," maintain close contact with the states. Within the Commission itself, close relations between the members and the planning staff are insured because each member is in charge of specific areas of the planning secretariat's work. One technical member is responsible for agriculture, a second for education, a third for industry, a fourth for natural resources and a fifth for perspective planning. The Minister of Finance is in charge of the Commission's work in finance.

pressure and some compromises would inevitably affect the final shape of the plan. If the Planning Commission looks upon itself as a technical and advisory body, it can make an effort to make the examination of individual proposals and its total recommendations as objective as possible. On the basis of such objective recommendations, the appropriate political authority will arrive at final decisions which are practicable in political terms. However, if in one and the same authority, both aspects of the process are inextricably mixed, one or the other must suffer. Inevitably, it is the objective approach that suffers. Both the composition and the situation of the Indian Planning Commission have resulted in pushing the aspect of technical expertise and objective examination into the background. To all intents and purposes, in the preparation of plans and examination of schemes and projects, the Planning Commission and its organs appear to act on the level of political practicability.[19]

Nor is it realistic to assume that political authorities will long countenance technicians who assert their legal right to equality in any controversy with government ministers in a mixed planning agency on the policy level. When, for example, the three civil service technicians on Turkey's High Planning Council attempted it, they ended up by resigning from the Council and the Government. When the State Control Commission, one of two planning agencies in Ghana,

> consisted of an equal number of ministers and senior civil servants, it did not work satisfactorily, as in practice the latter had no way of getting their opinions on technical questions accepted.[20]

Even the technical members of the Indian Planning Commission, who are often eminent and highly respected individuals from outside Government, have shown a tendency to defer to the political members. Besides, the first Prime Minister of India was the key figure in the Commission. Where a difference arose between the political and technical viewpoints there was little question that within the Planning Commission,

> the Prime Minister not only arbitrated the alternatives which flow from the two sides, but that his overriding person could make 'agreement' where the issues have not actually been resolved.[21]

[19] Gadgil, D. R. *Planning and Economic Policy in India,* p. 101.
[20] United Nations Meeting of Experts on Administrative Aspects of National Development Planning. *Administration of Planning in Ghana,* p. 5.
[21] Malenbaum, Wilfred. "Who Does the Planning?" pp. 305–306.

The ineffectiveness of Ghana's State Control Commission made it necessary to change it into an interministerial body. In Turkey, consideration is being given to converting the High Planning Council into a cabinet planning committee. In India, also, sentiment has developed for separating the technical and political aspects of planning. Whatever the eventual outcome of the continuing debate, it has produced an awareness that the merger of political and technical viewpoints in one planning agency on the policy level secures neither independent objectivity nor government responsibility in planning. Indeed, the results finally reached in such an agency by political bargaining and negotiation often obscure what was originally considered to be technically desirable and confound attempts to fix responsibility. When everything goes well, everyone takes credit. But when things go wrong, the technicians blame the politicans and the politicians blame the technicians, with no one the wiser since the role played by each is buried in the archives of the planning agency. It then becomes plain that a government must assume ultimate responsibility for development and, hence, for planning. For this, there must be a clear division between the political and technical tiers. This brings us back to the point made at the beginning of this chapter. In most countries, a cabinet planning committee has been found to be the most effective means by which a government can exercise authority commensurate with its responsibility for planning development.

THE TECHNICAL PLANNING AGENCY

Where a separate planning agency on the policy level exists, provision must also be made for a group of planners on the technical level. This group, as we have seen, may be located in various places: in the office of a chief executive, in an old-line agency like finance or economic affairs, in a ministry of planning or in an autonomous planning agency. It may be headed by one man or several. In Pakistan, for example, the Planning Board was a three-man body composed of full-time members. Each member of the three-man Board was nominally responsible for supervising the day-to-day activities of designated sections of the Board. In theory, the members of the Board collectively made all major decisions. But the Board almost never met as a body and the Chairman, an exceptionally able senior civil servant with great prestige, was the *de facto* operating head of the agency. Later, when the Board became the

Planning Commission with the President as its Chairman, the Deputy Chairman assumed the prerogatives formerly exercised by the Chairman of the Board. Since the two regular members of the Board and, later, the Commission have always accepted the Chairman's and, later, the Deputy Chairman's pre-eminence, there has never been any problem about the relative position of each member. But in Colombia, where two of the four Council members worked full time and expected to supervise specific activities of the technical staff, serious problems developed because the Director of the technical staff felt he could not administer his organization efficiently with two additional, and nominally equal, supervisors at his elbow all the time. In India, the problem has not arisen although responsibility for running technical planning activities in the Planning Commission is divided among Commission members. But this was partly because the Deputy Chairman (until 1964), the Commission's operating head, was a busy man with many duties. He was responsible for the Commission's relations with Parliament as Minister for Planning, for the work of specific sections of the Commission's technical staff as a member of the Commission and, in addition, for the central Ministry of Labor and Employment, whose portfolio he held. But the pre-eminence of India's first Prime Minister was the most important reason why few problems arose from what superficially appeared to have been multiple direction of the Commission's technical planning activities. He was the effective head of the Commission and because of his personality, the other members were, in fact as in name, his subordinates. More recently, a new full-time Deputy Chairman assumed office. He has made it clear that he operates as the effective day-to-day head of the Planning Commission.

On the basis of the available experience, therefore, there is little to recommend a system which divides responsibility for directing a technical planning agency in a less developed country among several people. Collegiate executive groups do not work well in countries where personal leadership is the rule. Where, as in Pakistan and India, collegiate executive groups appear to have operated effectively, examination indicates that one member of the group was in fact the recognized head. But where, as in Colombia, the dominance of one of the group was not accepted by the others, it has led to dispersion of authority and conflict among members of the group.

The disadvantages of a group as the executive head for a technical planning agency must be widely apparent or suspected since one-man direction is by far the most common form. If the technical body is in a ministry, the head is generally either a minister or a subordinate. If it is an autonomous agency, its director or a subordinate usually heads the technicians. If the technicians are in a chief executive's office, one man is usually appointed as the head.

The question of what rank the head of a technical planning agency outside a ministry should have is one that has been much debated. In some countries, e.g., Pakistan and Indonesia, the operating head of the agency has the rank of minister without cabinet status. This may give some satisfaction to the one who possesses the title; it may also, as it does in Pakistan, insure that all important cabinet papers are made available to the head of the central planning agency and that he has an opportunity to comment on them and to present the planning agency's views at Cabinet meetings; [22] but it is doubtful whether it helps much in improving the standing of his agency. Indeed, a case can be made for the view that to put the head of a planning agency on the ministerial level weakens, not strengthens, his position vis-a-vis the other ministers. He needs no official rank if he draws his strength from the fact that he speaks to the ministers with the authority of the chief executive. In Pakistan and Indonesia, as in other countries, the position of the technical planning agency largely depends on the attitude of the Chief Executive toward it and the closeness of the relationship which the agency's operating head has established with the Chief Executive and his Cabinet.

Where a cabinet planning committee or mixed planning agency exists, the head of the technical planning agency should be its secretary and prepare its agenda, and the technical planning agency should be its secretariat. In the USSR, where the head of the *All-Union Gosplan* reports directly to the Council of Ministers, he always participates in the Council's economic deliberations. It is desirable, similarly, in mixed-economy countries, for the head of the technical planning agency to be invited to participate in cabinet discussions when they relate to planning matters.

Because of the close association which the head of a technical planning agency must have with a chief executive and his cabinet, it is much more important that he have the full confidence of the chief executive and know how to work well with ministers and heads of agencies than that he be an economist or a planning technician. He

---

[22] The same objectives, and more, can sometimes be achieved by designating the head of the central planning agency as the Economic Secretary of the Cabinet with responsibility for preparing its economic agenda.

need only know how to use the results produced by economists and planners and how to make them comprehensible and acceptable to the political authorities. There are economists and planning technicians who have the confidence of a chief executive and, more rarely, the co-operation of ministers and heads of agencies. Of course, when such a person is available, he can also head a technical planning agency. But well-trained economists and planning technicians are scarce, especially in less developed countries. Furthermore, the record unfortunately shows that the heads of technical planning agencies are expendable. When things go awry with plans or when a government changes, they are among the first to go. Some have even had their civil rights suspended, a few have been jailed, and one was executed. A question arises, therefore, whether it is not better for a planning technician, as well as for planning, if he seeks and holds the job next to the top one instead of the top job in a technical planning agency, leaving the top job to someone who is easier to replace. In some countries, e.g., Iran at one time, the head of the planning agency was primarily concerned with those tasks which required political contacts outside the agency.[23] While he engaged in discussions with ministers, politicians, businessmen and other persons and groups outside the agency, a technician was in charge of the technical aspects of plan preparation and execution within the agency. In this way, the holder of the top job acted as a buffer for the technician against the shafts which ministers and other politicians regularly aimed at the planning agency. There is, however, this difficulty in the way of widespread application of this formula: few planners have demonstrated the "passion for anonymity" required to forego the top job when the opportunity arose to get it.

SUMMARY AND CONCLUSIONS

The preparation and overseeing of national plans require machinery to carry out (1) procedures by which a plan's goals are approved and implemented and (2) the process by which a plan is prepared on the basis of the approved goals. The first set of tasks requires action on the political level, in most countries by the chief executive and his cabinet. The second set of tasks requires action on the technical level, usually by a body of technicians. In general, the more direct the connection between the political and technical levels, the better.

[23] Chile has a similar arrangement for its *Oficina Central de Planificación*.

Because the chief executive and cabinet of most mixed-economy countries are too overburdened to devote the time required by development planning, there is an increasing tendency toward establishing a planning committee of the cabinet as an intermediary group between a cabinet and a technical planning agency. The committee is generally headed by the chief executive and is composed of the ministers most concerned with development policy and the head of the central bank if he is responsible for monetary and credit policy. Some countries prefer to include in the committee's membership ministers who do not have large claims on investment resources, on the belief that this helps assure objective assessment of investment proposals submitted by spending ministries and agencies. But for several reasons, a committee with "neutral" ministers is likely to be less effective than one composed of ministers with the greatest stake in development.

A committee of the cabinet must be kept small if it is to operate efficiently. Other ministers can be invited to join committee meetings when subjects of direct concern to their ministries are being considered. It is important that the ministers themselves attend committee meetings, because if one minister begins to send a subordinate, other ministers are likely to follow suit—and the committee is likely to become a discussion group of civil servants without power to make basic decisions. Experience shows that in countries with a civil service tradition, a subministerial committee can perform a useful purpose in reviewing and criticizing proposals, but that it is an inadequate substitute for a cabinet planning committee.

It is important that a country's chief executive be the chairman of a cabinet planning committee. Although he may appoint a high official to act as vice-chairman for ordinary business, it is essential that the chief executive himself preside over committee meetings when major questions are discussed. If the top authorities do not have the necessary time to participate in major discussions, the country is unlikely to develop rapidly.

Some countries have tried planning bodies which combine ministers with members from outside a cabinet, but such planning bodies have generally been found to be less effective than cabinet planning committees. The inclusion of regional or provincial representatives, foreigners, legislators, and representatives of the public or business interests in planning agencies on the political level have generally inhibited close relationships between the agencies and their government authorities. This is because governments have been unwilling to entrust policy-making functions to outsiders who bear no public responsibility for governing a country. Because of this, it is preferable to obtain the participation of interested persons outside a cabinet in the planning process by setting them up in separate advisory groups.

The planning machinery in most countries has operated with only one level or tier, in the form of a cabinet planning committee or one of mixed composition, between the cabinet and the technical planning agency. But some operate with two or, with what seems to be a superfluity of steps, three tiers.

In contrast, other countries try to combine in one planning agency both policy and technical planning functions. Those who favor this kind of organization believe that it reconciles what would otherwise be incompatible objectives, i.e., a central planning agency's need for independence from political authorities and a government's obligation for maintaining its authority over the planning process. But a cabinet planning committee, composed only of ministers who control most public investment expenditures, automatically provides direct liaison with the most important spending ministries. Liaison with the technical planning body is obtained if the person in charge of the technical body acts as the cabinet planning committee's secretary. The introduction of technicians in a planning body, especially if they come from outside government, makes it more difficult to insure liaison and co-ordination with other parts of government.

Experience shows that a planning agency cannot be both autonomous and politically directed simultaneously. The two purposes are, in practice, irreconcilable. A government must assume ultimate responsibility for development and, hence, for planning, and this requires that there be a clear division between the political and technical planning levels.

Where a separate planning agency on the policy level exists, there must also be a group of planners on the technical level. This group may be located in one of several places. It may be headed by one man or several. A system which divides responsibility for directing a technical planning agency among several persons has little to recommend it. Experience shows that direction by one man is best.

The question of what rank this man should have has been much debated. But the question is usually unimportant since the status of the head of a technical planning agency is largely determined, not by his rank or title, but by the attitude of the chief executive toward him and the agency he directs. He need not be an economist or a planning technician. It is much more important that he have the full confidence of the chief executive and his ministers. And he needs to know how to use the results produced by economists and planners and how to make them comprehensible and acceptable to the political authorities. Well-trained economists and planners are scarce. Unfortunately, the heads of technical planning agencies are often made to bear the brunt when things go wrong. Due to the political perils of the job, it would appear better for the scarce planning technicians to hold the job next to the top one instead of the top job in a technical planning agency, leaving a buffer for the technicians, who would be free to concentrate on the technical aspects of planning for which only they are fitted by training and experience.

Chapter XV

Organization of a Central Planning Agency

It is tempting to 'solve' the administrative
tasks involved in planning by drawing and
redrawing organization charts.—Anon.

STAFFING DIFFICULTIES

THERE IS an acute shortage of trained and experienced planning
technicians and, as will be seen later, the shortage is exacerbated in
most countries by the way in which technicians are organized in central
planning agencies. Despite the establishment of United Nations' institutes in Africa, Asia and Latin America for training planners, as well as
the expansion of the World Bank's Economic Development Institute to
increase the number of planning personnel trained each year, the
shortage is not likely to be greatly alleviated in the immediate future. It
takes time to train planners and the demand for them is expanding
more rapidly than the supply can be increased.

Planning is a multidisciplinary process which requires many skills.
Technicians with a knowledge of mathematics, statistics, econometrics
and research techniques are essential to carrying out the planning
function. In addition, the planner should be well acquainted with the
political and administrative organization in the country in which he
works if he is to judge correctly the possibilities of implementing the
plans he prepares.[1]

Besides administrators who are necessary for co-ordination, central
planning agencies use many kinds of technicians, including accountants, agronomists, architects, engineers, physical and social scientists,
lawyers, educational experts, mathematicians, statisticians and even
physicians and dentists. These technicians can provide technical infor-

[1] Abdel-Rahman, I. H. and Ramzi, M. *Organizational and Administrative Aspects
of Development Planning*, p. 25.

mation and appraisals which are very useful in planning. But since the core of a central planning agency's work is to ascertain alternative choices for using resources, a task which is basically economic, a planning agency's greatest need is for economists. The establishment of a central planning agency also tends to accentuate the demand for economists in operating departments, ministries and agencies in a government. It is, therefore, the scarcity of qualified economists which is especially noticeable when a country attempts to plan.

Even when a central planning agency locates suitable economists and other specialists, it may be unable to recruit them or keep those who have been engaged. There may be several reasons for this. A position with a planning agency, especially when it is new, normally confers less prestige, power and opportunities for advancement than do comparable positions in operating organizations. Because of this, most technicians who want to work for a government prefer the greater security and superior status of regular government jobs, especially since a planning agency's salaries and personnel policies are often no better than those in other parts of government.

Nor are planning agencies able to compete successfully for personnel with autonomous public corporations or private firms. Technicians in many countries prefer, as a matter of principle, not to work for government. Some specifically object to working for a central planning agency, especially if it becomes evident that its proposals are largely disregarded by a government. But even where technicians have no aversion to working for a government or a planning agency, they can frequently earn more in private industry or in autonomous public corporations than in a planning agency. In Pakistan, for example, the Planning Board followed cumbersome civil service rules for establishing positions and for selecting, training and promoting personnel which seriously impeded the acquisition and retention of qualified technicians. Under these rules, salaries were determined on the basis of seniority instead of merit or performance. The salaries which the Board offered well-trained candidates without seniority were not high enough to compete with those paid by private industry, autonomous entities or international agencies and attempts to get government approval for higher salaries met with little success.[2] The Iraqi Development Board at first was able to obtain a staff of well-qualified technicians by paying higher wages than those prevailing in the rest of the government. But

[2] Waterston, Albert. *Planning in Pakistan*, p. 22.

when the Board was reorganized in 1953, Iraqi employees were incorporated into the regular civil service and salaries were reduced accordingly. This action induced staff resignations and resulted in reduced efficiency. In Nigeria, low starting salaries and low-level positions have made it difficult to attract and retain competent economists and planning technicians in regional and federal planning agencies.

Sometimes a central planning agency is set up on a temporary basis. When this happens it finds it especially difficult to acquire a qualified staff. Pakistan's Planning Board was greatly handicapped because it was a temporary organization for the first three years of its existence in an environment in which civil servants considered job security, seniority, rank and status to be of prime importance. Because it was a temporary agency, the Board could not offer jobs with permanent civil service status and had to obtain people either on short-term contracts or on loan from other agencies.[3]

Central planning agencies have generally found that if they are not to attract only "the rich, the crooked or the incompetent," they must be exempted from the unduly restrictive civil service regulations which prevail in many countries and pay salaries above those paid to regular government employees. But since it has not been easy to change the rules, planning agencies have often had to resort to subterfuge to acquire competent personnel. A central bank or other autonomous agency may be prevailed upon to put, or retain, a planning agency's employees on its payroll with higher salaries than those paid in government or to pay a part of their salaries; persons from other government agencies may be temporarily assigned from their regular jobs to the planning agency; temporary or part-time employees may be engaged; or full-time employees may be appointed to paid posts on committees or permitted to hold second jobs elsewhere.

---

[3] *Ibid.* A temporary planning agency is also undesirable for reasons other than personnel difficulties. Indeed, a temporary planning agency is an anomaly because planning is a continuous process. Indonesia's Eight-Year Development Plan was drawn up by a temporary National Planning Council assisted by *ad hoc* staffs of civil servants in each operating department and working parties. When their tasks were completed there was no planning body left to review the Plan and make necessary recommendations to the authorities for appropriate action. Norway has found that its practice of using temporary planning secretariats to formulate multi-annual plans "is not a satisfactory system. Problems connected with long-term planning are so numerous and complicated that it is essential that there be a permanent organization to attend to and take the responsibility for this work." (Norway. Royal Norwegian Ministry of Finance. *Extension of Economic Planning,* p. 4.)

' These ways of staffing a planning agency are hardly ideal. While the use of part-time, borrowed or temporary personnel may be justified occasionally as an expedient to supplement a regular staff, a central planning agency must have a strong nucleus of regular, full-time technicians to insure planning continuity. In some countries, e.g., Colombia and Greece, the only way such a nucleus could be obtained was by engaging technicians by contract, a system of employment which circumvents civil service salary regulations. In other countries, e.g., Israel, more than the usual number of senior positions were established and exempted from restrictive civil service regulations. Only rarely do governments accept the need for central planning agencies to establish salary levels and other conditions of employment which will attract qualified technicians in sufficient number. When salary levels are high enough to attract competent personnel, other factors may intervene to interfere with the building up of a body of qualified technicians. In the Philippines, for example, salaries paid by the National Economic Council (NEC)

> are generally on a much higher level than those in government corporations. . . . There is every reason to expect, therefore, that the NEC has among the best brains of the country on its staff. Yet, the very wide gap between NEC salary scales compared to the rates obtaining generally in the government service has been a source of trouble for personnel management in the agency. Positions in the NEC have been subject to political bargaining. The result is that, with respectable exceptions, technical jobs are now held by persons whose main qualification is political backing.[4]

Governments with well-developed civil services find it desirable, as part of the regular civil service rotation system, to add to the regular staff of a planning agency personnel with general administrative experience. For example, out of 49 staff members in Japan's Economic Planning Agency, 28 civil servants seconded from economic ministries were assigned for two-year periods.[5] While many positions in a planning agency require technical training, administrators are also needed. In the Indian Planning Commission, for example, co-ordination work is often done by general administrators. Experience has shown that such general administrators are as useful as specialists for management and

[4] Philippine Delegation. *Administration of Economic Planning and Programs in the Philippines,* p. 3.
[5] Abdel-Rahman, I. H. and Ramzi, M. *Organizational and Administrative Aspects of Development Planning,* p. 10.

administrative jobs, and for some technical jobs.[6] In Pakistan, civil servants with general administrative experience who are scheduled for assignment with the Planning Commission may go through a period of technical instruction at a university at home or abroad before taking up their duties with the Commission. Rotation is considered desirable in Pakistan because the Planning Commission is believed to offer too circumscribed an opportunity for a permanent career. Even more important, rotation of civil servants helps institutionalize planning in the government administration by providing the Planning Commission with personnel who have close connections in other parts of Government and by providing operating organizations with civil servants who have acquired planning experience in the Commission.

In the United Kingdom's semiautonomous National Economic Development Council (NEDC), the inclusion of some civil servants seconded by government departments in a staff largely drawn from industry and universities was considered an asset because it provided NEDC with people who are directly linked to the regular government administration and to the civil servants who are responsible for its operation. A Venezuelan decree [7] classifies officials anywhere in the Government who perform programing or planning work as planning officials and provides for their rotation between the central planning agency and the operating organization; while in France, the fact that some staff members of the Commissariat Général du Plan are only temporarily detached from their regular departments is considered to provide assurance to every one that

> the Plan is not the citadel of a clan or a group, but a meeting place where all people are welcome.[8]

LEGAL AUTHORITY

Some public administration experts believe that a central planning agency which has been established by statute has advantages over one that has been created by executive decree or resolution. Thus, a study prepared by the International Institute of Administrative Sciences for the United Nations contends:

[6] UN. ECAFE. *Planning Machinery in India*, p. 16.
[7] No. 492.
[8] Massé, Pierre. "French Methods of Planning," p. 3.

Since planning and economic development involve the allocation and use of scarce resources, they usually result in political pressures from various groups which seek to maintain or increase their economic advantages. Establishment of the development organization by law offers some protection against selfish political pressures.[9]

But the available evidence does not support this view. Thus, on the one hand, Iran's Plan Organization, which was duly established by statute, was for a long time subjected to unremitting political pressure to which it eventually surrendered; while on the other hand, India's Planning Commission, which was set up by a resolution of the Government, has proved itself well able to resist political pressure. Nor does the manner of establishment seem to have much bearing on the status of a central planning agency. The Indian Planning Commission has enjoyed great prestige while the Philippines' National Economic Council and Thailand's National Economic Development Board, which are statutory bodies, have yet to win full acceptance by their respective Governments. If a central planning agency is supported by its government, the way it was set up appears to matter little; if it does not have that support, it is unlikely to be helped much because it was created by law.

Planning is a dynamic process involving many imponderables which only become apparent in operation. As the Indian experience shows, a planning agency which is not bound by legal rigidities can adapt itself easily to changing circumstance. In contrast, a legally constituted planning agency may lack flexibility since it must operate within the confines provided by law.[10] If the law has been couched in broad terms, this is not a serious handicap. But in some countries, laws creating central planning agencies go into such great detail that they unduly restrict the agency's freedom of action. For example, the law which established Costa Rica's Planning Office [11] not only spelled out the Office's organizational subdivisions and minutely defined their functions and interrelationships within the Planning Office; [12] it also specified that the Office's Department of Long and Medium Term

[9] Stone, Donald C. and Associates. *National Organization for the Conduct of Economic Development Programs*, p. 46.

[10] Natarajan, B. *Plan Coordination in India*, p. 4.

[11] Asamblea Legislativa Decreta, "Ley de Planificación," p. 413.

[12] Thus, Article 12 of the law provides that the Department of Annual Plans in the Planning Office must present the Office's Director with an annual plan not later than January 31 each year.

Plans must prepare ten-year and four-year development plans, that they must be rolling plans and that the ten-year plan must be based on a "permanent study of the supply and demand of manpower." [13]

THE ORGANIZATION CHART

Whenever possible, the internal organization of a central planning agency should not be fixed in detail in the law establishing the agency. Experience reveals that the initial concept of a central planning agency's internal structure rarely endures for long. In a surprisingly large number of cases, it is not put into practice from the start. Changed circumstances, the progress of planning or the replacement of a director frequently make it necessary to alter an agency's organization. Where the organizational setup has been fixed by law, this is not easy to accomplish. It is therefore preferable to leave to administrative determination what the detailed internal organization should be at any time.

Changes in organization, both minor and major, are so common in most planning agencies that it is hard to keep organization charts up to date. Shifts in the structure of power—within a government, in a planning agency or in both—may bring about basic realignments in command which are only inadequately reflected in an agency's chart of organization. In practice, therefore, few organization charts accurately represent the actual form of organization of a central planning agency.[14] What is more important, charts do not show how personnel are distributed, whether the agencies work and, if they do, how they work. In the UAR's National Planning Commission, for example, a separate evaluation unit was unable to produce useful progress reports. It was therefore incorporated in the annual planning section, which was best able to compare results with plan targets. Actually, evaluation and progress reports were first made in each sectoral unit of the Planning Commission and then combined into a consolidated report by the evaluation unit. In the same way, both the form and function of other parts of the planning agency have evolved until they differ substantially from those included in the original law. The statute which

[13] *Ibid.* Articles 7 and 8.
[14] This is why only a few central planning agency charts are reproduced in the Appendices. Those shown are intended mainly to be illustrative rather than precise statements of organization.

created Turkey's State Planning Organization provided it with three Departments: Economic Planning, Social Planning and Coordination. But from the beginning, the Economic Planning Department has dominated the activities of the State Planning Organization. There is, in fact, no real division among the three Departments, and technicians in Social Planning and Coordination usually join forces with those in Economic Planning in working parties dealing with all problems.

The kind of organization which a central planning agency has depends on the kind of planning it does, the extent to which it engages in executive activity, and on requirements which are peculiar to the country concerned. The more detailed the planning, the more complex and unwieldy the organization must be, and the more inefficient it is bound to become. A plan including targets for the production of everything from tractors to vest buttons, as is sometimes the case in the socialized countries, needs a more elaborate organization than if it were limited to government action in a few key sectors, as is frequently the case in mixed-economy countries. If a plan lays out details of projects and programs, organization has to be more elaborate than if it simply formulates key policies and relies on operating organizations to work out details; more elaborate if the planning agency supervises execution of the plan, or carries out projects and programs, than if it limits itself to advisory function; and more elaborate if the agency prepares regional plans, or has to integrate them into a national plan, than if it does neither. The organization will also reflect special responsibilities which a planning agency may have to prepare, or supervise special programs, e.g., community development or village aid.

The size of a central planning agency's staff also depends on the kind of planning involved and the responsibilities assumed. Thus, the number of persons employed in central planning agencies in socialized countries is, on the average, much greater than in the mixed-economy countries. Bulgaria and Hungary, for example, have planning agencies with staffs of about 500 each, while Poland's numbers almost 800. Such large planning offices are to be expected in socialized countries since planning there is considerably more detailed and planning offices are more involved in executive activity than in the mixed-economy countries. Yugoslavia is again the exception among the socialized countries. When planning in that country followed the Soviet model, some 700 people were employed by its central planning agency; now that the planning agency is only an advisory body and draws up plans in broad outline, which republics, districts, communes and enterprises are expected to carry out, the number employed in the central planning agency amounts to about 180.

In the mixed economies, Iran's Plan Organization has had a force of about 1,000 because it implemented as well as formulated projects and plans. India's Planning Commission employed about 1,130 persons in 1964, not only because it is responsible for co-ordinating state and regional plans into the national plan, but also because it has frequently gone beyond the limits of an advisory body. Most central planning agencies in mixed-economy countries have staffs which range from 25 to 100 persons. The French Commissariat Général du Plan has a total planning staff of about 100 (of which 40 to 50 are professionals) but it relies heavily on other government agencies for many services. In contrast, Argentina's National Development Council, which carries out a considerable amount of research and also prepares sectoral programs, has a staff of about 375 persons.

Only about one-third to one-half of a central planning agency's staff is generally classified as professional, the rest being administrative and other supporting personnel. Among the professionals in the central planning agencies of the less developed countries, few can be considered to be adequately trained and experienced. A planning agency with 50 to 60 persons listed as professionals is fortunate if it can count on five or ten individuals who are qualified by training or experience to carry out planning tasks with reasonable competence. Many an accountant, lawyer, engineer or physicist in central planning agencies performs the tasks of an economist. Some do it well, but most do not.

Because of differences in approach to planning and in circumstances in each country, there is no standard organization chart for central planning agencies which can be used as a universal model. At one extreme, at least in mixed-economy countries, is the organization chart of Iran's Plan Organization (Appendix V), which includes bureaus for supervising and following up plan implementation, financial budgeting and control of development expenditures, and engineering review of projects and programs, as well as planning; at the other extreme is the exceedingly flexible organization of the French *Commissariat Général du Plan,* which essentially comprises three small task forces dealing with (1) general economic and planning problems, (2) financial problems related to planning, and (3) regional planning. In the Philippines, the National Economic Council has a secretariat divided into an Office of Statistical Coordination and Standards (to promote an orderly and efficient statistical system), an Office of Foreign Aid

Coordination (to co-ordinate foreign aid and technical assistance) and an Industrial Development Center (to assist in the establishment of new industrial enterprises and in increasing productivity in existing plants), as well as an Office of Planning (Appendix VI). In Morocco, the Division of Economic Coordination and Planning was more a central statistical office than a planning agency (Appendix VII); while in Mexico, a Bureau of Planning and a Bureau of Public Investment, existing at the same level in the Department of the Presidency have created

> a curious dichotomy . . . as the result of the coexistence of two parallel agencies independently occupied with two parts of what is essentially a single whole: national planning and the management of public sector investment.[15]

Nevertheless, most central planning agencies have basically similar organizations which include units, separately or in combination, for (1) planning, (2) progress reporting and plan evaluation, (3) co-ordination of plan formulation and execution, (4) technical assistance, (5) public relations and (6) administration.

The part concerned with planning is the heart of the organization. It is generally divided vertically (or sectorally) into sections dealing with specific sectors of the economy, and horizontally (or functionally) into sectors dealing with macro-economic and aggregative planning problems. The number of vertical sections varies with the importance attached in different countries to specific economic sectors or branches. The UAR's National Planning Commission has eighteen. The Indian Planning Commission has ten (Appendix VIII); Pakistan's Planning Commission has eight (Appendix IX); Ceylon's planning agency has only three. In the socialized economies, where heavy industry is important, industry is likely to be subdivided into sections dealing with ferrous and nonferrous metallurgical industries, mechanical construction and chemicals; fisheries are combined with industry in Portugal and with agriculture in Tunisia; in Yugoslavia tourism constitutes a separate section; and so on.

As previously indicated, authorities agree that operating organizations are primarily responsible for formulating sectoral programs and a central planning agency for reconciling them with each other and for integrating them into an aggregative plan. The establishment of sec-

---

[15] Wionczek, Miguel S. "Incomplete Formal Planning: Mexico," p. 166.

toral sections in a central planning agency therefore calls for a small staff of specialists to do work which operating organizations cannot or should not do. Specialists in operating organizations almost always look at problems from the limited point of view of their own sector, while specialists in a central planning agency generally take a broader, national point of view. If there is close co-operation and collaboration between the technicians in the sectoral units of the planning agency and the operating organizations, both views can be harmonized. Otherwise, differences can and frequently do lead to duplication of effort. In the Indian Planning Commission, for example, the sectoral sections are supposed to collect and analyze data required to help formulate sectoral policies and programs. They are also supposed to keep in close contact with their counterparts in the various ministries and with the various departments in the States to assure a constant exchange of technical knowledge and information about policies and programs.[16] Yet the view has been expressed that the sectoral sections in the Planning Commission sometimes duplicate the work in the central ministries and in state Governments, thereby divesting the ministries and states of a sense of responsibility for programing and for supervising execution in their respective fields.[17] The same thing could be said about the central planning agencies in other countries.

The functional sections have the task of combining and reconciling the sectoral programs which operating organizations are supposed to produce with the assistance of the specialists in the central planning agency's sectoral sections. They also make

> estimates of the value of total production in the economy; the flow of income to business enterprises, consumers, and the government; anticipated expenditures for goods and services by consumers, private business enterprises, and the government; the capacity of the economic system as a whole to supply the quantities of goods and services the three groups will wish to buy; and the capacity of the country's foreign earnings to finance the purchases the three groups will wish to make abroad. . . . [They make] estimates of changes in fiscal, monetary, and foreign exchange control policies on the aggregate demand for goods and services.[18]

One section may prepare long-term, medium-term and annual plans or there may be separate sections for each. In India, Pakistan and some

---

[16] Natarajan, B. *Plan Coordination in India*, p. 15.
[17] Gadgil, D. R. *Planning and Economic Policy in India*, pp. 107–108.
[18] Hagen, Everett (ed). *Planning Economic Development*, pp. 339–340.

other countries, a separate section prepares the long-term or perspective plans. There is also an increasing tendency to place manpower problems in a section of its own in keeping with the greater attention which planners are now giving to these problems. The Colombian and Honduran central planning agencies, in common with some others, have sections responsible for physical planning of urban and rural development. Where an agency engages in research, there may be a special research section. The UAR's National Planning Commission has two research units, one for Economic Research, the second for Operations Research.

Where a central planning agency has jurisdiction over the collection, arrangement and publication of government statistics, it will generally have a separate statistical section or division, with subunits, to carry out this function. In Tunisia, however, the central planning office in the Ministry of Planning and Finance chose to distribute the 150 members of the central statistical staff among its planning units. This approach may make it easier for each unit to control the statistical work for the economic sector with which it is concerned, but it greatly increases the need for, and difficulty of, co-ordinating all statistical activities. Even where there is an independent central statistical office, there may be a small statistical section in the planning agency to evaluate or regroup statistical data for planning purposes or to conduct quick surveys. The Indian Planning Commission, for example, has a Statistics and Surveys Division for these purposes. There may be advantages in having a few statisticians attached to a central planning agency to deal with short-range statistical estimations. They can collect information from other entities, including the central statistical office, and make analyses required by planners. Such an arrangement leaves the central statistical office free to continue its longer-term statistical programs without frequent interruptions from planners for *ad hoc* investigations and interpretations. But a statistical section of this kind in a central planning agency is likely to be more useful at a later than at an early planning stage. It is important, in any case, that the field of operation of the statistics section be clearly delimited. If it assumes too many functions, it may end up duplicating or usurping the work of a central statistical office.[19]

In some circles, there exists a strong conviction that the traditional

---

[19] This is avoided in India's Planning Commission by having the Director of the separate Central Statistical Office act, *ex officio*, as Chief of the Statistics and Surveys Division.

administrative structure of many governments in less developed countries usually has been oriented toward economic action, and, as a consequence, that this has retarded social planning. Thus, the Economic Commission for Asia and the Far East (ECAFE) has concluded that

> the persistence of the economic-biased machinery [in ECAFE countries] has tended to obstruct social development planning.[20]

This belief, shared by a number of countries, has led some to set up separate social planning entities within their central planning apparatus to redress what they considered to be an imbalance between social and economic development planning. At one time, for example, Burma established a Social Planning Commission as well as an Economic Planning Commission and, in Honduras, a Division of Social Planning was set up alongside a Division of Economic Planning in the central planning agency of that country. Iran and the Philippines also have established social planning units separately from economic planning units in their central planning agencies. A Social Planning Department, as well as an Economic Planning Department, was included on the same organizational level in Turkey's State Planning Organization because it was believed that planning for social projects and programs involved inherently different techniques from economic planning (Appendix X).

But the division between social and economic planning has proved to be an artificial one. In practice, it is difficult or impossible to distinguish between the two. Decisions made in economic planning generally determine results in the social field. Thus, if a target to increase production by, say, 8 per cent per annum is set in a plan, the resources required to achieve such a high target, and hence the resources remaining for social programs, are largely predetermined.

If a central planning agency is entrusted with the co-ordination of technical assistance, this function is almost always carried out by a special section. In most central planning agencies, a progress reporting and plan evaluation section is generally separated from a planning section. In Pakistan, for example, it was set up as an independent section; while in Turkey the function was included in a Coordination Department with three sections, one to follow up the implementation of plans, another to co-ordinate public and private plan execution, and

[20] UN. ECAFE. "The Interrelationships Between Social and Economic Development Planning," p. 21.

the third to recommend administrative, financial and legal measures to facilitate plan implementation. Tunisia has a similar form of organization, with an office for plan supervision and co-ordination (*Sous Direction du Contrôle du Plan*) set apart from the office concerned with the drafting of plans (*Direction du Plan*). Those who advocate separating progress reporting and plan evaluation from the planning function within a central planning agency believe it is important that planners should not be asked to report on, and evaluate the progress of, their own plans. But experience indicates that evaluation units separated from planners usually do not have enough knowledge of the plan to evaluate its progress effectively. In the UAR, for example, a separate evaluation unit set up in the central planning agency was eventually combined with the planning section because the planners were found to be best able to relate to the plan data received from operating organizations on the progress of their projects and programs.

With the growing interest in regional planning, central planning agencies are increasingly establishing a section concerned with the co-ordination of regional planning. India has for many years had a Programme Administration Division which acts as a secretariat for the three or four Advisors for Programme Administration whose responsibility it is to assist States in their planning activities and maintain liaison between the Planning Commission in the Central Government and the planning bodies in the states. Several of the emerging countries in Africa, including the Malagasy Republic, Mali and Senegal, also have sections in their central planning agencies which are responsible for co-ordinating regional with national plans. Like India, Madagascar and Senegal use touring representatives from their central planning agency to maintain close liaison with planning bodies in the regions.

Finally, all central planning agencies have an administrative section which performs the usual housekeeping functions for the agency. This section may also include units concerned with publications and public relations.

If a central planning agency composed of a series of interdependent functional and sectoral units is to perform satisfactorily and meet its planning deadlines, the activities of the various units must be co-ordinated and scheduled in accordance with a strict timetable. It is not unusual to find central planning agencies in which one section knows little about what other sections are doing. Two or more sections may send questionnaires on the same subject to other government offices or to an industry within a short period of time without being aware of the duplication. A system may not have been established to make available or even call attention to information obtained by one section to the others. As a result, much existing data needed to fill gaps in knowledge go unused. Duplication, wasted effort and the presentation of data in noncomparable forms are frequent. For example, in one Latin American country, the plan-frame included tables prepared by different sections of the central planning agency, some of which were in current prices and others in constant prices.

For effective planning, there is need to insure that basic production, income, investment, revenue, population and other data used by one section of a planning agency are the same or consistent with those used by other sections; that projections produced by one section are reconcilable with those produced by other sections; and that financial and physical targets are synchronous. For this purpose, there must be frequent meetings and consultations among the heads of the various units in a central planning agency. It may be desirable for a planning agency to set up a "consistency committee," composed of the chiefs of units engaged in substantive planning, with the task of achieving internal consistency in basic data and approach to planning. Such a committee is used with considerable success in Pakistan's Planning Commission. Pakistan's consistency committee not only attempts to insure that uniform basic data are used in all parts of the Planning Commission; it also produces preliminary evaluations of progress and other reports providing data for projections made by the various sections of the Commission.

Many central planning agencies operate on an *ad hoc* basis and unforeseen "rush jobs" frequently intervene to interrupt the regular course of work. Few planning agencies, even those which have existed for a long time, operate in accordance with well-defined operating procedures. Worksheets and other basic source materials are rarely maintained for reference purposes, filing systems are inadequate and even such a simple matter as getting copies of an important compilation of statistics may become a major task for heads of sections. There is little or no follow-up on matters of importance either inside or outside the planning agency because no one may have been made responsible for this. Liaison with other parts of government may be haphazard and personality problems, inevitably encountered in every organization, may make it impossible for appropriate liaison and co-ordination between a planning agency and other government offices to operate effectively.

There is, therefore, much need for "planning the planning" in central planning agencies. But the greatest need in most central planning agencies is for central co-ordination by a high official whose primary responsibility it is to perform this function. In many countries, the director of the planning agency attempts to do this job. The heads of sections, even at the lowest levels, may report directly to him, especially if there are vacancies in the upper echelons of the agency. Since the director of a planning agency has many responsibilities, coordination is frequently inadequate. In Indonesia, for example, the National Planning Bureau for the first year and a half of its existence was

> a kind of headless monster. General direction and co-ordination were provided by the Minister of Finance, Dr. Sumitro, who had been designated by the Prime Minister as co-ordinator of the Planning Bureau. Because of the wide range of his responsibilities, however, Dr. Sumitro was unable to give continuous attention to the affairs of the Bureau.[21]

In Pakistan, also, activities of the Planning Board and, later the Planning Commission, were poorly co-ordinated because the operating head of the planning agency could not, in the absence of a "chief of staff," cope with the task and also discharge his other obligations. In Thailand, as in Pakistan, vacancies in the upper levels of the central planning agency aggravated the problem of co-ordination. At one time, Thailand's National Economic Development Board (NEDB) included a Technical Cooperation Office, a Central Statistical Office and a National Income Office, as well as a Planning Office. But the post of Planning Director had not been filled and all section heads in the Planning Office reported directly to the Secretary General of the NEDB or to one of his two Deputies. Only the Secretary General made an attempt at co-ordinating the work of the sections in the Planning Office. Since he also had at least nominal supervisory responsibility over the three other offices in the NEDB, served on the NEDB Executive Committee and had to carry out various other time-consuming tasks, co-ordination within the Planning Office was weak.

THE TASK FORCE APPROACH

The typical central planning agency starts operating with an organization chart which provides for the familiar arrangement of sections

[21] Higgins, Benjamin. *Economic Development, Principles, Problems, and Policies,* p. 734.

along functional and sectoral lines. But the organizational pattern is likely to reflect what the first director and his advisers consider ideal, rather than one which can be staffed immediately. Since planning talent is very scarce, attempts to fill vacancies are generally haphazard and only partially successful. Positions are filled whenever suitable technicians can be obtained, not necessarily in the order of priority dictated by planning requirements. For some units, only candidates for low-level positions may be engaged; for others, only a chief may be found. Some units may have only one or two technicians, some may have none, and others may have more than enough to get the unit's work done in time. Even when some units are individually under-staffed, poor definition of their respective roles or lack of adequate internal co-ordination may lead to duplication of effort so that, taken as a whole, more people than necessary are employed in getting a job done. Thus, overstaffing and understaffing may exist side by side in the same agency. In India, for example,

> there is a view within the Planning Commission as much as outside that some sections, if not the Commission as a whole, are overstaffed. This may be true to a degree, but taking all factors into account, . . . the Commission is probably not . . . over-expanded. . . .[22]

Indeed, it has been estimated that nearly 20 per cent of the Commission's posts are vacant because of the shortage of qualified personnel.[23]

But with a total staff of 1,000, of whom, well over a third are professionally trained, India's central planning agency is incomparably better off than most planning agencies. In many countries, the planning agency has only a handful of qualified technicians who cannot operate effectively unaided by outside technical assistance. In Nigeria, the central planning agency had a staff of only nine Nigerian civil servants, mostly very young and inexperienced, when the National Development Plan was being prepared, for the most part, by three foreign advisers.[24] When Ghana's Seven-Year Plan was being formulated, the Ghanaian staff of the Office of the Planning Commission included only four senior civil servants with adequate qualifications

[22] Venkatasubbiah, H. *Hindu Weekly Review*, p. 10.
[23] *Ibid.*
[24] United Nations Meeting of Experts on Administrative Aspects of National Development Planning. *Administration of Planning in Nigeria*, p. 3.

who were reinforced by no less than 16 foreigners obtained through a variety of national and international technical assistance agencies.[25] Thirty Afghans work in Afghanistan's Ministry of Planning, but most of the significant work is carried out by 20 foreign and international advisers. Pakistan's Planning Commission, like India's, has an elaborate organization chart with a large number of sections and subsections, but they have been lightly manned because the Commission has been unable to staff them adequately. Foreign advisers were largely responsible for preparing Pakistan's First Five Year Plan and, to a somewhat lesser extent, for preparing the Second Plan. After more than a decade, the Commission still has need for foreign technical assistance. Latin American central planning agencies generally have only a small complement of technicians who are distributed more or less according to a table of organization with only one or two men per section and often with no staff in some sections.

Frequently, the shortage of planners, which is real, is made to appear greater than it is because of the size and complexity of the organization chart. An agency with many sections naturally requires a larger and more specialized staff, and is therefore likely to have more vacancies than one with fewer sections. This can give an impression that the agency with the more elaborate organization chart is more seriously understaffed than the one with the smaller and simpler organization, even if the first agency has more technicians than the second. The larger agency may, moreover, be less effective than the smaller because its staff is more specialized and dispersed. It may be working on many more subjects than the smaller planning agency but, because of inadequate staffs in many sections, the end results may be less timely and hence less useful than the output of a smaller and more concentrated staff. There may, therefore, be virtues in keeping a central planning agency small and its organization simple, especially at the beginning. This has been Mexico's experience:

> Our country's experience in the matter of State investment had demonstrated the advisability of not creating large scale agencies with an excess of staff when they have to deal with definite problems which, nevertheless, have great repercussion on the public sector or on the national economy. There are great advantages in starting an agency in a modest way, with a small technical

[25] United Nations Meeting of Experts on Administrative Aspects of National Development Planning. *Administration of Planning in Ghana*, p. 9.

and administrative staff, and, particularly, with specific tasks which although apparently of limited scope at first, may, with experience, contemplate further steps. This is exactly the experience gained by the Federal Government in: (a) determining the appropriate level of public investment, bearing in mind the pertinent necessities and the available funds; (b) evaluating investment projects in order to determine their economic and social value; (c) coordinating different investments and according them priority in terms of funds and needs; (d) formulating the annual and six-year investment programs of the State, adjusting them to the trends of the national economy.[26]

In Mexico's case, planning has been limited to the public sector. But the experience has been the same in France, which plans comprehensively for a well-developed economy. In that country, it will be recalled, the size of the professional staff in the central planning agency is purposely limited to 40 or 50 persons. The organization chart of the Office of the Commissioner for the Plan originally provided for divisions along the usual functional and sectoral lines. However, the Commission has found that best results can be obtained from its small staff, not by dispersing it into sectoral and functional sections according to the prevailing stereotype for central planning agencies, but by consolidating it into three major task forces dealing with national planning, the financial aspects of planning and regional planning. By setting up a list of priority subjects for each task force and concentrating its efforts on the most important jobs first (as well as by delegating as much work as possible to operating, research and other outside entities), the Commissariat has been able to produce effective plans on schedule.

It may be that what the French planners do because they want to keep their staff small, most planning agencies would find profitable to do because they have no choice but to have small staffs. Rational use of available personnel in the agencies of many countries is often made difficult because of planners' preconceptions about what constitutes the proper organization for a central planning agency. As a result of these preconceptions, basically similar organizational structures are set up in countries which are basically dissimilar in their stage of development, the character of their planning problems and the rate at which their planning needs change. They also encourage the acquisition and dispersal of specialists into sections prescribed by an organization chart

---

[26] Salinas Lozano, Raul. "Comision de Inversiones," pp. 10–11.

to work on subjects which may or may not be of immediate use. The need in developing countries is for organizational flexibility to meet differing and changing situations. The virtue of the French system is that it embodies the flexibility of organization and mobility of staff required for the effective use of a small staff in varying circumstances.

If other countries adopted this approach, the number of task forces and the assigned subject areas might be different from country to country, depending in part on what was considered important and in part on how many competent leaders were available to head the task forces. Conceivably, four or five task forces might be better than three in some cases, although in an agency with a small staff even four task forces may disperse technicians unduly. There are advantages in having fewer task forces. The smaller their number, the greater the stimulation for planners to identify and concentrate on the highest planning priorities, postpone less important items and eliminate unnecessary frills. The fewer the task forces, also, the more compact the staff; hence, the smaller the need for supervisory, co-ordinative and administrative personnel and the easier to use the services of foreign consultants and technicians in training and advising the staff.

Many conventionally organized planning agencies have been driven by necessity to combine technicians and specialists from different sections into working parties to concentrate on specific rush jobs. But this practice has generally been viewed as a temporary expedient. Nor has it always worked well since it required the disruption of existing administrative arrangements and made it necessary for specialists to work outside their own fields. Experience has shown that for a task force to operate effectively, it must be composed of individuals who are capable of working in a variety of fields. This calls for personnel and organizational arrangements which differ materially from those prevailing in most central planning agencies. Thus, if technicians are to work in task forces without functional specialization in the formal organizational sense, many more general economists and other generalists must be engaged than sectoral or other specialists. A few specialists may be needed, but in the task force approach it is the generalists who have to acquire some degree of competence in several fields as may be required. The planning agency which employs task forces must also have a much more flexible organization than the conventional type, with a simple hierarchical structure placing stress on group activity and mobility.

SUMMARY AND CONCLUSIONS

There is a world-wide lack of qualified planners which is likely to persist for a long time. Even when a central planning agency can locate suitable candidates, it often does not succeed in recruiting them or keeping those it has engaged. There may be several reasons for this, but it is often a question of salary and/or archaic personnel regulations. Central planning agencies set up on a temporary basis find it especially difficult to acquire a good staff, but a temporary planning agency is undesirable in itself because planning is a continuous process which only a permanent body can carry out.

Because of civil service or other government restrictions, planning agencies often have to resort to the use of part-time, borrowed or temporary personnel. It is essential that a central planning agency have a strong nucleus of regular, full-time technicians to insure planning continuity. Governments with well-developed civil services have, however, found it desirable to add to the regular staff of a central planning agency general administrators as part of their regular civil service rotation system; among other advantages, rotation hastens the institutionalization of planning.

Some experts believe that a central planning agency which has been established by statute has advantages over one created by executive resolution. But this view is not confirmed by the record. If a central planning agency is supported by its government, how it was set up seems not to matter much. If it does not have that support, its position is not made better because it was established by statute.

Since experience shows that it is frequently necessary to alter a planning agency's organizational setup, it is desirable to leave the details of organization to administrative determination. Where the organization has been fixed by law, this is not easy to do. In practice, few organization charts provide a reliable indication of the way the organization actually works.

The kind of organization which a central planning agency has, and its size, depends on the kind of planning it does, the extent to which it exercises executive functions and on requirements which are peculiar to the country concerned. Generally, planning agencies in the mixed economies have staffs which range from 25 to 100 persons but some have much more; and the numbers are usually much greater still in the socialized countries. Only about one-third to one-half of a central planning agency's staff is generally classified as professional, the rest being administrative and other supporting personnel. Few of the professionals in the planning agencies of the less developed countries can be considered adequately trained and experienced.

While there is no standard organization chart for central planning agencies which can be used as a model for all countries, most planning agencies have basically similar organization. These usually include units for (1) planning, (2) progress reporting and plan evaluation, (3) co-ordination of plan formulation and execution, (4) technical assistance, (5) public relations and (6) administration. The heart of the organization is the part concerned with planning. It is generally divided into sectoral sections dealing with specific sectors of the economy and functional sections dealing with macro-economic planning problems.

The sections concerned with economic sectors in a central planning agency are supposed to do work which operating organizations cannot or should not do. Unless there is close co-operation between technicians in planning and operations, differences can and frequently do lead to duplication of effort. Besides being concerned with over-all economic and planning problems, the functional sections have the task of combining and reconciling sectoral programs. Each planning agency sets up functional sections which reflect the functions it performs. There has been a trend toward establishing separate perspective and manpower planning sections as a result of planners' increasing interest in these subjects. Sometimes, the inclusion of a small statistical section has also proved useful.

Some countries, including Burma, Honduras and Turkey, have considered it necessary to set up social planning units apart from economic planning units as a way of emphasizing the importance of social programs. But the division between social and economic planning is an artificial one and it is usually difficult to distinguish between the two.

In many countries, the director of the planning agency attempts to co-ordinate the work of the various functional and sectoral sections. But since he has many responsibilities, co-ordination is frequently inadequate. The greatest need is for central co-ordination by an individual or group within the agency whose primary job is to perform this function.

Although there is a shortage of planners, the shortage is often made to appear greater than it is because of the size and complexity of the organization. An agency with many sections may give the impression that it is more seriously understaffed than an agency with fewer sections, even if the former has more technicians than the latter. The larger agency may, moreover, be less effective than the smaller because its staff is more dispersed.

The French Commissariat Général du Plan has found that its small staff can be used most effectively by consolidating it into three task forces. It may be that other countries with small staffs would find it profitable to emulate the French task force system. It has the flexibility required for making the most efficient use of a small planning staff under varying circumstances. The system also is likely to stimulate planners to identify and concentrate on the most important planning tasks and postpone less important ones.

Many conventionally organized planning agencies have been compelled by necessity to combine technicians and specialists from different sections into working parties in order to concentrate on specific jobs which had to be done quickly. This has not always worked well since it required changes in existing organizational arrangements and made it necessary for specialists to work outside their fields of competence. Experience shows that if a task force is to operate effectively, a planning agency must make greater use of generalists than is usual and lay less emphasis on hierarchical authority and more on group activity and mobility.

Chapter XVI

Subnational Regional and Local Planning Bodies

REGIONAL development planning bodies within a country have been established either for political subdivisions or for economic regions. Systems of planning bodies covering all political subdivisions of a country have in the past generally been limited to socialized countries and to mixed-economy countries with federal governments which planned on a national scale. With the spread of national planning, mixed-economy countries with unitary governments have also begun to set up comprehensive planning machinery for their regional and, sometimes, for their subregional political subdivisions. Nevertheless, in the mixed economies, pervasive systems of planning bodies below the national level are still an exception. In contrast, planning machinery for economic regions, as distinguished from planning machinery for political subdivisions of a country, is almost entirely restricted to mixed-economy countries, where it may be found in nations with either federal or unitary governments.

PLANNING BODIES IN POLITICAL
REGIONS AND LOCALITIES

In Socialized Countries

Planning by bodies attached to regional and local political administrations constitutes an integral part of national planning in the socialized countries. By supplying data and by helping to execute national plans, regional and local planning bodies in political subdivisions permit central planners to take appropriate account of discrepancies in regional growth rates associated with structural changes in the economy and differences in resource endowment. Hence, regional and local planning bodies in political regions are important components of the planning machinery in these countries.

Besides the USSR *Gosplan* on the national level, the Soviet Union has planning bodies at the republican, territorial and district levels. Each republican planning body (*Gosplan*) is organized along horizontal and vertical lines with functional planning and sectoral sections. It is headed by a chairman who is assisted by a vice-chairman and section heads usually selected from among the ministers in the government of the republic concerned.

Planning bodies associated with territorial economic councils (*sovnarkhozy*) consist of five to seven members and have functional sections, as well as sections which correspond to branches of the economy operating within their territories. The size of their staffs also depends on the number of types of industries in their territories. The main function of the territorial planning bodies is to secure the economic development of their territories through the maximum use of resources. The planning bodies of small *sovnarkhozy* plan mainly for current output, but those in large *sovnarkhozy* engage in long-term as well as short-term planning and sectoral programing. One of their most important responsibilities is to insure that their territories fulfill the delivery quotas set for them in the national plan. With exceptions in the heavy industries, they also supervise the preparation of long-term and current plans by enterprises in their areas, which they may approve or modify. Councils established in 1962 in 18 major regions which cut across republican lines are supposed to co-ordinate the activities of the *sovnarkhozy* in their planning bodies.[1]

Finally, local planning bodies (*oblplan, gorplan, rayplan*) in towns and districts, each with a chairman and four to six members, function at the lowest planning level. Besides permanent employees, their staffs include consulting specialists employed in enterprises, institutions and other organizations in their towns or districts. Larger local planning bodies have sections for the various sectors of the local economy. Their function is mainly to plan for small enterprises and social welfare activities within their boundaries, since larger enterprises and activities come under the jurisdiction of territorial or republican planning bodies or recently reconstituted central ministries.

The planning bodies at the republican, regional, territorial and local levels are advisory bodies subordinate to their respective administrative authorities. The members of the planning bodies on each level

---

[1] At the time this is written, in the spring of 1965, there are strong indications that the powers of both the *sovnarkhozy* and the 18 councils are being reduced.

are appointed by these authorities. They supervise the work of the planning bodies and approve their plans before they are transmitted to higher authorities. Planning bodies at one level are therefore not formally linked to planning bodies at other levels and are not a part of an integrated system of planning bodies. But in practice, the lower planning bodies work closely with the planning bodies of the higher administrations. Since all plans must be integrated into one plan for each territory and region, as well as for each industry and, finally, into a national plan, direct links between planning bodies at the different levels have been established to avoid the delays which would occur if they had to work through their administrative authorities. The effect of this is that the planning bodies at each level are subject to the supervision of the administrations to which they are attached as well as to the planning bodies of the higher administrative authorities.[2]

Generally similar setups prevail in other Eastern European countries,[3] although on a smaller scale. In Poland, for instance, 17 regional planning offices prepare general regional plans for the basic political areas of the country (*voivodeships*), as well as detailed regional plans for areas of concentrated investment. Yugoslavia departs from the usual pattern. In that country, planning bodies at lower levels are, in fact as well as in principle, independent of those at higher levels. Cooperation between the Federal Planning Institute and republican planning bodies which, in turn, work closely with district and communal planning offices, manifests itself in many ways, especially in the drafting of plans. But since there is no requirement that plans at lower levels concur in every respect with those at the national level, there is less need than in other socialized countries for the integration of all planning bodies. There is also another basic difference between regional and local planning bodies in the USSR and other Eastern European countries, on the one hand, and Yugoslavia, on the other. In the Soviet Union, for example, republican, regional and, to a lesser extent, territorial planning bodies have much more important functions than local planning bodies; in Yugoslavia, the situation is reversed because the *commune*, the basic unit of government at the local

[2] UN. Department of Economic and Social Affairs. *Planning for Economic Development, Report of the Secretary-General Transmitting the Study of a Group of Experts*, p. 90.

[3] However, in Hungary, regional plans are prepared by the National Planning Office, partly on the basis of work performed by the planning bodies of territorial councils.

administrative level, and not the district or even the republic, has been assigned responsibilities whose proper execution is most important for the implementation of national plans. While planning in *communes* is closely related to proposals for expanding productive capacity in their areas, district planning bodies (which are intermediate political areas between *communes* and republics) have functions of considerably narrower scope.[4] Republican planning bodies play a more important role than those in districts because they plan for larger enterprises and co-ordinate communal plans with the national plan.[5]

In Mixed Economies with Federal Governments

In the mixed economies, national planning plays a lesser role than in the socialized countries and, hence, planning in political subdivisions below the national level is much less important than in the socialized countries. However, in mixed-economy countries with federal governments, constitutional provisions generally require the federal government to share responsibility for planning in varying measure with its political subdivisions. When a country with a federal government begins to plan, therefore, this usually leads to the establishment of planning machinery at the state (or provincial) level and, to a lesser extent, at the local level.

Nigeria. But in most cases, these subnational planning bodies are not yet able to perform their functions adequately. This is true, for example, of the planning bodies in three of the four regions of the Federation of Nigeria. Eastern Nigeria, where the political leadership is firmly committed to development, is a notable exception. Eastern and Northern Nigeria each has a Ministry of Economic Planning, Western Nigeria has a Ministry of Economic Planning and Community Development and Mid-Western Nigeria has a Ministry of Economic Development. The Nigerian staffs of these Ministries (again, except in Eastern Nigeria) are very small and, in all but the Mid-Western Region, have been supplemented by foreign advisers.

---

[4] District planning bodies may have research and investment sections, but for the rest of their work they are likely to have one technician in charge of several activities in the district.

[5] Republican planning bodies employ from 30 to 70 persons, typically distributed among the following seven sections: research, regional development, industry and mining, agriculture and forestry, investment and construction, other economic activities and administration.

Western Nigeria's Ministry of Economic Planning and Community Development is also responsible for Western Nigeria's Community Development Program. The Region is divided into provinces, divisions and blocks. There are 130 blocks, each with 10 villages. A program is prepared for each block, with the co-operation of civil servants and representatives of the villages in the block. Block plans are combined into divisional and provincial plans by the Ministry and the aggregate constitutes the regional community development plan.[6]

India. Among the mixed-economy nations with a long planning history, India has one of the most extensive systems of planning bodies in political subdivisions, associated with the 15 states. Each state has a planning and development department, usually under the direction of the chief minister of the state. The permanent secretary of this department, who is customarily designated as the development commissioner, sometimes is also the chief secretary of the state government.

The planning and development department is responsible for the preparation of the state plan and generally supervises its implementation through the various secretaries and heads of technical departments. To assist in this work, there may be a co-ordinating committee composed of secretaries and heads of departments. The planning and development department also co-ordinates district and village plans in its state and in many cases is also responsible for the state's community development program. As the state's liaison with the central Planning Commission on planning matters, it arranges for the preparation of suitable projects by the various state technical departments and for their approval by the central Planning Commission and the central ministries concerned.

The procedures for formulating a state plan are broadly similar to those in the Central Government. Beginning with the Third Five-Year

[6] In Eastern Nigeria, co-ordination of activities of the various regional ministries concerned with community development projects is obtained by committees at three levels. An interministerial committee is responsible for general problems, mobilization of resources, the provision of technical assistance and centralized co-ordination of training. Provincial rural development committees are responsible for co-ordination at the provincial level and county rural development committees co-ordinate development projects in the counties. In Northern Nigeria, where community development is less advanced than in Eastern and Western Nigeria, 13 provincial commissioners representing the Regional Government supervise, through 53 divisional officers, the work of about the same number of local administrations. (United Nations Meeting of Experts on Administrative Aspects of National Development Planning. *Administration of Planning in Nigeria*, pp. 26–27.)

Plan, each state sets up a series of functional and sectoral working groups which paralleled others set up in the Central Government. Arrangements were made for the working groups at the center and in the states to be in informal contact with each other. Each was composed of the heads of appropriate state development departments, to prepare functional and sectoral programs as a basis for the state plan. The proposals of all the working groups were screened by a steering committee,[7] which fixed priorities and reduced the total proposed investment to what it believed to be a realistic level. On the basis of the results obtained, a draft state plan was prepared and placed before a planning committee of the state cabinet and later before the state cabinet itself. After approval by the cabinet, the draft plan was discussed by a state advisory committee for planning composed of government and non-government representatives in the state. This committee may have operated with a series of subcommittees to study the draft plan and to prepare its own suggestions. When the plan was finally approved by the state government and legislature, it was discussed with the Planning Commission and the central ministries in New Delhi.

This procedure was not without problems since the preparatory phase on the state level had to be carried out without clear indications from the Government of India regarding the extent to which it would contribute to the execution of each state's plan. It was only after the state plan had been approved by its authorities that the Government of India made commitments to assist in its execution. At that time, each project in the state plan was scrutinized by the Planning Commission and the central ministries concerned and a determination was made concerning the extent to which the Central Government would contribute towards its completion.[8]

Below the state level are the districts, blocks and villages. At the district level, the district officer (also known as the district collector or magistrate) is responsible for formulating the district plan and its implementation. He usually chairs, and is assisted by, a district development board or council, with heads of district development departments as members. In areas of a district where development projects

[7] Typically, its members were the chief secretary to (the state) government, the development commissioner and the secretary of the department of finance.

[8] Natarajan, K. V. "State Plans," p. 546.

are being carried out there may be block planning committees (*panchayat samiti*) composed of the elected heads of village development councils (*panchayats*), at the lowest level. The block is considered to be the basic unit for development planning purposes.[9] At the village level, *panchayats* made up of villagers and officials emphasize self-help activities to construct local public works with contributions of land, labor or materials by villagers.

Despite what appears to be a finely articulated system, it does not work as well as it might, especially below the state level. Even in the states, the planning process is sometimes wanting. In most states,

> there is not a single officer in the service of the State Government who is specialized in the problems of planning. There is no machinery to draw on the intellectual resources of academic economists and for tackling the economic problems of the State.[10]

Despite growing responsibilities of the states, the situation has not improved appreciably in recent years. Pointing out that responsibility for power and transport had been turned over entirely to the states, Shri Tarlok Singh, a member of the Planning Commission, recently expressed the view that

> the existing planning establishments in the States would not be able to cope with the work of planning for the next [i.e., the fourth] plan.[11]

Pakistan. Regional planning bodies were established in both East and West Pakistan soon after independence. But they were slow in getting started and have only begun to operate reasonably well in recent years. In East Pakistan a Planning Department, headed by a Development Commissioner, was created in 1948; but its staff was too

[9] According to Natarajan, K. V. (*ibid.*), "The Block Plans are prepared in four parts—Part I indicating the block programme under Community Development; Part II giving out the block segment of the annual district plans; Part III furnishing the programmes of various departments proposed for execution in the block from the normal developmental budgets; and Part IV detailing schemes implemented by panchayat bodies (such as Khadi, handloom and village industries) and by voluntary organisations."

[10] "Planning at the State Level," *Economic Weekly*, p. 902.

[11] *Economic Times*, November 10, 1963.

small and its head held too low a rank in the civil service hierarchy to permit the department to carry out its functions. In 1960, the rank of the Development Commissioner of the then existing provincial Planning and Development Department was raised to the level of the third highest civil servant in the Provincial Government. This made it possible for him to deal effectively with the heads of provincial operating departments.[12] Difficulties in obtaining capable personnel were overcome by raising the level and salaries of division and section heads. The increase in staff which these changes made possible greatly improved the outlook for planning in East Pakistan.

The Planning and Development Department acts as the secretariat of three groups which participate in provincial planning: (1) A Planning Authority, composed of the Chief Secretary (the highest civil servant in the Province), the Development Commissioner and the Finance Secretary functions as a subcommittee of the Secretaries' Meeting, comprising the permanent secretaries of all the provincial departments, and is empowered to make final decisions on development matters. (2) A provincial Development Working Party, composed of one representative each of the Planning and Development Department, the Finance Department and the operating department sponsoring the project(s), reviews and reports on projects to the Planning Authority. (3) A Planning Board with three members, headed by the Development Commissioner, is visualized as the counterpart on the provincial level of the central Planning Commission. It has been given wide powers to assess development resources and requirements; prepare long-term and annual plans; devise and adopt measures for implementing plans, promote research, surveys and investigations; and maintain provincial liaison with the central Planning Division.

Provincial planning in West Pakistan has lagged even more than in East Pakistan. Because officials designated as development commissioners in West Pakistan were also frequently responsible for one or more operating departments, they usually had little time for planning; since their rank was often no higher than that of other secretaries and was sometimes lower, they did not have the status required to oversee the planning and implementing of development in operating departments. In 1961, West Pakistan finally separated the planning function

---

[12] The Planning and Development Department has two divisions: Planning and Projects. The first is concerned with over-all planning, the second with inspecting, reporting and evaluating the implementation of provincial projects and sector programs.

from operations by creating a Planning and Development Department headed by a Development Commissioner who, unlike his predecessors, was able to devote full time to planning.[13] A staff of nine professionals was assembled to assist him. Following the precedent set in East Pakistan, West Pakistan also raised the rank of its Development Commissioner. His higher status has also made it easier for him to deal effectively with provincial operating departments and agencies.

The Planning and Development Department, in collaboration with the provincial Finance Department and other entities, draws up the provincial annual development plan. It also evaluates and reports progress in executing plans and programs, engages in economic research and acts as liaison between provincial departments and central ministries and agencies on development matters.

Provincial operating departments and agencies send their proposals or projects to be included in provincial plans for review and comment to the Planning and Development Department and to the provincial Finance Department. As in East Pakistan, there is a provincial Development Working Party, chaired by the Development Commissioner, on which the Finance Department and the department or agency sponsoring the project under consideration are represented by their permanent secretaries. Decisions taken by the provincial Development Working Party are in the form of recommendations to the Governor of West Pakistan, who generally approves the recommendations as presented.

The inadequacies of the provincial planning agencies in East and West Pakistan prevented them from making significant contributions to the preparation of the First Plan for 1955–60 and the Second Plan for 1960–65. Pakistan's Constitution of 1962 gave effect to a growing realization in the country that in Pakistan, with its two separated and diverse Provinces, decentralized planning was likely to produce better results than centralized planning. As a consequence of the devolution of development functions from the Central to the Provincial Governments following adoption of the new Constitution, the importance of good planning has become more manifest to the provincial authorities. The staff and status of the provincial planning bodies have now

---

[13] West Pakistan's Planning and Development Department has three divisions: (1) an Economics and Progressing Cell, which prepares provincial plans and reports on the status of project execution, (2) a Bureau of Statistics, which collects and processes statistical data and (3) a Coordination and Administration Section, which provides the services indicated by its name.

reached levels which permit them to participate actively, if not always effectively, in both the formulation and execution of development plans and programs.

Since there is no line of authority from the central Planning Commission to the provincial planning bodies, machinery has been set up to improve communications between them. Because of the distance, East Pakistan's planning body in Dacca has found it particularly difficult to maintain contacts with the Planning Commission in Karachi. To provide a more formal and broader basis for consultation between the two organizations, the Central Government directed the Planning Commission to hold quarterly meetings with the heads of the provincial Planning and Development Departments to consider planning and implementation problems. The Planning Commission moves as a body to Dacca once each quarter for a two to three-week stay and the chiefs of the Planning Commission's Economic and Projects Divisions also visit Dacca at prescribed intervals.

Planning machinery on the local level in Pakistan is slowly evolving as part of the system of "Basic Democracies" instituted in 1959. This system set up five levels of councils. At the bottom are union councils (for towns and cities) and, in ascending order for larger geographic units, *tehsil* (in West Pakistan) or *thana* (in East Pakistan) councils, district councils, divisional councils and, finally, provincial development advisory councils. The councils at each level have economic as well as political functions. These include the preparation and execution of development plans at each level. Thus far, however, only a beginning has been made by these institutions to plan their development.

Malaya. Among mixed-economy countries, Malaya probably has the most effective comprehensive system for planning at state, district and local levels. In each of the 11 states constituting the former Federation, there is a state rural development committee, headed by the chief minister of the state (*mentri besar*). There is also a state development officer with wide powers of decision over the allocation of funds for federal and state projects, who acts as vice-chairman of the committee. The committee's members include three to five state legislators, as well as the representatives of all federal development ministries at the state level.[14] There is also a smaller committee, headed by the chief minister of the state, and including the state development officer, the director

---

[14] I.e., the state directors of agriculture, co-operatives, education, health, and finance, as well as the public works engineer, the drainage and irrigation officer and the state commissioner of lands and mines.

of finance, the commissioner of lands and mines and the public works officer, which acts as a subcommittee of the state rural development committee and does most of the work of vetting and supervising the execution of projects and programs. All but one of the states are divided into districts, *mukims* (groups of villages) and *kampongs* (villages). There are 70 districts, each headed by a district officer. Each district officer is chairman of a district rural development committee [15] and is responsible for setting up village development committees in the *kampongs* in his district.[16]

The district officer, assisted by members of the district rural development committee, prepares his district's development proposals after discussions with *kampong* development committees composed of *kampong* headmen, as well as with town councils or boards. District representatives of state and federal ministries are responsible for forwarding proposals which affect their respective ministries to officials of these ministries at the state level. Officials at the state level are, in turn, responsible for presenting the proposals to the state rural development committee. Each of these committees combines all district proposals it approves with state projects to form the state's plan or proposals. State representatives of federal ministries are then required to forward the projects and proposals in the state plan which affect their respective ministries to their head offices in Kuala Lumpur, the federal capital. Similar procedures are followed for forwarding municipal projects and programs which are to be financed wholly or partly with federal loans.[17]

The system works well, not only because of its pragmatic simplicity, but because of the drive and interest provided by an unusually dynamic Deputy Prime Minister who actively directs the entire operation. The stimulus he provides manifests itself not only in the formulation of state, district and local plans but even more in the effectiveness of procedures already described for executing regional and subregional plans and for reporting on their progress.

[15] The committee includes district representatives of the Federal Divisions of Public Works, Drainage and Irrigation, Agriculture, Cooperatives, Social Security, district members of Parliament and chiefs of technical services at the *mukim* level. Representatives of the Federal Departments of Health and Education also attend the monthly meetings of the District Committee. (United Nations Meeting of Experts on Administrative Aspects of National Development Planning. *Administration of Planning in Malaya*, pp. 27–28.)

[16] About one-third of the *kampongs* have such committees.

[17] Wilcox, Clair. *Planning and Execution of Economic Development in Southeast Asia*, pp. 26–28.

In Mixed Economies with Unitary Governments

The motives which have prompted socialized countries and mixed-economy countries with federal governments to establish planning bodies for their political subdivisions have, until recently, been absent in most mixed-economy countries with unitary governments. Where such governments have set up planning bodies for political subdivisions, they have generally played a minor role. Norway, which has engaged in regional planning for a longer period than most mixed-economy countries, is an example. Beginning as long ago as 1949, planning bodies, each with a staff of two or three persons, were established in each of Norway's 18 rural counties.[18] These planning bodies have played a certain role in the development of their areas; but while they have prepared surveys of county economies and contributed studies for long-term plans, most of their work has been related to individual projects rather than to economic planning.

But for most mixed economies with unitary governments, planning machinery for political subdivisions is a much more recent innovation. In Lebanon, for example, regional consultative councils and regional technical committees have only just been established. The council in each region is composed of the regional commissioner (*mohafez*) and representatives from each district (*caza*) within the region. The councils, in co-operation with a Regional Activities Division in the Ministry of Planning, advise the central planning policy body, the Development and Planning Council, about the needs of their regions with a view to helping bring about the best distribution of development programs and projects. The regional technical committees consist of the *mohafez* and regional representatives of the Ministries of Planning, Public Works, Education, Health and Agriculture, as well as the Office of Social Development. With the representative of the Ministry of Planning acting as secretary, each committee is responsible for assisting the *mohafez* to implement programs and projects in the region. In Tunisia, also, committees at the region (*gouvernate*) and local (*delegation*) levels have been set up recently to provide a wider base for national planning.[19] Senegal, too, has recently created regional planning

---

[18] These counties exclude only Oslo and Bergen.

[19] Each regional committee, which presided over by the governor of the region, includes members of the ruling (Neo-Destour) Party (renamed the Constitutional Socialist Party in October 1964), representatives of national organizations and cen-

machinery. The country has been divided into seven regions (subdivided into 28 *cercles* and 81 *arrondissements*), each headed by a director and each with a regional development committee and a regional assistance center for development. Each regional development committee is headed by the regional governor, who is assisted by two deputies, one for administration, the other for development. Each governor, aided by the regional development committee, is responsible for execution of the national plan in his region. But,

> the Senegalese authorities realize that the Governor is not yet in a position to carry out his task efficiently.[20]

Congo (Brazzaville) is another new nation which is attempting to plan regionally. The country has been divided into nine planning regions. The prefect who heads each region co-ordinates the planning activities of the area. He is assisted by a regional planning co-ordinator whose main function is to maintain liaison between the prefect and the central planning agency. The Sudan also has nine planning regions in as many provinces. Each province has a provincial council, whose chairman, appointed by the Central Government, is the head of the provincial administration. The provincial councils are responsible for co-ordinating planning activities on the provincial district and village levels, and for maintaining liaison with the Technical Committee of permanent secretaries in the Central Government on matters related to the local implementation of development projects.[21]

But while these and other attempts to establish regional planning machinery reveal a growing awareness in mixed-economy countries with unitary governments of the need for a regional approach to development planning, they are incipient and inchoate and will need much time before they produce significant results. This is even true of

---

tral operating organizations and other persons selected by reason of their competence in economic and social matters. The local planning committees are headed by delegates and include local representatives of the Party and national organizations, as well as persons outside government who are considered to be competent in economic and social fields. Regional and local planning committees have secretariats composed of officials from the Regional Planning Service in the central Ministry of Planning and Finance. These officials greatly influence the work of the committees. (United Nations Meeting of Experts on Administrative Aspects of National Development Planning. *Administration of Planning in Tunisia*, pp. 16–17.)

[20] United Nations Meeting of Experts on Administrative Aspects of National Development Planning. *Administrative Aspects of Planning in Developing Countries*, p. 21.

[21] *Ibid.*, pp. 21–22.

France, which has only recently begun to set up machinery for the 21 planning regions into which the country has been divided. In 1960, prefects of departments (*prefectures*) constituting each region were organized into interdepartmental conferences under the chairmanship of one of their members who was designated as "co-ordinating prefect." These conferences prepared investment projects. They were assisted by the chief administrators of the regions and by regional economic expansion committees, private bodies first established in 1955, comprising representatives of the various economic sectors and leading personalities in the regions who were considered able to attract wide support in economic and social circles.

Experience revealed the need to give the co-ordinating prefects a wider role and to remedy defects of the regional economic expansion committees, whose contributions were uneven and whose representative character was frequently disputed. Legislation approved in February 1964 introduced reforms. Co-ordinating prefects were given a higher status as "regional prefects." In each region, a regional economic development commission was established with a broader membership than that of the regional economic expansion committees, which continue to operate as private entities. The regional economic development commissions will be the primary media through which regional aspirations for development will be expressed. A National Territorial Development Commission also began operating in 1963. It works with the Commissariat Général du Plan and is to advise the Prime Minister on ways in which regional and national plans may be co-ordinated.

Regional planning on a country-wide basis is also receiving increasing attention in Belgium, where the establishment of a Council of Economic Regions was being discussed in 1964. The Council, which would be composed of representatives of the major economic and social bodies in each region, would advise the Central Government on regional economic planning and development matters. A draft law under discussion by the Government in 1964 also provided for the setting up of regional development companies (SDR's) as public law associations. The SDR's would have wide powers. They would co-operate in the preparation and execution of regional plans, seek to stimulate public or private action to promote regional development, engage in the preparation and execution of regional projects and programs in a number of fields and represent the region in national consultative bodies.

The idea that economic development must be tackled on a regional basis has developed rapidly in the United Kingdom in recent years and has led to the production of several regional studies. But these were made *ad hoc* and were largely directed by the Government. In December 1964, the United Kingdom's Labour Government set up permanent machinery for giving six regions in England a larger say in their own development.[22] The regions cover all but southeast England, about which decision was postponed. Similar planning machinery has been established for Scotland, Wales and Northern Ireland. The planning machinery in each of the regions consists of two bodies: an advisory planning council and a planning board. The membership of the councils is drawn from local authorities, industry, commerce, labor unions, universities and others who are concerned with improving the region. They are to study and analyze regional development problems and make recommendations to the planning boards. The boards are made up of local representatives of government departments concerned with economic and social matters and are headed by someone from the new central planning agency, the Ministry of Economic Affairs. They are each to have a staff for co-ordinating government activities in their region and they are to co-operate closely with local authorities in carrying out their functions. Final decisions are to be taken by the Government, but they are to be based on the advice of the councils and the work of the boards.[23]

There are also indications that a regional approach to development which cuts across state lines is in the making in the United States, a federally organized country. The regional concept was popular in the United States in the 1930's when the Tennessee Valley Authority was established. But little headway was made afterward by those who supported the idea. With the passage of the law in 1965 establishing a regional development authority for the 11 States of the so-called Appalachia Region, the Appalachian Regional Commission, the idea has again become popular. Members of Congress have indicated that they propose to advance proposals for other regions. The President has also let it be known that he considers the Appalachia program as the first of a series of regional development plans and that he proposes to improve the Government's area redevelopment program "to emphasize planning on a regional basis." [24]

[22] *Manchester Guardian,* December 17, 1964.
[23] *Financial Times,* November 9, 1964.
[24] *New York Times* and *Washington Post,* February 2, 1965.

In Individual Political Subdivisions

Growing interest in national planning, generally, as well as in regional planning in particular, has stimulated individual states and provinces in some countries to establish planning bodies for themselves. Thus, some states in the Federal Republic of Germany and most of the provinces in Canada have created planning, development or "productivity" agencies. A Lower St. Lawrence Council for Economic Planning (CREEGIM) was founded in the Province of Quebec in 1956. A Gaspé and Magdalen Islands Regional Council for Economic Development (COEB) was also established in Quebec in 1963. These councils, with memberships drawn from public corporations, socio-economic associations and private enterprises are concerned with the economic improvement of their areas. In 1963, also, both councils combined to form an Eastern Quebec Planning Bureau (*Bureau d'Amenagement de l'Est du Quebec Inc.,* or BAEQ).[25] In 1963, the Province of Nova Scotia also established regional planning machinery in the form of a Nova Scotia Voluntary Planning Board, composed of provincial government officials and representatives of labor and management for all sectors of the provincial economy. The Planning Board has prepared an eight-year development plan for the Province which is calculated to reduce unemployment to the Canadian average. The French planning system was used as a prototype. Planning committees were set up to prepare sectoral programs for the nine major sectors of the Province's economy.

PLANNING BODIES IN ECONOMIC REGIONS

Planning bodies for economic or functional regions [26] are usually created to meet special needs. They may be set up for the development

[25] BAEQ has a board of directors of ten members and shareholders, five of whom are appointed by CREEGIM and five by COEB. The staff, divided into three divisions for Development Research, Planning Research and Public Participation, is preparing a pilot program for the development of nine provincial counties.

[26] What constitutes an economic or functional region is a much debated subject. In the socialized countries, the limits of an economic region are largely determined by specialized production of an area. In the mixed economies, definitions of economic regions, although varied, give greater stress to the role of trade and services of an area. (UN. ECE. *Report by the Executive Secretary on the Third Meeting of Senior Economic Advisers to ECE Governments,* p. 45.)

of a single regional sector, e.g., agriculture, as with the Gezira Board in the Sudan; to build and operate co-ordinated regional power and water facilities, as with the Damodar Valley Corporation (DVC) in India and the Water and Power Development Authorities (WAPDA's) in East and West Pakistan; to promote the comprehensive development of virgin or relatively new regions, as in the case of the *Corporación Venezolana de Guayana;* or to help develop a relatively backward region in a country, as in the case of the *Cassa per il Mezzogiorno* (Cassa) in Italy or the *Superintendência do Desenvolvimento do Nordeste* (SUDENE) in Brazil.

In the socialized economies, these needs are almost always met through the existing planning bodies of their central and subordinate administrative units.[27] Where these units are considered inadequate, new administrative units are established, but these are likely to cover the entire country. Thus, with the increase in the number of *sovnarkhozy*,[28] Soviet authorities considered it necessary to divide the country into 18 major economic regions which cut across existing political subdivisions for the purpose of insuring better co-ordination of the *sovnarkhozy*. In mixed-economy countries, however, development planning bodies are usually established for one economic region at a time, even in countries with federal governments. In Colombia, where regional diversity in geography, climate and economics, as well as highly developed regional pride, make regional planning unusually attractive, three regional planning bodies have been established.[29] But the creation of three planning bodies for as many economic regions is unusual for a country of Colombia's size.

Some bodies established to further the development of an economic region, like the Council for the Development of the Extreme South (CODESUL) in Brazil, are primarily planning bodies with only advisory functions; but most are operational organizations which plan

---

[27] In Yugoslavia, where an attempt is made to channel public investment funds to enterprises in accordance with specified economic criteria calculated to increase economic yields, minimum amounts are nevertheless set aside in each plan for less developed political regions to be used for investment purposes even when they cannot compete on the basis of economic criteria applied to investments in more developed regions.

[28] This preceded the even more recent consolidation of *sovnarkhozy*.

[29] They are the: (1) *Corporación Autónima Regional del Cauca* (CVC); (2) *Corporación Autónima Regional de la Sabana de Bogotá y Valles de Chinqínquira y Ubate* (CAR); and (3) *Corporación Autónima Regional de los Valles de Magdalena y Sinú* (CVM).

for a region in conjunction with the projects and programs they prepare and execute or the responsibility they have for co-ordinating the work of other organizations operating in a region. The San Francisco Valley Commission in Brazil, the Commission for the Development of the Papaloápan Basin in Mexico and the Cauca Valley Corporation in Colombia (CVC) are examples of regional development bodies which plan mostly in connection with their operational responsibilities for executing development projects and programs in their regions. Italy's Cassa, which is concerned with problems of the country's Southern Region, is an example of a development body which draws up programs and plans which other organizations execute under its general supervision. SUDENE, whose concern is Brazil's Northeast Region, is another. But the Cassa has been better able than SUDENE to insure the proper execution of its plans and programs because it has had control over development funds to a much greater extent than SUDENE.[30] Unlike regular government ministries and departments, which find it difficult to have long-term programs because they must rely on annual budget appropriations, the Cassa relies instead on long-term and increasing commitments of the Italian Treasury to finance the Cassa's program. Experience shows that regional development bodies are most successful in carrying out plans when they have such long-term resources of their own and are permitted to administer their own budgets.

These resources sometimes come from the region concerned. For example, in the CVC area, a relatively well-to-do region in Colombia, most of the CVC's resources originate from a land tax levied on the region's landowners. But in most cases, central governments contribute a substantial part of the funds for regional development, at least at the beginning. Thus, in the case of the DVC in India, the Central Government contributed one-third of the capital cost of power projects, as well as other funds for flood control and other purposes; while in Brazil, the Constitution of 1946 provided that for 20 years not less than 3 per cent of the tax receipts of the National Government, as well as of state and municipal governments within the region, were to be set aside for investment in a comprehensive development plan for the Amazon Valley Region. Generally similar provisions were included in the Constitution for the Northeast and San Francisco Valley Regions.

---

[30] The General Administrator of the Salte (regional) Plan in Brazil has had even less control over regional development funds than SUDENE with correspondingly less control of the implementation of the Salte Plan by executing organizations.

Most planning or development bodies for economic regions are set up by national governments. These bodies may be national entities, independently administered and financed, but managed by government officials. Examples of this kind range from the long-established Tennessee Valley Authority in the United States to more recently created entities like the *Office du Niger*[31] in Mali. Public development planning bodies may also be set up by subnational states constituting an economic region without the intervention of a central government. For example, CODESUL, in Brazil, was established by agreement among the States of Rio Grande do Sul, Paraná and Santa Caterina;[32] or a regional body may be created by an association of local authorities or individuals in accordance with regulations set by law. Such bodies may then be made responsible by a government for executing and managing regional projects and programs. This system has been used by the Cassa in Italy for regional land improvement and irrigation, *"consorzi,"*[33] and in France, for intercommunal associations and syndicates concerned with the improvement of the Western Marshes.[34] Sometimes, the regional development planning body takes the form of a semipublic or mixed company which may include representatives of a national government, regional and local authorities, semipublic bodies like chambers of commerce, agriculture or trade, and private individuals. In Belgium, for example, 55 per cent of the shares in the regional development companies which the Government in 1964 was proposing to set up were to be held by the provinces and communes concerned, 15 per cent by the National Government, 15 per cent by the trade unions in the region and 15 per cent by any other subscribers. Semipublic companies have also been used to undertake major regional improvements in Provence, Corsica, Bas-Rhone and Languedoc, Landes, the Gascony Hills and in other provinces of France. These companies operate according to the provisions of company law but under government control.[35]

[31] Lamour, Philippe. "Legal and Administrative Problems in Regional Economic Development," p. 199.

[32] Bemis, George W. "Regional Government Organization in Brazil and Federal-State Public Adminstration," p. 131.

[33] The *consorzi* include representatives of enterprises interested in establishing themselves in an area. Their constitution must be approved by the President of the Republic and their plans, covering a 15-year period, by the Prime Minister.

[34] Lamour, Philippe. "Legal and Administrative Problems in Regional Economic Development," p. 199.

[35] *Ibid.*

Generally, legislation establishing planning bodies for economic regions provides that the national government and the subdivisions of a region are to be represented on the governing board or council of a regional planning body.[36] But regardless of legal requirements, a managing board or council of a planning body for an economic region is likely to contain representatives of both the national government and subdivisions of the region. Thus, although the Central Government legislation creating the DVC in India made no provision for representation from the States of Bihar and West Bengal, the two States composing the region, the Government of India by convention has appointed a representative of each State to the three-man Board of Directors. Conversely, the President of Brazil appoints a representative to CODESUL's management (*Directoria*), although CODESUL was created by agreement among the three States involved without the intervention of the National Government.[37]

Ideally, the number of members on the managing board of a regional planning body should be small. This is easy to arrange when there are only a few subdivisions in an economic region, but it becomes difficult when there are many. Thus, while the DVC in India has only three members, and the CVC in Colombia has seven, the *Corporación Venezolana de Guayana* has eight, the Cassa in Italy has 15, as has the Amazon Valley Authority in Brazil [38] and SUDENE, also in Brazil, has 20.[39] That there is no inherent necessity for such large management groups for regional development bodies is apparent from the fact that the Tennessee Valley Authority, whose activities involve seven States, as well as the U. S. Government, has a Board of Directors of only three members.

In the socialized countries, where regional planning experience (in

---

[36] Sometimes, a law may provide that the president or prime minister of a national government will appoint all members of a governing board, some of whom are to be nominated by regional authorities; in other cases, regional authorities may appoint their own representatives to the board.

[37] The Governor of each of the three States in the region appoints one Director and, jointly, they select CODESUL's President.

[38] Nine members on the Authority's Council represent states and territories; the remaining members include the administrative heads of the Authority's major operating sections.

[39] Not only is the size of SUDENE's Deliberative Council augmented by ten representatives, one from each of the ten States included wholly or partly in the region, but also by three representatives each from the Federal Ministry of Mines and Energy, the Ministry of Industry and Commerce and the Hydro-Electric Company of the San Francisco Valley.

political subdivisions) is based on many years of experience, reasonably effective links have been worked out between regional planning bodies, on the one hand, and central planning agencies and operating organizations in the central and regional governments, on the other hand. But, in the mixed economies, only beginnings have been made. Regional planning has been found to present especially knotty problems of co-ordination between regional planning bodies and operating ministries and agencies because regional representatives of operating organizations generally insist on referring back to their head offices in the capital a multitude of details for decision. This inevitably delays the process of regional plan formulation and execution. While co-ordination problems are commonly encountered in planning for political regions, they are particularly acute for economic or functional regions, where relationships between central operating organizations and regional planning bodies are likely to be less clearly defined than for political regions in a federal government.

Planning for economic or functional regions is also likely to encounter greater difficulties than planning for political regions on another score. Where the boundaries of an economic (or functional) region coincide with those of a political region, one political authority has the necessary legal power to formulate and carry out plans for the entire economic region. But where economic boundaries extend beyond the limits of political boundaries, as they frequently do, co-operation and co-ordination between two or more political authorities are required for effective planning of the economic region. Since such co-operation and co-ordination are hard to get, effective planning for economic regions is uncommon. A few countries plan for one or a few economic regions within their frontiers, but most regional planning is still limited to political regions. Thus, in India, regional planning is largely restricted to the states. This has its limitations. As one Indian writer sees it:

> Where we need regional planning most, we have not so far had any significant move in that direction. . . . In many cases Indian States do not constitute economic regions. A State depends on regions outside for its supply inputs. . . . For a vast country like India, where resources are distributed at a number of focal points, any efficient planning strategy must take into consideration the question of regional planning.[40]

[40] Chatterji, Manas. "Regional Economic Planning," p. 553.

The results obtained thus far from planning in India for economic regions have been disappointing. For example, when the DVC was established it was given wide authority to develop the power, irrigation and other facilities in Bihar and Bengal, now West Bengal. But the failure of these States to co-operate and the gradual replacement of development on the basis of regional planning by development on the basis of separate planning by both States have made it impossible for DVC to realize the potentialities for developing the Damodar Valley as an integrated region. Similar problems have been encountered in other countries. In Colombia, the Cauca Valley Authority (CVC) has had to restrict its planning activities largely to only one of the three (geographic) departments through which the Cauca Valley extends. Although CVC has accomplished much, it has proved difficult to attain the necessary co-operation among the three departments to permit implementation of development programs for the entire economic region.

The lack of competent planners also limits the effectiveness of regional planning bodies. For while there is almost always a serious shortage of qualified planners in central planning agencies in the capital of less developed, mixed-economy countries, there is a virtual absence of talent in the hinterland. In some countries, therefore, such regional planning as there is takes place in the capital. In Turkey, for example, where most economic decision-making is in any event centralized, regional planning is mostly carried out in the Ministry of Reconstruction and in the State Planning Organization. The Ministry of Reconstruction, with a staff of about 30 economists and planners, has prepared two regional studies.[41] The Social Planning Department of the State Planning Organization is currently engaged on much more ambitious regional studies of two areas.[42] In Greece,[43] Italy, Mexico, Spain, Thailand and the United Kingdom, among other countries, regional planning is also largely a function of national governments.

---

[41] Little has happened as a result of these studies, both of which were carried out with OECD assistance. One was of the Marmara Region, which includes Istanbul and some seven provinces; the second was of the Zonguldak Region, a coal and iron area.

[42] The first, sponsored by FAO, is of the Antalva Region, in the south, an agricultural area with some mining; the second, assisted by U.S. AID, is of the Cukurova Region, a cotton-producing province.

[43] Greece has a number of regional development plans (e.g., in the Ptolemais, Epirus and Western Peloponnese regions) which are carried out within the context of the national development plan and under the supervision of the Ministry of Coordination, the central planning agency.

Mauritania has established a series of regional commissions to prepare regional plans but these operate as a part of the central planning agency.

Some countries which are trying to promote planning within their regions, rather than plan for them in their capitals, have tried to alleviate the lack of qualified planners in the regions by establishing mobile teams of planners which travel around the country to assist regional planning authorities. Thus, Mali has a section in its Planning Department which is responsible for maintaining liaison with regions for this purpose. Madagascar and Senegal also employ mobile teams which operate out of their central planning agencies and co-operate with regional groups in the preparation of programs and plans.

Despite all efforts, however, the shortage of trained planners remains a much greater obstacle to effective planning on the regional level than it is on the national level. The widespread failure, thus far, of regional planning and regional planning bodies to relate themselves to national planning and planners also creates serious problems.

> It is when regional planning is elevated into a doctrine of its own, that its inherent dependence on national planning may easily be forgotten: it may then in fact divert attention from the need for national planning.[44]

At an international planning conference held in 1962, one expert summarized for the conference the current status of regional planning in general and SUDENE's plans and planning machinery in particular:

> A review of regional plans actually in operation shows how much we have still to learn about the process of regional planning. Few regions have attracted as much attention . . . as the Brazilian Northeast. . . . The organization of SUDENE . . . represents the major effort in the field of development planning by the Brazilian Government. . . . Yet the SUDENE plans are deficient in many respects. . . . There can be little doubt that SUDENE is staffed with hardworking, self-sacrificing, devoted and able people. However, very few of the SUDENE officials have training and experience appropriate for the task they are now undertaking. The SUDENE staff has limited knowledge of the process of regional planning. . . . Particularly disturbing is the tendency of

[44] Glass, Ruth. "The Evaluation of Planning: Some Sociological Considerations," p. 408.

SUDENE to regard the problems of the Northeast as something that has to be solved in the Northeast. The organization is set up as a species of super-state (even with its own diplomatic service) and the planning seems to proceed as though the Northeast were a separate country, completely cut off from the outside world.[45]

SUMMARY AND CONCLUSIONS

Regional development planning bodies have been established within countries for political subdivisions and for economic areas. Among the mixed-economy countries, federal governments which planned on a national scale have generally established planning bodies covering all political subdivisions of the country; and with the spread of national planning, countries with unitary governments have begun to set up comprehensive planning machinery for their regional and, sometimes, their subregional political subdivisions. Nevertheless, in the mixed economies, pervasive systems of planning bodies below the national level are an exception; in the socialized economies, they are the rule. Conversely, planning machinery for economic regions is almost entirely restricted to mixed-economy countries.

Planning by bodies attached to regional and subregional political administrations constitutes an integral part of national planning in socialized countries. In theory, subnational planning bodies in the socialized economies have no direct administrative links with each other or with the central planning agency, but in practice, planning bodies at each level are subject to supervision by planning bodies at higher levels as well as their own administrative authorities. Yugoslavia departs from the usual pattern. In that country, planning bodies at lower levels are, in fact as well as in principle, independent of those at higher levels.

Constitutions of mixed-economy countries with federal governments generally provide that each federal government must share responsibility for planning with its political subdivisions. Thus, when a country with a federal government begins to plan, planning machinery at the state (or provincial) level and, to a lesser extent, at the local level, is generally set up. But in most cases, these planning systems do not work

[45] Higgins, Benjamin. *Some Comments on Regional Planning*, pp. 6–7.

as well as they might, as, for example, in Nigeria, India and Pakistan. On the other hand, Malaya has a relatively effective system for planning at state, district and local levels.

Subnational planning in mixed economies generally is not an integral part of national planning. Many countries with unitary governments have established planning systems for their political regions, and individual subnational states or provinces have also begun to establish planning bodies for their areas. But all of these efforts are mostly incipient and inchoate attempts which will need much time before they produce significant results.

Planning bodies for economic or functional regions are generally established to meet special needs—to develop a single regional sector, carry out multipurpose water and electric power facilities, promote the comprehensive development of new regions or help raise the economic level of backward regions. In the socialized economies, these needs are almost always met through planning bodies of existing central and regional administrative units.

Most planning bodies for economic regions are established as a part of operating corporations or authorities which either prepare and execute projects and programs or co-ordinate the work of other organizations. Experience shows that regional development bodies are most successful when they have resources of their own and administer their own budgets. These resources may come from the region concerned; but in most cases, central governments contribute a substantial part of the funds for regional development, at least at the beginning.

Most planning or development bodies for economic regions are created by national governments, sometimes as national entities, independently administered or financed, and sometimes as a "mixed" company with national and regional officials, as well as nonofficial representation. They may also be set up by agreement among subnational states or provinces. Whatever the legal form, the managing board is likely to contain representatives of the national government and subdivisions of the region concerned. Where there are many subdivisions, it is desirable to find a formula which keeps the size of the board small.

Mixed economies have made only small beginnings in co-ordinating the work of planning bodies in economic regions with the activities of central planning agencies and central operating ministries and agencies. Where the boundaries of economic regions extend to two or more political subdivisions, as they frequently do, co-operation and co-ordination among the political subdivisions have also been hard to achieve. This is one reason why planning for economic regions is uncommon and frequently unsuccessful in countries where it has been tried. The lack of competent planners has also seriously limited the effectiveness of subnational regional planning bodies.

Chapter XVII

Programing Units in Operating Organizations

> . . . A journey of a thousand miles be-
> gins with one step.—Chinese proverb.

THE FUNCTION AND ROLE OF PROGRAMING UNITS

A PROGRAMING unit in an operating ministry, department or agency is essentially a microcosm of a central planning agency. This is perhaps an oversimplification, but it is a basically accurate and useful analogy. For a programing unit's relations with the operating units and the head of its own organization are fundamentally similar to, and raise the same issues as, a central planning agency's relations with a government's operating organizations and the national political authority. And while the relationship between a central planning agency and a programing unit is necessarily complementary, their respective functions differ more in degree than in substance.

The primary functions of a programing unit include (1) combining of the projects and proposals of its operating organization into sectoral or subsectoral programs for medium- and short-term (including annual) periods, either on a national or regional basis; (2) submitting and defending them before central planning and budgetary authorities;[1] (3) recommending policies, instruments of economic policy, administrative or other measures and machinery required to implement the programs of its organization; (4) reviewing and evaluating its organization's projects and programs; and (5) co-ordinating the or-

---

[1] Unlike a national government, an operating ministry, department or agency is generally too small, and qualified staff is too scarce, to permit programing to be separated from budgeting. Moreover, if programing and budgeting are combined within operating organizations, co-ordination between a central planning agency and a central budgetary authority is likely to be facilitated.

ganization's demand for, and the use of, outside technical skills, including consultants and consulting firms.

In addition, a programing unit must undertake *ad hoc* or special assignments, such as drafting loan applications for projects, preparing project reports for foreign aid missions and international agencies, or assessing the impact of a specific project or program on various elements, such as transport facilities, labor supply or administrative capacity. To permit the preparation of the required studies and reports, a programing unit must collect, record, process and analyze relevant statistical and other data obtained from operating units in its organization and elsewhere. It must also study ways of improving forms of organization, methods, standards and techniques for the efficient preparation and execution of projects and programs in its organization.

A programing unit therefore occupies a strategic position in a country's planning machinery. It should be the main channel of communication between a central planning agency and an operating organization. It should receive information from a central planning agency about planning objectives and directives which will permit its operating organization to prepare projects and programs for incorporation into national and regional plans. It must, in turn, transmit to the central planning agency information which the planning agency requires to formulate over-all plans, including the sector and subsector programs for its organization; and it must provide periodic progress reports on these programs to a central planning agency for inclusion into comprehensive reports covering the progress of national or regional plans. A sectoral or subsectoral program prepared by a programing unit is necessarily tentative until the central planning agency reconciles it with programs submitted by other operating organizations, approved plan targets and available resources. While the reconciliation of sector programs and their integration in an over-all plan is a central planning agency's responsibility, it is desirable that programing units participate in the process in which the final sectoral programs are evolved as part of the "planning-from-below" procedure already described.

To carry out these activities, close working relations must be established between programing units and a central planning agency. This is obvious enough, but difficult to achieve. Where a central planning agency has "vertical" or sectoral sections, one of these may be the point of contact. Frequently, more than one section in a central planning agency may need the same or related information from an operating organization. Unless co-ordination within the planning agency works better than it does in most, two or more sections of the agency are likely to request similar information from a programing unit. Moreover, since co-ordination within an operating organization may be no better, and may even be worse, than in a central planning agency, requests for data may be addressed directly to an operating unit in an organization without the knowledge of its programing unit. Deficiencies of co-ordination are common impediments to good working relationships between a central planning agency and programing units.

A programing unit should not prepare or execute projects, since these are functions of operating units. But while each operating unit should prepare and carry out its own projects, the programing unit has the responsibility for setting up suitable forms and standards for operating units to follow. These should provide, among other things, for (1) feasibility and engineering studies, and cost-benefit analyses; (2) the identification of major "milestones" in executing projects which permit the setting of realistic work schedules and the phasing of a project with other related ones; (3) building into the project suitable means for determining, on an up-to-date basis, unit and other costs, as well as physical progress during the execution of the project; (4) assigning responsibility for each task; (5) training programs required to produce personnel qualified to operate a project when it is completed; and (6) the creation of a suitable organization and management cadre to run the finished project.

It would be difficult to find many operating organizations in the governments of less developed countries which successfully manage some of these tasks; it might well be impossible to locate any which carry out all of them with reasonable efficiency. In many countries,

> the planning of development programs limps because some operating agencies fail to enter effectively into the process. The project proposals they present are so inadequately analyzed or prepared that it is impossible to determine the cost of each project, the benefits it will yield or the time it will require to execute.[2]

In order to obtain budgetary allocations for their projects and programs, operating agencies sometimes produce estimates of their financial requirement which have little value because they are not sufficiently based on physical programing of each project. In Burma, for example, the Ministry of National Planning found that

[2] Hagen, Everett (ed). *Planning Economic Development*, p. 353.

executing agencies have their operations so exceedingly oriented to financial planning that the physical aspects of project implementation are relegated to a minor position. The ways to overcome this are to insist on complete project proposals, cost-benefit studies, through assimilation of knowledge of physical inputs required accompanied by a schedule of sources of these inputs, and the formulation of realistic work-programmes.[3]

The need for similar reform is equally great in most less developed countries.

Because the work of a programing unit transcends organization lines in an operating organization, and because it must transmit directives to which operating units must conform in preparing and executing their projects, it is desirable that a programing unit be established as a staff unit headed by a high-ranking official who reports directly to the minister or head of an agency. As with a central planning agency, it is important that the head of the programing unit have the confidence of his minister or head of agency. The operating organization should also have a programing committee, made up of the minister or head of agency, his second in command and the chiefs of each of the operating divisions in the organization. The programing committee should be the planning group for the operating organization and, as such, should review policy proposals which the programing unit has prepared for the consideration of the minister or head of agency and, where appropriate, for the cabinet or planning committee of the cabinet. The programing committee should also endeavor to evolve means for achieving economy, avoiding waste and insuring efficient execution of projects. The programing unit should act as the secretariat of the programing committee and the head of the programing unit should be the committee's secretary.

It is also frequently desirable for a ministry or agency to have an advisory body composed of persons outside the organization to participate and help in the process of preparing and executing an organization's program.[4] For example, an advisory body to a ministry of agriculture would be composed of representatives of the important producer groups and regions in a country's agricultural sector. An

---

[3] Burma. Ministry of National Planning. *Second Four-Year Plan for the Union of Burma* (1961–62 to 1964–65), p. 88.

[4] This committee would differ from a working party composed of interested individuals within a government sometimes set up by a central planning agency to formulate a sectoral program.

advisory body's size should be determined on the basis of compromise. The ideal should be to obtain a group which is neither too large to be effective nor too small to be unrepresentative. The advisory body not only should prepare policy suggestions for the head of an operating organization, but should also be the sounding board for contemplated policies. It should perform an educational function as well, since the head of an operating organization should call upon it for co-operation in disseminating information about adopted policy. The advisory body's suggestions should be studied by the programing unit, which should also constitute the advisory body's secretariat. The head of the programing unit should be the secretary of the advisory body.

The size of the staff of a programing unit will depend on several factors, the two most important being the range of its organization's activities and the attitude of its head toward the work to be done. In most ministries and agencies, one programing unit usually suffices; but if a ministry has jurisdiction over two or more major sectors of an economy, for instance, industry and mining or industry and commerce, it may be advisable to set up separate programing units for each sector.[5] But even if there is only one programing unit, its staff need not be large if it is prepared to delegate as much work as possible to the operating units. A programing unit should avoid taking over operating functions for the same reasons that a central planning agency should. If its staff is to be kept small, it is desirable that it be organized in two loose, flexible groups or sections instead of in a rigid internal organization with more sections. One group or section should be concerned with research, surveys, studies and statistical collection and analysis. The second group or section should be concerned with project evaluation, the preparation of sectoral or subsectoral programs, submission of the operating organization's program for inclusion in government plans and budgets, reporting on the progress of project and program execution and co-ordination of technical skills within the organization.

The staff of a programing unit must be familiar with techniques of project appraisal and sector programing. These techniques require both economic and technical knowledge. Engineers (or other technicians) without economic training or economists without technical background are both, by themselves, unsuited to the task of project evaluation and sector programing. It is possible to include both

[5] United Nations Center for Industrial Development. *Organizational Aspects of Planning*, p. 38.

economists and technicians in a programing unit and this is sometimes done; but it is preferable, of course, to staff a programing unit with individuals who have both the required technical and economic knowledge. While economists generally make better central planners than technicians do, experience shows that engineers, agronomists or other technicians who have acquired some competency in economic techniques are more suitable than economists for project appraisal and sector programing. One authority, with considerable experience in Latin America, points out that

> actual programming work in Latin America has demonstrated that it is very difficult to become a good specialist in sectorial programming without a minimum technological knowledge of the field. . . . It is easier to train people possessing a technical background with some knowledge of economics to be good sectorial programmers than it is to provide economists with the minimum technical education necessary.[6]

THE ESTABLISHMENT OF PROGRAMING UNITS

In the USSR, every ministry and department in the Central Government and the republics has its own programing division which prepares draft plans for submission to the appropriate authorities. But as already indicated, in the governments of most less developed countries with central planning agencies, programing units in ministries, departments and agencies are unusual. In countries where these units exist, they generally have not been established for all or most operating organizations. In the former Federation of Malaya, for example, a few federal ministries have programing units, but most have only a development officer who acts as a channel of communication between the central planning agency and his ministry and also tries to carry out the programing function as best he can. Ceylon established Planning Committees in its ministries to prepare sector programs and to coordinate the implementation of projects in each ministry's program. These committees have not proved to be effective.

But in most countries not even a development officer or a planning committee exists in operating organizations, and central planning

---

[6] Ahumada, Jorge. "Problems of Specialized Training Requirements as Viewed from Inside a Country in Process of Economic Development," p. 16.

agencies have to deal separately with each operating unit in each ministry and agency. This system of operation may produce some results, but it is far from satisfactory. In Colombia, for instance,

> a great effort has been made by the planning bodies [in the central government] to promote and encourage planning activities in the executive public bodies, i.e., Ministries, autonomous agencies, and local government units, with some measure of success. In this respect the central planning organization has had a moderately successful 'demonstration effect' on other public bodies. The day is still far off, however, when the central planning bodies will play their proper role of merely guiding, analyzing, and coordinating the plans prepared by the various executive government agencies instead of having to prepare themselves much of the detailed plans of these agencies.[7]

The need for programing units is now well understood. Thus, the United Nations, after pointing out that programing units "act as channels through which the planning function permeates the executive ministries," admonishes:

> It will be advisable to establish them [i.e., programing units] at an early stage of the planning activity and to begin with the most important ministries. . . .[8]

Planners frequently urge that operating organizations establish programing units. Thus, Pakistan's First Five Year Plan counseled that ministries establish such units:

> The preparation of programmes and schemes in the different economic and social fields is and should be the responsibility of the administrative ministries concerned; for this purpose, each ministry should have a planning unit free to devote its whole time to the task.[9]

Ghana's draft Seven-Year Plan also called for the creation of programing units. In the Philippines, the Program Implementation Agency proposed the creation of programing units in each department and agency which would be staffed with individuals trained in economic analysis. Burma's central planners also exhorted ministries to establish viable programing units.

[7] Columbia University School of Law. *Public International Development Financing in Colombia*, p. 44.

[8] United Nations Center for Industrial Development. *Organizational Aspects of Planning*, p. 38.

[9] Pakistan. National Planning Board. *First Five Year Plan, 1955–1960*, p. 98.

In addition to the central planning organization there are or should be planning units in the Administrative Ministries. . . . The quality of the comprehensive plan depends on the quality of the basic sectoral plans. If the Administrative Ministries and executing agencies are deficient in formulation of plans for their respective fields the plan drawn up by the central planning agency may be unrealistic. It is essential for each Administrative Ministry to have a planning unit of its own. At present some of these Ministries have planning sections in name but are not staffed by technicians qualified to discharge the functions of these sections.[10]

But usually nothing comes of these exhortations. Where programing units have been established, as much in Afghanistan, El Salvador, Syria and the UAR as in Burma, they rarely function as they should and in co-operation with their central planning agencies; nor are their staffs likely to be familiar with the requisite techniques for sound project evaluation and sector programing. Frequently, they are understaffed and headed by junior officials or are established at too low a level in their organizations. In many cases, their functions are not defined with sufficient precision to permit them to carry them out effectively.

As mentioned earlier, the lack of viable programing units in the governments of less developed countries is at least partly due to the low priority assigned to them by planners when a country begins to plan. But even after central planners recognize the need for programing units and urge them upon operating organizations, progress in establishing them is usually painfully slow. In Pakistan, for example, only a few ministries, departments and agencies had taken the necessary measures to establish programing units two years after the Government, prompted by the Planning Commission, had issued directives for their establishment. Most departments and agencies eventually created programing units, but only three or four were reasonably effective several years afterward.

There are several reasons for the frequent and often extended delays in the establishment of workable programing units after central planning agencies urge that they be set up. Experience in Pakistan and elsewhere has revealed that few old-line ministries, departments or agencies have the technical capacity to establish and staff programing units. In many cases, the cause lies deeper than the lack of technical capacity. Within traditional ministries, a variety of organizational,

---

[10] Burma. Ministry of National Planning. *Second Four-Year Plan for the Union of Burma* (1961–62 to 1964–65), p. 87.

procedural and bureaucratic impediments to improved co-ordination, which is basic to the programing and planning process, generally interferes with the establishment and activity of effective programing units. Together, technical and administrative inadequacy constitute too great a hurdle for most old-line operating organizations to take without outside help.

There is also uncertainty about a central planning agency's role in establishing programing units. It is widely supposed that it is a planning agency's responsibility to help operating organizations establish programing units. Thus, the Organization of American States (OAS) has suggested that

> the central planning agency can be of crucial importance in assisting the operating departments in the establishment of their planning unit. . . . In countries where there is a healthy climate of mutual trust, a temporary exchange of technicians between operating ministries and the planning agency could help in the establishment of the planning units. It would also materially benefit the technicians of the central planning agency.[11]

But the fact is that few central planning agencies are in position to help establish programing units for operating organizations. Most planning agencies are themselves so understaffed and overworked that they cannot, and in practice almost never, assume this responsibility. Central planners are also generally inadequately equipped for this task because the talent required for evaluating projects and preparing sector programs "from-the-ground-up" is different from that required for aggregative planning. Of course, this does not mean that central planners have nothing to teach programers; rather, it implies that the kind of technical assistance needed to help establish programing units is not customarily found in central planning agencies. Moreover, even when a central planning agency has qualified technicians who are available to help set up programing units, they are likely to encounter suspicion if not open hostility in traditional ministries, where they have sometimes been looked upon as interlopers whose primary purpose it is to establish outposts of the central planning agency in operating organizations in order to meddle in operations.

In countries where, as the OAS says, "there is a healthy climate of mutual trust" between a central planning agency and operating organi-

---

[11] OAS. Inter-American Economic and Social Council, Special Committee I, etc. *Programming for Development: Five Urgent Problems*, p. 6.

zations, and the planning agency has the necessary staff, there is, of course, no good reason why a central planning agency should not assist operating organizations in establishing programing units. But where a central planning agency lacks the personnel or is likely to have to contend with opposition from operating organizations—and experience shows one or both factors prevail in most countries—it would be best if technical assistance for establishing programing units come from other sources than a central planning agency.

This brings into question the current practice of attaching foreign or international planning advisers, whether individuals or groups, to central planning agencies. Because of this association, they often find it difficult to advise operating ministries and agencies, either because the head of a central planning agency is opposed to it or because operating organizations tend to consider the advisers as partisans of a central planning agency. A more flexible arrangement would be for foreign or international planning advisers to be part of a resident mission to a government in general, to its chief executive or a training institute. This would allow them to assist both a central planning agency and operating organizations as circumstances required, without any semblance of partiality. If training institutes exist, or were established for the purpose, programing staffs could be trained in project evaluation and sector programing, as well as in planning techniques, in numbers far exceeding those who could be trained by being attached for a time to a central planning agency. Attempts to rationalize current public investment, through the "inventory technique" previously described, also could provide a means for establishing programing units and for in-service training of personnel to operate them effectively.

SUMMARY AND CONCLUSIONS

A programing unit in an operating organization is essentially a miniature central planning agency functioning within a more limited scope. Its relations with operating units and the head of its own organization are much like those of a central planning agency's with operating organizations and a nation's political leaders; and while the relationship between a central planning agency and a programing unit is necessarily complementary, their respective functions differ more in degree than in substance. A programing unit's main functions are to prepare sector and subsector programs for its organization for submission to both central planning and budgetary authorities, to recommend measures for implementing its organization's plans, to prepare periodic reports on the progress of projects and programs, and to co-ordinate technical assistance activities.

A programing unit occupies a crucial position in a country's planning apparatus. It should be the main channel of communication between a central planning agency and an operating organization. To establish the two-way flow of information required for this purpose, close working relations must be maintained between programing units and a central planning agency. This is frequently difficult to achieve. Deficiencies of co-ordination are common impediments to smooth working relations between a central planning agency and programing units.

Programing units should not prepare or execute projects; this is a job for operating units. Programing units should, however, set up forms and standards which operating units should follow—and there is great need for improved standards of project preparation and execution.

As with a central planning agency, it is important that a programing unit be set up as a staff unit closely associated with the head of an operating organization and that the official in charge of the unit have the confidence of the head of the organization. A programing committee composed of the highest officials of the operating organization should also be established to help formulate planning policy. The programing unit should act as the committee's secretariat, with the head of the programing unit serving as the committee's secretary. It is also frequently desirable for an operating organization to have an advisory body composed of outsiders to recommend policies and otherwise to assist in preparing and executing an organization's program. The advisory body's suggestions should be studied by the programing unit, which should also constitute the advisory body's secretariat. The head of the programing unit should be the secretary of the advisory body.

Generally, the staff of a programing unit can be kept small if it delegates as much work as possible to operating units. A desirable way to organize a programing unit is to set up two loose, flexible groups or sections. One of these should be concerned with general analysis, research and statistics; the second should be concerned with program-ing, co-ordination, progress reporting and evaluation. While econo-mists generally make better central planners than specialists do, experi-ence shows that engineers, agronomists or other technicians who have acquired some competency in economic techniques are more suitable than economists for working on project appraisal and sector programing.

The lack of viable programing units in less developed nations is at least partly explained by the low priority they usually have for planners when a country begins to plan. Another reason is the mistaken belief that a planning agency should help establish programing units. Most planning agencies are too undermanned and overburdened to undertake the task, and moreover, central planners generally do not have the technical competence required to evaluate projects and prepare sector programs "from-the-bottom-up." Finally, even when a planning agency has qualified technicians available, they are likely to meet with opposition in operating organizations. It is generally desirable, therefore, that technical assistance for establishing programing units come from sources other than a central planning agency.

Appendix I

Colombia: Questionnaire on Investment Programs of Public Entities

---

ENTITY

A. *Name of the Project*

    (1) Date on which it was or will be started (month and year):

    (2) If already started, probable date of completion (month and year):

        If not, time required for its entire execution:

B. *Investment*	Total	1955	1956	1957	1958	1959	1960
Total investment required:							
Amount of imported goods and services that will be used:							
C. Contribution to the project out of the ordinary funds of the entity:							
D. Additional financing required:							
I. Contributions by the national, departmental, or municipal governments and by other public or semi-public entities: [1]							
II. By private investors: [2]							
III. Loans: (a) domestic: [3] (b) foreign: [4]							

[1] Specify on a separate sheet what type of commitments or arrangements exist or are proposed; if none, so state.

[2] State whether the investors are Colombian or foreign.

[3] Supply on a separate sheet any information available on the manner in which the loans have been or are going to be obtained.

[4] If any information is possessed, fill in the separate questionnaire "FOREIGN FINANCING."

FOREIGN FINANCING

Name of the project:

Entity applying for the loan:

Lender: [1]

Amount of loan, by currencies:

Term of the loan and date when final repayment is due:

Cost of the loan:

    (a) rate of interest:
    (b) other costs, including commission:

System of amortization: [2]

Type of guarantee, if any: [3]

Present stage of negotiations relating to the loan: [4]

---

[1] Use a separate sheet for each loan.

[2] State the date on which amortization begins and the system or repayment.

[3] State the name of the entity that will furnish the guarantee and whether it includes the obligation to supply the necessary foreign exchange.

[4] Indicate one of the following stages:

    (a) preliminary discussions
    (b) negotiations commenced
    (c) loan agreement signed
    (d) loan agreement signed and approved by the National Government.

Appendix II

Argentina: Questionnaire on Public Investment Programs

GENERAL INSTRUCTIONS

With the aim of complying with the requirements of the present inventory, the information that is provided should conform to the following criteria:

I. All the contemplated works and those already in the process of execution which the organization expects will be carried out during the period of the plan (fiscal year 1963 to 1967 inclusive) shall be included.

II. The works and projects will be indicated following an order of priorities (see Table I) according to the judgment of the organization and taking account of the following indications: a) priority shall be given to works already under way; b) among the proposed works priority will be given to those which in the judgment of the organization promise greater economic and social benefit.

III. All the works or projects of remodeling, repair and reconditioning will also be computed.

IV. Projects and works with the same purpose and with influence in the same area may be grouped as a single investment, provided that the sum of each of the components of the group does not exceed 10 million pesos, or a total sum no greater than 50 million, according to justified criterion of the organization.

V. The organization will use the attached Table 1 to group all those works or projects which the organization considers to be related by some criterion of complementarity, regardless of the order of priority assigned to each individual work or project.

VI. It shall be understood that the amount of each work or project includes secondary and/or accessory investments which are indispensable to its operation.

Presidency of the Nation
National Development Council

Table No. 1

SURVEY OF INVESTMENTS IN THE PUBLIC SECTOR

Organization: ....

Division: ....

Project No. (1)	Name of Project	Location	Present Status (2)

(1) The numbering of the projects should be given by the priority assigned by the organization and/or division.
(2) Indicate whether the project is proposed, bidded upon, contracted, under way (estimate portion of project already completed).

Presidency of the Nation
National Development Council

Table No. 2

PHYSICAL APPRAISAL OF THE PROJECTS

Project No. (1)	Purpose of the Work (2)	Quantification of the Services		Estimate of Present Need for Services	Estimated Year of Completion	Remarks
		Unit/ Method	Quantity			

Presidency of the Nation
National Development Council

INVESTMENTS ALREADY MADE IN PESOS .... TOTAL INVESTMENT IN PESOS ....

Table No. 3

(Monetary figures in thousands)

Project No. (1)	Year Started	Investments Already Made (2) (a)			Investments to be Made (3) (b)			Total Investment (a + b)			Equipment Expenditures (4)	Operating Expenses (5)
		Pesos	US$	Total Expressed in Pesos	Pesos	US$	Total Expressed in Pesos	Pesos	US$	Total Expressed in Pesos		

(1) The numbering system used in previous tables should be used in this one.
(2) The amount ordered to be paid by October 31, 1962, should be given. In adding the part in foreign exchange to the part in pesos, convert the foreign exchange portion with the exchange rate actually used.
(3) The rate of exchange to be used is US$1.00 = 135 pesos.
(4) Note the additional expenditures not included in previous columns required to go forward with the investment.
(5) Estimate of annual expenses for financing the service. In the case of substitute projects or those extending works already in existence, only the additions to the existing budget are to be noted.

Table No. 4

Presidency of the Nation
National Development Council

PROPOSED INVESTMENTS AND FUTURE FINANCIAL COMMITMENTS

(Monetary figures in thousands)

Project No. (1)	1963		1964		1965		1966		1967		After 1967		Total Future Investment (2)		
	Pesos	US$	Pesos	US$	Pesos	US$	Pesos	US$	Pesos	US$	Pesos	US$	Pesos (a)	US$ (b)	Total Pesos (a + b)

(1) Repeat the numbering system used in previous tables.
(2) This should coincide with the column of investments to be realized according to Table No. 4.
NOTE: This table should include commitments contracted for but not ordered to be paid which apply in the fiscal years indicated in the tables and the future commitments determining their annual incidence.
The rate of exchange to be used is US$1.00 = 135 pesos.

Presidency of the Nation
National Development Council

Table No. 5

PROJECTION OF THE RESOURCES OF THE ORGANIZATION AND/OR DIVISION

(Monetary figures in thousands)

Year	General Income	Own Resources	Special Funds	Use of Credit (Domestic)	Foreign Credit	Other Resources (3)		Total Arranged Resources	Resources not Arranged
1963									
1964									
1965									
1966									
1967									

(3) Specify its source.

NOTE: The organization should attach a table showing resources allocated to specific purposes, indicating their source and destination.

Presidency of the Nation
National Development Council

Table No. 6

PROJECTION OF THE EXPENDITURES OF THE ORGANIZATION AND/OR DIVISION

(Monetary figures in thousands)

Year	Expenses		Patrimonial Investments		Transfers (2)	Total Expenses
	Personnel Expenses	Other Expenses	Investments	Public Works (1)		
1963						
1964						
1965						
1966						
1967						
After 1967						

(1) Each amount in the column on Public Works should coincide with the total of the sum of pesos plus US dollars in Table No. 4. The amounts in US dollars should be converted to pesos, utilizing the rate of exchange of US$1.00 = 135 pesos.
(2) Amounts transferred to other official and/or private organizations.

National Plans

Types of Plans Included

1. A list of long-, medium-, and short-term national plans of nations and dependent territories appears on the following pages.

2. The list is mainly a compilation of national development plans. However, in some cases other plans were included because they may be of interest to students of development planning. Thus, the list includes multi-annual financial plans of the Philippines and Puerto Rico, annual anticyclical plans of the Netherlands, as well as a development plan issued by Peru's central bank but never acknowledged as a national plan by that country's government.

3. Plans covering two or more sectors are included in the compilation; those covering only one sector are not. Regional plans, whether a part of a country or territory, or covering more than one country or territory, are also excluded.

4. Although an effort was made to compile as complete a list of plans as possible within the limitations set, it was recognized that completeness was not likely to be achieved because of time and resource restrictions. Nevertheless, it is believed that the compilation probably includes most of the national plans issued by countries and territories.

5. Whenever possible, titles of plans included in the compilation were taken from the plans themselves or, where this was not feasible, from library catalog listings. In many cases, however, the list contains references to plans derived from a variety of news media. These references include plans which were in course of preparation, as well as those whose preparation had been completed, by April 1, 1965, when the collection of information for the compilation terminated.

Key to the Listings

6. *Order of Listings.* Countries and dependent territories are listed alphabetically as shown in the Contents. Plans for each country or territory are listed chronologically.

7. *Titles of Plans.* All titles in languages other than English were translated into English. Where the exact title of a plan could not be ascertained,

the entry is not italicized. An italicized entry indicates that the title given is the one appearing on the plan itself. In some cases, two versions of the same plan have been listed where the plan has been issued in both the original language and an English translation. Any additions supplied to a title as it appeared on a plan are in brackets.

8. *Duration of Plans.* Whenever possible, the period covered by a plan is shown, whether or not it is part of the title. Where the period in the plan appears in terms of a non-Gregorian calendar, the corresponding Gregorian period is also shown. When the necessary information was available, the organization which formulated or issued a plan is also included.

9. *Reference Sources.* Wherever possible the source of an entry is indicated by two or more capital letters following the entry. The Reference Key which follows indicates the source, if it was a library or a book, report or similar publication. If the information came from a newspaper, magazine or other periodical, this is also indicated, but in brackets under the appropriate entry. "n.p." indicates that the place of publication could not be determined. "n.d." indicates that the date of publication could not be determined. The co-operation of the libraries listed, which made available plans or catalog listings, is gratefully acknowledged. Where plans were unavailable, references in the publications listed were frequently used.

SOURCE REFERENCE KEY

BEB   *Bibliography on Economic Planning with Special Reference to Long-Term Project* [Tokyo, National Diet Library, 1962].

CAR   Caribbean Organization. Library. *Bibliography of Development Plans.* Hato Rey, Puerto Rico, 1963.

CO   Colonial Office Library, Great Smith St., London.

CRO   Commonwealth Relations Office Library, Whitehall, London.

ECA   Library of the United Nations. Economic Commission for Africa. Addis Ababa, Ethiopia.

ECAFE   Library of the United Nations. Economic Commission for Asia and the Far East. Sala Santitham, Bangkok, Thailand.

GER   Bremer Ausschuss Für Wirtschaftsforschung. *Dokumente und Berichte über Entwicklungspläne; Ein Bibliographischer Nachweis.* Bremen, 1961.

JL   Joint Library of the International Bank for Reconstruction and Development/International Monetary Fund, 19th and H Sts., N.W., Washington, D.C. 20431.

LC   Library of Congress, Washington, D.C.

PAU   Columbus Memorial Library. Pan American Union. Washington, D.C.

SP   Spulber, Nicolas. "Planning and Development," in: Pounds, Norman J. G. and Spulber, Nicolas (eds). *Resources and Planning in Eastern Europe,* Vol. 4, Bloomington, Indiana University Publications, 1957, pp. 101–102.

TL   United States Treasury Department Library. *Postwar Plans for Economic Development Throughout the World.* Washington, D.C., January 1958.

UN   United Nations. Dag Hammarskjold Library. *Economic and Social Development Plans: Africa, Asia, Latin America.* New York, 1964 (ST/LIB/SER.B/9).

UNP   United Nations. Department of Economic Affairs. *Economic Development in Selected Countries: Plans, Programmes and Agencies,* 2 vols. New York, 1950 (ST/ECA/4).

UNS   United Nations. Economic Commission for Africa. *Outlines and Selected Indicators of African Development Plans.* New York, January 14, 1965 (E/CN.14/336).

YGC   Yale Growth Center. *Bibliography of National Economic Development Plans.* (Preliminary Version.) New Haven, Conn., Yale University, April 1, 1965.

CONTENTS

NATIONAL PLANS

Aden (United Kingdom)

Memorandum on Five-Year Development Plan, 1952/53–56/57. Aden, 1957. 33 p. JL
Financial Secretariat. *Draft Development Plan, 1955–1960.* Aden, January 1956. 13 p. CO
Financial Secretariat. *Development Plan, 1955–1960.* Aden, 22nd March 1956. 50 p. CO
Development Plan, 1960–64. Aden, 1960. 6 p.   CO–JL

Afghanistan

Ministry of National Economy. *The Five-Year Economic Development Plan of Afghanistan* [September 1956–August 1961]. Kabul, 1956. 247 p. ECAFE
Ministry of Planning. *Second Five-Year Plan, 1341–45* [March 1962– March 1967, Gregorian Calendar]. Kabul, 1963. 100 p.   UN

Albania

Albánský dvouletý hospodářsky plán [Albanian Two-Year Economic Plan]. Praha [Prague], Orbis, 1951.   LC
Pervyi piatiletnii plan narodnogo khoziaistva Narodnoi Respubliki Albanii [1951–1955]. [First Five-Year Plan for the Development of the National Economy of the People's Republic of Albania.] Tirana, 1952. 92 p.   BEB
Direktivat e kongresit të 3-të partisë së punës të shqiperisë mbi planin e dytë pesëvjecar të zhvilimit te ekonomisë popullore të republikës të shqiperisë në vjetët 1956–1960; Projekti komitet quëndror të PPSH [Directives of the 3rd Congress of the Albanian Workers Party for the Economic Development of the Albanian People's Republic in the years 1956–1960]. Tirana, 1956. 62 p.   BEB
Third Five-Year Plan, 1961–1965.   BEB

Algeria

Premier Plan Quadriennal d'Equipement (1949–1952). [First Four-Year Equipment Plan (1949–1952).]
        [Mentioned in Gouvernement Général de l'Algérie. *Rapport Général sur le Deuxième Plan Quadriennal de Modernisation et d'Equipement de l'Algérie* (1953–1956). Alger, 1953. p. 11.]
Deuxième Plan Quadriennal de Modernisation et d'Equipement de l'Algérie (1953–1956). [Second Four-Year Plan of Modernization and Equipment of Algeria (1953–1956).]
        [Mentioned on the title page of Gouvernement Général d'Algérie. *Rapport Général sur le Deuxième Plan Quadriennal de Modernisation et d'Equipement de l'Algérie* (1953–1956). Alger, 1953.]

France. Commissariat Général au Plan de Modernisation et d'Equipement. *Rapport Général de la Commission d'Etude et des Plans de Modernisation et d'Equipement de l'Algérie, de la Tunisie et du Maroc. Algérie* [1954–1957]. [General Report of the Study Commission and of the Modernization and Equipment Plans of Algeria, Tunisia, and Morocco. Algeria.] Paris, 1954. 137 p.   JL

France. Ministère de l'Algérie. *Perspectives Décennales de Développement Economique de l'Algérie* [1957–1966]. [Ten-Year Perspectives for the Economic Development of Algeria.] Alger, 1958. 455 p.   JL

France. Délégation Général du Gouvernement en Algérie. Direction du Plan et des Etudes Economiques. *Plan de Constantine, 1959–1963; Rapport Général.* [The Constantine Plan, 1959–1963; General Report.] Paris, 1960. 526 p.   JL

Annual Equipment Budget, 1963.   UNS

Annual Equipment Budget, 1964.   UNS

Angola (Portugal)

Plano do Fundo de Fomento de Angola, 1946–1955. [Plan for the Development Fund of Angola, 1946–1955.] Luanda [1947].   GER

Portugal. Ministério da Economia. *Plano de Fomento* [1953–1958]. [Development Plan.] Lisbon, 1953. pp. 78–84.   JL

Portugal. Ministério da Economia. *II Plano de Fomento, 1959–1964.* [The Second Plan of Development, 1959–1964.] Lisbon, 1959. pp. 191–209.   JL

Portugal. Presidência do Conselho. *Plano Intercalar de Fomento para 1965–1967.* [Transitional Development Plan for 1965–1967.] Lisbon, 1964. Vol. II. pp. 135–186.

Antigua (United Kingdom)

Presidency of Antigua. *Antigua Development Plan, 1951–1955.* Antigua, n.d. 51 p.   CO

Antigua Development Plan, 1963–1966. n.p., n.d. 9 p.   JL

Argentina

Presidencia de la Nación. *Plan de Gobierno, 1947 a 1951.* [Government Plan, 1947–1951.] Buenos Aires, 1946.   UNP

Secretaría de la Presidencia. Subsecretaría de Información y Prensa. *2° Plan Quinquenal de la Nación. Plan General de Gobierno 1953–1957.* Ley 14.184 (texto integral). [Second Five-Year Plan of the Nation. General Plan for 1953–1957.] Buenos Aires, 1955. 464 p.   PAU

Consejo Nacional de Desarrollo. *Informe sobre el Plan Nacional de Desarrollo, Años 1965–1969.* [Report on the National Development Plan, 1965–1969.] Buenos Aires, 1964. 3 parts.   JL
[Part 1, "Versión Preliminar"; Part 2, "Versión Preliminar Revisada"; Part 3, "Anexos."]

Bahamas (United Kingdom)

Development Programme. Approved by the House of Assembly, 1952. Bahamas, 1953. 32 p.   CO

Barbados (United Kingdom)

Ten-Year Development Plan for Barbados; Sketch Plan of Development, 1946–1956; Report of the Committee Appointed by His Excellency the Governor to Prepare a Sketch Plan to Provide the Framework for the Island's Development and Welfare Policy for the Period 1946–1956. n.p., 1945. 63 p.   JL
Five-Year Plan of Development and Taxation [1952/53–1956/57]. n.p., n.d. 28 p.   JL
Development Plan, 1955–1960. Barbados, n.d. 34 p.   JL
Development Plan, 1960–1965. [Bridgetown], n.d. 88 p.   JL
Development Programme, 1962–1965. n.p., n.d. 55 p.   CO–JL
Development Plan, 1965–1968. [Mentioned in *The Times* (London), May 12, 1965.]

Basutoland (United Kingdom)

Memorandum of Development Plans [1946–1955]. [Maseru, 1946.] 17 p.   CO
Five-Year Development Programme [1960–1964]. n.p., September 1960. 21 p.   JL
Office of the Secretariat. *Development Plan, 1963–1968.* Maseru, December 1963. 52 p.
        [Actual period of plan is 1963–1966.]

Bechuanaland Protectorate (United Kingdom)

Development Plan, 1956–1960.
        [Mentioned in *Development Plan, 1960–1964,* cited below, p. 1.]
Development Plan, 1960–1964 and Draft Colonial Development and Welfare Schemes, 1960–1964. n.p., 1960. 146 p.   JL
Draft Development Plan, 1963–1968. n.p., 1963. 59 p.   JL
Development Plan, 1963–1968. n.p., 1963. 72 p.   JL

Belgian Congo (See Congo, Democratic Republic of [Leopoldville] for post-independence plans)

Development Plan (1906).
        [Mentioned in Niculescu, Barbu, *Colonial Planning, A Comparative Study.* London, Allen and Unwin, 1958. p. 73.]
Franck Plan (1920).
        [Mentioned in Niculescu, Barbu, *Colonial Planning, A Comparative Study.* p. 73.]
Ministère Belge des Colonies. *Plan Décennal pour le Développement Economique et Social du Congo Belge* [1950–1959]. [Ten-Year Plan for the Economic and Social Development of the Belgian Congo.] Bruxelles, 1949. 2 vols.   JL
Belgian Congo. Conseil. *Session Générale 1958 du 23 Février au 2 Mars 1959; Annexe II: Avant-Projet Deuxième Plan Décennal, Notes Documentaires (1960–1969)* [General Session, February 23, 1958 to March 2, 1959; Annex II: Preliminary Draft of the Second Ten-Year Plan, Documentary Notes] [Leopoldville, 1959?]. 720 p.   ECA

Belgium

Ministère de la Coordination Economique et du Rééquipement National. *Programme Décennal des Investissements Publics, 1948–1957.* [Ten-Year Public Investment Program, 1948–1957.] Bruxelles [1948?]. 130 p. JL

Premier Programme d'Expansion Economique (1962–1965). [First Program of Economic Expansion (1962–1965).] Bruxelles, 1962. pp. 6–216. JL

> [In *Projet de Loi Portant Approbation du Premier Programme d'Expansion Economique (1962–1965).* Sénat de Belgique. Session de 1962–1963. 13 décembre 1962. 216 p.]

Five-Year Plan, 1965–1970.

> [Mentioned in *Neue Zürcher Zeitung.* June 14, 1964.]

Bermuda (United Kingdom)

The Next 20 Years; A Report on the Development Plan for Bermuda. Prepared for the Government of Bermuda by H. Thornley Dyer. n.p., May 13th, 1963. 29 p. United States Department of Labor Library, Washington, D.C.

Bhutan

Coordinated Five-Year Development Plan [1961–1966].

> [Mentioned in "Bhutan's Development Plan" in Colombo Plan Bureau. *Colombo Plan.* Vol. 8, No. 1. Colombo, Ceylon, 1963. p. 1.]

Bolivia

Ministerio de Relaciones Exteriores y Culto. *Plan Inmediato de Política Económica del Gobierno de la Revolución Nacional.* [Immediate Plan of Economic Policy of the National Revolutionary Government.] La Paz, 1955. 135 p. PAU

Junta Nacional de Planeamiento. *Plan Nacional de Desarrollo Económico y Social, 1962–1971; resumen.* [National Plan for Economic and Social Development, 1962–1971; summary.] La Paz, 1961. 328 p. JL

Junta Nacional de Planeamiento. *Plan Nacional de Desarrollo Económico y Social, 1962–1971.* [National Plan for Economic and Social Development, 1962–1971.] La Paz, 1961. pp. 16–288.

> [This constitutes Nos. 3–4–5, September 1961 of *Planeamiento, Revista Trimestral,* official publication of the Junta Nacional de Planeamiento.]

Secretaría Nacional de Planificación y Coordinación. *Plan Bienal de Desarrollo Económico y Social, 1963–1964.* [Two-Year Plan for Economic and Social Development, 1963–1964.] La Paz, 1963. 326 p. UN

> [This constitutes Nos. 6–7–8, September 1963 of *Planeamiento, Revista Trimestral.*]

Brazil

Conselho do Desenvolvimento. *Programa de Metas* [1957–1961]. [Program of Targets.] Rio de Janeiro, 1958. Tomo I, 103 p.; Tomo II, 260 p.; Tomo III, 394 p.   JL
Conselho do Desenvolvimento. *Program of Targets* [1957–1961]. Rio de Janeiro, January 1958. 145 p.
Presidência da Republica. *Plano Trienal do Desenvolvimento Economico e Social, 1963–1965.* [Three-Year Plan for Economic and Social Development, 1963–1965.] Brasilia, 1962. 195 p.
Presidência da Republica. *Three-Year Plan for Economic and Social Development, 1963–1965.* Rio de Janeiro, 1962. 146 p.   JL
Gabinete do Ministro Extraordinário para o Planejamento e Coordenação Econômico. *Programa de Ação Econômica do Govêrno, 1964–1966.* [Government Program of Economic Action, 1964–1966.] Rio de Janeiro, 1964.

> Vol. I: *Objectivos e Instrumentos de Ação, Redação Preliminar.* [Objectives and Instruments of Action, Preliminary Draft.]

> Vol. II: *Politicas e Programas Sectórias, Redação Preliminar.* [Policies and Sector Programs, Preliminary Draft.]

British Guiana (United Kingdom)

General Ten-Year Plan of Development and Welfare, 1947–1956; Papers Relating to Development Planning No. 1:

> Vol. I: *Report of the Main Development Committee of the Legislative Council.* Legislative Council Paper No. 8 of 1947. Georgetown, 1947. 70 p.   JL

> Vol. II: *Reports of the Subcommittees of the Main Development Committee of the Legislative Council.* Legislative Council Paper No. 11 of 1948. Georgetown, 1948. 396 p.   JL

> Vol. III: Maps.

Development Programme, 1956–1960. Legislative Council Paper No. 8 of 1956. Georgetown, 1956. 41 p.   JL
Development Programme, 1960–1964. Legislative Council Second Session, 1958–59. Paper No. 5. Demerara, 1959. 51 p.   JL
Five-Year Development Plan, 1966–1970.

> [Under preparation according to *The Times* (London). March 30, 1965.]

British Honduras (United Kingdom)

Development Planning Committee. *Report of the Development Planning Committee* [1947–1956]. Belize, 11 January 1946. 76 p.   JL
Immediate Plan, Part I [1946–1951].   CO

> [A summary of this plan appears on pp. 2–5 of *Immediate Plan, Part II,* below.]

Draft Development Plan [1950–1960]. Belize, 1950. 65 p.   UN

Immediate Plan, Part II, 1952–1956. Sessional Paper No. 12 of 1952. Belize, 1952. 58 p.   JL
Development Plan, Part III, 1955–1960. Belize, 1955. 48 p.   CO
Ministry of Finance. *Development Policy and Interim Expenditure Programme* [1961–1963]. Belize, May 1961. 94 p.   JL
Development Plan for British Honduras [1963–1970]. Prepared for the Government of British Honduras by Consultants appointed under the United Nations Programme of Technical Assistance. New York, 1963: Part I—157 p.; Part II—57 p.; Part III—89 p.; Part IV—207 p.   JL
Office of the First Minister. *Development Plan, 1964–1970.* Belize City, 30th September, 1963. 144 p.   JL

British Virgin Islands (United Kingdom)

Development Plan. Roadtown, Tortola, August 1951.   CAR
Administrator's Office. *Report of the Development Advisory Committee Relating to the Period, 1963–1966.* Tortola, 1963. 32 p.   JL
Administrator's Office. *Revised Development Plan, 1964–1966.* Tortola, 1st June 1964. 6 p.   CO

Brunei (United Kingdom)

Five-Year Development Plan; Summary of Proposals. Kuching, 1953. 6 p.   JL
Development Plan, 1953–1958. Brunei Town, 1958. 140 p.   ECAFE
National Development Plan, 1962–1966. Kuala Belait, 1962. 23 p.   JL

Bulgaria

First Bulgarian Two-Year Economic Plan [1947–1948]. Sofia, Foreign Information Service, 1947. 92 p.   JL
Zákon o pětiletém státním národnohospodářském plánu Lidové republiky bulharské, 1949–1953. [Law on the Five-Year National Economic Plan of the People's Republic of Bulgaria, 1949–1953]. Praha [Prague] Orbis, 1950. 32 p.   LC
Law on the Two-Year Economic Plan, 1947–48. Sofia, Ministry of Information and Arts, 1947.   SP
Terpeshev, Dobri. *Bulgaria's Five-Year Plan* [1949–53]; *Report submitted to the Congress of the Bulgarian Communist Party.* Sofia, Ministry of Foreign Affairs, 1949. 70 p.   LC
Bulgarska Komunisticheska Partiia. 6. Kongres, Sofia, 1954. *Directives on the Second Five-Year Plan for the Development of the People's Republic of Bulgaria from 1953 to 1957.* Sofia, 1954. 31 p.   LC
"Direktivy po tret'emu piatiletnemu planu razvitiia narodnogo khoziaistva Bolgarii (1958–1962 Gody)." [Directives on the Third Five-Year Plan for the Development of the National Economy of the People's Republic of Bulgaria (1958–1962)] in *Planovoe Khoziaistvo.* No. 10, 1958, pp. 87–89.   BEB
Bulgarska Komunisticheska Partiia. 8. Kongres, Sofia, 1962. *Direktivi na Osmiia kongres na Bulgarskata Komunisticheska partiia za razviteto na Narodna Republika Bulgariia prez perioda 1961–1980 g.* [Directives of

the 8th Congress of the Bulgarian Communist Party for the Development of the People's Republic of Bulgaria in the Period from 1961 to 1980.] Sofia, Bulgarian Communist Party, 1962. 48 p.   LC

Burma

Economic Planning Board. *Two-Year Plan of Economic Development for Burma* [1948–1949]. Rangoon, 1948. 55 p.   JL

Knappen-Tippetts-Abbett Engineering Co. associated with Pierce Management, Inc. and Robert R. Nathan Associates, Inc. *K.T.A. Preliminary Report on Economic and Engineering Survey of Burma for Burma Economic Council.* [New York], January 1952. 224 p.   JL

Knappen-Tippetts-Abbett Engineering Co. *Economic and Engineering Development of Burma, Comprehensive Report.* Prepared for the Government of the Union of Burma [by] Knappen-Tippetts-Abbett-McCarthy in association with Pierce Management Inc. and Robert R. Nathan Associates, Inc. [New York], 1953. 2 vols.   LC–JL

Economic and Social Board. *Pyidwatha, the New Burma; A Report from the Government to the People of the Union of Burma on Our Long-Term Programme for Economic and Social Development (1952–1960).* Rangoon, 1954. 128 p.   JL

Ministry of National Planning and Religious Affairs. *Comprehensive Development Plan, Supplement.* [Rangoon.] September 1955. 6 parts. JL

Ministry of National Planning. *Four-Year Plan of Capital Expenditures* [1956/57–1959/60]. [Rangoon], 14 June 1957. 1 vol.   JL

Ministry of National Planning. *Second Four-Year Plan for the Union of Burma* [1961–62 to 1964–65]. Rangoon, 1961. 215 p.   JL

Burundi (See Ruanda-Urundi for pre-independence plans)

Ministère des Finances et des Affaires Economiques. "Schéma d'Orientation d'un Plan Quinquennal de Développement Economique et Social du Royaume du Burundi" [Outline of the Five-Year Development Plan of the Kingdom of Burundi] in Royaume du Burundi. Ministère des Finances et des Affaires Economiques. Service de l'Information. *Bulletin Economique et Financier* (Bujumbura). No. 1. September 1964. pp. 22–26.   JL

Cabo Verde (Portugal)

Portugal. Ministério da Economia. *Plano de Fomento* [1953–1958]. [Development Plan.] Lisbon, 1953. pp. 72–74.   JL

Portugal. Ministério da Economia. *II Plano de Fomento, 1959–1964.* [The Second Plan of Development, 1959–1964.] Lisbon, 1959. pp. 169–175.   JL

Portugal. Presidência do Conselho. *Plano Intercalar de Fomento para 1965–1967.* [Transitional Development Plan for 1965–1967.] Lisbon, 1964. Vol. II. pp. 41–76.

Cambodia

Ministère du Plan. *Plan d'Equipement Biennal, 1956–1957.* [Two-Year Equipment Plan, 1956–1957.] Phnom-Penh, 1956. 277 p.   JL
Ministère du Plan. *Le Plan Quinquennal, 1960–1964.* [The Five-Year Plan, 1960–1964.] Phnom-Penh, 1960. 37 p.   UN
Second Five-Year Plan, 1965–1969.
> [Mentioned in Wilcox, Clair. *Planning and Execution of Economic Development in Southeast Asia.* Cambridge, Mass. Occasional Papers in International Affairs, No. 10, Harvard University Center for International Affairs, January 1965. p. 7.]

Cameroun (See French Cameroons for pre-independence plans)

Sociéte Générale d'Etudes et de Planification. *Cameroun; Plan de Développement Economique et Social, travaux préparatoires* [1960–1980]. [Cameroon: Economic and Social Development Plan, preliminary study.] Paris, 1960. 3 vols.   ECA
Ministère des Finances et du Plan. *Premier Plan Quinquennal de Développement Economique et Social* [1961–1965]. [First Five-Year Plan for Economic and Social Development.] Yaoundé, 1961. 271 p.   JL

Canada

Economic Council of Canada. *Economic Goals for Canada to 1970; First Annual Review.* Ottawa, December 1964. 213 p.

Canary Islands (Spain)

Spain. Presidencia del Gobierno. Comisaría del Plan de Desarrollo Económico. *Plan de Desarrollo Económico y Social, 1964–1967.* [Economic and Social Development Plan, 1964–1967.] Madrid, 1963. pp. 401–426.   JL

Cayman Islands (United Kingdom)

Development Plan. Kingston, 1947. 17 p.   CO
Development Plan for the Cayman Islands, 1960–64. Georgetown, 1960. 17 p.

Central African Republic (See Oubangui-Chari section, French Equatorial Africa for pre-independence plan)

Intermediate Three-Year Plan, 1960–1962.   UNS

Ceylon

National Planning Council. First Six-Year Plan, 1947/48–1952/53.
> [Mentioned in *The First Six-Year Plan, 1947/48–1952/53: An Assessement.* Colombo, Dept. of Information, June 1955.   GER]
Development Programme, 1951–1957.
> [Summary appears on pp. 28–32 and in Appendix 5 of Commonwealth Consultative Committee. *The Colombo Plan for Co-*

operative Economic Development in South and South-East Asia.
London, 1950. JL.]

Planning Secretariat. *Six-Year Programme of Investment, 1954/55 to 1959/60.* Colombo, 1955. 510 p. JL

Planning Secretariat. *Ten-Year Plan* [1959–1968]. Colombo, 1959. 490 p. JL

Department of National Planning. *Short-Term Implementation Programme* [1961/62–1963/64]. Colombo, 1962. 346 p. JL

Department of National Planning. *The Development Programme, 1964–1965.* Colombo, 1964. 65 p. JL

Chad (See French Equatorial Africa for pre-independence plans)

Société Générale d'Etudes et de Planification. *Tchad; Plan de Developpement Economique et Social, avant-projet.* [Chad; Economic and Social Development Plan, First Draft.] Paris [1959]. 2 vols. ECA

Commissariat Général au Plan. *Programme Intérimaire de Développement Economique et Social, 1964–1965.* [Interim Program of Economic and Social Development, 1964–1965.] Fort Lamy, 1964. 8 vols. ECA

Chile

Corporación de Fomento de la Producción. *Programa de Inversiones para 1952.* [Program of Investments for 1952.] Santiago, 1952. 53 p. PAU

Corporación de Fomento de la Producción. *Plan de Desarrollo Agrícola y de Transporte.* [Agricultural and Transportation Development Plan.] Santiago, 1954. 191 p. PAU

Inversión Pública 1963. [Public Investment 1963.] Santiago, 1962. 9 vols. PAU

Corporación de Fomento de la Producción. *Programa Nacional de Desarrollo Económico, 1961–1970.* [National Program of Economic Development, 1961–1970.] Santiago, 1961. 186 p. JL

Five-Year Plan, 1966–1970.
[Under preparation]

China, People's Republic of

First Five-Year Plan for Development of the National Economy of the People's Republic of China in 1953–1957. Peking, Foreign Languages Press, 1956. 231 p. BEB

Proposals of the Eighth National Congress of the Communist Party of China for the Second Five-Year Plan for Development of the National Economy (1958–1962). Peking, 1956. GER

State Planning Commission. Third Five-Year Plan, 1963–1967. YGC

Five-Year Plan [1966–1970].
[Mentioned in *The Economist* (London). February 20, 1965.]

China, Republic of

Economic Stabilization Board. Four-Year Economic Development Plan of Taiwan [1953–1956].

Economic Stabilization Board. *Highlights of the Second Four-Year Plan for the Economic Development of Taiwan* [1957–1960]. Taipei, 1957. 30 p.

Ministry of Economic Affairs. *Third Four-Year Economic Development Plan of Taiwan* [1961–1964]. Abridged edition. Taipei, December 1961. 82 p. JL

Council for International Economic Cooperation and Development. Fourth Four-Year Economic Development Plan for Taiwan, 1965–1968.

Council for International Economic Cooperation and Development. Ten-Year Perspective Plan 1965–1974.

Colombia

Ministerio de la Economía Nacional. *El Plan de Fomento de la Economía Nacional.* [The Development Plan for the National Economy.] Bogotá, 1940. UNP

Consejo Nacional de Política Económica y Planeación [y] Departamento Administrativo de Planeación y Servicios Técnicos. *Plan Cuatrienal de Inversiones Públicas Nacionales, 1961–1964.* [Four-Year National Public Investment Plan, 1961–1964.] Bogotá, 1960. 278 p. JL

Consejo Nacional de Política Económica y Planeación [y] Departamento Administrativo de Planeación y Servicios Técnicos. *Plan General de Desarrollo Económico y Social* [1961–1970]. [General Plan of Economic and Social Development.] Bogotá, 1962. 2 vols. JL

Three-Year Public Investment Plan, 1965–1967.

> [Under preparation according to Inter-American Development Bank. *Social Progress Trust Fund; Fourth Annual Report 1964.* Washington, D.C., 1965. p. 24.]

Congo, Democratic Republic of (Leopoldville) (See Belgian Congo for pre-independence plans)

Ministère du Plan et du Développement Industriel. *Plan Quinquennal de Développement Economique et Social de la République du Congo; Principes Généraux* [1963–1967?]. [Economic and Social Development Plan of the Republic of the Congo; General Principles.] [Leopoldville], 1963. 23 p. JL

Congo, Republic of (Brazzaville) (See French Equatorial Africa for pre-independence plans)

Commissariat au Plan. *Loi-Programme du Plan Triennal du Développement de la Republique du Congo* [1961–1963]. [Law-Program of the Three-Year Plan of Development of the Republic of the Congo.] Brazzaville, 1961. 12 p. JL

Ministère du Plan. *Projet du Premier Plan Quinquennal de Développement Economique et Social, 1964–1968.* [Draft of the First Five-Year Plan of Economic and Social Development, 1964–1968.] Brazzaville, 1963. 191 p.

Plan Intérimaire de Développement Economiaue et Social, 1964–1968. [Interim Plan of Economic and Social Development, 1964–1968.] Brazzaville, mars 1964. 191 p.

Costa Rica

"Ley de Planificación" [No. 3087]. *La Gaceta, Diario Oficial.* ["Planning Law" (No. 3087), The Gazette, Official Diary.] San José, Año LXXXV, No. 27, febrero 2, 1963.   JL
Oficina de Planificación. *Programa de Inversiones Públicas, para 1965–1966.* [Public Investment Program, 1965–1966.] San José, August 1964. 28 p.
Oficina de Planificación. *Programa Cuadrienal de Inversiones Publica, 1965–1968.* [Four-Year Program of Public Investment, 1965–1968.] San José, January 1965. [Preliminary Draft]

Cuba

Plan Trienal de Cuba o Plan de Reconstrucción Económico Social (P.R.E.S.). [Cuba's Three-Year Plan or Plan For Economic and Social Reconstruction (P.R.E.S.).] Habana [1937]. 127 p.   PAU
Ministerio de Gobernación. *Líneas Básicas del Programa del Plan Trienal.* [Basic Lines of the Program for the Three-Year Plan.] Habana [1937?]. 415 p.   LC
Ministerio de Obras Públicas. *El Plan de Obras Públicas del Gobierno del Dr. Ramón Grau San Martin, 1944–1948: un Informe a la Nación.* [The Plan of Public Works of the Government of Dr. Ramón Grau San Martin, 1944–1948: Report to the Nation.] Habana, n.d. 121 p.   JL
Consejo Nacional de Economía. *Programa Nacional de Acción Económica.* [National Program of Economic Action.] Habana, 1951. 239 p.   JL
Consejo Nacional de Economía. *El Programa Económico de Cuba.* [Cuba's Economic Program.] Habana, 1955. 84 p.   JL
Junta Central de Planificación. *Plan Perspectivo para el Desarrollo de Economía Nacional* [1962–1965]. [Perspective Plan for the Development of the National Economy.] Habana, 1962.
       [Mentioned in Bettelheim, C., "La Planificación de la Economía Cubana" in *Comercio Exterior.* marzo 1963. p. 154.]
Junta Central de Planificación. "Resumen del Plan de Desarrollo Económico de Cuba para 1962." [Summary of the Economic Development Plan of Cuba for 1962]: in Fondo de Cultura Económica. *El Trimestre Económico.* Vol. XXIX(1), Núm. 113. enero-marzo de 1962. pp. 160–162.   PAU
Junta Central de Planificación. El Plan de la Economía Nacional de Cuba para 1963. [The National Economic Plan of Cuba for 1963.]
       [Mentioned in Boti, Regino G., "El Plan de la Economía Nacional de Cuba para 1963" in *Cuba Socialista.* pp. 24–40.]

Cyprus

Secretariat. *A Ten-Year Programme of Development of Cyprus* [1946–1955]. Nicosia, October 1946. 143 p.   JL
Professor Sir Patrick Abercrombie. *Preliminary Planning Report: July 1947.* Nicosia, 1947. 24 p.   CRO
Central Planning Commission. *The Five-Year Programme of Economic Development, 1962–1966.* Nicosia, 1962. 37 p.

Czechoslovakia

První československý plán, předpoklady a úkóly zákona o dvouletém hospodářském plánu [1947–1948]. [First Czechoslovak Plan, Targets and Requirements of the Law of the Two-Year Plan.] Praha [Prague], Orbis, 1956. 153 p. LC

Czechoslovak Economic Two-Year Plan Act [1947–1948]. Prague, Orbis, 1947. 24 p. LC

First Czechoslovak Economic Plan [1947–1948]. Prague, Orbis, 1948. [123 p.] JL
  [Includes Explanatory Memorandum on the Bill and the Text of the Two-Year Economic Plan Act.]

První pětiletý hospodářský plán rozvoje československé republiky [1949–1953]. [First Five-Year Plan for the Development of the Czechoslovak Republic.] Praha [Prague], 1949. 276 p. LC

First Czechoslovak Economic Five-Year Plan; Act and Government Memorandum [1949–1953]. Prague, Orbis, 1949. 258 p. JL

"Revised First Five-Year Plan" [1949–1953] in *Rudé Pravo* (Red Right). Prague, February 25, 1951. SP

Annual Plan, 1954. BEB

Annual Plan, 1955. BEB

Metodické pokyny pro sestavení návrhu druhého pětiletého plánu rozvoje národního hospodářství ČSR na leta 1956–1960. [Methodical Compilation of the Targets for the Draft for the Second Five-Year Plan for the Development of the National Economy of CSR in the Years 1956–1960.] Praha [Prague], 1956. 1 vol. LC

Second Five-Year Plan, 1956–1960. BEB

Two-Year Plan, 1959–1960.

"Zakon o třetim petiletém plánu rozvoje národního hospodářství ČSR" [1961–1965]. [The Law of the Third Five-Year Plan for the Development of the National Economy of the CSR.] *Planovane Hospodarstvi.* Vol. 13 (1960). pp. 881–894. BEB

Annual Plan, 1963.

Annual Plan, 1964.
  [Mentioned in *Economic Times* (India), January 6, 1965.]

Seven-Year Plan, 1965–1970.

Five-Year Plan, 1966–1970.
  [Mentioned in *Prague Newsletter,* Prague, 5 December 1964, p. 3.]

Dahomey (See French West Africa for pre-independence plans)

Perspective Plan, 1960–1980. UNS

Société Générale d'Etudes et de Planification. *Plan de Développement Economique et Social du Dahomey, 1962–1965.* [Economic and Social Development Plan of Dahomey, 1962–1965.] Paris, 1962. 2 vols. JL

Société Générale d'Etudes et de Planification. *Plan de Développement Economique et Social du Dahomey, 1963–1967.* [Economic and Social Development Plan of Dahomey, 1963–1967.] Paris, 1963. 3 vols.

Denmark

Public Investment Plan [1965–1967].
  [Mentioned in *Neue Zürcher Zeitung.* January 26, 1965.]

Dominica (United Kingdom)

Sketch Plan for Development, 1946–1956. Roseau, n.d. 58 p. CO
Development Programme, 1959–1964. n.p., n.d. 17 p. JL

Dominican Republic

Plan Nacional de Desarrollo. [National Development Plan.] Santo Domingo,
  1963. 1 vol. PAU

Eastern Aden Protectorate (United Kingdom)

Revised Development Plan, Eastern Aden Protectorate, 1961–1964. n.p., n.d.
  [25 p.] CO

Ecuador

Ministerio de Economía. *Plan de Fomento Inmediato de la Economía Na-
  cional.* [Immediate Development Plan for the National Economy.]
  [Quito, 1945.] 44 p. PAU
Ministerio de Economía. *Plan de Fomento de la Producción; Proyecto de
  Ley Sometido a la Consideración del Consejo Nacional de Economía.*
  [Plan for Development of Production. Draft Submitted for the Con-
  sideration of the National Economic Council.] Quito, 1948. 143 p. JL
Junta Nacional de Planificación y Coordinación Económica. *Bases y Di-
  rectivas para Programar el Desarrollo Económico del Ecuador* [1955–
  1965]. [Bases and Directives for an Economic Development Program
  for Ecuador.] Quito, 1958. 2 parts. UN
Junta Nacional de Planificación v Coordinación Económica. *Plan Inmediato
  de Desarrollo* [1961–1965]. Ed. preliminar. [Immediate Development
  Plan.] Quito, 1961. 2 vols. JL
Junta Nacional de Planificación y Coordinación Económica. *Plan General de
  Desarrollo Económico y Social; versión preliminar.* [1964–1973.] [Gen-
  eral Plan of Economic and Social Development; preliminary version.]
  Quito, 1963. 6 vols. of 20 books. UN

El Salvador

Instituto Salvadoreño de Fomento de la Producción. *Programa Quinquenal,
  1961–1965.* [Five-Year Program, 1961–1965.] San Salvador, 1961. 2
  vols.
Consejo Nacional de Planificación y Coordinación Económica. *Primer Programa Bienal de Inversiones Públicas, 1964–1965.* [First Two-Year
  Public Investment Program, 1964–1965.] San Salvador, 1963. 2 vols.
Consejo Nacional de Coordinación Económica. Development Plan, 1965–
  1969.
    [Under preparation according to Inter-American Development
    Bank. *Social Progress Trust Fund; Fourth Annual Report.* Wash-
    ington, D.C., 1965, p. 93.]

Ethiopia

Planning Board Office. *Five Year Development Plan, 1957–1961.* Addis
    Ababa, 1959. 181 p.   UN
Office of the Planning Board. *Second Five Year Development Plan, 1955–*
    1959 E.C. [Ethiopian Calendar.] [1963–1967 Gregorian Calendar.]
    Addis Ababa, October 1962. 363 p.   JL

Federation of Rhodesia and Nyasaland (See Northern Rhodesia, Southern
    Rhodesia and Nyasaland for pre-Federation plans. See Zambia, South-
    ern Rhodesia and Malawi for post-Federation plans)

Development Plan 1954–1957: Presented to the Federal Assembly by the
    Prime Minister, G. M. Huggins on the 29th June 1954. [Salisbury,
    1954.] [12 p.]   ECA
Economic and Financial Working Party. *Development Plans, 1954–1957.*
    Salisbury, 3rd September 1953. 4 vols.   JL
        [Vol. I—Summary and Analysis
        Vol. II—Southern Rhodesia
        Vol. III—Northern Rhodesia
        Vol. IV—Nyasaland.]
Development Plan, 1955–1959, presented to the Federal Assembly by the
    Prime Minister on 28th June 1955. Salisbury, 1955. 7 p.   JL
Development Plan, 1957–1961, presented to the Federal Assembly by the
    Acting Prime Minister on the 27th June 1957. Salisbury, 1957. 12 p.
    JL
Ministry of Economic Affairs. *Development Plan, 1959–1963.* Salisbury,
    1959. 17 p.   JL
Ministry of Economic Affairs. *Federal Government Development Plan,*
    1962–1965. Salisbury, 1962. 40 p.   JL

Federation of South Arabia (United Kingdom)

Government of the Federation of South Arabia. *Development Plan, 1963–*
    1966. n.p., 1st April 1963. [80 p.]   CO

Fiji (United Kingdom)

Report of the Postwar Planning and Development Committee. Suva, August
    1945. 27 p.   CO
Secretariat. *Draft Development Plan, 1961–1970.* Suva, June 1960. 5 p.
    CO
        [Based on recommendations made in the *Report of the Burns*
        Commission, Council Paper No. 1 of 1960.]
Financial Secretariat. *Development Plan, 1961–1965.* Legislative Council of
    Fiji, Council Paper No. 6 of 1961. Suva, 1961. 12 p.   JL
Financial Secretariat. *Development Plan, 1964–1968.* Legislative Council of
    Fiji, Council Paper No. 33 of 1963. Suva, 1963. 21 p.   JL
Central Planning Office. Economic Development Plan for the Period 1966–
    1970.
        [Under preparation according to *Development Planning in Fiji.*
        Legislative Council of Fiji, Council Paper No. 43 of 1964. p. iii.]

Finland

Ten-Year Plan, 1960–1970.
  [Mentioned in United Nations. *Economic Bulletin for Europe.*
  Vol. 14, No. 2. November 1962. p. 59.]

France

Commissariat Général du Plan de Modernisation et d'Equipement. *Rapport
  Général sur le Premier Plan de Modernisation et d'Equipement* [1947–
  1952/53]. [General Report on the First Modernization and Equipment
  Plan.] Paris, 1946. 198 p.   JL
Commission de Modernisation des Territoires d'Outre-Mer. *Premier Rapport
  de la Commission de Modernisation des Territoires d'Outre-Mer.* [First
  Report of the Modernization Commission for the Overseas Territories.]
  Paris, January 1948. 155 p.   JL
    [Also known as Plan Pleven.]
Commissariat Général du Plan de Modernisation et d'Equipement. *Deuxième
  Plan de Modernisation et d'Equipement (1954–1957).* [Second Mod-
  ernization and Equipment Plan (1954–1957).] Paris, 1954. 139 p.   JL
    [Annex to the *Projet de Loi portant approbation du deuxième plan
    de modernisation et d'equipement.* Assemblée Nationale. No. 8555.
    Session de 1954.]
Commissariat Général du Plan de Modernisation et d'Equipement. *Rapport
  Général de la Commission d'Etude et de Coordination des Plans de
  Modernisation et d'Equipement des Territoires d'Outre-Mer.* [General
  Report of the Coordination and Study Commission of the Modernization
  and Equipment Plans of the Overseas Territories.] Paris, avril 1954.
  187 p.   JL
Commissariat Général du Plan de Modernisation et d'Equipement. *Troisième
  Plan de Modernisation et d'Equipement (1958–1961).* [Third Moderni-
  zation and Equipment Plan (1958–1961).] Paris, 1959. pp. 3421–3499.
  JL
    [Ministère des Finances et des Affaires Economiques. "Décret
    No. 59–443 du 19 mars 1959 portant approbation du troisième
    plan de modernisation et d'équipment," as published in *Journal
    Officiel de la République Française.* 22 mars 1959. Vol. 91. No.
    69. pp. 3421–3499.]
Plan Intérimaire, 1960–1961. [Interim Plan, 1960–1961.] Paris, 1960. 84 p.
  JL
Commissariat Général du Plan de Modernisation et d'Equipement. *Quatri-
  ème Plan de Développement Economique et Social (1962–1965).*
  [Fourth Economic and Social Development Plan (1962–1965).] Paris,
  1962. 493 p.   JL
    [Includes *Loi* No. 62–900 du 4 août 1962 portant approbation du
    Plan de développement économique et social (*Journal Officiel* du
    7 août 1962). pp. iii–iv.]
Five-Year Plan, 1966–1970.
    [Under preparation.]

French Cameroons (See Cameroun for post-independence plans)

Plan de Développement Economique et Social du Territoire [1947–1952]. [Economic and Social Development Plan of the Territory.] Yaoundé, 1946. 24 p. UN

Le Plan de Développement Economique et Social [1947–1952]. [The Economic and Social Development Plan.] Yaoundé, 1952. 198 p. UN

Second Plan Général de Développement Economique et Social [1953–1957]. [Second General Economic and Social Development Plan.] Yaoundé, 1952. 98 p.

French Equatorial Africa (See Chad, Central African Republic, Congo [Brazzaville] and Gabon for post-independence plans) [1]

Grand Conseil. *Plan Décennal d'Équipement et de Développement, années 1947 à 1956.* [Ten-Year Equipment and Development Plan, 1947–1956.] Brazzaville, 1948. 31 p. JL
[Adopté par le Grand Conseil le 27 Octobre 1948, délibération No. 85/48.]

Troisième Plan Quadriennal 1958–1962 de l'Afrique Equatoriale Française; Section Commune. [Third Four-Year Plan of French Equatorial Africa, 1958–1962 Common Section.] n.p., n.d. 74 p. JL

Projet de Troisième Plan Quadriennal (1958–1962) Section Territoriale du Moyen-Congo. [Draft of the Third Four-Year Plan, 1958–1962, Section on the Territory of the Middle Congo.] n.p., n.d. 185 p. JL

Projet de Programme, Troisième Plan Quadriennal; Section Territoriale de l'Oubangui-Chari. [1958–1962.] [Draft Program, Third Four-Year Plan; Section for the Territory of Oubangui-Chari.] n.p., n.d. 2 vols. JL

French Guiana (France)

France. Département de la Guyane Française. *Plan Quinquennal de Développement Economique et Social pour la Guyane Française, 1952–1956.* [Five-Year Economic and Social Development Plan for French Guiana, 1952–1956.] Cayenne, 1952. CAR

France. Commissariat Général du Plan de l'Equipement et de la Productivité. *Rapport Général de la Commission de Modernisation et d'Equipement des Départements d'Outre-Mer (Guadeloupe et dépendances, Guyane Française, Martinique, Réunion) 3me Plan, 1958–1961.* [General Report of the Modernization and Equipment Commission for the Overseas Territories (Guadeloupe and dependencies, French Guiana, Martinique, Réunion) Third Plan, 1958–1961.] Paris, 1959. 452 p. CAR

Comité Departemental d'Action Economique de la Guyane. *Plan de Développement Economique de la Guyane Française.* [Economic Development Plan for French Guiana.] Cayenne, 1960. 109 p. JL

French West Africa (See Senegal, Mauritania, Upper Volta, Niger, Guinea, Ivory Coast and Dahomey for post-independence plans)

[1] In 1960, the territory of Tchad became Chad; Moyen-Congo became the Republic of the Congo (Brazzaville), Oubangui-Chari became the Central African Republic and Gabon remained Gabon.

Plan Quadriennal, 1953–1957. [Four-Year Plan, 1953–1957.]
    [Mentioned in Haut-Commissariat en A.O.F. Direction Générale
    des Services Economiques et du Plan. *Le Financement du Plan,
    1953–1957.* (The Financing of the Plan, 1953–1957.) Paris juillet
    1957. p. 13.]

Gabon (See French Equatorial Africa for pre-independence plans)

Ministère d'Economie Nationale du Plan et des Mines. *Programme Intéri-
    maire, 1963–1965.* [Interim Program of Development, 1963–1965.] Li-
    breville, 1963. 14 p.
*Loi No. 11–63 du 12/1/63, portant approbation du Programme Intéri-
    maire de Développement* [1963–1965]. [Law No. 11–63 of 12/1/63,
    giving approval to the Interim Development Program.] Libreville, 1963.
    18 p.   JL
Five-Year Plan, 1965–1970.   UNS
    [Under preparation.]

Gambia, The

Development Committee. *Development and Welfare in the Gambia.* Bath-
    urst, June 1943. [XX chapters, each separately numbered.]   CO
Gambia Report on Development and Welfare, 1947. Bathurst, 1948. 10 p.
    JL
Gambia Report on Development and Welfare, 1948. Bathurst, 1949. 6 p.
    CRO
Gambia Report on Development and Welfare, 1949. Bathurst, 1950. 1 p.
    CRO
Gambia Report on Development and Welfare, 1950–1952. Sessional Paper
    No. 1/53. Bathurst, 1953. 4 p.   CRO
Gambia Government Development Programme, 1964–1967. Sessional Paper
    No. 10 of 1964. Bathurst, 1964. 39 p.   JL

German Democratic Republic

Der Deutsche Zweijahrplan für 1949–1950. [The German Two-Year Plan
    for 1949–1950.] Berlin, Dietz, 1948. 199 p.   BEB
    [Also includes the Economic Plan for 1948.]
First Five-Year Plan, 1951–1955.   BEB
*Direktive für den zweiten Fünfjahrplan zur Entwicklung der Volkswirtschaft
    der Deutschen Demokratischen Republik 1956 bis 1960.* [Directives for
    the Second Five-Year Plan for the Development of the National Econ-
    omy in the German Democratic Republic from 1956 to 1960.] Berlin,
    Dietz, 1956. 96 p.   BEB
People's Chamber. *Law on the Seven-Year Plan for the Development of the
    National Economy of the German Democratic Republic from 1959 to
    1965.* n.p., n.d. 80 p.   BEB
*Gesetz über den Siebenjahrplan zur Entwicklung der Volkwirtschaft der
    Deutschen Demokratischen Republik in den Jahren 1959 bis 1965.*
    [Statute concerning the Seven-Year Plan for the Development of the
    National Economy of the German Democratic Republic in the Years
    1959 to 1965.] Berlin, Junge Welt, 1959. 103 p.   BEB

Ghana (See Gold Coast for pre-independence plans)

Ministry of Finance. *The Consolidation Development Plan* [1957/58–1958/59]. Accra [1957–1958]. 2 vols. JL

Second Development Plan, 1959–1964. Accra, 1959. 124 p. JL

Planning Commission. Twenty-One Year Plan.

Office of the Planning Commission. *Seven-Year Development Plan, A Brief Outline* [1963/64–1969/70]. Accra, December 1963. 29 p. CRO

Planning Commission. *Seven-Year Plan for National Reconstruction and Development, Financial Years 1963/64–1969/70, presented by the President to Parliament, January 1964.* Accra, 1964. 303 p. JL

Gilbert and Ellice Islands Colony (United Kingdom)

Ten-Year Plan of Reconstruction and Development and Welfare [1946–1955]. n.p., 30th November 1946. 24 p. CO

Gôa (formerly Portuguese State of India)

Portugal. Ministério da Economia. *Plano de Fomento* [1953–1958]. [Development Plan.] Lisbon, 1953. pp. 91–93. JL

Portugal. Ministério da Economia. *Il Plano de Fomento, 1959–1964.* [The Second Plan of Development, 1959–1964.] Lisbon, 1959. pp. 224–232. JL

Gold Coast (See Ghana for post-independence plans)

Ten-Year Development Plan, 1920–1930.

> [Also known as The (Sir Gordon) Guggisberg Ten-Year Development Plan. Mentioned in Greenstreet, D. K., "The Guggisberg Ten-Year Development Plan." *The Economic Bulletin of Ghana.* Vol. VIII, No. 1. 1964. p. 1.]

Colonial Secretary's Office. *A Ten-Year Plan of Development and Welfare for the Gold Coast, 1946/47–1956/57* [Draft]. Accra, 1946. 57 p. CRO

Colonial Secretary's Office. *Memoranda on the Colony's Ten-Year Development Plan* [1946–1956]. Accra, 1st July 1946. 54 p. CRO

The Development Plan, 1951; Being a Plan for the Economic and Social Development of the Gold Coast. Accra, 1951. 34 p. JL

Revised Draft Ten-Year Plan for the Economic and Social Development of the Gold Coast, 1950–1960. Accra, 1951. 112 p. CRO

Greece

Greek Board of Reconstruction. [*Programme of Reconstruction.* Athens, 1947.] 2 vols. JL

> ["For the total application of the . . . programme, it has been estimated twenty years will be required. . . ." Introduction.]

Diomedes Commission. First Four-Year Program for Economic Rehabilitation. [1948–1952.]

> [Mentioned in Columbia University Law School. *Public International Development Financing in Greece.* New York, September 1964. The Diomedes Commission, also known as the Marshall Plan

Committee, was charged with studying the needs of the Greek
economy for the four-year period of the Economic Cooperation Administration Program.]

Ministry of Coordination. Preliminary Five-Year Programme for the Economic Development of Greece [1959–1963].
[Mentioned in Columbia University Law School. *Public International Development Financing in Greece.* New York, September
1964. p. 38.]

Ministry of Coordination. *Five-Year Programme for the Economic Development of Greece 1960–1964.* Athens, April 1960. 99 p.   JL

Ministère de la Coordination. *Memorandum sur le Programme de Développement Economique de la Grece* [1962–1966]. Athens, 1962. 133 p.   JL

Five-Year Plan, 1966–1970.
[Under preparation according to The Economist Intelligence Unit.
Quarterly Economic Review: Greece. No. 49. March 1965. p. 7.]

Greenland (Denmark)

Greenland Technical Organization. Five-Year Plan for Greenland.
[Mentioned in *Neue Zürcher Zeitung.* May 20, 1964.]

Grenada (United Kingdom)

Development Committee. *A Plan of Development for the Colony of Grenada,
1946–1956.* n.p., n.d. 48 p.   CO

Revised Development Plan for Grenada [1950–1956]. n.p., n.d. 18 p.   CO

Grenada: Economic Survey and Development Plan, 1960–1964. n.p.
[1960?] 143 p.   JL

Grenada Development Plan, 1964–1966. n.p., n.d. 23 p.   CO

Guadeloupe (France)

France. Commissariat Général du Plan de l'Equipement et de la Productivité.
*Rapport Général de la Commission de Modernisation et d'Equipement
des Département d'Outre-Mer (Guadeloupe et dépendances, Guyane
Française, Martinique, Réunion) 3me Plan, 1958–1961.* [General Report of the Modernization and Equipment Commission for the Overseas
Departments (Guadeloupe and dependencies, French Guiana, Martinique, Réunion) 3rd Plan, 1958–1961.] Paris, 1959. 452 p.   CAR

Guatemala

Consejo Nacional de Planificación Económica. *Plan de Desarrollo Económico
de Guatemala, 1955–1960,* segunda edición. [Economic Development
Plan for Guatemala, 1955–1960, second edition.] Guatemala, 1957.
204 p.   JL

Consejo Nacional de Planificación Económica. *Plan de Inversiones Públicas,
1960–1964.* [Public Investment Plan, 1960–1964.] Guatemala, 1961.
1 vol.   PAU

*Anteproyecto de un Plan para el Desarrollo Socio-Económico de Guate-
mala en 21 Años. Preliminar.* [Draft of a Plan for the Socio-Economic
Development of Guatemala in 21 years.] Guatemala, 1964. 58 p.   JL

Breve Descripción de los Programas de Inversión, 1960/61–1963/64. [Short Description of the Investment Programs, 1960/61–1963/64.] Guatemala City, May 1963. 31 p.

Five-Year Plan for Economic and Social Development, 1965–1969.
[Under preparation according to *Alliance for Progress, Weekly Newsletter.* Vol. III, No. 4. January 25, 1965.]

Guinea (See French West Africa for pre-independence plans)

Plan Triennal de Développement Economique et Social de la République de Guinée [1960–1962]. [A Three-Year Plan of Economic and Social Development of the Republic of Guinea.] Conakry, 1960. 436 p.   JL

Seven-Year Plan, 1964–1971.
[Mentioned in "Former French Tropical Africa, Liberia," *Quarterly Economic Review.* July 6, 1964. p. 9.]

Haiti

Conseil National de Développement et de Planification. *Un Plan d'Urgence de Démarrage Economique et Social.* [Emergency Plan for Launching Economic and Social Development.] Port au Prince, août 1963. 97 p. JL
[This is a two-year plan, but the years are not given.]

Honduras

Consejo Nacional de Economía. *Programa Cuatrienal de Inversiones Públicas, 1962–1965.* [Four-Year Program of Public Investment, 1962–1965.] Tegucigalpa, julio de 1961. 107 p.   JL

Consejo Nacional de Economía. *Plan Nacional de Inversiones Públicas del Gobierno de Honduras, 1963–1964.* [National Plan of Public Investment of the Government of Honduras, 1963–1964.] [Tegucigalpa, 1962.] 181 p.   PAU

Consejo Nacional de Economía. *Inventario Revisado de Inversiones del Sector Público, 1965–1966.* [A Revised Inventory of Public Sector Investments, 1965–1966.] [Tegucigalpa, 1964.] 12 p.

Secretaría del Consejo Nacional de Economía. *Lineamientos del Plan de Desarrollo Económico y Social de Honduras, 1965–1969.* [Main Aspects of the Economic and Social Development Plan of Honduras, 1965–1969.] Tegucigalpa, 1964. 18 p.

Hungary

Hungarian Three-Year Plan [1947–1949]. Budapest, Hungarian Bulletin, 1947. 60 p.   LC

Five-Year Plan of Hungary [1950–1954]. Budapest, Hungarian Bulletin, 1949. 31 p.   LC

"Law No. 25 of 1949 on the First Economic Five-Year Plan of the Hungarian People's Republic" [1950 1954] in *Torvenyek es Torvenyereju Rendeletek 1949.* [Laws and Decrees with the Force of Law 1949.] Budapest, 1950.
[Cited in Helmreich, Ernst C. (ed). *Hungary.* New York, F. A. Praeger, 1957. pp. 437–438.]

Planirovanie narodnogo khoziaistva Vengrii, Sbornik materialov [1950–
     1954]. [Planning the People's Economy of Hungary, Collection of Ma-
     terials.] Moscow, Publishing House of Foreign Literature, 1950.   SP
Five-Year Plan of the Hungarian People's Republic [1950–1954]. Buda-
     pest, 1950. 53 p.   LC
Annual Plan, 1954.
          [Mentioned in Talabar, A. "Planned Economy in Hungary" in
          United Asia. Vol. XVI, No. 3, May–June 1964.]
Annual Plan, 1955.
          [Mentioned in Talabar, A. "Planned Economy in Hungary" in
          United Asia. Vol XVI, No. 3, May–June 1964.]
"Principles of the Second Five-Year Plan of the Hungarian People's Econ-
     omy" [1956–1960]. *Szabad Nép* [Free People]. April 27, 1956.
          [Cited in Helmreich, Ernst C. (ed). *Hungary.* New York, F. A.
          Praeger, 1957. p. 439.]
Annual Plan, 1956.
          [Mentioned in Talabar, A. "Planned Economy in Hungary" in
          United Asia. Vol. XVI, No. 3, May–June 1964.]
Three-Year Plan of Hungary's National Economy, 1958–1960. Budapest,
     Hungarian Review, 1958. 79 p.   LC
Long-Range Plan, 1960–1980.
          [Mentioned in Talabar, A. "Planned Economy in Hungary" in
          United Asia. Vol. XVI, No. 3, May–June 1964.]
New Second Five-Year Plan, 1961–1965.   BEB
Annual Plan, 1965.
          [Mentioned in *The Times* (London). February 11, 1965.]

Iceland

General Memorandum [for O.E.E.C.] *on the 1950–51 and 1951–52 Pro-
     grammes.* Paris, 1950. 25 p.   JL
Economic Institute. *Economic Program, 1963–1966.* Reykjavík, 1963. 86 p.
     JL

India

Development Programme, 1951–1957.
          [Summary appears on pp. 12–20 and in Appendix 3 of Common-
          wealth Consultative Committee. *The Colombo Plan for Co-
          operative Economic Development in South and South-East Asia.*
          London, 1950.   JL]
Planning Commission. *First Five-Year Plan* [1951/52–1955/56]. New
     Delhi, 1952. 2 vols.   JL
Planning Commission. Thirty-Year Perspective Plan [1951–1981].
Planning Commission. *Second Five-Year Plan* [1956/57–1960/61]. New
     Delhi, 1956. 653 p.   JL
Planning Commission. Fifteen-Year Perspective Plan [1956–1971].
Planning Commission. Perspective Planning Division. Notes on Perspective
     of Development, India, 1960–61 to 1975–76.

[Mentioned in The *Economic Weekly* (India). January 23, 1965. p. 129.]
Planning Commission. *Third Five-Year Plan; A Draft Outline* [1961/62–1965/66]. New Delhi, 1960. 265 p.
Planning Commission. *Third Five-Year Plan* [1961/62–1965/66]. New Delhi, 1961. 774 p.   JL
Planning Commission. Fourth Five-Year Plan [1965/66–1970/71].
[Mentioned in Planning Commission. *Memorandum on the Fourth Five-Year Plan.* New Delhi, October 1964. 97 p.]
Planning Commission. Fifteen-Year Perspective Plan [1966–1981].

Indonesia

Biro Perantjang Negara. *Broad Outlines of the Five-Year Development Plan, 1956–1960.* Djakarta [1958?]. 290 p.   JL
Madjelis Permusjawaratan Rakjat Sementara. *Garis-garis Besar Pola Pembangunan Nasional-Semesta-Berentjana Tahapan Pertama 1961–1969.* [Broad Outlines Formulated for the Over-all National Plan for the First Phase, 1961–1969.] Djakarta, n.d. 17 vols. [4638 p.]   LC
[Supplement to *Ketetapan Madjelis Permusjawaratan Rakjat Sementara Republik Indonesia No. I/–II/MPRS/1960.* Djakarta, n.d. 2 vols. (375 p.)   LC]
National Planning Council. *Broad Outlines of the National Overall Development Plan, 1961–1969.* Djakarta, 1961. 43 p.   LC
National Planning Council. *List of Projects of National Overall Development Plan, 1961–1969.* Djakarta, 1961. 70 p.   ECAFE

Iran

Plan Organization. "The Seven-Year Development Plan Act" [1948/49–1954/55]. Teheran, 26 Bahman 1327 [i.e., 1948], included as Exhibit 2 in Vol. 1 of the Overseas Consultants, Inc., *Report on Seven-Year Development Plan for the Plan Organization of the Imperial Government of Iran* [1948–1954]. New York, 1949. 5 vols.   JL
Plan Organization. *Second Seven-Year Development Plan of Iran* [1955/56–1961/62]. Teheran, 1956. 31 p.   JL
Plan Organization. *Revised Second Seven-Year Development Plan, September 1955–September 1962.* (From Mehr 1334 thru the end of Shahrivar 1341). n.p., 1959. 76 p.   JL
Division of Economic Affairs, Plan Organization. *Third Plan Frame, 1341–1346* [September 1962–March 1968]. Teheran, 1961. 9 vols.   JL
[V. 1—Outline, 211 p.; V. 2—Agriculture, 234 p.; V. 3—Education, 106 p.; V. 4—Electricity, 43 p.; V. 5—Health, 192 p.; V. 6—Industry and Mining, 154 p.; V. 7—Manpower, 99 p.; V. 8—Statistics, 45 p.; V. 9—Transport and Communications, 102 p.]
Third Five-Year Development Plan Law, approved by the Council of Ministers in Session dated Shahrivar 15, 1341 [September 6, 1962 Gregorian Calendar]. Teheran, 1962. 23 p.   JL
Development Plan [April 1965–March 1969].
[Under preparation.]

Iraq

Development Board. First Development Plan, 1951–1956.
Second Five-Year Plan, 1955–1959.
Third Five-Year Plan.
Interim Economic Plan, 1959/60–1962/63. Law No. 181 of 1959.   GER
Five-Years Detailed Economic Plan, 1961/62–1965/66. Baghdad, Issued by
    Ministry of Guidance, 1961. 656 p.   JL
Five-Year Development Plan, 1966–1970.
        [Mentioned in *The Financial Times.* August 25, 1965.]

Ireland

First Programme for Economic Expansion [1959–1963]. Dublin, November
    1958. 48 p.   JL
Second Programme for Economic Expansion; Part I [1964–1970]. *Laid by
    the Government before each House of the Oireachtas, August 1963.*
    Dublin, August 1963. 67 p.
Second Programme for Economic Expansion; Part II [1964–1970]. *Laid by
    the Government before each House of the Oireachtas, July 1964.* Dub-
    lin, 1964. 340 p.

Israel

Economic Planning Authority. *Targets and Outlines of the Four-Year Plan,
    1963/64–1966/67, Draft Proposal.* Jerusalem, July 1962. 58 p.
Development Plan, 1965/66–1969/70.

Italian Somaliland (See also Somalia and Somaliland Protectorate)

Administration Italienne de Tutelle de la Somalie. *Plans de Développement
    Economique de la Somalie, Années 1954–1960.* [Economic Develop-
    ment Plans of Somalia, 1954–1960.] Roma, 1954. 94 p.   JL
United States Operations Mission to Italy. *Plans and Schedules for Somalia
    Economic Development,* by W. E. Corfitzen. Rome, 1954. 34 p.   ECA
        [For the years 1953/54; 1954/55.]
Somaliland (Italian Administration). Amministrazione Fiduciaria Italiana
    della Somalia. *Programma per lo Sviluppo Produttivo ed Industriale
    della Somalia, 1956–1958; Relazione Illustrativae Piano Operativo di
    Attuazione.* [Program for the Productive and Industrial Development
    of Somalia, 1956–1958; Report on the Operational Plan of Execution.]
    Mogadiscio, 1956. 65 p.   UN

Italy

Comitato Interministeriale per la Ricostruzione. Segreteria per il Programma
    di Sviluppo Economico. *Lineamenti del Programma di Sviluppo dell-
    'Occupazione e del Reddito in Italia* [1955–1964]. [Outline of the Pro-
    gram for the Development of Employment and Income in Italy.] Roma
    [1956]. 77 p.   JL
        [The Vanoni Plan]

Ministero del Bilancio. *Outline of Development of Income and Employment in Italy in the Ten-Year Period 1955–1964.* Paris, 1955. 108 p.   JL
[The Vanoni Plan]
Ministero del Bilancio. *Progetto di Programma di Sviluppo Economico per il Quinquennio, 1965–1969.* [Draft Program of Economic Development for the Five Years, 1965–1969.] Roma, 1965. 179 p.   JL

Ivory Coast (See French West Africa for pre-independence plans)

Ministère du Plan. *Troisième Plan Quadriennal de Développement Economique et Social, 1958–1962.* [Third Four-Year Plan of Economic and Social Development, 1958–1962.] Abidjan, 1958. 227 p.   UN
Ten-Year Plan for Economic and Social Development, 1960–1970.   UNS
Two-Year Intermediate Plan, 1962–1963.   UNS
Ministère des Finances, des Affaires Economiques et du Plan. *Plan Quinquennal de Développement Economique et Social, 1965–1970.* [Five-Year Plan of Economic and Social Development, 1965–1970.] Abidjan, 1964. 232 p.
[Cited in: OECD. Development Center. *Essai d'une Bibliographie sur la Cote d'Ivoire.* Paris, 1964. p. 9.]

Jamaica

Secretariat. *Memorandum on Colonial Development and Welfare Schemes,* Revised in accordance with Estimates as passed by the House of Representatives. Kingston, July 1945. 24 p.   CRO
A Ten-Year Plan of Development for Jamaica [1946/47–1955/56]. Kingston, 1945. 46 p.   JL
Finance Branch of the Secretariat. *Report on the Revision of the Ten-Year Plan of Development for Jamaica.* Kingston, 1951. 28 p.   JL
Five-Year Development Programme, 1955/56–1959/60, as laid on the *Table of the House of Representatives, October 1954.* Kingston, 1954. 15 p.   JL
Central Planning Unit. *A National Plan for Jamaica, 1957–1967.* Kingston, 1957. 70 p.   JL–ECA
Central Planning Unit. *Ten-Year Plan, 1962–1971.* Kingston, 1962. 31 p.
Central Planning Unit. *A Five-Year Independence Plan, 1963–1968.* Kingston, 1963. 240 p.   JL

Japan

Economic Planning Board. *Economic Self-Support 5-Year Plan; Decided by the Cabinet Meeting on 23 December 1955.* [1956–1960.] Tokyo, 1955. 36 p.   JL
Economic Planning Agency. *New Long-Range Economic Plan of Japan, FY 1958–FY 1962.* Tokyo, 1957. 196 p.   JL
Economic Planning Agency. *New Long-Range Economic Plan of Japan, (1961–1970); Doubling National Income Plan.* Tokyo, 1961. 127 p.   JL
Keizaishingikai [Economic Council]. *Chuki Keizai Keikaku* [FY 1964–1968]. [Medium-Range Economic Plan.] Tokyo, January 21, 1965. 59 p.

Jordan

Development Board. *Five-Year Phased Programme of Economic Development as Revised October 1954.* Ammān, 1954. 17 p.   JL
Development Board. *Five-Year Programme for Economic Development,
1962–1967.* Ammān, 1961. 367 p.   JL

Kenya

The Development Programme, 1954–1957. [1st January 1954—30th June
1957.] Legislative Council, Sessional Paper 51 of 1955. Nairobi, 1955.
126 p.   JL
The Development Programme, 1957–1960. Legislative Council, Sessional
Paper 77 of 1956/57. Nairobi, 1957. 100 p.   JL
The Development Programme, 1960–1963. Legislative Council, Sessional
Paper 4 of 1959/60. Nairobi, 1960. 57 p.   JL
Ministry of Finance. *Development Plan, 1964–1970.* Nairobi, 1964. 137
p.   JL

Korea, Democratic People's Republic (North)

Trekhletnii narodnokhoziaistvennyi plan KNDR na 1954–1956 gg. [Three-
year National Economic Plan of the KDPR in the years 1954–1956.]
Pkhen'ian [Pyongyang], Ministr. kul't. i prop. [Ministry of Culture and
Propaganda] KNDR, 1954. 99 p.   BEB
Pervyi piatiletnii plan razvitiia narodnogo khoziaistva KNDR (1957–1961).
[The First Five-Year Plan for the Development of the National
Economy of the KDPR, 1957–1961.] Pkhen'ian [Pyongyang], Izd-vo
lit. na inostr. iaz. [Foreign Languages Publishing House], 1958. 100 p.
BEB
*Control Figures for the Seven-Year Plan (1961–1967) for the Development
of the National Economy of the Democratic People's Republic of Korea.*
Pyongyang, Korean Central News Agency, 1961. 39 p.   BEB
Semiletnii plan, 1961–1967. [Seven-Year Plan, 1961–1967.] Pkhen'ian
[Pyongyang], Izd-vo lit. na inostr. iaz. [Foreign Languages Publishing
House], 1962. Unpaged.
     [Mentioned in *Journal of Asian Studies.* Vol. XXIII, No. 5.
     September 1964. p. 92.]

Korea, Republic of (South)

Economic Development Council. *Three-Year Economic Development Plan*
[1960–1962]. Seoul, 1960. 116 p.
Overall Economic Reconstruction Plan (draft) from 1962 to 1966. Seoul,
1961. 44 p.   JL
     [Appears as an appendix to *Explanatory Note for Five-Year
     Economic Reconstruction Plan.* Seoul, 1961. 38 p.]
Economic Planning Board. *Draft First Five-Year Economic Plan, 1962–
1966.* [Seoul], 1961. 349 p.   JL
Economic Planning Board. *Summary of the First Five-Year Economic Plan,
1962–1966.* Seoul, 1962. 88 p.   ECAFE
Economic Planning Board. *First Five-Year Plan for Technical Development;*

Supplement to First Five-Year Economic Plan. Seoul, 1962. 71 p. JL
Economic Planning Board. *First Five-Year Economic Development Plan
(1962–1966); Adjusted Version.* [Seoul], March 1964. 107 p. JL

Kuwait

Planning Board. Five-Year Plan for Economic and Social Development.
[Under preparation according to *Middle East and African Economist.* Vol. XIX, No. 1. January 1965.]

Laos

Commissariat au Plan. *Projet du Plan de Développement Economique et
Social du Laos.* [Draft Plan of Economic and Social Development of
Laos.] [Vientiane?], 1958. 158 p. LC
Commissariat au Plan. *Plan de Développement Economique et Social du
Laos; Période de 5 ans du 1er Juillet 1959 au 30 Juin 1964.* [Plan of
Economic and Social Development of Laos; Five-Year period from
1 July 1959 to 30 June 1964.] [Vientiane?], 1959. 162 p. JL
Ministère de l'Economie Nationale et du Plan. *Plan de Développement
Economique et Social du Laos; Année Fiscale 1962–1963.* [Economic
and Social Development Plan for Laos; Fiscal Year 1962–1963.]
Vientiane, 17 September 1962. 47 p.
Ministère de l'Economie Nationale et du Plan. *Plan d'Urgence Pour le
Premier Semestre 1963: Dernier Semestre de l'Année Fiscale 1962–
1963.* [Urgent Plan for the First Six Months of 1963; the Last Six
Months of the Fiscal Year 1962 1963.] Vientiane, 2 Février 1963. 8 p.

Lebanon

Five-Year Plan, 1962–1966.
Ministère du Plan. Projet du Plan Quinquennal 1964–1968. [Draft of the
Four-Year Plan 1964–1968.]
[Mentioned in Corm, Georges G., *Politique Economique et
Planification au Liban, 1953–1963.* Beyrouth, n.d. p. 87.]

Leeward Islands (United Kingdom)

Development Plan, 1946–1956. n.p., 1947. 160 p. CO

Liberia

Five-Year Development Program, 1951–1956.
*Supplement. An Act Approving the Nine-Year Program for the Economic
Development of the Republic of Liberia.* [1951–1959.] In: Liberian
Code of Laws of 1956. GER
Office of National Planning. Five-Year Plan, 1964–1969. YGC

Libya

Ministry of Planning and Development. *Khuttat el Tanmeya el Iqtisadeya
wa el Ijtimaeya Lil-Sanawat el Khams, 1963–1968.* [Five-Year Economic and Social Plan for the Period, 1963–1968.] Tripoli [1964?].
108 p.

Ministry of Planning and Development. *Five-Year Economic and Social Development Plan, 1963–1968.* [Tripoli], n.d. 153 p.   JL–ECA
> [Also contains Law No. 8 of 1963 approving the over-all Five-Year Development Programme, 1963–1968 and Law No. 5 of 1963 for the Organisation of Planning and Development Affairs.]

Second Five-Year Plan.
> [Under preparation.]

Macão (Portugal)

O Plano de Fomento en Macão e as Obras Levadas a Efeito nos Ultimos Três Años (1951–1954). [The Plan of Development for Macão and the Works Carried out during the Last Three Years (1951–1954).] Três anos de governo. . . . (Conférencia . . . pelo José Dos Santos Baptista). Macão, Círculo cultural de Macão, 1955.   GER

Portugal. Ministério da Economia. *Plano de Fomento* [1953–1958]. [Development Plan.] Lisbon, 1953. pp. 93–94.   JL

Portugal. Ministério da Economia. *II Plano de Fomento, 1959–1964.* [The Second Plan of Development, 1959–1964.] Lisbon, 1959. pp. 233–244.   JL

Portugal. Presidência do Conselho. *Plano Intercalar de Fomento para 1965–1967.* [Transitional Development Plan for 1965–1967.] Lisbon, 1964. Vol. II. pp. 227–252.

Malagasy Republic

Haut Commissariat de la République Française à Madagascar et Dépendances. Plan Décennal d'Equipement Economique et Social. [Ten-Year Economic and Social Equipment Plan.]
> [Mentioned in *Plan Décennal d'Equipement Economique et Social. Rapport d'Exécution de la Section de Madagascar.* Tananarive, n.d. 1 vol.   LC]

Haut Commissariat à Madagascar et Dépendances. Direction du Service du Plan. *Plan de Développement Economique et Social, 1958–1962; Bilan de la Période 1946–1956.* [Economic Development and Social Plan, 1958–1962: Evaluation of the Period 1946–1956.] [Tananarive, 1957.] 335 p.   ECA

Ministère de l'Industrie et du Plan. *Programme Triennal de Développement Economique et Social, 1959–1962.* [Three-Year Program of Economic and Social Development, 1959–1962.] Tananarive, 1959. 180 p.   UN

Commissariat Général au Plan. Plan Quadriennal, 1963–1967.   YGC

Commissariat Général au Plan. *Plan Quinquennal, 1964–1968.* [Five-Year Plan, 1964–1968.] Tananarive, 1964. 253 p.   ECA

Malawi (See Nyasaland for pre-independence plans)

Ministry of Finance. *Development Plan, 1965–1969.* Zomba, 1964. 20 p.   JL

Malaya (See Malaysia for post-independence plans)

High Commissioner's Office. *Draft Development Plan of the Federation of Malaya* [1950–1955]. Kuala Lumpur, 1950. 174 p.   CRO

Development Programmes, 1951–1957.
> [Summary appears on pp. 33–39 and Appendix 6 of Common-wealth Consultative Committee. *The Colombo Plan for Co-operative Economic Development in South and South-East Asia,* London, 1950. JL]

National Development Planning Committee. The First Five-Year Capital Expenditure Plan [1956–1960].
> [Mentioned in *Fact Sheet on the Federation of Malaya* (Issued by Information Services), Federation of Malaya, No. 11, March 1958.]

National Development Planning Committee. *Second Five-Year Plan, 1961–1965.* Kuala Lumpur, 1961. 67 p. JL

Malaysia (See Malaya, North Borneo, Sabah, Sarawak and Singapore for pre-Federation plans)

National Development Planning Committee. First Malaysia Five-Year Plan for Economic and Social Development, 1966–1970.
> [Under preparation according to *Address by His Majesty the Yang Di-Pertuan Agong* at the First Meeting of the First Session of the Second Parliament, 19 May 1964.]

Mali

Ministère du Plan et de l'Economie Rurale. *Rapport sur le Plan Quinquennal de Développement Economique et Social de la République du Mali, 1961–1965.* [Report on the Five-Year Economic and Social Develop-ment Plan of the Republic of Mali, 1961–1965.] Bamako, 1960. 42 p. JL

Malta

Schemes of Development for the Period 1955–1960. Valletta, n.d. 19 p. CRO

Colin Bruce. *The Economic Development of Malta; A Report Containing a Revision of the 5 Year Development Programme, 1956/57 to 1960/61.* Valletta, October 1957. 127 p. CRO

The Secretariat. *Development Plan for the Maltese Islands, 1959–1964.* Valletta, 1959. 96 p. JL

Development Plan for the Maltese Islands, 1964–1969. Valletta, 1964. 113 p. JL

Martinique (France)

France. Commissariat Général du Plan de l'Equipement et de la Productivité. *Rapport Général de la Commission de Modernisation et d'Equipement des Départements d'Outre-Mer (Guadeloupe et dépendances, Guyane Française, Martinique, Réunion) 3me Plan, 1958–1961.* [General Report of the Modernization and Equipment Commission for the Overseas Departments (Guadeloupe and dependencies, French Guiana, Martinique, Réunion) 3rd Plan, 1958–1961.] Paris, 1959. 452 p. CAR

Programme d'Industrialisation, 1963–1965. [Industrialization Program, 1963–1965.] Fort-de-France, 1963. 54 p. JL

Mauritania (See French West Africa for pre-independence plans)

Ministère de l'Expansion Economique et du Plan; Service du Plan. *Troisième Plan Quadriennal, 1958–1962.* [Third Four-Year Plan, 1958–1962.] Saint Louis, 1958. [Pagination not consecutive.]
Intermediate Three-Year Plan, 1960–1962. UNS
Plan Quadriennal de Développement Economique et Social, 1963–1966. [Four-Year Economic and Social Development Plan, 1963–1966.] n.p., 1964. 246 p. JL
  [Includes "Loi 63–149, portant approbation du Plan Quadriennal de développement économique et social (1963–1966)." p. 9.]

Mauritius (United Kingdom)

Governor. *Memorandum on Mauritius Development and Welfare: Ten-Year Plan.* Port Louis, 1946. 10 p. CO
Capital Expenditure Programme, 1955/56–1959/60. Legislative Council; Sessional Paper 6 of 1956. Port Louis, 1956. 22 p. JL
Economic Planning Committee. *Plan for Mauritius; the Final Report of the Committee, being a Programme for Capital Expenditure for the Period 1 July 1957 to 30 June 1962.* Port Louis, 1958. 97 p. JL
Economic Planning Committee. *Reconstruction and Development Programme, 1960–1965.* Port Louis, 1961. 90 p. JL
Extension of the Reconstruction and Development Programme to Cover the Six-Year Period, 1960–1966. Legislative Assembly; Sessional Paper No. 3 of 1964. Port Louis, April 1964. 32 p. JL

Mexico

Plan Sexenal de Gobierno del Partido Nacional Revolucionario, 1934–1940. [Six-Year Plan of the Government of the National Revolutionary Party, 1934–1940.]
Partido Revolucionario Institucional. *Segundo Plan Sexenal, 1941–1946.* [The Second Six-Year Plan, 1941–1946.] Texto aprobado en la Asamblea Nacional celebrada en la Ciudad de México los días lo., 2 y 3 de Noviembre de 1939. Y varios discursos documentales pronunciados por el Gral. Manuel Avila Camacho y por el Gral. Herberto Jara. [Mexico? 1939?] 160 p. PAU
Partido Revolucionario Institucional. *The Second Six-Year Plan, 1941–1946.* Text approved in the National Assembly held in the city of Mexico on the 1st, 2nd and 3rd days of November 1939, and several documental speeches, delivered by General Manuel Avila Camacho . . . and General Herberto Jara . . . [Mexico? 1939?] 144 p. PAU
Secretarías de la Presidencia y de Hacienda y Crédito Público. *Mexico, Plan de Accion Inmediata, 1962–1964.* [Mexico, Immediate Action Plan, 1962–1964.] Mexico City, June 1962. 88 p.
  [Mentioned by Victor Urquidi in *The Statist* (Review of Mexico). February 1965.]

Mongolia

First Five-Year Plan, 1948–1952. BEB

Second Five-Year Plan, 1953–1957. BEB
Three-Year Plan, 1958–1960. BEB
Five-Year Plan, 1961–1965. YGC
Five-Year Plan 1966–1970. [Mentioned in *Novosti Mongolii,* June 6, 1965.]

Montserrat (United Kingdom)

Presidency of Montserrat. *Plan for Development and Welfare* [1946–1956].
n.p., n.d. 17 p. CO
Office of the Chief Minister. *Five-Year Development Plan, 1964–1968.* n.p.,
n.d. 89 p. CO

Morocco

Commissariat Général au Plan de Modernisation et d'Equipement. *Rapport*
Général sur le Premier Plan de Modernisation et d'Equipement,
Novembre 1946–Janvier 1947. [General Report on the First Mod-
ernization and Equipment Plan, November 1946–January 1947.] Paris,
1947. 198 p. UN
Division du Commerce et de la Marine Marchande. *Programme d'Equipe-*
ment à Long Terme, 1949–1952. [Long-Term Equipment Program,
1949–1952.] Rabat, 1949. 328 p. UN
Rapport Général de la Commission d'Etude et de Coordination des Plans de
Modernisation et d'Equipement de l'Algérie, de la Tunisie et du Maroc.
Maroc: Deuxième Plan de Modernisation et d'Equipement [1954–
1957]. [Morocco: Second Modernization and Equipment Plan.] Paris,
1954. 357 p. JL
Division de la Coordination Economique et du Plan. *Plan Biennal d'Equipe-*
ment, 1958–1959. [Two-Year Equipment Plan, 1958–1959.] Rabat,
1958. 78 p. JL
Division de la Coordination Economique et du Plan. *Plan Quinquennal,*
1960–1964. Rabat, 1960. 401 p. JL
Plan Triennal, 1965–1967. [Three-Year Plan, 1965–1967.] UNS

Mozambique (Portugal)

Portugal. Ministério da Economia. *Plano de Fomento* [1953–1958]. [De-
velopment Plan.] Lisbon, 1953. pp. 84–91. JL
Portugal. Ministério da Economia. *II Plano de Fomento, 1959–1964.* [The
Second Plan of Development, 1959–1964.] Lisbon, 1959. pp. 210–223.
JL
Portugal. Presidência do Conselho. *Plano Intercalar de Fomento para 1965–*
1967. [Transitional Development Plan for 1965–1967.] Lisbon, 1964.
Vol. II. pp. 187–224.

Nepal

National Planning Council. *Draft Five-Year Plan: A Synopsis* [1956/57–
1960/61]. Katmandu, 1956. 82 p. JL
National Planning Council. *Three-Year Plan (1962–1965) Summary.*
Katmandu, 1962. 31 p. JL

National Planning Council. *Interim Plan, 1961/62: Planning and Policy Development.* Katmandu, June 1961. 17 p.
Five-Year Plan, 1965–1970.

Netherlands

First Memorandum on the Central Economic Plan 1946 and National Budget 1947. The Hague, 1946. 65 p. JL
Central Planning Bureau. The 1946–1952 Plan.
[Mentioned in United Nations. *Report on the World's Social Situation 1961, Planning for Balanced Social and Economic Development in the Netherlands with particular reference to the Postwar Years.* No. E/CW5/346/Add 6, 27 September 1961.]
Centraal Planbureau. *Centraal Economisch Plan, 1947.* [Central Economic Plan, 1947.] 's-Gravenhage, 1946. 64 p. JL
Centraal Planbureau. *Centraal Economisch Plan 1949.* [Central Economic Plan, 1949.] 57 p. JL
Central Planning Bureau. Twenty-Year Long-Term Plan, 1950–1970. BEB
Centraal Planbureau. *Centraal Economisch Plan 1950.* [Central Economic Plan, 1950.] 52 p. JL
Centraal Planbureau. *Centraal Economisch Plan 1951.* [Central Economic Plan, 1951.] 53 p. JL
Centraal Planbureau. *Centraal Economisch Plan 1952.* [Central Economic Plan, 1952.] 47 p. JL
Centraal Planbureau. *Central Economic Plan 1952.* The Hague, 1952. 44 p. BEB
Centraal Planbureau. *Centraal Economisch Plan 1953.* [Central Economic Plan, 1953.] 73 p. JL
Centraal Planbureau. *Centraal Economisch Plan 1954.* [Central Economic Plan, 1954.] 42 p. JL
Centraal Planbureau. *Centraal Economisch Plan 1955.* [Central Economic Plan, 1955.] 127 p. JL
Centraal Planbureau. *Central Economic Plan 1955.* The Hague, 1955. 97 p. BEB
Centraal Planbureau. *Centraal Economisch Plan 1956.* [Central Economic Plan, 1956.] 106 p. JL
Centraal Planbureau. *Centraal Economisch Plan 1957.* [Central Economic Plan, 1957.] 153 p. JL
Centraal Planbureau. *Centraal Economisch Plan, 1958.* [Central Economic Plan, 1958.] 's-Gravenhage, 1958. 156 p. JL
Centraal Planbureau. *Centraal Economisch Plan, 1959.* [Central Economic Plan, 1959.] 's-Gravenhage, 1959. 136 p. JL
Centraal Planbureau. *Centraal Economisch Plan, 1960.* [Central Economic Plan, 1960.] 's-Gravenhage, 1960. 132 p. JL
New Long-Term Plan, 1960–1980.
[Mentioned in United Nations. *Report on the World's Social Situation 1961. Planning for Balanced Social and Economic Development in the Netherlands with particular reference to the Postwar Years.* No. E/CW5/346/ Add 6. 27 September 1961.]

Centraal Planbureau. *Central Economic Plan, 1961.* 's-Gravenhage, 1961. 156 p.
Centraal Planbureau. *Centraal Economisch Plan, 1962.* [Central Economic Plan, 1962.] 's-Gravenhage, februari 1962. 136 p.   JL
Centraal Planbureau. *Centraal Economisch Plan, 1964.* [Central Economic Plan, 1964.] 's-Gravenhage, maart 1964. 165 p.   JL
Centraal Planbureau. *Centraal Economisch Plan, 1965.* [Central Economic Plan, 1965.] The Hague, 1965. 177 p.   JL
Central Planning Bureau. Five-Year Plan, 1966–1970.
  [Mentioned in *The Financial Times.* April 8, 1964.]

Netherlands Antilles (Aruba Island)

Ontwikkelingsplan Aruba. [Development Plan for Aruba.] n.p., [1961?]. 49 p.   JL

Netherlands Antilles (Curaçao)

Tienjarenplan Curaçao. [Ten-Year Plan for Curaçao.] [Willemstad], 1962. 14 parts.   JL
Ten-Year Plan Curaçao 1962–1971, General Survey. Willemstad, February 1962. 39 p.   CAR

Nicaragua

Instituto de Fomento Nacional. *Suggestions for a Five-Year Industrial Development Program in Nicaragua* [1961–1965]. Managua, April 1962. 49 p.   JL
Outline of an Economic and Social Development Plan, 1965–1969.
  [Mentioned in Inter-American Development Bank. *Social Progress Trust Fund; Fourth Annual Report, 1964.* Washington, D.C., 1965. p. 394.]

Niger (See French West Africa for pre-independence plans)

Présidence de la République. *Plan de Développement Economique et Social, 1961–1963, Plan Intérimaire.* [Economic and Social Development Plan, 1961–1963, Interim Plan.] Niamey, 1961. 299 p. [in 2 vols.]   JL
Summary Translation of the Niger Republic's Economic and Social Development Plan: Interim Plan, 1961–1963. Niamey, 1962. 29 p.   JL
Commissariat Général au Plan. *Plan Intérimaire, 1964.* [Interim Plan, 1964.] Niamey, février 1964. 46 p.   JL

Nigeria

Ten-Year Plan of Development and Welfare for Nigeria. Sessional Paper No. 24 laid on the table of the Legislative Council on the 13th December 1945. Lagos, 1945. 157 p.   CRO
Ten-Year Plan of Development and Welfare for Nigeria, 1946. Sessional Paper No. 24 laid on the table of the Legislative Council on 13th December 1945 as amended by the Select Committee of the Council and approved by the Legislative Council on 7th February 1946. Lagos, 1946. 157 p.   JL

Revised Plan of Development and Welfare for Nigeria, 1951–1956. Legislative Council. Sessional Paper No. 6 of 1951. Lagos, 1951. 146 p.   JL
Economic Programme of the Government of the Federation of Nigeria, 1955–1960. Sessional Paper No. 2 of 1956. Lagos, 1956. 75 p.   JL
Federal Government Development Programme, 1962–1968. Sessional Paper No. 1 of 1962. Lagos, 1962. 46 p.   JL
Federal Ministry of Economic Development. *National Development Plan, 1962–1968.* Lagos, 1962. 362 p.   JL

North Borneo (United Kingdom) (See Sabah for 1965–1970 plan)

Development Committee. *Reconstruction and Development Plan for North Borneo, 1948–1955.* Jesselton, 1948. 128 p.   JL
Four-Year Plan, 1957–1960.
> [Mentioned in United Nations. Economic Commission for Asia and the Far East. "Economic Development and Planning in Asia and the Far East," *Economic Bulletin for Asia and the Far East.* Vol. XII, No. 3. December 1961. p. 51.]
Development Committee. *Development Plan, 1959–1964.* Jesselton, n.d. 20 p.   JL

Northern Ireland (United Kingdom)

Comprehensive Five-Year Economic Growth Programme, 1965–1969.
> [Mentioned in *The Financial Times.* August 24, 1964.]

Northern Rhodesia (See Zambia for post-independence plans. See Federation of Rhodesia and Nyasaland for Federation plans)

Development Authority. *Ten-Year Development Plan for Northern Rhodesia, as approved by Legislative Council on 11th February 1947* [1947–1956]. Lusaka, 1948. 88 p.   JL
Revision of the Northern Rhodesia Ten-Year Development Plan, November 1953. Presented to the Legislative Council on 30th November 1953 by the Development Secretary. Lusaka, 1953. 23 p.   CRO
Development Plan for the Period 1st July 1961 to 30th June 1965. Lusaka, 1962. 63 p.   JL

Norway

Om Utarbeidelse av et Langtidsprogram til Organisationen for Europeisk Okonomisk Samarbeid [1949–1952]. [On the Preparation of a Long-Term Program to the Organization for European Economic Cooperation.] St. meld. nr. 54 (1948).
> [Cited in Bourneuf, Alice., *Norway, The Planned Revival.* Cambridge, Mass., Harvard University Press, 1958. p. 214. The Program was published in English in the *Interim Report on the European Recovery Program.* Vol. II. Paris, Organization for European Economic Cooperation, December 30, 1948.]
Statsministeren. *Norwegian Long-Term Program, 1954–1957.* Storting Report No. 62 presented by the Prime Minister on April 29, 1953. Oslo, 1953. 334 p.   JL

Statsministeren. *Om et Langtidsprogram for 1954–1957*. [On a Long-Term Program for 1954–1957.] Oslo, 1953. St. meld. nr. 62 (1953). 2 vol. JL

Statsministeren. *Om Langtidsprogrammet for 1958–1961*. [On the Long-Term Program for 1958–1961.] Oslo, 1957. St. meld. nr. 67 (1957). 101 p. JL

Finans-og Toll-Departementet. *Langtidsprogrammet 1962–1965*. [Long-Term Program 1962–1965.] Oslo, 1961. St. meld. nr. 60 (1960–61). 110 p. JL

Royal Norwegian Ministry of Finance. *Norwegian Long-Term Programme 1962–1965*. n.p., n.d. 62 p. JL

> [This is an English translation of extracts from the *Langtidsprogrammet 1962–1965* published on 19th April 1961 as St. meld. nr. 60 (1960–61). Cited above.]

Finans-og Toll-Departementet. *Langtidsprogrammet 1966–1969*. [Long-Term Program 1966–1969.] Oslo, 1965. St. meld. nr. 63 (1964–65). 163 p. JL

Nyasaland (See Malawi for post-independence plans. See Federation of Rhodesia and Nyasaland for Federation plans)

Colonial Development Advisory Committee. *Development Programme, 1931–1934*. Zomba, 13th September 1930. 65 p. CRO

Development Committee. *Report of the Post-War Development Committee* [1946–1955]. Zomba, 1946. 139 p. JL

Revised Report of the Post-War Development Committee [1946–1955]. Zomba, January 1947. 42 p. JL.

The Nyasaland Development Programme. Zomba, n.d. 30 p. JL

Ministry of Finance. *Capital Development Plan, 1957–1961*. Zomba, 1957. 91 p. JL

Ministry of Finance. *Development Plan, 1962–1965*. Zomba, 1962. 143 p. JL

Pakistan

Ministry of Economic Affairs. *Six Year Development Programme of Pakistan, July 1951 to June 1957*. Karachi, n.d. 67 p. JL

Planning Board. *First Five Year Plan, 1955–60 (Draft)*. Karachi, 1956. 524 p. JL

National Planning Board. *The First Five Year Plan, 1955–1960*. Karachi, 1958. 652 p. JL

Planning Commission. *The Second Five Year Plan, 1960–1965*. Karachi, 1960. 414 p. JL

Planning Commission. *Development Programme* [1st July 1960 to 30th June 1961]. Karachi, June 1960. 147 p.

Planning Commission. *Development Programme, 1964–1965*. Karachi, 1964. 686 p. ECAFE

Perspective Plan, 1965–1985.

> [Under preparation according to *The Financial Times*. July 9, 1964.]

Planning Commission. *The Third Five Year Plan (1965–1970)*. [Karachi],
  1965. 533 p. JL

Panama

Dirección General de Planificación y Administración. *Programa de Desarrollo
  Económico y Social de la República de Panamá* [1963–1970]. [Eco-
  nomic and Social Development Program of the Republic of Panama.]
  Panama, April 1963. 935 p. Preliminary edition.
Dirección General de Planificación y Administración. *Revisión del Programa
  de Desarrollo Económico y Social de la República de Panamá* [1964–
  1966]. [Revised Program of Economic and Social Development for the
  Republic of Panama.] Panama, n.d. 99 p.

Paraguay

Departamento Nacional de Prensa y Propaganda. *Plan Quinquenal 1944–
  1948 de Reconstrucción Nacional*. [Five-Year Plan, 1944–1948, of
  National Reconstruction.] [Asunción, 1944.] 25 p. PAU
Plan Cuatrienal de Obras Publicas, 1956–1959. [Four-Year Plan of Public
  Works, 1956–1959.] Asunción, 1955. GER
Technical Secretariat for Planning. Two-Year Development Plan, 1965–
  1966.
        [Mentioned in Inter-American Development Bank. *Social Progress
        Trust Fund; Annual Report, 1964*. Washington, D.C., 1965. p.
        432.]

Peru

Partido del Pueblo. Secretaría Nacional del Plan de Gobierno. *Bases para el
  Plan de Gobierno del Partido, 1962–1968*. [Guidelines for The Gov-
  ernment Party's Plan, 1962–1968.] [Lima?] 1962. 1 vol. PAU
Banco Central de Reserva del Perú. *Plan Nacional de Desarrollo Económico
  y Social del Perú, 1962–1971*. [National Plan for the Economic and
  Social Development of Peru, 1962–1971.] [Lima, 1962?] 292 p. JL
Instituto Nacional de Planificación. *Programa de Inversiones Públicas, 1964–
  1965*. [Public Investment Program, 1964–1965.] Lima, 1964. 3 vols.
Instituto Nacional de Planificación. Investment Program, 1964–1970.
        [Mentioned in International Monetary Fund. *International News
        Financial Survey*. Vol. XVI, No. 46. Nov. 20, 1964.]

Philippines

Joint Philippine-American Finance Commission. *Philippine Economic Development; A Technical Memorandum* [1947–1951]. Manila, 1947.
  66 p. LC
        [Prepared by Thomas E. Hibben.]
National Development Company. *Proposed Program for Industrial Rehabilitation and Development of the Republic of the Philippines*. Manila,
  1947. 247 p. JL
        [Prepared by the Technical Staff of the National Development
        Co. under the supervision of the H. E. Beyster Corp., consulting
        engineers.]

Joint American-Philippine Finance Commission. *Report and Recommendations of the Joint Philippine-American Finance Commission.* Washington, D.C., 1947. 222 p. LC

National Economic Council. *Government Program of Economic Rehabilitation and Development* [1949–1953]. Manila, 1949.
> [Known as the Cuaderno Plan after the then Secretary of Finance Miguel Cuaderno. Mentioned in Golay, Frank H., *The Philippines: Public Policy and National Economic Development.* Ithaca, New York, Cornell University Press, 1961. p. 350.]

Economic Survey Commission. *Philippine Agricultural and Industrial Development Program. Revised 1950.* Manila, 1950. 516 p. JL
> [Known as the Yulo Plan after its chairman, Jose Yulo.]

Economic Survey Mission to the Philippines. *Report to the President of the United States.* Washington, D.C., 1950. 107 p. JL
> [Known as the Bell Mission Report after its Chairman, Daniel W. Bell.]

Economic Survey Commission. *Revised Philippine Economic Development Program.* Manila, 1950. 107 p. LC

National Economic Council. *The Five-Year Economic Development Program for FY 1955–1959.* [First Draft.] Manila, 1954. 1 vol. JL
> [Known as the Rodriguez Plan after Filemon C. Rodriguez, Acting Executive Director of the National Economic Council.]

Montelibano Plan (1956).
> [Mentioned in Crucillo, Cornelio V., "Foreign Aid in Planned Economic Development." *Economic Research Journal.* Vol. XI, No. 1. June 1964.]

Puyat-Romualdez Plan [1957?].
> [Mentioned in Crucillo, Cornelio V., "Foreign Aid in Planned Economic Development." *Economic Research Journal.* Vol. XI, No. 1. June 1964. This became the FY 1957–1961 Programme.]

National Economic Council. *Five-Year Economic and Social Development Programme for FY 1957–1961. Adopted by the Council on January 3, 1957.* Manila, 1957. 292 p. JL

Locsin, Senator Jose C., *Three-Year Production Program.* [FY 1957–1959.] Manila, 1957. pp. 133–190. JL
> [Supplement to National Economic Council. *Five-Year Economic and Social Development Program for FY 1957–1961.* Manila, 1957. Cited above.]

Budget Commission. "The Five-Year Fiscal Program" [1957–1961] in President of the Philippines. *Budget for the Fiscal Year 1958.* Manila, 1957. pp. 8A–12A. JL

Budget Commission. "The Five-Year Fiscal Plan" [1958–1962] in President of the Philippines. *Budget for the Fiscal Year 1959.* Manila, 1958. pp. 3A–14A. JL

Budget Commission. "The Five-Year Fiscal Plan" [1959–1963] in President of the Philippines. *Budget for the Fiscal Year 1960.* Manila, 1959. pp. 3A–20A. JL

National Economic Council. *Three-Year Programme for Economic and*

Social Development; (FY 1959–60 to FY 1961–62) Adopted by the Council on January 2, 1959. Manila, 1959. 171 p.   LC-UN

Budget Commission. "The Five-Year Fiscal Plan" [1960–1964] in President of the Philippines. *Budget for the Fiscal Year 1961.* Manila, 1960. pp. 4A–20A.   JL

Budget Commission. "The Five-Year Fiscal Plan, 1961–1965" in President of the Philippines. *Budget for the Fiscal Year 1962.* Manila, 1961. pp. 7A–14A.   JL

Budget Commission. "The Five-Year Fiscal Program, 1963–1967" in President of the Philippines. *Budget for the Fiscal Year 1963.* Manila, 1962. p. 4A.   JL

Proposed Five-Year Integrated Program for Socio-Economic Development (FY 1963–1967). Manila, 1962. 171 p.   JL
[*Annex A* to the State of the Nation Message of President Diosdado Macapagal, January 22, 1962.]

Budget Commission. "The Five-Year Fiscal Program" [1964–1968] in President of the Philippines. *Budget for the Fiscal Year 1964.* Manila, 1963. pp. 8A–10A.   JL

Poland

Central Board of Planning. *Polish National Economic Plan. Resolution of the National Council Concerning the National Economic Plans and the Plan of Economic Reconstruction for the Period of January 1, 1946–December 31, 1949.* Warszawa, 1946. 108 p.   LC

Central Planning Board. *Government Investment Plan for the Year 1947.* Warsaw, 1947.   UNP

Plan sześcioletni [1950–1955]. [Six-Year Plan.] Warszawa, Książka i Wiedza, 1950. 227 p.   LC

Sejm uchwala plan sześcioletni [1950–1955]. [The Sejm (Parliament) Approves the Six-Year Plan.] Warszawa, Książka i Wiedza, 1951. 266 p.   LC

The Six-Year Plan of Building the Foundations of Socialism in Poland, 1950–1955. Warsaw, Polskie Wydawnictwa Gospodarcze, 1951. 37 p.   LC

Ustawa o piecioletnim planie rozwoju gospodarki narodowej w latach 1956–1960. [The Law on the Five-Year Plan for the Development of the National Economy in the Years 1956–1960.] Warszawa, 1956. 116 p.   LC

Seven-Year Plan, 1959–1965.   BEB

Pięcioletni plan rozwoju gospodarki narodowej na lata 1961–1965. [Five-Year Plan for the Development of the National Economy in the Years 1961–1965.] Warszawa, Książka i Wiedza, 1961. 205 p.   LC

Secomski, Kazimierz. Perspektywiczny plan rozwoju gospodarczego Polski [1961–1975]. [Perspective Plan for the Development of Polish Economy.] *Ekonomista*, No. 6, 1958. pp. 1346–1374.   BEB

Five-Year Plan, 1966–1970.
[Mentioned in *The New York Times*. February 12, 1965.]

Portugal

Law of Economic Reconstruction of May 24, 1935 (No. 1914), 1935–1950.
Lisbon, 1935.
[Mentioned in *The Portuguese Economic Development Drive.*
Lisbon, Central Bureau for the Development Plan, 1963.
pp. 7–8. JL]
General Memorandum on the 1950–51 and 1951–52 Programmes. Paris,
Organization for European Economic Cooperation, April 1950. 32 p.
JL
Ministério da Economia. *Plan de Fomento* [1953–1958]. [Development
Plan.] Lisbon, 1953. 2 vols. JL
Plano de Fomento (Lei No. 2058) Revisão de 1955 (Lei No. 2077). [De-
velopment Plan (Law No. 2058) Revision of 1955 (Law No. 2077).]
Lisbon, 1955. 67 p. JL
Ministério da Economia. *II Plano de Fomento, 1959–1964.* [The Second
Plan of Development, 1959–1964.] Lisbon, 1959. 3 vols. JL
Presidência do Conselho. *Plano Intercalar de Fomento para 1965–1967.*
[Transitional Development Plan for 1965–1967.] Lisbon, 1964. 2 vols.
[Com. a Lei No. 2123, de Dezembro de 1964, Autorizando a sua
Organização e Execução.]

Portuguese Guinea (Portugal)

Portugal. Ministério da Economia. *Plano de Fomento* [1953–1958]. [Devel-
opment Plan.] Lisbon, 1953. pp. 74–76. JL
Portugal. Ministério da Economia. *II Plano de Fomento, 1959–1964.* [The
Second Plan of Development, 1959–1964.] Lisbon, 1959. pp. 176–
183. JL
Portugal. Presidência do Conselho. *Plano Intercalar de Fomento para 1965–
1967.* [Transitional Development Plan for 1965–1967.] Lisbon, 1964.
Vol. II. pp. 77–104.

Puerto Rico

Planning, Urbanizing and Zoning Board. *Development Plan for Puerto Rico.*
Technical Paper No. 1. Santurce, 1944. 66 p. JL
Planning, Urbanizing and Zoning Board. *Second Six-Year Financial Program
for the Fiscal Years 1945–46 to 1950–51.* Santurce, 1945. 55 p. LC
Planning, Urbanizing and Zoning Board. *Third Six-Year Financial Program
for the Fiscal Years 1946–47 to 1951–52.* Santurce, 1946. 69 p. LC
Planning, Urbanizing and Zoning Board. *Fourth Six-Year Financial Pro-
gram for the Fiscal Years 1947–48 to 1952–53.* Santurce, 1947. 79 p.
LC
Planning, Urbanizing and Zoning Board. *Fifth Six-Year Financial Program
for the Years 1948–49 to 1953–54.* Santurce, 1948. 63 p. LC
Planning, Urbanizing and Zoning Board. *Sixth Six-Year Financial Program
for the Years 1949/50 to 1954/55.* Santurce, March 1949. 60 p. PAU

Planning Board. *Seventh Six-Year Financial Program for the Years 1950–51 to 1955–56.* Santurce, 1950. 67 p. JL

Planning Board. *Eighth Six-Year Financial Program for the Years 1951–52 through 1956–57.* Santurce, 1951. 69 p. JL

Planning Board. *Noveno Programa Económico de Seis Años, 1952–53 à 1957–58.* [Ninth Six-Year Economic Program, 1952–53 to 1957–58.] Santurce, 1952. 65 p. JL

Planning Board. *Decimo Programa Económico de Seis Años, 1953–54 à 1958–59.* [Tenth Six-Year Economic Program, 1953/54–1958/59.] Santurce, 1953. 69 p.   JL

Planning Board. *Undécimo Programa Económico de Seis Años, 1955–1960.* [Eleventh Six-Year Economic Program, 1955–1960.] San Juan, 1954. 82 p. JL

Planning Board. *Eleventh Six-Year Financial Program, 1955–1960.* Santurce, 1954. 80 p. LC

Planning Board. *Duodécimo Programa Económico de Seis Años Fiscales 1956 à 1961.* [Twelfth Six-Year Economic Program; Fiscal Years 1956 to 1961.] Santurce, 1955. 69 p.   UN

Planning Board. *Decimotercer Programa Económico de Seis Años; Años Fiscales 1957 à 1962.* [Thirteenth Six-Year Economic Program; Fiscal Years 1957–1962.] Santurce, 1956. 62 p. JL

Planning Board. *Decimocuarto Programa Económico de Seis Años; Años Fiscales 1958 à 1963.* [Fourteenth Six-Year Economic Program; Fiscal Years 1957–1962.] Santurce, 1957. 150 p. JL

Junta de Planificación. *Decimoquinto Programa Económico de Seis Años; Años Fiscales 1959 à 1964.* [Fifteenth Six-Year Economic Program; Fiscal Years 1959–1964.] Santurce, 1958. 115 p. JL

Junta de Planificación. *Decimosexto Programa Económico de Seis Años; Años Fiscales 1960 à 1965.* [Sixteenth Six-Year Economic Program; Fiscal Years 1960–1965.] [Santurce], 1959. 87 p. JL

Junta de Planificación. *Decimoseptimo Programa Económico de Seis Años; Años Fiscales 1961 à 1966.* [Seventeenth Six-Year Economic Program; Fiscal Years 1961 to 1966.] Santurce, 1960. 89 p. JL

Planning Board. *Decimoctavo Programa Económico de Seis Años; Años Fiscales 1962 à 1967.* [Eighteenth Six-Year Economic Program, 1962–1967.] n.p., 1961. 92 p. JL

Planning Board. *Decimonoveno Programa Económico de Seis Años; Años Fiscales 1963 à 1968.* [Nineteenth Six-Year Economic Program; Fiscal Years 1963–1968.] n.p., 1962. 103 p. JL

Planning Board. *Programa Económico de Cuatro Años; Años Fiscales 1964 à 1967.* [Four-Year Economic Program; Fiscal Years 1964 to 1967.] San Juan, 1963. 143 p. LC

Réunion (France)

France. Commissariat Général du Plan de l'Equipement et de la Productivité. *Rapport Général de la Commission de Modernisation et d'Equipement des Départements d'Outre-Mer (Guadeloupe et dépendances, Guyane Française, Martinique, Réunion) 3me Plan, 1958–1961.* [General

Report of the Modernization and Equipment Commission for the Overseas Departments (Guadeloupe and dependencies, French Guiana, Martinique, Réunion) 3rd Plan, 1958–1961.] Paris, 1959. 452 p.   CAR

Ruanda-Urundi (See Burundi for post-independence plans)

Belgium. Ministère des Colonies. *Plan Décennal pour le Développement Economique et Social du Ruanda-Urundi* [1950–1959]. [Ten-Year Plan for the Economic and Social Development of Ruanda-Urundi.] Bruxelles, 1951. 598 p.   JL

Rumania

"Zákon o vseobecném hospodářském plánu Lidové Republiky Rumunské na rok 1949." [Law on the One-Year Economic Plan of the Rumanian People's Republic for the Year 1949] in *Rumunské Hospodářské Plány.* [Rumanian Economic Plans.] Praha [Prague], Orbis, 1951. pp. 17–60.   LC
[Translated into Czech by Jaroslav Minař.]
"Romania's Economic One-Year Plan" [1949] in *Rumanian News.* Washington, D.C., January 16, 1949.   SP
"Zákon o státnim plánu Lidové Republiky Rumunské na rok 1950." [Law on the State Plan of the Rumanian Republic for the Year 1950] in *Rumunské Hospodářské Plány.* [Rumanian Economic Plans.] Praha [Prague], Orbis, 1951. pp. 63–103.   LC
[Translated into Czech by Jaroslav Minař.]
"Bill on the State Plan of the RPR" [1950] in *Planned Development of the RPR.* [Rumanian People's Republic.] Bucharest, 1950.   SP
"Zákon o pětiletem plánu rozvoje národniho hospodářstvi Lidové Republiky Rumunské na léta 1951–55." [Law on the Five-Year Plan for the Economic Development of the Rumanian People's Republic in the Years 1951–1955] in *Rumunské Hospodářské Plány.* [Rumanian Economic Plans.] Praha [Prague], Orbis, 1951. pp. 133–167.   LC
[Translated into Czech by Jaroslav Minař.]
Zakon o piatiletnem plane razvitiia narodnogo khoziaistva Rumynskoi Narodnoi Republiki v 1951–1955 gg. [Law on the Five-Year Plan for the Economic Development of the Rumanian People's Republic in the Years 1951–1955.] Moskva, 1951. 30 p.   BEB
[In Russian.]
Stroitel'stvo socializma v Rumynii: sbornik dokladov i materialov [1951–1955]. [Building Socialism in Rumania: Collection of Reports and Basic Materials.] Bucharest, Gos. Izd., 1951. 133 p.   BEB
[In Russian.]
Second Five-Year Plan, 1956–1960.   BEB
Perspective Program, 1960–1975.   BEB
Six-Year Plan, 1960–1965.   BEB
[A summary of the Six-Year Plan, 1960–1965, appears in La Documentation Française. *Notes et Etudes Documentaires.* No. 2.700. Paris, 16 September 1960.]

Economic Plan for 1965.
[Mentioned in *The Financial Times*. February 5, 1965.]
Five-Year Plan, 1966–1970.
[Mentioned in *East Europe*. Vol. 14, No. 7. July 1965.]

Ryukyu Islands (United States)

United States Civil Administration. Office of Plans and Programs. *Joint Economic Plan for the Ryukyu Islands, FY 1962–1966*. Naha, Okinawa, 1960. 363 p.   JL

Sabah (See North Borneo for plans before 1965)[2]

Financial Secretary's Office. *First Draft of the Sabah State Development Plan, 1965–1970*.
[Prepared for inclusion in the First Malaysian Five-Year Plan, 1966–1970.]

St. Christopher-Nevis-Anguilla (United Kingdom)

Draft Ten-Year Plan of Development: St. Christopher-Nevis-Anguilla in the Colony of the Leeward Islands, 1946–1956. n.p., n.d. 49 p.   CO
Ten-Year Plan of Development: St. Christopher-Nevis-Anguilla in the Colony of the Leeward Islands, 1946–1956.   CAR
Presidency. *Development Plan, 1955–1960*. Antigua, 24 June 1956. 9 p.   CO

St. Helena (United Kingdom)

Ten-Year Plan of Economic Development and Social Welfare, 1947–1956. [Preliminary.] The Castle, St. Helena, 15 July 1946. 19 p.

St. Lucia (United Kingdom)

Development Sketch Plan, 1946–1950. [Prepared under the direction of the Administrator, Mr. E. F. Twining, C.M.G., M.B.E.] Castries, 1945. 31 p.   CO
Development Committee. *Revised Development Sketch Plan, 1946–1956*. n.p., 1947. 32 p.   CO
Five-Year Development Plan, 1960–1964.
[Mentioned in Caribbean Organization. *Planning for Economic Development in the Caribbean*. Hato Rey, Puerto Rico, 1963. p. 209.]

St. Vincent (United Kingdom)

St. Vincent Development Committee. *A Plan of Development for the Colony of St. Vincent* [1946–1956]. n.p., 1947. 821 p.   JL
Memorandum on the Revision of the Development Plan. Legislative Council Paper No. 2 of 1951. n.p., 1951. 26 p.   CO

[2] The Crown Colony of North Borneo became the State of Sabah with internal self-government on August 31, 1965. On September 16, 1965, the State of Sabah joined the Federation of Malaysia.

São Tomé and Príncipe Islands (Portugal)

Portugal. Ministério da Economia. *Plano de Fomento* [1953–1958]. [Development Plan.] Lisbon, 1953. pp. 76–78. JL

Portugal. Ministério da Economia. *II Plano de Fomento, 1959–1964.* [The Second Plan of Development, 1959–1964.] Lisbon, 1959. pp. 184–190. JL

Portugal. Presidência do Conselho. *Plano Intercalar de Fomento para 1965–1967.* [Transitional Development Plan for 1965–1967.] Lisbon, 1964. Vol. II. pp. 105–134.

Sarawak (See Malaysia for plan after Federation)

Development Programme for Sarawak for the Period 1951–1957. Kuching, 1950. 15 p. CO

Development Board. *Revised Development Plan of Sarawak, 1951–1957.* Kuching, 1952. [17 p.] JL

Development Board. *Development Plan of Sarawak, 1955–1960.* Kuching, 1954. 53 p. JL

Council Negri. *Revision of 1955–1960 Development Plan; Approved on the 26th August 1957.* Kuching, 1957. 14 p. JL

Sarawak Development Plan, 1959–1963: Approved by the Council Negri on the 25th August 1959. Kuching, 1959. 25 p. JL

National Development Planning Committee. *Development Plan, 1964–1968.* Kuching, 1963. 64 p. ECAFE
[Prepared for inclusion in the First Malaysian Five-Year Plan, 1966–1970.]

Senegal (See French West Africa for pre-independence plans)

Long-term Perspective Plan, 1960–1985. UNS

Ministère du Plan, du Développement et de la Coopération Technique. *Plan Quadriennal de Développement, 1961–1964.* [Four-Year Development Plan, 1961–1964.] Dakar, 1961. 209 p. JL

Second Five-Year Plan, 1965–1969. UNS

Seychelles (United Kingdom)

Ten-Year Development Plan, 1947–1956. Report of the Committee appointed to draw up a ten-year development programme and to advise on various representations for reduction of taxation. Mahé, 1947. 29 p. CO

Seychelles 5-Year Development Plan, 1956–1960 and Estimates of Revenue and Expenditure for the 1st Phase Year 1956. Mahé, n.d. [9 p.] JL

Seychelles Development Plan, 1st April 1959 to 31st March 1962. [Draft.] Mahé, April 1959. 103 p. CO

A Plan for Seychelles. Mahé, 1959. 58 p. JL

Sierra Leone

Development Council. *Outline of the Ten-Year Plan for the Development of Sierra Leone.* Freetown, 1946. 23 p. LC

H. Childs, Dept. of Agriculture. *Plan of Economic Development for Sierra Leone.* Freetown, 1949. 56 p.   JL
     [". . . measures to . . . increase production . . . during the next four or five years." (*Plan of Economic Development for Sierra Leone, p. 1*).]
Ministry of Development. *Ten-Year Plan of Economic and Social Development for Sierra Leone, 1962/63–1971/72.* Freetown, 1962. 105 p.
Five-Year Development Plan [April 1, 1965–March 31, 1970].   UNS
     [Under preparation.]

Singapore (See Malaysia for post-Federation plan)

Ministry of Finance. *State of Singapore Development Plan, 1961–1964.* Singapore, 1961. 134 p.   JL

Somalia (See Italian Somaliland and Somaliland Protectorate for pre-independence plans)

Planning and Coordinating Committee for Economic and Social Development. *First Five-Year Plan, 1963–1967.* Mogadiscio, 1963. 161 p.   JL
Planning and Coordinating Committee for Economic and Social Development. *First Five-Year Plan, 1963–1967.* Mogadiscio, 1963. 209 p.   ECA

Somaliland Protectorate (See also Somalia and Italian Somaliland)

Secretariat. *Somaliland Protectorate Development Plan.* Colonial Development and Welfare Acts, 1940 and 1945. Hargeisa, 8th December 1950. 18 p.   JL
Somaliland Protectorate; Financial Statement of Proposed Development, 1955–1960. n.p., n.d. 35 p.   CO

South Africa

Department of Planning. *Economic Development Programme for the Republic of South Africa, 1964–1969.* Pretoria, 1964. 81 p.   JL

Southern Rhodesia (See Federation of Rhodesia and Nyasaland for Federation plans)

Four-Year Plan, 1949–1953. Salisbury, n.d.   GER
Second Four-Year Plan: Capital Expenditure from Loan Funds, April 1951 to March 1955. [Salisbury, 1951?] 32 p.   JL
Development Plan, 1955–1959. [Salisbury], 1955. 6 p.   JL
Development Plan, 1957–1961. [Salisbury], 1957. 8 p.   JL

South-West Africa

Ten-Year Development Plan (Odendaal Plan).
     [Mentioned in *The New York Times.* January 25, 1965.]

Spain

Presidencia del Gobierno. Comisaría del Plan de Desarrollo Económico. *Plan de Desarrollo Económico y Social, 1964–1967.* [Economic and Social Development Program, 1964–1967.] Madrid, 1963. 494 p.   JL

Spanish Guinea (Spain. Includes island of Fernando Póo and territory of Río Muni)

Comisión para el Desarrollo Económico de Fernando Póo y Río Muni. *Guinea Ecuatorial; Anexo al Plan de Desarrollo Económico y Social Años 1964–1967.* [Equatorial Guinea; Annex to the Economic and Social Development Program, 1964–1967.] Madrid, 1964. 240 p. JL

Sudan

Development Priorities Committee. First Five-Year Development Programme [1946–1951].
Finance Department. Development Branch. *Sudan Development Programme, 1951–1956.* Khartoum, 1953. 27 p. JL
Ministry of Finance and Economics. Economic Planning Secretariat. *Ten-Year Plan of Economic and Social Development, 1961/62–1970/71.* Khartoum, 1962. 180 p. JL

Surinam

Stichting Planbureau Suriname. *De Grondslagen van een Tienjarenplan voor Suriname* [1953–1962]. [The Principles for a Ten-Year Plan for Surinam.] Paramaribo, 1952. 191 p. JL
Surinam Planning Bureau. *Ten-Year Plan for Surinam; Revised Programme;* by order of the Government of Surinam and in close co-operation with the Government and the Contact Committee of the Legislative Council of Surinam [1955–1964]. Paramaribo, October 1954. 83 p. JL
Ministerie van Opbouw. *Development Plan for Agriculture, Animal Husbandry and Fisheries, 1960–1965.* Paramaribo, 1960. 41 p. CAR
Stichting Planbureau Suriname. *Raamwerk Integraal Opbouwplan Suriname, 1963–1972.* [Draft Integrated Surinam Development Plan, 1963–1972.] Paramaribo, 1963. 208 p. JL

Swaziland (United Kingdom)

Secretariat. *Eight-Year Development Plan Covering the Period 1st April 1948 to 31st March 1956.* Mbabane, 17th July 1948. 32 p. CO
Secretariat. *Eight-Year Development Plan, 1st April 1948 to 31st March 1956; Financial Report on the First Four Years of the Plan and Revision of the Plan for the Remaining Four Years.* Mbabane, 17th February 1953. 83 p.
Office of the Secretariat. *Development Plan, 1960–1964.* Mbabane, March 1960. 21 pieces in 1 vol. JL
Office of the Secretariat. *Development Plan, 1963–1966; Revised July 1964.* Mbabane, 1964. 100 p.

Sweden

Finansdepartementet. *Ekonomiskt Langtidsprogram, 1951–1955.* [Long-Term Economic Program, 1951–1955.] Stockholm, 1951. 200 p. JL

Syria

Extraordinary Budget for Economic Development [1955–1961]. Law No.
116. August 29, 1955.
    [Seven-Year Plan, 1955–1961. Later extended into the ten-year
    program cited below.]
United Arab Republic. Economic Development Organisation. *Bernamej el
Inmaa el Iqtisadi, 1958–1967.* [Economic Development Program, 1958–
1967.] n.p. [1958]. 380 p. JL
United Arab Republic. Economic Development Organisation. *Report on Economic Development Plan, 1958–1967.* [Syrian Region.] Cairo, 1959.
297 p. JL
    [Translation of Economic Development Program, 1958–1967 by
    Ragheb Abdou.]
Ministry of Planning. *Syrian Five-Year Plan for Economic and Social Development, 1960/61–1964/65.* n.p., 1961. 142 p. JL

Tanganyika (See Tanzania and Zanzibar)

Development Commission. *A Ten-Year Development and Welfare Plan for
Tanganyika Territory* [1947–1956]. Dar es Salaam, 1946. 67 p. JL
Revised Development and Welfare Plan for Tanganyika, 1950–1956. Dar
es Salaam, 1951. 40 p. JL
Member for Communications, Works and Development Planning. *Develop-
ment Plan, 1955–1960; Capital Works Programme.* Dar es Salaam,
1955. 29 p. JL
Development Committee of the Council of Ministers. *Development Plan for
Tanganyika, 1961/62–1963/64.* Dar es Salaam, 1961. 95 p. JL
Ministry of Development Planning. *Tanganyika Five-Year Plan for Economic
and Social Development, 1st July 1964–30th June 1969.* Dar es Salaam,
1964. 2 vols. ECA

Tanzania (See Tanganyika and Zanzibar)

Thailand

National Economic Development Board. "National Economic Development
Plan for the Period BE 2504 to BE 2506 and to BE 2509" [1961–1963–
1966] in: *Royal Thai Government Gazette.* Vol. 2, No. CCVIII, Octo-
ber 28, 1960. pp. 481–506.
Sum-Naggan-Sapa-Setakit Hang Chart. Sumnag-Nayog-Ratamontri. *Pan-
Patanakarn-Setakit-Hang-Chart: BE 2504–2506–2509: Raya-Tee-
Song: BE 2507–2509.* [National Economic Development Plan for the
period BE 2504 to BE 2506 and to BE 2509: Second Phase BE 2507–
2509.] Bangkok, 1964. 218 p.
National Economic Development Board. *National Economic Development
Plan, 1961–1966, Second Phase: 1964–1966.* Bangkok, 1964. 171
p. ECAFE
National Economic Development Board. Second Economic and Social De-
velopment Plan for 1967–72.
    [Under preparation according to *Bangkok World,* July 8, 1965.]

Timor (Portugal)

Portugal. Ministério da Economia. *Plano de Fomento* [1953–1958]. [Development Plan.] Lisbon, 1953. pp. 94–95. JL

Portugal. Ministério da Economia. *II Plano de Fomento, 1959–1964.* [The Second Plan of Development, 1959–1964.] Lisbon, 1959. pp. 245–256. JL

Portugal. Presidência do Conselho. *Plano Intercalar de Fomento para 1965–1967.* [Transitional Development Plan for 1965–1967.] Lisbon, 1964. Vol. II. pp. 253–274.

Tobago

Great Britain. Development and Welfare Organization in the West Indies. *Development Plan for Tobago; Report of the Team which visited Tobago in March–April, 1957.* Bridgetown, 1957. 172 p. JL

Togo

Long-Term Perspective Plan, 1965–1984. UNS
Five-Year Plan, 1965–1969. UNS
       [Under preparation.]

Trinidad and Tobago

Five-Year Economic Programme [1950–1955]. Laid in the Legislative Council on the 16th June 1950. Port of Spain, 1950. 2 vols. JL

Planning and Development Unit. *Five-Year Development Programme, 1958–1962.* Port of Spain, 1957. 118 p. JL

Economic Planning and Development Department. *Five-Year Development Programme, 1958–1962; Projects for 1959.* Trinidad, 1959. 59 p. UN

Economic Planning Division. *Five-Year Development Programme, 1958–1962; Report of the Premier on Development Projects for the Year 1960.* Trinidad, 1962. 115 p. UN

Five-Year Development Programme, 1958–1962; Projects for 1961. Trinidad, 1961. 79 p. UN

Five-Year Development Programme, 1958–1962; Projects for 1962. Trinidad, 1962. 90 p. UN

Prime Minister's Office. *Programme of Development Projects for the Year 1963.* Port of Spain, 1963. 54 p. CRO

National Planning Commission. *Draft. Second Five-Year Plan, 1964–1968.* Port of Spain, 1963. 340 p. JL-ECA

Tunisia

Direction des Travaux Publics. *Plan d'Equipement et de Reconstruction d'Outillage Public; Tranche 1948.* [Public Industrial Development and Reconstruction Plan for 1948.] Tunis, 1948. 67 p. JL

France. Commissariat Général au Plan de Modernisation et d'Equipement. *Rapport Général de la Commission d'Etude et de Coordination des Plans de Modernisation et d'Equipement de l'Algérie, de la Tunisie et du Maroc. Tunisie* [1954–1957]. [General Report of the Commission of Study and Coordination of the Modernisation and Equipment Plans of Algeria, Tunisia and Morocco. Tunisia.] Paris, juin 1954. 125 p. JL

Sécrétariat d'Etat au Plan et aux Finances. *Perspectives Décennales de Développement, 1962–1971.* [Ten-Year Prospects of Development, 1962–1971.] Tunis, 1962. 365 p.   JL
Sécrétariat d'Etat au Plan et aux Finances. *Plan Triennal, 1962–1964.* [Three-Year Plan, 1962–1964.] Tunis, 1962. 452 p.   JL
Sécrétariat d'Etat au Plan et aux Finances. *Plan Triennal, 1962–1964.* [Three-Year Plan, 1962–1964.] [Tunis, 1962?] 505 p. ECA
Deuxième Plan de Développement, 1965–1968. [Second Development Plan, 1965–1968.]

Turkey

State Planning Organization. *Program for the Year 1962 (For Transition into the Plan-Period).* [Draft.] Ankara, October 1961. 192 p.   JL
State Planning Organization. *Program for the Year 1962 (For Transition into the Plan-Period); Draft Implementation Plan.* Ankara, October 1961. 25 p.   JL
Devlet Plânlama Teşkilâti. *Kalkinma Plâni; Birinci beş Yil, 1963–1967.* [First Five-Year Development Plan, 1963–1967.] Ankara, 1963. 528 p.   LC
State Planning Organization. *First Five-Year Development Plan, 1963–1967.* Ankara, 1963. 497 p.   UN

Turks and Caicos Islands (United Kingdom)

Sketch Plan; Turks and Caicos Islands. Grand Turk, 17th July 1945. 65 p. CO
Development Plan. Kingston, 1947. 11 p.   CO
Memorandum on Revised Form of the Turks and Caicos Islands Development Plan. Kingston, 1947.   GER

Uganda

E. B. Worthington. *A Development Plan for Uganda* [1947–1956]. Entebbe, 1947. 112 p.   JL
Sir Douglas Harris, Development Commissioner. *The 1948 Revision of the Plan* [1947–1956]. Entebbe, 1949. 146 p.   JL
  [This document also includes the 1947–1956 Development Plan.]
Development Council. *A Five-Year Capital Development Plan, 1955–1960.* Entebbe, 1954. 73 p.   JL
A Five-Year Capital Development Plan, 1955–1960, The First Revision. Sessional Paper No. 13 of 1956/57. Entebbe, 1957. 130 p.   JL
First Five-Year Development Plan, 1961/62–1965/66; A plan for development in the public sector and an estimate of private sector investment during the period 1st July 1961 to 30th June 1966. Entebbe, 1963. 113 p.   JL

Union of Soviet Socialist Republics

State Planning Commission. *The Soviet Union Looks Ahead; The Five-Year Plan for Economic Reconstruction* [1928/29–1932/33]. New York, Horace Liveright, 1930. 271 p.   BEB

Piatiletnii plan narodnokhoziaistvennogo stroitel'stva SSSR [1928/29–1932/1933]. [Five-Year Plan for the National Economy of the USSR.] Tom 1–3. Moskva, Planovoe Khoziaistvo [Planned Economy], 1929. 3 vols. in 4 parts. BEB

State Planning Commission. *The Second Five-Year Plan for the Development of the National Economy of the USSR (1933–1937)*. New York, International Publishers, n.d. 671 p. BEB

Gosudarstvennaia Planovaia Komissiia. *Vtoroi piatiletnii plan razvitiia narodnogo khoziaistva SSSR, 1933–1937 gg.* [Second Five-Year Plan for the Development of the National Economy of the USSR, 1933–1937.] Moskva, Izd. Gosplana, 1934. 2 vols. BEB

Trelii piatiletnii plan razvitiia narodnogo khoziaistva soiuza SSR (1938–1942 gg). [Third Five-Year Plan for the Development of the National Economy of the USSR (1938–1942).] Moskva, Gosplanizdat, 1939. 238 p. BEB

Voznesenskii, Arsenii N., *Economic Results of the U.S.S.R. in 1940 and the Plan of National Economic Development for 1941; report delivered at the 18th All-union Conference of the C.P.S.U. (b.)* February 18, 1941. Moscow, Foreign Languages Publishing House, 1941. 39 p. LC

Law on the Five-Year Plan for the Rehabilitation and Development of the National Economy of the U.S.S.R., 1946–1950. (Adopted at the first session of the Supreme Soviet of the U.S.S.R. on March 18, 1946.) London, Soviet News, 1946. 103 p. BEB

Communist Party of the Soviet Union. 19th Congress, Moscow, 1952. *Directives of the XIX Party Congress for the Fifth Five-Year Plan of the Development of the U.S.S.R. in 1951–1955;* resolution adopted on the report of M. Z. Saburov, chairman of the State Planning Committee. Moscow, Foreign Languages Publishing House, 1952. 41 p. BEB

Bulganin, Nikolai A., *Report by N. A. Bulganin to the 20th Congress of the Communist Party of the Soviet Union on the Directives of the Sixth Five-Year Plan for the Development of the USSR, 1956–1960;* as approved by the 20th Congress of the CPSU, February 1956. London, Soviet News, 1956. LC

Kontrol'nye cifri razvitiia narodnogo khoziaistva SSSR na 1959–1965 gody: Utverzhdeny Edinoglasno XXI S'ezdom KPSS 5 Fevralia 1959 goda. [Control Figures for the Development of the National Economy of the USSR in the Years 1959–1965: Unanimously Approved at the 21st Congress of the CPSU, February 5, 1959.] Moskva, Gospolitizdat, 1959. 111 p. BEB

Control Figures for the Economic Development of the U.S.S.R., 1959–1965. Theses of N. S. Krushchov's [sic] *Report to the Twenty-First Congress of the C.P.S.U.* Moscow, Foreign Languages Publishing House, 1958. 130 p. BEB

Twenty-Year Perspective Plan, 1961–1980.

Five-Year Plan, 1966–1970.

[Under preparation according to *The New York Times.* April 20, 1965.]

United Arab Republic

Ten-Year Perspective Plan, 1960–1970. UNS.

Etar. El Khuta el Amma Ultanmiyeh el Iqtisadieh wa el Ijtimaeih 1960–1965. [Framework. Five-Year Plan, July 1960–June 1965, for Economic and Social Development.] Cairo, 1960. 496 p. JL

National Planning Committee. *Comprehensive Five-Year Plan for the Economic and Social Development of the U.A.R., 1960–1965.* Cairo, 1960. 108 p. UN

Second Five-Year Plan, 1965/66–1971/72.
   [Mentioned in *Middle East and African Economist.* June 1965.]

United Kingdom

National Economic Development Council. *Growth of the United Kingdom Economy to 1966.* London, 1963. 149 p. JL

National Economic Development Council. *Conditions Favourable to Faster Growth.* London, 1963. JL

Ministry of Economic Affairs. Five-Year Economic Development Plan.
   [Under preparation according to *The Financial Times.* February 19, 1965.]

Upper Volta (See French West Africa for pre-independence plans)

Long-Term Perspective Plan, 1963–1975. UNS

Projet de Plan Quinquennal 1963–1967. [Draft Five-Year Plan, 1963–1967.] Paris, 1963. 2 vols. UNS

Ministère de l'Economie Nationale. *Plan Intérimaire, 1963–1964.* [Interim Plan, 1963–1964.] Ouagadougou, 1963. 217 p. JL

Uruguay

Comisión de Inversiones y Desarrollo Económico. Ten-Year Perspective Plan 1964–1974.
   [Under preparation.]

Comisión de Inversiones y Desarrollo Económico. Three-Year Plan 1964–1966.
   [Under preparation.]

Venezuela

Three-Year Plan of Venezuela (1938–1941). Extracts from Special Message of the President of the Republic to the National Congress of May 6, 1938.
   [Extracts appear as Appendix C to Lorwin, Lewis L., *National Planning in Selected Countries.* Washington, D.C., National Resources Planning Board, 1941. JL]

Presidente. *Plan de Obras Públicas Nacionales para el Período Presidencial, 1941 à 1946.* [National Public Works Plan for the Presidential Term, 1941–1946.] Caracas, 1942. 40 p. JL

Coordination and Economic Planning Office. *Plan de la Nación, 1960–1964.* [National Plan, 1960–1964.] Caracas, 1960. 166 p. JL

Oficina Central de Coordinación y Planificación. *Plan de Desarrollo Económico y Social para 1962.* [Economic and Social Development Plan for 1962.] Caracas, 1961. UN

Oficina Central de Coordinación y Planificación. *Plan de la Nación, 1963– 1966.* [National Plan, 1963–1966.] Caracas, 1963. 495 p. JL

Oficina Central de Coordinación y Planificación. *Plan de Inversiones Adicionales, 1964–1967.* [Supplementary Investment Plan, 1964–1967.] Caracas, May 11, 1964.

> [Mentioned by Dr. Raul Leoni in an address to the Venezuelan National Congress. *Mensaje Especial presentado por el Ciudadano Presidente de la República, Dr. Raul Leoni al Congreso Nacional.* Caracas, 11 May 1964.]

Oficina Central de Coordinación y Planificación. Plan de la Nación, 1965– 1968. [National Plan, 1965–1968.]

> [Mentioned in *La República* (Bogotá). March 27, 1965.]

Viet Nam, Democratic Republic of (North)

Directorate-General of Planning. Two-Year Rehabilitation Plan [1953– 1956].

Projet de Plan Quinquennal, 1957–1961. [Draft of a Five-Year Plan, 1957– 1961.]

Three-Year Plan, 1958–1960. BEB

Five-Year Plan [1960–1964].

> [Mentioned in Jones, P. H. M. "Under Two Plans," *Far Eastern Economic Review.* May 4, 1961. p. 220.]

Viet Nam, Republic of (South)

Direction Général du Plan. *Projet du Plan Quinquennal* [1957–1961]. [Draft Five-Year Plan.] Saigon, 1957. 330 p.

Three-Year Plan, 1961–1963. Saigon, 1961. 28 p.

Direction Générale du Plan. *Deuxième Plan Quinquennal, 1962–1966.* [Second Five-Year Plan, 1962–1966.] [Saigon], 1962. 271 p. JL

Virgin Islands (United States)

Economic Development Board. *Overall Economic Development Program of the Economic Development Board.* Charlotte Amalie, St. Thomas, June 1962. 60 p. CAR

Western Samoa

Economic Development Program.

> [Under preparation according to *The New York Times.* February 7, 1965.]

Yugoslavia

Zakon o petogodišnjem planu razvitka narodne privrede Federativne Narodne Republike Jugoslavije u godinama 1947–1951. [Law on the Five-Year Plan for the Development of the National Economy of the People's Republic of Yugoslavia in the Years 1947–1951.] Beograd, Izd. "Sluzbenog lista FNRJ," 1949. 100 p. LC

Law on the Five Year Plan for the Development of the National Economy of the Federative People's Republic of Yugoslavia in the period from 1947 to 1951. Beograd, Office of Information, 1947. 166 p.   LC

Prijedlog društvenog plana FNRJ za godinu 1952 sa dokumentacijom. [Proposal of Social Plan of FPRY for 1952 with Documents.] Belgrade, 1952.

> [Cited in, Mid-European Studies Center. *Yugoslavia.* New York, F. A. Praeger, 1957. p. 459.]

"Zakon o društvenom planu FNRJ za 1952." [Law on the Social Plan of FPRY for 1952.] *Službeni List FNRJ.* [Official Gazette of FPRY.] April 1, 1952.

> [Cited in, Mid-European Studies Center. *Yugoslavia.* New York, F. A. Praeger, 1957. p. 459.]

Prijedlog društvenog plana FNRJ za godinu 1953 sa dokumentacijom. [Proposal of Social Plan of FPRY for 1953 with Documents.] Belgrade, 1953.

> [Cited in, Mid-European Studies Center. *Yugoslavia.* New York, F. A. Praeger, 1957. p. 459.]

"Zakon o društvenom planu FNRJ za 1953." [Law on the Social Plan of FPRY for 1953.] *Službeni List FNRJ.* [Official Gazette of FPRY.] December 30, 1952.

> [Cited in, Mid-European Studies Center. *Yugoslavia.* New York, F. A. Praeger, 1957. pp. 459–460.]

"Dokumentacija uz Zakon o društv. planu za 1953g." [Documents Accompanying Law on The Social Plan for 1953.] *Službeni List FNRY.* [Official Gazette of FPRY.] January 28, 1953.

> [Cited in, Mid-European Studies Center. *Yugoslavia.* New York, F. A. Praeger, 1957. p. 458.]

Prijedlog društvenog plana FNRJ za godinu 1954 sa dokumentacijom. [Proposal of Social Plan of FPRY for 1954 with Documents.] Belgrade, 1954.

> [Cited in, Mid-European Studies Center. *Yugoslavia.* New York, F. A. Praeger, 1957. p. 459.]

"Savezni društveni plana za 1954g." [Federal Social Plan for 1954.] *Službeni List FNRJ.* [Official Gazette of FPRY.] March 24, 1954.

> [Cited in, Mid-European Studies Center. *Yugoslavia.* New York, F. A. Praeger, 1957. p. 459.]

Nacrt saveznog društvenog plana za 1955. [Draft of Federal Social Plan for 1955.] Belgrade, 1954.

> [Cited in, Mid-European Studies Center. *Yugoslavia.* New York, F. A. Praeger, 1957. p. 458.]

Annual Plan, 1956.

Društveni plan privrednog razvoja Jugoslavije, 1957–1961. [Social Plan for the Economic Development of Yugoslavia, 1957–1961.] Beograd, Kultura, 1957. 237 p.   LC

Društveni plan privrednog razvoja Jugoslavije, 1961–1965. [Social Plan for the Economic Development of Yugoslavia, 1961–1965.] Beograd, Kultura, 1961. 164 p.   BEB

Five-Year Plan of Economic Development of Yugoslavia, 1961–1965. Beograd, Secretariat for Information of the Federal Executive Council, 1961. 121 p.   LC
Seven-Year Plan, 1964–1970.
> [Mentioned in Yugoslav Information Center. *Yugoslavia News Bulletin* (New York). Vol. III, No. 295. July 21, 1964.]

Zambia (See Northern Rhodesia for pre-independence plans)

Office of the President. Central Planning Office. *An Outline of the Transitional Development Plan* [1st January 1965–30th June 1966]. Lusaka, 1965. 104 p.   JL-ECA
> [This plan is "transitional in the sense that it bridges the time period between the past plan with its emergency extension and the full Four- or Five-Year Plan which will be prepared in the course of this year. Although it covers a period of eighteen months from 1st January 1965 to 30th June 1966, the first six months of that period formed part of the previous plan, while the last six months will be absorbed into the larger and longer plan, once that is determined and promulgated." p. 3.]

Development Plan, 1966–1970.
> [Under preparation according to *The Financial Times.* January 2, 1965.]

Zanzibar (See Tanganyika for 1964–1969 Plan for Tanzania)

Programme of Social and Economic Development in the Zanzibar Protectorate for the Ten-Year Period 1946–1955. Legislative Council, Sessional Paper No. 1 of 1946. Zanzibar, 1946. 35 p.

Programme of Social and Economic Development in the Zanzibar Protectorate for the Five-Year Period 1st January 1955 to 31st December 1959 as approved by the Legislative Council on the 24th of August 1955. Sessional Paper No. 8 of 1955. Zanzibar, 1955. 16p.   JL

Development Plan, 1960–1964. Sessional Paper No. 24 of 1959.   JL
> [In Zanzibar. Legislative Council. Papers laid before the Legislative Council, 1959. pp. 62–80, 148–166.]

Revised Development Programme for the Three-Year Period, July 1961 to June 1964. Legislative Council. Sessional Paper No. 3 of 1962. Zanzibar, 1962. 6 p.   CRO

Central Planning Agencies

ADEN
Financial Secretariat
Aden Colony

AFGHANISTAN
Ministry of Planning,
Government of Afghanistan
Kabul

ALBANIA
Komisjoni Planit
[Planning Commission]
Tirana

ALGERIA
Département de Planification,
Ministère de l'Economie Nationale de la République Al-
gérienne Démocratique et Po-
pulaire [Department of Planning, Ministry of National
Economy of the Algerian
Democratic and People's Re-
public]
Algiers

ARGENTINA
Consejo Nacional de Desarrollo,
Presidencia de la Nacion [Na-
tional Development Council,
Presidency of the Nation]
Hipolito Irigoyen 250, 8 Piso
Buenos Aires

BARBADOS
Planning Unit, Ministry of Finance
Bridgetown

BASUTOLAND
Office of the Secretariat
Maseru

BECHUANALAND
The Secretariat
P.O. Box 106
Mafeking, C.P.

BELGIUM
Bureau de Programmation, Mini-
stère des Affaires Economiques
[Programming Bureau, Minis-
try of Economic Affairs]
Brussels

BOLIVIA
Secretaría Nacional de Planificación y Coordinación [Na-
tional Secretariat of Planning
and Coordination]
La Paz

BRAZIL
Ministério de Planejamento
[Ministry of Planning]
Edifício do Ministério da Fazenda
6° andar
Rio de Janeiro, GB

BRITISH GUIANA
Central Planning Office
Georgetown

BRITISH HONDURAS
Economics Section, Ministry of Finance and Development
Belize

BRITISH VIRGIN ISLANDS
Administrator's Office
Tortola

BRUNEI
State Development Board
Brunei Town

BULGARIA
Dŭrzhaven Komitet za Planirane [State Planning Committee]
Bul. Dondukov 21
Sofia

BURMA
Ministry of National Planning
Secretariat Post Office
Rangoon

BURUNDI
Plan de Développement et Assistance Technique, Cabinet du Premier Ministre [Development Plan and Technical Assistance, Prime Minister's Cabinet]
Bujumbura

CAMBODIA
Ministère du Plan [Planning Ministry]
Government of Cambodia
Phnom-Penh

CAMEROUN
Ministère des Finances et du Plan [Ministry of Finance and of the Plan]
Yaoundé

CANADA
Economic Council of Canada
P.O.B. 527
Ottawa, Ontario

CENTRAL AFRICAN REPUBLIC
Haut Commissariat au Plan, Presidence de la République [High Planning Commission, Presidency of the Republic]
Bangui

CEYLON
Ministry of Planning and Economic Affairs
Office of the Prime Minister
Senate Building
Colombo

CHAD
Commissariat Général au Plan [General Planning Commission]
Fort Lamy

CHILE
Oficina de Planificación Nacional, Presidencia de la Republica [Central Planning Office, Presidency of the Republic]
Santiago

CHINA (Taiwan)
Council for International Economic Cooperation and Development
Executive Yuan
118 Hwai-Ning Street
Taipei, Taiwan

COLOMBIA
Departamento de Planeación y Servicios Técnicos [Department of Planning and Technical Services]
Edificio Bochica, Piso 9°
Bogotá

CONGO (Leopoldville)
Ministère du Plan et de la Co-
ordination Economique
[Ministry of Planning and Eco-
nomic Coordination]
Leopoldville

CONGO (Brazzaville)
Ministère des Finances du Budget
et du Plan
[Ministry of Finance, of the
Budget and of the Plan]
Brazzaville

COSTA RICA
Oficina de Planificación, Presi-
dencia de la Republica
[Planning Office, Presidency of
the Republic]
San José

CUBA
Junta Central de Planificación
[Central Planning Board]
Paseo y Liñea
Vedado
Havana

CYPRUS
Central Planning Commission
Nicosia

CZECHOSLOVAKIA
Státní Plánovací Komise
[State Planning Commission]
Nábřeží Kpt. Jaroše 1000
Praha-Holešovice
Praha

DAHOMEY
Ministère des Finances, des Af-
faires Economiques et du Plan
[Ministry of Finance, Economic
Affairs and the Plan]
Porto Novo

DENMARK
Ministeriet for Økonomiske og
Nordiske Anliggender
[Ministry for Economic and
Nordic Affairs]
Copenhagen

DOMINICAN REPUBLIC
Junta Nacional de Planificación y
Coordinación [National Plan-
ning and Coordination Board]
Manuel Ma. Castillo, esquina Julio
Verne Street
Santo Domingo

ECUADOR
Junta Nacional de Planificación y
Coordinación Económica, Pres-
idencia de la República
[National Board of Planning
and Economic Coordination,
Presidency of the Republic]
Quito

EL SALVADOR
Consejo Nacional de Planificación
y Coordinación Económica
[National Council of Planning
and Economic Coordination]
San Salvador

ETHIOPIA
Planning Board of Ethiopia
P.O. Box 1037
Prime Minister's Office
Addis Ababa

FIJI
Central Planning Office
Suva

FRANCE
Commissariat Général du Plan de
Modernisation et d'Equipement
[High Commission of the Plan,
Modernization and Equipment]
18, rue de Martignac
Paris

FRENCH GUIANA
Comité Départemental d'Action
Economique de la Guyane
[Departmental Committee for
Economic Action of Guiana]
Cayenne

GABON
Ministère de l'Economie National-
ale du Plan et des Mines
[Ministry of National Economy,
Plan and Mines]
Libreville

GERMAN DEMOCRATIC REPUBLIC
Staatliche Plankommission [State
Planning Commisson]
Leipziger Strasse 5/7
Berlin, W.1

GHANA
National Economic Planning Com-
mission
Accra

GREECE
Ministry of Coordination
Athens

GREENLAND
Ministeriet for Grønland
[Ministry for Greenland]
Kultorvet
Copenhagen

GUATEMALA
Consejo Nacional de Planificación
Económica [National Council
of Economic Planning]
Guatemala City

GUINEA
Ministry of Economic Develop-
ment
Conakry

HAITI
Commissariat National de ,Dé-
veloppement et de Planification
[National Development and
Planning Commission]
Palais des Finances
Port au Prince

HONDURAS
Consejo Nacional de Economía
[National Economic Council]
Tegucigalpa

HUNGARY
Országos Terzhizatal
[National Planning Board]
Nádor-Utcā 9–15
Budapest 5

ICELAND
Efnahagsstofnunin
[Economic Institute]
Hverfisgata 4
Reykjavík

INDIA
Planning Commission
Yojana Bhavan
Parliament Street
New Delhi

INDONESIA
Dwan Perantjang Nasional
[National Planning Council]
Djalan Asia–Africa
Djakarta

IRAN
Plan Organization
Khiaban Daneshkadeh
Teheran

IRAQ
The Planning Board,
Ministry of Planning
Baghdād

IRELAND
Department of Finance
Upper Merrion St.
Dublin 2

ISRAEL
Economic   Planning   Authority,
Prime Minister's Office
P.O.B. 2075
Jerusalem

ITALY
Ufficio del Programma, Ministero
del Bilancio [Programming Of-
fice, Budget Ministry]
Via XX Settembre
Roma

IVORY COAST
Ministère des Finances, des Af-
faires Economiques et du Plan
[Ministry of Finance, Economic
Affairs and the Plan]
Abidjan

JAMAICA
Central Planning Unit
P.O. Box 512
Kingston

JAPAN
Economic Development Agency
3–2, Kasumigaseki
Chiyoda-ku
Tokyo

JORDAN
Development Board
P.O. Box 555
Ammān

KENYA
Directorate of Planning,
Ministry of Finance and Eco-
nomic Planning
P.O. Box 30266
Nairobi

KOREA (North)
Kukka Kyehoek Wiwonhoe
[State Planning Commission]
Pyongyang

KOREA (South)
Economic Planning Bureau,
Economic Planning Board
Seoul

KUWAIT
The Planning Board
P.O. Box 15
Kuwait

LAOS
Ministère de l'Economie Nation-
ale et du Plan
[Ministry of National Economy
and the Plan]
Vientiane

LEBANON
Ministère du Plan
[Planning Ministry]
Beirut

LIBYA
Ministry of Planning and Devel-
opment, Government of Libya
Tripoli

LUXEMBOURG
Ministère les Affaires Economiques
[Ministry of Economic Affairs]
Luxembourg

MALAGASY
Commissariat Général au Plan
[General Commission for the
Plan]
Tananarive

MALAWI
Office of the Permanent Secretary,
Ministry of Finance
Zomba

MALAYSIA
Economic Planning Unit,
   Office of the Prime Minister
Jalan Brockman
Kuala Lumpur

MALI
Ministère du Plan et de l'Econo-
   mie Rurale [Ministry of the
   Plan and Rural Economy]
Bamako

MALTA
The Secretariat
Valletta

MAURITANIA
Ministère du Plan des Domaines
   et de l'Habitat
   [Ministry of the Plan, Public
   Lands and Housing]
Nouakchott

MAURITIUS
Economic Planning Committee
Port Louis

MEXICO
Secretaría de la Presidencia
   [Secretariat of the Presidency]
Mexico, D.F.

MONGOLIA
Gosudarstvennaia Planovaia Ko-
   missiia
   [State Planning Commission]
Ulan-Bator

MONTSERRAT
Office of the Chief Minister
Montserrat

MOROCCO
Division de la Coordination
   Economique et du Plan, Cabi-
   net du Royaume [Division of
   Economic Coordination and the
   Plan, Royal Cabinet]
Rabat

NEPAL
Ministry of Economic Planning,
   His Majesty's Government
Singha Durbar
Katmandu

NETHERLANDS
Centraal Planbureau
   [Central Plan Bureau]
's-Gravenhage

NICARAGUA
Oficina de Planificación Econó-
   mica
   [Economic Planning Office]
Managua

NIGER
Commissariat Général au Plan,
   Présidence [General Planning
   Commission, Presidency]
Niamey

NIGERIA
Economic Planning Unit, Federal
   Ministry of Economic Devel-
   opment
Lagos

NORWAY
Finans-og Toll-Departementet
   [Finance and Customs Depart-
   ment]
Oslo

PAKISTAN
Planning Commission
K.I.T. Building
Karachi

PANAMA
Departamento de Planificación,
   Dirección General de Plan-
   ificación y Administración,
   Presidencia de la República
   [Department of Planning, Di-
   rectorate of Planning and Ad-
   ministration, Presidency of the
   Republic]
Panama City

PAPUA-NEW GUINEA
Central Policy and Planning Committee
Port Moresby

PARAGUAY
Secretaría Técnica de Planificación del Desarrollo Económico y Social de la Presidencia de la Republica [Technical Secretariat of Planning for Economic and Social Development]
Asunción

PERU
Instituto Nacional de Planificación, Cámara Legislativa [National Planning Institute, Legislative Chamber]
Plaza Bolívar
Lima

PHILIPPINES
National Economic Council
Padre Faure
Manila

Program Implementation Agency
1440 Arlegui Street
Manila

POLAND
Komisja Planowania przy Radzie Ministrów [Planning Commission attached to the Council of Ministers]
Plac Trzech Krzyzy 5
Warszawa

PORTUGAL
Ministério da Economía [Ministry of Economy]
Lisbon

PUERTO RICO
Junta de Planificación [Planning Board]
Santurce

RUMANIA
Comitetul de Stat al Planificării [State Planning Committee]
Calea Victoriei 152
Bucharest

RWANDA
Ministère du Plan, de la Coopération et de l'Assistance Technique [Ministry of the Plan, Cooperation and Technical Assistance]
Kigala

RYUKYU ISLANDS
Office of Plans and Programs, United States Civil Administration
Naha, Okinawa

SABAH
Financial Secretary's Office
Jesselton

ST. CHRISTOPHER-NEVIS-ANGUILLA
Central Housing and Planning Authority
Basseterre

ST. LUCIA
Development Committee
Castries

SARAWAK
Development Board
Kuching

SAUDI ARABIA
Supreme Planning Board
Riyadh

SENEGAL
Ministère du Plan et du Développement [Ministry of the Plan and Development]
Dakar

SIERRA LEONE
The Development Office
Ministerial Office Block
George St.
Freetown

SINGAPORE
Economic Planning Unit
Prime Minister's Office
Singapore 6

SOMALIA
Planning and Coordinating Com-
mittee for Economic and Social
Development
Mogadiscio

SOUTH AFRICA
Department of Planning
Pretoria

SOUTHERN RHODESIA
Development Planning Committee
Salisbury

SPAIN
Comisaria de Plan de Desarrollo
Económico, Presidencia del Go-
bierno [Economic Development
Planning Commission, Presi-
dency of the Government]
Madrid

SPANISH GUINEA
Comision para el Desarrollo Eco-
nómico de Fernando Póo y
Río Muni [Fernando Póo and
Río Muni Economic Develop-
ment Planning Commission]
Madrid

SUDAN
Economic Planning Secretariat,
Ministry of Finance and Eco-
nomics
P.O.B. 298
Khartoum

SURINAM
Stichting Planbureau Suriname
[Surinam Planning Bureau]
Paramaribo

SWAZILAND
The Secretariat
P.O. Box 57
Mbabane

SWEDEN
Finansdepartementet
[Department of Finance]
Stockholm

SYRIA
Supreme Planning Council, Min-
istry of Planning (Secretariat)
Damascus

TANZANIA
Directorate of Development Plan-
ning
P.O. Box 9242
Dar es Salaam

THAILAND
National Economic Development
Board
Krung Kasem Road
Bangkok

TOGO
Ministère des Finances des Af-
faires Economiques et du Plan
[Ministry of Finance, Economic
Affairs and the Plan]
Lomé

TRINIDAD AND TOBAGO
Development Plan Secretariat,
Prime Minister's Office
Whitehall
Port of Spain

TUNISIA
  Secretariat d'Etat au Plan et aux
  Affaires Economiques
  [Secretariat of State of the Plan
  and Economic Affairs]
  Tunis

TURKEY
  Devlet Plânlama Teskilâti
  [State Planning Organization]
  Government of Turkey
  Ankara

UNITED ARAB REPUBLIC
  Ministry of Planning
  Cairo

UNITED SOVIET SOCIALIST REPUBLIC
  Gosudarstvennyi Planovyi Komitet
  Soveta Ministrov SSR
  [State Planning Committee of
  the Ministers of the U.S.S.R.]
  Prospekt Marksa 12
  Moskva

UGANDA
  Central Planning Bureau, Ministry
  of Planning and Community
  Development
  Entebbe

  Ministry of Planning and Community Development
  Kampala

UNITED KINGDOM
  Ministry of Economic Affairs
  Storey's Gate
  London, S.W.1

UPPER VOLTA
  Ministère de l'Economie Nationale
  [Ministry of National Econ-
  omy]
  Ouagadougou

URUGUAY
  Comisión de Inversiones y Desar-
  rollo Económico
  [Investment and Economic De-
  velopment Commission]
  Convención 1523
  Montevideo

VENEZUELA
  Oficina Central de Coordinación y
  Planificación, Presidencia de la
  República [Central Office of
  Planning and Coordination,
  Presidency of the Republic]
  Palacio Blanco
  Caracas

VIET NAM, REPUBLIC OF (South)
  Direction Général du Plan
  [Planning Department]
  46 Bên Chuong Duong
  Saigon

VIRGIN ISLANDS (United States)
  Economic Development Board
  Charlotte Amalie, St. Thomas

YUGOSLAVIA
  Savezni Zavod za Privredno Plan-
  iranje [Federal Economic Plan-
  ning Institute]
  Kn. Milosa 20
  Beograd

ZAMBIA
  Office of National Development
  and Planning
  P.O. Box 340
  Lusaka

Appendix V

ORGANIZATION CHART OF IRAN'S PLAN ORGANIZATION
(MARCH 1963)

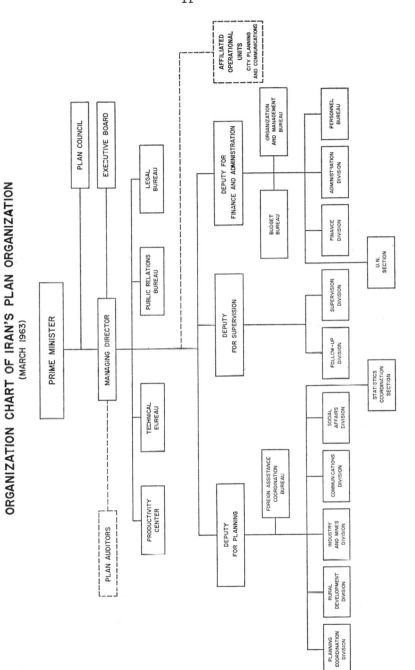

SOURCE: Plan Organization

THE PHILIPPINE NATIONAL ECONOMIC COUNCIL (1959)

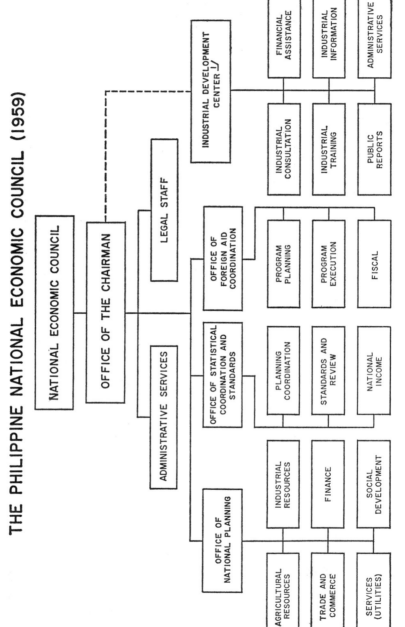

NATIONAL ECONOMIC COUNCIL

OFFICE OF THE CHAIRMAN

LEGAL STAFF

ADMINISTRATIVE SERVICES

INDUSTRIAL DEVELOPMENT CENTER 1/

- FINANCIAL ASSISTANCE
- INDUSTRIAL INFORMATION
- ADMINISTRATIVE SERVICES
- INDUSTRIAL CONSULTATION
- INDUSTRIAL TRAINING
- PUBLIC REPORTS

OFFICE OF FOREIGN AID COORDINATION

- PROGRAM PLANNING
- PROGRAM EXECUTION
- FISCAL

OFFICE OF STATISTICAL COORDINATION AND STANDARDS

- PLANNING COORDINATION
- STANDARDS AND REVIEW
- NATIONAL INCOME

OFFICE OF NATIONAL PLANNING

- INDUSTRIAL RESOURCES
- FINANCE
- SOCIAL DEVELOPMENT
- AGRICULTURAL RESOURCES
- TRADE AND COMMERCE
- SERVICES (UTILITIES)

1/ Temporarily placed under the office of the Chairman.

Source: From material in World Bank files.

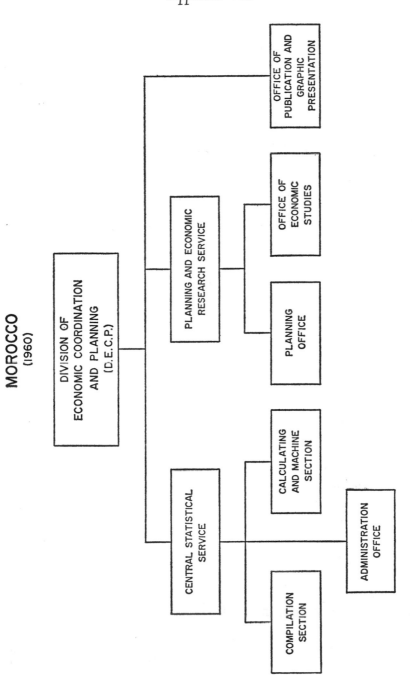

MOROCCO
(1960)

DIVISION OF
ECONOMIC COORDINATION
AND PLANNING
(D.E.C.P.)

PLANNING AND ECONOMIC
RESEARCH SERVICE

OFFICE OF
PUBLICATION AND
GRAPHIC
PRESENTATION

OFFICE OF
ECONOMIC
STUDIES

PLANNING
OFFICE

CENTRAL STATISTICAL
SERVICE

CALCULATING
AND MACHINE
SECTION

ADMINISTRATION
OFFICE

COMPILATION
SECTION

SOURCE: Albert Waterston, Planning in Morocco, (Baltimore:Johns Hopkins Press, 1962), p. 55.

Appendix VIII

India's Planning Commission

DIVISIONS, SECTIONS, UNITS AND BRANCHES[1]
(AS OF JULY 1964)

Co-ordination Divisions

1. Programme Administration Division
2. Plan Co-ordination Section

General Divisions

3. Economic Division
   a. Financial Resources
   b. Economic Policy and Growth
   c. Foreign Exchange and International Trade
   d. Price Policy
   e. Inter-Industries Studies
4. Perspective Planning
5. Labour and Employment
6. Statistics and Surveys
7. Resources and Scientific Research
   a. Natural Resources
   b. Scientific Research
8. Management and Administration

---

[1] "The terms 'Division,' 'Section,' 'Unit' and 'Branch' have not always been used in the Commission with clear and identifiable distinctions drawn among them. Broadly speaking, a Division connotes a unit which is somewhat larger than a Section, Unit or Branch, deals with imported subjects and is headed by a 'Chief' or similar officer. A Section may either be a part of a Division or may be independent but it is usually small and headed by an officer of a lower status (Assistant Chief or Director). The term 'Branch' has been principally confined to describing the house-keeping units in the Commission. In a few cases (for example, Inter-Industries Unit), the term 'Unit' has also been used." (Paranjape, H. K., *Planning Commission, A Descriptive Account*, p. 64. The functions of the principal units in the Commission are described in detail in Chapter V, pp. 77–135 of the work cited.)

Subject Divisions

9. Agriculture (including Community Development, Cooperatives and Panchayat, Raj)
10. Irrigation and Power
    a. Irrigation
    b. Power
11. Land Reforms
12. Industry and Minerals
    a. Metals
    b. Industry and Minerals
    c. Oil and Minerals
    d. Engineering
13. Village and Small Industries
14. Transport and Communications
15. Education
16. Health
17. Housing (including Urban Development)
18. Social Welfare

Divisions Concerned with Specific Development Programmes

19. Rural Works
20. Public Co-operation

Housekeeping Organs

21. Administration
22. General Co-ordination
23. Plan Co-ordination and Charts and Maps
24. Information, Publicity and Publications
25. Library

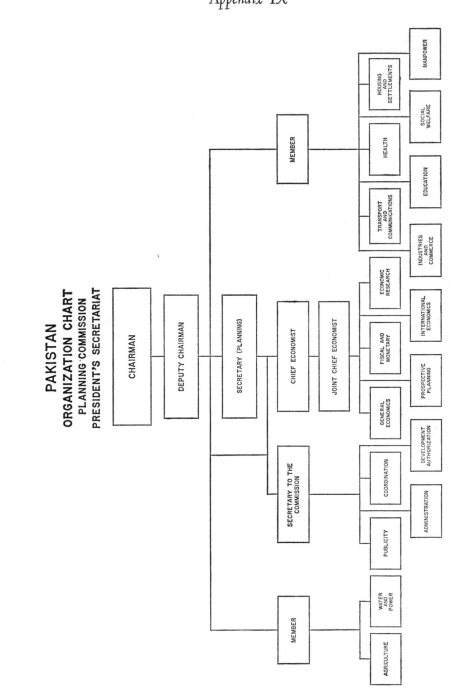

PAKISTAN
ORGANIZATION CHART
PLANNING COMMISSION
PRESIDENT'S SECRETARIAT

CHAIRMAN

DEPUTY CHAIRMAN

SECRETARY (PLANNING)

MEMBER

MEMBER

SECRETARY TO THE COMMISSION

CHIEF ECONOMIST

JOINT CHIEF ECONOMIST

AGRICULTURE

WATER AND POWER

PUBLICITY

ADMINISTRATION

COORDINATION

DEVELOPMENT AUTHORIZATION

GENERAL ECONOMICS

PROSPECTIVE PLANNING

FISCAL AND MONETARY

INTERNATIONAL ECONOMICS

ECONOMIC RESEARCH

INDUSTRIES AND COMMERCE

TRANSPORT AND COMMUNICATIONS

EDUCATION

HEALTH

SOCIAL WELFARE

HOUSING AND SETTLEMENTS

MANPOWER

Source: Albert Waterston, *Planning in Pakistan* (Baltimore: Johns Hopkins Press, 1963), p. 80.

Appendix X

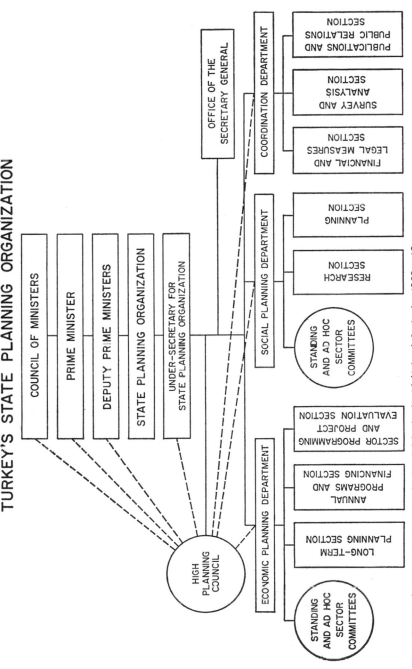

TURKEY'S STATE PLANNING ORGANIZATION

COUNCIL OF MINISTERS

PRIME MINISTER

DEPUTY PRIME MINISTERS

STATE PLANNING ORGANIZATION

UNDER-SECRETARY FOR STATE PLANNING ORGANIZATION

OFFICE OF THE SECRETARY GENERAL

HIGH PLANNING COUNCIL

ECONOMIC PLANNING DEPARTMENT

LONG-TERM PLANNING SECTION

ANNUAL PROGRAMS AND FINANCING SECTION

SECTOR PROGRAMMING AND PROJECT EVALUATION SECTION

STANDING AND AD HOC SECTOR COMMITTEES

SOCIAL PLANNING DEPARTMENT

RESEARCH SECTION

PLANNING SECTION

STANDING AND AD HOC SECTOR COMMITTEES

COORDINATION DEPARTMENT

FINANCIAL AND LEGAL MEASURES SECTION

SURVEY AND ANALYSIS SECTION

PUBLICATIONS AND PUBLIC RELATIONS SECTION

SOURCE: Planning, State Planning Organization, Publication No.14, (Ankara), September 1962, p.18.

659

Works Cited

ABDEL-RAHMAN, I. H. and RAMZI, M. *Organizational and Administrative Aspects of Development Planning* [Memo No. 87]. Cairo, U.A.R. Institute of National Planning, November 15, 1961.

ABDULGANI, ROESLAN. "The Lessons of Indonesia's Experience of Planning," *United Asia* (Bombay). Vol. 12, No. 5, 1960.

ADHIN, J. H. *Development Planning in Surinam in Historical Perspective.* Leiden, H. E. Stenfert Kroese N.V., 1961.

AHUMADA, JORGE. "Problems of Specialized Training Requirements as Viewed from Inside a Country in Process of Economic Development," in: *Aspects of Training in Economic Development.* Papers and proceedings of the first Meeting of Directors of Training Institutes in the field of Economic Development [September 11–14, 1961, The Hague]. Paris, O.E.C.D. Publications, January 1962.

APPLEBY, PAUL H. *Re-Examination of India's Administrative System, with Special Reference to Administration of Government's Industrial and Commercial Enterprises.* n.p., 1956.

APPLEBY, PAUL H. "Role of the Budget Division," *Public Administration Review* (Washington, D.C.). Vol. XVII, No. 3, Summer 1957.

ARANETA, SALVADOR. "The Planning, Approval and Implementation of Economic Policy," in: MILNE, R. S. (ed). *Planning for Progress; The Administration of Economic Planning in the Philippines.* Manila, University of the Philippines, 1960.

Asamblea Legislativa. Decreta, "Ley de Planificación" [No. 3087], *La Gaceto, Diario Oficial* (San José, Costa Rica). Año LXXXV, No. 27, febrero 2, 1963.

AUKRUST, ODD. "Factors of Economic Development: A Review of Recent Research," *Weltwirtschaftliches Archiv* (Hamburg). Band 96, Heft 1, 1964.

BAILEY, STEPHEN K. "The Place and Functioning of a Planning Agency Within the Government Organization of Developing Countries," in: *Organization, Planning, and Programming for Economic Development*, Vol. VIII [of] United States Papers Prepared for the United Nations Conference on the Application of Science and Technology for the Benefit of the Less Developed Areas. Washington, D.C., United States Government Printing Office, 1963.

BALDWIN, CLAUDE DAVID. *Economic Planning: Its Aims and Implications.* Urbana, Ill., University of Illinois, 1962.

Bangkok Post (Bangkok).

Bank of Baroda Weekly Review (Baroda, India). Vol. 2, No. 17, April 24, 1964.

BANSAL, G. L. "Liaison Between Government and the Private Sector," *Indian Journal of Public Administration* (New Delhi). Vol. 11, No. 1, January–March 1956.

BELL, DAVID E. "Allocating Development Resources: Some Observations Based on Pakistan Experience," in: *Public Policy: A Yearbook of the Graduate School of Public Administration.* Cambridge, Mass., Graduate School of Public Administration, Harvard University, 1959.

BELL, DAVID E. "Planning for Development in Pakistan," *Pakistan Economic Journal* (Lahore). Vol. XII, No. 1, March 1962.

BEMIS, GEORGE W. "Regional Government Organization in Brazil and Federal-State Public Administration," in: DALAND, ROBERT T. (ed). *Perspectives of Brazilian Public Administration,* Volume I. Los Angeles, Getúlio Vargas Foundation and University of Southern California, June 1963.

BHAGAT, B. R. *Economic Times* (Bombay). November 10, 1963.

BHALERAO, C. N. "Substantive Forces in Indian Administration," *Economic Weekly* (Bombay). Vol. XVI, No. 42, October 17, 1964.

BLASS, WALTER P. "Economic Planning European-Style," *Harvard Business Review* (Cambridge, Mass.). Vol. 41, No. 5, September-October 1963.

BOGNAR, J. "The Importance of Devising Effective Machinery for the Implementation of Development Plans," *Economic Bulletin* (Ghana). Vol. II, No. 4, April 1963.

Bolivia. Junta Nacional de Planeamiento. *Plan Nacional de Desarrollo Económico y Social, 1962–1971: Resumen.* La Paz, 1961.

BOND, FLOYD A. "The Nature and Goals of Soviet Planning," *Michigan Business Review* (Ann Arbor). Vol. XIII, No. 2, May 1961.

BOR, MIKHAIL ZAKHAROVICH. "The Organization and Practice of National Economic Planning in the Union of Soviet Socialist Republics," in: *Planning for Economic Development,* Vol. II (Studies of National Planning Experience, Part 2, Centrally Planned Economies). New York, United Nations Publications, 1965 (A/5533/Rev. 1/Add.2).

BURKHEAD, JESSE. *Government Budgeting.* New York, John Wiley and Sons, 1956.

Burma. Ministry of National Planning. *Second Four-Year Plan for the Union of Burma* (1961–62 to 1964–65). Rangoon, 1961.

CAIRNCROSS, A. K. "Programmes as Instruments of Coordination," *Scottish Journal of Political Economy* (Edinburgh). Vol. VIII, No. 2, June 1961.

CALDWELL, LYNTON K. "Turkish Administration and the Politics of Expediency," in: SIFFIN, W. J. (ed). *Toward the Comparative Study of Public Administration.* Bloomington, Ind., Indiana University, 1957.

"Canada's Planners Walk a Tightrope," *Business Week.* March 14, 1964.

Caribbean Organization. *Report of Joint Meeting of Planners and Planning Experts and Standing Advisory Committee of the Caribbean Plan* [San Juan, Puerto Rico, May 1–8, 1962]. Hato Rey, P.R., 1962.

CHAIGNEAU, YVES. *Réflexions Sur La Planification Au Sénégal.* Exposé fait au Séminaire d'Economie Appliquée du Vendredi, Institut de Science Economique Appliquée, février 15, 1963.

CHATTERJI, MANAS. "Regional Economic Planning," *Economic Weekly* (Bombay), Vol. 15, No. 13, March 30, 1963.

Christian Science Monitor (Boston).

CLARK, PETER BENTLEY. "Economic Planning for a Country in Transition: Nigeria," in: HAGEN, EVERETT (ed). *Planning Economic Development.* Homewood, Ill., Richard D. Irwin, Inc., 1963.

COLLETT AND CLAPP, INC. *Organización y Administración de la Función de Planeación.* San Juan, Puerto Rico, 1963.

COLM, GERHARD. "Economic Planning in the United States," *Weltwirtschaftliches Archiv* (Hamburg). Band 92, Heft 1, 1964.

COLM, GERHARD and GEIGER, THEODORE. "Country Programming as a Guide to Development," in: *Development of the Emerging Countries.* Washington, D.C., Brookings Institution, 1962.

Colony and Protectorate of Kenya. *Development Programme, 1954–57* [Sessional Paper, No. 51, 1955]. Nairobi, Government Printer, 1955.

Columbia University School of Law. *Public International Development Financing in Chile* (Report No. 8). A Report prepared in Co-operation with the Institute of International Studies and Overseas Administration, University of Oregon. New York, March 1964.

Columbia University School of Law. *Public International Development Financing in Colombia* (Report No. 6). A Report prepared in Co-operation with the Institute of International Studies and Overseas Administration, University of Oregon. New York, June 1963.

Columbia University School of Law. *Public International Development Financing in Greece* (Report No. 10), by PSIBOS, DIOMEDES D. and WESTEBBE, RICHARD M. New York, September 1964.

DALAND, ROBERT T. "Chapter IV. The Politics of the Plano Trienal," in: *Brazilian Planning: Politics and Administration.* University of North Carolina, n.d. (manuscript).

DALAND, ROBERT T. "Chapter V. The Future and Brazilian Planning," in: *Brazilian Planning: Politics and Administration.* University of North Carolina, n.d. (manuscript).

DAVIES, R. W. *Development of the Soviet Budgetary System.* Cambridge, Cambridge University Press, 1964.

Dawn (Karachi).

DEMUTH, RICHARD H. *Planning, Projects and People.* Paper prepared for the African Conference on Some Aspects of Development, Cambridge University, September 22–October 5, 1963.

DEVONS, ELY. "Economic Planning in War and Peace," *Manchester School of Economic and Social Studies* (Manchester). Vol. XVI, No. 1, January 1948.

DEVONS, ELY. *Planning in Practice.* Cambridge, Cambridge University Press, 1950.

"Dhanam" in *Economic Times* (Bombay).

"Economic News," *Review of International Affairs* (Belgrade). Vol. XV, No. 339, May 20, 1964.

Economic Times (Bombay).

Economic Weekly (Bombay).

Economist (London).

Ecuador. National Board of Economic Planning and Coordination. "Chapter IV. The Organization for the Plan for Economic Development and the Administrative Reform," in: *General Plan for Economic and Social Development*. Quito, 1963.

ELLIOTT, JOHN E. "Economic Planning Reconsidered," *Quarterly Journal of Economics* (Cambridge, Mass.). Vol. LXXVI, No. 1, February 1958.

EMMERICH, HERBERT. "Administrative Roadblocks to Co-ordinated Development," in: DEVRIES, EGBERT and MEDINA ECHAVARRÍA, JOSÉ (eds). *Social Aspects of Economic Development in Latin America*. Vol. 1, Papers submitted to the Expert Working Group on Social Aspects of Economic Development in Latin America [December 12–21, 1960, Mexico, D.F.]. Paris, UNESCO, 1963.

Ethiopia. Office of the Planning Board. *Second Five-Year Development Plan, 1955–1959 E.C.* [1963–1967 Gregorian Calendar]. Addis Ababa, 1962.

"Experiment 52," *East Europe* (New York). Vol. 14, No. 1, January 1965.

FAINSOD, MERLE. "The Structure of Development Administration," in: SWERDLOW, IRVING (ed). *Development Administration; Concepts and Problems*. Syracuse, Syracuse University Press, 1963.

Financial Times (London).

FRANCO HOLGUIN, JORGE. "Politica, Económica y Planeación," *La Nueva Economia* (Bogotá). Vol. 1, No. 3, June 1961.

FRANKS, OLIVER. *Central Planning and Control in War and Peace*. London, Longmans, Green and Co., 1947.

FRIEDMANN, JOHN. "Introduction" (to) The Study and Practice of Planning. *International Social Science Journal, UNESCO* (Paris). Vol. XI, No. 3, 1959.

FURNIVALL, J. S. *Governance of Modern Burma*. New York, Institute of Pacific Relations, 1958 (mimeographed).

GADGIL, D. R. *Planning and Economic Policy in India*. Poona, Asia Publishing House, 1962.

GALBRAITH, JOHN K. *Economic Development in Perspective*. Cambridge, Mass., Harvard University Press, 1962.

Ghana. *Second Development Plan, 1959–64*, Accra, 1959.

GHOSH, O. K. *Problems of Economic Planning in India*. Allahabad, Kitabistan, 1957.

GLASS, RUTH. "The Evaluation of Planning: Some Sociological Considerations," *International Social Service Journal, UNESCO* (Paris). Vol. XI, No. 3, 1959.

GOLAY, FRANK. *Environment of Philippine Economic Planning*. Paper presented at Conference on Economic Planning in Southeast Asia, February 1–5, 1965, Honolulu, Hawaii.

GOLDMAN, MARSHALL I. "Economic Controversy in the Soviet Union," *Foreign Affairs* (New York). Vol. 41, No. 3, April 1963.

GOODE, RICHARD and BIRNBAUM, EUGENE A. "Government Capital Budgets," *International Monetary Fund Staff Papers* (Washington, D.C.). Vol. V, No. 1, February 1956.

Great Britain. Chancellor of the Exchequer. *Public Expenditure in 1963–64 and 1967–68*. London, HMSO, 1963. Cmnd. 2235.

Great Britain. *East African Royal Commission, 1953–1955, Report*. Presented by the Secretary of State for the Colonies to Parliament. London, HMSO, June 1955. Cmd 9475.

GREENSTREET, D. K. "The Guggisberg Ten-Year Development Plan," *Economic Bulletin of Ghana* (Accra). Vol. VIII, No. 1, 1964.

GROSS, BERTRAM M. *Activating National Plans.* CAG Occasional Papers, American Society for Public Administration. Indiana University International Development Research Center, July 1964.

GROSS, BERTRAM M. "When is a Plan Not a Plan," *Challenge* (New York). Vol. 10, No. 3, December 1961.

GULILAT, TAYE. "Approach to Economic Planning in Ethiopia," in: Sachs, Ignacy (ed). *Planning and Economic Development.* Warszawa, PWN-Polish Scientific Publishers, 1964.

HAGEN, EVERETT (ed). *Planning Economic Development.* Homewood, Ill., Richard D. Irwin, Inc., 1963.

HAPGOOD, DAVID. "Africa's New Elite," *Harper's Magazine.* Vol. 227, No. 1363, December 1963.

HAQ, MAHBUB UL. *Planning Agencies.* Paper presented at the Organization for Economic Co-operation and Development Fourth Study Conference on Problems of Economic Development, Government Organization and Economic Development. Paris, September 7–11, 1964.

HAQ, MAHBUB UL. *Strategy of Economic Planning: A Case Study of Pakistan.* Karachi, Oxford University Press, 1963.

HARTOG, FLOOR. "Economic Development And Cooperation In Africa," in: TINBERGEN, JAN (ed). *Shaping the World Economy, Suggestions for an International Economic Policy.* New York, Twentieth Century Fund, 1962.

HARWOOD, WILSON R. *Advice to the Plan Organization of Iran, 1956–61.* Washington, D.C., Government Affairs Institute, 1961.

HASAN, SAID. *Dawn* (Karachi), August 14, 1963.

HELLER, WALTER W. "The Commitment to Growth," an Address at the 46th Annual Meeting of the American Council on Education. Washington, D.C., October 4, 1963.

HERMAN, ROBERT S. "Two Aspects of Budgeting," *Indian Journal of Public Administration* (New Delhi). Vol. III, No. 3, July–September 1962.

HERRERA, FELIPE. "The Financing of Latin American Integration," *International Development Review* (Washington, D.C.). Vol. V, No. 3, September 1963.

HIGGINS, BENJAMIN. *Economic Development, Principles, Problems and Policies.* New York, W. W. Norton & Company, Inc., 1959.

HIGGINS, BENJAMIN. *Some Comments on Regional Planning.* Paper prepared for the International Conference on Comprehensive Planning, October 17–27, 1962. Berlin, Deutsche Stiftung Für Entwicklungsländer, 1962.

Hindu Weekly Review (Madras).

HIRSCHMAN, ALBERT O. "Comments on 'A Framework for Analyzing Economic and Political Change,'" in: *Development of the Emerging Countries, An Agenda for Research.* Washington, D.C., Brookings Institution, 1962.

HIRSCHMAN, ALBERT O. "Economics and Investment Planning: Reflections Based on Experience in Colombia," in: *Investment Criteria and Economic Growth*. Bombay, Asia Publishing House, 1961 [Papers presented at a Conference sponsored jointly by the Center for International Studies and the Social Science Research Council, Massachusetts Institute of Technology, October 15–17, 1954].

HIRSCHMAN, ALBERT O. "Ideologies of Economic Development in Latin America," in: *Latin American Issues, Essays and Comments*. New York, Twentieth Century Fund, 1961.

HIRSCHMAN, ALBERT O. *Journeys Toward Progress: Studies of Economic Policy-Making in Latin America*. New York, Twentieth Century Fund, 1963.

HOLESOVSKY, VACLAV. "Czechoslovakia's Economic Debate," *East Europe* (New York). Vol. 13, No. 12, December 1964.

HULIČKA, KAREL. "Political and Economic Aspects of Planning of the National Economy in the U.S.S.R. and the Soviet Bloc," *South African Journal of Economics* (Johannesburg). Vol. 29, No. 1, March 1961.

Hungary. "The Main Features of National Economic Planning in Hungary," in: *Planning for Economic Development, Vol. II* (Studies of National Planning Experience, Part 2, Centrally Planned Economies). New York, United Nations Publications, 1965 (A/5533/Rev.1/Add.2).

HURTADO, HECTOR. "Planning for the 70's," *Financial Times* (London), April 9, 1964.

HUSSAIN, Z. "Organization and Responsibilities of the Pakistan Planning Board," in: Pakistan National Training Center on Economic and Financial Appraisal of Agricultural Plans and Prospects, *Digest of Lectures*. Rome, Food and Agriculture Organization of the United Nations, December 1955 (FAO/55/11/8509).

HYNEMAN, CHARLES S. *Bureaucracy in a Democracy*. New York, Harper & Brothers, 1950.

India. Planning Commission. *Third Five-Year Plan* (1961–1966). New Delhi, 1961.

India. Planning Commission. *Third Plan Mid-Term Appraisal*. New Delhi, November 1963.

International Bank for Reconstruction and Development. *A Public Development Program for Thailand*. Baltimore, Johns Hopkins Press, 1959.

International Bank for Reconstruction and Development. *Basis of a Development Program for Colombia*. Baltimore, Johns Hopkins Press, 1950.

International Bank for Reconstruction and Development. *Economic Development of Ceylon*. Baltimore, Johns Hopkins Press, 1953.

International Bank for Reconstruction and Development. *Economic Development of Iraq*. Baltimore, Johns Hopkins Press, 1952.

International Bank for Reconstruction and Development. *Economic Development of Jordan*. Baltimore, Johns Hopkins Press, 1957.

International Bank for Reconstruction and Development. *Economic Development of Libya*. Baltimore, Johns Hopkins Press, 1960.

International Bank for Reconstruction and Development. *Economic Development of Mexico*. Baltimore, Johns Hopkins Press, 1963.

International Bank for Reconstruction and Development. _Economic Development of Nicaragua._ Baltimore, Johns Hopkins Press, 1953.

International Bank for Reconstruction and Development. _Economic Development of Spain._ Baltimore, Johns Hopkins Press, 1963.

International Bank for Reconstruction and Development. _Economic Development of Syria._ Baltimore, Johns Hopkins Press, 1955.

International Bank for Reconstruction and Development. _Economic Development of Tanganyika._ Baltimore, Johns Hopkins Press, 1961.

International Bank for Reconstruction and Development. _Economic Development of Uganda._ Baltimore, Johns Hopkins Press, 1962.

International Bank for Reconstruction and Development. _Economic Development of Venezuela._ Baltimore, Johns Hopkins Press, 1961.

International Bank for Reconstruction and Development. _Economy of Turkey._ Baltimore, Johns Hopkins Press, 1951.

IONIDES, MICHAEL G. "The Objects and Implications of Economic Development," in: _Administrative Organization for Economic Development._ Report of the Conference, Pembroke College, Cambridge, July 13–24, 1959. Organized by the Royal Institute of Public Administration.

Iran. Plan Organization. _Review of the Second Seven Year Plan Program of Iran._ Teheran, Division of Economic Affairs, March 10, 1960.

JOHNSON, A. W. "Planning and Budgeting," _Canadian Public Administration_ (Toronto). Vol. II, No. 3, September 1959.

KANNAPPAN, SUBBIAH. "Planning Pitfalls in India," _Journal of Asian Studies_ (Ann Arbor). Vol. XXII, No. 3, May 1963.

KHAN, JEHANQIR. _Progress Reporting—How Can We Achieve the Contemplated Objectives._ Lahore, Office of the Director of Public Instructions, n.d.

KHILIUK, F. "Some Questions on Improving the Organization of Planning" [Planovoe Khoziaistva, 1962, No. 7], _Problems of Economics_ (New York). Vol. V, No. 10, February 1963.

KOVALEV, N. I. "The Problems in Introducing Mathematics and Electronic Computers in Planning," _Problems of Economics_ (New York). Vol. 5, No. 4, August 1962.

KRAUSE, WALTER. _Economic Development: The Underdeveloped World and the American Interest._ San Francisco, Wadsworth Publishing Company, Inc., 1961.

KRAUSE, WALTER. "Observations on National Economic Planning," _Economic Research Journal_ (Manila). Vol. VI, No. 3, December 1959.

LAMOUR, PHILIPPE. "Legal and Administrative Problems in Regional Economic Development," in: ISARD, WALTER and CUMBERLAND, JOHN H. (eds). _Regional Planning, Techniques of Analysis for Less Developed Areas._ Papers and proceedings of the Organization for Economic Cooperation and Development. First Study Conference on Problems of Economic Development [June 19—July 1, 1960, Bellazio, Italy]. Paris, O.E.C.D. Publications, 1961.

LANGE, OSKAR. "Economic Planning and Management in the Socialist Economy of Poland," in: Indian Statistical Institute. _Planning and Statistics in Socialist Countries._ Bombay, Asia Publishing House, 1963.

LANGE, OSKAR. "The Tasks of Economic Planning in Ceylon," in: *Papers by Visiting Economists*. Colombo, Ceylon, National Planning Council, 1959.

LEMERLE, PAUL. "Planning for Economic Development in France," in: *Planning for Economic Development, Vol. II* (Studies of National Planning Experience, Part 1, Private Enterprise and Mixed Economies). New York, United Nations Publications, 1965 (A/5533/Rev.1/Add.1).

LEWIS, JOHN P. "India," in: HAGEN, EVERETT (ed). *Planning Economic Development*. Homewood, Ill., Richard D. Irwin, Inc., 1963.

LEWIS, JOHN P. *Quiet Crisis in India*. Washington, D.C., Brookings Institution, 1962.

LEWIS, W. ARTHUR. "On Assessing a Development Plan," *Economic Bulletin* (Ghana). Vol. 3, Nos. 6, 7, June–July 1959.

LEWIS, W. ARTHUR. *Planning Public Expenditure*. Paper presented at Conference on Economic Planning, Princeton, N.J., November 27–28, 1964. Sponsored by Universities—National Bureau Committee for Economic Research.

LEWIS, W. ARTHUR. *Principles of Economic Planning*. [New ed. with a new introduction.] London, George Allen and Unwin Ltd., 1952.

LEWIS, W. ARTHUR. "Sponsored Growth: A Challenge to Democracy," in: HALDAR, M. K. and GHOSH, ROBIN (eds). *Problems of Economic Growth (Report of a Seminar held in Tokyo)*. New Delhi, Parabhakar Padhye for the Congress for Cultural Freedom, July 1960.

LEWIS, W. ARTHUR. *Theory of Economic Growth*. London, George Allen and Unwin Ltd., 1955.

LIBERMAN, YEVSEI G. Letter to *Economist*, October 31, 1964.

LLERAS CAMARGO, ALBERTO. "The Alliance for Progress: Aims, Distortions, Obstacles," *Foreign Affairs* (New York). Vol. 42, No. 1, October 1963.

MACASPAC, ISIDRO. "National Economic Planning," *Economic Research Journal* (Manila). Vol. VI, No. 3, December 1959.

MAHALANOBIS, P. C. *Perspective Planning in India*. Paper presented to the Thirty-Fourth Session of the International Statistical Institute, Ottawa, Canada, August 1963.

MALENBAUM, WILFRED. "Who Does the Planning?" in: PARK, RICHARD L. and TINKER, IRENE (eds). *Leadership and Political Institutions in India*. Princeton, Princeton University Press, 1959.

Management Group. Committee on Plan Projects. "Management Planning in Public Enterprises," *Indian Journal of Public Administration* (New Delhi). Vol. X, No. 3, July–September 1964.

Manchester Guardian (Manchester).

MANNE, ALAN S. "Key Sectors in the Mexican Economy, 1960–1970," in: MANNE, ALAN S. and MARKOWITZ, HARRY M. (eds). *Studies in Process Analysis*. Proceedings of a Conference Sponsored by the Cowles Foundation for Research in Economics [April 24–26, 1961, Yale University]. New York, John Wiley & Sons, Inc., 1961.

MASON, EDWARD S. *On the Appropriate Size of a Development Program*. Occasional Papers in International Affairs, No. 8, Harvard University Center for International Affairs, August 1964.

MASON, EDWARD S. "Some Aspects of the Strategy of Development Planning—Centralization versus Decentralization," *Organization, Planning, and Programming for Economic Development*. Vol. VIII [of] United States Papers Prepared for the United Nations Conference on the Application of Science and Technology for the Benefit of the Less Developed Areas, Washington, D.C., United States Government Printing Office, 1963.

MASSÉ, PIERRE. "French Economic Planning," *French Affairs* (New York). No. 127, Ambassade de France, Service de Presse et d'Information, December 1961.

MASSÉ, PIERRE. "French Methods of Planning," *Journal of Industrial Economics* (Oxford). Vol. XI, No. 1, November 1962.

MASSÉ, PIERRE. "Planning in France," in: *Planning*. Papers read at the Business Economists Conference at New College, Oxford, April 5–8, 1962. London, Business Economists Group, 1962.

MAYNE, ALVIN. "Designing and Administering a Regional Economic Development Plan with Specific Reference to Puerto Rico," in: *Regional Economic Planning*. Paris, Organization for European Economic Cooperation, July 1961.

MAYNE, ALVIN. *Perspective Planning in India* [Memorandum to Statistical Advisor of India] n.p., Puerto Rico Planning Board, Bureau of Economics and Statistics. April 11, 1957.

MEIER, G. M. *Role of an Expert Advisory Group in a Young Government.* Paper presented to the Nyasaland Economic Symposium, Zomba, July 18–28, 1962 (mimeographed).

MELLO E SOUZA, NELSON. "Public Administration and Economic Development," in: DALAND, ROBERT T. (ed). *Perspectives of Brazilian Public Administration*. Volume 1, Los Angeles, Getúlio Vargas Foundation and University of Southern California, June 1963.

MILLIKAN, MAX F. "Criteria for Decision-Making in Economic Planning," in: *Organization, Planning, and Programming for Economic Development*. Vol. VIII [of] United States Papers Prepared for the United Nations Conference on the Application of Science and Technology for the Benefit of the Less Developed Areas. Washington, D.C., United States Government Printing Office, 1963.

MIROSHNICHENKO, B. "Some Problems of National Economic Planning at the Present Stage," *Problems of Economics* (New York). Vol. IV, No. 2, June 1961.

MITRA, ASHOK. "Underdeveloped Statistics," *Economic Development and Cultural Change* (Chicago). Vol. XI, No. 3, Part 1, April 1963.

MONTGOMERY, ARTHUR. *How Sweden Overcame the Depression, 1930–1933.* Stockholm, Alb. Bonniers Boktryckeri, 1938.

MONTIAS, JOHN M. *Central Planning in Poland.* New Haven, Yale University Press, 1962.

MONTIAS, JOHN M. *Evolution of the Czech Economic Model, 1949–1961* (draft). Yale University, September 1962 (mimeographed).

MORGAN, THEODORE. *Economic Planning—Points of Success and Failure.*

Paper presented at the Conference of Economic Planning in Southeast Asia, February 1–5, 1965, Honolulu, Hawaii.

MORGENSTERN, OSKAR. *On the Accuracy of Economic Observations.* Princeton, N.J., Princeton University Press, 1963.

MORRISON, HERBERT. *Economic Planning.* London, Institute of Public Administration, 1947.

MOYNIHAN, M. H. *Ops. Room Technique.* A Note with Special Reference to Regional Economic Development, n.p., n.d. (mimeographed).

MUNOZ AMATO, PEDRO. *Introducción a la Administración Pública.* Mexico, Fondo de Cultura, 1954.

NATARAJAN, B. *Plan Coordination in India* [Memo No. 67]. Cairo, U.A.R. Institute of National Planning, October 15, 1961.

NATARAJAN, K. V. "State Plans," *Yojana* (New Delhi), August 30, 1964.

National Bank of Egypt. *Economic Bulletin* (Cairo). Vol. XIV, No. 1, 1961.

National Planning Association. "Aerial Photography and Development Planning," Memorandum of the Center for Development Planning. Washington, D.C. (M-7703, November 12, 1963.)

NEGANDI, ANANT R. "GOI's Decision-Making Apparatus," *Economic Weekly* (Bombay). Vol. XVIII, No. 4, January 23, 1965.

NEHRU, JAWAHARLAL. "Annual Address by the Prime Minister," *Indian Journal of Public Administration* (New Delhi). Vol. VII, No. 4, October–December 1961.

NEHRU, JAWAHARLAL. "Strategy of the Third Plan," in: *Problems of the Third Plan.* New Delhi, Published by the Government of India, 1961.

NELSON, JOAN MARIE. *Central Planning for National Development and the Role of Foreign Advisors: The Case of Burma.* Unpublished thesis presented to the Department of Government. Radcliffe College, Cambridge, Mass., May 1960.

Nepal. National Planning Council, Ministry of National Guidance. *Policy Statement on Planning and Development,* by Shah, Rishikest. Katmandu, n.d.

Newsletter of the Caribbean Organization (Hato Rey, Puerto Rico). Vol. III, Nos. 2, 3, 4, October, November, December 1963.

New York Times (New York).

NICULESCU, BARBU. *Colonial Planning, A Comparative Study.* London, George Allen and Unwin Ltd., 1958.

Nigeria. Federal Ministry of Economic Development. *National Development Plan, 1962–1968.* Lagos, 1962.

Norway. Royal Norwegian Ministry of Finance. *Extension of Economic Planning* [Government Bill No. 1, Supplement No. 1 (1962–63)]. Oslo, 1963.

NOVE, ALEC. *Soviet Economy, An Introduction.* London, George Allen and Unwin Ltd., 1961.

NOVE, ALEC. "The Industrial Planning System: Reforms in Prospect," *Soviet Studies* (Oxford). Vol. XIV, No. 1, July 1962.

OLSEN, P. BJØRN and RASMUSSEN, P. NØRREGAARD. "An Attempt at Planning in a Traditional State: Iran," in: HAGEN, EVERETT (ed). *Planning Economic Development.* Homewood, Ill., Richard D. Irwin, Inc., 1963.

Organization of American States. Department of Economic Affairs. *Planning Organization and Implementation in Guatemala.* August 27, 1962 [UP/G.5/1(Eng.)].

Organization of American States. Department of Economic Affairs. *Rio Organization and Methods Workshop, Development Administration Program, Public Administration Unit.* February 4, 1964 (UP/G.16/2).

Organization of American States. Fourth Inter-American Statistical Conference [November 5–16, 1962, Washington, D.C.]. *Factors Affecting the Statistical Development of America.* By the General Secretariat of the Inter-American Statistical Institute. October 11, 1962 (OAS/Ser. K/IV.4.1).

Organization of American States. Fourth Inter-American Statistical Conference [November 5–16, 1962, Washington, D.C.]. *Final Report.* March 1963 (OAS/Ser.C/VI.6.4).

Organization of American States. Inter-American Economic and Social Council [First Annual Meetings, October 1962, Mexico, D.F.]. *Development Planning and Budgeting* (Reference Document No. 33). October 5, 1962 (OEA/Ser.H/X.3).

Organization of American States. Inter-American Economic and Social Council [First Annual Meetings, October 1962, Mexico, D.F.]. *Present State of Economic Development Planning in Latin America* (Reference Document No. 9). July 21, 1962 (OEA/Ser.H/X.3).

Organization of American States. Inter-American Economic and Social Council [First Annual Meetings, October 1962, Mexico, D.F.]. *Report of the Panel of Experts to the Inter-American Economic and Social Council* (Reference Document No. 17). September 30, 1962 (OEA/Ser.H/X.3).

Organization of American States. Inter-American Economic and Social Council [First Annual Meetings, August 1962, Mexico, D.F.]. "Summary of Mr. Diaz's Remarks on Chile's Experience with an Autonomous Planning Agency" [Appendix to Annex II] in: *Consultation on Economic and Social Development Planning* [*Santiago, Chile, February 26–March 3, 1962*] *Report of the Meeting* (Reference Document No. 1). July 1, 1962 (OEA/Ser.H/X.3).

Organization of American States. Inter-American Economic and Social Council, Special Committee I: Planning and Project Formulation [First Meeting, February 15–23, 1963, Buenos Aires, Argentina]. *Programming for Development: Five Urgent Problems.* March 10, 1963 [OEA/Ser.H/XIII (English) CIES/Com.I/3 Rev.].

Organization of American States. Pan American Union. *Alliance for Progress, A Weekly Report on Activities and Public Opinion* (Washington, D.C.). No. 33, April 15, 1963 [PAU Clearing House for Information on the Alliance for Progress].

Organization of American States. Pan American Union. *Alliance for Progress, A Weekly Newsletter* (Washington, D.C.). Vol. II, No. 46, November 16, 1964.

Overseas Consultants, Inc. *Report on Seven-Year Development Plan for the*

Plan Organization of the Imperial Government of Iran. Vol. V, New York, 1949.

Pakistan. National Planning Board. *First Five Year Plan, 1955–1960.* Karachi, 1958.

Pakistan. Planning Board. *Report of the Special Conference of Economists of East Pakistan on the Draft Five-Year Plan and Connected Papers.* Dacca, Government of Pakistan Press, 1956.

Pakistan. Planning Commission. *Outline of the Second Five Year Plan (1960–65).* Karachi, 1960.

Pakistan. Planning Commission. *Report of the Panel of Economists on the Second Five Year Plan (1960–65).* Karachi, Government of Pakistan Press, 1959.

Pakistan. Planning Commission. *Second Five Year Plan, 1960–1965.* Karachi, 1960.

PANT, Y. P. "Nepal's Economic Development: A Study in Planning Experience," *Economic Weekly* (Bombay). Vol. XIV, Nos. 44, 45, November 10, 1962.

PANT, Y. P. "Nepal's Planned Development," *Far Eastern Economic Review* (Hong Kong). Vol. XXXVI, No. 9, May 31, 1962.

PANT, Y. P. "The Process of Planning in Nepal," *Karachi Commerce.* Vol. XVI, No. 24, June 13, 1964.

PARANJAPE, H. K. *Planning Commission, A Descriptive Account.* New Delhi, Indian Institute of Public Administration, 1964.

PARSONS, MALCOLM B. "Performance Budgeting in the Philippines," *Public Administration Review* (Washington, D.C.). Vol. XVII, No. 3, Summer 1957.

PATEL, H. M. "Some Administrative Problems," in: TANDON, B. C. (ed). *Third Five Year Plan and India's Economic Growth.* Allahabad, Chaitanya Publishing House, 1962.

"Paths to Plenty." *Financial Mail* (Johannesburg), December 18, 1964.

PECK, H. AUSTIN. "Economic Planning in Jamaica: A Critique," *Social and Economic Studies* (Jamaica). Vol. 7, No. 4, December 1958.

P.E.P. (Political and Economic Planning). *Planning in Pakistan* (London). Vol. XXV, No. 433, April 20, 1959.

P.E.P. (Political and Economic Planning). *Town Planning and the Public* (London). Vol. XVII, No. 316, August 8, 1950.

PERKINS, DWIGHT H. "Centralization Versus Decentralization in Mainland China and the Soviet Union," *Annals of the American Academy of Political and Social Science* (Philadelphia). Vol. 349, September 1963.

PERLOFF, HARVEY S. and SAEZ, RAUL. "National Planning and Multinational Planning Under the Alliance for Progress," in: *Organization, Planning, and Programming for Economic Development.* Vol. VIII [of] United States Papers Prepared for the United Nations Conference on the Application of Science and Technology for the Benefit of the Less Developed Areas. Washington, D.C., United States Government Printing Office, 1963.

Philippine Delegation. *Administration of Economic Planning and Programs in the Philippines.* Paper prepared for the Regional Conference on

Public Administration, Manila and Baguio, June 7–21, 1958.

"Planning at the State Level," *Economic Weekly* (Bombay) (Special number). Vol. XII, Nos. 23, 24, 25, June 1960.

"Planning in a Vacuum," *New Statesman* (London). Vol. LXIV, No. 1650, October 26, 1962.

"Progress of National Plans," *Colombo Plan* (Ceylon). Vol. 8, No. 1, 1960.

Public Administration Service. *A Program of Administrative Improvements for the Government of the Republic of El Salvador.* Report conducted by Molkup, Joseph J., Slattengren, Alden W., Solano, Richard V. and Ricketts, Edmond F., October 15, 1962.

RAM, BHARAT. "Government and the Private Sector," *Indian Journal of Public Administration* (New Delhi). Vol. IX, No. 3, July–September 1963.

REDDAWAY, W. B. "Importance of Time Lags for Economic Planning," *Economic Weekly* (Bombay). Vol. XII, Nos. 4, 5, 6, January 1960.

Report of the Study Team on Five-Year Plan Publicity [Appointed under a Resolution of the Government of India, Ministry of Information and Broadcasting No. 9 (70)/59–PP, April 3, 1963] (mimeographed).

RIGGS, FREDERICK W. "Public Administration: A Neglected Factor in Economic Development," *Annals of the American Academy of Political and Social Science* (Philadelphia). Vol. 305, May 1956.

RIGGS, FREDERICK W. "Relearning an Old Lesson: The Political Context of Development Administration," *Public Administration Review* (Washington, D.C.). Vol. XXV, No. 1, March 1965.

RIJKEN VAN OLST, HENRI. "Economic Development and Cooperation in Latin America," in: TINBERGEN, JAN (ed). *Shaping the World Economy, Suggestions for an International Economic Policy.* New York, Twentieth Century Fund, 1962.

ROMERO KOLBECK, GUSTAVO. "La Inversion del Sector Publico," an Address at the Ciudad Universitaria, Mexico, D.F., February 4, 1960.

ROSE, E. MICHAEL. *Some Political and Administrative Problems of Economic Development in the Middle East.* Cambridge, Mass., Center for International Affairs, Harvard University, June 1959 (manuscript).

ROXAS, SIXTO K. *Lessons from Philippine Experience in Development Planning.* Paper prepared for Conference on Economic Planning in Southeast Asia, February 1–5, 1965, Honolulu, Hawaii.

ROXAS, SIXTO K. *Organizing the Government for Economic Development Administration.* Report to His Excellency, President Diosdado Macapagal, Manila, February 29, 1964.

Royal Thai Government Gazette (Bangkok).

SALINAS LOZANO, RAUL. "Comision de Inversiones," *Revista de Administracion Publica* (Mexico, D.F.). No. 5, enero-marzo, 1957.

SALTER, JAMES ARTHUR. *Development of Iraq, A Plan of Action.* London, Caxton Press, 1955.

SCHATZ, SAYRE P. "The Influence of Planning on Development: The Nigerian Experience," *Social Research* (New York). Vol. 27, No. 4, Winter 1960.

SEERS, DUDLEY. "The Role of National Income Estimates in the Statistical Policy of an Under Developed Area," *Review of Economic Studies* (London). Vol. XX(3), No. 53, 1952–53.

SHAFFER, HARRY G. "New Tasks for the Enterprise Director?" *East Europe* (New York). Vol. 13, No. 8, August 1964.

SHAH, RISHIKESH. *On Planning and Development.* Kathmandu, Department of Publicity and Broadcasting, Ministry of National Guidance, HMG, n.d.

SHARP, WALTER R. "Some Observations on Public Administration in Indo-China," *Public Administration Review* (Washington, D.C.). Vol. XIV, No. 4, Winter 1954.

SHEHAB, FAKHRI. "Kuwait: A Super-Affluent Society," *Foreign Affairs* (New York). Vol. 42, No. 3, April 1964.

SINGER, H. W. *Co-ordination of Technical Assistance and Development Planning: Determination of Priorities.* Paper prepared for Organization for Economic Co-operation and Development, Seminar on Technical Assistance Programming, Paris, November 16–19, 1964 (mimeographed).

SINGH, TARLOK. "Administrative Assumptions in the Five-Year Plan," *Indian Journal of Public Administration* (New Delhi). Vol. IX, No. 3, July–September 1963.

SINGH, TARLOK. *Planning Process.* New Delhi, Government of India Planning Commission, 1963.

SIROTKOVIC, JAKOV. "Drafting of the Seven-Year Plan," *Review of International Affairs* (Belgrade). Vol. XIV, No. 328, December 5, 1963.

SKEOCH, L. A. and SMITH, DAVID C. *Economic Planning: The Relevance of Western European Experience for Canada.* Private Planning Association of Canada, 1963.

SMOLENSKI, LEON. "What Next in Soviet Planning?" *Foreign Affairs* (New York). Vol. 42, No. 4, July 1964.

SNODGRASS, DONALD R. *Ceylon: An Export Economy in Transition* (draft). Economic Growth Center, Yale University, June 1964.

Sociedad Interamericana de Planificación. *Ensenânza de la Planificación en la América Latina.* San Juan, Puerto Rico, 1960 (mimeographed).

SPITZ, A. A. and WEIDNER, E. W. *Development Administration, An Annotated Bibliography.* Honolulu, East-West Center Press, 1963.

SPULBER, NICOLAS. "Planning and Development," in: POUNDS, NORMAN J. G. and SPULBER, NICOLAS (eds). *Resources and Planning in Eastern Europe,* Vol. 4. Bloomington, Indiana University Publications, 1957.

STALEY, EUGENE. *Political Implications of Economic Development and Pitfalls to be Avoided.* Paper presented to the Nyasaland Economic Symposium, Zomba, July 18–28, 1962 (mimeographed).

Statesman Overseas Weekly (Calcutta).

Statist (London).

STAVRIANOPOULOS, ALEXANDER. *Co-ordination in the Administration of Technical Assistance: The Point of View of a Recipient Country.* Paper prepared for Organization for Economic Co-operation and Development, Seminar on Technical Assistance Programming, Paris, November 16–19, 1964 (mimeographed).

STOLPER, WOLFGANG F. "The Development of Nigeria," *Scientific American.* Vol. 209, No. 3, September 1963.

STONE, DONALD C. "Government Machinery Necessary for Development," in: Kriesberg, Martin (ed). *Public Administration in Developing Countries.* Washington, D.C. Brookings Institution, 1965.

STONE, DONALD C. and Associates. *National Organization for the Conduct of Economic Development Programs.* Brussels, International Institute of Administrative Sciences, 1954.

SWAN, D. and McLACHLAN, D. L. "Programming and Competition in the European Communities," *Economic Journal* (London). Vol. LXXIV, No. 293, March 1964.

Syrian Arab Republic. Ministry of Planning. *Annual Report on the Economic and Social Development Plan, 1960/1961.* Damas, Bureau des Documentations Syriennes et Arabes, n.d.

TESDELL, LOREN. "Planning for Technical Assistance: Iraq and Jordan," *Middle East Journal* (Washington, D.C.). Vol. 15, No. 4, Autumn 1961.

Thailand. National Economic Development Board. *National Economic Development Plan, 1961–1966, Second Phase: 1964–1966.* Bangkok, 1964.

THET TUN, U. *A Review of Economic Planning in Burma.* Rangoon, Central Statistical and Economic Department, 1959 (mimeographed).

THONG YAW HONG. *Building Institutions for Preparing and Executing Development Plans, the Malaysian Experience.* Paper presented at Conference on Economic Planning in Southeast Asia, February 1–5, 1965, Honolulu, Hawaii.

Times (London).

TINBERGEN, JAN. *Central Planning.* New Haven, Yale University Press, 1964.

TINBERGEN, JAN and Bos, HENDRICS C. *Mathematical Models of Economic Growth.* New York, McGraw-Hill Book Co., Inc. 1962.

TINTNER, GERHARD and DÁVILA, OSWALDO. "Un Modelo Econometrico para el Ecuador," *Planificación* (Quito). Vol. 1, No. 3, October 1964.

TRAPEZNIKOV, VADIM A. "For Flexible Economic Management of Enterprises," *Problems of Economics* (White Plains, N.Y.). Vol. VII, No. 9, January 1965.

TRESS, R. C. "The Practice of Economic Planning," *Manchester School of Economic and Social Studies* (Manchester). Vol. 26, No. 2, May 1948.

TREVES, GIUSEPPINO. *Government Organization for Economic Development.* Report of XIIth International Congress of Administrative Sciences [July 16–20, 1962, Vienna]. Brussels, International Institute of Administrative Sciences, 1963.

TSURU, SHIGETO. "Formal Planning Divorced from Action: Japan," in: HAGEN, EVERETT (ed). *Planning Economic Development.* Homewood, Ill., Richard D. Irwin, Inc., 1963.

Turkey. State Planning Organization. *Planning in Turkey, Summary of the First Five Year Plan.* Ankara, 1963.

Turkey. State Planning Organization. *Program for the Year 1962 (For Transition into the Plan-Period)* [draft]. Ankara, October 1961.

United Nations. Bureau of Technical Assistance Operations. *Report of the Inter-Regional Workshop on Problems of Budget Classification and Man-*

agement in *Developing Countries* [August 31–September 11, 1964, Copenhagen, Denmark]. 1964 (ST/TAO/SER.C/70).

United Nations. Bureau of Technical Assistance Operations. *Report of the Third Workshop on Problems of Budget Reclassification and Management in the ECAFE Region* [August 17–26, 1960, Bangkok and August 28–September 2, 1960, Manila]. 1961 (ST/TAO/SER.C/48).

United Nations. Bureau of Technical Assistance Operations. *Report of the Workshop on Budgetary Classification and Management in South America* [September 3–14, 1962, Santiago, Chile]. 1962 (ST/TAO/SER.C/58).

United Nations. Bureau of Technical Assistance Operations. *Report of the Workshop on Problems of Budget Reclassification and Management in Africa* [September 4–15, 1961, Addis Ababa, Ethiopia]. 1962 (ST/TAO/SER.C/53).

United Nations. Consultative Group on Planning for Economic Development [Second Session, March 25–April 5, 1963]. "The Political and Administrative Organization of the Planning System in France," by VIOT, PIERRE. *Planning for Economic Development.* January 9, 1963 (EPPC/EDP/R.3).

United Nations. Department of Economic and Social Affairs. *A Handbook of Public Administration, Current Concepts and Practices with Special Reference to Developing Countries.* 1961 (ST/TAO/M/16).

United Nations. Department of Economic and Social Affairs. *A Manual for Economic and Functional Classification of Government Transactions.* 1958 (ST/TAA/M/12).

United Nations. Department of Economic and Social Affairs. *Economic Survey of Africa Since 1950.* 1959 (E/CN.14/28).

United Nations. Department of Economic and Social Affairs. *Planning for Economic Development, Report of the Secretary-General Transmitting the Study of a Group of Experts.* 1963 (A/5533/Rev.1). [The first of a two-volume study (the second volume contains two parts).]

United Nations. Department of Economic and Social Affairs. *Public Administration in Venezuela 1958–1961.* Prepared for the Government of Venezuela by EMMERICH, H., MYER, D. S., WALSH, D. P., LOUW, M. H. H., and SMITH, J. D. M. November 1, 1961 (TAO/VEN/13).

United Nations. Department of Economic and Social Affairs. "Some Problems of Financial Administration in African Countries," in: United Nations. Economic Commission for Africa. *Report of the Seminar on Urgent Administrative Problems of African Governments.* December 18, 1962 (E/CN.14/180) (Annex IV).

United Nations. Department of Economic and Social Affairs. "Chapter 1, Problems and Policies in the Development Decade," p. 8. in: *World Economic Survey, 1964: Part I, World Economic Trends, Economic Planning and Projections, Development Plans: Appraisal of Targets and Progress in Developing Countries.* May 18, 1965 (E/4046) [preliminary mimeographed edition].

United Nations. Economic Commission for Africa. *Comprehensive Development Planning,* by STOLPER, WOLFGANG F. November 15, 1961 (E/CN.14/ESD/6).

United Nations. Economic Commission for Africa. *Economic Bulletin for Africa* [Part B: Special Articles]. Vol. IV, No. 1, January 13, 1964 (E/CN.14/239 Part B).

United Nations. Economic Commission for Africa. *Meeting of Experts on Techniques of Development Programming in Africa, 30 November to 5 December 1959, Executive Secretary's Report.* December 23, 1959 (E/CN.14/42).

United Nations. Economic Commission for Africa. *Memorandum on Statistical Development.* December 31, 1962 (E/CN.14/29).

United Nations. Economic Commission for Africa. *Outlines and Selected Indicators of African Development Plans.* January 14, 1965 (E/CN.14/336).

United Nations. Economic Commission for Africa. *Problems Concerning Techniques of Development Programming in African Countries* [Prepared by the Secretariat for the Meeting of Experts on Techniques of Development Programming in Africa, November 30–December 5, 1959, Addis Ababa, Ethiopia]. December 18, 1959 (E/CN.14/42/Add. 1).

United Nations. Economic Commission for Africa. *Report of the First Conference of African Statisticians* [September 28–October 8, 1959, Addis Ababa]. October 8, 1959 (E/CN.14/25).

United Nations. Economic Commission for Africa. *Report of the Meeting of the Expert Group on Comprehensive Development Planning.* January 4, 1963 (E/CN.14/182).

United Nations. Economic Commission for Africa. *Report of the Working Party on Economic and Social Development* (draft). February 12, 1962 (E/CN.14/127).

United Nations. Economic Commission for Asia and the Far East [Conference of Asian Economic Planners, Second Session, October 19–26, 1964, Bangkok, Thailand]. *Statement by Dr. Douglas S. Paauw, Member of U.S. Delegation on Agenda Item 4.* October 20, 1964 (mimeographed).

United Nations. Economic Commission for Asia and the Far East. *Draft Report of the Conference of Asian Economic Planners* [Conference of Asian Economic Planners, Second Session, October 19–26, 1964, Bangkok, Thailand]. October 26, 1964 (E/CN.11/673).

United Nations. Economic Commission for Asia and the Far East. "Economic Development and Planning in Asia and the Far East," *Economic Bulletin for Asia and the Far East.* Vol. VI, No. 3, November 1955.

United Nations. Economic Commission for Asia and the Far East. "Economic Development and Planning in Asia and the Far East," *Economic Bulletin for Asia and the Far East.* Vol. XII, No. 3, December 1961.

United Nations. Economic Commission for Asia and the Far East. "Economic Development and Planning in Asia and the Far East," *Economic Bulletin for Asia and the Far East.* Vol. XV, No. 3, December 1964.

United Nations. Economic Commission for Asia and the Far East. *Economic Survey of Asia and the Far East 1961.* Bangkok, March 1962 [Also issued as *Economic Bulletin for Asia and the Far East.* Vol. XII, No. 4].

United Nations. Economic Commission for Asia and the Far East. *Planning Machinery in India* [Conference of Asian Economic Planners, First Session, September 26–October 3, 1961, New Delhi, India]. September 15, 1961 [CAEP. 1/Background document (India) 12].

United Nations. Economic Commission for Asia and the Far East. "Problems and Techniques of Foreign Exchange Budgeting," *Economic Bulletin for Asia and the Far East.* Vol. XIV, No. 3, December 1963.

United Nations. Economic Commission for Asia and the Far East. *Problems of Long-Term Economic Projections with Special Reference to Economic Planning in Asia and the Far East.* Report of the Third Group of Experts on Programming Techniques. December 26, 1962 (E/CN. 11/L.112).

United Nations. Economic Commission for Asia and the Far East. *Programming Techniques for Economic Development with Special Reference to Asia and the Far East* [Development Programming Techniques Series No. 1]. Bangkok, 1960 (E/CN.11/535).

United Nations. Economic Commission for Asia and the Far East. *Report of the Seminar on Basic Statistics for Economic and Social Development.* January 9, 1963 (E/CN.11/602).

United Nations. Economic Commission for Asia and the Far East. "Some Social Aspects of Development Planning in the ECAFE Region," *Economic Bulletin for Asia and the Far East.* Vol. XIV, No. 2, September 1963.

United Nations. Economic Commission for Asia and the Far East. *Speed and Efficiency in Development Administration* [Conference of Asian Economic Planners, First Session, September 26–October 3, 1961, New Delhi, India]. October 1961 (CAEP. 1/Country Paper 8).

United Nations. Economic Commission for Asia and the Far East. "The Interrelationships Between Social and Economic Development Planning," *Economic Bulletin for Asia and the Far East.* Vol. XIV, No. 2, September 1963.

United Nations. Economic Commission for Europe. *A Study of Determinants of Growth During the Nineteen-Fifties.* March 2, 1961 (ECON. ADVISERS/CONF/13).

United Nations. Economic Commission for Europe. "Long-term plans in Western Europe," *Economic Bulletin for Europe.* Vol. 14, No. 2, November 1962.

United Nations. Economic Commission for Europe. *Report by the Executive Secretary on the Third Meeting of Senior Economic Advisers to ECE Governments* [November 2–6, 1964, Geneva]. November 9, 1964 (E/ECE/561).

United Nations. Economic Commission for Latin America. *A Manual for Programme and Performance Budgeting* (draft). Prepared by The Fiscal and Financial Branch, Department of Economic and Social Affairs. May 14, 1962 (E/CN.12/BRW.2/L.5).

United Nations. Economic Commission for Latin America. *Experience of the Advisory Groups and the Practical Problems of Economic Development* [May 1961, Santiago, Chile]. April 18, 1961 (E/CN.12/584).

United Nations. Economic Commission for Latin America. *Fiscal Budget as an Instrument in the Programming of Economic Development.* April 25, 1959 (E/CN.12/BRW.1/L.3).

United Nations. Economic Commission for Latin America. "Planning in France," by LeGuay, François. *Economic Bulletin for Latin America.* Vol. VIII, No. 1, March 1963.

United Nations. Economic Commission for Latin America. *Report of the Latin American Seminar on Planning* [Santiago, February 19–24, 1962]. February 14, 1963 (E/CN.12/644).

United Nations. Economic Commission for Latin America. *Use of National Accounts for Economic Analysis and Development Planning.* April 16, 1963 (E/CN.12/671).

United Nations. Inter-Regional Workshop on Problems of Budget Classification and Management in Developing Countries [August 31–September 12, 1964, Copenhagen, Denmark]. *Budgetary Developments in the Philippines Since the Early 1950's,* by Sy-Changco, Fastino. August 1964 (IBRW.1/P.20).

United Nations. Inter-Regional Workshop on Problems of Budget Classification and Management in Developing Countries [August 31–September 12, 1964, Copenhagen, Denmark]. *Relationship Between Planning and Government Budgeting in Developing Countries* [Parts I and II]. July 23, 1964 (IBRW.1/L.5).

United Nations. Inter-Regional Workshop on Problems of Budget Classification and Management in Developing Countries [August 31–September 12, 1964, Copenhagen, Denmark]. *Review of Developments in the Budget Field.* June 10, 1964 (IBRW.1/L.4).

United Nations. Seminar on Industrial Programming [March 4–15, 1963, São Paulo, Brazil]. *India's Experience in Industrial Planning.* February 5, 1963 (ST/ECLA/CONF. 11/L.9).

United Nations. Statistical Commission. *Basic Statistics for Economic and Social Development.* Memorandum prepared for the Secretary-General, March 24, 1958 (E/CN.3/248).

United Nations. Statistical Commission. *Report of the Commission to the Economic and Social Council on its 10th Session, held in New York from 28 April to 15 May, 1958.* July 1958 (E/CN.3/255).

United Nations. Statistical Office. *A System of National Accounts and Supporting Tables.* rev. ed., 1964 (ST/STAT/SER.F/2/Rev.2).

United Nations. Technical Assistance Administration. *Economic Planning in Ceylon,* by Newman, P. K. August 14, 1958 (TAA/CEY/11).

United Nations. Technical Assistance Administration. *Introduction to Public Administration in Development Policy, Preliminary survey of the experience of several Latin American countries,* by Tejera Paris, Enrique. December 12, 1957 (TAA/LAT/17).

United Nations. Technical Assistance Administration. *Standards and Techniques of Public Administration with Special Reference to Technical Assistance for Under-developed Countries* [Report by the Special Committee on Public Administration Problems]. November 20, 1951 (ST/TAA/M/1).

United Nations Center for Industrial Development. *Organizational Aspects of Planning* [Background document No. 11, prepared for the United Nations Seminar on Industrial Programming, March 4–15, 1963, São Paulo, Brazil]. February 1963.

United Nations Conference on the Application of Science and Technology for the Benefit of the Less Developed Areas [February 4–20, 1963, Geneva]. *Organization of Planning Machinery: Lessons from Burmese Experience*, by THET TUN, U. February 1963 (H/88).

United Nations Conference on the Application of Science and Technology for the Benefit of the Less Developed Areas [February 4–20, 1963, Geneva]. *Organization of Statistical Services*, by SEARLE, W. F. October 6, 1962 (E/CONF. 39/4/3).

United Nations Conference on the Application of Science and Technology for the Benefit of the Less Developed Areas [February 4–20, 1963, Geneva]. *Planning Machinery in Afghanistan*, by YAFTALI, ABDULLAH. October 22, 1962 (E/CONF.39/H/40).

United Nations Conference on the Application of Science and Technology for the Benefit of the Less Developed Areas [February 4–20, 1963, Geneva]. *Science and Technology for Development*. Vol. VII, Science and Planning. 1963 (E/CONF.39/1, Vol. VII).

United Nations Meeting of Experts on Administrative Aspects of National Development Planning [June 8–19, 1964, Paris]. *Administration of Planning in Colombia*. February 1964 (Country Paper: Colombia).

United Nations Meeting of Experts on Administrative Aspects of National Development Planning [June 8–19, 1964, Paris]. *Administration of Planning in Ghana*. February 1964 (Country Paper: Ghana).

United Nations Meeting of Experts on Administrative Aspects of National Development Planning [June 8–19, 1964, Paris]. *Administration of Planning in Malaya*. February 1964 (Country Paper: Malaya).

United Nations Meeting of Experts on Administrative Aspects of National Development Planning [June 8–19, 1964, Paris]. *Administration of Planning in Nigeria*. February 1964 (Country Paper: Nigeria).

United Nations Meeting of Experts on Administrative Aspects of National Development Planning [June 8–19, 1964, Paris]. *Administration of Planning in Tunisia*. February 1964 (Country Paper: Tunisia).

United Nations Meeting of Experts on Administrative Aspects of National Development Planning [June 8–19, 1964, Paris]. *Administrative Aspects of Planning in Developing Countries*. February 1964.

United States. Agency for International Development. *Modernizing Government Budget Administration*. Prepared by the Public Administration Service, Chicago, 1962.

United States. Agency for International Development. *Report of the United States Delegation to the Second Session of the Conference of Asian Economic Planners* [United Nations Economic Commission for Asia and the Far East, Bangkok, Thailand, October 19–26, 1964]. Submitted to the Secretary of State by ROBERT S. SMITH, U.S. Representative, November 25, 1964.

United States Senate. Committee on Government Operations, Subcommittee on National Policy Machinery. *Organizing for National Security.* 86th Congress, 2nd Session, Washington, D.C. 1960.

VAN DER KROEF, JUSTUS M. "Indonesia's New Development Plan," *Eastern World* (London). Vol. XV, No. 2, February 1961.

VEDAGIRI, T. S. "Planning and Programming of Projects Since Independence," in: *Administrative Reforms Since Independence,* Supplement to Indian Journal of Public Administration (New Delhi). Vol. IX, No. 3, July–September 1963.

VENKATASUBBIAH, H. *Hindu Weekly Review* (Madras). Vol. XII, No. 31, August 5, 1963.

VERGNER, ZDENEK. "Economic Planning in Czechoslovakia," in: *Planning for Economic Development, Vol. II* (Studies of National Planning Experience, Part 2, Centrally Planned Economies). New York, United Nations Publications, 1965 (A/5533/Rev.1/Add.2).

VISVESWARAYA, M. *Planned Economy for India.* Bangalore City, Bangalore Press, 1934.

WALDBY, ODELL. "Chapter 5, Performance Budgeting," in: WALDBY, ODELL (ed). *Philippine Public Fiscal Administration, Reading and Documents.* Manila, Institute of Public Administration, University of the Philippines, 1954.

WALINSKY, LOUIS J. "Burma," in: HAGEN, EVERETT (ed). *Planning Economic Development.* Homewood, Ill., Richard D. Irwin, Inc., 1963.

WALINSKY, LOUIS J. *Economic Development in Burma 1951–1960.* New York, Twentieth Century Fund, 1962.

WALKER, DAVID. *Balanced Social and Economic Development in Uganda: A Case Study.* Study prepared at the request of the Bureau of Social Affairs of the United Nations. January 25, 1960 (dittoed).

WARD, BARBARA. *Plan Under Pressure: An Observer's View.* London, Asia Publishing House, 1963.

Washington Post (Washington, D.C.).

WATERSTON, ALBERT. *Planning in Morocco.* Baltimore, Johns Hopkins Press, 1963.

WATERSTON, ALBERT. *Planning in Pakistan.* Baltimore, Johns Hopkins Press, 1963.

WEINER, MYRON. *Politics of Scarcity.* Chicago, University of Chicago Press, 1962.

WHEELOCK, KEITH. *Nasser's New Egypt: A Critical Analysis.* New York, Frederick A. Praeger, 1960.

WICKHAM, S. "French Planning: Retrospect and Prospect," *Review of Economics and Statistics* (Cambridge, Mass.). Vol. XLV, No. 4, November 1963.

WILCOX, CLAIR. "Pakistan," in: HAGEN, EVERETT (ed). *Planning Economic Development.* Homewood, Ill., Richard D. Irwin, Inc., 1963.

WILCOX, CLAIR. *Planning and Execution of Economic Development in Southeast Asia.* Cambridge, Mass. Occasional Papers in International Affairs, No. 10, Harvard University Center for International Affairs, January 1965.

WIONCZEK, MIGUEL S. "Incomplete Formal Planning: Mexico," in: HAGEN, EVERETT (ed). *Planning Economic Development*. Homewood, Ill., Richard D. Irwin, Inc., 1963.

WORSWICK, G. D. N. "A Technically Advanced Country: England," in: HAGEN, EVERETT (ed). *Planning Economic Development*. Homewood, Ill., Richard D. Irwin, Inc., 1963.

YOINGCO, ANGEL Q. "Performance Budgeting for the Philippine Government," in: WALDBY, ODELL (ed). *Philippine Public Fiscal Administration, Reading and Documents*. Manila, Institute of Public Administration, University of the Philippines, 1954.

ZAUBERMAN, ALFRED. "New Phase Opens in Soviet Planning," *Times* (London), February 2, 1965.

ZIMMERMAN, VIRGIL B. "Comments on 'Performance Budgeting in the Philippines,'" *Public Administration Review* (Washington, D.C.). Vol. XVIII, No. 1, Winter 1958.

Name Index

Subject Index

Absorptive capacity: definition of, 300
Accounting, 216–17; financial controls, 264–67
Accounting prices, 322n. *See also* "Shadow" prices
Aden: plans listed, 592
Administration, 339–343; capacity, limit to project execution, 250; capacity, measurement of, 287–89, 343–50; delays, 279–80; inefficiency, estimating cost, 288; inertia, 257, 444n; obstacles to planning, 249–92; organization, need for, 271–74
Administrative reform, 272, 281–82: attempts, 279; comprehensive approach, 285–86; difficulties of, 278–85; nuclei approach, 285–87
Aerial photography: aid in data gathering, 198n
Afghanistan: feasibility studies, lack of technicians, 326; foreign aid, co-ordination problems, 405; Ministry of Planning, 219, 487, 533; object budgeting, 219; plans listed, 592; planning, reason for, 36; programing units, 572
AFL-CIO: proposal for national planning agency, 41
Africa, 301; administrative improvements, 282; "Africanization," 255; linear programing, limitations, 100; postwar planning, 36–38; statistics for planning, 67. *See also individual country*
Agency for International Development (US), 86, 238n; study of Cukurova Region (Turkey), 560n
Aggregative planning. *See* Comprehensive plans
Agricultural targets, failure to achieve, 297–98, 365
Albania: plans listed, 592
Algeria: plans listed, 592

Alliance for Progress: Committee of Nine, 26, 111, 127; Declaration of Punta del Este, 67, 86; duration of plans, 123; influence on planning, 36, 103; investment projects, shortage, 85–86; partial planning, experience with, 100; Tripartite groups, 97
Amersfoort (Netherlands): five-year rolling plan, 139n
Angola: plans listed, 593
Annual plans: description of, 141–44, 201–2; formulation, responsibility for, 387–89, 429–30; relation to budget, 201–2, 244–45
Anticyclical planning, 14–15
Antigua: plans listed, 593
Argentina: GNP estimates, competing sets, 178; investment inventory, 97, 579; plans listed, 593
—National Development Council, 97n; national income accounts, preparation of, 443; staff, size of, 524
Asia: agriculture, performance, 297; early plans, 71; economic projections, 294; growth rates, decline in, 294; postwar planning, 32–34. *See also individual country*
Asian Economic Planners: *1961* Conference, 189–90, 278; *1964* Conference, 82, 86, 340
Auditing procedures: delays, 246; outmoded, 266
Autonomous agencies: advantages, 272–73; limitations, 272–73; problems, 273–74
Average capital-output ratio. *See* Capital-output ratios

Bahamas: plan listed, 593
Bakshish (India), 276
Barbados: plans listed, 594
Basutoland: plans listed, 594
Bechuanaland: plans listed, 594